D1432150

Psychopathia
Sexualis

Psychopathia Sexualis

*With Especial Reference to the
Antipathic Sexual Instinct*

A MEDICO-FORENSIC STUDY

BY

Richard von Krafft-Ebing

*Professor of Psychiatry and Neurology
University of Vienna*

TRANSLATED FROM THE TWELFTH GERMAN EDITION AND
WITH AN INTRODUCTION BY
Franklin S. Klaf, M.D., M.P.H.

INTRODUCTION TO THE ARCADE EDITION BY
Joseph LoPiccolo, Ph.D.

FOREWORD BY
Daniel Blain, M.D., F.A.C.P., F.A.P.A.

Complete English-language Edition

ARCADE PUBLISHING • NEW YORK

FIRST ARCADE EDITION

Library of Congress Cataloging-in-Publication Data
Krafft-Ebing, R. von (Richard), 1840–1902.
    [Psychopathia sexualis. English]
    Psychopathia sexualis : with especial reference to the antipathic
sexual instinct : a medico-forensic study / by Richard von Krafft-Ebing ;
translated from the twelfth German edition and with an introduction by
Franklin S. Klaf ; introduction by Joseph LoPiccolo, Ph.D. ; foreword by
Daniel Blain. — Complete English-language ed., 1st Arcade ed.
        p.   cm.
    Originally published: New York : Stein and Day, [1965].
    Includes bibliographical references and index.
    ISBN 1-55970-426-8 (hc)
    ISBN 1-55970-425-X (pb)
    1. Sexual deviation.   I. Klaf, Franklin S.   II. Title.
HQ71.K91213   1998
616.85'83—dc21   98-13156

Published in the United States by Arcade Publishing, Inc., New York
Distributed by Little, Brown and Company

10 9 8 7 6 5 4 3 2 1

BP

PRINTED IN THE UNITED STATES OF AMERICA

CONTENTS

      The manifestations of pathological sexual life in the various
      forms and conditions of mental disturbance, 308—Inhibition

INTRODUCTION TO THE ARCADE EDITION

Although there is no doubt that the original publication of *Psychopathia Sexualis* was a landmark in the history of psychiatry, many have felt over the subsequent decades a temptation to regard this comprehensive study as merely an artifact of a previous era. In fact, Daniel Blain, introducing this translation of the book in 1965, wrote, "Today's reader should clearly recognize that the conclusions and opinions given in this nineteenth-century textbook have little scientific value today." However, even though some of the book's statements reflect both the culture and the limited scientific-medical knowledge base of Krafft-Ebing's time, contemporary readers of this volume will, upon a close and objective look, be struck by the relevance, farsightedness, and "modernity" of his views.

One of Krafft-Ebing's major contributions to the study of sexual deviance was the development of a rather complete typology of sexually deviant behaviors. Indeed, he saw so many cases of so many types that it has been said that "every sexual deviation you can think of and many more you would never think of are all there in Krafft-Ebing"! Indeed, his concern about possible prurient interest in the book caused him to publish the original editions with the case material in Latin to prevent the general public from reading it. (It is rumored that there was a marked increase in sales of Latin dictionaries in Germany and Austria after the publication of *Psychopathia Sexualis.*)

Krafft-Ebing's work offers useful information to the modern reader and clinician both in dealing with obscure and uncommon sexual deviations and in describing sexual problems that are all too common. The clinical material is presented in a remarkably objective fashion, not constantly shaped by a theoretical orientation. Krafft-Ebing even includes instructive autobiographical material written by the patients themselves.

Psychopathia Sexualis addresses therapeutic, societal, and legal responses to sexual deviation, and its author was ahead of his time in suggesting that the mental condition of the individual must be considered — not just the nature of the act. Krafft-Ebing anticipated such current issues as the "insanity defense," irresistible impulses, and the question of diminished responsibility. He also made the observation, unfortunately still true today, that child molesters are imprisoned without treatment and thus typically re-offend upon release. Krafft-Ebing cautioned that while we may need to lock such individuals away, we must also treat them — or it will never be safe to release them. It is amazing that Krafft-Ebing wrote about this problem more than a hundred years ago, and despite the accumulation of supporting evidence in the intervening decades, social policy still has not changed. If society had only listened to Krafft-Ebing, thousands of children may well have been spared molestation over the past century.

In addition to writing about responses to sexual deviations, Krafft-Ebing had some remarkable insights into the causes of such conditions. In a statement that was revolutionary at the time, he suggested that sexual deviations were not reflections of "moral defect" but were issues of mental disease. While this idea may seem self-evident today, some of our current laws regarding sexual crimes actually suggest that we have not even now entirely embraced this concept.

Krafft-Ebing noted that many male sexual offenders have in common a fear of adult women and a resulting inability to utilize normal sexual outlets. In this he anticipated modern cognitive behavioral thinking. Allowing for differences in terminology, he cogently described these men as having what we now label "heterosocial anxiety and heterosocial skills deficits."

Krafft-Ebing anticipated modern thinking about what is now called "accidental conditioning" as a factor in some sexual deviations. For example, he mentions that boys being spanked may experience incidental penile sensations (if held face down across the lap of the adult, or simply from friction against their own trousers), and consequently come to associate erotic pleasure with spanking, leading to a spanking fetish, and perhaps in some cases to sadism or masochism. However, he points out that most boys who experience such things do not become fixated on these chance experiences but go on to "normal" sexuality. This conceptualization demonstrates his clear thinking, as there are some clinicians even today who simplistically argue that accidental conditioning is always powerful enough to produce a deviation. Probing deeper into the issue, Krafft-Ebing attempted to identify personality and life experience factors that could render some people more vulnerable than others to the effects of such conditioning.

Krafft-Ebing's thinking on homosexuality, both from a clinical and societal point of view, was in some ways on the cutting edge of today's clinical work. He suggested that there are different types of homosexuality and proposed that some cases seemed to be inherited and biologically based. Genetic research in recent years does seem to support this view for at least some instances of male homosexuality. Krafft-Ebing wrote about male homosexuals, for example, who from early childhood had strong preferences for female attire and toys, an observation that has since been well substantiated by the longitudinal studies of Dr. Richard Green and others.

Krafft-Ebing argued that outlawing private homosexual behavior serves no useful societal purpose but rather creates a harmless "criminal class" that is often victim to blackmail, social ostracism, and professional prejudice. He noted, correctly, that homosexual men are no more likely than heterosexual men to be child molesters. While legalization remains a debate to this day (twenty-three states still have laws against consensual sodomy on their books), it is remarkable to see Krafft-Ebing advocating such reform at his time in history.

Furthermore, Krafft-Ebing anticipated the current debate about both the efficacy and the ethics of "treating" individuals who voluntarily seek out help in altering their sexual orientation from homosexuality to heterosexuality. He suggested that therapy for homosexuals can at most make them celibate—it cannot change them into heterosexuals. His belief has been supported by contemporary research, which indicates that such therapy is generally not successful unless the patient has at least moderate bisexual tendencies.

Krafft-Ebing went further and questioned whether it is even ethically proper in the first place to try to aid homosexuals who wish to become heterosexual, a dilemma that continues to divide clinicians today. One side argues that such an attempt merely reflects society's homophobia and fosters self-hatred, and that patients in this situation should simply be counseled to accept their sexual orientation and placed in contact with appropriate social support networks. The other side argues that it is improper for a therapist to set a new goal for a patient (of accepting one's sexual orientation) rather than help the patient reach his or her desired goal (of altering one's sexual orientation). Krafft-Ebing took a sensible, empirical approach to this politically loaded question. In the case material, he mentions encouraging patients to seek out the company of members of the opposite sex and see to what extent they enjoy this contact. He seemed to realize that sometimes the only way to make a diagnostic decision is to try the treatment intervention and see if it does have the intended effect. Some modern clinicians resist this point of view, as it forces them to face the fact that there are not always easy answers to complex questions in their field.

Psychopathia Sexualis made great advances in the classification and investigation of what we now diagnostically label "sexual dysfunctions." These include lack of sexual drive, failure to become aroused, and failure to reach orgasm, in both men and women. In Krafft-Ebing's age, there was no study or even discussion of female sexual dysfunction—normal, decent women were not supposed to be sexual. Therefore, despite some prescient comments about the pleasure women should ideally derive from sexual activity, the focus in Krafft-Ebing's work (as well as that of his contemporaries) was upon men suffering from "loss of the power"—impotence—now diagnostically referred to as "erectile dysfunction."

Krafft-Ebing's theories foresaw modern sex therapy work on the causes and treatment of these sexual dysfunctions. For example, in 1970 Masters and Johnson were hailed as innovative with their theory that erectile dysfunction is caused by performance anxiety and the taking of a self-evaluative, spectator role. Yet almost a century earlier, Krafft–Ebing had stated that "fear of unsuccessful coitus . . . may inhibit the occurrence of erection, and cause it, when present, to disappear." Despite the total lack of knowledge of the physiology of erection at the time, his speculation that both a lack of adequate physical stimulation of the genitals and possible neurological problems may contribute to erectile failure are similar to concepts that are now standard assessment and treatment procedures.

In a few of the case studies, Krafft-Ebing mentions patients going to houses of prostitution during the course of treatment. (It is not known whether Krafft-Ebing himself encouraged or even suggested this behavior.) As usual, Krafft-Ebing reports the results objectively: some of these patients had good experiences with prostitutes; for others the effect was negative. While the use of "surrogate partners" for unmarried erectile dysfunction patients remains a highly controversial topic in the sex therapy field, with most current sex therapists arguing that surrogates are either always good or always bad, Krafft-Ebing seems more open to using clinical experience as a guide.

Any historical document, however forward-thinking or free of theoretical bias, will reveal some faults and shortcomings when analyzed critically from a century's distance. *Psychopathia Sexualis* is certainly no exception. The book does articulate a number of "politically incorrect" racial, ethnic, and gender stereotypes, to be sure. In Krafft-Ebing's time, Africans, Pacific Islanders, Asians, and even southern Europeans were seen by dominant northern Europeans as "inferior" in any number of ways. Women of that era, though much admired for their beauty and purity, were certainly not respected for intelligence or valued for their sexuality. They were primarily judged on the basis of their physical attractiveness.

Some of Krafft-Ebing's statements reflect these outlooks, but it is important to note that he never uses such bias to explain his case material. In fact, he often rejects the stereotyped thinking of his time when seeking to evaluate cases and disorders. A prime example is his discussion of nymphomania (unbridled lust in a woman). While he does allow in the book for the possibility that this can be classified as a deviation, he also suggests that when a woman dearly loves her husband, a high level of mutually enjoyed sexual activity should be viewed positively. Although it sounds a bit prudish to twentieth-century ears, this was a remarkably liberated statement for the late nineteenth century.

Another topic upon which Krafft-Ebing's writing betrays the limitations of the beliefs and clinical knowledge of his time is the discussion of the consequences of masturbation. In several cases, he attributes the causality of a patient's problem, at least in part, to masturbation during the patient's childhood, adolescence, or adulthood. In particular, he refers to masturbation as a causal mechanism for deviations and for erectile dysfunction, which it was commonly considered at the time. We now understand that masturbating with deviant thoughts does not cause someone to become deviant. Even if such fantasies are eventually acted out, masturbation is not the cause but merely a reflection of fantasies that are already present. As for erectile dysfunction, it has since been determined by research that childhood and adolescent masturbation does not "use up" some store of erectile capabilities and lead to eventual erectile dysfunction; it is simply normal behavior.

The merits of *Psychopathia Sexualis* as a valuable source work and classification, as well as a highly objective set of case studies offering much information to modern-day clinicians, far outweigh the limitations that sometimes chain the work to the author's time and culture. The thoughtful reader will certainly find this volume of far more than merely historical interest.

Joseph LoPiccolo, Ph.D.
July, 1998

INTRODUCTION
Richard von Krafft-Ebing
and "Psychopathia Sexualis"

RICHARD von Krafft-Ebing, who ended his career as Professor of Psychiatry
at the University of Vienna, was a man of restless energy and diffuse
talents. When heart disease suddenly removed him on December 22, 1902,
at the height of his productivity, modern psychiatry lost one of its most
creative meistersingers, the one physician who investigated every aspect
of mental pathology.

Krafft-Ebing's multifaceted ability was the result of natural endowment plus parental (and even grandparental) encouragement. He was
born in Mannheim on August 14, 1840, and received his elementary
education in Germany and in Switzerland. The most significant early
influence was that of his mother, a cultured, kindly woman who came
from the Mittermaier family, long distinguished as lawyers and
intellectuals.

When Krafft-Ebing reached university age, his parents moved from
Mannheim to Heidelberg, where he came under the direct tutelage of
his maternal grandfather, who practiced law and lived in that city. Dr.
Mittermaier was the German attorney for the damned, championing the
legal rights of those condemned to ostracism by a still puritanical society.
One such group were sexual deviates, who received harsh treatment in the
courts.

These Heidelberg experiences influenced Krafft-Ebing's professional
choice, but did not determine his future career. His compassionate nature
led him to the study of medicine, which was interrupted by a severe
attack of typhus. Before returning to school, Krafft-Ebing recuperated in
Switzerland, that land of magic mountains where all afflictions were supposed to disappear.

The Swiss interlude not only helped the young student regain his
health, but it decided his medical specialty. The famous mid-nineteenth-
century psychiatrist, Greisinger, was delivering a series of lectures in
Zurich. Krafft-Ebing happened to attend, and was deeply impressed by
the immensity and fascination of human psychopathology. After completing his recovery from typhus, he quickly shifted his plans and applied
as a volunteer at Illenau to commence his psychiatric training.

On September 1, 1863, Krafft-Ebing's forty-year career in psychiatry
and neurology began. He chose the theme "Mental Delirium" for his
doctoral dissertation, and then departed for Berlin to seek further experience. Between 1864 and 1869, he started his association with the

courts and worked on bodily changes resulting from psychotic abnormality, one of the precursors of psychosomatic medicine. Krafft-Ebing viewed each patient as an individual, long before this point was belabored by twentieth-century academicians.

By 1870, Krafft-Ebing was the best trained neuropsychiatrist on the continent, and his youthful industriousness was rewarded by a professorship at Strasbourg after Alsace-Lorraine became Prussian territory. In the years that followed, he investigated hereditary anthropological and functional factors to discover the causes of mental illness. Krafft-Ebing's clinical research led him into hypnosis, hysteria, criminal psychopathy, geriatrics, epilepsy, menstrual psychoses, migraine, and masochism. He was widely traveled and in constant demand as a consultant from Russia to England.

With such a background and diversity of interests, we can understand Krafft-Ebing's later distrust of the early pronouncements of the young and then inexperienced Sigmund Freud. Actually, Krafft-Ebing and Freud shared a fascination with sexual problems, and each risked social and professional disapproval for his ideas and publications. The two psychiatric leaders differed in emphasis and approach. Freud spent his time studying sexual development while Krafft-Ebing tried to explain the phenomenological facts of daily sexual existence. Krafft-Ebing carried with him the old German conviction of hereditary predisposition, which Freud disavowed in his angry protest against tradition. The truth, as usual, lay somewhere between the two viewpoints, and both Freud and Krafft-Ebing succeeded in making essential contributions to the advancement of psychiatric knowledge.

Today, Krafft-Ebing is remembered mainly for his book on sexual deviation, *Psychopathia Sexualis*, a study based on years of forensic experience and having the same aim as the pioneering work of Alfred Kinsey. Krafft-Ebing's *Psychopathia Sexualis* has remained our most informative scientific volume on sexual deviation for nearly a hundred years. His insight into the underworld of the deviate has been emulated but never surpassed.

Unfortunately, a curtain enveloped Krafft-Ebing during the Victorian era, and his name still carries a disreputable connotation in some circles. The paucity of published information about his life and achievements may be attributable to this notoriety. Krafft-Ebing himself seems to have anticipated the furor his book on sexual deviation created. After resigning from his professorship at Strasbourg, he founded the Sanatorium Marigrum near Graz, Austria, where he lived in peaceful seclusion during the 1880's. Finally, the call came from Vienna, and Krafft-Ebing assumed the highest academic position by taking over Meynert's clinic and teaching activities.

Increasing responsibility did not stop Krafft-Ebing from revising *Psychopathia Sexualis* through its twelfth edition. Each edition contains new case material, gathered from colleagues throughout the world. The book covers the full spectrum of sexual deviations, including fetichism, nymphomania, satyriasis, sadism, and incest. Krafft-Ebing defined masochism and emphasized the importance of clitoral orgasm. Also, he had the courage to begin the scientific discussion of homosexuality. While *Psychopathia Sexualis* contains macabre sections and descriptions of tortured people, it is a medical work designed to enlighten, not to stimulate sensationalism. It appeared more than twenty years before Freud's *Three Contributions to the Theory of Sex*, and it helped to prepare the public for the open investigation of previously forbidden territory.

Early editions, both in German and in English translation, contained parts rendered obscure by keeping them in Latin. In the translation of these passages, I have had the valued assistance of a leading Latinist; other sections have been clarified from the twelfth German edition. Krafft-Ebing completed revisions for this edition just prior to his death. Medical and psychiatric terminology has been explained whenever necessary.

This is the first complete translation of Krafft-Ebing's indispensable book, (there have been many bowdlerized versions, of course). Krafft-Ebing richly deserves his place in the library of every person interested in the science of human behavior.

—Franklin S. Klaf, M.D., M.P.H.

FOREWORD

THE casual observer, glancing curiously through the pages of this book, now brought again to the attention of the public in a new and more up-to-date translation, may be more concerned with the details of case histories commonly found only in medical libraries than with any sense of the place this book has in the gradual enlightenment of the public on problems of behavioral abnormalities not uncommon in the psychiatric consultation room or in the courtroom. Richard von Krafft-Ebing wrote *Psychopathia Sexualis* as a textbook in a branch of medicine which needed documentation. He was a highly reputable and accredited scientist of the day and illuminated through this book a hitherto neglected area of human propensity. This aspect of the author's varied scientific contributions has been held to be controversial in some quarters. The positive values of advancing further social and medical inquiries in this dark corner of knowledge and understanding has more than compensated for the feelings of morbid curiosity in some persons and the harm that may have been done. To the student of today the book is primarily of historical value. The body of the text and the comments of various translators in the succeeding editions serve as a valuable reflection of advanced thinking of the time and the social and professional reactions to the subject matter, a mixture of moral and professional judgment.

The teachers who influenced Krafft-Ebing most were Friedrich at Heidelberg, who gave him a bent toward neurology, and Griesinger, under whom he worked at Zurich. Krafft-Ebing also based his work on Jacoby's inexhaustible studies of mental disorders, Spielmann's thoughtful work on diagnosis, Jensen's brilliant and thorough articles in the *Berlin Encyclopedia*, and the works of Pinel and Esquirol; he was inspired, too, by Windt's lectures on the soul of man and animals, Fechner's technique of psycho-physics, the discovery of vascular nerves, and Morel's theory of heredity.

Several significant things can be construed from the obituary of Krafft-Ebing which appeared in *The British Medical Journal*. The obituary appeared on January 3, 1903, only eleven days after Krafft-Ebing's death, which attests to his importance. But the obituary's reference to the present work reflects attitudes toward its subject matter. It says: "He was a copious contributor to the literature of his specialty. Among his works are a textbook of psychiatry which has gone through six editions; a textbook of medico-legal and psycho-pathology . . . His name was brought into unfortunate prominence by his book entitled *Psychopathia*

Sexualis, of which an unfavorable opinion was expressed in *The British Medical Journal* some time ago. . . . Krafft-Ebing, however, made many valuable contributions to neurology for which his name must be held in honor."

The *Allgemeine Weine Medezinische Zeitung* said: "By 1889, he was world famous, he had a high title, and he was known as an extraordinary lecturer. His textbook of psychiatry was most important; even more so was his textbook of judicial psychopathology. There was much controversy about his work as he had attacked so many institutions and superstitions. He revolutionized popular attitudes about sexual inverts by seeing them as persons of unusual development rather than as degenerates or invalids."

Perhaps because Krafft-Ebing's name is associated almost exclusively with the subject of sexual psychopathy, even most physicians today are unaware of the great work in his *Textbook of Psychiatry* which was translated in 1904 by Charles Gilbert Chaddock, M.D. Frederick Peterson, M.D., President of the New York State Lunacy Commission, said of Krafft-Ebing in his Foreword to the American edition: "During his stay at Graz in 1873, he began to interest himself in hypnotism and sketched out that volume on psychopathia sexualis which brought him both recognition and criticism. In 1886 his *Textbook of Psychiatry* was published. There is perhaps no other work in psychiatry, in any language, which has had the vogue, the wide distribution, and the popularity of this of Krafft-Ebing. Following his accession to the chair of psychiatry at the Royal University of Vienna, he entered into his golden period. Honors and recognitions were showered upon him, not only in his own country but by many professional bodies and associations abroad.

"He became a careful and most painstaking clinician. He weighed every psychic and somatic symptom seeking the inner connections in the evolution of mental disorder by the minutist study of the changes in physical and mental conditions, and by the preparation of the most complete histories of his cases."

Robinson, in his introduction to the English version of the twelfth edition of *Psychopathia Sexualis*, says: "He did not want the public to read his book; it was meant for doctors, lawyers, and judges exclusively. He, therefore, used technical language and put the specific descriptions of sexual acts in Latin. With each edition of the book he attempted to make it more obscure to the public . . . Krafft-Ebing's opinions were realistic and sensible. . . . He felt that civilization has spread many such unnatural evils and linked civilization and socialization. He called sexual inverts the stepchildren of nature."

Krafft-Ebing was one of the first to face the anticipated criticism over bringing the matter of sexuality into the open. Two other prominent persons joined him in this endeavor, Sigmund Freud and Havelock Ellis.

Freud says little about Krafft-Ebing except for one or two notable comments. In Ernest Jones's life of Freud, we find: "On May 2, 1896,

Freud gave an address to the Society of Psychiatry and Neurology in Vienna entitled 'The Etiology of Hysteria.' It was published in amplified form later in the year. According to Freud, the paper met with an icy reception. Krafft-Ebing, who was in the chair, contented himself with saying, 'It sounds like a scientific fairy tale.' " Jones then quotes Freud himself in regard to this episode: "I did not at first perceive the peculiar nature of what I had discovered. Without thinking, I sacrificed at this inception my popularity as a physician and the growth of a large consulting practice among nervous patients, by inquiries relating to the sexual factors involved in the causation of the neurosis; this brought me a great many new facts which definitely confirmed my conviction of the practical importance of the sexual factor. Unsuspectingly, I spoke before the Vienna Neurological Society, then under the presidency of Krafft-Ebing, expecting to be compensated by the interest and recognition of my colleagues for the material loss I had willingly undergone. I treated my discoveries as ordinary contributions to science and hoped they would be met with the same spirit, but the silence with which my addresses were received, the void which formed itself about me, the insinuations that found their way to me, caused me gradually to realize that one can't count upon views about the part played by sexuality in the etiology of the neuroses meeting with the same reception as other communications. I understood that from now on I belong to those who have 'troubled the sleep of the world,' as Habbel says, and that I could not count upon objectivity and tolerance."

Freud speaks with gratitude of Krafft-Ebing, however, in connection with Freud's desire for a higher rank at the University of Vienna, and Krafft-Ebing, along with Nothnagel and Frankel-Hochaart worked actively to obtain the position of Associate Professor for Freud.

Freud also referred once to Krafft-Ebing's work itself: "With regard to a case where the childhood remembrances were confirmed by seeing an old nurse, this provided new valuable evidence that the soundness of my material is provided by its agreement with the perversions described by Krafft-Ebing."

Havelock Ellis has contributed the most searching comments on Krafft-Ebing. He says in *Studies in the Psychology of Sex:* "Of much more importance in the history of the theory of sexual inversion is the work of Dr. R. von Krafft-Ebing. . . . his great work, *Psychopathia Sexualis,* in the eleventh edition, contains over two hundred histories. They are not all original cases, however, and they cover not only sexual inversion but all forms of sexual perversion. *Psychopathia Sexualis* is the best known work on the subject and the chief storehouse of facts. Krafft-Ebing's methods are open to some objection. His mind is not of a severly critical order. He has poured out new and ever enlarged editions of his great work with extraordinary rapidity . . . The various editions . . . have been remodeled from time to time, and interesting material sometimes has been thrown out. . . .

"Krafft-Ebing's great service lies in the clinical enthusiasm with which he has approached the study of sexual perversion, with the firm conviction that he is conquering a great neglected field of morbid psychology, which rightly belongs to the physician. He has accumulated, without any false shame, a vast mass of detailed histories, and his reputation has induced sexually abnormal individuals in all directions to send him their autobiographies in the desire to benefit their fellow men.

"It is as the great clinician of sexual inversion rather than a psychologist we must regard Krafft-Ebing."

With regard to the public criticism which would come at the publication of such personal material as was contained in the case histories, Krafft-Ebing himself was quite well aware. You will find in his own author's preface to this work, his defense well worked out in advance.

Krafft-Ebing's defensiveness was warranted by the prevailing attitudes. For instance, *The British Medical Journal,* in 1893, said of *Psychopathia Sexualis:* "We have considered at length whether we should notice this book or not, but we deem the importance of the subject and the position of the author make it necessary to refer to it in consideration of the feelings with which it has been discussed by the public. We have questioned whether it should have been translated into English at all. Those concerned could have gone to the original. Better if it had been written entirely in Latin, and thus veiled in the decent obscurity of a dead language. . . ."

The translator's preface to the seventh edition quotes at length from Dr. Schrenck-Notzing of Munich: "It may be questioned whether it is justifiable to discuss the anomalies of the sexual instinct apart, instead of treating them in their proper place in psychiatry. . . . Moreover, attention has been ascribed to the baneful influence possibly exerted by such publications as *Psychopathia Sexualis.* To be sure the appearance of seven editions of that work could not be accounted for were its circulation confined to psychiatric readers. . . . But . . . the injury done by implanting knowledge of sexual pathology in unqualified persons is not to be compared with the good accomplished. . . . For the physician himself, sexual anomalies, treated as they are in a distant manner in textbooks on psychiatry, are in greater part a 'terra incognita.' . . . a thorough knowledge of the obscuration of the sexual instinct is indispensable to the jurist."

In the preface to the tenth edition, translated by F. J. Rebman in 1901, he says, "The exceptionally favorable criticisms are guarantee that the book exercises a beneficent influence upon legislation and jurisprudence and will assist in removing erroneous ideas and superannuated laws.

"Its commercial success is the best proof that large numbers of unfortunate people find in its pages instruction and relief in the frequently enigmatical manifestations of sexual life. . . ."

I have presented to the reader a good sampling of the opinions of Krafft-Ebing's colleagues and contemporaries—perhaps the most appropriate judgment of his historically important work. Today's reader should

clearly recognize that the conclusions and opinions given in this nineteenth century textbook have little scientific value today, though some
broad generalities may still hold true. The case histories represent the
general level of descriptive approach of the day but do not contain the
exhaustive study that has made Sigmund Freud's contributions, often on
similar subjects, of far more lasting value. Krafft-Ebing is recognized as
one who has pushed forward the understanding of the homosexual individual, to some degree giving him a somewhat more favorable opportunity
to be understood by the public.

This historical document is, then, a relic of the attempts in the late
nineteenth century to bring the facts on man's psychopathic sexuality to
the light of thoughtful exposure.

Dr. Klaf has rendered a service in preparing a translation as much
as possible in keeping with demands of accuracy in modern English.

Daniel Blain, M.D., F.A.C.P., F.A.P.A.
Philadelphia, February, 1965

AUTHOR'S PREFACE TO THE FIRST EDITION

FEW people are conscious of the deep influence exerted by sexual life upon the sentiment, thought and action of man in his social relations to others. *Schiller*, in his essay "Die Weltweisen," touches upon this subject in these memorable words: "So long as philosophy keeps together the structure of the Universe so long does it maintain the world's machinery by hunger and love."

From the standpoint of the philosopher sexual life takes a subordinate position.

Schopenhauer ("Die Welt als Wille und Vorstellung," third edition, vol. ii, p. 586, etc.) considers it peculiar that love has hitherto offered material to the poet only and not also to the philosopher, the scant researches by *Plato, Rousseau* and *Kant* always excepted.

Whatever *Schopenhauer*, and after him *E. von Hartmann*, the philosopher of the unknown, discuss about sexual relationship, is so thoroughly incorrect and illogical that, so far as science is concerned, empirical psychology and the metaphysics of man's sexual existence are simply virgin soil. *Michelet's* "L'amour" and *Mantegazza's* "Physiology of Love" are merely clever causeries, and cannot be considered in the light of scientific research.

The poet is the better psychologist, for he is swayed rather by sentiment than by reason, and always treats his subject in a partial fashion. He cannot discern deep shadows, because he is dazed by the blazing light and overcome by the benign heat of the subject. Although the "Physiology of Love" provides inexhaustible material for the poetry of all ages and of all peoples, nevertheless the poet will not discharge his arduous task adequately without the active co-operation of natural philosophy and, above all, that of medicine, a science which ever seeks to trace all psychological manifestations to their anatomical and physiological sources.

In these efforts medicine succeeds, perhaps, in forming a connection between the pessimistic reflections of the philosopher of the stamp of *Schopenhauer* and *Hartmann*,[1] and the gay and naïve creations of the poet.

It is not intended to build up in this book a system of the psychology of sexual life, still from the close study of psychopathology there arise most important psychological facts which it behooves the scientist to notice.

The object of this treatise is merely to record the various psycho-pathological manifestations of sexual life in man and to reduce them to their lawful conditions. This task is by no means an easy one, and the author is well aware of the fact that, despite his (varied) far-reaching experience in psychiatry and criminal medicine, he is yet unable to offer anything but an imperfected system.

The importance of the subject, however, demands scientific research on account of its forensic bearing and its deep influence upon the common weal. The medical barrister only then finds out how sad the lack of our knowledge is in the domain of sexuality when he is called upon to express an opinion as to the responsibility of the accused whose life, liberty and honour are at stake. He then begins to appreciate the efforts that have been made to bring light into darkness.

Certain it is that so far as sexual crimes are concerned erroneous ideas prevail, unjust decisions are given, and the law as well as public opinion are on first view prejudiced against the offender.

The scientific study of the psychopathology of sexual life necessarily deals with the miseries of man and the dark sides of his existence, the shadow of which contorts the sublime image of the deity into horrid caricatures, and leads astray aestheticism and morality.

It is the sad privilege of medicine, and especially that of psychiatry, to ever witness the weaknesses of human nature and the reverse side of life.

The physician finds, perhaps, a (satisfaction) solace in the fact that he may at times refer those manifestations which offend against our ethical or aesthetical principles to a diseased condition of the mind or the body. He can save the honour of humanity in the forum of morality, and the honour of the individual before the judge and his fellow-men. It is from the search of truth that the exalted duties and rights of medical science emanate.

The author adopts the saying of *Tardieu* ("Attacks upon morals"): "No physical or moral misery, no wound, no matter how infected, should frighten someone who has dedicated himself to the science of man; and the sacred ministry of the physician, while obliging him to see everything, also permits him to say everything."

Psychopathia
Sexualis

I. FRAGMENTS OF A SYSTEM OF PSYCHOLOGY OF SEXUAL LIFE

THE propagation of the human race is not left to mere accident or the caprices of the individual, but is guaranteed by the hidden laws of nature which are enforced by a mighty, irresistible impulse. Sensual enjoyment and physical fitness are not the only conditions for the enforcement of these laws, but higher motives and aims, such as the desire to continue the species or the individuality of mental and physical qualities beyond time and space, exert a considerable influence. Man puts himself at once on a level with the beast if he seeks to gratify lust alone, but he elevates his superior position when by curbing the animal desire, he combines with the sexual functions ideas of morality, of the sublime, and the beautiful.

Placed upon this lofty pedestal, he stands far above nature and draws from inexhaustible sources material for nobler enjoyments, for serious work and for the realization of ideal aims. *Maudsley* ("Deutsche Klinik," 1873, 2, 3) justly claims that sexual feeling is the basis upon which social advancement is developed.

If man were deprived of sexual fulfillment and the nobler enjoyments arising therefrom, all poetry and probably all moral tendency would be eliminated from his life.

Sexual life no doubt is the one mighty factor in the individual and social relations of man which discloses his powers of activity, of acquiring property, of establishing a home, of awakening altruistic sentiments towards a person of the opposite sex, and towards his own issue as well as towards the whole human race.

Sexual feeling is really the root of all ethics, and no doubt of aestheticism and religion.

The sublimest virtues, even the sacrifice of self, may spring from sexual life, which, however, on account of its sensual power, may easily degenerate into the lowest passion and basest vice.

Love unbridled is a volcano that burns down and lays waste all around it: it is an abyss that devours all—honour, substance and health.

It is of great psychological interest to follow up the gradual development of civilization and the influence exerted by sexual life upon habits and morality.[1] The gratification of the sexual instinct seems to be the primary motive in man as well as in beast. Sexual intercourse is done openly, and men and women are not ashamed of their nakedness. The savage races, *e.g.*, Australasians, Polynesians, Malays of the Philippines are still in this stage (see *Ploss*). Woman is the common property of man, the spoil of the strongest and mightiest, who chooses the most winsome for his own, a sort of instinctive sexual selection of the fittest.

Woman is a "chattel," an article of commerce, exchange or gift, a vessel for sensual gratification, an implement for toil. The presence of shame in the manifestations and exercise of the sexual functions, and of modesty in the mutual relations between the sexes are the foundations of morality. Thence arises the desire to cover the nakedness ("and they saw that they were naked") and to perform the act in private.

The development of this grade of civilization is furthered by the conditions of frigid climes which necessitate the protection of the whole body against the cold. It is an anthropological fact that modesty can be traced to much earlier periods among northern races.[2]

Another element which tends to promote the refined development of sexual life is the fact that woman ceases to be a "chattel." She becomes an individual being, and, although socially still far below man, she gradually acquires rights, independence of action, and the privilege to bestow her favours where she inclines. She is wooed by man. Traces of ethical sentiments pervade the rude sensual appetite, idealization begins and community of woman ceases. The sexes are drawn to each other by mental and physical merits and exchange favours of preference. In this stage woman is conscious of the fact that her charms belong only to the man of her choice. She seeks to hide them from others. This forms the foundation of modesty, chastity and sexual fidelity so long as love endures.

This development is hastened wherever nomadic habits yield to the spirit of colonization, where man establishes a household. He feels the necessity for a companion in life, a housewife in a settled home.

The *Egyptians*, the *Israelites*, and the *Greeks* reached this level at early periods, as did the *Teutonic* races. Its principal characteristics are high appreciation of virginity, chastity, modesty and sexual fidelity in strong contrast to the habits of other peoples, where the host places the personal charms of the wife at the disposal of the guest.

The history of Japan furnishes a striking proof that this high grade of civilization is often the last stage of moral development, for in that country twenty years ago prostitution was not considered to impair in any way the social status of the future wife.

Christianity raised the union of the sexes to a sublime position by making woman socially the equal of man and by elevating the bond of love to a moral and religious institution.[3] Thence emanates the fact that the love of man, if considered from the standpoint of advanced civilization, can only be of a monogamic nature and must rest upon a stable basis. Even though nature should claim merely the law of propagation, a community (family or state) cannot subsist without the guarantee that the offspring thrive physically, morally and intellectually. From the moment when woman was recognized the peer of man, when monogamy became a law and was consolidated by legal, religious and moral conditions, the Christian nations attained a mental and material superiority over the polygamic races, and especially over Islam.

Mohammed strove to raise woman from the position of the slave and mere handmaid of enjoyment, to a higher social and matrimonial grade; yet she remained still far below man, who alone could obtain divorce, and that on the easiest terms.

Above all things Islamism excludes woman from public life and enterprise, and stifles her intellectual and moral advancement. The Mohammedan woman is simply a means for sensual gratification and the propagation of the species; whilst in the sunny balm of Christian doctrine, blossom forth her divine virtues and her qualities of housewife, companion and mother. What a contrast!

Compare the two religions and their standard of future happiness. The Christian expects a heaven of spiritual bliss absolutely free from carnal pleasure; the Mohammedan, an eternal harem, a paradise among lovely houris. Yet, in spite of the aid which religion, law, education and the moral code offer him, the Christian (to subdue his sensual inclination) often drags pure and chaste love from its sublime pedestal and wallows in the quagmire of sensual enjoyment and lust.

Life is a never-ceasing duel between the animal instinct and morality. Only will-power and a strong character can emancipate man from the meanness of his corrupt nature, and teach him how to enjoy the pure pleasures of love and pluck the noble fruits of earthly existence.

It is an open question whether the moral status of mankind has undergone an improvement in our times. No doubt society at large shows a greater veneer of modesty and virtue, and vice is not as flagrantly practiced as of yore.

The reader of *Scherr* ("Deutsche Culturgeschichte") will gain the impression that our moral code is not so gross as was that of the middle ages, even if only more refined manners have taken the place of former coarseness.

In comparing the various stages of civilization it becomes evident that, despite periodical relapses, public morality has made steady progress, and that Christianity is the chief factor in this advance.

We are certainly far beyond sodomitic idolatry, the public life, legislation and religious exercises of ancient Greece, not to speak of the worship of Phallus and Priapus, in vogue among the Athenians and Babylonians, or the Bacchanalian feasts of the Romans and the privileged position held by the courtesans of those days.

There are stagnant and fluctuating periods in this slow progress, but they are only like the ebb- and flood-tide of sexual life in the individual.

The episodes of moral decay always coincide with the progression of effeminacy, lewdness and luxuriance of the nations. These phenomena can only be ascribed to the higher and more stringent demands which circumstances make upon the nervous system. Exaggerated tension of the nervous system stimulates sensuality, leads the individual as well as the masses to excesses, and undermines the very foundations of society, and the morality and purity of family life. The material and moral ruin of the community is readily brought about by debauchery, adultery and luxury. Greece, the Roman Empire, and France under Louis XIV. and XV., are striking examples of this assertion. In such periods of civic and moral decline the most monstrous excesses of sexual life may be observed, which, however, can always be traced to psycho-pathological or neuro-pathological conditions of the nation involved.[4]

Large cities are hotbeds in which neuroses and low morality are bred, as is evident in the history of Babylon, Nineveh, Rome and the mysteries of modern metropolitan life. It is a remarkable fact that among savages and half-civilized races sexual intemperance is not observed (except among the Aleutians and the Oriental and Nama-Hottentot women who practice masturbation).[5]

The study of sexual life in the individual naturally deals with its various phases, beginning with the stage of puberty to the extinction of sexual feeling.

Mantegazza ("Physiology of Love") draws a beautiful picture of the bodings and yearnings of awakening love, of the mysterious sensations, foretastes and impulses that fill the heart, long before the period of puberty has arrived. Psychologically speaking, this is, perhaps, the most momentous epoch of life, for the wealth of ideas and sentiments engendered through it, forms the standard by which psychic activity may be measured.

The advance of puberty develops the impulses of youth, hitherto vague and undefined, into conscious realization of the sexual power. The psychological reactions of animal passion manifest themselves in the irresistible desires of intimacy, and the longing to bestow the strange affections of nature upon others.

Religion and poetry frequently become the temporary haven of rest, even after the period of storm and stress is passed. Religious enthusiasm is more commonly met with in the young than the old. The lives of the saints [6] are replete with remarkable records of temptations. The religious feasts of the ancients often degenerated into orgies, or into mystic cults of a voluptuous character. Even the meetings of certain modern sects dissolve themselves simply into obscene practices.

On the contrary we find that the sexual instinct, when disappointed and unappeased, frequently seeks and finds a substitute in religion.

Even where psycho-pathological conditions are diagnosed beyond dispute, this relation between religious and sexual feelings can easily be established. The cause of religious insanity is often to be found in sexual aberration. In psychosis a motley mixture of religious and sexual delusions is observable, *viz.*, in female lunatics who imagine that they are or will be the mother of God, and especially in persons slaves to masturbation. The cruel, sensual acts of chastisement, violation, emasculation and even crucifixion perpetrated upon self by religious maniacs, bear out this assertion.[7]

Any attempt to explain the psychological relations between religion and love must needs meet with difficulties, for analogous instances are met with in great numbers.

Sexual inclinations and religious leanings (if considered as psychological factors), are composed of two elements.

Schleiermacher recognized the primary feeling of dependence as the paramount element in religion, long before modern anthropological and ethnographic research in the domain of primitive causes, arrived at the same conclusions.

The secondary and truly ethical element, *i.e.*, the love of God, enters the religious sentiment only when a higher stage of culture is attained. At first, the double-faced, now benevolent, now angry, chimeras of complicated mythologies, take the place of the evil spirits, until they in turn are dislodged by the benign form of the deity, the giver of perpetual happiness, whether it be in the shape of Jehovah as the author of all earthly blessings, or Allah who bestows physical delight in Paradise, or Christ who is gone before to prepare mansions of eternal light and bliss, or Nirvana who reigns in the heaven of the Buddhist.

The primary element of *sexual preference* is love, *i.e.*, the expectation of unsurpassed pleasure. The secondary element is the feeling of dependence, although it is in reality the root from which both arise, as the former may be entirely absent. It certainly exists in a stronger measure in woman, on account of her social position, and the passive part which she takes in the act of procreation; but at times it is also found in men who are of a feminine type.

Religion as well as sexual love is mystical and transcendental. In sexual love the real object of the instinct, *i.e.*, propagation of the species, is not always present in the mind during the act, and the impulse is much stronger than could be justified by the gratification that can possibly be derived from it. Religious love strives for the possession of an object that is absolutely ideal, and cannot be defined by experimental knowledge. Both are metaphysical processes which give unlimited scope to imagination.

They converge, however, in a similar *indefinite* focus; for the gratification of the sensual appetite promises a boon which far surpasses all other conceivable pleasures, and faith has in store a bliss that endures for ever.

In either condition the mind is conscious of the enormous importance of the object to be obtained; thus impulses often become irresistible and overcome all opposing motives. But because neither of them can at times grasp the real object of their existence, they easily degenerate into fanaticism, in which intensity of emotion overbalances clearness and stability of reason. Expectation of unfathomed bliss is now coupled with reckless resignation and unconditional submission.

Owing to this conformity it happens that under high tension one dislodges the other, or that both make their appearance together; for every violent upheaval in the soul must necessarily sweep along its surroundings. Nature, always the same, draws alike upon these two spheres of conception, now forcing one, then the other into stronger activity, which degenerates even into acts of cruelty either actively exercised, or passively endured.

In religious life this may assume the shape of self-sacrifice or self-destruction, prompted by the idea that the victim is necessary for the material sustenance of the deity. The sacrifice is brought as a sign of reverence or submission, as a tribute, as an atonement for sins committed, or as a price wherewith to purchase happiness.

If, however, the offering consists in self-punishment—and that occurs in all religions!—it serves not only as a symbol of submission, or an equivalent in the exchange of present pain for future bliss, but everything that is thought to come from the deity, all that is done in obedience to divine mandates or to the honour of the Godhead, is felt directly as pleasure. Thus religious exuberance leads to ecstasy, a condition in which consciousness is so preoccupied with feelings of mental pleasure, that distress is stripped of its painful quality.

Exaggerated religious enthusiasm also finds pleasure in the sacrifice of another person, when rapture combines with sympathy.

Similar manifestations may be observed in sexual life, as will be shown later on under the headings of Sadism and Masochism.

Thus the relations existing between religion, lust, and cruelty may be condensed into the formula: Religious and sexual hyperaesthesia at the zenith of development show the same volume of intensity and the same quality of excitement, and may therefore, under given circumstances, interchange. Both will in certain pathological states degenerate into cruelty.

Sexual influence is just as potent in the awakening of aesthetic sentiments. What other foundation is there for sculpture or poetry? From (sensual) love arises that warmth of fancy which alone can inspire the creative mind, and the fire of sensual feeling kindles and preserves the glow and fervour of art.

This explains the sensual natures of great poets and artists.

The world of fancy keeps pace with the development of sexual power. Whoever during that period cannot be animated by the ideals of all that is great, noble and beautiful remains a "Philistine" all his life. Even the dolt tries his hand at poetry when in love.

On the borders of physiological reaction may be observed those mysterious processes of maturing puberty, which give origin to obscure yearnings and moods of despondency and *Weltschmerz*, rendering life tedious, and coupled with the impulse to inflict pain and sorrow upon others (weak analogies of a psychological connection between lust and cruelty).

First love always looks in a romantic idealizing direction. It wraps the beloved object in the halo of perfection. In its incipient stages it is of a platonic character, and turns rather to forms of poetry and history. With the approach of puberty it runs the risk of transferring the idealizing powers upon persons of the opposite sex, even though mentally, physically and socially they be of an inferior station. To this may easily be traced many cases of misalliance, abduction, elopement and errors of early youth, and those sad tragedies of passionate love that are in conflict with the principles of morality or social standing, and often terminate in murder, self-destruction, and double suicide.

Purely sensual love is never true and lasting, for which reason first love is, as a rule, but a passing infatuation, a fleeting passion.

True love is rooted in the recognition of the moral and mental qualities of the beloved person, and is equally ready to share pleasures and sorrows and even to make sacrifices. True love shrinks from no dangers or obstacles in the struggle for the undisputed possession of the beloved.

Deeds of daring and heroism lie in its wake. But unless the moral foundation be solid, it will lead to crime, and jealousy often mars its beauty.

The love of the feeble-minded is based upon sentimentality, and when unrequited, results in suicide.

Sentimental love is likely to degenerate into a burlesque, especially when the sensual element lacks force (e.g., the Knight of Joggenburg, Don Quixote, and many of the minstrels and troubadours of the middle ages).

This kind of love is nauseating and has a repulsive or ludicrous effect on others, whilst true love and its manifestations command sympathy, respect, and even fear.

Love when weak is frequently turned away from its real object into different channels, such as voluptuous poetry, bizarre aesthetics, or religion. In the latter case it readily falls a prey to mysticism, fanaticism, sectarianism or religious mania. A smattering of all this can always be found in the immature love of early puberty. The poetical effusions of that period of life are only then worthy of perusal when emanating from the pen of the truly endowed genius.

Ethical surroundings are necessary in order to elevate love to its true and pure form, but, notwithstanding, sensuality will ever remain its principal basis.

Platonic love is a platitude, a misnomer for "kindred spirits."

Since love implies the presence of sexual desire it can only exist between persons of different sex capable of sexual intercourse. When these conditions are wanting or destroyed, it is replaced by friendship.

The sexual functions of man exercise a very marked influence upon the development and preservation of character. Manliness and self-reliance are not the qualities which adorn the impotent onanist.

Gyurkovechky ("Männl. Impotenz," Wien, 1889) is correct in his observation that virility establishes the ratio of difference between old men and young, and that impotence impairs health, mental freshness, activity, self-confidence and imagination. The damage stands in proportion to the age of the subject and the extent of his debauchery.

The sudden loss of the virile powers often produces melancholia, or is the cause of suicide when life without love is a mere blank.

In cases where the reaction is less pronounced, the victim is morose, peevish, egotistical, jealous, narrow-minded, cowardly, devoid of energy, self-respect and honour.

The Skoptzi, for instance, after castration rapidly degenerate.

This matter will be further elucidated under the heading of "Effemination" (see below).

In the sedate matron this condition is of minor psychological importance, though it is noticeable. The biological change affects her but little if her sexual career has been successful, and loving children gladden the maternal heart. The situation is different, however, where sterility has denied that happiness, or where enforced celibacy prevented the performance of the natural functions.

These facts characterize strongly the differences that prevail in the psychology of sexual life in man and woman, and the dissimilarity of sexual feeling and desire in both.

Man has beyond doubt the stronger sexual appetite of the two. From the period of pubescence he is instinctively drawn towards woman. His love is sensual, and his choice is strongly prejudiced in favour of physical attractions. A mighty impulse of nature makes him aggressive and impetuous in his courtship. Yet the law of nature does not wholly fill his psychic being. Having won the prize, his love is temporarily eclipsed by other vital and social interests.

Woman, however, if physically and mentally normal, and properly educated, has but little sensual desire. If it were otherwise, marriage and family life would be empty words. As yet the man who avoids women, and the woman who seeks men are sheer anomalies.

Woman is wooed for her favour. She remains passive. Her sexual organization demands it, and the dictates of good breeding come to her aid.

Nevertheless, sexual consciousness is stronger in woman than in man. Her need of love is greater; it is continual not periodical, but her love is more spiritual than sensual. Man primarily loves woman as his wife, and then as the mother of his children; the first place in woman's heart belongs to the father of her child, the second to him as husband. Woman is influenced in her choice more by mental than by physical qualities. As mother she divides her love between offspring and husband. Sensuality is merged in the mother's love. Thereafter the wife accepts marital intercourse not so much as a sensual gratification as a proof of her husband's affection.

Woman loves with her whole soul. To woman love is life, to man it is the joy of life. Misfortune in love bruises the heart of man; but it ruins the life of woman and wrecks her happiness. It is really a psychological question worthy of consideration whether woman can truly love twice in her life. Woman's mind certainly inclines more to monogamy than that of man.

In the sexual demands of man's nature will be found the motives of his weakness towards woman. He is enslaved by her, and becomes more and more dependent upon her as he grows weaker, and the more he yields to sensuality. This accounts for the fact that in the periods of decline and luxury sensuousness was the predominant factor. From this arises the social danger when courtesans and their dependents rule the State and finally encompass its ruin.

History shows that great (states)men have often been the slaves of women in consequence of the neuropathic conditions of their constitution.

It shows a masterly psychological knowledge of human nature that the Roman Catholic Church enjoins celibacy upon its priests in order to emancipate them from sensuality, and to concentrate their entire activity in the pursuit of their calling. Nevertheless it is a pity that the celibate state deprives the priest of the ennobling influence exercised by love and marital life upon the character.

From the fact that by nature man plays the aggressive *rôle* in sexual life, he is exposed to the danger of overstepping the limits set by law and morality.

The unfaithfulness of the wife, as compared with that of the husband, is morally of much wider bearing, and should always meet with severer punishment at the hands of the law. The unfaithful wife not only dishonours herself, but also her husband and her family, not to speak of the possible uncertainty of paternity.

Natural instincts and social position are frequent causes of disloyalty in man (the husband), whilst the wife is surrounded by many protecting influences.

Sexual intercourse is of different import to the spinster and to the bachelor. Society claims of the latter modesty, but exacts of the former chastity as well. Modern civilization concedes only to the wife that exalted position, in which woman sexually furthers the moral interests of society.

The ultimate aim, the ideal, of woman, even when she is dragged in the mire of vice, ever is and will be marriage. Woman, as *Mantegazza* properly observes, seeks not only gratification of sensual desires, but also protection and support for herself and her offspring. No matter how sensual man may be, unless also thoroughly depraved, he seeks for a consort only that woman whose chastity he cannot doubt.

The emblem and ornament of woman aspiring to this state, truly worthy of herself, is modesty, so beautifully defined by *Mantegazza* as "one of the forms of physical self-esteem."

To discuss here the evolution of this, the most graceful of virtues in woman, is out of place, but most likely it is an outgrowth of the gradual rise of civilization.

A remarkable contrast may be found in the occasional exposure of physical charms, conventionally sanctioned by the world of fashion, in which even the most discreet maiden will indulge when robed for the ball-room, theatre, or similar social function. Although the reasons for such a display are obvious, the modest woman is fortunately no more conscious of them, than of the motives which underlie periodical fashions that bring certain forms of the body into undue prominence, to say nothing of corsets, etc.

In all times, and among all races, the women are fond of toilet and finery. In the animal kingdom nature has distinguished the male with the greater beauty. Men designate women as the beautiful sex, a gallantry which clearly arises from their sensual requirements. So long as woman seeks only self-gratification in personal adornment, and so long as she remains unconscious of the psychological reasons for thus making herself attractive, no objection can be raised against it, but when done with the fixed purpose of pleasing men, it degenerates into coquetry.

Under analogous circumstances man would make himself ridiculous.

Woman far surpasses man in the natural psychology of love, partly because evolution and training have made love her proper element, and partly because she is animated by more refined feelings (*Mantegazza*).

Even the best of breeding concedes to man that he looks upon woman mainly as a means by which to satisfy the cravings of his natural instinct, though it confines him only to the woman of his choice. Thus civilization establishes a binding social contract which is called marriage, and grants by legal statutes protection and support to the wife and her issue.

It is important, and on account of certain pathological manifestations (to be referred to later on) indispensable, to probe into those psychological events which draw man and woman into that close union which concentrates the fullness of affection upon the beloved one only to the exclusion of all other persons of the same sex.

If one could demonstrate design in the processes of nature—adaptation cannot be denied them—then the fact of fascination by one person of the opposite sex with indifference towards all others, as it occurs between true and happy lovers, would appear as a wonderful provision to ensure monogamy for the promotion of its object.

The scientific observer finds in this loving bond of hearts by no means simply a mystery of souls, but he can refer it nearly always to certain physical or mental peculiarities by which the attracting power is qualified.

Hence the words FETICH and FETICHISM. The word fetich signifies an object, or parts or attributes of objects, which by virtue of association to sentiment, personality, or absorbing ideas, exert a charm (the Portuguese "fetisso") or at least produce a peculiar individual impression which is in no wise connected with the external appearance of the sign, symbol or fetich.[9]

The individual valuation of the fetich extending even to unreasoning enthusiasm is called *fetichism*. This interesting psychological phenomenon may be explained by an empirical law of association, *i.e.*, the relation existing between the notion itself and the parts thereof which are essentially active in the production of pleasurable emotions. It is most commonly found in *religious* and *erotic* spheres. *Religious* fetichism finds its original motive in the delusion that its object, *i.e.*, the idol, is not a mere symbol, but possesses divine attributes, and ascribes to it peculiar wonder-working (relics) or protective (amulets) virtues.

Erotic fetichism makes an idol of physical or mental qualities of a person or even merely of objects used by that person, etc., because they awaken mighty associations with the beloved person, thus originating strong emotions of sexual pleasure. Analogies with religious fetichism are always discernible; for, in the latter, the most insignificant objects (hair, nails, bones, etc.) become at times fetiches which produce feelings of delight and even ecstasy.

The germ of sexual love is probably to be found in the individual charm (fetich) with which persons of opposite sex sway each other.

The case is simple enough when the sight of a person of the opposite sex occurs simultaneously with sexual excitement, whereby the latter is intensified.

Emotional and optical impressions combine and are so deeply embedded in the mind that a recurring sensation awakens the visual memory and causes renewed sexual excitement, even orgasm and pollution (often only in dreams), in which case the physical appearance acts as a fetich.

Binet, on the other hand, contends that mere peculiarities, whether physical or mental, may have the effect of the fetich, if their perception coincides with sexual emotion.

Experience shows that chance controls in a large measure this mental association, that the nature of the fetich varies with the personality of the individual, thus arousing the oddest sympathies or antipathies.

These physiological facts of fetichism often account for the affections that suddenly arise between man and woman, the preference of a certain person to all others of the same sex. Since the fetich assumes the form of a distinctive mark, it is clear that its effect can only be of an individual character. Being accentuated by the strongest feelings of pleasure, it follows, that existing faults in the beloved are overlooked ("Love is blind") and an infatuation is produced which appears incomprehensible or silly to others. So it happens that the devoted lover who worships and invests his love with qualities which in reality do not exist, is looked upon by others simply as ludicrous. Thus love exhibits itself now as a mere passion, now as a pronounced psychical anomaly which attains what seemed impossible, renders the ugly beautiful, the profane sublime, and obliterates all consciousness of existing duties towards others.

Tarde ("Archives de l'Anthropologie Criminelle," vol. v, No. 30) argues that the type of this fetich (ism) varies with persons as well as with nations, but that the ideal of beauty remains the same among civilized peoples of the same era.

Binet has more thoroughly analyzed and studied this *fetichism of love.*

From it springs the particular choice for slender or plump forms, for blondes or brunettes, for particular form or colour of the eyes, tone of the voice, odour of the hair or body (even artificial perfume), shape of the hand, foot or ear, etc., which constitute the individual charm, the first link in a complicated chain of mental processes, all converging in that one focus, love, *i.e.,* the physical and mental possession of the beloved.

This fact establishes the existence of *physiological* fetichism.

Without showing a pathological condition the fetich may exercise its power so long as its leading qualities represent the integral parts, and so long as the love engendered by it comprises the entire mental and physical personality.

Max Dessoir (pseudonym Ludwig Brunn) [10] in an article, "The Fetichism of Love," cleverly says:

"Normal love appears to us as a symphony of tones of all kinds. It is roused by the most varied agencies. It is, so to speak, polytheistic. Fetichism recognizes only the tone-colour of a single instrument; it issues forth from a single motive; it is monotheistic."

Even moderate thought will carry the conviction that the term real love (so often misused) can only apply where the entire person of the beloved becomes the physical and mental object of veneration.

Of course, there is always a sensual element in love, *i.e.*, the desire to enjoy the full possession of the beloved object, and, in union with it, to fulfil the laws of nature.

But where the body of the beloved person is made the sole object of love, or if sexual pleasure only is sought without regard to the communion of soul and mind, true love does not exist. Neither is it found among the disciples of Plato, who love the soul only and despise sexual enjoyment. In the one case the body is the fetich, in the other the soul, and love is fetichism.

Instances such as these represent simply transitions to pathological fetichism.

This assumption is enhanced by another criterion of true love, *viz.*, the mental satisfaction derived from the sexual act.[11]

A striking phenomenon in fetichism is that among the many things which may serve as fetiches there are some which gain that significance more commonly than others; for instance, the HAIR, the HAND, the FOOT of woman, or the expression of the EYE. This is important in the pathology of fetichism.

Woman certainly seems to be more or less conscious of these facts. For she devotes great attention to her hair and often spends an unreasonable amount of time and money upon its cultivation. How carefully the mother looks after her little daughter's hair! What an important part the hairdresser plays! The falling out of the hair causes despair to many a young lady. The author remembers the case of a vain woman who fell into melancholia on account of this trouble, and finally committed suicide. A favourite subject of conversation among ladies is *coiffures*. They are envious of each other's luxuriant tresses.

Beautiful hair is a powerful fetich with many men. In the legend of the Lorelei, who lured men to destruction, the "golden hair" which she combs with a golden comb appears as a fetich. Frequently the *hand* or the *foot* possesses an attractiveness no less powerful; but in these instances masochistic and sadistic feelings often—though not always—assist in determining the peculiar kind of fetich.

By a transference through association of ideas, *gloves* or *shoes* obtain the significance of a fetich.

Max Dessoir (*op. cit.*) points out that among the customs of the middle ages drinking from the shoe of a beautiful woman (still to be found in Poland) played a remarkable part in gallantry and homage. The shoe also plays an important *rôle* in the legend of Aschenbrödel.

The *expression of the eye* is particularly important as a means of kindling the spark of love. A neuropathic eye frequently affects persons of either sex as a fetich. "Madame, your beautiful eyes cause me to die of love" (*Molière*).

There are many examples showing that *odours* of the body become fetiches.

This fact is taken advantage of in the "Art of Loving" by woman either consciously or unconsciously. Ruth sought to attract Boaz by perfuming herself. The *demi-monde* of ancient and modern times is noted for its lavish use of strong scents. *Jäger*, in his "Discovery of the Soul," calls attention to many olfactory sympathies.

Cases are known where men have married ugly women solely because their personal odours were exceedingly pleasing.

Binet makes it probable that the voice also may act as a fetich.

Belot in his novel "Les baigneuses de Trouville" makes the same assertion. *Binet* thinks that many marriages with singers are due to the fetich of their voices. He also observes that among the singing birds the voice has the same sexual significance as odours among the quadrupeds. The birds allure by their song, and the male that sings most beautifully is joined at night by the charmed mate.

The pathological facts of masochism and sadism show that mental peculiarities may also act as fetiches, but in a wider sense.

Thus the fact of idiosyncrasies is explained, and the old proverb, "There is no disputing about tastes," retains its force.

With regard to fetichism in women, science must at least for the present time be content with mere conjectures. This much seems to be certain, that since it is a physiological factor, its effects are analogous to those in men, *i.e.*, it produces sexual sympathies towards persons of the same sex.

Details will come to our knowledge only when medical women enter into the study of this subject.

We may take it for granted that the physical as well as the mental qualities of man assume the form of the female fetich. In most cases, no doubt, physical attributes in the male exercise this power without regard to the existence of conscious sensuality. On the other hand, it will be found that the mental superiority of man constitutes the attractive power where physical beauty is wanting. In the upper "strata" of society this is more apparent, even if we disregard the enormous influence exercised by "blue blood" and high breeding. The possibility that superior intellectual development favours advancement in social position, and opens the way to a brilliant career, does not seem to weigh heavily in the balance of judgment.

The fetichism of body and mind is of importance in progeneration; it favours the selection of the fittest and the transmission of physical and mental virtues.

Generally speaking the following masculine qualities impress women, *viz.*, physical strength, courage, nobility of mind, chivalry, self-confidence, even self-assertion, insolence, bravado, and a conscious show of mastery over the weaker sex.

A "Don Juan" impresses many women and elicits admiration, for he establishes the proof of his virile powers, although the inexperienced maiden can in no wise suspect the many risks of lues and chronic urethritis she runs from a marital union with this otherwise interesting rake.

The successful actor, musician, or vocal artist, the circus rider, the athlete, and even the criminal, often fascinate the young miss as well as the maturer woman. At any rate women rave over them, and inundate them with love letters.

It is a well-known fact that the female heart has a predominant weakness for military uniforms, that of the cavalry-man ever having the preference.

The hair of man, especially the beard, the emblem of virility, the secondary symbol of generative power—is a predominant fetich with woman. In the measure in which women bestow special care upon the cultivation of their hair, men who seek to attract and please women, cultivate the elegant growth of the beard, and especially that of the moustache.

The eye as well as the voice exert the same charm. Singers of renown easily touch woman's heart. They are overwhelmed with love letters and offers of marriage. Tenors have a decided advantage.

Binet (*op. cit.*) refers to an observation of this character made by *Dumas* in his novel "La maison du vent." A woman who falls in love with a tenor-voice loses her virtue.

The author has thus far not succeeded in obtaining facts with regard to pathological fetichism in woman.

II. PHYSIOLOGICAL FACTS

DURING the time of the maturation of physiological processes in the reproductive glands, desires arise in the consciousness of the individual, which have for their purpose the perpetuation of the species (sexual instinct).

Sexual desire during the years of sexual maturity is a physiological law. The duration of the physiological processes in the sexual organs, as well as the strength of the sexual desire manifested, vary, both in individuals and in races. Race, climate, heredity and social circumstances have a very decided influence upon it. The greater sensuality of southern races as compared with the sexual needs of those in the north is well known. Sexual development in the inhabitants of tropical climes takes place much earlier than in those of more northern regions. In women of northern countries ovulation, recognizable in the development of the body and the occurrence of a periodical flow of blood from the genitals (menstruation), usually begins about the thirteenth to the fifteenth year; in men puberty, recognizable in the deepening of the voice, the appearance of hair on the face and mons veneris, and the occasional occurrence of pollutions, etc., takes place at about the fifteenth year. In the inhabitants of tropical countries, however, sexual development occurs several years earlier in women—sometimes as early as the eighth year.

It is worthy of note that girls who live in cities develop about a year earlier than girls living in the country, and that the larger the town the earlier, other things being equal, the development takes place.

Heredity, however, has no small influence on *libido* and sexual power. Thus there are families in which, with great physical strength and longevity, great desire and virility are preserved until a great age, while in other families the sexual life develops late and is early extinguished.

In woman the period of activity of the reproductive glands is shorter than in man, in whom sexual power may last until a great age; ovulation ceases about thirty years after puberty. The period of waning activity of the ovaries is called the change of life (*climacterium, menopause*). This biological phase does not represent merely a cessation of functional potency and final atrophy of the reproductive organs, but a transformation of the whole organism.

In Middle Europe the sexual maturity of man begins about the eighteenth year, and virility reaches its acme at forty. After that age it slowly declines. The power of procreation ceases usually at the age of sixty-two, but the power of intercourse may be present much longer.

The existence of the sexual instinct is continuous during the time of sexual life, but it varies in intensity. Under physiological conditions it is never periodical in the human male, as it is in animals; it manifests an organic variation of intensity in consonance with the collection and expenditure of semen. In women the degree of sexual desire coincides with the process of ovulation in such a way that sexual passion is intensified after the menstrual period.

Sexual instinct—as emotion, idea and impulse—is a function of the cerebral *cortex*. Thus far no definite region of the cortex has been proved to be exclusively the seat of sexual sensations and impulses. This psychosexual centre is nothing more than a junction and crossing of principal paths leading on the one hand to the sensitive motor apparatus of the sexual organs, and on the other hand to those nerve centres of the visual and olfactory organs which are the carriers of that consciousness distinguishing between the "male" and the "female."

Owing to the close relations which exist between the sexual instinct and the olfactory sense,[1] it is to be presumed that the sexual and olfactory centres lie close together in the cerebral *cortex*. The development of sexual life has its beginning in the organic sensations which arise from the maturing reproductive glands. These excite the attention of the individual. Reading and the experiences of every-day life (which, unfortunately, are now-a-days too early and too frequently suggestive), convert these notions into clear ideas, which are accentuated by organic sensations of a pleasurable character. With this accentuation of erotic ideas through lustful feelings, an impulse to induce them is developed (sexual desire).

Thus there is established a mutual dependence between the cerebral cortex (as the place of origin of sensations and ideas), and the reproductive organs. The latter, by reason of physiological processes (hyperaemia, secretion of semen, ovulation) give rise to sexual ideas, images, and impulses.

The cerebral cortex, by means of preconceived or reproduced sensual ideas, reacts on the reproductive organs, including hyperaemia, production of semen, erection, ejaculation. This is effected by means of centres for vasomotor innervation and ejaculation, which are situated in the lumbar regions of the cord, and lie close together. Both are reflex centres.

The centre of erection (*Goltz, Eckhard*) is an intermediate station placed between the brain and the genital apparatus. The nervous paths which connect it with the brain probably run through the *pedunculi cerebri* and the *pons*. This centre may be excited by central (psychical and organic) stimuli, by direct irritation of the nerve-tract in the *pedun-*

culis cerebri, pons, or cervical portion of the cord, as well as by peripheral irritation of the sensory nerves (penis, clitoris and annexa). It is not directly subordinated to the will.

The excitation of this centre is conveyed to the *corpora cavernosa* by means of nerves (*nervi erigentes—Eckhard*) running into the first three sacral nerves.

The action of the nervi erigentes, which renders erection possible, is inhibitory in so far as it inhibits the ganglionic nervous mechanism in the *corpora cavernosa,* upon the action of which the erectile tissue of the *corpora cavernosa* is dependent (*Kölliker* and *Kohlrausch*). Under the influence of the action of the excited nerves, these fibres of the *corpora cavernosa* become relaxed, and their spaces fill with blood. Simultaneously, as a result of the dilatation of the capillary net-work of the *corpora cavernosa,* pressure is exerted upon the veins of the penis and the return of blood is impeded. This effect is aided by the contraction of the *bulbo cavernosus* and *erector penis* muscles, which extend by means of an aponeurosis over the dorsal surface of the penis.

The erection-centre is under the influence of both exciting and inhibitory innervation arising from the cerebrum. Ideas and sense-perceptions of sexual content have an exciting effect. According to observations made on men that have been hung, it is evident that the erection-centre may also be aroused by excitation of the tract of the spinal cord. Observations on the insane and those suffering with cerebral disease show that this is also possible as a result of organic irritation in the cerebral cortex (psycho-sexual centre?). Spinal diseases (tabes, especially myelitis) affecting the lumbar portion[2] of the cord, in their earlier stages, may directly excite the erection-centre.

Reflex excitation of the centre is possible and frequent in the following ways: by irritation of the (peripheral) sensory nerves of the genitals and surrounding parts by friction; by irritation of the uretha (gonorrhoea), of the rectum (haemorrhoids, oxyuris), of the bladder (distension with urine, especially in the morning; irritation of calculi); by distension of the seminal vesicles with semen; by increased blood supply to the genitals, occasioned by lying on the back and thus inducing pressure of the intestines upon the blood-vessels of the pelvis.

The erection-centre may also be excited by irritation of the nervous ganglia which are so abundant in the prostatic tissue (prostatitis, introduction of catheter, etc.).

The experiment of *Goltz,* according to whom, when (in dogs) the lumbar portion of the cord is severed, erection is more easily induced, shows that the erection-centre is also subject to inhibitory influences from the brain.

In men the fact that will-power and emotions (fear of unsuccessful coitus, surprise in the midst of the sex act, etc.) may inhibit the occurrence of erection, and cause it, when present, to disappear, also indicates this.

The duration of erection is dependent upon the duration of its exciting causes (sensory stimuli), the absence of inhibitory influences, the nervous energy of the centre, and the early or late occurrence of ejaculation (see below).

The central point of the sexual mechanism is the cerebral cortex. It is justifiable to presume that there is a definite region of the cortex (cerebral centre), which gives rise to sexual feelings, ideas and impulses, and is the place of origin of the psycho-somatic processes which we designate as *sexual life, sexual instinct,* and *sexual desire.* This centre is susceptible to both central and peripheral stimuli.

Central stimuli, in the form of organic excitation, may be due to diseases of the cerebral cortex. Physiologically they are dominated by psychical impressions (memory and sensory perceptions, lascivious stories, touch, pressure of the hand, kiss, etc.). Auditory and olfactory perceptions certainly play but a very subordinate *rôle.* Under pathological conditions (see below), the latter have a very decided influence in inducing sexual excitement.[3]

In beasts the influence of olfactory perception on the sexual sense is unmistakable. *Althaus* ("Beiträge zur Physiol. und Pathol. des Olfactorius," "Archiv. für Psych." xii., H. 1) declares that the sense of smell is important with reference to the reproduction of the species. He shows that animals of opposite sexes are drawn to each other by means of olfactory perception, and that almost all animals, at the time of rutting, emit a specially distinct odour from their genitals. An experiment by *Schiff* is confirmatory of this. He extirpated the olfactory nerves in puppies, and found that, as the animals grew up, the male was unable to distinguish the female. Again, an experiment by *Mantegazza* ("Hygiene of Love"), who removed the eyes of rabbits and found that the defect constituted no obstacle to procreation, shows how important in animals the olfactory sense is for sex life.

It is also remarkable that many animals (musk-ox, civet-cat, beaver), possess on their sexual organs, glands which secrete substances having a very strong odour.

Althaus also shows that in man there are certain relations existing between the olfactory and sexual senses. He mentions *Cloquet* ("Osphrésiologie," Paris, 1826), who calls attention to the sensual pleasure excited by the odour of flowers, and tells how *Richelieu* lived in an atmosphere laden with the heaviest perfumes, in order to excite his sexual functions.

Zippe ("Wien. Med. Wochenschrift," 1879, No. 24), in connection with a case of kleptomania in an onanist, likewise establishes such relations, and cites *Hildebrand* as authority, who in his popular physiology says: "It cannot be doubted that the olfactory sense stands in remote connection with the sexual apparatus. Odours of flowers often occasion pleasurable sensual feelings, and when one remembers the passage in the 'Song of Solomon,' 'And my hands dropped with myrrh, and my fingers with sweet-smelling myrrh, upon the handles of the lock,' one finds that it did not escape Solomon's observation. In the Orient the pleasant perfumes are esteemed for their relation to the sexual organs, and the women's apartments of the Sultan are redolent with the fragrance of flowers."

Most, professor in Rostock (*cf. Zippe*), relates: "I learned from a sensual young peasant that he had excited many a chaste girl sexually, and easily gained his end, by carrying his handkerchief in his axilla for a time, while dancing, and then wiping his partner's perspiring face with it."

The case of Henry III. shows that contact with a person's perspiration may be the exciting cause of passionate love. At the betrothal feast of the King of Navarre and Margaret of Valois, he accidentally dried his face with a garment of Maria of Cleves, which was moist with her perspiration. Although she was the bride of the Prince of Condé, Henry conceived immediately such a passionate love for her that he could not resist it, and made her, as history shows, very unhappy. An analogous instance is related of Henry IV., whose passion for the beautiful Gabriel is said to have originated at the instant when, at a ball, he wiped his brow with her handkerchief.

Professor *Jäger*, the "discoverer of the soul," refers to the same thing in his well-known book (2nd. ed., 1880, chap. xv., p. 173); for he regards the sweat as important in the production of sexual effects, and as being especially seductive.[4]

One learns from reading the work of *Ploss* ("Das Weib"), that attempts to attract a person of the opposite sex by means of the perspiration, may be discerned in many forms in popular psychology.

In reference to this, a custom which holds among the natives of the Philippine Islands when they become engaged, as reported by *Jagor*, is remarkable. When it becomes necessary for an engaged pair to separate, they exchange articles of wearing-apparel, by means of which each becomes assured of faithfulness. These objects are carefully preserved, covered with kisses, and smelled.

The love of certain libertines and sensual women for perfumes[5] indicates a relation between the olfactory and the sexual senses.

A case mentioned by *Heschl* ("Wiener Zeitschrift f. pract. Heilkunde," 22d March, 1861), is remarkable, where the absence of both olfactory lobes was accompanied by imperfectly developed genitals. It was the case of a man aged forty-five, in all respects well developed, with the exception of the testicles, which were not larger than beans and contained no seminal canals, and the larynx, which seemed to be of feminine dimensions. Every trace of olfactory nerves was wanting, and the olfactory trigones and the furrow on the under surface of the anterior lobes were absent. The perforations of the ethmoid plate were sparingly present, and occupied by nerveless processes of the dura instead of by nerves. In the mucous membrane of the nose there was also an absence of nerves.

Finally, the clearly defined relation of the olfactory and sexual senses in mental diseases is worthy of notice, for in the psychoses of both sexes superinduced by masturbation, as well as in insanity due to disease of the female organs, or during the climacterium, olfactory hallucinations are especially frequent, while in cases where a sexual cause is wanting they are very infrequent.

I am inclined to doubt[6] that, under normal conditions, olfactory impressions in man, as in animals, play an important *rôle* in the excitation of the sexual centre. On account of the importance of this sensation for the understanding of pathological cases, it is necessary here to thoroughly consider the relations existing between the olfactory and sexual senses.

With reference to these physiological relations it may be mentioned as an interesting fact that there exists a certain histological conformity between the nose and the genitals, for both have erectile tissue (likewise the nipple).

Interesting physiological and clinical observations by *J. N. Mackenzie* may be found in the "Journal of Medical Science," April, 1884. He finds: (1) that in certain women with normal olfactory organs, regularly with menstruation a swelling of the erectile tissue of the nose occurs which disappears again with the flooding; (2) that menstruation is at times replaced by nosebleeds, which disappear when the uterine flow begins, but in some cases always recur with the menstrual functions; (3) irritations of the nasal organs such as violent sneezing, etc., occur at the time of sexual excitement; (4) stimulation of the genital tracts is occasioned by affections of the nasal organs.

He also observes that nasal affections in women grow worse during the time of menstruation; that venereal excesses produce inflammation of the Schneiderian membrane, or intensify it where it already exists.

He also points out that masturbators very frequently suffer from nasal disease, are troubled with abnormal sensations of olfaction, and are subject to nosebleeds. According to his experience there are affections of the nose which stubbornly resist all treatment until the concomitant (and causal) genital disease is removed.

Other interesting observations and elucidations about the connection between the nose and the genitals may be found in a book by *Fliess* recently published: "Die Beziehungen zwischen Nase und weiblichen Geschlechtsorganen," Vienna (Deuticke), 1897.—*Cerviset*, contribut. a l'étude

du tisses érectile des fosses nasales. Thèse de Lyon 1887. *Joal*, revue men-
suelle de laryngologie 1888 Fevr.—*Peyer*, Münch. med. Wochenschr, 1889.
4;—*Eudriss*, Dissertat., Würzburg 1892.

The sexual sphere of the cerebral cortex may be excited, in the sense
of an excitation of sexual concepts and impulses, by processes in the generative organs. This is possible as a result of all conditions which excite
the erection-centre by means of centripetal influence (stimulus resulting
from distension of the seminal vesicles; enlarged Graafian follicles; any
sensory stimulus, however produced, about the genitals; hyperaemia and
turgescence of the genitals, especially of the erectile tissue of the corpus
cavernosum of the penis and clitoris, as a result of luxurious, sedentary
life; abdominal plethora, high external temperature, warm beds, clothing;
taking of cantharides, pepper and other spices).

Sexual libido may also be induced by stimulation of the gluteal region
(castigation, whipping).[7]

This fact is important for the proper understanding of certain pathological manifestations. It sometimes happens that in boys the first excitation of the sexual instinct is caused by a spanking, and they are thus
incited to masturbation. This should be remembered by those who have
the care of children.

On account of the dangers to which this form of punishment of children gives rise, it would be better if parents, teachers and nurses were to
avoid it entirely.

Passive flagellation may excite sensuality, as is shown by the sects of
flagellants,[8] so widespread in the thirteenth and fifteenth centuries. They
were accustomed to whip themselves, partly as an atonement and partly
to mortify the flesh (in accordance with the principle of chastity promul-
gated by the Church—*i.e.*, the emancipation of the soul from sensuality).

These sects were at first favoured by the Church; but, since sensuality
was only the more excited by flagellation, and this fact became apparent
in unpleasant occurrences, the Church was finally compelled to oppose it.
The following facts from the lives of the two heroines of flagellation,
Maria Magdalena of Pazzi and Elizabeth of Genton, clearly show the
significance of flagellation as a sexual excitant. The former, the daughter of distinguished parents, was a Carmelite nun in Florence (about
1580), and, by her flagellations, and still more through the results obtained
by them, she became quite celebrated, and is mentioned in the "Annals."
It was her greatest delight to have her hands bound by the prioress behind
her back, and her naked loins whipped in the presence of the assembled
sisters.

But the whippings, continued from her earliest youth, quite destroyed
her nervous system, and, perhaps, no other heroine of flagellation had so
many hallucinations ("Entzückungen"). While she was being whipped,
her thoughts were of love. The inner fire threatened to consume her,
and she frequently cried, "Enough! Fan no longer the flame that consumes

me. This is not the death I long for; it comes with all too much pleasure and delight." Thus it continued. But the spirit of impurity wove the most sensual, lascivious fancies, and several times she came near losing her chastity.

It was the same with Elizabeth of Genton. As a result of whipping she actually passed into a state of bacchanalian madness. As a rule, she raved when, excited by unusual flagellation, she believed herself united with her "ideal." This condition was so exquisitely pleasant to her that she would frequently cry out, "O love, O eternal love, O love, O you creatures! cry out with me: 'Love, Love!'"

It is known, on the authority of *Taxil* (*op. cit.*, p. 175), that rakes sometimes have themselves flagellated, or pricked until blood flows, just before the sexual act, in order to stimulate their diminished sexual power.

These facts find an interesting confirmation in the following experiences, taken from *Paullini's* "Flagellum Salutis" (1st ed., 1698; reprint, Stuttgart, 1847):

"There are some nations, *viz.*, the Persians and Russians, where the women regard blows as a peculiar sign of love and favour. Strangely enough, the Russian women are never more pleased and delighted than when they receive hard blows from their husbands, as *John Barclarus* relates in a remarkable narrative. A German, named Jordan, went to Russia, and, pleased with the country, settled there and took a Russian wife, whom he loved dearly, and to whom he was always kind in everything. But she always wore an expression of dissatisfaction, and went about with sighs and downcast eyes. The husband asked the reason, for he could not understand what was wrong. 'Aye,' she said, 'though you love me, you do not show me any sign of it.' He embraced her, and begged to be told what he had carelessly and unconsciously done to hurt her feelings, and to be forgiven, for he would never do it again. 'I want nothing,' was the answer, 'but what is customary in our country—the whip, the real sign of love.' When Jordan adopted the custom, his wife began to love him dearly.

Similar stories are told by *Peter Petreus*, of Erlesund, who adds that husbands, immediately after the wedding, "among other indispensable household articles, provide themselves with a whip."

On page 73 of this remarkable book, the author says further: "The celebrated Count of Mirandula, *John Picus*, relates of one of his intimate acquaintances that he was an insatiable fellow, but so lazy and incapable of love that he was practically impotent until he had been roughly handled. The more he tried to satisfy his desire, the heavier the blows he needed, and he could not attain his desire, unless he had been whipped till the blood came. For this purpose he had a suitable whip made, which was placed in vinegar the day before using it. He would give this to his companion, and on bended knees beg her not to spare him, but to strike blows with it, the heavier the better. The good count thought this singular man found the pleasure of love in this punishment. Not being a bad man in other respects he understood and hated his weakness."

Coelius Rhodigin relates a similar story, as does also the celebrated jurist, *Andreas Tiraquell*. In the time of the skilful physician, *Otten Brunfelsen*, there lived in Munich, then the capital of the Bavarian electorate, a debauchee who could never perform his (sexual) duties without a severe preparatory beating. *Thomas Barthelin* knew a Venetian, who had to be beaten and driven before he could have intercourse, just as reluctant Cupid was driven by his followers with sprays of hyacinths. A few years ago there was in Lübeck a cheesemonger, living on Mill Street, who, on a complaint to the authorities of unfaithfulness, was ordered to leave the city. The prostitute with whom he had been, went to the judges and begged on his behalf, telling how difficult all intercourse had become for him. He could do nothing until he had been mercilessly beaten. At first the fellow, from shame and to avoid disgrace, would not confess, but after earnest questioning he could not deny it. There is said to have been a man in the Netherlands who was similarly incapable, and could do nothing without blows. On the decree of the authorities, however, he was not only removed from his position, but also severely punished. A reliable friend, a physician in an important city of the kingdom, related to me how a woman of bad character had told a companion, who had been in the hospital a short time before, that she, with another woman of like character, had been sent to the woods by a man who followed them there, cut rods for them, and then exposed his naked buttocks, commanded them to beat him thoroughly. They obeyed, and it is easy to conjecture what he then did with them. Not only men have thus been excited and inflamed to lasciviousness, but also women, that they too might experience greater intensity of pleasure.[9] For this reason the Roman woman had herself whipped and beaten by the followers of Pan. Thus Juvenal writes:

> They die sterile, and they are not
> Helped by the contents of Lyde's medicine box
> Nor by holding out their palms for an agile Lupercus to beat.

In men, as well as in women, erection and orgasm, or even ejaculation, may be induced by irritation of various other regions of the skin and mucous membrane. These "hyperaesthetic" zones in woman are, while she is a virgin, the clitoris, and, after defloration, the vagina and cervix uteri.

In woman the nipple particularly seems to possess this quality. Tickling of the nipple region plays an important part in the art of love. In his "Typographical Anatomy," 1865, Bd. i., p. 552, *Hyrtl* cites Val. Hildenbrandt, who observed a peculiar anomaly of the sexual instinct in a girl, which he called masturbation by sucking. She had her breasts sucked by her lover, and after a while, by constantly pulling her nipples, she was enabled to suck them herself, an act that gave her most intense pleasure. *Hyrtl* also calls attention to the fact that cows sometimes suck the milk from their own udders. *L. Brunn* ("Zeitg. f. Literatur," etc., d. Hamburg, Correspondent, 1889, No. 21), in an interesting article on "Sensuality and Love of Kin," points out how zealously the nursing mother gives herself to the nursing of the babe, "for love of the weak, undeveloped, helpless being."

It is easy to assume that, along with the ethical motives, the fact that the sucking may be attended by feelings of physical pleasure plays a part. The remark of *Brunn*, although correct in itself, but one-sided, that, according to *Houzeau's* experience, among the majority of animals the relations between mother and offspring are close only during the time of nursing, and thereafter indifferent, also speaks in favour of this assumption.

Bastian found the same thing (blunting of the feeling for the offspring after weaning) among savages.

Under pathological conditions, as is shown by *Chambard*, among others, in his thesis for the doctorate, other portions of the body (in hysterical persons) about the breasts and genitals may attain the significance of "hyperaesthetic" zones.

In man, physiologically, the only "hyperaesthetic" zone is the penis and perhaps the skin of the external genitals.

Under pathological conditions the anus may become a "hyperaesthetic" area. Thus anal automasturbation, which seems to be only too frequent, and passive pederasty would be explained. (*Cf. Garnier*, "Anomalies sexuelles," Paris, p. 514; *A. Moll*, "Conträre Sexualempfindung," 3rd ed., p. 369; *Frigerio*, "Archivio di Psichiatria," 1893; *Cristiani*, "Archivio delle Psicopatie sessuali," p. 182, "autopederastia in un alienato, affetto da follia periodica.")

The psycho-physiological process comprehended in the idea of sexual instinct is composed of

(1) concepts awakened centrally or peripherally;

(2) the pleasurable feelings associated with them.

The longing for sexual satisfaction (sexual libido) arises from them. This desire grows stronger constantly in proportion as the excitation of the cerebral sphere accentuates the feeling of pleasure, by appropriate concepts and activity of the imagination; and the pleasurable sensations are increased to lustful feeling by excitation of the erection centre and the consequent excess of blood in the genitals (entrance of prostatic fluid into the urethra, etc.).

If circumstances favour the satisfactory performance of the sexual act, the ever-increasing desire is gratified; if, however, conditions are unfavourable, inhibition occurs, checks the central erectile power, and prevents the sexual act.

To civilized man the ready presence of ideas which inhibit sexual desire is of distinct import. The moral freedom of the individual, and the decision whether, under certain circumstances, excess, and even crime, be committed or not, depend, on the one hand, upon the strength of the instinctive impulses and the accompanying organic sensations; on the other, upon the power of the inhibitory ideas. Constitution, and especially organic influences, have a marked effect upon the instinctive impulses; education and cultivation of self-control counteract the opposing influences.

The exciting and inhibitory powers are variable quantities. For instance, over-indulgence in alcohol is very fatal in this respect, since it awakens and increases sexual libido, while at the same time it weakens moral resistance.

THE ACT OF COHABITATION.[10]

The essential condition for the man is sufficient erection. *Augel* ("Arch. für Psych., viii., H. 2) calls attention to the fact that in sexual excitement not alone the erection centre is influenced but the nervous excitement is distributed over the entire vasomotor system of nerves. The proof of this is the turgescence of the organs in the sexual act, injection of the conjunctiva, prominence of the eyeballs, dilation of the pupils, cardiac palpitation (resulting from paralysis of the vasomotor nerves of the heart, which arise from the cervical sympathetic, and the resulting dilation of the cardiac arteries, and the increased stimulation of the cardiac ganglia induced by the consequent hyperaemia of the cardiac walls). The sexual act is accompanied by a pleasurable feeling, which, in the male, is evoked by the passage of semen through the ejaculation ducts to the urethra, in consequence of the sensory stimulation of the genitals. This pleasurable sensation occurs earlier in the male than in the female, grows rapidly in intensity up to the moment of commencing ejaculation, reaches its acme in the instant of free emission, and disappears quickly after the ejaculation.

In the female the pleasurable feeling occurs later and comes on more slowly, and generally outlasts the act of ejaculation.

The distinctive event in coitus is ejaculation. This function is dependent on a centre (genito-spinal), which *Budge* has shown to be situated at the level of the fourth lumbar vertebra. It is a reflex centre. The stimulus that excites it, is the ejection of semen from the seminal vesicles into the urethral membrane, a reflex effect of stimulation of the penis. As soon as the collection of semen, with ever-increasing pleasurable sensation, has reached a sufficient amount to be effectual as a stimulus of the ejaculation-centre, this centre acts. The reflex motor path lies in the fourth and fifth lumbar nerves. The action consists of a convulsive excitation of the bulbo-cavernosus muscle (innervated by the third and fourth sacral nerves), which forces the semen out.

In the female as well, at the height of sexual and pleasurable excitement, a reflex movement occurs. It is induced by stimulation of the sensory genital nerves and consists of a peristaltic movement in the tubes and uterus as far down as the entrance to the vagina, which presses out the mucous secretions of the tubes and uterus. Inhibition of the ejaculation centre is possible as a result of cortical influence (want of desire in coitus, emotions in general, influence of the will).

Under normal conditions, with the completion of the sexual act, sexual libido and erection disappear, and the psychical and sexual excitement gives place to a comfortable feeling of lassitude.

III. ANTHROPOLOGICAL FACTS [1]

EVERY individual whose sexual development has been in accordance with the normal process, represents physical and metaphysical attributes which, as experience shows, are typical of the sex to which the individual belongs. These sexual characteristics are either primary (sexual glands and organs of propagation) or secondary. The latter are bodily and psychical and are developed only during the period of puberty. Now and then cases of precocious as well as retarded sexual development are reported. As a rule they may be found to be due to abnormal evolutionary conditions in them, chiefly in individuals with a heavy neurotic taint.

The secondary sexual characteristics differentiate the two sexes; they present the specific male and female types. The higher the anthropological development of the race, the stronger these contrasts between man and woman, and vice versa.

Important somatic secondary sexual characteristics are, the skull, skeleton, pelvis (particularly), facial types, hair, larynx (voice), breasts, thighs, etc.

Important psychical characteristics are sexual consciousness (i.e., the knowledge of a special sexual individuality as man or woman) and a congruous sexual instinct, from both of which a long series of special features and individual peculiarities are evolved, such as psychical dispositions, inclinations, etc.

This differentiation of the sexes and the development of sexual types is evidently the result of an infinite succession of intermediary stages of evolution. The primary stage undoubtedly was bi-sexuality, such as still exists in the lowest classes of animal life and also during the first months of foetal existence in man. The type of the present stage of evolution is mono-sexuality, that is to say, a congruous development of the secondary bodily and psychical sexual characteristics belonging to the respective sexual glands.

Observation teaches that the pure type of the man or the woman is often enough missed by nature, that is to say that certain secondary male characteristics are found in woman and vice versa, to wit, men with an inclination for female occupations (embroidery, toilet, etc.), and women with a decided predilection for manly sports (without the influencing elements of early education). In both instances particular cleverness in the inverted and pronounced awkwardness in the originally proper occupation will be noticed. In this class belong castrates, women with a bass voice (abnormal development of the larynx), a narrow pelvis, a beard, undevelopment of the breasts, etc.

Of special scientific interest are the cases of *Gynecomastia, i.e.*, the development of breasts in the male individual, with concomitant inhibited development of the testicles during the period of puberty. *Galen* described and named this anomaly. *Laurent's* monograph [2] on this subject is worthy of mention.

As a rule the *gynecomast* is slender in build, has a smooth face and stunted testicles, is devoid of the secondary sexual characteristics of the man, has but little sexual desire for the opposite sex, is in short a sort of a man-woman of moral and metaphysical inferiority.

It is a remarkable fact that *Gynecomastia* only occurs in neurotically degenerated families, and must be looked upon as the manifestation of an anatomical and functional degeneration.

Castration never produces *Gynecomastia*, in which the glandular tissue but rarely develops, whilst the nipple becomes erogenous and capable of erection as in woman. Lactation has but seldom been observed. With involution even the mammae disappear. The true *Gynecomast* betrays signs of effemination—the voice is soft and has a high pitch, the hair on the mons veneris is that of a woman, the skin is soft, the pelvis wide, potency though weak is yet heterosexual and libido is wanting. It cannot be denied that in these cases through the interruption of evolutionary processes the sexual characteristics of the man have been replaced by those of the woman and that by this substitution the development also of other physical and psychical sexual characteristics has been influenced in the sense of inversion. The possible combinations, of course, vary greatly.

An interesting and important question now arises, viz.: "What determines the development of an individual of that definite sexual type which possesses all the characteristics of a man, or a woman?"

One is tempted to look upon the development of the genital glands as the determining factor which may be recognized even in the apparently bisexual foetus. For the primary sexual characteristics in the form of the sexual organs are present and may be with puberty developed into the secondary sexual characteristics.

That the sexual glands are important so far as the sex itself is concerned is hardly open to controversy, but they are not necessarily the determining factor. For we shall see later on that the secondary characteristics (sexual sensations, attraction by the physical and psychical properties of the opposite sex, and the instinct to have sexual intercourse with persons of the opposite sex) may be inverted even at the very beginning of sexual development.

Again the experience of gynecologists allows of the following deductions: *Hegar* (Nothnagel's Pathologie, xx. Part I., p. 371) points out:

(1) that despite congenital defects and rudimentary development of the ovaries the feminine type may be thoroughly preserved;

(2) that the female sexual characteristics are relatively independent of the ovaries as is proved by transverse Hermaphroditism. The old axiom "It is only her ovary that makes woman what she is," therefore falls.

The sex-determining momentum is unknown.

The form of the sexual glands is therefore not the qualifying element of sex-determination, but we must look rather to sexual sensations and the sexual instinct.

All this directs our attention to the central domains of that nervous plexus which dominates the sexual functions and which renders intermediary sexual gradations between the pure type of man and woman possible, quite in accordance with the original bisexual predisposition of the foetus. These grades may be due to some interference in the evolution of our present mono-sexuality (corresponding physical and psychical sexual characteristics) based upon degenerative, especially hereditary degeneration conditions.

The science of to-day can boast of but little positive knowledge about the evolutionary influence which the various departments of the sexual apparatus exercise upon each other. It is natural that we should study the influence exercised by the removal or total loss of the sexual glands upon the development or course of the sexual life. That such an influence exists cannot be doubted; but the extent of the controlling power of peripheral factors might largely depend on whether the elimination of the sexual glands took place before or after the development of puberty; and again due regard must be given to the fact that the rise of psychical sexual characteristics may have considerably preceded physical development. Facts seem to prove that with the loss of the genital glands *previous* to puberty the development of somatic and psychical sexual characteristics is stunted even unto *Asexuality*. This is true as to the male and female of the human kind as well as of domestic animals.

Matters are different if the injury occurs *after* this biological phase. Here we are bound to find physical as well as psychical characteristics already existing, but their further development becomes stunted. The manner in which these organs succumb (through illness or surgical interference) is of no import, neither is the sex itself. The only condition needed is that the development of the secondary sexual characteristics had already begun as this is plainly dependent upon central spheres. How far then sexual development will go, depends chiefly upon the condition and the developing powers of these central factors; whilst its direction is governed by the biological energy of these bisexually predisposed centres.

If the development ran hitherto in heterosexual channels, but was lacking in force, the sex experiences simply a check; but if the original bisexual predisposition had not yet received a definite sexual direction, and possessed strength, sexual characteristics of the opposite sex and under circumstances even of an inverted nature may unfold. In most cases there is but a partial development of the characteristics of the opposite sex.

Analogous experiences are made in cases in which the sexual glands were lost long after matured puberty. For instance, bearded women are frequently found in the *post mortem*, minus ovaries (Dict. de méd. et de chirurg. prat. art. "ovario"). In a similar manner pheasant hens are found with degenerated ovaries, but with the plumage and voice of the male.[3] (Discuss. de la societé zoologique de Londres).

It is a well-known fact that many women grow a beard after the climacterium and that the voice drops to a lower register. If the climax be reached very early and vitality remains very strong even another (opposite) sex may be developed. See page 162 and cases 128 and 129.

A sharp difference may also be found in eunuchs, according to whether castration took place before or after psychical puberty. In the latter case the sexual life is by no means a blank page, for sexual feeling and sexual instinct for the opposite sex are present, although physical and psychical sexual characteristics of the male are stunted and femininism may take its place.

In rare cases—apparently in strongly developed bisexuality—signs of inverted sexuality may appear (*Bedor's* case in Cadiz of a eunuch with developed breasts).

These facts are not in favour of the exclusive effects exercised by the sexual glands upon the development of the sexual life, especially of the psychical sexual characteristics, which no doubt belong to those central spheres which normally come into functional force with arriving puberty and thus determine the essential criterion of the sex (sexual instinct).

IV. GENERAL PATHOLOGY [1]
(Neurological and Psychological)

ANOMALIES of the sexual functions are met with especially in civilized races. This fact is explained in part by the frequent abuse of the sexual organs, and in part by the circumstance that such functional anomalies are chiefly the signs of an inherited diseased condition of the central nervous system ("functional signs of degeneration").

Since the generative organs stand in important functional relation to the entire nervous system, and especially to its psychical and somatic functions, the frequency of general neuroses and psychoses arising in sexual (functional or organic) disturbances, is easy to understand.

SCHEDULE OF THE SEXUAL NEUROSES.

I. PERIPHERAL.
1. *Sensory.*
(*a*) Anaesthesia; (*b*) Hyperaesthesia; (*c*) Neuralgia.
2. *Secretory.*
(*a*) Aspermia; (*b*) Polyspermia.
3. *Motor.*
(*a*) Pollutions (spasm); (*b*) Spermatorrhoea (paralysis)
II. SPINAL NEUROSES.
1. *Affections of the Erection Centre.*

(*a*) *Irritation* (priapism) arises from reflex action of peripheral sensory irritants (*e.g.,* gonorrhoea); directly, from organic irritation of the nerve-tracts leading from the brain to the erection centre (spinal disease in the lower cervical and upper dorsal regions), or of the centre itself (certain poisons); or from psychical irritation.

In the latter case satyriasis exists, *i.e.,* abnormal duration of erection, with *libido.* In reflex or direct organic irritation, *libido* may be wanting, and the priapism may even give rise to disgust.

(*b*) *Paralysis* arises from the destruction of the centre, or of the nerve-tracts (nervi erigentes), in diseases of the spinal cord (paralytic impotence).

A milder form is that of lessened excitability of the centre, resulting from over-stimulation (sexual excess, especially onanism), or from alcoholic intoxication, abuse of bromides, etc. It may also originate from cerebral anaethesia, or that of the external genitals. Cerebral hyperaesthesia is more frequent in such cases (increased libido).

A peculiar form of diminished excitability is shown in those cases where the centre responds only to certain stimuli. Thus there are men to whom sexual contact with their virtuous wives does not supply the necessary stimulus for an erection, but in whom it occurs when the act is attempted with a prostitute, or in the form of some unnatural sexual act. So far as psychical stimuli are concerned, they may be inadequate (see below, paraesthesia and perversion of sexual instinct).

(*c*) *Inhibition.* The erection centre may become incapable of function through cerebral influence. This inhibitory influence is an emotional process (disgust, fear of contagion), or fear [2] of impotence. There are men who have an unconquerable antipathy to woman, or fear of infection, or are suffering with perverse sexual instinct. In the latter condition are those neuropathic individuals (neurasthenics, hypochondriacs), frequently weakened sexually (masturbators), who have reason, or think they have, to mistrust their sexual power. This idea acts as an inhibitory impulse, and makes the act with the person of the opposite sex temporarily or absolutely impossible.

(*d*) *Irritable Weakness.* In this condition there is abnormal impressionability of the centre, but accompanied by rapid diminution of its energy. There may be functional disturbance of the centre itself, or weakness of the innervation through the nervi erigentes; or there may be weakness of the erector penis muscle. Cases in which erection is abortive on account of abnormally early ejaculation, form a transition to the following anomalies:—

2. *Affections of the Ejaculation Centre.*

(*a*) *Abnormally easy ejaculation* from absence of cerebral inhibition, resulting from excessive psychical excitement or irritable weakness of the centre. In this case, under certain circumstances, the simple conception of a lascivious situation is sufficient to set the centre in action (high degree of spinal neurasthenia, usually resulting from sexual abuse). A third possibility is excessive sensitivity of the urethra, by virtue of which the escaping semen induces an immediate and excessive reflex action of the ejaculation centre. In such cases simple proximity to the female genitals may be sufficient to induce ejaculation.

In cases of excessive sensitivity of the urethra (as a cause), ejaculation may be accompanied by painful, instead of pleasurable sensations. Usually in cases where there is excessive sensitivity of the urethra, there is at the same time irritable weakness of the centre. Both these functional disturbances are important in the production of excessive and daily pollution.

The accompanying pleasurable feeling may be pathologically absent.

This occurs in defective men and women (anaesthesia, aspermia?), and, further, as a result of disease (neurasthenia, hysteria); or (in prostitutes) it follows over-stimulation and the blunting this induced. The intensity of the pleasurable feeling accompanying the sexual act depends on the degree of psychical and motor excitement. Under pathological conditions this may become so pronounced, that the movements of coitus assume the character of involuntary convulsive actions, and even pass into general convulsions.

(b) *Abnormally difficult ejaculation.* It is occasioned by inexcitability of the centre (absence of *libido*, paralysis of the centre: organic, from disease of brain or spinal cord; functional, from sexual abuses, marasmus, diabetes, morphinism), and, in this case, for the most part, in connection with anaesthesia of the genitals and paralysis of the erection centre. Or, it is the result of a lesion of the reflex arc or of peripheral anaesthesia (urethra), or of aspermia. The ejaculation occurs either not at all, or tardily, in the course of the sexual act, or only afterward, in the form of a pollution.

III. CEREBAL NEUROSES.

(1) *Paradoxia, i.e.,* sexual excitement occurring independently of the period of the physiological processes in the generative organs.

(2) *Anaesthesia* (absence of sexual instinct). Here all organic impulses arising from the sexual organs, as well as all impulses, and visual, auditory and olfactory sense impressions fail to sexually excite the individual. This is a physiological condition in childhood and old age.

(3) *Hyperaesthesia* (increased desire, satyriasis). In this state there is an abnormally increased impressionability of the sexual life to organic, psychical and sensory stimuli (abnormally intense *libido*, lustfulness, lasciviousness). The stimulus may be central (nymphomania, satyriasis) or peripheral, functional or organic.

(4) *Paraesthesia* (perversion of the sexual instinct, *i.e.,* excitability of the sexual functions to inadequate stimuli).

Sub-divisions of *paraesthesia* are:

(a) *Sadism.* It consists in this that the association of lust and cruelty, which is indicated in the physiological consciousness, becomes strongly marked on a psychically degenerated basis, and that this lustful impulse coupled with presentations of cruelty rises to the height of powerful affects. This generates a force that seeks to materialize these presentations of fancy, and which is accomplished when hyperaesthesia supervenes as a complication, or inhibitory moral counter-presentations fail to act,

The quality of sadistic acts is defined by the relative potency of the tainted individual. If potent, the impulse of the sadist is directed to coitus, coupled with preparatory, concomitant or consecutive maltreatment, even murder, of the consort (*"Lust murder"*), the latter occurring chiefly because sensual lust has not been satisfied with the consummated coitus.

If the sadist is psychically or spinally impotent, as an equivalent of coitus, there will be noticed strangling, stabbing, flagellating (of women), or under circumstances ridiculously silly and mean, acts of violence on the other person (*symbolical sadism*), or also—for want of something better—on any living and feeling object (whipping of school children, recruits, apprentices, cruel acts on animals, etc.).

(*b*) *Masochism* is the counterpart of sadism in so far as it derives the zenith of pleasure from reckless acts of violence at the hands of the consort. It springs from the impulse to create a situation by means of external physical force, which is in accordance with the individual psychical and spinal stage of potency, as a preparatory and concomitant means to experience the voluptuous sensation of coitus, to increase it or to make it a substitute for cohabitation. In direct ratio of the intensity of the perverse instinct and the remaining power of moral and aesthetic counter motives, it forms a gradation of the most abhorrent and monstrous to the most ludicrous and absurd acts (the request for personal castigation, humiliations of all sorts, passive flagellation, etc.).

(*c*) *Fetichism* invests imaginary presentations of separate parts of the body or portions of raiment of the opposite sex, or even simply pieces of clothing-material, with voluptuous sensations. The pathological aspect of this manifestation may be deduced from the fact that fetichism of parts of the body never stands in direct relation to *sex*, that it concentrates the whole sexual interest in the one part abstracted from the entire body.

As a rule, when the individual fetish is absent coitus becomes impossible or can only be managed under the influence of the respective imaginary presentation, and even then grants no gratification. Its pathological condition is strongly accentuated by the circumstance that the fetichist does not find gratification in coitus itself, but rather in the manipulation of that portion of the body or that object which forms the interesting and effective fetich.

The fetich varies individually and is, no doubt, occasioned by some incident which determines the relation between a single impression and the voluptuous feeling.

(*d*) *Antipathic Sexuality* is the total absence of sexual feeling toward the opposite sex. It concentrates all sexuality in its own sex. The physical and psychical properties of persons of the same sex alone exercise an aphrodisiac effect and awaken a desire for sexual union. It is purely a psychical anomaly, for the sexual instinct does in no wise correspond with the primary and secondary physical sexual characteristics. In spite of the fully differentiated sexual type, in spite of the normally developed and active sexual glands, man is drawn sexually to the man, because he has, consciously or otherwise, the instinct of the female toward him, or vice versa.

From the clinical and anthropological standpoint this abnormal manifestation offers various grades of development.

(*a*) In predominant homosexual instinct traces of heterosexual (psychical) hermaphrodisia are to be found.

(*b*) If there is only inclination to the own sex (homosexuality) the secondary physical sexual characteristics are normal, but the psychical ones may point to incipient inversion.

(*c*) The psychical sexual characteristics are inverted, *i.e.*, they are shaped in accordance with the existing abnormal sexuality (women who behave like men).

(*d*) Also the secondary physical sexual characteristics approach that sex to which the individual, according to his instinct, belongs (pseudo-hermaphroditism).

These cerebral anomalies fall within the domain of psychopathology. The spinal and peripheral anomalies may occur in combination with the former; but as a rule they affect persons free from mental disease. They may occur in various combinations, and become the cause of sexual crimes, for which reason they demand consideration in the following description. However, the cerebral anomalies claim the principal interest, since they very frequently lead to the commission of perverse and even criminal acts.

A. PARADOXIA. SEXUAL INSTINCT MANIFESTING ITSELF INDEPENDENTLY OF PHYSIOLOGICAL PROCESSES.

1. *Sexual Instinct Manifested in Childhood.*

Every physician conversant with nervous affections and diseases incident to childhood is aware of the fact that manifestations of sexual instinct may occur in very young children. The observations of *Ultzmann* concerning masturbation in childhood [3] are worthy of attention in relation to it. It is necessary here to differentiate between the numerous cases, in which, as a result of phimosis (elongation of the prepuce), balanitis (inflammation of the penis), or oxyuris (infestation of the rectum or the vagina), young children have itching of the genitals and experience a kind of pleasurable sensation from manipulations occasioned thereby, and thus come to practice masturbation, and those cases in which sexual ideas and impulses occur in the child as a result of cerebral processes without peripheral causes. It is only in this latter class of cases that we have to do with premature manifestations of sexual instinct. In such cases it may always be regarded as an accompanying symptom of a neuropsychopathic constitutional condition.

A case of *Marc's* ("Die Geisteskrankheiten," etc., *von Ideler*, i., p. 66) illustrates very well these conditions. The subject was a girl of eight years of age, of respectable family, who was devoid of all child-like and moral feelings, and had masturbated from her fourth year; at the same time she consorted with boys of the age of ten or twelve. She had thought of killing her parents, that she might become her own mistress and give herself up to pleasure with men.

In these cases of premature manifestation of *libido* the children begin early to masturbate; and, since they are greatly predisposed constitutionally, they often sink into dementia, or become subjects of severe degenerative neuroses or psychoses.

Lombroso ("Archivio di Psichiatria," iv., p. 22) has collected a number of cases of children affected with very decided hereditary taint, which belong to this category. One was that of a girl who masturbated shamelessly and almost constantly at the age of three. Another girl began at the age of eight, and continued to practise masturbation when married, and even during pregnancy. She was pregnant twelve times. Five of the children died early, four were hydrocephalic, and two boys began to masturbate—one at the age of seven, the other at the age of four.

Zambaco ("L'Encéphale," 1882, Nr. 1, 2) tells the disgusting story of two sisters affected with premature and perverse sexual desire. The elder, R., masturbated at the age of seven, practiced lewdness with boys, stole wherever she could, seduced her four-year-old sister into masturbation, and at the age of ten was given up to the practice of the most revolting vices. Even a white hot iron applied to the clitoris had no effect in overcoming the practice, and she masturbated with the cassock of a priest while he was exhorting her to reformation.

Cf. also *Magnan*, "Lectures on Psychiatry," (in German by *Möbius*, vols. ii. and iii., p. 27), giving the case of premature and perverse sexual life in a girl of twelve with hereditary taint. Other cases, ibidem p. 120-121.

2. Re-awakening of Sexual Instinct in Old Age.[4]

Cases in which the sexual instinct prevails until a great age are rare. "Indeed, vigor brings greater esteem for old age than years do." (*Zittmann*). *Oesterlen* (*Maschka*, Handb.," iii., p. 18) mentions the case of a man aged eighty-three, who was sentenced to three years' imprisonment by a court in Würtemberg on account of sexual misdemeanours. Unfortunately nothing is said of the nature of the crime or of the mental condition of the criminal.

The manifestation of sexual instinct in old age is not in itself pathological.

Presumption of pathological conditions must necessarily be entertained when the individual is decrepit and his sexual life has already long become extinct; and when the impulse, in a man whose sexual needs were in his early life, perhaps, not very marked, manifests itself with greater strength, and strives for even perverse satisfaction in a shameless and impulsive manner.

In such cases a presumption of pathological conditions suggests itself at once. Medical science recognizes the fact that such an impulse depends upon the morbid alterations of the brain which lead to senile dementia. This abnormal manifestation of sexual life may be the precursor of senile dementia, and make its appearance even long before there are any well-defined manifestations of intellectual weakness. The attentive and experienced observer will always be able to detect in this prodromal stage an alteration of character in the beginning, and a deterioration of the moral sense accompanying the peculiar sexual manifestation.

The *libido* of those passing into senile dementia is at first expressed in lascivious speech and gesture. The first objects for the attempts of these senile subjects of brain atrophy and psychical degeneration are children. This sad and dangerous fact is explained by the better oportunity they have in succeeding with children, but more especially by a feeling of imperfect sexual power. Defective sexual power, and greatly diminished moral sense, explain the additional fact of the perversity of the sexual acts of such aged men. They are the equivalents of the impossible physiological act.

The annals of legal medicine distinguish as such, exhibition of the genitals,[5] lustful handling of the genitals of children, inducing them to perform masturbation on the seducer, and performing masturbation [7] or flagellation on the victim.

In this stage the intellect may still be sufficiently intact to allow avoidance of publicity and discovery, while the moral sense is too far gone to allow consideration of the moral significance of the act, and resistance to the impulse. With the progress of dementia, these acts are more and more shamelessly committed. Then care on account of defective sexual power disappears, and adults also become the objects of the senile passion; but the defective sexual power necessitates equivalents for coitus. Not infrequently sodomy results, and, as *Tarnowsky* (*op. cit.*, p. 77) points out, in the sexual act performed with geese, chickens, etc., the sight of the dying animal and its death-struggles at the time of coitus afford complete gratification. The perverse sexual acts with adults are quite as horrible, and may be explained psychologically in the same way.

Case 49, in the author's "Text-Book of Legal Psychopathology," second edition, p. 161, demonstrates how enormously increased sexual lust may be during the course of senile dementia. A lustful old man killed his own daughter out of jealousy and took delight in the sight of the dying girl's wounded breast.

Erotic delirium and states of satyriasis may occur in the course of the malady, with or without maniacal episodes, as the following case shows:—

CASE 1. J. René, always given to indulgence in sensuality and sexual pleasures, but always with regard for decorum, had shown, since his seventy-sixth year, a progressive loss of intelligence and increasing perversion of his moral sense. Previously bright and outwardly moral, he now wasted his property in concourse with prostitutes, frequented brothels only, asked every woman on the street to marry him or allow coitus, and thus became publicly so obnoxious that it was necessary to place him in an asylum. There the sexual excitement increased to a veritable satyriasis, which lasted until he died. He masturbated continuously, even before others; took delight only in obscene ideas; thought the men about him were women, and followed them with indecent proposals (*Legrand du Saulle*, "La Folie," p. 533).

Moreover, women previously moral, when affected with senile dementia, may manifest similar conditions of great sexual excitement (nymphomania, furor uterinus).

It may be seen from a reading of *Schopenhauer*,[8] that, as a result of senile dementia, the abnormally excited and perverse instinct may be directed exclusively to persons of the same sex (see below). Gratification is obtained by passive pederasty, or, as I ascertained in the following case, by mutual masturbation:—

CASE 2. Mr. X., aged eighty, of high social standing, born of a family with hereditary taint. He was always very sensual and a cynic, of uncontrollable temper, and, according to his own confession, as a young man preferred masturbation to coitus. However, he never showed signs of sexual perversion, and kept mistresses, raising a child by one. At the age of forty-eight he married, out of inclination, and begat six children, and never gave his wife cause for complaint. I could obtain but an incomplete history of his family. It was certain that his brother was suspected of love for men, and that a nephew became insane as a result of excessive masturbation.

The patient's temper, always peculiar and quick, had for years been growing more violent. He had become exceedingly suspicious, and slight opposition to his wishes induced attacks of anger which turned at times into actual raving, when he would raise his hand even against his wife. For a year there had been unmistakable signs of incipient senile dementia. The patient had become forgetful, localized past events incorrectly, and had false ideas of time. For fourteen months it was noticed that he manifested affection for certain male servants, especially for a gardener's boy. Otherwise rude and overbearing to servants, he surfeited his favourite with favours and presents, and commanded his family and his house officials to treat the boy with the greatest respect. The aged patient awaited the hour of rendezvous in true sexual excitement. He sent his family away, that he might be with his favourite undisturbed, and remained shut up with him for hours; and when the doors were opened again, he was found lying on the bed exhausted. Besides this object of his passion, the patient had intercourse episodically with other servants. It is certain that he enticed them, asked them for kisses, exhibited himself, allowed manipulation of the genitals, and practiced mutual masturbation. By these practices absolute demoralization was brought about in the household. The family was powerless; for any opposition caused violent outbreaks of anger and even threats against his relatives. The patient was completely without appreciation of his perverse sexual acts; and therefore the only course left to the afflicted family was to remove all authority from his hands and place him in an asylum. No erotic inclination towards the opposite sex was observed, though the patient occupied a sleeping-apartment with his wife. With reference to the perverse sexuality and the defective moral sense of this unfortunate man, it is worthy of note that he questioned the servants of his daughter-in-law as to whether she had lovers.

B.—ANAESTHESIA SEXUALIS (ABSENCE OF SEXUAL FEELING).

1. As a Congenital Anomaly.

Only those cases can be regarded as unquestionable examples of absence of sexual instinct dependent on cerebral causes, in which, in spite of generative organs normally developed and the performance of their functions (secretion of semen, menstruation), the corresponding emotions of sexual life are absolutely wanting. These functionally sexless individuals are rare cases, and, indeed, always persons having degenerative defects, in whom other functional cerebral disturbances, states of psychical degeneration, and even anatomical signs of degeneration, may be observed.

CASE 3. K., aged 29, civil servant, consulted me on account of his abnormal sexual condition. Being without relatives he wanted to marry, but only on rational grounds. He claimed never to have experienced a sensual emotion. Sexual life was known to him only from what he had heard other men say about it or from what he had read in erotic novels, which, however, had never made any impression upon him. He had no dislike for the opposite sex, or special inclination towards his own sex, and had never masturbated. Since his seventeenth year he had at intervals nocturnal pollutions, but without concomitant lascivious dreams. Erections occurred in the morning when waking which, however, disappeared at once after emptying the bladder. Excepting this want of sexual instinct K. considered himself quite normal. No psychical defects could be detected. He was fond of solitude, but of a frigid nature, without interest in the arts or the beautiful, but a highly efficient and esteemed official.

CASE 4. W., aged 25, merchant, claimed to be untainted, never had a severe illness, never had masturbated, since his nineteenth year had but rarely pollutions, mostly with sensual dreams. Since his twenty-first year he had rarely enjoyed coitus; his act, inside the female body, had been almost masturbatory and had given him no pleasure. W. declared to have made these attempts solely through curiosity, and soon gave them up altogether as desire, gratification, and ultimately even erection were wanting. He never had any leaning towards his own sex. His deficiency did not seem to cause him any worry. In the ethical and aesthetical field there were no abnormal manifestations.

CASE 5. P., aged thirty-six, common labourer, was received at my clinic in the beginning of November on account of spastic spinal paralysis. He declared he came of a healthy family. A stutterer from his youth. Cranium microcephalic (cf. 53 cm.). Patient somewhat imbecilic. He was never sociable, never had a sexual emotion. The sight of a woman never had anything enticing for him. He never had a desire to masturbate. Erections frequent, but only on awakening in the morning with a full bladder, and without a trace of sexual feeling. Pollutions very infrequent —about once a year, in sleep—and usually while dreaming that he was concerned with a female. These dreams, however, as his dreams in general, were not markedly erotic. He said the act of pollution was not accompanied by any pleasurable sensation. Patient did not feel this absence of sexual sensation. He gave the assurance that his brother, aged thirty-four, was in exactly the same sexual condition as himself, and made it seem probable that a sister, aged twenty-one, was in a similar state. A younger brother, he said, was sexually normal. The examination of his genitals revealed nothing abnormal beyond phimosis.

Further cases see V. *Krafft*, "Arbeiten," iv., p. 178, 179.

Hammond ("Sexual Impotence"), even with his wide experience, reports only the following three cases of anaesthesia sexualis:—

CASE 6. Mr. W., aged thirty-three; strong, healthy, with normal genitals. He had never experienced *libido*, and had vainly sought to awaken his defective sexual instinct by means of obscene stories and intercourse with prostitutes. On the occasion of such attempts he experienced only disgust, with even a feeling of nausea, and became nervously and mentally exhausted. Only once, when he forced the situation, did he have a transitory erection. W. had never masturbated, and had had pollutions about once every two months from his seventeenth year. Important interests demanded that he should marry. He had no terror of women, and longed for a home and a wife, but felt that he was incapable of the sexual act. He died unmarried in the American Civil War.

CASE 7. X., aged twenty-seven, genitals normal; never felt *libido*. Mechanical or thermic stimuli easily induced erection, but sexual desire was regularly replaced by a desire for alcoholic indulgence. Such excesses also induced erections, and he then sometimes masturbated. He had a disinclination for women and a loathing of coitus. If, with an erection, he made an attempt at coitus, it disappeared at once. Death in coma during a cerebro-vascular accident.

CASE 8. Mrs. O., normally developed, healthy, menstruated regularly; aged thirty-five; fifteen years married. She never experienced *libido*, and never had any erotic excitement in sexual intercourse with her husband. She was not averse to coitus, and sometimes seemed to experience pleasure in it, but she never had a wish for repetition of cohabitation.

In connection with such genuine cases of anaesthesia,[9] there should be considered other cases in which the mental side of the sex life is a blank leaf in the life of the individual, but where elementary sexual sensations manifest themselves at least in masturbation (*cf.* the transitional *case* 7). According to *Magnan's* ingenious classification—which, however, is not strictly correct and somewhat too dogmatic—in such cases the sexual life is so limited as to be designated spinal. Possibly in some such cases there exists virtually a mental side of the sex life, but it is very weak, and undermined by masturbation before it attains development. These represent the transitional cases from the congenital to the acquired (psychical) sexual anesthesia. This danger threatens many masturbators of vitiated constitution. It is psychologically interesting that when the sexual element is early vitiated, then an ethical defect is manifested.

The two following cases, previously published by me in the "Archiv für Psychiatrie," vii., are given here as illustrations worthy of consideration:—

CASE 9. F. J., aged nineteen, student; mother was nervous, sister epileptic. At the age of four, acute brain affection, lasting two weeks. As a child he was not affectionate, and was cold towards his parents; as a student he was peculiar, retiring, preoccupied with self, and given to much reading. Well endowed mentally. Masturbation from fifteenth year. Eccentric after puberty, with continual vacillation between religious enthusiasm and materialism—now studying theology, now natural sciences. At the university his fellow-students took him for a fool. He read Jean Paul almost exclusively, and wasted his time. Absolute absence of sexual feeling towards the opposite sex. Once he indulged in intercourse, experienced no sexual feeling in the act, found coitus absurd, and did not repeat it. Without any emotional cause whatever, he often had thought of suicide. He made it the subject of a philosophical dissertation, in which he contended that it was, like masturbation, a justifiable act. After repeated experiments which he made on himself with various poisons, he attempted suicide with fifty-seven grains of opium, but he was saved and sent to an asylum.

Patient was destitute of moral and social feelings. His writings disclosed incredible frivolity and vulgarity. His knowledge was of a wide range, but his logic peculiarly distorted. There was no trace of emotionality. He treated everything (even the sublime) with incomparable cynicism and irony. He pleaded for the justification of suicide with false philosophical premises and conclusions, and, as one would speak of the most indifferent affair, he declared that he intended to accomplish it. He regretted that his penknife had been taken from him. If he had it, he would open his veins as Seneca did—in the bath. At one time a friend had given him instead of a poison as he supposed, a cathartic. Instead of sending him to the other world, it sent him to the water-closet. Only the Great Operator could eradicate his foolish and fatal idea with the scythe of death, etc.

The patient had a large, rhombic, distorted skull, the left half of the forehead being flatter than the right. The occiput was very straight. Ears far back, widely projecting, and the external meatus formed a narrow slit. Genitals very lax; testicles unusually soft and small.

Now and then the patient suffered with compulsive word repetition. He was compelled to think of the most useless problems and give himself up to interminable, distressing and worrying thoughts, and became so fatigued that he was no longer capable of any rational thinking. After some months the patient was sent home unimproved. There he spent his time in reading and frivolities, and busied himself with the thought of founding a new system of Christianity because Christ had been subject to grand delusions and had deceived the world with miracles(!). After remaining at home some years the sudden occurrence of a maniacal outbreak brought him back to the asylum. He presented a mixture of primordial delirium of persecution (devil, antichrist, persecution, poisoning, persecuting voices) and delusions of grandeur (Christ, redemption of the world), with impulsive, incoherent actions, After five months there was a remission of this intercurrent acute mental disease, and the patient returned to the level of his original intellectual peculiarity and moral defect.

CASE 10. E., aged thirty, journeyman painter, was arrested while trying to cut off the scrotum of a boy he had caught in the woods. He gave as a motive for this act that he wished to cut it off in order that the world should not multiply. Often in his youth, with like purpose, he had cut into his own genitals.

It is impossible to learn anything of his ancestry. From his childhood he was mentally abnormal, violent, never lively, very irritable, irascible, selfish and weak minded. He hated women, loved solitude, and read much. He sometimes laughed to himself and did silly things. Of late years his hatred of women had increased, especially of those that were pregnant, they being responsible for the misery of the world. He also hated children, and cursed his father. He entertained communistic ideas, and berated the rich and the ministry and God, who had allowed him to come into the world so poor. He declared that it would be better to castrate all children than to allow others to come into the world fated only to endure poverty and misery. He had always had the intention, from his fifteenth year, of castrating himself, in order that he might have no part in increasing unhappiness and adding to the number of men. He hated the female sex because it was a means of procreation. Only twice in his life had he allowed women to practice masturbation on him, and with the exception of this he had never had anything to do with them. Occasionally he had sexual desire, but never for a natural gratification of it. When nature did not help him, he occasionally helped himself by means of masturbation.

He was a powerful, muscular man. The formation of the genitals presented no abnormality. On the scrotum and penis were numerous scars, the results of his attempts at self-emasculation, which, he asserted, were not carried out on account of pain. Knock-kneed. No evidence of onanism could be discovered. He was moody, defiant, irritable. Social feelings were absolutely foreign to him. With the exception of imperfect sleep and frequent headaches, there were no functional disturbances.

From cases of this kind, depending on cerebral causes, there must be distinguished others in which the absence of function arises from an absence of malformation of the generative organs, as in certain hermaphrodites, idiots and cretins.

Ultzmann's [10] observations show sexual anaesthesia is not caused simply by *aspermia.* He shows that even in congenital *aspermia* the sex life and sexual power may be entirely satisfying; an additional proof that the origins of defective *libido* are to be sought for in cerebral conditions.

The frigid nature of *Zacchias* are examples of a milder form of anaesthesia. They are met with more frequently in women than in men. The characteristic signs of this anomaly are: slight inclination to sexual intercourse, or pronounced disinclination to coitus without sexual equivalent, and failure of corresponding psychical, pleasurable excitation during coitus, which is indulged in simply from sense of duty. I have often had occasion to hear complaints from husbands about this. In such cases the wives have always proved to be neuropathic from birth. Some were at the same time hysterical.

2. Acquired Anaesthesia.

Acquired diminution of sexual instinct, extending through all degrees to extinction, may depend on various causes. These may be organic and functional, psychical and somatic, central and peripheral. The diminution of *libido*, as age advances, and its temporary disappearance after the sexual act, are physiological. The variations with reference to the duration of the sexual instinct are dependent upon individual factors. Education and manner of life have a great influence upon the intensity of the sexual life. Intense mental activity (hard study), physical exertion, emotional depression, and sexual continence decidedly diminish sexual inclination. Continence at first induces an increase, but sooner or later, according to constitutional conditions, the activity of the generative organs decreases, and with it *libido*. At all events, in a person sexually mature, a close connection exists between the activity of the generative glands and the degree of *libido*. That this relation is not determined is shown by the cases of sensual women, who, after the climacterium, continue to have sexual intercourse, and may manifest states of sexual excitement (cerebral). Also in eunuchs it is seen that *libido* may long outlast the production of semen.

On the other hand, however, experience teaches that *libido* is essentially conditioned by the functions of the generative glands, and that the facts mentioned are exceptional manifestations. As peripheral causes of diminution or extinction of *libido*, may be mentioned castration, degeneration of the sexual glands, marasmus, sexual excesses in the form of coitus and masturbation, and alcoholism and abuse of cocaine. In the same way, the disappearance of *libido* in general disturbances of nutrition (diabetes, morphinism, etc.) may be explained. Finally, the atrophy of the testicles should be remembered, which has sometimes been observed to follow focal lesions of the brain (cerebellum).

A diminution of the sexual life from degeneration of the tracts of the cord and genito-spinal centre, occurs in diseases of the spinal cord and brain. A central interference with the sexual instinct may be organically induced by cortical disease (dementia paralytica in its advanced stages); functionally, by hysteria (central anaesthesia?) and emotional insanity (melancholia, hypochrondria).

C. HYPERAESTHESIA (ABNORMALLY INCREASED SEXUAL DESIRE).

One of the most important anomalies of sexual life is an abnormal presence of sexual sensations and presentations from which necessarily arise frequent and violent impulses for sexual gratification. No doubt it is the outcome of the education, or rather the breeding of many centuries that the sexual instinct which is indispensable for the preservation of the race and therefore congenital in every normal individual, is not the predominant key in the chord of human sentiments, but rather forms episodes in the physical and psychical life of cultured man with periods of ebb and flood tide; is the generating element of higher and nobler social and moral sentiments, and leaves room for other spheres of activity, the object of which is the furtherance of interests affecting the individual as well as society at large.

It is, moreover, a statute of the moral code and of the common law that civilized man satisfy his sexual instinct only within the barriers (established in the interests of the community) of modesty and morality, and that man should, under all circumstances, control this instinct so soon as it comes in conflict with the altruistic demands of society.

If the normally constituted civilized individual were unable to comply with this rule, family and state would cease to exist as the foundations of a moral, lawful community.

Practically speaking the sexual instinct never develops in the normal, sane individual that has not been deprived by intoxication (alcohol, etc.) of his reason or good senses, to such an extent that it permeates all his thoughts and feelings, allowing of no other aims in life, tumultuously, and in rut-like fashion demanding gratification without granting the possibility of moral and righteous counter-presentations, and resolving itself into an impulsive, insatiable succession of sexual enjoyments.

For the latter would at once betray a pathological condition, which episodically might produce such a high degree of sexual affection, that self-consciousness becomes clouded, sanity impaired, and a true psychical calamity established which would lead to an irresistible impulse to commit sexual acts of violence.

Such psycho-sexual extravagances have been but little probed scientifically, though they are of great importance for the criminal court since the individual so affected can scarcely be held mentally responsible. It is fortunate for society and for the criminal doctor, who is called upon to make the diagnosis, that these cases, in which irresistible hypersen-

suality leads to the gravest and indisputably pathological sexual aberrations, are only encountered in that category of human beings whom we
class among the degenerates infected with hereditary taint.

Alas, their number is by no means small in modern society, which
shows many marks of physical and psychical degeneration, especially in
the centres of culture and refinement.

Coupled with perversions of sexual life and sexual imbecility springing from the same degenerated soil, often with the aiding influence of
alcohol, the most monstrous and horrible sexual excesses (cf. *Sadism*)
are perpetrated which would disgrace humanity at large, could they be
committed by normal man.

The commission of these atrocious acts by degenerated and partially
defective individuals is the outcome of an irresistible impulse or delirium.
The mechanism of these actions is indeed the property of psychical
degeneration.

The special act follows the direction given by the hereditary or
acquired impulse and in many instances is determined by the relative
potency or impotence of the agent. This pathological sexuality is a
dreadful scourge for its victim, for he is in constant danger of violating
the laws of the state and of morality, of losing his honour, his freedom
and even his life. Alcohol and prolonged sexual abstinence are apt
to produce in such degenerated persons at any time powerful sexual
affections.

Besides these graver manifestations of pathological sexuality we
find also milder and more numerous gradations of hypersexuality, to the
lowest of which, perhaps, belong those individuals who, impecunious
though they be whilst sexually potent, move in the better classes of
society and have no other aim in life than to gratify their sexual desires.
These are not afflicted with a pathological sexual condition, know how to
control themselves in a measure, observe the acknowledged rules of
decency, do not compromise themselves, but allow no opportunity to
pass by without utilizing it to the utmost. Another grade are the *apron-
hunters*, the Don Juans, whose whole existence is an endless chain
of sensual enjoyment and whose blunted moral sense does not keep
them from seduction, adultery and even incest.

CASE 11. P., Caretaker, age 53; married; no evidence of hereditary
taint; no epileptic antecedents; moderate drinker; no sign of senile
degeneration; appeared, according to the statement of his wife during
the whole time of their married life covering a period of 28 years,
hypersexual, extremely libidinous, ever potent, in fact insatiable in his
marital relations. During coitus he became quite bestial and wild,
trembled all over with excitement and panted heavily. This nauseated
the wife who by nature was rather frigid and rendered the discharge
of her conjugal duty a heavy burden. He worried her with his jealous

behaviour, but he himself soon after the marriage seduced his wife's sister, an innocent girl, and had a child by her. In 1873 he took mother and child to his home. He now had two women, but gave preference to the sister-in-law, which the wife tolerated as a lesser evil. As years went by his *libido* increased, though his potency decreased. He often resorted to masturbation even immediately after coitus, and without in the least minding the presence of the women. Since 1892 he committed immoral acts with a girl of 16 years, who was his ward, *i.e.*, he was in the habit of going with the girl and masturbating. He even tried to force her at the point of a revolver to have coitus with him. The same attempts he made on his own illegitimate child, so that both often had to be protected from him. At the clinic he was quiet and well-behaved. His excuse was hypersexuality. He acknowledged the wrongfulness of his actions, but said he could not help himself. The frigidity of the wife had forced him to commit adultery. There was no disturbance of his mental faculties, but the ethical elements were utterly wanting. He had several epileptic fits but no signs of degeneration.

We must concede that the degree of sexual libido is subject to rise and fall in the untainted individual, according to age, constitutional conditions, mode of life and the various influences of health and illness of the body, etc. Sexual desire rapidly increases after puberty, until it reaches a marked degree; it is strongest from the twentieth to the fortieth year, and then slowly decreases. Married life seems to preserve and control the instinct. Sexual intercourse with many persons increases the desire.

Since woman has less sexual need than man, a predominating sexual desire in her arouses a suspicion of its pathological significance. Those living in large cities, who are constantly reminded of sexual things and incited to sexual enjoyment, certainly have more sexual desire than those living in the country. A dissipated, luxurious, sedentary manner of life, preponderance of animal food, and the consumption of spirits, spices, etc., have a stimulating influence on the sexual life. In woman the sexual inclination is post-menstrually increased. At this period, in neuropathic women, the excitement may reach a pathological degree.

The great *libido* of consumptives is remarkable, even during the very latest stages of the disease. Sexual hyperaesthesia is in my opinion a functional manifestation of degeneration. Whether it may occur as an acquired, accidental, episodical condition in the untainted is worthy of scientific research. Excessive *libido* may be peripherally or centrally induced. The former manner of origin is the more infrequent. Pruritus and eczema of the genitals may cause it, and likewise certain substances, like cantharides, which powerfully stimulate sexual desire.

Not infrequently in women at the climacteric period sexual excitement occurs, occasioned by pruritus, and also in cases where there is neuropathic taint. *Magnan* ("Annales médico-psychol.," 1885, p. 157) reports the case of a lady who was afflicted in the mornings with attacks of frightful increased irritability of the genitals, and the case of a man aged fifty-five who was tormented at night by unbearable persistent erection. In each case there was a neurosis present.

The central origin of sexual excitement can often be traced [11] in persons having neurotic taint or hysteria and in conditions of psychical exaltation. When the cortex and the psycho-sexual centre are in a condition of hyperaesthesia (abnormal excitability of the imagination, increased ease of association), not only visual and tactile impressions, but also auditory and olfactory sensations, may be sufficient to call up lascivious conceptions.

Magnan (*op. cit.*) reports the case of a young woman who had an increasing sexual desire from puberty, and satisfied it by masturbation. Gradually she grew to become sexually excited at the sight of any man pleasing to her; and, since she was unable to control herself, she would sometimes shut herself up in a room until the storm had passed. At last she gave herself up to men of her choice, that she might get rest from her tormenting desire, but neither coitus nor masturbation brought relief, and she went to an asylum.

The case of a mother of five children is added, who, in despair about her inordinate sexual impulse, attempted suicide, and then sought an asylum. There her condition improved, but she never trusted herself to leave it.

There are several illustrative cases in men and women in the author's article, "On Certain Anomalies of Sexual Instinct," cases 6 and 7 ("Archiv für Psychiatrie," vii., 2).

The two following cases show how powerful, dangerous and painful sexual hyperaesthesia may become in those afflicted with this anomaly:—

CASE 12. Excessive sexual desire. One who masturbated in the presence of his pupils in school.

Z., 36 years of age, father of seven children, president of the school, confessed that he committed masturbation in school whilst sitting at his desk which, however, prevented the act being seen by the pupils as it was encased all around. He drank more than usual on the preceding evening, had been provoked to anger before going to school, and had been excited by the sight of some very pretty girls attending his lecture. This produced a violent erection and led to masturbation. After the act he became conscious at once of his compromising position, but the thought that the pupils had not noticed his excitement had helped him to regain self-possession.

His previous conduct being without a blemish, the authorities suspected a pathological condition and insisted upon a medical examination by the author.

The facts elicited were the following: Z. came from healthy parents. Two close relations were epileptics. At the age of 13 Z. suffered from a severe concussion of the brain, which produced an acute dementia lasting three weeks. Since that time frequent spells of irritability and intolerance of alcohol.

At the age of 16 awakening of sex life with abnormal vigor and pronounced sexual emotions. Lascivious literature and pictures of women produced satisfying ejaculation. From the age of 18 onward he indulged now and then in coitus. But as a rule the touching of a woman's arm sufficed to produce orgasm and ejaculation. He married at the age of 24 and indulged in coitus three or four times daily, and besides practiced masturbation, coupled with normal coitus.[11]

With the birth of his fourth child (three years ago) Z. was forced, for economical reasons, to restrain himself from sexual intercourse as he despised anticonceptional means. The touch of a woman, which produced daily pollution, proved unsatisfactory as did also masturbation. He suffered much from incessant sexual excitement, which at the end of periods of six weeks became so strong that it affected his mind and will power. Only masturbation kept him from committing sexual violence on women. He became very irritable and easily flew into passion, yelled and raged about the house and even beat wife and children.

It often happened now that at the height of such a spell he would fall over and become unconscious, rattling from the throat in a peculiar manner. After a few minutes he would recover again with complete amnesia of what had happened. An attack of this kind had, however, not preceded the act with which he now stood charged, but had occurred three days afterward.

Z. was an intelligent, decent man, most penitent and filled with shame.

He understood quite well that he could no longer teach at a girl's school and bewailed his unnatural, unbridled sensuality.

He made no attempt to in any way excuse his action, but pointed out that his nervous system had been thoroughly shaken of late by insatiable desire and overwork (lessons up to twelve hours daily).

Vegetative functions normal; parietal protuberance of cranium; genitals large, lax, but normal.

Patellar reflexes much exaggerated.

In my report I pointed out that Z. suffered from a pathologically exaggerated sex life and most probably from epilepsy, and had committed the act whilst subject to a sexual affection which depressed the power of self-control to a minimum.

Further legal proceedings were withdrawn. Z. was pensioned off.

CASE 13. On 11th July, 1884, R., aged thirty-three, servant, was admitted suffering with delusions of persecution and neurotic sexual impulses. Mother was neuropathic; father died of spinal disease. From childhood he had an intense sexual desire, of which he became conscious as early as his sixth year. From this age, masturbation; from fifteenth year, for want of anything better, pederasty; occasionally, sodomitic indulgences. Later, he indulged in abusive coitus in marriage, with his wife, i.e., presumably he used her anal passage. Now and then even perverse impulse to commit *cunnilingus* and to administer cantharides to his wife, because her *libido* did not equal his own. His wife died after a short period of married life. Patient's circumstances became strained, and he had no means to indulge himself sexually. Then masturbation again; employment of the tongue of a dog to induce ejaculation. At times, priapism and conditions approaching satyriasis. He was then driven to masturbate in order to avoid rape. With gradually predominating sexual neurasthenia and hypochondria came beneficial diminution of excessive desire.

A particular species of excessive sexual urge may be found in females in whom a most impulsive desire for sexual intercourse with certain men imperatively demands gratification. No doubt "unrequited love" for another man may often affect the married woman who does not either psychically or physically (because of impotence of the husband) experience connubial satisfaction; but the normal, untainted wife guided by ethical reasons knows how to conquer herself.

Of course, pathological conditions change the situation.

Fetichism must here be considered. Sexual impulse is overpowering, at times periodically recurrent. The very attempt to overcome it produces most painful attacks of worry and anxiety. This pathological want becomes so powerful that all considerations of shame, conventionality and womanly honour simply disappear, and it reveals itself in the most shameless manner even to the husband, whilst the normal woman, endowed with full moral consciousness, knows how to conceal the terrible secret.

Magnan ("Psychiatr. Vorlesungen") quotes two striking instances from his own experience. One is specially instructive. A young woman, mother of three children, with a blameless past, but daughter of a lunatic, tells her husband one day openly that she is in love with a certain young man and that she would kill herself if her intimate relations with him were interfered with. She begs permission to live with him for six months in order to quench the fire of her passion, when she would return to her family again. Husband and children have no place in her heart with her present love. The husband took her to a foreign country and placed her there under medical treatment.

This pathological love of married women for other men is a phenomenon in the domain of *psychopathia sexualis* which sadly stands in need of scientific explanation. The author has had the opportunity of observing five cases belonging to this category. The pathological conditions were paroxysmal, in one case repeatedly recurrent; but always sharply distinct from the unaffected, healthy period, during which deep sorrow and contrition over the occurrence were manifested. But it was the sorrow over an unavoidable fatality caused by psychically abnormal conditions.

Whilst the pathological conditions lasted, absolute indifference, even hatred, prevailed towards husband and children; and an utter want of understanding of the bearings and consequences of the scandalous behaviour, jeopardizing the honour and dignity of wife and family, were noticeable. It is remarkable that in all these cases the husband and relatives had come to the conclusion that the condition was caused by psychopathia, even before they had obtained expert opinion.

As against the "non-psychopathical" but otherwise abnormally libidinous nymphomaniacs, it is well worthy of note that this sexual aberration is only an episode in the life of the otherwise honourable woman, and that the illicit intercourse was of a strictly monogamic character. This, and particularly the circumstance that the unfortunate woman was not the woman of many men, but only the mistress of one man, establishes a distinct difference from nymphomania. In three of the cases mentioned above, the grossly sensual momentum was missing, the real motive for marital infidelity was to be found in a fetich-like charm, in mental superior qualities,—in one case the voice of the charmer.

In two cases unmistakable proofs of excessive sexual desire and of absolute impotence towards the husband were found, whilst the merest touch of the other man produced orgasm, and the sexual act the zenith of pleasure. Of course, in these latter cases absolute sexual abandonment followed.

D. PARAESTHESIA OF SEXUAL FEELING
(PERVERSION OF THE SEXUAL INSTINCT).

In this condition there is perverse emotional colouring of the sexual ideas. Ideas physiologically and psychologically accompanied by feelings of disgust, give rise to pleasurable sexual feelings; and the abnormal association finds expression in passionate, uncontrollable emotion. The practical results are perverse acts (perversion of the sexual instinct). This is more easily the case if the pleasurable feelings, increased to passionate intensity, inhibit any opposing ideas with corresponding feelings of disgust; or the influence of such opposing conceptions may be rendered impossible on account of the absence or loss of all ideas of morality, aesthetics and law. This loss, however, is only too frequently found where the wellspring of ethical ideas and feelings (a normal sexual instinct) has been poisoned from the beginning.

With opportunity for the natural satisfaction of the sexual instinct, every expression of it that does not correspond with the purpose of nature—*i.e.*, propagation—must be regarded as perverse. The perverse sexual acts resulting from paraesthesia are of the greatest importance clinically, socially, and forensically; and, therefore, they must here receive careful consideration; all aesthetic and moral disgust must be overcome.

Perversion of the sexual instinct, as will be seen farther on, is not to be confounded with *perversity* in the sexual act; since the latter may be induced by conditions other than psycho-pathological. The concrete perverse act, monstrous as it may be, is clinically not decisive. In order to differentiate between disease (*perversion*) and vice (*perversity*), one must investigate the whole personality of the individual and the original motive leading to the perverse act. Therein will be found the key to the diagnosis (see below).

Paraesthesia may occur in combination with hyperaesthesia. This association seems to be frequent clinically. Sexual acts are then confidently to be expected. The perverse direction of sexual activity may be toward sexual satisfaction with the opposite or the same sex. Thus two great groups of perversions of sexual life may be distinguished.

I. SEXUAL INCLINATION TOWARDS PERSONS OF THE OPPOSITE SEX, WITH PERVERSE ACTIVITY OF THE INSTINCT.

1. *Sadism.*[12] *Association of Active Cruelty and Violence with Lust.*

Sadism, especially in its rudimentary manifestations, seems to be of common occurrence in the domain of sexual perversion. Sadism is the experience of sexual pleasurable sensations (including orgasm) produced by acts of cruelty, bodily punishment afflicted on one's own person or when witnessed in others, be they animals or human beings. It may also consist of an innate desire to humiliate, hurt, wound or even destroy others in order thereby to create sexual pleasure in one's self.

Thus it will happen that one of the consorts in sexual heat will strike, bite [13] or pinch the other, that kissing degenerates into biting. Lovers and young married couples are fond of teasing each other, they wrestle together "just for fun," indulge in all sorts of horseplay. The transition from these atavistic manifestations, which no doubt belong to the sphere of physiological sexuality, to the most monstrous acts of destruction of the consort's life can be readily traced.

Where the husband forces the wife by menaces and other violent means to the conjugal act, we can no longer describe such as a normal physiological manifestation, but must ascribe it to sadistic impulses. It seems probable that this sadistic force is developed by the natural shyness and modesty of woman towards the aggressive manners of the male, especially during the earlier periods of married life and particularly where the husband is hypersexual. Woman no doubt derives pleasure from her innate coyness and the final victory of man affords her intense and refined gratification. Hence the frequent recurrence of these little love comedies.

A further development of these sadistic traces may be found in men who demand the sexual act in unusual places, for this seems to offer an opportunity to him to show his superiority over woman, to provoke her defense and delight in her subsequent confusion and abashment.

CASE 14. One of my patients, hereditarily tainted, a crank, married to an extremely handsome woman of very vivacious temperament, became impotent when he saw her beautiful, pure white skin and her elegant toilet, but was quite potent with an ordinary wench, no matter how dirty (*Fetichism*). But it would happen that during a lonely walk with her in the country he would suddenly force her to have coitus in a meadow, or behind a shrub. The stronger she refused the more excited he became with perfect potency. The same would happen in places where there was a risk of being discovered in the act, for instance, in the railway train, in the lavatory of a restaurant. But at home in his own bed he was quite devoid of desire.

In the civilized man of to-day, in so far as he is untainted, associations between lust and cruelty are found, but in a weak and rather rudimentary degree. If such therefore occur and in fact even light atrocious manifestations thereof, they must be attributed to distorted dispositions (sexual and motoric spheres).

They are due to an awakening of latent psychical dispositions, occasioned by external circumstances which in no way affect the normal individual. They are not accidental deviations of sentiment or instinct in the sense as given by the modern doctrine of association. Sadistic sensations may often be traced back to early childhood and exist during a period of life when their revival can by no manner of means be attributed to external impressions, much less to sexual temper.

Sadism must, therefore, like Masochism and the antipathic sexual instinct, be counted among the primitive anomalies of the sexual life. It is a disturbance (a deviation) in the evolution of psychosexual processes sprouting from the soil of psychical degeneration.

That lust and cruelty often occur together is a fact that has long been recognized and is frequently observed. Writers of all kinds have called attention to this phenomenon.[14]

Blumröder ("Ueber Irresein," Leipzig, 1836, p. 51) saw a man who had several wounds in the pectoral muscle, which a woman, in great sexual excitement, had bitten at the height of lustful feeling during coitus. The same author ("Ueber Lust und Schmerz," *Friedreich's* "Magazin für Seelenkunde, 1830, ii., 5) calls especial attention to the psychological connection between lust and murder. In relation to this, he especially refers to the Indian myths of Siva and Durga (Death and Lust); to human sacrifice with voluptuous mysteries; and to sexual instinct at puberty with a lustful impulse to suicide, with whipping, pinching, and pricking of the genitals, in the blind impulse to satisfy sexual desire. *Lombroso* ("Verzeni e Agnoletti," Rome, 1874) also cites numerous examples of the occurrence of a desire to murder with greatly increased lust.

Ball quotes in his "Clinique St. Anne" the case of a powerful epileptic who during coitus bit off pieces of his consort's nose and swallowed them.

Ferriani (Archiv. delle psicopatie sessuali I. 1896, p. 106) speaks of a young man who used to wrestle with his inamorata before coitus, bit and pinched her during the act "because he felt otherwise no gratification." One day, however, he hurt the girl too much and she brought an action against him.

On the other hand, when homicidal mania has been excited, lust often follows. *Lombroso* (*op. cit.*) alludes to the fact mentioned by *Mantegazza*, that to the terrors of spoliation and plunder by bandits generally are added those of brutal lust and rape.[15] These examples form transitions to the pronounced pathological cases.

The examples of the degenerate Caesars (Nero, Tiberius) are also instructive. They took delight in having youths and maidens slaughtered before their eyes. Not less so is the history of that monster, Marschalls Gilles de Rays (*Jacob*, "Curiosités de l'histoire de France," Paris, 1858), who was executed in 1440, on account of mutilation and murder, which he had practiced for eight years on more than 800 children. As the monster confessed it, it was from reading Suetonius and the descriptions of the orgies of Tiberius, Caracalla, etc., that the idea was gained of locking children in his castles, torturing them, and then killing them. This inhuman wretch confessed that in the commission of these acts he enjoyed inexpressible pleasure. He had two assistants. The bodies of the unfortunate children were burned, and only a number of heads of particularly beautiful children were preserved—as memorials.

Cf. Eulenburg, op. cit. p. 58, where he gives satisfactory proofs of Rays' insanity; —— also, in "Die Zukunft, vii., Jahrg. No. 26; —*Bossard et Maulle*, Gilles de Rays, dit Barbe-Bleu, Paris, 1886 (*Champion*); *Michelet*, histoire de France, Tome vi., p. 316-326; Bibliothèque de Criminologie, t. xix., Paris, 1899, p. 245.

In an attempt to explain the association of lust and cruelty, it is necessary to return to a consideration of the quasi-physiological cases, in which, at the moment of most intense lust, very excitable individuals, who are otherwise normal, commit such acts as biting and scratching, which are usually due to anger. It must further be remembered that love and anger are not only the most intense emotions, but also the only two forms of robust emotion. Both seek their object, try to possess them-selves of it, and naturally exhaust themselves in a physical effect on it; both throw the psycho-motor sphere into the most intense excitement, and thus, by means of this excitation, reach their normal expression.

From this standpoint it is clear how lust impels to acts that other-wise are expressive of anger.[16] The one, like the other, is a state of exal-tation, an intense excitation of the entire psycho-motor sphere. Thus there arises an impulse to react on the object that induces the stimulus, in every possible way, and with the greatest intensity. Just as maniacal exaltation easily passes to raging destructiveness, so exaltation of the sexual emotion often induces an impulse to spend itself in senseless and apparently harmful acts. To a certain extent these are psychical accom-paniments; but it is not simply an unconscious excitation of innervation of muscles (which also sometimes occurs as blind violence); it is a true hyperbole, a desire to exert the utmost possible effect upon the individual giving rise to the stimulus. The most intense means, however, is the infliction of pain.

Through such cases of infliction of pain during the most intense emotion of lust, we approach the cases in which a real injury, wound, or death is inflicted on the victim.[17] In these cases the impulse to cruelty which may accompany the emotion of lust, becomes unbounded in a psychopathic individual; and, at the same time, owing to defect of moral feeling, all normal inhibitory ideas are absent or weakened.

Such monstrous, sadistic acts have, however, in men, in whom they are much more frequent than in women, another source in physiological conditions. In the intercourse of the sexes, the active or aggressive *rôle* belongs to man; woman remains passive, defensive.[18] It affords man great pleasure to win a woman, to conquer her; and in the art of love making, the modesty of woman, who keeps herself on the defensive until the moment of surrender, is an element of great psychological significance and impor-tance. Under normal conditions man meets obstacles which it is his part to overcome, and for which nature has given him an aggressive character. This aggressive character, however, under pathological conditions may likewise be excessively developed, and express itself in an impulse to subdue absolutely the object of desire, even to destroy or kill it.[19]

If both these constituent elements occur together—the abnormally intensified impulse to a violent reaction towards the object of the stimu-lus, and the abnormally intensified desire to conquer the woman,—then the most violent outbreaks of sadism occur.

Sadism is thus nothing else than an excessive and monstrous patho-logical intensification of phenomena—possible, too, in normal conditions in rudimental forms—which accompany the psychical sexual life, par-ticularly in males. It is of course not at all necessary, and not even the rule, that the sadistic individual should be conscious of his instinct. What he feels is, as a rule, only the impulse to cruel and violent treatment of the opposite sex, and the colouring of the idea of such acts with lustful feelings. Thus arises a powerful impulse to commit the imagined deeds. In as far as the actual motives of this instinct are not comprehended by the individual, the sadistic acts have the character of impulsive deeds.

When the association of lust and cruelty is present, not only does the lustful emotion awaken the impulse to cruelty, but *vice versâ*; cruel ideas and acts of cruelty cause sexual excitement, and in this way are used by perverse individuals.[20]

A differentiation of original and acquired cases of sadism is scarcely possible. Many individuals, tainted from birth, for a long time do everything to conquer the perverse instinct. If they are potent, they are able for some time to lead a normal sex life, often with the assistance of fanciful ideas of a perverse nature. Later, when the opposing motives of an ethical and aesthetic kind have been gradually overcome, and when oft-repeated experience has proved the natural act to give but incomplete satisfaction, the abnormal instinct suddenly bursts forth. Owing to this late expression, in acts, of an originally perverse disposition, the appearances are those of an acquired perversion. As a rule, it may be safely assumed that this psychopathic state exists from birth.

Sadistic acts vary in monstrousness according to the power exercised by the perverse instinct over the individual thus afflicted, and in accordance with the strength of opposing ideas that may be present, which nearly always are more or less weakened by original ethical defects, hereditary degeneracy, or moral insanity. Thus there arises a long series of forms which begins with capital crime and ends with paltry acts affording merely symbolic satisfaction to the perverse desires of the sadistic individual.

Sadistic acts may be further differentiated according to their nature; either taking place after consummated coitus which leaves the excessive desire unsatisfied; or, with diminished virility, being undertaken to merely stimulate the diminished power; or, finally, where virility is absolutely wanting, as becoming simply an equivalent for impossible coitus, and for the induction of ejaculation. In the last two cases, notwithstanding impotence, there is still intense *libido*; or there was, at least, intense *libido* in the individual at the time when the sadistic acts became a habit. Excessive sexual desire must always be regarded as the basis of sadistic inclinations. The impotence which occurs so frequently in psychopathic and neuropathic individuals here considered, resulting from excesses practiced in early youth, is usually dependent upon spinal weakness. Often, too, there is a kind of psychical impotence, superinduced by concentration of thought on the perverse act with simultaneous fading of the idea of normal satisfaction. No matter what the external form of the act may be, the mentally perverse predisposition and instinct of the individual are essential to an understanding of it.

(a) *Lust-Murder*[21] (*Lust Potentiated as Cruelty, Murderous Lust Extending to Anthropophagy*).

The most horrible example, and one which most pointedly shows the connection between lust and a desire to kill, is the case of Andreas Bichel, which *Feuerbach* published in his "Aktenmässige Darstellung merkwürdiger Verbrechen."

He killed and dissected the ravished girls. With reference to one of his victims, at his examination he expressed himself as follows: "I opened her breast and with a knife cut through the fleshy parts of the body. Then I arranged the body as a butcher does beef, and hacked it with an axe into pieces of a size to fit the hole which I had dug up in the mountain for burying it. I may say that while opening the body I was so greedy that I trembled, and could have cut out a piece and eaten it."

Lombroso, too ("Geschlechtstrieb und Verbrechen in ihren gegenseitigen Beziehungen." "*Goltdammer's* Archiv." Bd. xxx), mentions cases falling in the same category. A certain Philippe indulged in strangling prostitutes, after the sex act, and said: "I am fond of women, but it is sport for me to strangle them after having enjoyed them."

A certain Grassi (*Lombroso, op. cit.*, p. 12) was one night seized with sexual desire for a relative. Irritated by her remonstrance, he stabbed her several times in the abdomen with a knife, and also murdered her father and uncle who attempted to hold him back. Immediately thereafter he hastened to visit a prostitute in order to cool in her embrace his sexual passion. But this was not sufficient, for he then murdered his own father and slaughtered several oxen in the stable.

It cannot be doubted, after the foregoing. that a great number of so-called lust murders depend upon a combination of excessive and perverted desire. As a result of this perverse colouring of the feelings, further acts of bestiality with the corpse may result—*e.g.*, cutting it up and wallowing in the intestines. The case of Bichel points to this possibility.

A modern example is that of Menesclou ("Annales d'hygiène publique"), who was examined by *Lasègue, Brouardel* and *Motet*, declared to be mentally sound, and executed.

CASE 15. A four-year-old girl was missing from her parents' home, 15th April, 1880. On 16th April, Menesclou, one of the occupants of the house, was arrested. The forearm of the child was found in his pocket, and the head and entrails, in a half-charred condition, were taken from the stove. Other parts of the body were found in the water-closet. The genitals could not be found. M., when asked their whereabouts, became embarrassed. The circumstances, as well as an obscene poem found on his person, left no doubt that he had violated the child and then murdered her. M. expressed no remorse, asserting that his deed was an unhappy accident. His intelligence was limited. He presented no anatomical signs of degeneration; somewhat deaf and scrofulous.

Age twenty.

Convulsions at the age of nine month. Later he suffered from disturbed sleep (nocturnal bedwetting); was nervous, and developed tardily and imperfectly. With puberty he became irritable, showed evil inclinations, was lazy, intractable, and in all trades proved to be of no use. He grew no better even in the House of Correction. He was made a marine, but there, too, he proved useless. When he returned home he stole from his parents, and spent his time in bad company. He did not run after women, but gave himself up passionately to masturbation, and occasionally indulged in sodomy with bitches. His mother suffered with violent desire during menstrual periods. An uncle was insane, and another a drunkard. The examination of M.'s brain showed morbid changes of the frontal lobes, of the first and second temporal convolutions, and of a part of the occipital convolutions.

CASE 16. Alton, a clerk in England, went for a walk out of town. He lured a child into a thicket. Afterwards at his office he made this entry in his note-book: "Killed to-day a young girl; it was fine and hot." The child was missed, searched for, and found cut into pieces. Many parts, and among them the genitals, could not be found. A. did not show the slightest trace of emotion, and gave no explanation of the motive or circumstances of his horrible deed. He was a psychopathic individual, and occasionally subject to fits of depression and boredom. His father had had an attack of acute mania. A near relative suffered from mania with homicidal impulses. A. was executed.

CASE 17. Jack the Ripper.—On December 1, 1887, July 7, August 8, September 30, one day in the month of October and on the 9th of November, 1888; on the 1st of June, the 17th of July and the 10th of September, 1889, the bodies of women were found in various lonely quarters of London ripped open and mutilated in a peculiar fashion. The murderer has never been found. It is probable that he first cut the throats of his victims, then ripped open the abdomen and groped among the intestines. In some instances he cut off the genitals and carried them away; in others he only tore them to pieces and left them behind. He does not seem to have had sexual intercourse with his victims, but very likely the murderous act and subsequent mutilation of the corpse were equivalents for the sexual act. (*McDonald*, le criminal type, 2 edit., Lyon, 1884;—*Spitzka*, The Journal of Mental and Nervous Diseases, 1888, December;—*Kierman*, The Medical Standard, 1888, Nov. and Dec.)

CASE 18. Vacher, the Ripper.—On the 31st August, 1895, Portalier, seventeen years old, a shepherd, was found naked in the field. The belly was ripped open and the body bore other wounds besides. Examination showed that the victim had been strangled first. On the 4th August, 1897, a tramp, named Vacher, was arrested on suspicion of having committed this crime. He confessed to it as well as to numerous other acts of a similar nature that had been perpetrated in various parts of France since 1894. He claimed that at the time when he committed the crimes he suffered from temporary insanity and irresistible impulse, in fact, was a madman. Medical examination, however, proved that Vacher was mentally competent when he committed these atrocious deeds, fled after their commission and had a very clear memory of the facts.

V. was born in 1869 of honourable parents and belonged to a mentally sound family. He never had a severe illness, was from his earliest infancy vicious, lazy and shy of work. When twenty he had immorally assaulted a small child. During his military service he had gained for himself a very bad reputation and was in 1893 discharged from his regiment on account of "psychical disturbances" (confused talk, persecution-mania, threatening language, extreme irritability). In 1893 he wounded a girl because she refused to marry him, then made an attempt at suicide (he shot himself through the right ear, which left him deaf on that side and produced facial paralysis). He was sent to an insane asylum and there treated for persecution-mania. On April 1, 1894, he was dismissed as cured. He began to tramp about the country and committed the following horrible crimes: On March 20, 1894, he strangled Delhomme, twenty-one years old, cut her throat, trampled upon her abdomen, tore out a portion of her right breast and then had coitus with the corpse. The same atrocity, but without ravaging the bodies, he committed on November 20, 1804, on a girl of the name of Marcel, 13 years of age, and on May 12, 1895, on another girl named Mortureux, 17 years of age. On August 24, 1895, he strangled and then ravaged a lady of the name of Morand, 58 years old, and on the 22d he cut the throat of Allaise, a sixteen year old girl and attempted to rip her abdomen open. On September 29, he committed the same crime—as later on on Portalier—on Palet, a fifteen-year-old boy, but in this instance he also cut off the genitals of the boy and sexually assaulted the corpse.

On the 1st of March, 1896, he attempted rape on Deronet, a girl eleven years old, but was scared off by the field police. On the 10th of September, he committed his usual atrocity on a Mrs. Mounier, just married, nineteen years of age, and on the 1st of October, on Rodier, a shepherdess, fourteen years of age. He cut out her genitals and carried them away. Toward the end of May, 1897, he killed a tramp boy, fourteen years old, named Beaupied, by cutting his throat. The corpse he threw down into a well. On June 18th he murdered a shepherd boy, thirteen years old, named Laurent, and committed pederasty on the corpse. Soon afterward he made an attempt on a Mrs. Plantier, but she was rescued. Unfortunately they allowed him to go unpunished.

Lacassagne, Professor of Forensic Medicine in Lyon, *Pierrel*, Professor of Psychiatry, and *Rebatel*, specialists on insanity, were the experts in this atrocious murder trial. They found no hereditary taints, no cerebral disease, nor traces of epilepsy. V. was not particularly bright, very irascible from his earliest years, vicious and fond of maltreating animals. No one retained him long in service. He entered a monastery, but was soon dismissed as he began to masturbate his comrades. He could not find employment on account of immorality and ill temper. He was not a drinker. In the army he was feared and shunned. One day when he was disappointed by not being made a corporal, he flew into a passion, attacked his superior and became delirious. He was taken to the infirmary and thence sent to the insane asylum. His comrades did not consider him normal. During his spells of rage he was uncontrollable and considered dangerous. He always threatened others with cutting their throats, and was thought capable of doing such an act. He slept badly, constantly dreamed of murder, and often was delirious during the night, so that no one cared for sleeping near him.

At the asylum he was found to suffer from persecution-mania and was considered a dangerous character. Nevertheless he was dismissed as cured.

Subsequently he became guilty of eleven murders, which are acts of sadism, lust murders. They consisted of strangling, cutting of the throat and ripping open of the abdomen, mutilation of the corpse, especially the genitals, eventually gratification of the sexual lust on the corpse.

It was definitely proved that V. acted in cold blood, was quite conscious of his actions and suffered from no psychical abnormality.

He committed the crimes in various sections of France, traversing the country in every direction.

There were no marks of anatomical degeneration. His genitals were normally developed. In confinement he was lazy, irascible and quite intractable. Out of sheer stubbornness and because he thought he had been slighted, he refused on one occasion all food for a period of seven days. On another occasion he flew into a frightful rage when permission to go to church was refused him. He spoke cynically of his crimes, showed no remorse, insisted that they were the outcome of madness and insanity, played the insane, hoping thus to be sent to an insane asylum whence escape is easier. The experts could establish no symptoms of mental disturbance.

Resumé of the experts: "V. is neither an epileptic nor subject to an impulsive disease. He is an immoral, passionate man, who once temporarily suffered from a depressing persecution-mania, coupled with an impulse to suicide. Of this he was cured, and thereafter became responsible for his actions. His crimes are those of an antisocial, sadistic, bloodthirsty being, who considers himself privileged to commit these atrocities because he was once upon a time treated in an asylum for insanity, and thereby escaped well merited punishment. He is a common criminal and

there are no ameliorating circumstances to be found in his favour."—
V. was sentenced to death. (Archives d'anthropologie criminelle, xiii.,
No. 78.)

In such cases it may even happen that appetite for the flesh of the
murdered victim arises, and in consequence of this perverse colouring of
the idea, parts of the body may be eaten.

CASE 19. Leger, vine-dresser, aged twenty-four. From youth moody,
silent, shy of people. He started out in search of a situation. Wandering
about eight days in the forest he there caught a girl twelve years old,
violated her, mutilated her genitals, tore out her heart, ate of it, drank
the blood, and buried the remains. Arrested, at first he lied, but finally
confessed his crime with cynical cold-bloodedness. He listened to his
sentence of death with indifference, and was executed. At the *post-mortem*
examination *Esquirol* found morbid adhesions between the cerebral
membranes and the brain (*Georget*, "Darstellung der Prozesse *Leger,
Feldtmann*," etc., Darmstadt, 1827).

CASE 20. Tirsch, hospital beneficiary of Prag, aged fifty-five, always
silent, peculiar, coarse, very irritable, grumbling, revengeful, was sentenced
to twenty years' imprisonment for violating a girl ten years old. He had
attracted attention on account of outbursts of anger from insignificant
causes, and also on account of weariness with life. In 1864, on account
of the refusal of an offer of marriage which he made to a widow, he
developed a hatred toward women, and on the 8th of July he went
about with the intention of killing one of this hated sex. He waylaid
a wretched old woman as she was hurrying through a wood, demanded
coitus of her, and when she refused, threw her to the ground and
strangled her, "possessed by fury." He then cut a branch off a birch-tree
and wanted to beat the corpse with it, but did not do so, because his
conscience forbade him to do such a thing He therefore cut off the dead
woman's breasts and genitalia with a knife, cooked them at home and,
in the course of the next few days, ate them. On the 12th of September,
when he was arrested, the remains of this meal were found. He gave
as the motive of this act "inner impulse." He himself wished to be executed, because he had always been an outcast. In confinement he showed
great emotional irritability and occasional outbursts of fury, preceded
by refusal of food, which made isolation, lasting several days, necessary.
It was authoritatively established that most of his earlier excesses
were coincident with outbreaks of excitement and fury (*Maschka*, "Pra-
ger Vierteljahrsschrift," 1886, i., p. 79. "*Gauster* bei Maschka, Handb. der
gerichtl. Medicin," iv., p. 489).

In other cases of lust-murder, for physical and mental reasons (vide
supra), violation is omitted, and the sadistic crime alone becomes the

equivalent of coitus. The prototype of such cases is the following one of Verzeni. The life of his victim hung on the rapid or retarded occurrence of ejaculation. Since this remarkable case presents all the peculiarities which modern science knows concerning the relation of lust to lust-murder with cannibalism, and especially since it was carefully studied, it receives detailed description here:

CASE 21. Vincenz Verzeni, born in 1849; since January 11th, 1872, in prison; was accused (1) of an attempt to strangle his nurse Marianne, four years ago, while she lay sick in bed; (2) of a similar attempt on a married woman, Arsuffi, aged twenty-seven; (3) of an attempt to strangle a married woman, Gala, by grasping her throat while kneeling on her abdomen; (4) on suspicion of the following murders:—

In December a fourteen-year-old girl, Johanna Motta, set out for a neighbouring village between seven and eight o'clock in the morning. As she did not return, her master set out to find her, and discovered her body near the village, lying by a path in the fields. The corpse was frightfully mutilated with numerous wounds. The intestines and genitals had been torn from the open body, and were found near by. The naked-ness of the body and erosions on the thighs made it seem probable that there had been an attempt at rape; the mouth, filled with earth, pointed to suffocation. In the neighborhood of the body, under a pile of straw, were found a portion of flesh torn from the right calf, and pieces of clothing. The perpetrator of the deed remained undiscovered.

On 28th August, 1871, a married woman, Frigeni, aged twenty-eight, set out into the fields early in the morning. As she did not return by eight o'clock, her husband started out to fetch her. He found her a corpse, lying naked in the field, with the mark of a thong, with which she had been strangled, around her neck, and with numerous wounds. The abdomen had been ripped open, and the intestines were hanging out.

On August 29th, at noon, as Maria Previtali, aged nineteen, went through a field, she was followed by her cousin, Verzeni. He dragged her into a field of grain, threw her to the ground and began to choke her. As he let her go for a moment to ascertain whether any one was near, the girl got up and, by her supplicating entreaty, induced Verzeni to let her go, after he had pressed her hands together for some time.

Verzeni was brought before a court. He was then twenty-two years old. Cranium of more than average size, but asymmetrical. The right frontal bone narrower and lower than the left, the right frontal promi-nence being less developed, and the right ear smaller than the left (by 1 centimetre in length and 3 centimetres in breadth); both ears defective in the inferior half of the helix; the right temporal artery somewhat atheromatous. Bull-necked; enormous development of the cheek bone and inferior jaw bone; penis greatly developed, frenulum missing; slight divergent alternating strabismus (insufficiency of the internal rectus muscle, and myopia). *Lombroso* concluded from these signs of degeneration, that there was a congenital arrest of development of the right frontal bone. As seemed probable, Verzeni had a bad ancestry—two uncles were cretins; a third, microcephalic, beardless, one testicle missing, the other atrophic. The father showed traces of pellagrous degeneration, and had an attack of pellagrous hypochondria. A cousin suffered from cerebral hyperaemia; another was a confirmed thief.

Verzeni's family was bigoted and low-minded. He himself had ordinary intelligence; knew how to defend himself well; sought to prove an *alibi* and cast suspicion on others. There was nothing in his past that pointed to mental disease, but his character was peculiar. He was silent and inclined to be solitary. In prison he was cynical. He masturbated, and made every effort to gain sight of women.

Verzeni finally confessed his deeds and their motive. The commission of them gave him an indescribably pleasant (lustful) feeling, which was accompanied by erection and ejaculation. As soon as he had grasped his victim by the neck, sexual sensations were experienced. It was entirely the same to him, with reference to these sensations, whether the women were old, young, ugly, or beautiful. Usually, simply choking them had satisfied him, and he then had allowed his victims to live; in the two cases mentioned, the sexual satisfaction was delayed, and he had continued to choke them until they died. The gratification experienced in this garrotting was greater than in masturbation. The abrasions of the skin on Motta's thighs were produced by his teeth, whilst sucking her blood in most intense lustful pleasure. He had torn out a piece of flesh from her calf and taken it with him to roast at home; but on the way he hid it under the straw-stack, for fear his mother might suspect him. He also carried pieces of the clothing and intestines some distance, because it gave him great pleasure to smell and touch them. The strength which he possessed in these moments of intense lustful pleasure was enormous. He had never been a fool; while committing his deeds he saw nothing around him (apparently as a result of intense sexual excitement, annihilation of perception—instinctive action). After such acts he was always very happy, enjoying a feeling of great satisfaction. He had never had pangs of conscience. It had never occurred to him to touch the genitals of the martyred women, or to violate his victims. It had satisfied him to throttle them and suck their blood. These statements of this modern vampire seem to rest on truth. Normal sexual impulses seemed to have remained foreign to him. Two sweethearts that he had, he was satisfied to look at; it was very strange to him that he had no inclination to strangle them or press their hands, but he had not had the same pleasure with them as with his victims. There was no trace of moral sense, remorse and the like.

Verzeni said himself that it would be a good thing if he were to be kept in prison, because with freedom he could not resist his impulses.

Verzeni was sentenced to imprisonment for life (*Lombroso,* "Verzeni e Agnoletti," Rome, 1873). The confessions which Verzeni made after his sentence are interesting:

"I had an unspeakable delight in strangling women, experiencing during the act erections and real sexual pleasure. It was even a pleasure only to smell female clothing. The feeling of pleasure while strangling them was much greater than that which I experienced while masturbating. I took great delight in drinking Motta's blood. It also gave me the greatest pleasure to pull the hair-pins out of the hair of my victims.

"I took the clothing and intestines, because of the pleasure it gave me to smell and touch them. At last my mother came to suspect me, because she noticed spots of semen on my shirt after each murder or attempt at one. I am not crazy, but in the moment of strangling my victims I saw nothing else. After the commission of the deeds I was satisfied and felt well. It never occurred to me to touch or look at the genitals or such things. It satisfied me to seize the women by the neck and suck their blood. To this very day I am ignorant of how a woman is formed. During the strangling and after it, I pressed myself on the entire body without thinking of one part more than another."

Verzeni arrived at his perverse acts quite independently, after having noticed, when he was twelve years old, that he experienced a peculiar feeling of pleasure while wringing the necks of chickens. After this he had often killed great numbers of them and then said that a weasel had been in the hen-coop (*Lombroso,* "*Goltdammer's* Archiv," Bd. xxx., p. 13).

Lombroso mentions an analogous case ("*Goltdammer's* Archiv") which occurred in Vittoria (Spain):—

CASE 22. A certain Gruyo, aged forty-one, with a blameless past life, having been three times married, strangled six women in the course of ten years. They were almost all public prostitutes and quite old. After the strangling he tore out their intestines and kidneys through the vagina. Some of his victims he violated before killing, others, on account of the occurrence of impotence, he did not. He set about his horrible deeds with such care that he remained undetected for ten years.

(b) *Mutilation of Corpses.*

Following on the preceding horrible group of perversions, come naturally the necrophiles; in these cases, just as with lustful murderers and analogous cases, an idea which in itself awakens a feeling of horror, and before which a sane person would shudder, is accompanied by lustful feelings, and thus leads to the impulse to indulge in acts of necrophilia.

The cases of mutilation of bodies mentioned in literature seem to be of a pathological character; but, with the exception of that of Sergeant Bertrand (see below), they are far from being described and observed with accuracy. In certain cases there may be nothing more than the possibility that unbridled desire sees in the idea of death no obstacle to its satisfaction. The seventh case mentioned by *Moreau*, perhaps, belongs here.

A man, aged twenty-three, attempted to rape a woman, aged fifty-three. Struggling, he killed her, and then violated her, threw her in the water, and fished her out again for renewed violation. The murderer was executed. The meninges of the anterior lobes were thickened and adherent to the *cortex*.

French writers have recorded numerous examples of necrophilia.[22] Two cases concerned monks performing the watch for the dead. In a third case the subject was an idiot, who also suffered from periodical mania, and after commission of rape was sent to an insane asylum, where he mutilated female bodies in the mortuary.

In other cases, however, there is undoubtedly direct preference for a corpse to the living woman. When no other act of cruelty—cutting into pieces, etc.—is practiced on the cadaver, it is probable that the lifeless condition itself forms the stimulus for the perverse individual. It is possible that the corpse—a human form absolutely without will—satisfies an abnormal desire, in that the object of desire is seen to be capable of absolute subjugation, without possibility of resistance.

Brierre de Boismont ("Gazette médicale," July 21st, 1859) relates the history of a corpse-violator who, after bribing the watchman, had gained entrance to the corpse of a girl of sixteen belonging to a family of high social position. At night a noise was heard in the death-chamber, as if a piece of furniture had fallen over. The mother of the dead girl effected an entrance and saw a man dressed in his night-shirt springing from the bed where the body lay: It was at first thought that the man was a thief, but the real explanation was soon discovered. It afterwards transpired that the culprit, a man of good family, had often violated the corpses of young women. He was sentenced to imprisonment for life.

The story of a prelate, reported by *Taxil* [23] ("La prostitution contemporaine," p. 171), is of great interest as an example of necrophilia. From time to time he would visit a certain brothel in Paris and order a prostitute, dressed in white like a corpse, to be laid out on a bier. At the appointed hour he would appear in the room, which, in the meantime had been elaborately prepared as a room of mourning; then he would act as if reading a mass for the soul, and finally throw himself upon the girl, who, during the whole time, was compelled to play the *rôle* of a corpse.[24]

The cases in which the perpetrator injures and cuts up the corpse are clearer. Such cases come next to those of lust-murder, in so far as cruelty, or at least an impulse to attack the female body, is connected with lust. It is possible that a remnant of moral sense deters from the cruel act in a living woman, and possibly the fancy passes beyond lust-murder and rests on its result, the corpse. Here also it is possible that the idea of defenselessness of the body plays a *rôle*.

CASE 23. Sergeant Bertrand, a man of delicate physical constitution and of peculiar character; from childhood silent and inclined to solitude.

The details of the health of his family were not satisfactorily known; but the occurrence of mental diseases in his ancestors was ascertained. It was said that while he was a child he was affected with destructive impulses, which he himself could not explain. He would break whatever was at hand. In early childhood, without teaching, he learned to masturbate. At nine he began to feel inclinations towards persons of the opposite sex. At thirteen the impulse to sexual intercourse became powerfully awakened in him. He now masturbated excessively. When he did this, his fancy always created a room filled with women. He would imagine that he carried out the sexual act with them and then killed them. Immediately thereafter he would think of them as corpses, and of how he defiled them. Occasionally in such situations the thought of carrying out a similar act with male corpses would come up, but it was always attended with a feeling of disgust.

In time he felt the impulse to carry out such acts with actual corpses. For want of human bodies, he obtained those of animals. He would cut open the abdomen, tear out the entrails, and masturbate during the act. He declared that in this way he experienced inexpressible pleasure. In 1846 these bodies no longer satisfied him. He now killed dogs, and proceeded with them as before. Toward the end of 1846 he first felt the desire to make use of human bodies.

At first he had a horror of it. In 1847, being by accident in a grave-yard, he ran across the grave of a newly buried corpse. Then this impulse, with headache and palpitation of the heart, became so powerful that, although there were people near by, and he was in danger of detection, he dug up the body. In the absence of a convenient instrument for cutting it up, he satisfied himself by hacking it with a shovel.

In 1847 and 1848, during two weeks, as reported, the impulse, accompanied by violent headache, to commit brutalities on corpses actuated him. Under the greatest difficulties and dangers he satisfied this impulse some fifteen times. He dug up the bodies with his hands, in nowise sensible in his excitement to the injuries he thus inflicted on himself. When he had obtained the body, he cut it up with a sword or pocket-knife, tore out the entrails, and then masturbated. The sex of the bodies is said to have been a matter of indifference to him, though it was ascertained that this modern vampire had dug up more female than male corpses.

During these acts he declared himself to have been in an indescribable state of sexual excitement. After having cut them up, he reinterred the bodies.

In July, 1848, he accidentally came across the body of a girl of sixteen. Then, for the first time, he experienced a desire to carry out coitus on a cadaver.

"I covered it with kisses and pressed it wildly to my heart. All that one could enjoy with a living woman is nothing in comparison with the pleasure I experienced. After I had enjoyed it for about a quarter of an hour, I cut the body up, as usual, and tore out the entrails. Then I buried the cadaver again." Only after this, as B. declared, had he felt the impulse to use the bodies sexually before cutting them up, and thereafter he had done it in three instances. The actual motive for exhuming the bodies, however, was then, as before, to cut them up; and the enjoyment in so doing was greater than in using the bodies sexually. The latter act had always been nothing more than an episode of the principal one, and had never quieted his desires; for which reason he had later on always mutilated the body.

The medico-legal examiners gave an opinion of "monomania." Court-martial sentence to one year's imprisonment. (*Michéa,* "Union méd.," 1849; *Lunier,* "Annal. méd.-psycho." 1849, p. 153; *Tardieu,* "Attentats aux moeurs," 1878, p. 114; *Legrand,* "La folie devant les tribun.," p. 524.)

CASE 24. Ardisson, born 1872, belonged to a family of criminals and insane. At school he learned readily; he was not addicted to drink, had no epileptic antecedents, never had an illness, but was rather weak-minded. The man who adopted him and with whom he lived, was a moral outcast. When A. came of puberty he practiced masturbation. He was in the habit of devouring his own sperm because "it would be a pity to lose it." He ran after the girls, but could not understand why they shunned him. In places where women went to urinate, he would drink the urine. He did not think that there was anything wrong about this. He was looked upon in the village as a venal felon. With his adopter he shared the favours of the beggar women that stayed over night at their house. He was fond of fornication, was a breast fetichist and he loved to suck breasts. Later on he fell to necrophily. He exhumed cadavers of females ranging from three to sixty years of age, sucked their breasts, practiced cunnilingus on them, but rarely coitus or mutilation. Once he carried away the head of a woman, at another time the whole corpse of a little girl three and one-half years old. After his ghoulish deeds he would re-arrange the grave properly. He lived isolated by himself, was at times very morose, never showed signs of heart. As a rule, however, he was not of an evil disposition even when in prison. Several times he worked as a stonemason. Remorse and shame over his misdeeds were unknown to him. In 1892 he had for a while acted as a gravedigger. He deserted from the army and then took to begging from house to house. He loved to eat rats and cats. When arrested and returned to the regiment he deserted again. He was not punished because he was not held responsible. Dismissed from the army he again became a gravedigger. When a girl of seventeen who had very prominent breasts was buried his old passion awoke again. He unearthed the cadaver and profaned it in his usual manner. This happened from now on very frequently. The head of one woman which he took home with him, he covered with kisses and called it his bride. He was caught after he had taken home the body of a child three and one-half years of age which he secreted in the straw. On this he gratified his sexual desires even whilst the putrid body was falling to pieces. The stench filling the house betrayed him. Laughingly he admitted everything.—A. was small of stature, had a protruding jaw, and was feeble; skull symmetrical; general tremor; genitals normal, without sexual emotion; intelligence very limited; devoid of all moral sense.—A. was pleased with prison life. (*Epaulard op. cit.*)

(c) Injury to Women (Stabbing, Flagellation, etc.).

Following lust-murder and violation of corpses, come cases closely allied to the former, in which injury of the victim of lust and sight of the victim's blood are a delight and pleasure. The notorious Marquis de Sade,[25] after whom this combination of lust and cruelty has been named, was such a monster. Coitus only excited him when he could prick the object of his desire until the blood came. His greatest pleasure was to injure naked prostitutes and then dress their wounds.

The case of a captain belongs here, mentioned by *Brierre de Boismont,* who always compelled the object of his affection to place leeches to the genitals before coitus, which was very frequent. Finally this woman became very anaemic and, as a result of this, insane.

The following case, from my own practice, very clearly shows the connection between lust and cruelty, with desire to shed and see blood:—

CASE 25. Mr. X., aged twenty-five; father syphilitic, died of paretic dementia; mother hysterical and neurasthenic. He was a weak individual, constitutionally neuropathic, and presented several anatomical signs of degeneration.

When a child, hypochondria and impulsiveness; later, constant alternation of exaltation and depression. While yet a child of ten the patient felt a peculiar lustful desire to see blood flow from his fingers. Thereafter he often cut or pricked himself in the fingers, and took great delight in it. Very early, erections were added to this, and also if he saw the blood of others; for example, when he once saw the servant-girl cut her finger it gave him an intense lustful feeling. From this time his sexual life became more and more active. Without any teaching he began to masturbate, and always during the act there were memory-pictures of bleeding women. It now no longer sufficed him to see his own blood flow; he longed to see the blood of young females, especially those that were attractive to him. He could scarcely overcome the impulse to violate two cousins and a certain servant.

Any young woman, although not attractive, induced this impulse when she excited him by some peculiarity of dress or adornment, especially coral jewelry. At first he succeeded in overcoming these desires; but in his imagination thoughts of blood were ever present, inducing lustful excitement. An inner relation existed between thoughts and feelings. Often there were other cruel fantasies. He imagined himself in the *rôle* of a tyrant who had the people shot in crowds with grape-shot. He would imagine a scene as it would be, if enemies were to take a city and mutilate, torture, kill and rape the young women.

When in his normal state this patient, who had a mild disposition and was not morally defective, was ashamed of and horrified by such cruel, lustful fancies, which became at once latent, when his sexual excitement was satisfied by masturbation.

After a few years the patient became neurasthenic. Then simple imaginary representations of blood and scenes of blood sufficed to induce ejaculation. In order to free himself from his vice and his cruel imagination, he began to indulge in sexual intercourse with females. Coitus was possible, but only when the patient called up the idea that the girl's fingers were bleeding. Without the assistance of this idea no erection was possible. The cruel thought of cutting was limited to the woman's hand. At the time of greatest sexual excitement, simply the sight of the hand of an attractive woman was sufficient to induce most violent erections. Frightened by the popular stories about the injurious results of onanism, he abstained and fell into a condition of severe general neurasthenia, with melancholia and weariness with life. Careful and watchful medical treatment cured the patient for a few months. He remained mentally well for three years; but became again very sensual, though very seldom was he troubled by his earlier ideas of flowing blood. He gave up masturbation altogether, and found satisfaction in natural sexual indulgence, remained virile, and it was no longer necessary for him to call up ideas of blood.

The following case, reported by *Tarnowsky* (*op. cit.*, p. 61), shows that such lustful, cruel impulses may be simply episodical, and occur in certain exceptional states of mind in neurotic individuals:—

CASE 26. Z., physician; neuropathic constitution, reacting badly to alcohol. Under ordinary circumstances capable of normal coitus, but as soon as he had indulged in wine he found that his increased *libido* was no longer satisfied by simple coitus. In this condition he was compelled to prick the genitals of the girl, or to make stabs with the lancet, to see blood, and feel the entrance of the blade into the living body, in order to have ejaculation and experience complete satiety of his lust.

The majority of those afflicted with this form of perversion seem insensible to the normal stimulus of woman. In the first case (25), the assistance of the idea of blood was necessary to obtain erection. The following is that of a man who, by masturbation, etc., in early youth, had diminished his power of erection so that the sadistic act took the place of coitus:

CASE 27. *The girl-stabber of Bozen* (reported by *Demme*, "Buch der Verbrechen," Bd. ii., p. 341). In 1829, H., aged thirty, soldier, became the subject of legal investigation. At different times and in different places, he had wounded girls with pocket-knives or penknives, by stabbing them in the abdomen, preferably in the genitals. He gave as a motive for these acts heightened sexual impulse, increasing to the intensity of fury, which found satisfaction only in the thought and act of stabbing persons of the female sex. This impulse would pursue him for days at a time. He would then pass into a confused mental state, which would clear away only when the impulse had been satisfied by the deed. In the act of stabbing he experienced the same satisfaction as that produced by completed coitus. This was increased by the sight of blood dripping from the knife. In his tenth year the sexual instinct became powerfully manifest. At first he yielded to masturbation, and felt physically and mentally weakened by it. Before he became a girl-stabber, he had satisfied his sexual lust in violation of immature girls, by causing them to practice masturbation on him, and by sodomy. Gradually the thought came to him how pleasurable it would be to stab a young and pretty girl in the genitals, and take delight in the sight of the blood running from the knife.

Among his effects were found copies of the objects of phallic cult and obscene pictures painted by himself of Mary's conception, and of the "thought of God injected" into the lap of the Virgin. He was considered a peculiar, very irritable man, shy of people, fond of women, moody and glum. Of shame and regret for his deeds no traces were ever found. He was apparently a person [26] who had become impotent through early sexual excesses, and was thus predisposed, by the continuance of intense sexual desire and heredity, to perversion of sexual life.

CASE 28. In the "sixties" the inhabitants of Leipzig were frightened by a man who was accustomed to attack young girls on the street, stabbing them in the upper-arm with a dagger. Finally arrested, he was recognized as a sadist, who at the instant of stabbing had an ejaculation, and with whom the wounding of the girls was an equivalent for coitus. (*Wharton*, "A Treatise on Mental Unsoundness," § 623. Philadelphia, 1873.)[27]

Impotence exists likewise in the next three cases. It may be psychical, however, since the principal tone of the sexual life lies in sadistic inclination and the normal elements are distorted:—

CASE 29. *The girl-cutter of Augsburg* (reported by *Demme* "Buch der Verbrechen," vii., p. 281). Bartle, wine-merchant. He was subject to lively sexual excitement at the age of fourteen, though decidedly opposed to its satisfaction by coitus, his aversion going so far as disgust for the female sex. At that time he already had the idea to cut girls, and thus satisfy his sexual desire. He refrained from it, however, because of lack of opportunity and courage. He disdained masturbation, but now and then had pollutions with erotic dreams of girls who had been cut. At the age of nineteen he for the first time cut a girl. During the act he had a seminal emission and experienced intense pleasure. From that time the impulse grew constantly more powerful. He chose only young and pretty girls, and, as a rule, asked them before the deed whether they were still single. The ejaculation or sexual satisfaction occurred only when he was sure that he had actually wounded the girls. After such an act he always felt tired and bad, and was also troubled with qualms of conscience. Up to his thirty-second year he pursued this process of cutting, but was always careful not to wound the girls dangerously. From that time until his thirty-sixth year he was able to control his impulse. Then he sought to satisfy himself by simply pressing the girls on the arm or neck, but this gave rise to erections only and not to ejaculation. Then he sought to attain his object by pricking the girls with the knife left in its sheath, but this did not suffice. Finally, he stabbed with the open knife, and had complete success, for he thought that a girl when stabbed bled more and suffered more pain than when merely cut. In his thirty-seventh year he was detected and arrested. In his lodgings were found a collection of daggers, sword-canes, and knives. He said that the mere sight of these weapons, and still more the grasping of them, gave him an intense feeling of sexual pleasure, with violent excitement. According to his own confession, he had injured in all fifty girls. His external appearance was rather pleasing. He lived in very good circumstances, but was peculiar and shy.

CASE 30. During the month of June, 1896, quite a number of young girls had been stabbed in the genitals in the street in broad daylight. On the 2nd of July the perpetrator was caught in the act. V., twenty years of age, was hereditarily heavily tainted; when fifteen years old he had been sexually excited to a high degree at the sight óf a woman's buttocks. From that time on it was this part of the female body which attracted him in a sensuous manner and became the object of his erotic fancies and dreams, accompanied by pollutions. Soon this was coupled with the lascivious desire to slap, pinch or cut the genitals of women. At the moment when he in his dreams performed this act, pollution took place. Soon he was tempted to transfer his dreams into real practice. For a while he succeeded in mastering his morbid craving, but this produced feelings of anxiety and a copious perspiration would break out over his entire body. When orgasm and erection became very vehement, he would be overcome with fear and confusion to such an extent that the impulse to cut became irresistible. At that psychical moment ejaculation would take place, and he felt relieved in body and mind. *Magnan* in *Thoinot's op. cit.* p. 451.—For more detailed account see *Garnier* in Annales d'hygiène publique, 1900, Feb., p. 112.)

CASE 31. J. H., aged twenty-six, in 1883 came for consultation concerning severe neurasthenia and hypochondria. Patient confessed that he had practiced onanism since his fourteenth year, infrequently up to his eighteenth year, but since that time he had been unable to resist the impulse. Up to that time he had no opportunity to approach females, for he had been anxiously cared for and never left alone on account of being an invalid. He had had no real desire for this unknown pleasure, but he accidentally learned what it was when one of his mother's maids cut her hand severely on a pane of glass, which she had broken while washing windows. While helping to stop the bleeding he could not keep from sucking up the blood that flowed from the wound, and in this act he experienced extreme erotic excitement, with complete orgasm and ejaculation.

From that time on, he sought, in every possible way to see and, where practicable, to taste the fresh blood of females. That of young girls was preferred by him. He spared no pains or expense to obtain this pleasure. At first he availed himself of a young servant, who allowed her finger to be pricked with a needle or lancet at his request. When his mother discovered this, she discharged the girl. Then he was driven to prostitutes as a substitute, with success frequently enough, though with some difficulty. In the intervals he practiced onanism and incomplete coitus with a woman, which, however, never afforded him complete satisfaction, but, on the contrary, caused listlessness and self-reproach. On account of his nervous difficulties he visited many sanatoria, and was twice a voluntary patient in institutions. He used hydrotherapy, electricity, and strengthening cures, without particular success. For a time it was possible, by means of cold sitz-baths, monobromate of camphor, and bromides, to diminish his sexual excitability and onanistic impulse. However, when the patient felt himself free again, he would immediately fall into his old passion, and spare no pains or money to satisfy his sexual desire in the abnormal manner described.

Of special interest for the scientific proof of sadism is a case related by *Moll* (see case 29, ninth edition of this work (German) and recently published by *Moll* himself in his book on "Libido Sexualis," p. 500.).

It discloses clearly one of the hidden roots of sadism—the impulse to complete subjugation of the woman, which here became consciously entertained. This is the more remarkable since it occurred in an individual decidedly timid, and in other respects modest and even apprehensive. The case also shows clearly that powerful *libido* which even impels the individual to overcome all obstacles, may be present, while at the same time coitus is not desired, because the principal intensity of feeling is, from the beginning, connected with the cruel part of the sadistic (lustful and cruel) circle of ideas. This case also contains weak elements of masochism (see below).

Cases are by no means infrequent in which men with perverse inclinations induce prostitutes, by paying them high prices, to allow themselves to be whipped and even wounded by them. Works on prostitution contain reports of them (see *Coffignon*, "La Corruption à Paris," etc.).

(d) *Defilement of Women.*

The perverse sadistic impulse, to injure women and put contempt and humiliation upon them, is also expressed in the desire to defile them with disgusting or, at least, foul things.

The following case, published by *Arndt* ("Vierteljahrsschr. f. ger. Medicin," N. F. xvii., H. 1), belongs here:—

CASE 32. A., a medical student at Greifswald, was accused of repeatedly exhibiting his genitals in public to girls of virtuous family; he would allow his private parts to hang, completely naked, out of his trousers, previously keeping them covered under his overcoat. Sometimes he followed the girls as they fled and, drawing them towards him, would defile them with urine. All this happened in broad daylight, and he never spoke a word as he performed these actions.

A. was twenty-three years old, well built, neat in dress, and polite in manners. Indication of under-developed brain; chronic pneumonia of the apex of the right lung; emphysema. Pulse, 60; in excitement not more than 70 to 80. Genitals normal. Occasional disturbances of digestion, and hardness of the abdomen, vertigo, excessive excitement of sexual desires, early led to onanism. The sexual desire never was directed towards a natural method of satisfaction. Occasional attacks of depression, or thoughts of deprecation of self, and of perverse impulses, for which he could find no motive, such as laughing at serious things, throwing his money in the water, and running about in the pouring rain. The father of the culprit was of a nervous temperament, the mother subject to nervous headaches. A brother was subject to epileptic convulsions.

From his youth the culprit presented a nervous temperament, was inclined to convulsions and attacks of syncope, and when severely scolded would fall into a state of momentary stiffness. In 1869 he studied medicine in Berlin. In 1870 he went to the war as a hospital assistant. His letters at this time betray peculiar torpidity and softness. On his return home, in 1871, his emotional irritability was noticed at once by those about him. Thereafter frequent complaints of bodily ailments; unpleasantness resulting from a love affair. In November, 1871, he pursued his studies diligently in Greifswald. He was considered very gentlemanly. In confinement he was quiet, calm, and sometimes self-absorbed. His acts he attributed to painful sexual excitement, which of late had become excessive. He declared that he had been fully conscious of his perverse acts, and after committing them had always been ashamed of them. He had not experienced actual sexual satisfaction in their commission. He obtained no correct insight into his position. He considered himself a kind of martyr—a victim to an evil power. Presumption of irresponsibility, as a result of absence of free will.

The impulse to defile occurs also, paradoxically, in the aged, when there is a reappearance of sexual instinct, which, under such circumstances, is so often expressed in perverse acts. Thus *Tarnowsky* reports (p. 76) the following case:

CASE 33. I knew such a patient, who had a woman dressed in a *décolleté* ball-dress lie down on a low sofa in a brightly lighted room. He, himself, stood near the door of another room, which was in darkness; he gazed at the woman for a little while, then sprang excitedly on top of her and defecated onto her bosom. He declared that in doing this he experienced a sort of ejaculation.

An officer of Vienna informed me that men, by means of large sums of money, induce prostitutes to suffer the men to spit, defecate and urinate into their mouths.[28]

The following case by *Dr. Pascal* ("Igiene dell' amore") seems also to belong here:—

CASE 34. A man had an inamorata who would allow him to blacken her hands with coal or soot. She then had to sit before a mirror in such a way that he could see her hands in it. While conversing with her, which was often for a long time, he looked constantly at her mirrored hands, and finally, after a time, he would take his leave, fully satisfied.

The following case, communicated by a physician, may be of interest in relation to this subject:—

An officer was known in a brothel in K. only by the name of "Oil." "Oil induced erection and ejaculation only by having a nude girl step into a tub filled with oil, while he rubbed the oil all over her body."

These acts lead to the presumption that certain cases of injury to the clothing of females (*e.g.*, sprinkling them with sulphuric acid, ink, etc.) depend upon a perverse sexual impulse; at any rate the motive seems to be to inflict an injury, or pain of some sort, and those injured are always females, and the perpetrators males. In crimes of this kind, pains should always be taken to examine into the sexual life of the culprits.

The case of Bachmann, Case 120, below, throws a clear light on the sexual nature of such crimes; for, in this case, the sexual motive in the deed is proven.

CASE 35. B., age twenty-nine, merchant, married, heavily tainted, since his sixteenth year masturbation by means of a pocket electric battery, neurasthenic, impotent at the age of eighteen, for a while absynth drinker on account of unrequited love. One day meeting a nurse-maid wearing a white apron such as his love used to wear, he could not resist the temptation to steal the white apron. He took it home and after masturbating into it, burned it with renewed masturbation. Returning to the street he met a woman wearing a white dress. The sight of it produced an impulse to stain the dress with ink. Having done it he went home revelling in the sensual situation thus provoked and again masturbated. At another time, strolling about the street, he amused himself with cutting the dresses of women with a penknife. He was arrested as a pick-pocket. At other times a stain on a lady's dress caused orgasm and ejaculation in him. He obtained the same results while burning with a cigar a hole into the clothing of women whom he passed. (*Magnan*, reported by *v. Thoinot*, Attentats aux moeurs, p. 434, and by *Garnier*, Annales d' hygiène publ., 1900, March, p. 237.)

Garnier (Annales d' hygiène 1900, Feb'y-March) has given these cases of sadism special attention, reducing them to fetichism (see below). This is particularly apparent in case 35 in which the fetich consisted in a blue dress covered with a white apron. The personality of the wearer was a matter of indifference; it was the fetich that fascinated, the impulse being irresistible. Garnier calls these cases Sadi-Fetichism and points out their social and forensic importance, suggesting confinement of such unfortunate individuals in an insane asylum. Destructive actions like these towards the fetich which, properly speaking, is an object of desire and possession, this sadism on lifeless objects, may be explained by the fact that the fetich awakens sensual sensations coupled in sadistic natures with the pleasure derived from acts of cruelty and destruction.

In fetichism, well-developed, the fetich itself—abstracted from the personality of the wearer—dominates by itself the whole sexual life, brings it into action and may under circumstances awaken kindred regions of a sadistic nature which find gratification in the field of the (impersonal) fetich. The sadistic act in itself is often enough an equivalent for coitus rendered impossible by physical and psychical impotence. It may be practiced on boys, animals, persons of the same sex, without relation to paedophilia, zoophilia or homosexuality.

It is remarkable and seems to prove the connection with lust-cruelty that at the moment of the destroying act against the fetich (cutting off girl's tresses, stabbing women, defiling ladies' toilets, etc.) orgasm and ejaculation take place in the "sadi-fetichist."

A. *Moll* (Zeitschr. f. Medicinalbeamte) has recently published a case which may be considered classical:—

An academically cultured man, age thirty-one years, heavily tainted by heredity, offspring from a marriage between blood-relations, always shy and retired, used to romp about when growing into puberty (17) with the play-fellows of his sister, girls about eleven years of age, and from the sight of their white underwear became a "laundry fetichist." He began to masturbate thinking of girls clad in white garments and manipulating during the act light-coloured pieces of clothing belonging to his female relatives.

When twenty-three years of age he began coitus with girls dressed in white. At the age of twenty-five he saw a girl's white dress being bespattered with mud. This produced a very strong sexual emotion in him and from that time on he felt an irresistible impulse to defile the apparel of women, to crush and tear it. This impulse was particularly provoked at the sight of women clad in white. He used a solution of sesquichlorate of iron (ferrus) or ink and thus produced orgasm and ejaculation. At times he had dreams of white female underwear which were accompanied by pollution at the moment of touching or crushing it. Insanity could not be established. He was fined the sum of 50 marks for unlawfully causing damage to personal property.

(e) *Other Kinds of Assault on Females—Symbolic Sadism.*

The foregoing groups do not exhaust the forms in which the sadistic impulse toward women is expressed. If the impulse is not overmastering, or if there is yet sufficient moral resistance, it may happen that the perverse inclination is satisfied by an act that is apparently quite senseless and silly, but which has nevertheless a symbolic meaning for the perpetrator. This seems to be the meaning of the two following cases:—

CASE 36. (*Dr. Pascal*, "Igiene dell' amore.") A man was accustomed to go, on a certain day once a month, to an inamorata and cut her "fringe." This gave him the greatest pleasure. He made no other demands on the girl.

CASE 37. A man in Vienna regularly visited several prostitutes only to lather their faces and then to remove the lather with a razor, as if he were shaving them. He never hurt the girls, but became sexually excited and ejaculated during the procedure.[29]

(f.) *Ideal Sadism.*

Sadism may eventually manifest itself solely in the imagination, *i.e.,* in dream pictures which accompany the act of masturbation or accompany the process of pollution in sadistic fancies.

That it remains an ideal act only may be due to want of opportunity or courage to put it into practical action or that latent ethics forbid violence, or it may be that when debility of the centre of ejaculation is pronounced, a vivid sadistic impression suffices to provoke ejaculatory gratification. In this case sadism is merely an equivalent for coitus.

CASE 38. D., agent, age twenty-nine years, family heavily tainted, masturbation at the age of fourteen, coitus at twenty, but without pronounced libido or satisfaction, thereafter masturbation preferred. At first these acts were accompanied by the thought of a girl whom he could maltreat and subject to humiliating and infamous actions.

Reading of acts of violence on women excited him sexually. But he did not like to see blood either on himself or on others. He hated the sight of a naked woman.

He never felt inclined to put his sadistic ideas into actual practice for he disliked unnatural sexual intercourse.

He could not account for his sadistic ideas. These statements he made at a consultation for neurasthenia.

CASE 39. Ideal sadism with "Podex-Fetichism." P., aged twenty-two, of independent means, heavily tainted by heredity, by accident saw the governess chastising his sister (fourteen years of age) on the buttocks, holding the girl between her knees. This made a deep impression on him and henceforth he had a constant desire to see and touch his sister's buttocks. By some clever stratagem he succeeded. When seven years old he became the play-fellow of two small girls, of which one was tiny and lean, the other rather plump. He played the *rôle* of the father chastising his children. The lean girl he simply spanked over the clothes. The other, however, allowed him to smack her bare bottom (she was then ten years old). This gave him great sexual pleasure and caused erection.

One day, after being chastised in this manner the girl asked him to look at her genitalia. But he refused the invitation, as this view did not interest him in the least.

At the age of nine he became acquainted with a boy a little older than himself. One day they came across a picture representing the scene of flagellation in a monk's monastery. P. soon persuaded his companion to enact the scene. The latter consented to playing the passive *rôle* and found delight in it. This was often repeated. On one occasion P. assumed the passive *rôle* but it gave him no pleasure. This relation between the two continued till they grew up into manhood, and P. always ejaculated during the flagellation. He dominated his friend, who looked upon him as a superior being. Only twice whilst this friendship lasted did P. attempt this procedure on other persons; once on a nurse-maid whose bare bottom he smacked, and once in the street on a girl, eleven years old, whose cries, however, drove him to hasty flight.

He never felt any inclination to masturbation, coitus with girls, nor antipathic sexual sensations. He confined himself to touching the buttocks of women when in a crowd, or of girls whilst mixing with them on the playground, to looking under the dresses of women climbing the stairs of an omnibus or watching little girls undressing themselves.

He practiced "Sadism-Fetichism." His fancy revelled in situations in which he flagellated his younger brother, a nurse-maid or a nun; he invented stories which always ended in a scene of flagellation; answered advertisements such as: "Severe lady requires pupil" and derived the utmost delight from the correspondence that followed; made drawings of flagellation scenes, of bare female buttocks, ransacked the libraries for books containing sadistic writings, made abstracts of the whole literature, collected pictures referring to this favourite subject and designed such himself in keeping with the progress he made in developing his perversion.

The flights of his fancy rose from the exhibition of the naked buttocks, to smacking, flagellating and even teasing them, even to the murder of the owner. The latter act, however, frightened him. The ever recurring ejaculations finally brought on severe neurasthenia. He never could make up his mind to seek medical advice. At last he found a woman with whom he could have coitus as she permitted him to flagellate her during the act.

(*Regis*, Archives d' anthropologie criminelle, N. 82, July, 1899.)

CASE 40. Merchant, forty years of age, abnormally early hetero- and hypersexuality. From his twentieth year occasionally coitus and for want of something better, masturbation. In consequence of fright (surprise during coitus) psychical impotence. Treatment unsuccessful. This affected his mind and he came near to despair. He now tried immature girls with whom impotence could not put him to shame. His moral will power, still unimpaired, enabled him to resist this impulse, however, and he found satisfaction in going with girls legally of age and no longer innocent, but they must in appearance be younger than their years. In such cases his impotence disappeared. One day he saw a lady smiting the face of her daughter, fourteen years old. This produced at once violent erection and orgasm in him. The thought of it had the same result. From that time he found a mighty stimulant in seeing girls, no matter how young, beaten; even reading or hearing of maltreatment of females had the same result.

That the retarded sadism in this case was not acquired but only latent is evident from the fact that it ever existed in an ideal form. It was part of the sensual idea predominant in him that he introduced "the upper extremity into the vagina of a woman up to the hilt" and groped about within. [Other cases of ideal sadism see *Moll* (Libido sexualis, pp. 324 and 500); *Krafft,* "Arbeiten," iv. p. 163.]

(g) *Sadism with Any Other Object—Whipping of Boys.*

The sadistic acts with females just now described are also practiced on other living, sensitive objects,—children and animals. There may be a full consciousness that the impulse is really directed towards women, and that only for want of something better the nearest attainable objects (pupils) are abused. But the condition of the perpetrator may be such that the impulse to cruel acts enters consciousness accompanied only by lustful excitement, while its real object (which alone can explain the lustful coloring of such acts) remains latent.

The first alternative suffices as an explanation of the cases which *Dr. Albert* describes (*Friedreich's* "Blätter f. ger. Med.," p. 77, 1859),—cases in which lustful teachers whipped their pupils on the naked buttocks without cause. We must think of the second alternative, the sadistic impulse with unconsciousness of its object, when the sight of punishment causes spontaneous sexual excitement in the witness and thus becomes the determining factor in his future sexual life, as in the following cases:—

CASE 41. K., aged twenty-five, merchant, applied to me in the fall of 1889 for advice concerning an anomaly of his sexual life, which made him fear invalidism and impossibility of future happiness in marriage.

Patient came from a nervous family. As a child he was delicate, weak and nervous. Healthy except for measles; later on he became more robust.

At the age of eight, while at school, he saw the teacher punish the boys by taking their heads between his thighs and spanking them with a ferule. This sight caused the patient lustful excitement. "Without any idea of the danger and enormity of onanism," he satisfied himself with it, and from that time often masturbated, always calling up the memory-picture of a boy being punished.

Thus it continued until his twentieth year. Then he learned the significance of onanism, was terribly frightened, and tried to overcome his impulse to masturbate; but he fell into the practice of psychical onanism, which he regarded as innocuous and morally defensible, and for which he made use of the memory-pictures of boys being whipped, previously mentioned.

Patient now became neurasthenic, suffered with pollutions, and tried to cure himself by visiting brothels; but he could not induce erection. Then he sought to obtain normal sexual feelings by means of social intercourse with ladies; but he recognized that he was entirely insensible to the charms of the fair sex.

The patient was an intelligent man, normally developed, and of aesthetic taste. There was no inclination to persons of his own sex. My advice consisted of means to combat the neurasthenia and pollutions; interdiction of psychical and manual onanism; avoidance of all sexual excitants; and, possibly, hypnotic treatment to ultimately induce a return of the sexual life to its normal condition.

CASE 42. Abortive sadism. N., student, came under observation in December, 1890. He had practiced masturbation from early youth. According to his statements, he became sexually excited when he saw his father whip the children, and, later, when he saw his companions whipped by the teacher. When a spectator of such scenes, he always experienced lustful feelings. He could not say exactly when this first occurred, but it may have been at about the age of six. He could not tell exactly when he began to masturbate, but he stated with certainty that his sexual instinct was first awakened by the punishment of others, and thus he unconsciously came to practice masturbation. The patient remembered clearly that from the age of four to the age of eight he was frequently spanked, and that this caused him pain, never lustful pleasure.

Since he did not always have opportunity to see others whipped, he began to *imagine* how others were punished. This excited his lust, and he would then masturbate. Whenever he could, he managed to see others punished at school. Now and then he also felt desire to whip others. At the age of twelve he induced a comrade to allow him to whip him. He found great sexual pleasure in it. When, however, his companion beat him in return he experienced nothing but pain.

The impulse to beat others was never very strong. The patient experienced more satisfaction in filling his imagination with scenes of whipping. He never indulged in any other sadistic acts, and never had any desire to see blood, etc. Up to his fifteenth year his sexual indulgence consisted of masturbation, coupled with such fancies. After that (dancing lessons, association with girls) the early fancies disappeared almost entirely and were accompanied by only weak lustful feelings; then the patient gave them up entirely. In their place came thoughts of coitus in a natural way, without anything sadistic.

The patient indulged in coitus for the first time "on account of his health." He was potent, and the act gratified him. He then tried to abstain from masturbation, but was not successful, though he often indulged in coitus, and with more pleasure than he had in masturbation. He wished to be freed from masturbation as something vicious. He had coitus once a month, but masturbated once or twice every night. He was sexually normal, excepting the masturbation. There was no neurasthenia; genitals normal.

CASE 43. P., aged 15, of high social position, came of an hysterical mother whose brother and father died in an asylum. Two children of the family died in early childhood of convulsions. The patient was talented, virtuous, and quiet; but at times he was very disobedient, stubborn, and of violent temper. He had epilepsy, and practiced masturbation. One day it was learned that P., with money, induced a comrade of fourteen, B., to allow himself to be pinched in the arms, genitals, and thighs. When B. cried, P. became excited and struck at B. with his right hand, while with his left he made manipulations in the left pocket of his trousers. P. confessed that to maltreat his friend, of whom he was very fond, gave him peculiar delight; and that ejaculation while hurting his friend gave him much more pleasure than when he masturbated alone. (v. Gyurkovechky, "Pathol. und Therapie der männl. Impotenz.," p. 80, 1889.)

CASE 44. K., fifty years of age, without occupation, heavily tainted, satisfied his perverse sexual feelings exclusively on boys of ten to fifteen years of age, whom he seduced to mutual masturbation. At the climax of the act he would pierce the lobe of the boy's ear. When this, later on, proved inefficient, he cut off the lobe of a boy's ear. He was arrested and sentenced to five years' imprisonment. (Thoinot, op. cit., p. 452.)

That in all these cases of sadistic abuse of boys there can be no thought of a combination of sadism and antipathetic sexual instinct, as often occurs (see below) in individuals of inverted sexuality, is shown —aside from the absence of all positive signs of it—by a study of the next group, where, in association with the object of injury—animals,— the instinct for women is seen to appear repeatedly.

(h) Sadistic Acts with Animals.

In numerous cases, sadistically perverse men, afraid of criminal acts with human beings, or who care only for the sight of the suffering of a sensitive being, make use of the sight of dying animals,[30] or torture animals, to stimulate or excite their lust.

The case of a man in Vienna, which is reported by Hofmann in his "Text-Book of Legal Medicine," is noteworthy in relation to this. According to the evidence of several prostitutes, before the sexual act he was accustomed to excite himself by torturing and killing chickens and pigeons and other birds, and, therefore, was called "Hendlherr" (chickenmister).

For the elucidation of such cases the observation of *Lombroso* is of value, according to whom two men had ejaculations when they killed chickens or pigeons, or wrung their necks.

The same author, in his "Uomo delinquente," p. 201, speaks of a poet of some reputation, who became powerfully excited sexually whenever he saw calves slaughtered, and also at the sight of bloody meat.

Mantegazza (op. cit. p. 114) relates that among degenerate Chinese the practice prevails to sodomize geese and at the moment of ejaculation to cut off their heads.

Mantegazza ("Fisiologia del piacere," fifth ed., pp. 394, 395) mentions the case of a man who once saw chickens killed, and from that time had a desire to wallow in their warm, steaming entrails, because he experienced a feeling of lust while doing it.

Thus, in these and similar cases, the sexual life is so constituted from the beginning that the sight of blood, death, etc., excites lustful feeling. It is so in the following case:—

CASE 45. C. L., aged forty-two, engineer, married, father of two children; from a neuropathic family; father irascible, a drinker; mother hysterical, subject to eclamptic attacks. The patient remembers that in childhood he took particular pleasure in witnessing the slaughtering of domestic animals, especially swine. He thus experienced lustful pleasure and ejaculation. Later he visited slaughterhouses, in order to delight in the sight of flowing blood and the death throes of the animals. When he could find opportunity, he killed the animals himself, which always afforded him a vicarious feeling of sexual pleasure.

At the time of full maturity he first attained to a knowledge of his abnormality. The patient was not exactly opposed in inclination to women, but close contact with them seemed to him repugnant. On the advice of a physician, at twenty-five he married a woman who pleased him, in the hope of freeing himself of his abnormal condition. Although he was very partial to his wife, it was only seldom, and after great trouble and exertion of his imagination, that he could perform coitus with her; nevertheless, he begat two children. In 1866 he was in the war in Bohemia. His letters written at that time to his wife were composed in an exalted, enthusiastic tone. He was missed after the battle of Königgrätz.

If, in this case, the capability of normal coitus was much impaired by the predominance of perverse ideas, in the following it seems to have been entirely repressed:—

CASE 46. (*Dr. Pascal,* "Igiene dell' amore") A gentleman visited prostitutes, had them purchase a living fowl or rabbit, and made them torture the animal. He particularly revelled in the sight of cutting off the heads and tearing out the eyes and entrails. If he found a girl who would consent, and go about it right cruelly, he was delighted, and paid her and went his way without asking anything more or touching her.

Interesting is the awakening of sadistic feelings toward animals as related in the following case of *Féré:*—

CASE 47. B., thirty-seven years of age, tanner, tainted, began masturbation at the age of nine. One day, as he was about to masturbate with another boy at the corner of a street, where the gradient was very steep, a heavily laden dray pulled by four horses came along. The driver yelled at the horses and whipped them. The horses slipped about a good deal and made the sparks fly from the cobble stones. This excited B. very much and he ejaculated as one of the horses fell. Ever afterwards a similar occurrence would have the same effect on him and he went in search of it. If the difficulty was overcome without extra exertion on the part of the horse, or without the use of the whip, B. became only excited and he had to resort to masturbation or coitus to find final satisfaction. Even after he was married and had children, sadism continued. When one of his children fell ill with chorea, B. had hysterical attacks. (*Féré, l'instinct sexuel*, p. 255.)

The last two sections, *g* and *h*, show that the suffering of any living being may become a source of perverse sexual enjoyment to sadistically constituted persons, and that there may be sadism with almost any [living] object. However, it would be erroneous and an exaggeration to try to explain by sadistic perversion all the remarkable and surprising acts of cruelty that occur, and to assume sadism as the motive underlying all the horrors recorded in history or found in certain psychological manifestations among the peoples of the present time.

Cruelty arises from various sources and is natural to primitive man. Compassion, in contrast with it, is a secondary manifestation and acquired late. The instinct to fight and destroy, so important an endowment in prehistoric conditions, is long afterwards operative; and, in the ideas engendered by civilization, like that of "the criminal," it finds new objects, so long as its original object—"the enemy"—still exists. That not simply the death, but also torture of the conquered is demanded, is in part explained by the sense of power, which satisfies itself in this way, and in part by the insatiableness of the impulse of vengeance. Thus all horrors and historical enormities may be explained without recourse to sadism (which may often enough have been the motive, but should not be assumed as such, since it is a relatively rare perversion).

At the same time, there is still another powerful psychical element to be taken into consideration, which explains the attraction which is still exerted by executions, etc.; *viz.*, the pleasure which is produced by intense and unusual impressions and rare sights, in contrast to which, in coarse and blunted beings, pity is silent.

But undoubtedly there are individuals for whom, in spite or even by reason of their lively compassion, all that is connected with death and suffering has a mysterious attraction who, with inward opposition, and yet following a dark impulse, occupy themselves with such things, or at least with pictures and notices of them. Still, this is not sadism, so long as no sexual element enters into consciousness; and yet it is possible that, in unconscious life, slender threads connect such manifestations with the hidden depths of sadism.

(i) *Sadism in Woman.*

That sadism—a perversion, though often met with in men—is less frequent in women, may be easily explained. In the first place, sadism, in which the need of subjugation of the opposite sex forms a constituent element, in accordance with its nature represents a pathological intensification of the masculine sexual character; in the second place, the obstacles which oppose the expression of this monstrous impulse are, of course, much greater for woman than for man. Yet sadism occurs in women, and it can only be explained by the primary constituent element—the general hyper-excitation of the motor sphere. Only two cases have thus far been scientifically studied.

CASE 48. A married man presented himself with numerous scars of cuts on his arms. He told their origin as follows: When he wished to approach his wife, who was young and somewhat "nervous," he first had to make a cut in his arm. Then she would suck the wound and during the act become violently excited sexually.

This case recalls the widespread legend of the vampires, the origin of which may perhaps be referred to such sadistic facts.[31]

In the second case of feminine sadism, for which I am indebted to *Dr. Moll*, of Berlin, by the side of the perverse impulse, as so frequently happens, there is anaesthesia in the normal activities of sexual life; and three are also traces of masochism (see below).

CASE 49. Mrs. H., of H., aged twenty-six, came of a family in which nervous or mental diseases are said not to have been observed; but the patient herself presented signs of hysteria and neurasthenia. Although married eight years and the mother of a child, Mrs. H. never had desire to perform coitus. Very strictly educated as a young girl, until her marriage she remained almost innocent of any knowledge of sexual matters. She had menstruated regularly since her fifteenth year. Essential abnormality of the genitals was not apparent. To the patient coitus was not only not a pleasure, but even an unpleasant act, and repugnance to it had constantly increased. The patient could not understand how any one could call such an act the greatest delight of love, which to her was something far sublimer and unconnected with sensual impulse. At the same time it should be mentioned that the patient really loved her husband. In kissing him, too, she experienced a decided pleasure, which she could not exactly describe. But she could not conceive how the genitals can have anything to do with love. In other respects Mrs. H. was a decidedly intelligent woman of feminine character.

If she kissed her husband, she experienced the greatest pleasure in biting him. It was extremely gratifying to her to bite her husband so hard that she drew blood. She was pleased at being bitten in lieu of coitus, and also if she herself was allowed to bite him. However, she would be sorry if the biting caused great pain. (*Dr. Moll.*) [32]

In history there are examples of famous women who, to some extent, had sadistic instincts. These nymphomaniacs are particularly characterized by their thirst for power, lust, and cruelty. Among them are Valeria Messalina herself, and Catherine de' Medici, the instigator of the Massacre of St. Bartholomew, whose greatest pleasure was to have the ladies of her court whipped before her eyes, etc.[33]

2. MASOCHISM.[34] THE ASSOCIATION OF PASSIVELY ENDURED CRUELTY AND VIOLENCE WITH LUST.

Masochism is the opposite of sadism. While the latter is the desire to cause pain and use force, the former is the wish to suffer pain and be subjected to force.

By masochism I understand a peculiar perversion of the psychical sexual life in which the individual affected, in sexual feeling and thought, is controlled by the idea of being completely and unconditionally subject to the will of a person of the opposite sex; of being treated by this person as by a master, humiliated and abused. This idea is colored by lustful feeling; the masochist lives in fantasies, in which he creates situations of this kind and often attempts to realize them. By this perversion his sexual instinct is often made more or less insensible to the normal charms of the opposite sex—incapable of a normal sexual life—psychically impotent. But this psychical impotence does not in any way depend upon a horror of the opposite sex, but upon the fact that the perverse instinct finds an adequate satisfaction differing from the normal—in woman, to be sure, but not in coitus.

But cases also occur in which with the perverse impulse there is still some sensibility to normal stimuli, and intercourse under normal conditions takes place. In other cases the impotence is not purely psychical, but physical, *i.e.*, spinal; for this perversion, like almost all other perversions of the sexual instinct, is developed only on the basis of a psychopathic and, for the most part, hereditarily tainted individuality; and as a rule such individuals are given to excesses, particularly masturbation, to which the difficulty of attaining what their fancy creates drives them again and again.

I feel justified in calling this sexual anomaly "Masochism," because the author *Sacher-Masoch* frequently made this perversion, which up to his time was quite unknown to the scientific world as such, the substratum of his writings. I followed thereby the scientific formation of the term "Daltonism," from *Dalton*, the discoverer of colour-blindness.

During recent years facts have been advanced which prove that Sacher-Masoch was not only the poet of Masochism, but that he himself was afflicted with this anomaly.[35] Although these proofs were communicated to me without restriction, I refrain from giving them to the public. I refute the accusation that I have coupled the name of a revered author with a perversion of the sexual instinct, which has been made against me by some admirers of the author and by some critics of my book. As a man Sacher-Masoch cannot lose anything in the estimation of his cultured fellow-beings simply because he was afflicted with an anomaly of his sexual feelings. As an author he suffered severe injury so far as the influence and intrinsic merit of his work is concerned, for so long and whenever he eliminated his perversion from his literary efforts, he was a gifted writer, and as such would have achieved real greatness had he been actuated by normally sexual feelings. In this respect he is a remarkable example of the powerful influence exercised by the sexual life—be it in the good or evil sense—over the formation and direction of man's mind.

The number of cases of undoubted masochism thus far observed is very large. Whether masochism occurs associated with normal sexual instincts, or exclusively controls the individual; whether or not, and to what extent, the individual subject to this perversion strives to realize his peculiar fancies; whether or not, he has thus more or less diminished his virility—depends upon the degree of intensity of the perversion in the single case, upon the strength of the opposing ethical and aesthetic motives, and the relative power of the physical and mental organization of the affected individual. From the psychopathic point of view, the essential and common element in all these cases is *the fact that the sexual instinct is directed to ideas of subjugation and abuse by the opposite sex.*

Whatever has been said with reference to the impulsive character (indistinctness of motive) of the resulting acts and with reference to the original (congenital) nature of the perversion in sadism, is also true in masochism.

In masochism there is a gradation of the acts from the most repulsive and monstrous to the silliest, regulated by the degree of intensity of the perverse instinct and the power of the remnants of moral and aesthetic countermotives. The extreme consequences of masochism, however, are checked by the instinct of self-preservation, and therefore murder and serious injury, which may be committed in sadistic excitement, have here in reality, so far as known, no passive equivalent. But the perverse desires of masochistic individuals may in imagination attain these extreme consequences (see below, case 50).

Moreover, the acts to which masochists resort are in some cases performed in connection with coitus, *i.e.*, as preparatory measures; in others, as substitutes for coitus when this is impossible. This, too, depends only upon the condition of sexual power, which has been diminished for the most part physically and mentally by the activity of the sexual ideas in the perverse direction, and not upon the nature of the act itself.

(A) THE DESIRE FOR ABUSE AND HUMILIATION AS A MEANS OF SEXUAL SATISFACTION.

CASE 50. Mr. Z., age twenty-nine, technologist, came for consultation because of fear of syphilis. Father nervous, died tabetic. Father's sister insane. Several relatives very nervous and peculiar. On closer examination the patient was found to have sexual, spinal and cerebral asthenia. He presented no symptoms of *tabes dorsalis*. Questions concerning abuse of the sexual organs brought out a confession of masturbation practiced since youth. In the course of the examination the following interesting psycho-sexual anomalies were discovered: At the age of five the sexual life began with the impulse to whip himself, as well as with the desire to see others whipped. In this he never thought of individuals as of the one sex or the other. For want of something better he practiced flagellation on himself, and, in time, this induced ejaculation. Long before this he had begun to satisfy himself with masturbation, and always during the act revelled in imaginary scenes of whipping. He twice visited brothels to have himself flogged by prostitutes. For this purpose he chose the prettiest girl he could find; but he was disappointed, and did not even have an erection, to say nothing of ejaculation. He recognized that the flagellation was subsidiary, and that the idea of subjection to the woman's will was the important thing. He realized this on the second trial. When he had the "thought of subjection" he was perfectly successful. In time, by straining his imagination with masochistic ideas, he performed coitus without flagellation;

but he found little satisfaction in it, so that he performed sexual inter-course in a masochistic way. He found pleasure in masochistic scenes, in the sense of his original desire for flagellation, only when he was flagellated on the buttocks, or, at least, only when he called up such a situation in imagination. At times of great excitability it was even suffi-cient if he told stories of such scenes to a pretty girl. He would thus have an orgasm, and usually ejaculation.

A very effectual fetichistic idea was early associated with this. He noticed that he was attracted and satisfied only by women wearing high heels and short jackets ("Hungarian fashion"). He did not know how he arrived at this fetichistic idea. Boys' legs with high heels also pleased him; but this charm was purely aesthetic without any sensual colouring; and he said he had never noticed anything homosexual in himself. The patient referred his fetichism to his partiality for calves (legs). He was charmed by ladies' calves only when elegant shoes were on the feet. Nude legs—feminine nudity in general—did not in the least affect him sexually. A subordinate fetichistic idea for the patient was the human ear. It was a lustful pleasure for him to caress the handsome ears of people. With men this pleasure was slight, but with women it gave him great enjoyment.

He also had a weakness for cats. He thought them simply beautiful, and their movements were very attractive to him. The sight of a cat could raise him from a feeling of the deepest depression. Cats seemed to him sacred; he saw something divine in them! He did not know the reason for this idiosyncrasy.

Of late he also frequently had sadistic ideas about punishing boys. In these imaginary flagellations both men and women played a part, but particularly the latter, and then his enjoyment was much more intense.

The patient found that, besides what he recognized and felt as masochism, there was something else which he preferred to designate "pageism."

While his masochistic fancies and acts were entirely of a coarse, sensual nature, his "pageism" consisted of the idea of being a page to a beautiful girl. His conception was perfectly chaste, but piquant; his relation to her that of a slave, but absolutely pure—a mere platonic submission. This revelling in the idea of serving such a "beautiful crea-ture" as a page was coloured by a pleasurable feeling, but this was in no way sexual. He experienced in it an exquisite feeling of moral satisfac-tion, in contrast to sensually coloured masochism, and therefore he could but regard it as something of a different nature.

At first sight there was nothing remarkable in the patient's appear-ance; but his pelvis was abnormally broad, the ilia were flat, and the pelvis, as a whole, tilted and decidedly feminine. Eyes, neuropathic. He also mentioned that he often had itching and lustful irritation at the anus, and that in this ("erogenous" area) he could satisfy himself by means of a finger.

The patient was troubled about his future. Help would be possible for him if he could but excite in himself an interest in women, but his will and imagination were too weak for that.

What the patient designated as "pageism" does not differ in any way from masochism, as may be seen when it is compared with the following cases of symbolic masochism and others; and, further, upon the consideration that in this perversion coitus is avoided as an inadequate act, and from the fact that in such cases there is often a fantastic exaltation of the perverse ideal:

CASE 51. *Ideal Masochism.* Mr. X., technologist, twenty-six years old. Mother of nervous disposition; suffered from neuralgia. In the father's family a case of spinal disease and one of psychosis. A brother suffered from nervousness. Mr. X. had only slight infantile affections; he learned easily at school, and developed normally. He was of manly appearance, but rather weakly and under medium size. The descent of the right testicle was imperfect, but could be noticed in the inguinal canal. Penis normally formed, but rather small.

At the age of five he felt sexual excitement whilst swinging on the cross-bar with legs crossed, and stretched out at full length. He repeated the exercise several times, but forgot about the sensation until he grew up to maturer age. He then tried to induce this pleasurable feeling by repeating the exercise, but without success.

At the age of seven he took part in a general fight between the pupils of the school which he attended, after which the victors rode on the backs of the vanquished. This impressed X. considerably.

He thought the position of the prostrate boys a pleasant one, wanted to put himself in their place, imagining how by repeated efforts he could move the boy on his back near his face so that he might inhale the odor of his genitals. These thoughts, coupled with pleasurable feelings, often recurred to him afterwards, although they never occasioned real sensations of lust; in fact, he considered these thoughts sinful and bad, and sought to repulse them. He claimed to have had no knowledge at that time of sexual matters. It is remarkable that the patient up to his twentieth year was periodically troubled with nocturnal bedwetting.

Up to the time of puberty these masochistic fancies to lie under the thighs of others, boys as well as girls, recurred periodically. Now the objects were chiefly girls, but these exclusively when puberty was completed. Little by little these situations gained a different meaning, for soon the culminating point was the consciousness to be absolutely subject to the will and whims of a fully developed girl, coupled with corresponding humiliating acts and attitudes.

For instance, X. says:—

"I am lying on my back on the floor. The mistress stands over my head with one foot on my breast or she holds my head between her feet so that her genitals are directly in a line with my vision. Or she sits a-straddle on my chest or on my face, using my body as a table. If I do not obey her commands promptly she locks me up in a dark W.C. and leaves the house to find pleasure elsewhere. She introduces me to her friends as her slave and turns me over as such to them as a loan.

"She makes me perform the lowest menial work, wait upon her when she arises, in the bath and when she urinates. At times she uses my face for the latter purpose and makes me drink of the voidance."

X. claimed that he never practically put these ideas into effect for fear of not realizing the anticipated pleasure.

Once only he sneaked into the room of a pretty housemaid in order to drink the girl's urine; but he was too much disgusted to carry out the purpose.

He stated that he fought in vain against these masochistic impulses, considering them of a painful and disgusting nature. They were still prevalent. He pointed out particularly that the *humiliation* connected with these imaginary acts was the principal attraction, and that the pleasure derived from causing pain to others was never associated with them.

He preferred as "mistress" a slender maiden of about twenty years of age, with a pretty face, and wearing short light dresses.

The ordinary intercourse with young women, dancing, or mixed society, never impressed him.

With the period of puberty these masochistic ideas were at times accompanied by pollutions, but only weak emotions of lust.

At one time the patient resorted to friction of the penis, but he could not induce erection, much less ejaculation, and instead of pleasure he produced disagreeable paralytic feelings. This saved him from masturbation. But after the age of twenty he often experienced lustful emotions with ejaculation when performing gymnastic exercises on the horizontal bar, or when climbing poles or ropes. He never had a desire for sexual intercourse with women or for inverted sexual actions. At the age of twenty-six a friend urged him to coitus, but already on the way to the house "anxiety, restlessness, and decided disgust" crept over him. He became so excited, trembled all over, and broke out into a profuse perspiration, that he could not command an erection. Repeated attempts proved complete failures, but he was able to control his mental and physical excitement a little better than the first time.

Libido was never present. Masochistic imaginations gave no assistance, because his mental faculties at such times were "as if paralyzed," and he "could not call up those intense imaginary representations which he found necessary for an erection." Thus he gave up all attempts at coitus, partly because *libido* was absent, and partly on account of his utter want of confidence in success. Only now and then he satisfied his weak sexual desires by the aid of gymnastic exercises. Occasionally, however, spontaneous or superinduced masochistic fancies (when awake) would cause erection, but never ejaculation.

Pollutions occurred at periods of six weeks.

The patient was highly intellectual, of refined manners, and a little neurasthenic. He complained that when he was in society the feeling obtruded itself constantly that he was being observed. This caused him worry and embarrassment, although he was fully aware that all this was naught but imagination. He loved solitude, for fear that others might find out his sexual abnormality.

This impotence did not cause him pain, for he had scarcely any desire. Nevertheless he would consider the cure of his sexual life a great boon, since so much depended upon it in social life, and he would be more self-possessed and manlier when among others.

His present existence he considered a misery, and his life a burden.

CASE 52. X., man of letters, aged twenty-eight, tainted. Sexually hyperaesthetic from childhood. At the age of six he had dreams of being whipped on the buttocks by a woman. Upon awakening, he felt intense lustful excitement; thus he came to practice onanism. When eight years old he once asked the cook to whip him. From his tenth year, neurasthenia. Until his twenty-fifth year he had dreams of flagellation or similar fancies when awake, and indulged in onanism. Three years ago he had an impulse to have himself whipped by a girl. The patient was disappointed, for neither erection nor ejaculation occurred. At twenty-seven he made another effort, with the thought of enforcing erection and ejaculation. This was finally made possible by the following artifice: While coitus was attempted the girl had to tell him how she flogged mercilessly· other impotent men, and threaten him with the same. Besides this, it was necessary for him to fancy that he was bound, entirely in the woman's power, helpless, and most painfully beaten by her. Occasionally, in order to become potent, it was necessary to have himself actually bound. Thus coitus was possible. Pollutions were accompanied by lustful feeling only when he (infrequently) dreamed that he was abused, or that he looked on while one girl whipped the other. He never had a real lustful pleasure in coitus. The only things in women that interested him were the hands. Powerful women with big fists were his preference. At the same time, his desire for flagellation was only ideal; for with his great cutaneous sensitiveness at the most a few strokes were sufficient. Blows from men were repugnant to him. He wished to marry. From the impossibility of asking a decent woman to perform flagellation and the doubt about being potent without flagellation sprang his embarrassment and desire to recover.

CASE 53. D., age thirty-two, sculptor, hereditarily tainted, marks of degeneration, constitutionally neuropathic, neurasthenic, weakly in his earlier years. First emotions of sexuality at the age of seventeen; it developed slowly and exclusively in a hetero-sexual, but masochistic direction. He craved for floggings at the hands of a pretty woman (but no hand-fetichism). He preferred women of haughty and imperious appearance. He never sought to put his masochistic desires into real practice. He could not explain them.

On four occasions he tried coitus but without success. He practiced masturbation, which caused severe neurasthenia, accompanied by phobia, whereupon he sought medical advice.

Passive Flagellation and Masochism.

In three of the foregoing cases for the most part passive flagellation serves him that is subject to this perversion of masochism as an expression of the desired situation of subjection to the woman. The same means is needed by a large number of masochists. But passive flagellation is a process which, as is known, has a tendency to induce erection reflexly by irritation of the nerves of the buttocks.[36] This effect of flagellation is used by weakened debauchees to help their diminished power; and this perversity—not perversion—is very common. It is, therefore, necessary to ascertain in what relation the passive flagellation of the masochists stands to those dissipated individuals who are not psychically perverse, but physically weakened.

It is not difficult to show that masochism is something essentially different from flagellation, and more comprehensive. For the masochist the principal thing is subjection to the woman; the punishment is only the expression of this relation—the most intense effect of it he can bring upon himself. For him the act has only a symbolic value, and is a means to the end of mental satisfaction of his peculiar desires. On the other hand, the individual that is weakened and not subject to masochism and who has himself flagellated, desires only a mechanical irritation of his spinal centre.

Whether in a given case it is simple (reflex) flagellation or masochism is made clear by the individual's statements, and often by the secondary circumstances. The determination depends upon the following facts:—

In the *first* place, the impulse to passive flagellation exists in the masochist from the beginning. The desire is felt before there has been any experience of the reflex effect, often first in dreams, as, for example, in case 55, see below. *Secondly*, with the masochist, as a rule, flagellation is only one of many and various punishments which come into his mind as fancies and are often realized. In these other punishments and the frequent acts expressing purely symbolic humiliations which occur by the side of flagellations, there can, of course, be no thought of a reflex physical irritative effect. *Thirdly*, it is significant that, in the masochist when the desired flagellation is carried out, it need have no aphrodisiac effect at all. Very often, indeed, there is a more or less defined dis-apopintment, in fact, always, if the masochist is not successful in his desire to create by means of the prearranged program the illusion of the desired situation (to be in the woman's power), so that the woman ordered to carry out the act seems to be nothing more than the executive agent of his own will. In reference to this important point, compare the three foregoing cases and case 58.

Between masochism and simple (reflex) flagellation, there is a relation somewhat analogous to that existing between inverted sexual instinct and acquired pederasty. It does not lessen the value of this opinion that, in the masochist, the flagellation may also have the known reflex effect; or that a whipping received in childhood may have aroused lust for the first time, and thus simultaneously excited the latent masochistically constituted sex life. In this event, the case must be characterized by the conditions mentioned above under the heads of *"secondly"* and *"thirdly,"* in order to be masochistic. If the details of the origin of the case are not known, other circumstances, such as those mentioned above under *"secondly"* would make it clearly masochistic. This is illustrated in the following two cases:—

CASE 54. A patient of *Tarnowsky's* had a person in his confidence rent a house during his attacks, and instruct its *personnel* (three prostitutes) in what was to be done with him. Whenever he came there he was undressed, manustuprated and flagellated as ordered. He pretended to offer resistance, and begged for mercy; then, as ordered, he was allowed to eat and sleep. But in spite of protest he was kept there, and beaten if he did not submit. Thus the affair would go on for some days. When his attack was over he was dismissed, and he returned to his wife and children, who had no suspicion of his disease. The attacks occurred once or twice a year (*Tarnowsky, op. cit.*).

CASE 55. X., aged thirty-four, greatly predisposed, suffered with antipathic sexual instinct. For various reasons he had no opportunity to satisfy himself with men, in spite of great sexual desire. Occasionally he dreamed that a woman whipped him, and then had a pollution.

Through this dream he came to have prostitutes beat him as a substitute for love with men. Occasionally he would obtain a prostitute, undress himself completely (while she was not to take off her chemise), and have her tread upon him, whip and beat him. He was filled with the greatest pleasure while this was being done and would lick the woman's foot, which was the only thing that could increase his passion;

he then achieved ejaculation. Then disgust at the morally debasing situation occurred, and he retired as quickly as possible.

CASE 56. A gentleman of high standing, age twenty-eight years, would go to a house of prostitution once a month. He always announced his coming, with a note reading thus: "Dear Peggy, I shall be with you tomorrow evening between 8 and 9 o'clock. Whip and knout! Kindest regards. . . ."

He always arrived at the appointed time carrying a whip, a knout and leather straps. After undressing he had himself bound hand and foot, and then flogged by the girl on the soles of his feet, his calves and buttocks until ejaculation ensued. Other desires or wishes he never expressed. The fact that he disdained coitus seems to point to the fact that he resorted to this method simply as a means to gratify his masochistic inclination and not as a ruse to restore potency.

Cases occur, however, in which passive flagellation alone constitutes the entire content of the masochistic fancies, without other ideas of humiliation, etc., and without well-defined consciousness of the real nature of this expression of submission. Such cases are difficult to differentiate from those of simple reflex flagellation. A knowledge of the primary origin of the desire, before any experience of reflex stimuli (see above, under "*first*"), is the only thing that renders the differential diagnosis certain, if weighed with the circumstance that genuine masochists are perverse from early youth, and that the realization of their desires is scarcely ever accomplished or proves a disappointment (see below, under "*thirdly*"); for the whole thing chiefly belongs to the realm of imagination.

The following is a case of typical masochism in which the whole circle of ideas peculiar to this perversion appears completely developed. This case, in which there is a detailed personal description of the whole psychical state, is different from case 49 in the 11th edition only in that there is here no thought of a realization of the perverse fancies, and that, notwithstanding the perversion of the sexual life, normal stimuli are so far effectual that sexual intercourse is really possible under normal conditions.

CASE 57. "I am thirty-five years old, mentally and physically normal. Among all my relatives, in the direct as well as in the lateral line, I know of no case of mental disorder. My father, who at my birth was thirty years old, as far as I know had a preference for voluptuous, large women.

"Even in my early childhood I loved to revel in ideas about the absolute mastery of one man over others. The thought of slavery had something exciting in it for me, alike whether from the standpoint of master or servant. That one man could possess, sell or whip another, caused me intense excitement; and in reading 'Uncle Tom's Cabin' (which I read at about the beginning of puberty) I had erections. Particularly exciting for me was the thought of a man being hitched to a wagon in which another man sat with a whip, driving and whipping him. Until my twentieth year these ideas were purely objective and sexless—i.e., the one in subjugation in my fancy was another (not myself), and the master was not necessarily a woman. These ideas were, therefore, without effect on my sexual desires—i.e., on the way in which they took practical shape. Although these ideas caused erections, yet I have never masturbated in my life, and from my nineteenth year I had coitus without the help of these ideas and without any relation to them. I always had a great preference for elderly, voluptuous, large women, though I did not scorn younger ones.

"After my twenty-first year my ideas became objective, and it became an essential thing that the 'mistress' should be a woman over forty years old, tall and powerful. *From this time I was always in my fancies the subject*; the 'mistress' was a rough woman, who made use of me in every way, also sexually; who harnessed me to a carriage and made me take her for a drive, whom I must follow like a dog, at whose feet I must lie naked and be punished—i.e., whipped—by her. This was the constant element in my ideas, around which all others were grouped. In these fancies I always found endless pleasurable comfort which caused erection, but never ejaculation. As a result of the induced sexual excitement, I would immediately seek a woman, preferably one corresponding exteriorly with my ideal, and have coitus with her without any actual aid of my fancies, and sometimes also without any thought of them during the act. I had, however, also inclination towards women of a different kind, and had coitus with them without being impelled to it by my fancy.

"Notwithstanding all this, my life was not exceedingly abnormal sexually; yet these ideas were certain to occur periodically, and they have remained essentially unchanged. With growing sexual desire, the intervals constantly grew shorter. At the present time the attacks come every two or three weeks. If I previously were to have coitus, the occurrence of the fancies would, perhaps, be postponed. I have never attempted to realize my very definite and characteristic ideas—i.e., to connect them with the world without me—but I have contented myself with revelling in the thoughts, because I was convinced that my ideal would not allow even an approach to realization. The thought of a comedy with paid prostitutes always seemed so silly and purposeless, for a person hired by me could never take the place of my imagination of a 'cruel mistress.' I doubt whether there are sadistically constituted women like *Sacher-Masoch's* heroines. But, if there were such women, and I had the fortune (!) to find one, still, in a world of reality, intercourse with her would ever seem only a farce to me. Indeed, I can say that, were I to become the slave of a nymphomaniac, I believe that owing to the other necessary renunciations, my desired manner of life would soon pall on me, and in my lucid intervals I should make every effort to obtain my freedom at all hazards.

"Yet I have found a way in which to induce, in a certain sense, a realization. After my sexual desire has been intensely excited by revelling in my fancy, I go to a prostitute and there call up before my mind's eye with great intensity some scene of the kind mentioned, in which I play the principal *rôle*. After thinking of such a situation for about half an hour, with a constantly resulting erection, I perform coitus with increased lustful pleasure and strong ejaculation. After the latter, the vision fades away. Ashamed, I depart as quickly as possible, and try not to think of the affair. Then for about two weeks I have no more such ideas! indeed, after a particularly satisfactory coitus, it may happen that until the next attack I have not even any sympathy whatever with masochistic ideas. But the next attack is sure to come sooner or later. I must, however, state that I also have coitus without being prepared by such ideas, especially, too, with women that are acquainted with me and my position, and in whose presence I abhor such fantasies. *Under the latter circumstances, however, I am not always potent, while, with masochistic ideas, my virility is perfect.* It does not seem superfluous to add that otherwise in my thought and feeling I am very aesthetic, and despise anything like maltreatment of a human being. Finally, I will not leave unmentioned the fact that the form of address is of importance. In my fancies it is essential that the 'mistress' address me in the second person (*Du*), while I must address her in the third (*Sie*). This circumstance of being thus familiarly addressed (*Du*) by a person so inclined, as the expression of absolute mastery, has from my youth given me lustful pleasure, and does today.

"I had the fortune to find a wife who is in everything, but especially sexually, attractive to me; though, as I scarcely need say, she in no way resembles my masochistic ideals. She is gentle, but voluptuous, for without the latter characteristic I cannot conceive such a thing as sexual charm. The first few months of married life were normal sexually; the masochistic attacks did not occur, and I had almost lost all thought of masochism. Then came the first confinement and the necessary abstinence. Punctually, then, with the occurrence of *libido* came the masochistic fancies again, which, in spite of my great love for my wife, necessitated coitus with another, with the accompaniment of masochistic ideas. It is here worthy of note that marital coitus, which was later resumed, did not prove sufficient to banish the masochistic ideas, as masochistic coitus always does. As for the essential element in masochism, I am of the opinion that the ideas—*i.e.*, the mental element—are the end and aim.

"If the realization of the masochistic ideas (*i.e.*, passive flagellation, etc.) be the desired end, then it is in opposition to the fact that the majority of masochists never attempt realization; or when this is attempted great disappointment occurs, or at any rate the desired satisfaction is not obtained.

"Finally, I should mention that, according to my experience, the number of masochists, especially in big cities, seems to be quite large. The only sources of such information are—since men do not reveal these things—statements by prostitutes, and since they agree on the essential points, certain facts may be assumed as proved.

"Thus there is the fact that every experienced prostitute keeps some suitable instrument (usually a whip) for flagellation, but it must be remembered that there are men who have themselves whipped simply to increase their sexual pleasure. These, in contrast with masochists, regard flagellation as a means to an end.

"On the other hand, almost all prostitutes agree that there are many men who like to play 'slave'—i.e., like to be so called, and have themselves scolded and trod upon and beaten. As has been said, the number of masochists is larger than has yet been dreamed.

"As you can imagine, your chapter on this subject has made a deep impression on me. I should like to have faith in a cure, in a logical cure, so to speak, in accordance with the motto: 'To understand all is to cure all.'

"Of course the word cure is to be taken with some limitation, and there must be a distinction made between general feelings and concrete ideas. The former can never be removed; they come like a streak of lightning, are there, and one does not know whence or how.

"But the practice of masochism in imagination by means of concrete associated ideas can be avoided, or at least restricted.

"Now the thing is changed. I say to myself: What! you busy your mind with things which not only the aesthetic sense of others, but also your own, disapproves? You regard that as beautiful and desirable which, in your own judgment, is at once ugly, coarse, silly, and impossible? You long for a situation which in reality you can never attain? This opposing idea has an immediate inhibitory and undeceiving effect, and breaks the point of the fancy. In fact, since reading your book (early this year) I have not actually revelled in my fancy, though the masochistic tendencies have recurred at regular intervals.

"I must also confess that, in spite of its marked pathological character, masochism is not only incapable of destroying my pleasure in life, but it does not in the least affect my outward life. When not in a masochistic state, as far as feeling and action are concerned, I am a perfectly normal man. During the activity of the masochistic tendencies there is, of course, a great revolution in my feeling, but my outward manner of life suffers no change; I have a calling that makes it necessary for me to move much in public, and I pursue it in the masochistic condition as well as ever."

The author of the foregoing lines also sends me the following notes:—

I. "Masochism, according to my experience, is under all circumstances congenital, and never acquired by the individual. *I know positively that I was never spanked;* that my masochistic ideas were manifested from my earliest youth, and that, as long as I have been capable of thinking, I have had such thoughts. If the origin of them had been the result of a particular event, especially of a beating, I should certainly not have forgotten it. It is characteristic that *the ideas were present before there was any libido.* At that time the ideas were absolutely sexless. I remember that when I was a boy it affected (not to say excited) me intensely when an older boy addressed me in the second person (*Du*) while I spoke to him in the third (*Sie*). I would keep up a conversation with him and have this exchange of address (*Du* and *Sie*) take place as often as possible. Later, when I had become more mature sexually, such things affected me only when they occurred with a woman, and one relatively older than myself.

II. "Physically and mentally I am in all respects masculine. I have a superabundant growth of beard, and my whole body is very hairy. In my relations to the female sex that are not masochistic, the dominating position of the man is an indispensable condition, and any attempt to change it would meet with my energetic opposition. I am energetic, if not over-courageous; but the want of courage is not manifest when my pride is injured. I am not sensitive to events in nature (thunder storms, storms at sea, etc.).[37]

"Again, my masochistic tendencies have nothing feminine or effeminate about them (?). To be sure, in these, the inclination to be sought and desired by the woman is dominant; but the general relation desired with her is not that in which a woman stands to a man, but that of the slave to the master, the domestic animal to its owner. If one regards the ultimate aim of masochism without prejudice, it must be acknowledged that its ideal is the position of a dog or horse. Both are owned by masters and punished by them, and the masters are responsible to no one. Just this unlimited power of life and death, as exercised over slaves and domestic animals, is the aim and end of all masochistic ideas.

III. "The foundation of all masochistic ideas is *libido*, and as this ebbs and flows, so do the masochistic fancies. On the other hand, as soon as the ideas are present, they greatly intensify the *libido*. I am not by nature excessively sensual. However, when the masochistic ideas occur I am impelled to coitus at any cost (for the most part I am driven to the lowest women); and if these impulses are not soon obeyed, *libido* soon becomes almost satyriasis. One is almost justified in looking upon this as a vicious circle.

"*Libido* occurs either in the course of time or as the result of especial excitement (also of a kind that is not masochistic—*e.g.,* kissing). In spite of its manner of origin, this *libido*, by virtue of the masochistic ideas it engenders, is soon transformed into a masochistic and impure *libido*.

"Moreover, there is no doubt that external accidental impressions, particularly loitering in the streets of a large city, greatly intensify the desire. The sight of beautiful and imposing female forms, *in nature* as well as in art, is exciting. For those subject to masochism—at least during the attacks—the whole external world becomes masochistic. The box on the ear administered by the teacher to the pupil and the crack of the driver's whip make deep impressions on the masochist, while they leave him indifferent or annoy him when he is not in the masochistic state.

IV. "In reading *Sacher-Masoch* it struck me that in masochists now and then there was also an undercurrent of sadistic feeling. I have now and then discovered in myself sporadic feelings of sadism. I must remark, however, that the sadistic feelings are not so marked as the masochistic. Apart from the fact that they appear but seldom, and then only in a manner as accessories, these sadistic fancies never leave the sphere of abstract feeling, and, above all, never take the form of concrete, connected ideas. The effect on *libido*, however, is the same with both."

If this case is remarkable on account of the complete development of the psychical state which constitutes masochism, the following is noteworthy because of the great extravagance of the acts resulting from perversion. The case is also particularly suited to make clear the reason for the subjection and humiliation at the hands of the woman, and the peculiar sexual colouring of the resulting situations:—

CASE 58. Mr. Z., official, aged fifty; tall, muscular, healthy. Said to come of healthy parentage, but his father was thirty years older than his mother. A sister, two years older than Z., suffered with delusions of persecution. There was nothing remarkable in Z.'s external appearance. Skeleton entirely masculine; abundant beard, but no hair on trunk. He characterized himself as a man of sanguine temperament, who could not refuse others anything; though irascible and quick-tempered, he was quick to regret outbursts.

Z. claimed that he had never masturbated. From his youth there had been nightly pollutions, in which girls played a part, but the sexual act never. For example, he dreamed that a pleasing woman lay heavily on him, or that as he lay sleeping on the grass she playfully walked up his back. Z. had always been averse to coitus with women. This act seemed bestial to him. Nevertheless, he was drawn to women. It was only in the society of beautiful women and girls that he felt well and in his place. He was very gallant, without being forward.

A voluptuous woman of beautiful form, and particularly with a pretty foot, when seated, had the power to throw him into intense excitement. He was impelled to offer himself as a chair, in order "to support such grand beauty." A kick, a box on the ear from her, would be heaven to him. He had a horror at the thought of coitus with her. He felt the need to serve woman. He thought how much ladies liked to ride. He revelled in the thought how fine it would be to be wearied by the burden of a beautiful woman in order to give her pleasure. He painted the situation in all colours; thought of the beautiful foot armed with spurs, the beautiful calves, the soft, full thighs. Every beautiful mature woman, every pretty female foot, always excited his imagination; but he never betrayed the peculiar feelings that seemed to him abnormal, and was able to control himself. But he felt no need to fight against them; on the contrary, it would have grieved him to be compelled to give up the feelings that had become so dear to him.

At the age of thirty-two Z. happened to make the acquaintance of an attractive woman, aged twenty-seven, who had been separated from her husband, and whom he found in need. He took her and worked for her without any selfish motive, for months. One evening she impatiently demanded sexual satisfaction from him, and almost used violence. Coitus was successful. Z. took the woman, lived with her, and indulged in coitus moderately, but coitus was more a burden than a pleasure; erections became weak, and he could no longer satisfy the woman. She finally declared that she would not have intercourse with him, because he only excited without satisfying her. Though he loved the woman very much, he could not give up his peculiar fancies. After this he lived with her only in friendly relations, and deeply regretted that he could not serve her in the way she desired.

Fear of how she would receive his propositions and a feeling of shame kept him from confessing. He found a substitute in his dreams. Thus, for example, he dreamed that he was a proud, fiery steed, ridden by a beautiful lady. He felt her weight, the bit he had to obey, the pressure of the thighs on his flanks; he heard her beautiful, joyous voice. The exertion threw him into a perspiration, the touch of the spurs did the rest, and always induced pollution with great lustful pleasure. Under the influence of such dreams, seven years ago Z. overcame his reluctance, in order to experience such things in reality. He was successful in creating a suitable opportunity. He speaks of it as follows: "I knew how to arrange it so that on an occasion she would of her own will seat herself on my back. Then I endeavored to make this situation as pleasant as possible, and easily arranged it so that on the next occasion she said spontaneously, 'Come, give me a little ride!' Being of tall stature, both hands braced on a chair, I made my back horizontal, and she mounted astride, after the manner of a man. I then did the best I could to imitate the movements of a horse, and loved to have her treat me like a horse, without consideration. She could beat, prick, scold, or caress me, just as she felt inclined. I could carry on my back persons weighing from sixty to eighty kilos. for half or three-quarters of an hour, without interruption. At the end of this time I usually asked for a rest. During this the intercourse between the mistress and me was perfectly harmless, and without any relation to what had preceded. After about a quarter of an hour I was rested and placed myself again at the disposal of the mistress. When time and circumstances allowed it, I did this three or four times in succession. It sometimes happened that I practiced it both in the morning and afternoon. After it I never felt weary or had uncomfortable feelings, but on such days I had very little appetite. When possible, I liked best to bare my trunk, that I might feel the riding-whip more sharply. The mistress had to be decent. I liked her best in pretty shoes and stockings, with short closed drawers reaching to the knee; with the upper portion of her person completely dressed, and with hat and gloves."

Mr. Z. further said he had not performed coitus in seven years, but he thought he was potent. The riding was a perfect substitute for that "bestial act," even when ejaculation was not induced.

For eight months Z. had determined to give up his masochistic play, and had kept his determination. But he thought that if a woman only moderately pretty were to address him directly and say, "Come, I want to ride you," he would not be strong enough to withstand the temptation. Z. wished to know whether his abnormality was curable, whether he was unworthy as a vicious man, or an invalid deserving pity.

Even in the foregoing series of cases, with other things, the act of being walked upon has played a *rôle* as a means of expressing the masochistic situations of humiliation and pain. The exclusive and most extensive use of this means for perverse excitation and satisfaction, which has caused me to arrange a special group, because it forms the transition to another kind of perversion (see below (*b*)), is shown in the following classical case of masochism, reported by *Hammond* (*op. cit.*, p. 28) from an observation by *Dr. Cox* [38] of Colorado:

CASE 59. X., a model husband, very moral, the father of several children, had times—*i.e.*, attacks—in which he visited brothels, chose two or three of the largest girls, and shut himself up with them. He bared the upper portion of his body, lay down on the floor, crossed his hands on his abdomen, closed his eyes, and then had the girls walk over his naked breast, neck and face, urging them at every step to press hard on his flesh with the heels of their shoes. Sometimes he wanted a heavier girl, or some other act still more cruel than this procedure. After two or three hours he had enough. He paid the girls with wine and money, rubbed his blue bruises, dressed himself, paid his bill, and went back to his business, only to give himself the same strange pleasure again after a few weeks.

Occasionally it happened that he had one of the girls stand on his breast, and the others then turn her around until his skin was torn and bleeding from the turning of the heels of her shoes. Frequently one of the girls had to stand on him in such a way that one shoe was over the eyes, with its heel pressing on one eye, while the other shoe rested across his neck. In this position he endured the pressure of a person weighing about 150 pounds for four or five minutes. The author speaks of dozens of similar cases that are known to him. Hammond presumes, with reason, that this man had become impotent for intercourse with women; that in this strange procedure he found an equivalent for coitus; and that, when the heels drew blood, he had pleasant sexual feelings, accompanied by ejaculations.

CASE 60. X., gentleman belonging to upper class of society; age sixty-six; father hypersexual; two brothers said to be masochists. X. claimed that his masochism dates back to early childhood. At the age of five he asked little girls to undress him and spank his naked bottom. Later on he arranged with other boys or girls in playing teacher with him to flog him. With the age of fifteen he began to imagine that girls ambushed and then beat him. At that time he had no idea as yet of the sexual meaning of such proceedings, in fact he was still unaware of the sexual life. His craving for being beaten by women steadily increased. At the age of eighteen he learned how to satisfy it and had the first pollution during the act. When nineteen he engaged in first coitus with complete satisfaction and potency and without masochistic representations. Normal sexual intercourse until he was twenty-one, when a girl suggested a masochistic scene. He accepted, and from that time never had coitus without a masochistic adventure preceding it. He soon recognized the fact that the stimulus proceeded from the idea of being in the power of a woman rather than from the act of violence itself. He succeeded in making a happy marriage, free from masochistic ideas, but admitted that from time to time he had to seek relief in some masochistic act with a girl, even though he then had grandchildren. The masochistic scene was always the prelude to coitus. He showed no psychopathic symptoms and was free from other perversions. He pointed out the frequency of masochism and the clever methods often applied by so-called masseuses. According to his experience masochism is of frequent occurrence in England, and English women are easily persuaded to practice it.

CASE 61. L., artist, age twenty-nine; nervous disease and tuberculosis of frequent occurrence in family. Sex desire suddenly arose in him at the age of seven whilst being caned on the buttocks; at ten, masturbation. During the act he always thought of someone flagellating him. In later years nocturnal pollutions were always accompanied by dreams of flagellation. The wish to be flogged was ever present in his mind since he was ten years old. From eleven to eighteen he had inclinations to persons of his own sex, though they never overstepped the bounds of boyish friendship. During this homosexual period he was always agitated by the desire to be beaten by his companion.

At nineteen he had coitus, but without sufficient erection or gratifying pleasure. His heterosexual inclinations were always towards women older than himself. He was indifferent towards young girls. His craving for flagellation increased with the years.

At twenty-five he fell violently in love with a woman much older than himself, but marriage he refused. The woman made every effort in her power to win him over to natural sexual intercourse. Although he detested the state of affairs and professed undying love for the woman he insisted that his sexual feelings for her were only of a masochistic character. Now and then he succeeded in persuading her to flagellate him.

His sexual needs being strong, he had girls flagellate him. He claimed that flagellation was the only adequate sexual act during which he could experience really pleasurable ejaculation. Coitus was of minor importance and only on rare occasions did he couple it with the act of flagellation, probably on account of psychical impotence.

Nevertheless the two acts affected him in a different manner. Coitus seemed to improve him both mentally and physically, whilst flagellation had bodily exhaustion and moral depression in its wake. He was persuaded that masochism in him was a pathological condition; on that ground he came for advice.

His appearance was undeniably masculine, his conduct decent and beyond criticism. He complained of cerebral neurasthenia (weakness of mind, of will power, absent-mindedness, irritability, shyness, anxiety of mind, pressure in the head, etc.). Genitals normal. Erections only in the morning.

He inclined to the belief that if he could find a woman whom he could love, he might strip off his masochistic inclination in wedlock.

Therapeutic advice: auto-combating of masochistic thoughts, impulses and acts, if necessary, with the aid of hypnotic suggestion;

strengthening of the nervous system, and removing manifestations of irritating weakness by antineurasthenic treatment.

· The cases of masochism thus far described, and the numerous analogous cases mentioned by those who report them, form a counterpart to the previously described Group *"c"* of sadism. Just as in sadism men excite and satisfy themselves by maltreating women, so in masochism the same effect is sought in the passive reception of similar abuse.[39] But Group *"a"* of the sadists—that of lust-murder—strange as it may seem, is not without its counterpart in masochism. In its extreme consequences, masochism must lead to the desire to be killed by a person of the opposite sex, in the same way that sadism has its acme in active lust-murder. But the instinct of self-preservation opposes such a result, so that the extreme is not actually carried out. When, however, the whole structure of masochistic ideas is purely psychical, in the imagination of such individuals even the extreme may be reached, as the following case shows:—

CASE 62. A middle-aged man, married, and the father of a family, who had always led a normal sexual life, but who came of a very nervous family, made the following communication: In his early youth he was powerfully excited sexually at the sight of a woman slaughtering an animal with a knife. From that time, for many years, he had revelled in the lustfully colored idea of being stabbed and cut, and even killed, by women with knives. Later on, after the beginning of normal sexual intercourse, these ideas lost completely their perverse stimulus for him.

This case should be compared with the statements according to which men find sexual pleasure in being lightly pricked with knives in the hands of women, who at the same time threaten them with death.

Such fancies, perhaps, give the key to an understanding of the following strange case, for which I am indebted to a communication from Dr. *Körber*, of Rankau, in Silesia:—

CASE 63. "A lady relates to me the following: While still a young and innocent girl, she was married to a man of about thirty years. On their wedding night he forced a bowl with soap into her hands, and without any expression of endearment wanted her to lather his chin and neck (as if for shaving). The inexperienced young wife did it, and was not a little astonished during the first weeks of married life to learn its secrets in absolutely no other form. Her husband always told her that it gave him the greatest delight to have his face lathered by her. Later, after she had sought the advice of friends, she induced her husband to perform coitus, and had three children in the course of time (by him, she states with every assurance). The husband was industrious and reliable, but a moody man, with short temper; by occupation a merchant."

It may be inferred that this man conceived the act of being shaved (*i.e.*, the lathering as a preparatory measure) as a rudimentary, symbolic realization of ideas of injury or death, or of fancies about knives, like those the man previously mentioned had had in his youth, and by means of which he had been sexually excited and satisfied. The perfect sadistic counterpart to this case, looked upon in the same light, is offered by observation 37, which is a case of symbolic sadism.

Symbolic Masochism.

At any rate, there is a whole group of masochists who satisfy themselves with the symbolic representations of situations corresponding with their perversion; a group which corresponds with Group "*a*" and "*e*" of sadism. Thus, just as the perverse longings of the masochist may on the one hand advance to "passive lust-murder" (to be sure, only in imagination), so, on the other hand, they may be satisfied with simple symbolic representations of the desired situations, which otherwise are expressed in acts of cruelty (this, of course, taken objectively, goes much farther than the idea of being murdered, but in fact not so far, owing to the determining subjective conditions). Cases similar to 63 may be here described, in which the acts desired and planned by the masochists have a *purely symbolic* character, and to a certain extent serve to define the desired situation.

CASE 64. (*Pascal*, "Igiene dell' amore.") Every three months a man of about forty-five years old would visit a certain prostitute and pay her ten francs for the following act. The girl had to undress him, tie his hands and feet, bandage his eyes, and draw the curtains of the windows. Then she would make her guest sit down on a sofa, and leave him there alone in a helpless position. After half an hour she had to come back and unbind him. Then the man would pay her and leave perfectly satisfied, to repeat his visit in about three months.

In the dark this man seems to have extended this situation of being helpless in the hands of a woman by the aid of imagination. The following case, in which again a complicated comedy in the sense of masochistic desires is played, is still more peculiar:—

CASE 65. (*Dr. Pascal, ibid.*) A gentleman in Paris was accustomed to call on certain evenings at a house where a woman, the owner, acceded to his peculiar desire. He entered the *salon* in full dress, and she, likewise in evening *toilette*, had to receive him with a very haughty manner. He addressed her as "Marquise," and she had to call him "dear Count." Then he spoke of his good fortune in finding her alone, of his love for her, and of a lover's interview. At this the lady had to feel insulted. The pseudo-count grew bolder and bolder, and asked the pseudo-marquise for a kiss on her shoulder. "There is an angry scene; the bell is rung; a servant, prepared for the occasion, appears, and throws the count out of the house. He departs well satisfied, and pays the actors in the farce handsomely."

CASE 66. X., age thirty-eight, engineer, married, father of three children, married life unmarred. Visited periodically a prostitute who had to enact, previous to coitus, the following comedy. As soon as he entered her compartment she took him by the ears, and pulled him all over the room, shouting: "What do you want here? Do you know that you ought to be at school? Why don't you go to school?" She would then slap his face and flog him soundly, until he knelt before her begging pardon. She then handed him a little basket containing bread and fruit, such as children carry with them to school. He remained penitent until the girl's harshness produced orgasm in him, when he would call out: "I am going! I am going!" and then performed coitus.

It is probable that this masochistic comedy may have arisen from some scenes enacted during his schooltime and that in this wise *libido* became associated with them. Further details of X.'s sexual life are not known. (*Dr. Carrara*, in Archivio di Psichiatria xxix., 4.)

Ideal Masochism.

A distinction must be made between "symbolic" and "ideal" masochism. In the latter the psychical perversion remains entirely within the spheres of imagination and fancy, and no attempt at realization is made. (*Cf.* cases 57 and 62.) Two other cases of ideal masochism are quoted here. The first is that of an individual mentally and physically tainted, bearing degenerative signs, in whom mental and physical impotence occurred early:—

CASE 67. Mr. Z., aged twenty-two, single, was brought to me by his father for medical advice, because he was very nervous and plainly sexually abnormal. Mother and maternal grandmother were insane. His father begat him at a time when he was suffering severely from nervousness.

Patient was said to have been a very lively and talented child. At the age of seven he was noticed to practice masturbation. After his ninth year he became inattentive, forgetful, and did not progress in his studies, constantly requiring help and protection. With difficulty he got through the Gymnasium, and during his time of freedom had attracted attention by his indolence, absent-mindedness, and various foolish acts.

Consultation was occasioned by an occurrence in the street, in which Z. had forced himself on a young girl in a very impetuous manner, and in great excitement had tried to have a conversation with her.

The patient gave as a reason that by conversing with a respectable girl he wished to excite himself so that he could be potent in coitus with a prostitute!

His father characterized him as a man of perfectly good disposition, moral but lazy, dissatisfied with himself, often in despair about his want of success in life, indolent, and interested in nothing but music, for which he possessed great talent.

The patient's exterior—his malformed head, his large, prominent ears, the deficient innervation of the right facial muscle about the mouth, the neuropathic expression of the eyes—indicated a degenerate, neuropathic individual.

Z. was tall, of powerful frame, and in all respects of masculine appearance. Pelvis masculine, testicles well developed, penis remarkably large, *mons veneris* with abundant hair. The right testicle much lower than the left, the cremasteric reflex weak on both sides. The patient was intellectually below the average. He felt his deficiency, complained of his indolence, and asked to have his will strengthened. His awkward, embarrassed manner, timid glances, and relaxed attitude pointed to masturbation. The patient confessed that from his seventh year until a year and a half ago he practiced it, years at a time, from eight to ten times daily. Until a few years ago, when he became neurasthenic (cephalic pressure, loss of mental power, spinal irritation, etc.) he said he always found great sensuous pleasure in it. Since then this had been lost, and the desire to masturbate had disappeared. He had constantly grown more bashful and indolent, less energetic, and more cowardly and apprehensive. He had lost interest in everything, and attended to his business only from a sense of duty, feeling very low-spirited. He had never thought of coitus, and from his standpoint as an onanist, he could not understand how others could find pleasure in it.

Investigation in the direction of inverted sexual instinct gave a negative result. He said he never was drawn toward persons of his own sex; he rather thought he had now and then had a weak inclination for females. He asserted that he came to masturbate independently. In his thirteenth year he first noticed ejaculations as a result of masturbatic manipulations.

It was only after long persuasion that Z. consented to unveil his sexual life entirely. As his statements which follow show, he may be classified as a case of ideal masochism, with rudimentary sadism. The patient distinctly remembered that at the age of six, without any cause, he had "ideas of violence." He was compelled to imagine that a servant girl spread his legs apart and showed his genitals to another; that she tried to throw him into cold or hot water in order to cause him pain. These "ideas of violence" were attended with lustful feelings, and became the cause of masturbatic manipulations. Later the patient called them up voluntarily, in order to incite himself to masturbation. They also played a part in his dreams; but they never induced pollution, apparently because the patient masturbated excessively during the day.

In time, to these masochistic "ideas of violence" others of a sadistic nature were added. At first they were scenes in which boys forcibly practiced onanism on one another, or cut off the genitals. He often imagined himself such a boy, now in an active, now in a passive *rôle*. Later he busied himself with mental pictures of girls and women exhibiting themselves to one another. He revelled in the thought, for example, of a servant girl spreading another girl's legs apart and pulling the genital hair; or in the thought of boys treating girls cruelly, and pricking and pinching their genitals.

Such ideas also always induced sexual excitement, but he never experienced any impulse to carry them out actively or to have them performed on himself passively. It satisfied him to use them for masturbation. Later on, with diminishing sexual imagination and *libido* these ideas and impulses had become infrequent, but their content remained unchanged. The masochistic "ideas of violence" predominated over the sadistic. Whenever he saw a lady, he had the thought that she had sexual ideas like his own. In this way, in part, he explained his embarrassment in social intercourse. Having heard that he would get rid of his burdensome sexual ideas if he were to accustom himself to natural sexual indulgence, he had twice attempted coitus, though he only experienced repugnance, and was not confident of success. On both occasions the attempt was a fiasco. The second time he made the attempt he felt such aversion that he pushed the girl away and fled.

The second case is the following observation placed at my disposal by a colleague. Even though it be aphoristic, it seems particularly suited to throw a clear light on the distinctive element of masochism—the consciousness of subjection, in its peculiar psycho-sexual effect:—

CASE 68. Z., aged twenty-seven, artist, powerfully built, of pleasing appearance, said to be free from hereditary taint. Healthy in youth, since his twenty-third year he had been nervous and inclined to be hypochondriacal. Although he bragged of sexual indulgence he was not very virile. In spite of associations with females, his relations with them were limited to innocent attentions. At the same time, his covetousness for women who were cold towards him was remarkable. Since his twenty-fifth year he had noticed that females, no matter how ugly, always excited him sexually whenever he discovered anything domineering in their character. An angry word from the lips of such a woman was sufficient to give him the most violent erections. Thus, one day he sat in a *café* and heard the (ugly) female cashier scold the waiters in a loud voice. This threw him into the most intense sexual excitement, which soon induced ejaculation. Z. required the women with whom he was to have sexual intercourse to repulse and annoy him in various ways. He thought that only a woman like the heroines of *Sacher-Masoch's* romances could charm him.

These cases of ideal masochism plainly demonstrate that the persons afflicted with this anomaly do not aim at actually suffering pain. The term "algolagnia," therefore, as applied by *Schrenck-Notzing* and by *v. Eulenburg* to this anomaly, does not signify the essence, *i.e.*, the psychical nucleus of the element of masochistic sentiment and imagination. This essence consists rather of the lustfully coloured consciousness of being subject to the power of another person. The ideal, or even actual, enactment of violence on the part of the controlling person, is only the means to the end, *i.e.*, the realization of the feeling.

Cases like this, in which the whole perversion of the sexual life is confined to the sphere of imagination—to the inner world of thought and instinct—and only accidentally comes to the knowledge of others, do not seem to be infrequent. Their *practical* significance, like that of masochism in general (which has not the great forensic importance of sadism), is confined to the psychical impotence to which such individuals, as a rule, become subject; and to the intense impulse to solitary indulgence, with adequate imaginary ideas, and all its consequences.

That masochism is a perversion of uncommonly frequent occurrence is sufficiently shown by the relatively large number of cases that have thus far been studied scientifically, as well as by the agreement of the various statements reported.

The works concerning prostitution in large cities also contain numerous statements concerning this matter.[40]

It is interesting and worthy of mention that one of the most celebrated of men was subject to this perversion and describes it in his autobiography (though somewhat erroneously). From "Jean Jacques Rousseau's Confessions" it is evident that he was affected with masochism.

Rousseau, with reference to whose life and malady *Möbius* ("J. J. Rousseau's Krankheitsgeschichte." Leipzig, 1890) and *Chatelain* ("La folie de J. J. Rousseau," Neuchâtel, 1891) may be consulted, tells in his "Confessions" (part i., book i.) how Miss Lambercier, aged thirty, greatly impressed him when he was eight years old and lived with her brother as his pupil. Her solicitude when he could not immediately answer a question, and her threats to punish him if he did not learn well, made the deepest impression on him. When one day he had blows at her hands, with the feeling of pain and shame he also experienced sensuous pleasure, that incited a great desire to be whipped by her again. It was only for fear of disturbing the lady that *Rousseau* failed to make other opportunities to experience this lustful, sensual feeling. One day, however, he unintentionally gave cause for a whipping at Miss Lambercier's hands. This was the last; for Miss Lambercier must have noticed something of the peculiar effect of the punishment, she did not allow the eight-year-old boy to sleep in her room any more. From this time *Rousseau* felt a desire to have himself punished by ladies pleasing to him, *à* la Lambercier, but he asserts that until he became a youth he knew nothing of the relation of the sexes to each other. As is known, Rousseau was first introduced to the real mysteries of love in his thirteenth year, and lost his innocence through Madame de Warrens. Till then he had only feelings and impulses attracting him to woman in the nature of passive flagellation, and other masochistic ideas.

Rousseau describes extensively how he suffered, with his great sexual desires, by reason of his peculiar sensuousness, which had undoubtedly been awakened by his whippings, for he revelled in desire, and could not disclose his longings. It would be erroneous, however, to suppose that *Rousseau* was concerned merely with flagellation. Flagellation only awakened ideas of a masochistic nature. At least in these ideas lies the psychological nucleus of his interesting study of self. The essential element with *Rousseau* was the feeling of subjection to the woman. This is clearly shown by the "Confessions," in which he expressly emphasizes that "To be at the knee of an imperious mistress, to obey her orders, to have to ask her pardon, this for me was a very tender pleasure."

This passage proves that the consciousness of subjection to and humiliation by the woman was the most important element.

To be sure, *Rousseau* was himself in error in supposing that this impulse to be humiliated by a woman had arisen by association of ideas from the idea of flagellation:—

"Never daring to declare my tastes, I amused myself at least by relationships which reminded me thereof."

It is only in connection with the numerous cases of masochism, the existence of which has now been established, and among which there are so many that are in no wise connected with flagellation, showing the primary and purely psychical character of this instinct of subjection—it is only in connection with these cases that a complete insight into *Rousseau's* case is obtained and the error detected into which he necessarily fell in the analysis of his own condition.

Binet ("Revue Anthropologique," xxiv., p. 256), who analyzes Rousseau's case in detail, justly calls attention to its masochistic significance when he says: "What Rousseau likes in women is not only the furrowed brow, the upraised hand, the severe look, the imperious attitude, but also the emotional state of which these facts are the external signs; he loves the proud, scornful woman crushing him under her feet by the weight of her royal wrath."

The solution of this enigmatical psychological fact *Binet* finds in his assumption that it is an instance of fetichism, only with the difference that the object of the fetichism—*i.e.*, the object of individual attraction (fetich)—is not a portion of the body like a hand or foot, but a mental peculiarity. This enthusiasm he calls "spiritual love," in contract with "earthly love," as manifested in ordinary fetichism.

This deduction is acute, but it is only a term by which to designate a fact, not a solution of it. Whether an explanation is possible, will later occupy our attention.

There were also elements of masochism (and sadism) in the French writer *C. P. Baudelaire*, who died insane.

Baudelaire came of an insane and eccentric family. From his youth he was psychically abnormal. His sexual life was decidedly abnormal. He had love-affairs with ugly, repulsive women—negresses, dwarfs, giantesses. About a very beautiful woman he expressed the wish to see her hung up by her hands and to kiss her feet. This enthusiasm for the naked foot also appears in one of his fiercely feverish poems as the equivalent of sexual indulgence. He said women were animals who had to be shut up, beaten and fed well. The man displaying these masochistic and sadistic inclinations died of paretic dementia. (*Lombroso,* "The Man of Genius.")

In scientific literature, the conditions constituting masochism have not received attention until recently. *Tarnowsky,* however ("Die krankhaften Erscheinungen des Geschlechtssinns," Berlin, 1886), relates that he has known happily married, intellectual men, who from time to time felt an irresistible impulse to subject themselves to the coarsest, cynical treatment—to scoldings or blows from passive or active pederasts or prostitutes. It is worthy of remark that, as *Tarnowsky* observes, in certain cases blows, even when they draw blood, do not bring the desired result (virility, or at least ejaculation during flagellation) by those given to passive flagellation. "The individual must then be undressed by force, his hands tied, fastened to a bench, etc., during which he shams opposition, scolds, and pretends to resist. Only under such circumstances do the blows induce excitement leading to ejaculation."

O. Zimmerman's work, "Die Wonne des Leids," Leipzig, 1885, also contributes much to this subject,[41] taken from history and literature.

More recently this matter has attracted fuller attention.

A. Moll, in his work, "Die Conträre Sexualempfindung," pp. 133 and 151 *et seq.*, Berlin, 1891, quotes a number of cases of complete masochism in individuals of inverted sexuality, and among them that of a man suffering with sexual perversion, who sent written instructions, containing twenty paragraphs, to a man engaged for this purpose, who was to treat and abuse him like a slave.

In June, 1891, Mr. *Dimitri von Stefanowsky*, Deputy Government Attorney in Jaroslaw, Russia, informed me that, about three years before, he had given his attention to the perversion of the sexual life designated "masochism" by me, and called "passivism" by him; that a year and a half previously he had prepared a paper on the subject for *Professor von Kowalewsky* for the Russian "Archives of Psychiatry"; and that in November, 1888, he had read a paper on this subject, considered in its legal and psychological aspects, before the Law Society of Moscow (printed in the "Juridischer Boten," the organ of the society, in Nos. 6 to 8).[42]

V. *Schrenck-Notzing* devotes in his work "Therapeutic Suggestions in *Psychopathia Sexualis*" (Stuttgart, 1892), several paragraphs to masochism and sadism and quotes several observations of his own.

Professor *E. Deak* of Buda Pesth, points out that the favourite thought of the masochist, viz.: to be used by a female person as a beast of burden, may be found in the old-Indian Literature, *e.g.,* in "Pantschatandra" (Benfey, Vol. ii., Book iv.) in the form of a narrative: "Woman's Wiles," the gist of which is: The wife of King Nenda (in consequence of some love quarrel) was very angry with her husband, but despite of his most earnest entreaties would not be reconciled. He says to her: "Love, without thee I cannot exist. I throw myself at thy feet and implore thee to be kind to me." She replies: "If thou wilt let me put a bit in thy mouth, mount thee and goad thee on to run and neigh like a horse, I will forgive thee." He did it. (*Cf.,* Case 58 of this book!)

Benfey found a similar story in a Buddhistic narrative which is published in "Memoires sur les contrées occidentales par Hionen Thsang, traduit du Chinois par St. Julien," i., 124.

Sacher-Masoch's writings have repeatedly been mentioned in this book.

Many perverts refer to this author as having given typical descriptions of their psychical conditions.

Zola has a masochistic scene in his "Nana," also in "Eugène Rougon." The "decadent" literature of recent times in France and Germany often has for a theme sadism and masochism. According to *v. Stefanowsky* the tendency of the Russian novel lies in the same direction. *Johann George Forster* (1754-94) mentions in his "Travels" that the same idea underlies the Russian folklore. *Stefanowsky* finds the type of the "Passivist" in an English tragedy by *Otway:* "Venice preserved," and refers also to *Dr. Luiz's* "Les fellatores. Moeurs de la décadence," Paris, 1888 (Union des bibliophiles).

Johannes Wedde (social-democrat agitator, died 1890), of Hamburg, advocates in his lyrics the subjection of man to woman who should be mistress instead of handmaid. (*Cf. Max Hoffmann*, "Magazin," v. 29, 2, 96.)

A striking example of masochism may also be found in northern literature by *J. P. Jacobsen*, "Niels Lyne."

(b) Latent Masochism—Foot- and Shoe-Fetichists.

Following the group of masochists is the very numerous class of foot- and shoe-fetichists. This group forms the transition to the manifestations of another independent perversion, *i.e.*, fetichism itself; but it stands in closer relationship to masochism than to the latter, for which reason it is placed here.

By fetichists (see page 143) I understand individuals whose sexual interest is concentrated exclusively on certain parts of the female body, or on certain portions of female attire. One of the most frequent forms of this fetichism is that in which the female foot or shoe is the fetich, and becomes the exclusive object of sexual feeling and desire. It is highly probable, and shown by a correct classification of the observed cases, that the majority—and perhaps all—of the cases of shoe fetichism, rest upon a basis of more or less conscious masochistic desire for self-humiliation.

In *Hammond's* case (case 59) the satisfaction of a masochist was found in being trod upon. In cases 55 and 58 they also had themselves trod upon. In case 59, erotic horse, the person loved a woman's foot, etc. In the majority of cases of masochism the act of being trod upon with feet plays a part as an easily accessible means of expressing the relation of subjection.[43]

CASE 69. Z., age 28, hereditarily and constitutionally neuropathic, claimed to have had pollution at the age of eleven, when he was chastised by his mother on the buttocks. He often recalls the scene as a pleasurable experience. At the age of thirteen he developed a weakness for ladies' boots with high heels. He pressed them between his thighs and thus produced ejaculation. The very thought of it sufficed to effect the desired result. He soon added to this fancy the idea that he lay at the feet of a pretty girl and allowed her to kick him with her pretty boots. This caused ejaculation. Until he was twenty-one he never had desire for coitus or the female genitals. From twenty-one to twenty-five he suffered from tuberculosis, during which period the masochistic inclination almost disappeared. After recovery he tried coitus for the first time, but when he saw the nude form of the girl, his desire vanished completely. He now confined himself to his masochistic fancies, but hoped that some day he would meet with the ideal woman who by means of sadistic acts might lead him to normal sexual intercourse.

Such cases are numerous in which, within a fully developed circle of masochistic ideas, the foot and the shoe or boot of a woman, conceived as a means of humiliation, have become the objects of special sexual interest. Through numerous degrees that are easily discriminated they form the demonstrable transition to other cases in which the masochistic inclinations retreat more and more to the background, and little by little pass beyond the threshold of consciousness, while the interest in women's shoes, apparently absolutely inexplicable, alone remains in consciousness. Frequent cases of shoe-lovers, which, like all cases of fetichism, possess forensic interest (theft of shoes), occupy a position midway between masochism and fetichism. The majority or all may be looked upon as instances of latent masochism (the motive remaining unconscious) in which *the female foot or shoe, as the masochist's fetich,* has acquired an independent significance.

In cases 70 and 71 the female shoe possesses a subordinate interest, but unmistakable masochistic desires play an important part:—

CASE 70. Mr. X., aged twenty-five, parents healthy, never ill before, placed the following autobiography at my disposal: "I began to practice onanism at the age of ten, without ever having any lustful thoughts during the act. Yet at that time—I am sure of this—the sight and touch of girls' elegant boots had a peculiar charm for me; my greatest desire was also to wear such shoes, a wish that was occasionally fulfilled at masquerades. But I was also troubled by a very different thought: *my ideal was to see myself in a position of humiliation; I would gladly have been a slave,* and whipped; in short, I wished to receive the treatment that one finds described in many stories of slavery. I do not know whether the reading of such stories gave rise to my wish, or whether it arose spontaneously.

"Puberty began at the age of thirteen; with the occurrence of ejaculation lustful pleasure increased, and I masturbated more frequently, often two or three times a day. From my twelfth to my sixteenth year, during the act of onanism, I always had the idea that I was forced to wear girls' boots. The sight of an elegant boot, on the foot of a girl at all pretty, intoxicated me; I inhaled the odor of the leather with avidity. In order to smell leather during the act of onanism, I bought a pair of leathern cuffs, which I smelled while I masturbated. My enthusiasm for ladies' leathern shoes remains the same today; once, since my seventeenth year, it has been coupled with the *wish to become a servant, to blacken shoes for distinguished ladies, to put on and take off their shoes for them, etc.*

"My dreams at night are made up of shoe-scenes: either I stand before the show-window of a shoe-shop regarding the elegant ladies' shoes—particularly buttoned shoes—or I lie at a lady's feet and lick her shoes. For about a year I have given up onanism and gone to girls;

coitus takes place by means of intense thought of ladies' buttoned shoes; or, if necessary, I take the shoe of the girl to bed with me. I have never suffered from my former onanism. I learn easily, have a good memory, and have never had a headache in my life. This much concerning myself.

"A few words about my brother: I am thoroughly convinced that he is also a shoe-fetichist. Of the many facts that demonstrate this to me, it is only necessary to mention that it is a great pleasure for him to have a certain cousin (a very beautiful girl) tread upon him. As for the rest, I might undertake to tell whether a man who stands before a shoe-shop and regards the shoes on exhibition is a "foot-lover" or not. This anomaly is uncommonly frequent. When in the circle of my acquaintance I turn the conversation to the question of what woman's charm is, I very frequently hear it said that it is much more in attire than in nudity; but every one is careful not to reveal his especial fetich. I think an uncle of mine is also a shoe-fetichist."

CASE 71. Z., twenty-eight years, official, comes from neuropathic mother. Father died early; as to his family and health no information available. Z. was from early childhood nervous and impressionable; began early to masturbate on his own accord; with puberty he became neuras-thenic, avoided onanism for a while, but was troubled with pollutions very frequently; recovered somewhat at a hydropathic institute; experi-enced strong *libido* towards woman, but never succeeded in coitus partly on account of diffidence in his power, partly from fear of infection. This upset him very much, especially as he relapsed for want of some-thing better into his secret habit.

Z., during a searching consultation about his sexual life, proved to be fetichist as well as masochist, and revealed interesting relations between these two anomalies. He asserted that since his ninth year he had a weakness for women's shoes. This, he claimed, was caused by seeing at that time a lady mounting a horse whilst an attendant held the stirrup for her. This sight excited him very much, it constantly recurred to his imagination, ever increasing his lustful feelings. Later on his sensations during pollution were connected with women in high boots. Laced boots with high heels charmed him most especially when this idea was associated with the lustful thought that a woman trod upon him with her heel, and that he, whilst kneeling, kissed a woman's shoes. The only interesting thing about a woman was her shoe. Impres-sions of odour did not play any part in this. The shoe as such was insuffi-cient; it must be worn by woman. Whenever he saw a woman with laced boots he became excited and masturbated. He believed that he could not command virile power with any woman unless her feet were clad with laced boots.

For want of something better he made a drawing of such a boot, and whilst masturbating, revelled in gazing at it.

The following case is not only instructive because of the relations shown therein to exist between shoe-fetichism and masochism, but is also of interest on account of the cure of the sexual life brought about by the patient himself.

CASE 72. Mr. M., thirty-three years of age, of good family, which on the maternal side for generations had shown manifestations of psychical degeneration, extending even to cases of moral insanity. The mother was neuropathic and characterologically abnormal. Himself strong, well built, but neuropathic; began as a small boy to practice onanism spontaneously. When twelve years of age he had peculiar dreams of being tortured, whipped and kicked by men and women, especially by the latter. When he was about fourteen a weakness for women's boots came over him. They caused sexual excitement; he was forced to kiss and press them to him; this produced erection and orgasm, followed by masturbation. But these acts were also accompanied by masochistic ideas of being kicked and tortured.

He recognized that his sexual life was abnormal, and at the age of seventeen he sought a cure in coitus. He found himself quite impotent. At eighteen another attempt proved a failure; he continued masturbation assisted by shoe-fetichism and masochistic fancies.

At the age of nineteen he heard by accident a man speak of flagellation by a girl as a means to bring about virility. He now felt that he had found his remedy, and hastened to carry out the advice just received, but was completely disappointed. The whole situation disgusted him so thoroughly that no erection resulted.

He made no more similar attempts, and satisfied himself in the accustomed manner. When he was twenty-seven he met by accident a sympathetic and *galante* girl, became intimate, and complained to her about his impotence. She laughed at him, and said that at his age and with his constitution this was impossible.

He gained self-confidence, but only after fourteen days of the greatest intimacy and with the aid of shoe-fetichism and masochistic fancies he obtained power. This lasted several months. His condition improved, he could do without the secret aids, and his abnormal fancies became latent. Then for three years, on account of psychical impotence with other women, he yielded again to masturbation and his former fetichism. With his thirtieth year he entered again upon sympathetic relations with another girl; but as he felt himself incapable of coitus without the aid of masochistic situations, he instructed her to treat him as her slave. She played her part well, made him kiss her feet, whipped him with a switch, and trod upon him. But it was all in vain. He only felt pain and utter confusion, and soon had these assaults discontinued. Ideal masochistic situations, however, aided him at times to accomplish coitus.

But he found little satisfaction under these circumstances. Then he came across my book on "Psychopathia Sexualis," and found out the real condition of his anomaly. He wrote to his former acquaintance and entered again upon intimate relations with her, but told her definitely that the former absurd scenes of "slavery" must not be enacted again, and that under no circumstances, even though he request it himself, must she enter upon his masochistic ideas.

In order to free himself of shoe-fetichism he adopted the following plan. He bought a lady's elegant boot and made daily these suggestions to himself whilst kissing the boot repeatedly: "Why should I have erections when kissing this boot, which is after all only a piece of ordinary leather?" This practice little by little stripped the object of its fetichistic charm. The erections disappeared, and finally the boot impressed him only as a boot. Intimate intercourse with the sympathetic person ran parallel with this suggestive self-treatment, and although at first he could not produce virility without the assistance of masochistic ideas, these latter gradually disappeared.

He was so pleased with his cure that he came to thank me for the valuable help he had found in the perusal of my book, which had shown him the right way to remedy his defect.

Since then he wrote that he was completely cured, that he met with no difficulties in his sexual intercourse, although from time to time masochistic representations faintly reappeared without, however, leaving any impression on his mind.

CASE 73. Reported by *Mantegazza* in his "Anthropological Studies," 1886, p. 110. X., American, of good family, mentally and morally well constituted; from the beginning of puberty capable of being excited sexually only by a woman's shoe. Her body and naked or stockinged foot made no impression on him; but the foot, when covered with the shoe, or a shoe alone, induced erection and even ejaculation. Sight alone was sufficient for him in the case of elegant shoes—*i.e.*, shoes of black leather, buttoning up the side and having very high heels. His sexual desire was powerfully excited by touching, kissing, or putting such shoes on his feet. His enjoyment was increased by driving nails through the soles so that their points would penetrate his feet while walking. This caused him terrible pain, but he had real lustful feeling at the same time. His greatest enjoyment was to kneel down before the elegant clad feet of ladies and have them step on him. If the wearer be an ugly woman, the shoes would not affect him, and his fancy would cool. If the patient had empty shoes only at his disposal, his fancy would create a beautiful woman wearing them, and ejaculation would result. His nightly dreams were of the shoes of beautiful women. He considered the exposure of ladies' shoes in show-windows immoral, while talk about the nature of woman seemed to him harmless, but in bad taste. X. attempted coitus several times without success, ejaculation never occurred.

In the following case the masochistic as well as the sadistic element is in evidence (*cf.* "Torture of Animals," under "Sadism"):—

CASE 74. A young, powerful man, aged twenty-six. Nothing in the opposite sex excited his sensual feeling except elegant shoes on the feet of a buxom woman, especially when they were made of black leather, and had high heels. The shoes without the wearer were sufficient. It gave him the greatest pleasure to see, touch and kiss them. The feminine foot, when bare or covered with a stocking, had no effect on him. Since childhood he had a weakness for ladies' fine shoes.

X. was potent; during the sexual act the female must be elegantly dressed and, above all, have on pretty shoes. At the height of sexual excitement cruel thoughts about the shoes arose. He was forced to think with delight of the death agonies of the animal from which the leather was taken. Sometimes he was impelled to take chickens and other animals with him to Phryne, in order to have her tread on them with her pretty shoes for his pleasure. He called this "sacrificing to the feet of Venus." At other times he had the woman walk on him with her shoes on, the harder the better.

Until the previous year it was sufficient—since he did not take the slightest sensual pleasure in women—to caress ladies' shoes that pleased him, thus attaining ejaculation and complete satisfaction (*Lombroso,* "Arch. di psichiatria," ix., fascic. iii.).

The next case reminds one of case 73, on account of the interest in the nails of the shoes (as capable of inflicting pain); and of 74, on account of the slight accompanying sadistic element:—

CASE 75. X., aged thirty-four, married; of neuropathic parentage; suffered severely from convulsions as a child; remarkably precocious, but one-sided in development (could read at age of three); nervous from childhood. At the age of seven he manifested an inclination to finger shoes, especially the nails of women's shoes. The mere sight, but still more the touching of the shoe nails and counting them, gave him indescribable pleasure.

At night he gave himself up to imagining how his cousins had their measures taken for shoes; how he nailed horse-shoes on to one of them or cut her feet off. In time the shoe-scenes came upon him during the day, and involuntarily induced erection and ejaculation. Frequently he took the shoes of female occupants of the house; and if he touched them with his penis he had an ejaculation. For a long time, when a student, it was possible for him to control his ideas and inclinations; but there came a time when he was compelled to listen to female foot-steps on the pavement, which, like the sight of the nails being driven into ladies' shoes, or the sight of shoes in the windows of the boot-shops, always swayed him with feelings of lustful pleasure. He married, and during the first months of his married life was free from these desires. Gradually he became diseased and neurasthenic.

At this stage he began to have hysterical attacks when the shoe-maker spoke to him of nails in ladies' shoes or of driving nails in the same. The reaction was still greater if he chanced to see a pretty lady with shoes well beset with nails. In order to induce ejaculation it was only necessary for him to cut soles out of pasteboard and beset them with nails; or he would buy ladies' shoes, have them beset with nails in the shop, and at home scrape them on the ground, and finally touch them with the end of his penis. Moreover, lustful shoe-visions occurred spontaneously, in which he satisfied himself by masturbation.

X. was otherwise intelligent, skillful in his calling, but powerless in combating his perverse inclinations. He presented elongation of the pre-puce; penis short, expanded at the root, and incapable of complete erec-tion. One day the patient allowed himself to masturbate when excited by the sight of ladies' shoes beset with nails in front of the window, of a shoe-shop, and thus became a criminal (*Blanche* "Archiv. de Neu-rologie," 1882, No. 22).

Reference may be made here to a case of inverted sexuality, to be described later, Case 137, in which the principal sexual interest was in the boots of male servants. The desire was to be trod upon by them, etc.

CASE 76. (*Dr. Pascal*, "Igiene dell' amore.") X., merchant; from time to time (but particularly in bad weather) had the following desire: He would accost some prostitute and ask her to go to a shoe-shop with him, where he would buy her the handsomest pair of shoes made of patent leather, under the condition that she would put them on imme-diately. When this had taken place, she had to go about in the street, walking in manure and mud as much as possible, in order to soil the shoes. Then X. would lead the person to a hotel, and, almost before they had reached a room, he would cast himself upon her feet, feeling an extraordinary pleasure in licking them with his lips. When he had cleaned the shoes in this manner, he paid her and went his way.

From these cases it may be plainly seen that the shoe is the fetich of the masochist, and apparently because of the relation of the dressed female foot to the idea of being trod upon and other acts of humiliation. When, therefore, in other cases of shoe-fetichism, the female shoe appears alone as the excitant of sexual desire, one is justified in presuming that masochistic motives have remained latent. The idea of being trod upon, etc., remains in the depths of unconscious life, and the idea of the shoe alone, the means for such acts, rises into consciousness. Cases which would otherwise remain wholly inexplicable are sufficiently explained.[44] Here one has to do with latent masochism which may always be assumed as the unconscious motive, when not infrequently the origin of the fetichism can be proved to arise from an association of ideas with some particular event, as in cases 113 and 114.

Such cases of desire for ladies' shoes, without conscious motive and without demonstrable origin, are really innumerable.[45] Three cases are here given as examples:—

CASE 77. Minister, aged fifty. From time to time he went to houses of prostitution under the pretext of renting a room. He entered it with a girl. Then he lustfully regarded her shoes, took one off and kissed and bit the shoe, seized with ecstasy. He then pressed the shoe on to his genitals, ejaculated and, with the ejaculated semen rubbed his chest and nipples. Then he awoke from his sexual ecstasy. He begged the woman to allow him to keep the shoe for a few days, and always, at the appointed time, returned it with thanks (*Cantaranot*, "La Psichiatria," v., p. 205).

CASE 78. Z., student, aged twenty-three; of a tainted family. Sister was insane; brother suffered from hysteria. The patient, peculiar from childhood, had frequent attacks of hypochondriacal depression, weariness of life, and felt that he was being slighted. In a consultation on account of mental trouble, I found him to be a very perverse hereditarily predisposed man, with neurasthenic and hypochondriacal symptoms. A suspicion of masturbation was confirmed. Patient made interesting disclosures concerning his sexual life. At the age of ten he was powerfully attracted by the foot of one of his comrades. At twelve he became an enthusiast for ladies' feet. It gave him a delightful sensation to revel in the sight of them. At fourteen he began to masturbate, thinking, at the same time, of the beautiful foot of a lady. At this time he revelled in the sight of the feet of his three-year-old sister. The feet of other females that attracted him induced sexual excitement. Only women's feet—no other part of them—interested him. The thought of sexual intercourse with women excited his disgust. He had never attempted coitus. After his twelfth year he had no interest in the feet of male individuals. The style of covering of the female foot was indifferent to him; it was only necessary that the person seemed to be sympathetic. The thought of enjoying the feet of prostitutes was disgusting to him. For years he had been in love with his sister's feet. If he could but obtain her shoes, the sight of them powerfully excited his sensuality.

Kissing or embracing his sister did not have this effect. His greatest delight was to embrace and kiss the foot of a sympathetic woman, when ejaculation would result with a lively pleasurable sensation. Often he was impelled to touch his genitals with one of his sister's shoes; but he had been able, thus far, to master this impulse, especially for the reason that for two years (owing to progressive irritable weakness of the genitals) the simple sight of the foot had induced ejaculation. From his relatives it was ascertained that the patient had a silly admiration for the feet of his sister; so that she avoided him and sought to hide her feet from him. The patient looked upon his perverse sexual impulse as pathological, and was painfully affected by the fact that his vile fancy had for its object his sister's foot. He avoided opportunity as much as he could, and sought to help the matter by masturbation when, as in dreams accompanied by pollution, ladies' feet filled his imagination. However, when the impulse became too powerful he could not avoid gaining a partial sight of his sister's foot. Immediately after ejaculation he would become angry with himself at having been weak again. His partiality for his sister's foot had cost him many a sleepless night. He often wondered that he could still love his sister. Although it seemed right to him that she should conceal her feet from him, yet he was often irritated because the concealment caused him to have pollutions. The patient gave assurances, confirmed by his relatives, of being moral in other respects.

CASE 79. S., New York, was accused of being a street-thief. Numerous cases of insanity in his ancestry; father, brother and sister mentally abnormal. At seven years, violent cerebral concussion twice. At thirteen, struck by a beam. At fourteen S. had violent attacks of headache. Accompanying these attacks, or immediately after them, peculiar impulse to take the shoes of female members of the family—as a rule, only one at a time—and hide them in some out-of-the-way corner. Confronted with this, he would lie, or declare that he had no recollection of the affair. The passion for shoes was unconquerable, and made its appearance every three or four months. On one occasion he attempted to take a shoe from the foot of one of the servants, and on another he stole his sister's shoe from her bedroom. In the spring two ladies had their shoes torn from their feet in the open street. In August, S. left his home early in the morning to go to his work as a printer. A moment afterwards he tore the shoe from a girl's foot in the open street, fled to his place of work, and there was arrested as a street-thief. He declared that he did not know much of his act; that it had come upon him like a stroke of lightning, at the sight of the shoe, that he must possess himself of it, but for what purpose he did not know. He had acted while in a state of unconsciousness. The shoe, as he correctly indicated, was found in his coat. In confinement he was so much excited mentally that an outbreak of insanity was feared. Discharged, he stole his wife's shoes while she was asleep. His moral character and habits of life were blameless. He was an intelligent workman; but irregularity of employment, that soon followed, made him confused and incapable of work. Pardoned (*Nichols*, "Am. Journal of Insanity," 1859; *Beck*, "Med. Jurisprudence," vol. i., p. 732, 1860).

Dr. Pascal (*op. cit.*) has some similar cases, and many others have been mentioned to me by colleagues and patients.

(c) *Disgusting Acts for the Purpose of Self-Humiliation and Sexual Gratification—Latent Masochism—Coprolagnia.*

Whilst in the manifestations thus far described the aesthetic sentiment is at least, so far as appearances go, saved, and the lustful situation is kept within the confines of a symbolic or ideal character, there are many cases in which the desire for sexual gratification by self-humiliation before woman finds expression in acts which defile the moral and aesthetic feeling of the normal man.

Impressions obtained through the senses of smell and taste, which in the normal man produce only feelings of nausea and disgust, are made the basis of the most vivid emotions of lust, producing in the perverse subject mighty impulses to orgasm and even ejaculation.

An analogy with the excesses of religious enthusiasm can even be traced. The religious enthusiast, Antoinette Bouvignon de la Porte, used to mix with her food excreta in order to mortify herself (*Zimmermann, op. cit.*, p. 124). The beatified Marie Alacoque licked up with her tongue the excrement of sick people to "mortify" herself, and sucked their festering toes. The analogy with sadism is also of interest in this connection because here also manifestations in the sense of vampyrism and cannibalism arising from disgusting appetites of the organs of taste and olfaction produce lustful feelings (*cf.* case 59, *Bichel, Menesclou,* f. Beob. 18, 19, 20, 22). This impulse to disgusting acts might well be named COPROLAGNIA. Its relations to Masochism (as a subordinate form) have been indicated in case 51. The subsequent observation will render them clearer.

In some cases it would appear as if the masochistic element were unknown to the perverse subject and the instinct for nauseating acts alone were present (latent masochism). A striking instance of masochistic coprolagnia (combined with perverse sexuality) may be found in case 114 of the eighth edition of this work. The subject of this case revels not only in the thought of being the slave of the beloved, referring for this purpose to *Sacher-Masoch's* "Venus in Furs," but he even pretended to himself that he was asking the object of his love to let him smell his sweaty sandals and eat his excrement. And then he related how, not having what he had imagined to himself and so strongly desired, he contrived a substitute for them by smelling his own sweat-soaked sandals and consuming his own feces and, in doing all this, how his penis had been erect, how he had been seized with a feeling of great pleasure and had ejaculated.

CASE 80. *Masochism—Coprolagnia.* Z., fifty-two years of age; high position; father tubercular; family claimed to be untainted; always nervous, only child, disposed to having peculiar emotions since he was seven, when by chance he saw the servants take off their boots and stockings preparatory to scrubbing the floors of the house. Once he begged one of the maids to show him her toes and feet before she washed them. When he began going to school and reading books, he felt forcibly drawn to literature which contained descriptions of refined cruelty and tortures, especially when they were executed at the demands of women. He simply devoured novels dealing with slavery and bondage, and whilst reading them, he became so excited that he began masturbation. What excited him most was to imagine that he was the slave of a pretty young lady of his acquaintance who allowed him after a long walk to lick her feet,[46] especially the soles and the spaces between the toes. He thought of the young lady as particularly cruel and enjoying tortures and whippings meted out to him. These fancies were accompanied by masturbation. At the age of fifteen whilst revelling in such fiction, he let a poodle dog lick his feet. One day he noticed how a pretty servant girl in his own home let a poodle dog lick her toes whilst she was reading. This caused in him erection and ejaculation. He persuaded the girl to let this happen frequently while he looked on. After a while he took the place of the poodle and ejaculated every time.

From his fifteenth to his eighteenth year he was at a boarding-school and had no opportunity for practicing such evil habits. He was satisfied to excite himself every few weeks with the perusal of literature treating of cruelties committed by women, imagining all the time that he was licking the feet of such women. This produced ejaculation accompanied by the highest lustful excitement. The female organs had never any attraction for him, and he never felt sexually drawn towards men. When he had attained puberty he solicited girls and had coitus with them, but always sucked their feet before the act. He would do this also between acts (*i.e.*, not only immediately before the act), and asked the girls to tell him with what cruelties they would afflict him in case he did not lick their toes quite clean. Z. affirms that he very often succeeded in this, and that the whole action was always pleasing to the girls.

He was especially attracted by the feet of well-bred women that were deformed by narrow boots and had not been washed for several days, but he could stomach only "slight, natural deposits, such as one may find upon the feet of clean well-bred ladies, also discolorations from the stockings, whilst sweating feet excited him only in imagination, but in reality disgusted him." "Cruel tortures" also existed for him only in imagination as a means to excitement; he abhorred them and never craved for them in reality. Nevertheless they played a pre-eminent part in his fancy, and he never neglected to instruct the women with whom he kept in masochistic touch how they were to write him threatening letters. From the collection of such letters placed at my disposal by Z. one is given here because it clearly illustrates the line of thought and sentiment:—

"Let the sweat be licked from women's feet! I take the utmost delight in conjuring up the moment when you will lick my toes, especially after a long walk. A facsimile of my foot I shall send you soon. It will intoxicate me like nectar when you will lick up my foot sweat. And if you will not do it voluntarily, I shall force you to it; I shall treat you as my meanest slave. You shall witness how another favourite licks the sweat from my feet, whilst you shall whine like a dog under the lashes of my servants. I shall declare you outlawed. I shall find the most exquisite pleasure in seeing you in pain, breathing your last under the most cruel tortures, licking my toes in extreme agony. . . . You challenge my cruelty—very well, I shall crush you under my foot like a worm. . . . You ask me for a stocking? I shall wear it longer than usual. But I demand that you kiss it and lick it; that you soak the foot of it in water and then drink the latter. If you do not carry out my pleasure absolutely, I shall chastise you with my riding-whip. I demand unconditional obedience. If you do not obey, I shall have you whipped with the knout, I shall make you walk over a floor well-spiked with sharp nails, I shall have you bastinaded and cast to the lions in the cage. It will give me the utmost delight to see how the wild beasts enjoy your flesh."

In spite of such ridiculous tirades, ordered by himself, Z. looked upon them as a means to satisfy his perverse sexuality. These sexual monstrosities, which to him were only a congenital anomaly, he did not consider unnatural, although he admitted them to be disgusting to the normally constituted man. Otherwise he appeared to be a decent sort of a man with rather refined manners, but his otherwise meagre aesthetic sentiments were overbalanced by sensuality which gratified his perverse desires.

Z. gave me an insight into his correspondence with the literary champion of masochism, *Sacher-Masoch*.

One of these letters, dated 1888, shows as a heading the picture of a luxuriant woman, with imperial bearing, only half covered with furs and holding a riding-whip as if ready to strike. *Sacher-Masoch* contends that "the passion to play the slave" is widespread, especially among the Germans and Russians. In this letter, the history of a noble

Russian is related who loved to be tied and whipped by several beautiful women. One day he found his ideal in a pretty young French woman and took her to his home.

According to *Sacher-Masoch*, a Danish woman yielded her favour to no man until he acted the part of slave to her for a considerable time. She would force her lovers to lick her feet and buttocks. She had her adorers put in chains and whipped until they obeyed her by licking her feet. Once she had the "slave" fastened to her bedposts and thus made him witness her granting the highest favors to another. After the latter left her she had the fettered "slave" whipped by her servants until he yielded by licking his mistress' buttocks.

If these assertions were true which, of course, cannot be accepted from the poet without definite proof, they would constitute remarkable proofs of the sadism of women. At any rate they are psychologically interesting instances of thoughts and sentiments specific to masochism (my own observations, "Centralblatt für Krankheiten der Harn- und Sexualorgane," vi., 7).

CASE 81. Z., aged twenty-four; Russian civil servant; mother neuropathic, father psychopathic. Z. was intelligent, of refined manners, physically normal, of pleasing appearance and aesthetic tastes; never had a severe illness. Claimed to have been of a nervous disposition from infancy; had like his mother neuropathic eyes and latterly suffered from cerebral asthenic troubles. The perversion of his sexual life caused him much worry, bordering on despair, deprived him of self-esteem and tempted him to suicide.

What oppressed him was the unnatural desire recurring every four weeks that a woman should urinate into his mouth. As cause he gave the following facts, interesting on account of their genetic importance. When six years of age he put his hand by accident under the buttocks of a girl who sat next to him in school. This caused him pleasure and he repeatedly did so. The memory of these pleasant situations strongly aroused his fancy.

When he was a boy of ten years of age, his nurse, upon a libidinous impulse, held herself against him and inserted his finger in her vagina, and afterwards, when he happened, by chance, to touch his nose with his finger, he found its smell extremely pleasing.

This immoral act developed into a lustful fancy which made him believe that he was lying bound between a woman's thighs and forced to sleep beneath her posterior and drink her urine.

With the thirteenth year these fictions disappeared. At fifteen first coitus, at sixteen second, quite normal and without fanciful representations.

Since he lacked money and was tormented by strong sexual desire, he satisfied his needs by masturbation.

At seventeen perverse ideas recurred. They became more powerful and he struggled against them in vain.

At eighteen he yielded to the impulse. When a certain woman urinated into his mouth, he felt the greatest pleasure. He then had coitus with the vile woman. Since then, he felt the necessity to repeat the disgusting act every four weeks.

After indulging in this perverse action he was ashamed of himself and disgust overcame him. Ejaculations accompanied the act but seldom, but it produced erections and orgasm and whenever ejaculation missed, he gratified himself with coitus.

During the intervals between these excessive impulses he was quite free from perverse thoughts and desires as well as from ideal masochism and fetichistic relations. *Libido* during these intervals was but slight and easily gratified in the normal fashion without the assistance of perverse fiction. He often travelled miles from his country seat to the city to satisfy his cravings when these spells came over him.

Again and again the patient—refined as he was and disgusted with his own perversity—sought to resist the morbid impulse, but in vain; restlessness, anxiety, trembling and somnolence made life unbearable, until he found final release from the psychical tension in the gratification of his morbid cravings at any price. He attained this easily, but was at once overcome with self-reproach and contempt for himself bordering even on boredom. These mental struggles enervated the patient and he complained of debility of memory, absent-mindedness, mental impotence, and cerebral pressure. His last hope was that medical science might succeed in freeing him from this monstrous affliction and in re-establishing his moral self.

CASE 82. *Masochism*—Fetichism—Coprolagnia. B., aged thirty-one, official, family neuropathically tainted, nervous from early childhood, weakly, nocturnal frights. First pollution at the age of sixteen. At seventeen fell in love with a French woman, twenty-eight years old and anything but pretty. Had a special weakness for her shoes. Whenever he could do so without being observed, he would cover them with kisses. This gave him sensual delights; but it never caused ejaculation. At that time according to his statement, he had no knowledge of the difference in sexes. He could not understand his weakness for shoes. After he attained the age of twenty-two he had coitus about once a month, but did not derive psychical gratification from the act. One day he met a prostitute in the street whose haughty demeanor, fascinating eye and challenging mien made a peculiar impression on him. He felt an impulse to throw himself at her feet, kiss them, and follow her like a dog or slave. Her "majestic" feet clad in patent leather boots especially captivated him. He trembled with voluptuous excitement. During the night he could not find sleep for the thought of the woman haunted him.

He imagined that he was kissing this woman's feet. This fancy super-induced ejaculation. Shy by nature, he now resorted to psychical masturbation, and having a dislike for prostitutes, he shunned henceforth the society of women altogether. He revelled in the thought of the pretty foot of an imperious woman and associated this thought with the olfactory impression he would receive from its proximity. In erotic dreams he would follow such women. Rain would begin to fall and the woman raising her skirts would show her pretty foot, ankle and calf, encased in a silken stocking. As soon as he grasped and fondled the warm form, so soft and yet so firm, he would ejaculate. On rainy days he used to patrol the streets to see such scenes in reality. If he saw what he came for he would carry away the impression in his memory and it became the object of his nightly dreams and acts of psychical masturbation. To hasten the act he would sniff his own socks, kiss, bite and chew them. His dreams and libidinous ecstasies were also mingled with fancies of a purely masochistic character, e.g., a woman but slightly clad stood in front of him holding a whip in her hand, whilst he knelt at her feet like a slave. She would cut him with the whip, put her foot on his neck, face or mouth, till he consented to sniff at length the secretion between the naked toes of her feet and suck them clean. During this mental act he would smell of his own feet, the odor of which was repulsive to him when in his normal state. He would vary these practices with acts of "podexfetichism" by using a girl's drawers and holding his own dirt up to his nostrils. At other times the vagina (etc.) of a woman would be his fetich and he would practice ideal *cunnilingus*. For assistance he would use pieces cut from the armpits of a woman's undervest, or stockings, or shoes. After six years, during which neurasthenia had increased whilst the imaginative power had waned, he lost all power to accomplish these acts of psychical onanism and came down to the level of a common masturbator. He, later on, became acquainted with a girl of a similar masochistic tendency, and coitus became possible for both, but always by having recourse to some masochistic situation. But the old fetichistic fascinations reappeared and he found greater pleasures in appeasing this perverse appetite than in coitus, which he performed only for the sake of honour. The end of this cynical sexual existence was a marriage—after his mistress had forsaken him—with a woman who had the same perverse inclinations as himself. They had children, but found sexual gratification chiefly in masochistic marital acts. (Centralblatt für Krankheiten der Harn- und Sexualorgane, vi., 7.)

Other cases of *Cantarano's* (*loc. cit.*) belong here (urination and even defecation by the girl on to the man's tongue before the act), consumption of confects smelling like faeces, in order to become potent; and also the following case, likewise communicated to me by a physician:—

"A Russian prince, who was very decrepit, was accustomed to have his mistress turn her back to him and defecate on his breast; this being the only way in which he could excite the remnant of *libido*."

Another supported a mistress in unusually brilliant style, with the condition that she eat marchpane exclusively. So that he might be filled with sexual excitement and be able to ejaculate, he took the woman's excrement into his mouth. A Brazilian physician tells me of several cases of defecation of a woman in the mouth of a man that have come to his knowledge. Such cases occur everywhere, and are not at all infrequent. All kinds of secretions—saliva, nasal mucus, and even aural cerumen—are used in this way and swallowed with pleasure; and kissing the buttocks and even kissing the anus are indulged in. *Dr. Moll* (*op. cit.*, p. 135) reports the same thing of a man affected with inverted sexuality. The perverse desire to practice *cunnilingus*, which is very widespread, probably has its root frequently in masochistic impulses.

Evidently the case quoted by *Cantarano* ("La Psichiatria," v., p. 207) belongs here also, in which coitus is preceded by sucking of the woman's toes which have not been washed for some time. Also a case quoted by me in the eighth edition of this book, *cf. ibid.*, case 68.

Stefanowsky ("Archives de l'Anthropologie criminelle," 1892, vol. vii.) knows of a Russian merchant who was greatly delighted drinking what a girl in a brothel, at his request, spit into a dish.

Neri, "Archivio delle psicopatie sessuali," p. 198: Workman, aged twenty-seven, heavily tainted, tic in the face, troubled with phobia (especially agoraphobia) and alcoholism. It caused him the greatest pleasure if prostitutes deposited their faeces and urine on his mouth (or face). He would also pour wine over their bodies, and as it flowed down over their vagina he would lap it up with his mouth. He was greatly pleased if he could suck the menstrual blood seeping from their genitals. He is a fetichist of ladies' gloves and slippers; he would kiss his sister's slippers, although her feet sweated profusely. He achieved the greatest sexual satisfaction, if he was insulted by girls, or better, actually beaten until he bled. While he was being beaten he would go down on his knees, beseeching the girl for forgiveness and clemency, and would then begin to masturbate.

Pelanda ("Archivio di Psichiatria," x., fascicolo 3, 4) relates the following case:—

CASE 83. W., aged forty-five, predisposed, was given to masturbation at the age of eight. From his sixteenth year, he gave himself sexual satisfaction by drinking recent female urine. So great was his pleasure as he drank the urine that he could neither taste nor smell anything in doing so. After drinking he always experienced disgust and ill-feeling, and made firm resolutions to do it no more in the future. Once he had the same pleasure in drinking the urine of a nine-year-old boy, with whom he once practiced *fellatio*. The patient suffered from epileptic insanity.

Still older cases belong here, which *Tardieu* ("Etude médico-légale sur les attentats aux moeurs," p. 206) observed in senile individuals. He describes as "renifleurs" (sniffers) persons "who hasten to secret places, most probably convenient porticoes outside theatres, where various women go to urinate, and there [these men], stimulated by inhaling the smell of the urine, indulge in mutual masturbation." The "Stercoraires" that *Taxil* ("La prostitution contemporaine") mentions are, in relation to this subject, unique.

Eulenburg relates further monstrous facts belonging to this section. Cf. *Zülzer's* "Klin. Handbuch der Harn- und Sexualorgane," iv., p. 47.

(d) *Masochism in Woman.*

In woman voluntary subjection to the opposite sex is a physiological phenomenon. Owing to her passive *rôle* in procreation and long-existent social conditions, ideas of subjection are, in woman, normally connected with the idea of sexual relations. They form, so to speak, the harmonics which determine the tone-quality of feminine feeling.

Any one conversant with the history of civilization knows in what a state of absolute subjection woman was always kept until a relatively high degree of civilization was reached,[47] and an attentive observer of life may still easily recognize how the custom of unnumbered generations, in connection with the passive *rôle* with which woman has been endowed by Nature, has given her an instinctive inclination to voluntary subordination to man; he will notice that exaggeration of customary gallantry is very distasteful to women, and that a deviation from it in the direction of masterful behaviour, though loudly reprehended, is often accepted with secret satisfaction.[48] Under the veneer of polite society the instinct of feminine servitude is everywhere discernible.

Thus it is easy to regard masochism in general as a pathological growth of specific feminine mental elements—as an abnormal intensification of certain features of the psycho-sexual character of woman—and to seek its primary origin in the sex (see below, p. 132). It may, however, be held to be established that, in woman, an inclination to subordination to man (which may be regarded as an acquired, purposeful arrangement, a phenomenon of adaptation to social requirements) is to a certain extent a normal manifestation.

The reason that, under such circumstances, the "poetry" of the symbolic act of subjection is not reached, lies partly in the fact that man has not the vanity of that weakling who would improve the opportunity by the display of his power (as the ladies of the middle ages did towards the love-serving knights), but prefers to realize solid advantages. The barbarian has his wife plough for him, and the civilized lover speculates about her dowry; she willingly endures both.

Cases of pathological increase of this instinct of subjection, in the sense of feminine masochism, are probably frequent enough, but custom represses their manifestation. Many young women like nothing better than to kneel before their husbands or lovers. Among the lower class of Slavs it is said that the wives feel hurt if they are not beaten by their husbands. A Hungarian official informs me that the peasant women of the Somogyer Comitate do not think they are loved by their husbands until they have received the first box on the ear as a sign of love.

It would probably be difficult for the physician to find cases of feminine masochism.[49] Intrinsic and extraneous restraints—modesty and custom—naturally constitute in woman insurmountable obstacles to the expression of perverse sexual instinct. Thus it happens that, up to the present time, but two cases of masochism in woman have been scientifically established.

CASE 84. Miss X., twenty-one years of age; her mother was a drug addict and died some years ago from nervous disorders. Her uncle (mother's side) was also a morphia-eater. One brother of the girl was neurasthenic, another a masochist (wished to be beaten with a cane by proud, noble ladies). Miss X. had never had a severe illness, but at times suffered from headaches. She considered herself to be physically sound, but periodically insane, viz., when she was haunted by the fancies which she thus described:—

Since her earliest youth she fancied herself being whipped. She simply revelled in these ideas, and had the most intense desire to be severely punished with a rattan cane.

This desire, she claimed, originated from the fact that at the age of five a friend of her father's took her for fun across his knees, pretending to whip her. Since then she had longed for the opportunity of being caned, but to her great regret her wish was never realized. At these periods she imagined herself as absolutely helpless and fettered. The mere mention of the words "rattan cane" and "to whip" caused her intense excitement. Only for the last two years she associated these ideas with the male sex. Previously she only thought of a severe school-mistress or simply a hand.

Now she wished to be the slave of a man whom she loves; she would kiss his feet if he would only whip her.

She did not understand that these manifestations were of a sexual nature.

A few quotations from her letters are characteristic as bearing upon the masochistic character of this case:—

"In former years I seriously contemplated going into a lunatic asylum whenever these ideas worried me. I fell upon this idea whilst reading how the director of an insane asylum pulled a lady by the hair from her bed and beat her with a cane and a riding-whip. I longed to be treated in a similar manner at such an institute, and have therefore unconsciously associated my ideas with the male sex. I liked, however, best to think of brutal, uneducated female warders beating me mercilessly.

"Lying (in fancy) before him, he puts one foot on my neck whilst I kiss the other. I revel in the idea of being whipped by him; but this changes often, and I fancy quite different scenes in which he beats me. At times I take the blows as so many tokens of love—he is at first extremely kind and tender, and then, in the excess of his love, he beats me. I fancy that to beat me for love's sake gives him the highest pleasure. Often I have dreamed that I was his slave—but, mind you, not his female slave! For instance, I have imagined that he was Robinson and I the savage that served him. I often look at the pictures in which Robinson puts his foot on the neck of the savage. I now find an explanation of these strange fancies: I look upon woman in general as low, far below man; but I am otherwise extremely proud and quite indomitable, whence it arises that I think as a man (who is by nature proud and superior). This renders my humiliation before the man I love the more intense. I have also fancied myself to be his female slave; but this does not suffice, for after all every woman can be the slave of her husband.

CASE 85. Miss v. X., aged thirty-five; of greatly predisposed family. For some years she had been in the initial stages of *paranoia*. This sprang from cerebro-spinal neurasthenia, the origin of which was found to be sexual hyperexcitation. When twenty-four she was given to masturbation. As a result of disappointment in an engagement, she began to practice masturbation and psychical onanism. *Inclination towards persons of her own sex never occurred.* The patient says: "At the age of six or eight I conceived a desire to be whipped. Since I had never been whipped, and had never been present when others were thus punished, I cannot understand how I came to have this strange desire. I can only think that it is congenital. With these ideas of being whipped I had a feeling of actual delight, and pictured in my fancy how fine it would be to be whipped by one of my female friends. I never had any thought of being whipped by a man. I revelled in the idea, and never attempted any actual realization of my fancies, which disappeared after my tenth year. Only when I read "Rousseau's Confessions," at the age of thirty-four, did I understand what my longing for whippings meant, and that my abnormal ideas were like those of *Rousseau*.

On account of its original character and the reference to *Rousseau*, this case may with certainty be called a case of masochism. The fact that it is a female friend who is conceived in imagination as whipping her, is explained by the circumstance that the masochistic desire was here present in the mind of a child before the psychical sexual life had developed and the instinct for the male had been awakened. Antipathic sexual instinct is here expressly excluded.

CASE 86. A physician in the General Hospital of Vienna had his attention drawn to a girl who used to call on the medical assistants of the institution. When meeting one of them she would express great delight at meeting a medical man and ask him to at once undertake a gynecological examination on her. She said she would make resistance, but he must take no notice of that, on the contrary ask her to be calm and proceed with the examination. If X. consented, the scene would be enacted as she desired. She would resist, and thus work herself up into a high state of sexual excitement. If the medical man refused to proceed any further she would beg him not to desist. It was quite evident that the examination was only requested for the purpose of inducing the highest possible degree of orgasm. When the medical man refused coitus she felt deeply offended, but begged him to let her come again. Money she never accepted.

It is apparent that orgasm was not induced by the mere palpation of the genitals, but the exciting cause undoubtedly lay in the act of force, which was always demanded, and which became the equivalent of coitus. It is evidently a manifestation belonging in the province of masochism in woman.

AN ATTEMPT TO EXPLAIN MASOCHISM.

The facts of masochism are certainly among the most interesting in the domain of psychopathology. An attempt at explanation must first seek to distinguish in them the essential from the unessential. The distinguishing characteristic in masochism is certainly the unlimited subjection to the will of a person of the opposite sex (in sadism, on the contrary, the unlimited mastery of this person), with the awakening and accompaniment of lustful sexual feelings to the degree of orgasm. From the foregoing it is clear that the particular manner in which this relation of subjection or domination is expressed (see below), whether merely in symbolic acts, or whether there is also a desire to suffer pain at the hands of a person of the opposite sex, is a subordinate matter.

While sadism may be looked upon as a pathological intensification of the masculine sexual character in its psychical peculiarities, masochism rather represents a pathological degeneration of the distinctive psychical peculiarities of woman. But masculine masochism is undoubtedly frequent; and it is this that comes most frequently under observation and almost exclusively makes up the series of observed cases. The reason for this has been previously stated.

Two sources of masochism can be distinguished in the sphere of normal phenomena. The first is, that in the state of lustful excitement every impression made by the person giving rise to the sexual stimulus, independently of the nature of its action, is pleasing to the individual excited.

It is entirely physiological that playful taps and light blows should be taken for caresses,[50]

> Like the lover's pinch, which hurts and is desired.
> —*Antony and Cleopatra*, v., 2.

From here the step is not long to a state where the wish to experience a very intense impression at the hands of the consort leads to a desire for blows, etc., in cases of pathological intensification of lust; for pain is always a ready means for producing intense bodily impressions. Just as in sadism the sexual emotion leads to a state of exaltation in which the excessive motor excitement implicates neighbouring nervous tracts, so in masochism an ecstatic state arises, in which the rising flood of a single emotion ravenously devours and covers with lust every impression coming from the beloved person.

The second and, indeed, the most important source of masochism is to be sought in a wide-spread phenomenon, which, though it is extraordinary and abnormal, yet, by no means lies within the domain of sexual perversion.

I here refer to the very prevalent fact that in innumerable instances, which occur in all varieties, one individual becomes dependent on another of the opposite sex, in a very extraordinary and remarkable manner, —even to the loss of all independent will-power; a dependence which forces the party in subjection to acts and suffering which greatly prejudice personal interest, and often enough lead to offenses against both morality and law.

This dependence, however, differs from the manifestations of normal life only in the intensity of the sexual feeling that here comes in play, and in the slight degree of will-power necessary for the maintenance of its equilibrium. The difference is one of intensity, not of quality, as in masochistic manifestations.

This dependence of one person upon another of the opposite sex— abnormal but not perverse, a phenomenon possessing great interest when regarded from a forensic standpoint—I designate *"sexual bondage,"* [51] for the relations and circumstances attending it have in all respects the character of bondage. The will of the ruling [52] individual dominates that of the person in subjection, just as the master's does that of bondsmen.

This "sexual bondage," as has been said, is certainly an abnormal phenomenon. It begins with the first deviation from the normal. The degree of dependence of one person upon another, or of two upon each other, resulting from individual peculiarity in the intensity of motives that in themselves are normal, constitutes the normal standard established by law and custom. Sexual bondage is not a perverse manifestation, however; the instinctive activities at work here are the same as those that set in motion—even though it be with less violence—the psychical sexual life which moves entirely within normal limits.

Fear of losing the companion and the desire to keep him always content, amiable, and inclined to sexual intercourse, are here the motives of the individual in subjection. An extraordinary degree of love—which, particularly in woman, does not always indicate an unusual degree of sensuality—and a weak character are the simple elements of this extraordinary process.[53]

The motive of the dominant individual is egotism which finds unlimited room for action.

The manifestations of sexual bondage are various in form, and the cases are very numerous.[54] At every step in life we find men that have fallen into sexual bondage. Among married men, hen-pecked husbands belong to this category, particularly elderly men who marry young wives and try to overcome the disparity of years and physical defects by unconditional submission to the wife's every whim; and unmarried men of ripe maturity, who seek to better their last chance of love by unlimited sacrifice, are also to be enumerated here. Here belong, also, men of any age, who, seized by hot passion for a woman, meet coldness and calculation, and have to capitulate on hard conditions; men of loving natures who allow themselves to be persuaded to marriage by notorious prostitutes; men who, to run after adventuresses, leave everything and jeopardize their future; husbands and fathers who leave wife and child, to lay the income of a family at the feet of a harlot.

But, numerous as the examples of masculine "bondage" are, every observer of life who is at all unprejudiced must allow that they are far from equalling in number and importance the cases of feminine "bondage." This is easily explained. For a man, love is almost always only an episode, and he has many other and important interests; for a woman, on the other hand, love is the principal thing in life, and, until the birth of children, always her first interest. After this it is still oftener her first thought, but always takes at least the second place. But, what is still more important, man ruled by this impulse easily satisfies it in embraces for which he finds unlimited opportunities. Woman in the upper classes of society, if she have a husband, is bound to him alone; and even in the lower classes there are still great obstacles to polyandry. Therefore, *a woman's husband means for her the whole sex*, and his importance to her becomes very great. It must also be considered that the normal relation established by law and custom between husband and wife is far from being one of equality. In itself it expresses a sufficient predominance of woman's dependence. The concessions she makes to her lover, to retain the love which it would be almost impossible for her to replace, only plunge her deeper in bondage; and this increases the insatiable demands of husbands resolved to use their advantage and traffic in woman's readiness to sacrifice herself.

Here may be placed the fortune-hunter, who for money allows himself to be enveloped in the easily created illusions of a maiden; the seducer, and the man who compromises wives, calculating on blackmail; the gilded army officer and the musician with the lion's mane, who know so well how to stammer "Thee or death!" as a means to pay debts and provide a life of ease. Here, too, belong the kitchen-soldier, whose love the cook returns with love *plus* means to satisfy a different appetite; the drinker, who consumes the savings of the mistress he marries; and the man who with blows compels the prostitute on whom he lives to earn a certain sum for him daily. These are only a few of the innumerable forms of bondage into which woman is forced by her greater need of love and the difficulties of her position.

It was necessary to give the subject of "sexual bondage" here brief consideration, for in it may be clearly discerned the soil from which the main root of masochism springs. The relationship of these two phenomena of psychical sexual life is immediately apparent. Bondage and masochism both consist of the unconditional subjection of the individual affected with this abnormality to a person of the opposite sex, and of domination of the former by the latter.[55] The two phenomena, however, must be strictly differentiated; they are not different in degree, but in quality.

Sexual bondage is not a perversion and not pathological; the elements from which it arises—love and weakness of will—are not perverse; it is only their simultaneous activity that produces the abnormal result which is so opposed to self-interest, and often to custom and law. The motive, in obedience to which the subordinated individual acts and endures tyranny, is the normal instinct toward woman (or man), the satisfaction of which is the price of bondage. The acts of the person in subjection, by means of which the bondage is expressed, are performed at the command of the ruling individual, to satisfy selfishness, etc. For the subordinated individual they have no independent purpose; they are only the means to an end—to obtain or retain possession of the ruling individual. Finally, bondage is a result of love for a particular person; it first appears when this love is awakened.

In masochism, which is decidedly abnormal and a perversion, this is all very different. The motive underlying the acts and suffering of the person in subjection is here the charm afforded by the tyranny in itself. There may, at the same time, be a desire for coitus with the dominant person, but the impulse is directed to the acts which serve to express the tyranny, as the immediate objects of gratification. These acts in which masochism is expressed are, for the individual in subjection, not means to an end, as in bondage, but the end in themselves. Finally, in masochism the longing for subjection occurs at first before the occurrence of an inclination to any particular object of love.

The connection between bondage and masochism may be assumed by reason of the correspondence of the two phenomena in the objective condition of dependence, notwithstanding the difference in their motives; and the transformation of the abnormality into the perversion probably takes place in the following manner: Any one living for a long time in sexual bondage becomes disposed to acquire a slight degree of masochism. Love that willingly bears the tyranny of the loved one then becomes an immediate love of tyranny. *When the idea of being tyrannized is for a long time closely associated with the lustful thought of the beloved person, the lustful emotion is finally transferred to the tyranny itself, and the transformation to perversion is completed.* This is the manner in which masochism may be acquired by cultivation.[56]

Thus a mild degree of masochism may arise from "bondage"— become acquired; but genuine, complete, deep-rooted masochism, with its feverish longing for subjection from the time of earliest youth, is congenital.

The explanation of the origin of the perversion—infrequent though it be—of fully developed masochism is most probably to be found in the assumption that it arises from the more frequent abnormality of "sexual bondage," through which, now and then, *this abnormality is hereditarily transferred to a psychopathic individual in such a manner that it becomes transformed into a perversion.* It has been previously shown how a slight displacement of the psychical elements under consideration may effect this transition. Whatever effects associating habits may have on possible cases of acquired masochism, the same effects are produced by the varying tricks of heredity upon original masochism. No new element is thereby added to "bondage," but on the contrary the very element is deleted which cements love and dependence, and thereby distinguishes "bondage" from masochism and abnormality from perversion. It is quite natural that only the instinctive element is transmitted.

This transition from abnormality into perversion, through hereditary transference, takes place very easily where the psychopathic constitution of the descendant presents the other factor of masochism,—*i.e.*, what has been previously called its main root,—the tendency of sexually hyperaesthetic natures to assimilate all impressions coming from the beloved person with the sexual impression.

From these two elements,—from "sexual bondage" on the one hand and from the above-mentioned disposition to sexual ecstasy, which apperceives even maltreatment with lustful emotion, on the other,—the roots of which may be traced back to the field of physiological facts, masochism arises from the basis of psychopathic predisposition, in so far as its sexual hyperaesthesia intensifies first all the physiological accessories of the sexual life and, finally, only its abnormal accompaniments, to the pathological degree of perversion.[57]

At any rate, masochism, as a congenital sexual perversion, constitutes a functional sign of degeneration in (almost exclusively) hereditary taint; and this clinical deduction is confirmed in my cases of masochism and sadism. It is easy to demonstrate that the peculiar, psychically anomalous direction of the sexual life represented in masochism is an original abnormality, and not, so to speak, cultivated in a predisposed individual by passive flagellation, through association of ideas, as *Rousseau* and *Binet* contend. This is shown by the numerous cases of masochism—in fact, the majority—in which flagellation never appears, in which the perverse impulse is directed exclusively to purely symbolic acts expressing subjection without any actual infliction of pain. This is demonstrated by the whole series of observations, from case 50, given here.

The same result—namely, that passive flagellation is not the nucleus around which all the rest is gathered—is reached when closer study is given to the cases in which passive flagellation plays a *rôle*, as in cases 50 and 52. Case 58 is particularly instructive in relation to this; for in this instance there can be no thought of a sexually stimulating effect by punishment received in youth. Moreover, in this case, connection with an early experience is not possible; for the situation constituting the object of principal sexual interest is absolutely incapable of being carried out by a child.

Finally, the origin of masochism from purely psychical elements, on confronting it with sadism (see below), is convincingly demonstrated. That passive flagellation occurs so frequently in masochism is explained simply by the fact that it is the most extreme means of expressing the relation of subjection.

I repeat that the decisive points in the differentiation of simple passive flagellation from flagellation dependent upon masochistic desire are, that in the former the act is a means to render coitus, or at least ejaculation, possible; and that in the latter it is a means of gratification of masochistic desires.

As we have already seen, masochists subject themselves to all other kinds of maltreatment and suffering in which there can be no question of reflex excitation of lust. Since such cases are numerous, we must in these acts (as well as in flagellation in masochists, having like significance) seek to ascertain the relation in which pain and lust stand to each other. From the statement of a masochist it is as follows:—

The relation is not of such a nature that what causes physical pain is here simply perceived as physical pleasure; for the person in a state of masochistic ecstasy feels no pain, either because, by reason of his emotional state (like that of the soldier in battle), the physical effect on his cutaneous nerves is not apperceived, or because (as with religious martyrs and enthusiasts), in the preoccupation of consciousness with lustful emotion, the idea of maltreatment remains merely a symbol, without its quality of pain.

To a certain extent there is overcompensation of physical pain in the psychical pleasure, and only the excess remains in consciousness as psychical lust. This also undergoes an increase, since, either through reflex spinal influence or through a peculiar colouring in the sensorium of sensory impressions, a kind of hallucination of bodily pleasure takes place, with a vague localization of the objectively projected sensation.

In the self-torture of religious enthusiasts (fakirs, howling dervishes, religious flagellants) there is an analogous state, only with a difference in the quality of pleasurable feeling. Here the conception of martyrdom is also apperceived without its pain; for consciousness is filled with the pleasurably coloured idea of serving God, atoning for sins, deserving heaven, etc., through martyrdom.

In order to give masochism its proper place in the sphere of sexual perversion, we must proceed from the fact that it is a manifestation of psychical characteristics of the feminine type transcending into pathological conditions, in so far as its determining marks are suffering, subjection to the will of others, and to force. Among peoples of a lower class of culture the subjection of woman is extended even to brutality. This flagrant proof of dependence is felt by woman even with sensual pleasure and accepted as a token of love. It is probable that the woman of high civilization looks upon the *rôle* of being overshadowed by the male consort as an acceptable situation which forms a portion of the lustful feeling developed in the sexual act. The daring and self-confident demeanor of man undoubtedly exercises a sexual charm over woman. It cannot be doubted that the masochist considers himself in a passive, feminine *rôle* towards his mistress and that his sexual gratification is governed by the success his illusion experiences in the complete subjection to the will of the consort. The pleasurable feeling, call it lust, resulting from this act differs *per se* in no wise from the feeling which woman derives from the sexual act.

The masochistically inclined individual seeks and finds an equivalent for his purpose in the fact that he endows in his imagination the consort with certain masculine psychical sexual characteristics—*i.e.*, in a perverse manner, in so far as the sadistic female partner constitutes his ideal.

From this emanates the deduction that masochism is, properly speaking, only a rudimentary form of antipathic sexual instinct. It is a partial *effemination* which has only apperceived the secondary sexual characteristics of the psychical sexual life.

This assumption is supported by the fact that heterosexual masochists consider themselves merely as individuals endowed with feminine feelings.[58] Observation shows that they really possess feminine traits of character.[59] This renders it intelligible that the masochistic element is so frequently found in homosexual men.[60]

In the woman masochist also these relations to antipathic sexual instinct are to be found. *Cf.*, case 84. *Moll* quotes a typical case of homosexuality in a woman afflicted with passive flagellantism and coprolagnia:

Case 87. Miss X., age twenty-six. At the age of six mutual licking of the vulva; then up to seventeen for want of an opportunity solitary masturbation. Since then cunnilingus with various female friends, at times playing the passive, at others the active role, always producing ejaculation in herself. For years coprolagnia. She derived the greatest pleasure from licking the anus of the female objects of her affection and also from licking the menstrual blood of a friend. She obtained the same gratification from beating naked girl friends who were built on generous lines as to the buttocks. The thought of performing coprolagnia with a man was repulsive to her. Satisfaction in having her female genitals licked by a man could only be obtained when she imagined that the act was performed by a woman, not by a man. Coitus with a man she disdained. Erotic dreams were always of a homosexual nature and were confined to active or passive cunnilingus. In mutual kissing she derived the most pleasure from biting her partner . . . by preference in the lobe of the ear, causing pain and subsequent swelling.

X. always had leaning to male occupations, loved to be among men as one of their own. From her tenth to her fifteenth year she worked in the brewery of a relative, if possible clad in trousers and a leather apron. She was bright, intelligent and good-natured, and felt quite happy in her perverse, homosexual existence. She smoked and drank beer. Female larynx (*Dr. Flatau*), small, badly developed breasts, large hands and feet. (*Dr. Moll*, intern. Centralblatt f. Physiol. und Patholog. der Harn- und Sexual-organe. iv. 3).

MASOCHISM AND SADISM.

The perfect counterpart of masochism is sadism. While in the former there is a desire to suffer and be subjected to violence, in the latter the wish is to inflict pain and use of violence.

The parallel is perfect. All the acts and situations used by the sadist in the active *rôle* become the object of the desire of the masochist in the passive *rôle*. In both perversions these acts advance from purely symbolic acts to severe maltreatment. Even murder, in which sadism reaches its zenith, finds, as is shown in case 62,—of course, only in fancy,—its passive counterpart. Under favourable conditions, both perversions may occur with a normal sexual life; in both, the acts in which they express themselves are preparatory to coitus or substitutes for it.[61]

But the analogy does not exist simply in external manifestations; it also extends to the intrinsic character of both perversions. Both are to be regarded as original psychopathies in mentally abnormal individuals, who, in particular, are affected with psychical excessive sexual desire, and, as a rule, also with other abnormalities; and for each of these perversions two constituent elements may be demonstrated, which have their roots in psychical facts lying within physiological limits. In masochism, as shown above, these elements lie in the fact (1) that in the state of sexual emotion every impression produced by the consort, independently of the manner of its production, is, *per se*, attended with lustful pleasure, which, when accompanied by excessive sexual desire may go so far as to overcompensate all painful sensation; and in the fact (2) that "sexual bondage," dependent on mental factors—in themselves not perverse—may, under pathological conditions, become a perverse, pleasurable desire for subjection to the opposite sex, which—even if its inheritance from the female side need not be presupposed—represents a pathological degeneration of the character (really belonging to woman) of the instinct of subordination, physiological in woman.

In harmony with this, there are, likewise, two constituent elements explanatory of sadism, the origin of which may also be traced back within physiological limits. These are: the fact (1) that in sexual emotion, to a certain extent as an accompanying psychical excitation, an impulse may arise to influence the object of desire in every possible way and with the greatest possible intensity, which, in individuals sexually hyperaesthetic, may degenerate into a craving to inflict pain; and the fact (2) that, under pathological conditions, man's active *rôle* of winning woman may become an unlimited desire for subjugation.

Thus masochism and sadism represent perfect counterparts. It is also in harmony with this that the individuals affected with these perversions regard the opposite perversion in the other sex as their ideal, as shown by case 57, and also by "*Rousseau's* Confessions."

But the contrast of masochism and sadism may also be used to invalidate the assumption that the former has its origin in the reflex effect of passive flagellation, and that all the rest is the product of association of related ideas, as *Binet*, in his explanation of *Rousseau's* case, thinks, and as *Rousseau* himself believed. In the active maltreatment forming the object of the sadist's sexual desire there is, in fact, no irritation of his own sensory nerves by the act of maltreatment, so that there can be no doubt of the purely psychical character of the origin of this perversion. Sadism and masochism, however, are so related to each other, and so correspond in all points with each other, that the one allows, by analogy, a conclusion for the other; and this is alone sufficient to establish the purely psychical character of masochism.

According to the above-detailed contrast of all the elements and phenomena of masochism and sadism, and as a *résumé* of all observed cases, lust in the infliction of pain and lust in inflicted pain appear but as two different sides of the same psychical process, of which the primary and essential thing is the consciousness of active or passive subjection, in which the combination of cruelty and lustful pleasure has only a secondary psychological significance. Acts of cruelty serve to express this subjection; first, because they are the most extreme means for the expression of this relation; and, again, because they represent the most intense effect that one person, either with or without coitus, can exert on another.

Sadism and masochism are the results of associations, just the same as all complicated manifestations of psychical life are associations. For psychic life consists, after the production of the simplest elements of consciousness, simply of associations and disassociations of these elements.

The chief point gained by this analysis is that sadism and masochism are not merely the results of accidental associations, occasioned by chance or an opportune coincidence, but results of associations springing from causes existing under normal circumstances, easily produced under certain conditions—*e.g.*, sexual hyperaesthesia. An abnormally intensified sexual instinct spreads in every direction. It reaches into adjacent spheres, and amalgamates with their contents, thus producing the pathological associations which are the real essence of both these perversions.[62]

Of course, this need not always be so, for there are cases of hyperaesthesia without perversion. But these cases of pure excessive sexual desire—at least, those of striking intensity—seem to be of rarer occurrence than those of perversion.

The cases in which sadism and masochism occur simultaneously in one individual are interesting, but they present some difficulties of explanation. Such cases are, for instance, No. 47 of the seventh edition, also Nos. 57 and 67 of the present, but especially No. 29 of the ninth edition. From the latter it is evident that it is especially the idea of subjection that, both actively and passively, forms the nucleus of the perverse desires. Traces of the same thing are also to be observed, with more or less clearness, in many other cases. At any rate, one of the two perversions is always markedly predominant.

Owing to this marked predominance of one perversion and the later appearance of the other in such cases, it may well be assumed that the predominating perversion is *original*, and that the other has been *acquired* in the course of time. The ideas of subjection and maltreatment, coloured with lustful pleasure, either in an active or passive sense, have become deeply imbedded in such an individual. Occasionally the imagination is tempted to try the same ideas in an inverted *rôle*. There may even be realization of this inversion. Such attempts in imagination and in acts, are, however, usually soon abandoned as inadequate for the original inclination.

Masochism and sadism also occur in combination with antipathic sexual instinct, and, in fact, in association with all forms and degrees of this perversion. The individual of inverted sexuality may be a sadist as well as a masochist (*cf.* cases 55 of the present and 49 of the seventh edition and numerous cases in the subsequent series of cases of sexual inversion).

Wherever a sexual perversion has developed on the basis of a neuropathic individuality, sexual hyperaesthesia, which may always be assumed to be present, may induce the phenomena of masochism and sadism—now of the one, now of both combined, one arising from the other. Thus masochism and sadism appear as the fundamental forms of psycho-sexual perversion, which may make their appearance at any point in the domain of sexual aberration.[63]

FETICHISM.—THE ASSOCIATION OF LUST WITH THE IDEA OF CERTAIN PORTIONS OF THE FEMALE PERSON, OR WITH CERTAIN ARTICLES OF FEMALE ATTIRE.

In the considerations concerning the psychology of the normal sexual life in the introduction to this work it was shown that, within physiological limits, the pronounced preference for a certain portion of the body of persons of the opposite sex, particularly for a certain form of this part, may attain great psycho-sexual importance. Indeed, the especial power of attraction possessed by certain forms and peculiarities for many men—in fact, the majority—may be regarded as the real principle of individualism in love.

This preference for certain particular physical characteristics in persons of the opposite sex—by the side of which, likewise, a marked preference for certain psychical characteristics may be demonstrated—following *Binet* ("Du Fétischisme dans l'amour," "Revue Philosophique," 1887) and *Lombroso* (Introduction to the Italian edition of the second edition of this work), I have called "fetichism"; because this enthusiasm for certain portions of the body (or even articles of attire) and the worship of them, in obedience to sexual impulses, frequently call to mind the reverence for relics, holy objects, etc., in religious cults. This physiological fetichism has already been described in detail.

By the side of this physiological fetichism, however, there is, in the psycho-sexual sphere, an undoubted *pathological, erotic fetichism*, of which there is already a numerous series of cases presenting phenomena having great clinical and psychiatric interest, and, under certain circumstances also, forensic importance. This pathological fetichism does not confine itself to certain parts of the body alone, but it is even extended to inanimate objects, which, however, are almost always articles of female wearing-apparel, and thus stand in close relation with the female person.

This pathological fetichism is connected, through gradual transitions, with physiological fetichism, so that (at least in body-fetichism) it is almost impossible to sharply define the beginning of the perversion. Moreover, the whole field of body-fetichism does not really extend beyond the limits of things which normally stimulate the sexual instinct. Here the abnormality consists only in the fact that the whole sexual interest is concentrated on the impression made by a part of the person of the opposite sex, so that all other impressions fade and become more or less indifferent. Therefore, the body-fetichist is not to be regarded as a monster by virtue of his or her excesses, like the sadist or masochist, but rather as a monster by virtue of his or her deficiencies. What stimulates him is not abnormal, but rather what does not affect him,—the limitation of sexual interest that has taken place in him. Of course, this limited sexual interest, within its narrower limits, is usually expressed with a correspondingly greater and abnormal intensity.

It would seem reasonable to assume, as the distinguishing mark of pathological fetichism, the necessity for the presence of the fetich as an indispensable condition for the possibility of performance of coitus. But when the facts are more carefully studied, it is seen that this limitation is really only indefinite. There are numerous cases in which, even in the absence of the fetich, coitus is possible, but incomplete and forced (often with the help of fantasies relating to the fetich), and particularly unsatisfying and exhausting; and, too, closer study of the distinctive subjective psychical conditions in these cases shows that there are transitional states, passing, on the one hand, to mere physiological preferences, and, on the other, to psychical impotence, in the absence of the fetich.

It is therefore better, perhaps, to seek the pathological origins of body-fetichism in purely subjective psychical states. The concentration of the sexual interest on a certain portion of the body that has no direct relation to sex (as have the breasts and external genitals)—a peculiarity to be emphasized—often leads body-fetichists to such a condition that they do not regard coitus as the real means of sexual gratification, but rather some form of manipulation of that portion of the body that is effectual as a fetich. This perverse instinct of body-fetichists may be taken as the pathological criterion, no matter whether actual coitus is still possible or not.

Fetichism of inanimate objects or articles of dress, however, in all cases, may well be regarded as a pathological phenomenon, since its object falls without the circle of normal sexual stimuli. But even here, in the phenomena, there is a certain outward correspondence with processes of the normal psychical sexual life; the inner connection and meaning of pathological fetichism, however, are entirely different. In the ecstatic love of a man mentally normal, a handkerchief or shoe, a glove or letter, the flower "she gave," or a lock of hair, etc., may become the object of worship, but only because they represent a mnemonic symbol of the beloved person —absent or dead—whose whole personality is reproduced by them. The pathological fetichist has no such relations. The fetich constitutes the entire content of his idea. When he becomes aware of its presence, sexual excitement occurs, and the fetich makes itself felt.[64]

According to all observations thus far made, pathological fetichism seems to arise only on the basis of a psychopathic constitution that is for the most part hereditary, or on the basis of existent mental disease.

Thus it happens that it not infrequently appears combined with the other (original) sexual perversions that arise on the same basis. Not infrequently fetichism occurs in the most various forms in combination with inverted sexuality, sadism, and masochism. Indeed, certain forms of body-fetichism (hand- and foot-fetichism) probably have a more or less distinct connection with the latter two perversions (see below).

But if fetichism also rests upon a congenital general psychopathic disposition, yet this perversion is not, like those previously considered, essentially of an original nature; it is not congenitally perfect, as we may well assume sadism and masochism to be.

While in the sexual perversions described in the preceding chapters we have met only cases of a congenital type, here we meet only *acquired* cases. Aside from the fact that often in fetichism the causative circumstance of its acquirement is traced, yet the physiological conditions are wanting, which in sadism and masochism, by means of sexual hyperaesthesia, are intensified to perversions, and justify the assumption of congenital origin. In fetichism, every case requires an event which affords the ground for the perversion.

As has been said, it is, of course, physiological in sexual life to be partial to one or another of woman's charms, and to be enthusiastic about it; but concentration of the entire sexual interest on such partial impression is here the essential thing; and for this concentration there must be a particular reason in every individual affected. Therefore, we may accept *Binet's* conclusion that *in the life of every fetichist there may be assumed to have been some event which determined the association of lustful feeling with the single impression.* This event must be sought for in the time of early youth, and, as a rule, occurs in connection with the first awakening of the sexual life. This first awakening is associated with some partial sexual impression (since it is always a thing standing in some relation to woman),[65] and stamps it for life as the principal object of sexual interest. The circumstances under which the association arises are usually forgotten;

the result of the association alone is retained. The general predisposition to psychopathic states and the excessive sexual desire of such individuals are all that is original here.[66]

Like the other perversions thus far considered, erotic (pathological) fetichism may also express itself in strange, unnatural, and even criminal acts: gratification with the female person in an illicit place (i.e., part of the body), theft and robbery of objects of fetichism, pollution of such objects, etc. Here, too, it only depends upon the intensity of the perverse impulse and the relative power of opposing ethical motives, whether and to what extent such acts are performed.

These perverse acts of fetichists, like those of other sexually perverse individuals, may either alone constitute the entire external sexual life or occur parallel with the normal sexual act. This depends upon the condition of physical and psychical sexual power, and the degree of excitability to normal stimuli that has been retained. Where excitability is diminished, not infrequently the sight or touch of the fetich serves as a necessary preparatory act.

The great practical importance which attaches to the facts of fetichism, in accordance with what has been said, lies in two factors. In the first place, pathological fetichism is not infrequently a cause of *psychical impotence*.[67] Since the object upon which the sexual interest of the fetichist is concentrated stands, in itself, in no *immediate* relation to the normal sexual act, it often happens that the fetichist diminishes his excitability to normal stimuli by his perversion, or, at least, is capable of coitus only by means of concentration of his fancy upon his fetich. In this perversion, and in the difficulty of its adequate gratification, just as in the other perversions of the sexual instinct, lie conditions favouring psychical and physical onanism, which again reacts deleteriously on the constitution and sexual power. This is especially true in the case of youthful individuals, and particularly in the case of those who, on account of opposing ethical and aesthetic motives, shrink from the realization of their perverse desires.

Secondly, fetichism is of great *forensic importance*. Just as sadism may extend to murder and the infliction of bodily injury, fetichism may lead to theft and even to robbery for the possession of the desired articles.

Erotic fetichism has for its object either a certain portion of the body of a person of the opposite sex, or a certain article or material of wearing apparel of the opposite sex. (Only cases of pathological fetichism in men have thus far been observed, and therefore only portions of the female person and attire are spoken of here.) In accordance with this, fetichists fall into three groups.

(a) *The Fetich Is a Part of the Female Body.*

Just as, in physiological fetichism, the eye, the hand, the foot and the hair of woman frequently become fetiches, so, in the pathological domain, the same portions of the body become the sole objects of sexual interest. This exclusive concentration of interest on these parts, by the side of which everything else feminine fades, and all other sexual value of woman may sink to *nil*, so that, instead of coitus, strange manipulations of the fetich become the object of desire,—this it is that makes these cases pathological.

CASE 88. (*Binet, op. cit.*) X., aged thirty-four, teacher in a gymnasium. In childhood he suffered from convulsions. At the age of ten he began to masturbate, with lustful feelings, which were connected with very strange ideas. He was particularly partial to women's eyes; but since he wished to imagine some form of coitus, and was absolutely innocent in sexual matters, to avoid too great a separation from the eyes, he evolved the idea of making the nostrils the seat of the female sexual organs. Then his vivid sexual desires revolved around this idea. He sketched drawings representing correct Greek profiles of female heads, but the nostrils were so large that insertion of the penis would have been possible.

One day, in a bus, he saw a girl in whom he thought he recognized his ideal. He followed her to her home and immediately proposed to her. Shown the door, he returned again and again until arrested. X. never had sexual intercourse.

Nose fetichism is but seldomly met with. The following rare bit of poetry comes to me from England:—

"Oh! sweet and pretty little nose, so charming unto me;
Oh, were I but the sweetest rose, I'd give my scent to thee.
Oh, make it full with honey sweet, that I may suck it all;
T'would be for me the greatest treat, a real festival.
How sweet and how nutritious your darling nose does seem;
It would be more delicious, than strawberries and cream."

Hand-fetichists are very numerous. The following case is not really pathological. It is given here as a transitional one:—

CASE 89. B., of neuropathic family, very sensual, mentally intact. At the sight of the hand of a beautiful young lady he was always charmed and felt sexual excitement to the extent of erection. It was his delight to kiss and press such hands. As long as they were covered with gloves he felt unhappy. By pretexts he tried to get hold of such hands. He was indifferent to the foot. If the beautiful hands were ornamented with rings, his lust was increased. Only the living hand, not its image, caused him this lustful excitement. It was only when he was exhausted sexually by frequent coitus that the hand lost its sexual charm. At first, the memory-picture of female hands disturbed him even while at work (*Binet, op. cit.*).

Binet states that such cases of enthusiasm for the female hand are numerous. Here it may be recalled that, according to case 25, a man may be partial to the female hand as a result of sadistic impulses; and that, according to case 52, the same thing may be due to masochistic desires. Thus such cases have more than one meaning. But it does by no means follow that all, or even a majority, of the cases of hand-fetichism allow or require a sadistic or masochistic explanation.

The following interesting case, that has been studied in detail, shows that, in spite of the fact that at first a sadistic or masochistic element seems to have exercised an influence, at the time of the individual's maturity and the complete development of the perversion, the latter contained nothing of these elements. Of course, it is possible that, in the course of time, they disappeared; but here the assumption of the origin of the fetichism in an accidental association meets every requirement:—

CASE 90. A case of *hand-fetichism*, communicated by *Albert Moll*. P. L., aged twenty-eight, a merchant in Westphalia. Aside from the fact that the patient's father was remarkably moody and somewhat quick-tempered, nothing of an hereditary nature could be proved in the family. At school the patient was not very diligent; he was never able to concentrate his attention on any one subject for any length of time; on the other hand, from childhood he had a great inclination for music. His temperament was always nervous.

In August, 1890, he came to me complaining of headache and abdominal pain, which in every way gave the impression of being neurasthenic. The patient also said he was destitute of energy. Only after accurately directed questions did the patient make the following statements concerning his sexual life. As far as he could remember, the beginning of sexual excitement occurred in his seventh year. Whenever he saw a boy of his own age urinate and caught sight of his genitals, he became lustfully aroused. L. states with certainty that this excitement was associated with accentuated erections. Led astray by another boy, L. learned to masturbate at the age of seven or eight. "Being of a very excitable nature," said L., "I practiced masturbation very frequently until my eighteenth year, without gaining any clear idea of the evil results or the meaning of the practice." He was particularly fond of practicing mutual onanism with some of his school-friends, but it was by no means an indifferent matter who the other boy was; on the contrary, only a few of his companions could satisfy him in this respect. To the question as to what particularly caused him to prefer this or that boy, L. replied that a *white, beautifully formed hand* in his school-fellow impelled him to practice mutual onanism with him. L. further remembered that frequently, at the beginning of the gymnastic lesson, he would exercise by himself on a bar standing apart. He did this for the purpose of exciting himself as much as possible, and he was so successful that, without using his hand and without ejaculation—L. was still too young—he had lustful pleasure. Another early event which L. remembered is interesting. One day his favourite companion, N., who practiced mutual onanism with him, proposed that L. should try to get hold of his (N.'s) penis, and he would do all he could to prevent it. L. acquiesced. In this way onanism was directly combined with a struggle between both parties, in which N. was always conquered. The struggle was finally ended in N.'s being compelled to allow L. to practice onanism on him. L. assured me that this kind of masturbation had' given him, as well as N., especial pleasure. In this way L. continued to practice masturbation very frequently until his eighteenth year. Warned by a friend, he then began to struggle with all his might against this evil habit. He became more and more successful, and finally, after the first performance of coitus, he stopped the practice of onanism entirely. But this was only accomplished in his twenty-second year. It now seemed incomprehensible to the patient—and he said he was filled with disgust at the thought—how he could ever have found pleasure in performing masturbation with other boys. Now, nothing could induce him to touch another man's genitals, the sight of which was even unpleasant to him. He had lost all inclination for men, and felt attracted by women exclusively.

It must be mentioned, however, that although L. had a decided inclination for the female sex, he presented an abnormal phenomenon.

The essential thing in woman that excited him was the sight of her beautiful hands; L. was far more impressed when he touched a beautiful female hand than he would have been had he seen its possessor in a state of complete nudity. The extent to which L.'s preference for beautiful female hands went is shown by the following incident:—

L. knew a beautiful young lady possessed of every charm, but her hands were quite large and not beautifully formed, and often they were not as clean as L. could wish. For this reason it was not only impossible for L. to conceive a deeper interest in the lady, but he was not able even to touch her. L. believed that there was nothing more disgusting to him than dirty finger-nails; this alone would make it impossible for him to touch a woman who in all other respects was most beautiful. L. formerly, as a substitute for coitus, induced the girl to perform genital manipulation with her hand until ejaculation took place.

To the question as to what there was about a woman's hand that attracted him in particular, whether he saw in it a symbol of power, and whether it gave him pleasure to be directly humiliated by a woman, the patient answered that only the *beautiful form* of the hand charmed him;

that it afforded him no gratification to be humiliated by a woman; and that he had never had any thought to regard the hand as the symbol or instrument of a woman's power. The preference for the hand was still so great that the patient had greater pleasure when his genitals were touched by it than when he performed coitus in the vagina. Yet, the patient preferred to perform the latter, because it seemed to him to be natural, while the former seemed abnormal. The touch of a beautiful female hand on his body immediately caused him to have erection; he thought that kissing and other contacts do not exert nearly so strong an influence. It was only of late years that the patient had performed coitus frequently, but it had always been very difficult for him to determine to do it. Moreover, in coitus, he did not find the complete satisfaction he sought. However, when he found himself near a woman whom he would like to possess, sometimes, at mere sight of her, his sexual excitement became so intense that ejaculation resulted. L. said expressly that during this process he did not intentionally touch or press his genitals; ejaculation under such circumstances afforded him much more pleasure than he experienced in actual coitus.[68]

To go back, the patient's dreams were never about coitus. When he had pollutions at night, they were almost always associated with other thoughts than those that occur to the normal man. The patient's dreams were of events of his school-days, when, besides the mutual onanism described, he had ejaculations whenever he became anxiously excited. When, for example, the teacher dictated an extemporaneous exercise, and L. was unable to follow in translation, ejaculation often occurred.[69] The pollutions that now occurred occasionally, at night, were only accompanied by dreams that had the same or a similar subject—i.e., the events at school just mentioned. On account of his unnatural feeling and sensibility, the patient thought he was incapable of loving a woman permanently.

Treatment of the patient's perversion was not possible.

This case of hand-fetichism certainly does not depend on masochism or sadism, but is to be explained simply on the ground of early indulgence in mutual onanism. Neither is there antipathic sexual instinct. Before the sexual appetite was clearly conscious of its object, the hands of school-fellows were used. As soon as the instinct for the opposite sex became evident, the interest in the hand was transferred to a woman's hand.

In hand fetichists, who according to *Binet*, are numerous, it is possible that other associations lead to the same result.

Next to the hand-fetichists, naturally come the *foot-fetichists*. While glove-fetichism, which belongs to the next group of object-fetichism, seldom takes the place of hand-fetichism, we find shoe- and boot-fetichism, of which there are innumerable cases occurring everywhere, taking the place of enthusiasm for the naked female foot. It is easy to see the reason for this. The female hand is usually seen uncovered; the foot, covered. Thus the early associations which determine the direction of the sexual life are naturally connected with the naked hand, but with the foot when covered.

This assumption is certainly correct with regard to those who have grown up in large cities, and easily explains the scarcity of foot-fetichism,[70] which will be elucidated by the following cases.

CASE 91. *Foot-fetichism. Acquired inverted sexuality.*

Mr. X., civil servant, twenty-nine years of age; mother neuropathic, father diabetic.

Had good mental qualities, was of nervous disposition, but never suffered from nervous disease, showed no signs of degeneration. Patient distinctly recalled that even at the age of six he became sexually excited when he saw the naked feet of women, and was impelled to follow them, or watch them when at work.

At the age of fourteen he slipped one night into the room where his sister slept and kissed her foot. At the age of eight he began spontaneously to masturbate, thinking all the while of the naked feet of women.

When sixteen he often took shoes and stockings of servant girls to bed with him; and whilst fingering them excited himself into masturbation.

At the age of eighteen he began sexual intercourse with persons of the opposite sex. He had full power, and coitus satisfied him without the aid of a fetich. For males he had not the slightest sexual inclination, neither had the feet of men any attraction for him.

At the age of twenty-four a great change came over his sexual feelings and his physical condition.

Patient became neurasthenic and began to experience sexual inclination to males. No doubt excessive masturbation brought about neurosis and inverted sexuality to which he was led by excessive desire remaining unsated by coitus, and by the sight (accidental or otherwise) of female feet.

As neurasthenia (at first sexual) increased, a rapid cessation of *libido*, power and gratification, with regard to women set in. Parallel with this, inclination towards his own sex developed and his fetichism was transferred to males.

With the age of twenty-five he had rare coitus with a woman, and without satisfaction. He had lost nearly all interest in the foot of women. The craving to have sexual intercourse with men grew daily stronger. When he was transferred to a large city he found the long-wished-for opportunity and actually revelled with intense passion in this unnatural love.

He ejaculated during these acts with the utmost voluptuousness. By-and-by the sight of a sympathetic man, especially if he were barefooted, sufficed him.

His nocturnal pollutions had now for their object intercourse with men, and, to be sure, in the fetichistic sense (feet). Shoes did not interest him. The naked foot was his charm. He often felt impelled to follow men in the street, hoping to find occasion for taking off their shoes. As a substitute he went barefooted himself. At times he was driven to walk along the street in his bare feet, thereby experiencing the most intense lustful feelings. If he resisted, agony, trembling, and palpitation of the heart set in. Often at nights he yielded to this impulse for hours, even in stormy, rainy weather, not minding the many risks and personal dangers to which he exposed himself by so doing.

He would carry the shoes in his hand, became sexually excited, and only found satisfaction in spontaneous, or induced ejaculation. He felt envious of navvies and the poor who could go barefoot without attracting attention.

His happiest moments were the time which he spent in an hydropathic establishment, à la Kneipp, where he was allowed to go barefoot with the other men under treatment.

An awkward affair, the result of his perverse sexual practices sobered him. He sought safety from his unnatural sexual existence by consulting a physician who sent him to me.

The patient did his utmost to abstain from masturbation and perverse connection with men. He underwent treatment for neurasthenia in an hydropathic institute, regained some interest in the gentle sex—his foot-fetichism serving as a bridge—had once, with a degree of pleasure, coitus with a barefooted peasant girl who acceded to his wishes, and later on visited girls a few times but without gratification. Then he turned again to persons of his own sex, backslid totally, felt irresistibly drawn to tramps and farm labourers, whom he paid for the favour of kissing their feet. An attempt to rescue the unfortunate man by suggestive treatment was wrecked by the impossibility of removing an enervation which was beyond therapeutic aid.

CASE 92. *Foot-fetichism with continued hetero-sexuality.* Mr. Y., fifty years of age, bachelor, belonged to high society. Consulted a physician on account of "nervous" troubles. Tainted, from childhood nervous, very sensitive to cold and heat, troubled with delusions which assumed the character of transient delusions of persecution. For instance, when he sat in a restaurant he imagined that everybody stared at him, talked about, and made fun of him. As soon as he rose this feeling left him and he no longer believed his fancies.

He never felt settled for any length of time, and moved about from one place to another. At times it happened that he engaged rooms at a hotel, but never went there on account of his peculiar delusions.

He never had much *libido.* All his feelings were heterosexual. Now and then he found gratification in coitus which he claimed to have been normal.

Y. admitted that his sexual life was peculiar from early youth. Neither women nor men excited him sexually, but the sight of female feet, be they of children or grown-up women, would do so. All other parts of the female body had no attraction for him.

If by chance he could see the naked feet of female gypsies or tramps he could gaze at them by the hour and was driven by a "terrible" impulse to rub his own genitals against their feet. Thus far he had successfully resisted this impulse.

What annoyed him most was to see these feet covered with dirt. He would like to see them well washed and clean. He could not say how this fetichism originated in him (from a communication of Professor *Forel*).

Moll in his recent researches in *libido sexualis,* p. 288, relates a most interesting case of foot-fetichism which resembles case 91 above, in so far as the patient by force of the fetich became homosexual.

Shoe-fetichism also finds its place in the following group of dress-fetichism; however, on account of its demonstrable masochistic character in the majority of cases, it has been, for the most part, described already above.

Besides the *eye, hand* and *foot,* the *mouth* and *ear* often play the *rôle of a fetich.* Among others, *Moll* (*op. cit.*) mentions such cases. (*Cf. Belot's* romance, "La Bouche de Madame X.," which, B. states, rests upon actual observation.)

The following remarkable case comes under my personal observation:—

CASE 93. A gentleman of very bad heredity consulted me concerning impotence that was driving him almost to despair. While he was young, his fetich was women of plump form. He married such a lady, and was happy and potent with her. After a few months the lady fell very ill, and lost much flesh. When, one day, he tried to resume his marital duty, he was absolutely impotent, and remained so. If, however, he attempted coitus with plump women, he was perfectly potent.

Even bodily defects become fetiches.

CASE 94. X., twenty-eight years of age; family heavily tainted; neurasthenic; want of self-confidence and frequent depression of mind, with fits of suicidal intentions, which he had great trouble to ward off.

The smallest worries threw him out of temper, and filled him with despair. He was an engineer in a factory in Russian-Poland, a man of robust frame, without signs of degeneration. He complained of a peculiar mania, which caused him to doubt his sanity. Since his seventeenth year he became sexually excited at the sight of physical defects in women, especially lameness and disfigured feet. He was not conscious of the original associative connection between his *libido* and these defects in women.

Ever since puberty he had been under the bane of this fetishism, which was painful to himself. Normal women had no attraction for him. If a woman, however, was afflicted with lameness or with contorted or disfigured feet, she exercised a powerful sensual influence over him, no matter whether she was otherwise pretty or ugly.

In his dreams, accompanied by pollutions, the forms of halting women were ever before him. At times he could not resist the temptation to imitate their gait, which caused vehement orgasm, with lustful ejaculation. He claimed to have strong *libido*, and suffered intensely when his sexual desire remained unsatisfied. Despite these facts, he had coitus for the first time when he was twenty-two years of age, and then but five times. He felt, however, not the slightest satisfaction in spite of complete ability. He thought it would cause him intense pleasure if he had the chance to mate with a halting woman. At any rate, he could never marry any other than a lame woman.

Since his twentieth year the patient manifested fetishism for garments. It often sufficed him to put on female stockings, shoes and drawers. He bought such wearing apparel at times and, putting it on secretly, became lustfully excited and ejaculated. Garments which had been worn by women had no attraction for him. He would prefer to wear female garb, so as to keep up sensual emotions, but had not yet dared to do so for fear of being detected.

His sexual life was reduced to these practices. He was definite in asserting that he never was addicted to masturbation. Quite recently he had been, in consequence of his neurasthenic afflictions, much troubled with pollutions.

CASE 95. Z., gentleman, family tainted. Even in early childhood always felt great sympathy with the lame and the crippled. He used to limp about the room on two brooms in lieu of crutches, or when unobserved, go limping about the streets; but at that time no sexual significance was coupled with the idea. Gradually the thought supervened that he would like "as a pretty lame child" to meet a pretty girl who would express sympathy with his affliction. Sympathy from men he disdained. Z. was brought up in a rich man's house by a private tutor, and claimed that he was unaware of the difference in sexes up to his twentieth year. His feelings were confined to the idea of being pitied by a pretty girl for being lame, or extending the same sympathy himself to a lame girl.

Gradually erotic emotions associated themselves with this fancy and at the age of twenty he succumbed to a temptation and masturbated for the first time. This act he practiced henceforth very often. Sexual incapacity supervened and an irritable weakness took hold of him to such an extent that the very sight of a girl with a halting gait induced ejaculation. When masturbating, or in his erotic dreams, the idea of the limping girl was always the controlling element. The personality of the halting girl was a matter of indifference to Z., his interest being solely centered in the limping foot. He never had coitus with a girl thus afflicted. He never felt an inclination for doing so and did not think he could be potent under the circumstances. His perverse fancies only revolved around masturbation against the foot of a halting female. At times he anchored his hope on the thought that he might succeed in winning and marrying a chaste lame girl, that, on account of his love for her, she would take pity on him and free him of his crime by "transferring his love from the sole of her foot to the foot of her soul." He sought deliverance in this thought. His present existence was one of untold misery.

CASE 96. Mr. V., thirty years, civil servant; parents neuropathic. Since his seventh year he had for a playmate a lame girl of the same age.

At the age of twelve, being of a nervous disposition and hypersexually inclined, the boy began spontaneously to masturbate. At that period puberty set in, and it lies beyond doubt that the first sexual emotions towards the other sex were coincident with the sight of the lame girl.

For ever after only limping women excited him sexually. His fetich was a pretty lady who, like the companion of his childhood, limped with the *left* foot.

Always heterosexual but abnormally sensual, he sought early relations .with the opposite sex, but was absolutely impotent with women who were not lame. Virility and gratification were most strongly attained if the girl limped with the left foot, but he was successful also if the lameness was in the right foot. Since, in consequence of his fetichism the opportunities for coitus occurred but seldom, he resorted to masturbation, but found it a disgusting and miserable substitute. His sexual anomaly rendered him very unhappy, and he was often near committing suicide, but regard for his parents prevented him.

This moral affliction culminated in the desire for marriage with a sympathetic lame lady, but since he could not love the soul of such a wife, but only her defect of lameness, he considered such a union a profanation of matrimony and an unbearable, ignoble existence. On this account he had often thought of resignation and castration.

When V. came to me for advice I obtained, in my examination of him, only negative results as regards signs of degeneration, nervous disease, etc.

I enlightened the patient on the subject, and told him that it was difficult, if not absolutely impossible, for medical science to obliterate a fetichism so deeply rooted by old associations, but expressed the hope that if he made a limping maid happy in wedlock, he himself would find happiness also.

Descartes, who himself ("Traité des Passions," cxxxvi.) expresses some opinions concerning the origin of peculiar affections in associations of ideas, was always partial to cross-eyed women, because the object of his first love had such a defect (*Binet, op. cit.*).

Lydston ("A Lecture on Sexual Perversion," Chicago, 1890) reports the case of a man who had a love affair with a woman whose right lower extremity had been amputated. After separation from her he searched for other women with a like defect. A negative fetich!

A peculiar variety of body fetichism may be found in the following case (strongly complicated with sadistic elements), in which *fine white virgin skin* is the fetich, and sadism leads to lustful acts of cruelty (as an equivalent to coitus), even cannibalism (*cf.* p. 63 *et seq.*), for which the deeply degenerated and probably epileptic patient seeks to find a substitute in automutilation and autophagy.

CASE 97. L., labourer, was arrested because he had cut a large piece of skin from his left forearm with a pair of scissors in a public park.

He confessed that for a long time he had been craving to eat a piece of the *fine white skin of a maiden*, and that for this purpose he had been lying in wait for such a victim with a pair of scissors; but, as he had been unsuccessful, he desisted from his purpose and instead had cut his own skin.

His father was an epileptic, and his sister was an imbecile. Up to his seventeenth year he suffered from nocturnal enuresis, was dreaded by everybody on account of his rough and irascible nature, and dismissed from school because of his insubordination and viciousness.

He began onanism at an early age, and read by preference pious books. His character showed traits of superstition, proneness to the mystic, and ostentatious acts of devotion.

When thirteen his lustful anomaly awoke at the sight of a beautiful young girl who had a fine white skin. The impulse to bite off a piece of that skin and eat it became paramount with him. No other parts of the female body excited him. He never had any desire for sexual intercourse, and never attempted such.

He hoped to achieve his end easier with the aid of scissors than with his teeth, for which reason he always carried a pair with him for years. On several occasions his efforts were nearly successful. Since the previous year he found it most difficult to bear his failures any longer, when he decided upon a substitute—*viz.*, each time when he had unsuccessfully pursued a girl he would cut a piece of skin from his own arm, thigh or abdomen and eat it. *Imagining that it was a piece of the skin of the girl whom he had pursued,* he would whilst masticating his own skin obtain orgasm and ejaculation.

Many extensive and deep wounds and numerous scars were found on his body.

During the act of self-mutilation, and for a long time afterwards, he suffered severe pains, but they were overcompensated by the lustful feelings which he experienced whilst eating the raw flesh, especially if the latter dripped with blood, and when he succeeded in his illusion that it was the skin of a virgin. The mere sight of a knife or scissors sufficed to provoke this perverse impulse, which threw him into a state of anxiety, accompanied by profuse perspiration, vertigo, palpitation of the heart, craving for the skin of a woman. He must, with scissors in hand, follow the woman that attracted him, but he did not lose consciousness or self-control, for at the acme of the crisis he took from his own what was denied him from the body of the girl. During the whole crisis he had erection and orgasm, and at the very moment when he began to chew the piece of his skin ejaculation set in. After that he felt greatly relieved and comforted.

L. was quite conscious of the pathological aspect of his condition. Of course, this dangerous character was sent to an insane asylum, where he attempted suicide (*Magnan* "Psychiatrische Vorlesungen").

An interesting category is formed by the *hair-fetichists.* The transition from "admirer of woman's hair" within physiological limits to pathological fetichism is easy. The beginning of the pathological series is formed by those cases in which the hair of a woman simply makes a sensual impression and incites to cohabitation. Then follow those in which virility is only possible with a woman who posesses this individual fetich. Possibly various senses (sight, smell, hearing, crepitant sounds, also touch as with velvet- and silk-fetichists, see below) are drawn into activity in this hair-fetichism as they receive lustful impulses.

The end of the series is formed by those whom the hair of woman suffices even when severed from the body—so to speak, no longer a part of the living body, but only matter, even a mercantile article—to excite *libido* and sensual gratification by way of physical or psychical onanism, eventually by contact of the genitals with the fetich.[71] An interesting instance of a hair-fetichist belonging to the second category is related by *Dr. Gemy,* under the title of "Historie des peruques aphrodisiaques," in "La Médecine Internationale," September, 1894.

CASE 98. A lady told *Dr. Gemy* that in the bridal night and in the night following her husband contented himself with kissing her, and running his fingers through the wealth of her tresses. He then fell asleep. In the third night Mr. X. produced an immense wig, with enormously long hair, and begged his wife to put it on. As soon as she had done so, he richly compensated her for his neglected marital duties. In the morning he showed again extreme tenderness, whilst he caressed the wig. When Mrs. X. removed the wig she lost at once all charm for her husband. Mrs. X. recognized this as a hobby, and readily yielded to the wishes of her husband, whom she loved dearly, and whose *libido* depended on the wearing of the wig. It was remarkable, however, that a wig had the desired effect only for a fortnight or three weeks at a time. It had to be made of thick, long hair, no matter of what colour.

The result of this marriage was, after five years, two children, and a collection of seventy-two wigs.

The following case, observed by *Magnan* and reported by *Thoinot* (*op. cit.* p. 419), is that of a man with antipathic sexual instinct, to whom the actual existence of the fetich was an essential condition for potency.

CASE 99. X., aged twenty, inverted sexually. Only loved men with a large bushy mustache. One day he met a man who answered his ideal. He invited him to his home, but was unspeakably disappointed when this man removed an artificial mustache. Only when the visitor put the ornament on the upper lip again, he exercised his charm over X. once more and restored him to the full possession of virility.

In those cases in which the female hair as mere matter possesses the properties of a fetich, it not uncommonly happens that the fetichist seeks to possess himself of woman's hair by unlawful acts. These form the group of hair-despoilers, of no slight importance from the forensic aspect.[72]

CASE 100. A *hair-despoiler*. P., aged forty, artistic, locksmith, single. His father was temporarily insane, and his mother was very nervous. He was well developed and intelligent, but was early affected with *tics* and delusions. He had never masturbated. He loved platonically, and often busied himself with matrimonial plans. He had coitus with prostitutes but rarely, and never felt satisfied with such intercourse—rather, disgusted. Three years ago he was overtaken by misfortune (financial ruin), and besides, he had a febrile disease, with delirium. These things had a very bad effect on his hereditarily predisposed nervous system. On August 28, 1889, P. was arrested at the Trocadero, in Paris, caught in the act of forcibly cutting off a young girl's hair. He was arrested with the hair in his hand and a pair of scissors in his pocket. He excused himself on the ground of momentary mental confusion and an unfortunate, irresistible passion; he confessed that he had ten times cut off hair, which he took great delight in keeping at home. On searching his home, sixty-five switches and tresses of hair were found, assorted in packets. P. had already been once arrested, on 15th December, 1886, under similar circumstances, but was released for lack of evidence.

P. stated that, for the last three years, when he was alone in his room at night, he felt ill, anxious, excited and dizzy, and then was troubled by the impulse to touch female hair. When it happened that he could actually take a young girl's hair in his hand, he felt intensely excited sexually, and had erection and ejaculation without touching the girl in any other way. On reaching home, he would feel ashamed of what had taken place; but the wish to possess hair, always accompanied by great sexual pleasure, became more and more powerful in him. He wondered that previously, even in the most intimate intercourse with women, he had experienced no such feeling. One evening he could not resist the impulse to cut off a girl's hair. With the hair in his hand, at home, the sensuous process was repeated. He was forced to rub his body with the hair and envelop his genitals in it. Finally, quite exhausted, he grew ashamed, and could not trust himself to go out for several days. After months of rest he was again impelled to possess himself of female hair, indifferent as to whose it might be. If he attained his end, he felt himself possessed by a supernatural power and unable to give up his booty. If he could not attain the object of his desire, he became greatly depressed, hurried home, and there revelled in his collection of hair. He combed and fondled it, and thus had intense orgasm, satisfying himself by masturbation. Hair exposed in the show-cases of hair-dressers made no impression on him; it required hair hanging down from a female head.

At the height of his act, he was in such a state of excitement that he had only imperfect apperception and subsequent recollection of what he had done. When he touched the hair with the scissors he had an erection, and, at the instant of cutting it off, ejaculation. Since his misfortune, about three years ago, he had weakness of memory, was easily exhausted mentally, and troubled by sleeplessness and night-terrors. P. deeply regretted his crime.

Not only hair, but a number of hair-pins, ribbons and other articles of the feminine toilet, were found in his possession, which he had had presented to him. He had always had an actual mania for collecting such things, as well as newspapers, pieces of wood and other worthless trash, which he would never give up. He also had a strange, and, to him, inexplicable fear of passing a certain street; if he ever tried it, it made him ill.

The opinion (medico-legal) showed him to be hereditarily predisposed, and proved the imperative, impulsive and decidedly involuntary character of the criminal acts, which had the significance of an imperative act, induced by an imperative idea, with an accompaniment of overpowering abnormal sexual feeling. Pardon; asylum for insane (*Voisin, Socquet, Motet*, "Annales d'hygiène," April, 1890).

Following this case is a similar one, which also deserves attention, for it has been well studied, and may be called almost classical; and it places also the fetich, as well as the original associative awakening of the idea, in a clear light.

CASE 101. A *hair-despoiler*. E., aged twenty-five. Maternal aunt, epileptic; brother had convulsions. Was fairly healthy as a child, and learned quite easily. At the age of fifteen he had an erotic feeling of pleasure, with erection, at the sight of one of the village beauties combing her hair. Until that time persons of the opposite sex had made no impression on him. Two months later, in Paris, the sight of young girls with their hair flowing down over their shoulders ever excited him intensely. One day he could not resist an opportunity to twist a young girl's hair in his fingers. For this he was arrested and sentenced to imprisonment for three months. After that he served five years in the army. During this time hair was not dangerous for him, because not very accessible; but he dreamed sometimes of female heads with the hair braided or flowing. Occasional coitus with women, but without their hair being effective as a fetich. Once more in Paris, he again dreamed as before, and became greatly excited by female hair. He never dreamed about the whole form of a woman, only of heads with braids of hair. His sexual excitement due to this fetich had become so intense of late that he had resorted to masturbation. The idea of touching female hair, or, better, of possessing it to masturbate while handling it, grew more and more powerful. Of late, when he had female hair in his fingers, ejaculation was induced. One day he succeeded in cutting hair, about twenty-five centimetres long, from three little girls in the street, and keeping it in his possession, when he was arrested in a fourth attempt. Deep regret and shame. He was not sentenced. After spending some time in the asylum, he improved so far that female hair no longer excited him. Set at liberty, he thought of going to his native place, where the women wear their hair done up (*Magnan*, "Archiv. de l'anthropol. criminelle," v., No. 28).

A third case is the following, which is likewise suited to illustrate the psychopathic nature of such phenomena; and the remarkable means which induced a cure are worthy of note:—

CASE 102. *Hair-fetichism*. Mr. X., between thirty and forty years old; of the higher class of society; single. Came of a healthy family, but from childhood had been nervous, vacillating and peculiar; since his eighth year he had been powerfully attracted by female hair. This was particularly true in the case of young girls. When he was nine years old, a girl of thirteen seduced him. He did not understand it, and was not at all excited. A twelve-year-old sister of this girl also courted, kissed, and hugged him. He allowed this quietly, because this girl's hair pleased him so well. When about ten years old, he began to have erotic feelings at the sight of female hair that pleased him. Gradually these feelings occurred spontaneously, and memory-pictures of girls' hair were always immediately associated with them. At the age of eleven he was taught to masturbate by school-mates. The associative connection of sexual feelings and a fetichistic idea were already established, and always appeared when the patient indulged in evil practices with his companions. With advancing years, the fetich grew more and more powerful. Even false hair began to excite him, but he always preferred natural hair. When he could touch or kiss it, he was perfectly happy. He wrote essays and poems on the beauty of female hair; he sketched heads of hair and masturbated. After his fourteenth year he became so powerfully excited by his fetich that he had violent erections. In contrast with his early taste while a boy, he was now charmed only by luxuriant, thick black hair. He experienced intense desire to kiss such hair, particularly to suck it. To touch such hair afforded him but little satisfaction; he obtained much more pleasure in looking at it, but particularly in kissing and sucking it. If this were impossible, he would become unhappy, even to the extent of weariness with life. Then he would attempt to relieve himself, imagining fantastic "hair-adventures" and masturbating. Not infrequently, in the street and in crowds, he could not keep from imprinting a kiss on ladies' heads. He would then hurry home to masturbate. Sometimes he could resist this impulse; but it was then necessary for him, filled with feelings of fear, to run away as quickly as possible, in order to escape the domination of his fetich. He was only once impelled to cut off a girl's hair in a crowd. In the act he was seized with fear, and was not successful with his pocket-knife; and, by flight, he narrowly escaped detection.

When he became mature, he attempted to satisfy himself in coitus with girls. He induced powerful erection by kissing their tresses, but could not induce ejaculation, and coitus did not satisfy him. At the same time, his favourite idea was coitus with kissing of hair; but even this did not satisfy him, because it did not induce ejaculation. For want of something better, he once stole the combings of a lady's hair, put it in his mouth, and masturbated while calling its owner up in imagination. In the dark a woman could not interest him, because he could not then see her hair. Flowing hair also had no charm for him; nor did the hair about the genitals. His erotic dreams were all about hair. Of late the patient had become so excited that he had a kind of satyriasis. He was incapable of business, and felt so unhappy that he sought to drown his sorrow in alcohol. He drank large quantities, had alcoholic delirium, an attack of alcoholic epilepsy, and required hospital treatment. After the intoxication had passed away, under appropriate treatment, the sexual excitement soon disappeared; and when the patient was discharged, he was freed from his fetichistic idea, save for its occasional occurrence in dreams. The physical examination showed normal genitals and no degenerative signs whatever.

Such cases of hair-fetichism, which lead to attacks on female hair, seem to occur everywhere, from time to time. In November, 1890, according to reports in American newspapers, several cities in the United States were troubled by such hair-despoilers.

(b) The Fetich is an Article of Female Attire.

The great importance of adornment, ornament and dress in the normal sexual life of man is very generally recognized. Culture and fashion have, to a certain extent, endowed woman with artificial sexual characteristics, the removal of which, when woman is seen unattired, in spite of the normal sexual effect of this sight, may exert an opposite influence.[73] It should not be overlooked that female dress often shows a tendency to emphasize and exaggerate certain sexual peculiarities,—secondary sexual characteristics (bosom, waist, hips). In most individuals the sexual instinct awakes long before there is any possibility or opportunity of intimate intercourse, and the early desires of youth are concerned with the ordinary appearance of the attired female form. Thus it happens that not infrequently, at the beginning of the sexual life, ideas of the persons exerting sexual charms and ideas of their attire become associated. This association may be lasting—the attired woman may be always preferred—if the individuals dominated by this perversion do not in other respects attain to a normal sexual life, and find gratification in natural charms.

In psychopathic individuals, sexually hyperaesthetic, as a result of this, it actually happens that the dressed woman is always preferred to the nude female form. It may be recalled that in case 55 the woman was not to take off her chemise, and that in case 58, erotic horse (in which the man concerned liked his paramour to ride on his back as though he were a horse), the woman was preferred dressed. Further on a similar case will be referred to.

Dr. *Moll* (*op. cit.* second edition) mentions a patient who could not perform coitus with a nude girl; the woman had to have on a chemise, at least. The same author (*op. cit.*, p. 16) mentions a man affected with inverted sexuality, who is subject to the same dress-fetichism.

The reason for this phenomenon is apparently to be found in the mental onanism of such individuals. In seeing innumerable clothed forms, they have set desires before seeing nudity.[74]

A more marked form of dress-fetichism is that in which, instead of the dressed woman in general, a *certain kind of attire* in particular becomes a fetich. One can understand how, with an intense and early sexual impression, combined with the idea of a particular garment on the woman, in hyperaesthetic individuals, a very intense interest in this garment might be developed.

Hammond (*op. cit.*, p. 46) reports the following case, taken from *Roubaud* ("Traité de l'impuissance," Paris, 1876):—

CASE 103. X., son of a general. He was raised in the country. At the age of fourteen he was initiated into the pleasure of love by a young lady. This lady was a blonde, and wore her hair in ringlets; and, in order to avoid detection in sexual intercourse with her young lover, she always wore her usual clothing,—gaiters, a corset, and a silk dress on such occasions.

When his studies were completed, and he was sent to a garrison where he could enjoy freedom, he found that his sexual desire could be excited only under certain conditions. A brunette could not excite him in the least, and a woman in night-clothes would stifle every bit of love in him. In order to awaken his desire, a woman had to be a blonde, and wear gaiters, a corset and a silk dress,—in short, she had to be dressed like the lady who had first awakened his sexual desire. He was always compelled to give up thoughts of matrimony, because he knew he would be unable to fulfill his marital duty with a woman in night-clothes.

Hammond (p. 42) reports another case where marital coitus could be performed only by the help of a certain costume; and Dr. *Moll* mentions several similar cases in individuals of hetero- and homosexuality. The cause may often be shown to be an early association, and such may always be assumed. It is only in this way that one can explain why a certain costume is irresistible to such individuals, no matter who the person is that wears the fetich. Thus one can understand why, as *Coffignon* (*op. cit.*) relates, men at brothels demand that the women with whom they are concerned put on certain costumes, such as that of a ballet dancer, or a nun, etc.; and why these houses are furnished with a complete wardrobe for such purposes.

Binet (*op. cit.*) relates the case of a judge who was exclusively in love with Italian girls who came to Paris as artists' models, and their peculiar costume. The cause was here demonstrably an impression made at the time of the awakening of the sexual instinct.

There is but a step from such cases to the complete absorption of the whole sexual life by the fetich, the possession and manipulation of which may suffice to provoke orgasm and even ejaculation where irritable weakness of the centre of ejaculation prevails.

CASE 104. P., thirty-three years of age, business man, son of a mother who suffered from melancholia and committed suicide. He was tainted with several signs of anatomical degeneration, was looked upon by his neighbors as a "type," and had the nickname "the lover of nurses and nursemaids of children."

He became a nuisance to these girls by his obtrusive behaviour, picked a quarrel with one of them who wore his fetich, and was arrested.

He claimed to have always been vehemently excited at the sight of wet-nurses and nurse-maids, but not because they were of the female sex, but because they wore a certain costume. Again, it was not certain portions, but the costume as a whole which attracted him. To be in the company of such persons was his greatest happiness. When he returned home from such interviews it was sufficient for him to recall the impressions just received, in order to produce an orgasm of love.

An analogous case is related by *Motet*. It refers to a young man, who became sexually excited only at the sight of a woman attired in bridal costume. The individuality of the woman was a matter of indifference to him. In order to gratify his fetichistic cravings, he spent a great deal of his time at the door of a restaurant where many weddings were celebrated (*Garnier*, "Les Fétichistes, p. 59).

A third form of dress-fetichism, having a much higher degree of pathological significance, is by far the most frequent. In this form it is no longer the woman herself, dressed, or even dressed in a particular fashion, that constitutes the principal sexual stimulus, but the sexual interest is so concentrated on some particular article of female attire that the lustful idea of this object is entirely separated from the idea of woman, and thus obtains an independent value. This is the real domain of dress-fetichism, where an inanimate object—an isolated article of wearing-apparel—is alone used for the excitation and satisfaction of the sexual instinct. This third form of dress-fetichism is also the one used for the excitation and satisfaction of the sexual instinct. This third form of dress-fetichism is also the one which forensically is the most important.

In a large number of these cases the fetiches are articles of female underwear, which, owing to their private use, are suited to occasion such associations.

CASE 105. K., aged forty-five, shoemaker, was reported to be without hereditary taint. He was peculiar, and had small mental endowment. He was of masculine habits, and without signs of degeneration. Previously blameless in conduct, on the evening of 5th July, 1876, he was detected removing stolen female under-garments from a place of concealment. There were found with him about 300 articles of the female toilet, among them, besides chemises and drawers, night-caps, garters, and a female doll. When arrested he was wearing a chemise. Since his thirteenth year he had been a slave to an impulse to steal women's linen; but, after his first punishment for it, he became very careful, and stole with refinement and success. When this longing came over him, he would grow anxious, and his head would become heavy. Then he could not resist the impulse, cost what it might. It was a matter of indifference to him from whom he took the articles. At night, on going to bed, he would put on the stolen clothing and create beautiful women in his imagination, thus inducing pleasurable feeling and ejaculation. This was apparently the motive of his thefts; at least, he had never disposed of any of the articles, but had hidden them here and there.

He declared that, earlier in his life, he had indulged in normal sexual intercourse with women. He denied onanism, pederasty, and other sexual acts. He said he was engaged at twenty-five, but the engagement was broken through no fault of his. He was incapable of grasping the abnormality of his condition and the wrong of his acts. (*Passow,* "Vierteljahrsschrift f. ger. Medic.," N. F. xxviii., p. 61; *Krauss,* "Psychologie des Verbrechens," 1884, p. 190.)

CASE 106. J., a young butcher. When arrested he wore underneath his overcoat a bodice, a corset, a vest, a jacket, a collar, a jersey, and a chemise, also fine stockings and garters.

Since he was eleven he was troubled by the desire to wear a chemise of his elder sister. Whenever he could do it unnoticed, he indulged in this pleasure, and since the age of puberty the wearing of such a garment would bring on ejaculation. When he became independent he bought chemises and other articles of feminine toilet. In his room a complete outfit of female attire was found. To put on such garments was the great aim of his sexual instinct. This fetichism had financially ruined him. At the hospital he begged the attending physician to permit him to wear female attire. Inverted sexuality did not exist in him. (*Garnier,* "Les Fétichistes," p. 62.)

CASE 107. Z., thirty-six years of age, scholar; had never heretofore felt interested in woman, only in her attire, and never had sexual intercourse. Besides the elegance and smartness of the female toilet in general, certain underwear, chemises made of cambric and trimmed with lace, silk corsets, embroidered silk shirts and silk stockings formed his particular fetich. It caused him voluptuous feelings to inspect and finger such female garments at the draper's. His ideal was the female form in bathing costume, with silk stockings and corset, and clad in a mourning-dress with a long train.

He studied the costumes of the girls in the streets, but found them tasteless. He found more pleasure in gazing at the shop windows, but felt annoyed because the exhibits therein were not changed often enough. He found partial satisfaction in holding and studying fashion magazines, and in buying now and then single garments of exceptional beauty. It would be the height of pleasure for him if he had access to the toilet arts of the boudoir or the fitting rooms of the dressmaker, or if he could be the chamber maid of some wealthy lady of the world, and could arrange the toilet for her. There were no traces of masochism or homosexual inclination to be found on this peculiar fetichist. He was of thoroughly manly appearance. (*Garnier,* "La folie à Paris," 1890.)

Hammond (*op. cit.*) reports a case of passionate interest in single articles of female wearing-apparel. Here, also, the patient's pleasure consisted in wearing a corset and other female garments (without any traces of antipathic sexual instinct). The pain of tight lacing, experienced by himself or induced in women, was a delight to him—sadistic-masochistic element.

A case probably belonging here is one reported by *Diez* ("Der Selbstmord," 1838, p. 24), where a young man could not resist the impulse to tear female linen. While tearing it, he always had ejaculation.

A combination of fetichism with an impulse to destroy the fetich (in a certain sense, sadism with inanimate objects) seems to occur quite frequently (*cf.* case 120).

An article of dress, which, though it has not really a private character, by its material and colour, as well as by the place where it is worn, might be suggestive of under-garments, and hence has sexual relations, is the *apron* (*cf.* also the metonymic use of the word "apron" for "petticoat" in the saying, "To chase every apron," etc.). This explains the following case:

CASE 108. C., aged thirty-seven; of a badly tainted family; of small mental development; deformed skull. At fifteen his attention was attracted by an apron hung out to dry. He put it on and masturbated behind the fence. From that time on he could not see aprons without repeating the act. If he met any one—no matter whether man or woman—with an apron on, he was compelled to run after the person. In order to free him from this constant stealing of aprons, he was sent as a marine in his sixteenth year. In this calling he saw no aprons, and had continual rest. When, at nineteen, he returned home, he was again compelled to steal aprons, and, as a result, got into serious complications, and was several times locked up. He sought to free himself of his weakness by a sojourn of several years with the Trappists. When he left them, he was just as bad as before. As a result of a new theft, he underwent a medico-legal examination, and was committed to an asylum. He never stole anything but aprons. It was a pleasure to him to revel in the memory of the first apron he ever stole. His dreams were filled with aprons. He occasionally used the memory of his thefts to make coitus possible, or for masturbation (*Charcot-Magnan,* "Arch. de neurolog.," 1882, No. 12).

In a case reported by *Lombroso* ("Amori anomali precoci nei pazzi," "Arch. di psich.," 1883, p. 17), analogous to those of this series, a boy of very bad heredity, at the age of four, had erections and great sexual excitement at the sight of white garments, particularly underclothing. He was lustfully excited by handling and crumpling them. At the age of ten he began to masturbate at the sight of white, starched linen. He seemed to have been affected with moral insanity, and was executed for murder.

The following case of *petticoat-fetichism* is coupled with peculiar circumstances:

CASE 109. Z., aged thirty-five; civil servant; the only child of a nervous mother and a healthy father. From childhood he was "nervous," and at the consultation his neuropathic eyes, delicate, slender body, fine features, very thin voice, and sparse growth of beard attracted attention. The patient presented nothing abnormal except symptoms of slight neurasthenia. Genitals and sexual functions normal. Patient stated that he had only masturbated four or five times when he was very young. As early as at the age of thirteen, the patient was powerfully excited sexually by the sight of wet female dresses, while the same dresses, when dry, had no effect upon him. His greatest delight was to look at women with wet garments in the rain. If he met a woman with a pleasing face under such circumstances, he experienced an intense feeling of lustful pleasure, had erection and felt impelled to perform coitus. He stated that he had never had any desire to steal wet female dresses or to throw water on women. He could give no explanation of the origin of his peculiarity.

It is possible that, in this case, the sexual instinct was first awakened by the sight of a woman as she exposed her charms by raising her skirts in wet weather. The obscure instinct, not yet conscious of its object, then became directed to the wet garments, as in other cases.

Lovers of female handkerchiefs are frequent, and, therefore, important forensically. As to the frequency of handkerchief-fetichism, it may be remarked that the handkerchief is the one article of feminine attire which, outside of intimate association, is most frequently displayed, and which, with its warmth from the person and specific odours, may by accident fall into the hands of others. The frequency of early association of lustful feelings with the idea of a handkerchief, which may always be presumed to have occurred in such cases of fetichism, probably is due to this.

CASE 110. A baker's assistant, aged thirty-two, single, previously of good repute, was discovered stealing a handkerchief from a lady. In sincere remorse, he confessed that he had stolen from eighty to ninety such handkerchiefs. He had cared only for handkerchiefs, and, indeed, only for those belonging to young women attractive to him. In his outward appearance the culprit presented nothing peculiar. He dressed himself with much taste. His conduct was peculiar, anxious, depressed and unmanly, and he often lapsed into whining and tears. Lack of self-reliance, weakness of comprehension, and slowness of perception and reflection were noticeable. One of his sisters was epileptic. He lived in good circumstances; never had a severe illness; was well developed. In relating his history, he showed weakness of memory and lack of clearness; calculation was hard for him, though when young, he had learned and comprehended easily. His anxious, uncertain state of mind gave rise to a suspicion of onanism. The culprit confessed that he had been given to this practice excessively since his nineteenth year. For some years, as a result of his vice, he had suffered with depression, lassitude, trembling of the limbs, pain in the back, and disinclination for work. Frequently a depressed, anxious state of mind came over him, in which he avoided people. He had exaggerated, fantastic notions about the results of sexual intercourse with women, and could not bring himself to indulge in it. Of late, however, he had thought of marriage. With great remorse and in a weak-minded way, he now confessed that six months ago, while in a crowd, he became violently excited sexually at the sight of a pretty young girl, and was compelled to crowd up against her. He felt an impulse to compensate himself for the want of a more complete satisfaction of his sexual excitement, by stealing her handkerchief. Thereafter, as soon as he came near attractive females, with violent sexual excitement, palpitation of the heart, erection and impetus to intercourse, the impulse would seize him to crowd up against them and for want of something better, steal their handkerchiefs. Although the consciousness of his criminal act never left him for a moment, he was unable to resist the impulse. During the act he was uneasy, which was in part due to his inordinate sexual impulse, and partly to the fear of detection. The medico-legal opinion rightly gave weight to the congenital mental enfeeblement and the pernicious influence of masturbation, and referred the abnormal impulses to a perverse sexual impulse, calling attention to the presence of an interesting and well-known physiological connection between olfactory and sexual senses. The inability to resist the pathological impulse was recognized. X. was not punished (*Zippe,* "Wiener Med. Wochenschrift," 1879, No. 23).

I am indebted to the kindness of Dr. *Fritsch,* of Vienna, for further facts concerning this handkerchief-fetichist, who was again arrested in August, 1890, in the act of taking a handkerchief from a lady's pocket:—

When his house was searched, 446 ladies' handkerchiefs were found. He stated that he had already burned two bundles of them. In the course of the examination, it was further shown that X. had been punished with imprisonment for fourteen days in 1883 for stealing twenty-seven handkerchiefs, and again with imprisonment for three weeks in 1886 for a similar crime. Concerning his relatives, nothing more could be learned than that his father was subject to congestions and that a brother's daughter was an imbecile and constitutionally neuropathic. X. had married in 1879, and embarked in an independent business, and in 1881 he made an assignment. Soon after that his wife, who could not live with him, and with whom he did not perform his marital duty (denied by X.), demanded a divorce. Thereafter he lived as assistant baker to his brother. He complained bitterly of an impulse for ladies' handkerchiefs, and when opportunity offered, unfortunately, he could not resist it. In the act he experienced a feeling of delight, and felt as if some one were forcing him to it. Sometimes he could restrain himself, but when the lady was pleasing to him he yielded to the first impulse. He would be wet with sweat, partly from fear of detection, and partly on account of the impulse to perform the act. He said he had been sexually excited by the sight of handkerchiefs belonging to women since puberty. He could not recall the exact circumstances of this fetichistic association. The sexual excitement occasioned by the sight of a lady with a handkerchief hanging out of her pocket had constantly increased. This had repeatedly caused erection, but never ejaculation. After his twenty-first year, he said, he had inclination to normal sexual indulgence, and had coitus without difficulty without ideas of handkerchiefs. With increasing fetichism, the appropriation of handkerchiefs had afforded him much more satisfaction than coitus. The appropriation of the handkerchief of a lady attractive to him was the same to him as intercourse with her would have been. In the act he had true orgasm.

If he could not gain possession of the handkerchief he desired, he would become painfully excited, tremble and sweat all over. He kept separate the handkerchiefs of ladies particularly pleasing to him, and revelled in the sight of them, taking great pleasure in it. The odour of them also gave him great delight, though he states that it was really the scent peculiar to the linen, and not the perfume, which excited him sensually. He had masturbated but very seldom.

X. complained of no physical ailments except occasional headache and vertigo. He greatly regretted his misfortune, his abnormal impulse —the evil spirit that impelled him to such criminal acts. He had but one wish: that some one might help him. Objectively there were mild neurasthenic symptoms, anomalies of the distribution of blood, and unequal pupils.

It was proved that X. had committed his crimes in obedience to an abnormal, irresistible impulse. Pardon.

CASE 111. Z. began to masturbate at the age of twelve. From that time he could not see a woman's handkerchief without having orgasm and ejaculation. He was irresistibly compelled to possess himself of it. At that time he was a choir boy and used the handkerchiefs to masturbate with in the bell-tower close to the choir. But he chose only such handkerchiefs as had black and white borders or violet stripes running through them. At fifteen he had coitus. Later on he married. As a rule, he was only potent when he wound such a handkerchief around his penis. Often he preferred coitus between the thighs of a woman where he had placed a handkerchief. Wherever he espied a handkerchief he did not rest until he came in possession of it. He always had a number of them in his pockets and aroused his genitals (*Rayneau*, Annales médico-psychol., 1895).

Such cases of handkerchief-fetichism, where an abnormal individual is driven to theft, are very numerous. They also occur in combination with inverted sexuality, as is proved by the following case, which I borrow from page 162 of Dr. *Moll's* frequently cited work:— [75]

CASE 112. *Handkerchief-fetichism in a case of antipathic sexual instinct.* K., aged thirty-eight; mechanic; a powerfully built man. He made numerous complaints—weakness of the legs, pain in the back, headache, want of pleasure in work, etc. The complaints gave the decided impression of neurasthenia with tendency to hypochondria. Only after the patient had been under Dr. *Moll's* treatment for several months did he state that he was also abnormal sexually.

K. had never had any inclination whatever for women; but handsome men, on the other hand, had a peculiar charm for him. Patient had masturbated frequently until he came to Dr. *Moll.* He had never practiced mutual onanism or pederasty. He did not think that he would have found satisfaction in this, because, in spite of his preference for men, an article of *white linen* was his chief charm, though the beauty of its owner played a *rôle.* The *handkerchiefs* of handsome men particularly excited him sexually. His greatest delight was to masturbate in men's handkerchiefs. For this reason he often took his friends' handkerchiefs. In order to save himself from detection, he always left one of his own handkerchiefs with his friends in place of the one he stole. In this way he sought to escape the suspicion of theft, by creating the appearance of a mistake. Other articles of men's linen also excited K. sexually, but not to the extent that handkerchiefs did.

K. had often performed coitus with women, having erection and ejaculation, but without lustful pleasure. There was also nothing which could stimulate the patient to the performance of coitus. Erection and ejaculation occurred only when, during the act, he thought of a man's handkerchief; and this was easier for the patient when he took a friend's handkerchief with him and had it in his hand during coitus. In accordance with his sexual perversion, in his nightly pollutions with lustful ideas, men's linen played the principal *rôle.*[76]

Still far more frequent than the fetichism of linen garments is that of *women's shoes.* These cases are, in fact, almost innumerable, and a great many of them have been scientifically studied. I have but a few reports at third hand of similar glove-fetichism; not to speak of case 122 (see below), in which glove-fetichism develops itself merely into "stuff-fetichism." (Concerning the reason for the relative infrequency of glove-fetichism, see above *a*).

In shoe-fetichism the close relationship of the object to the feminine person, which explains linen-fetichism, is absolutely wanting. For this reason, and because there is a large number of well-observed cases at hand, in which the fetichistic enthusiasm for the female shoe or boot consciously and undoubtedly arises from masochistic ideas, an origin of a masochistic nature, even when it is concealed, may always be assumed in shoe-fetichism when, in the concrete case, no other manner of origin is demonstrable. For this reason the majority of the cases of shoe- or foot-fetichism have been given under "Masochism." There the constant masochistic character of this form of erotic fetichism has been sufficiently demonstrated by means of transitional conditions. This presumption of the masochistic character of shoe-fetichism is weakened and removed only where another accidental cause for an association between sexual excitation and the idea of women's shoes—the occurrence of which is quite improbable *a priori*—is capable of proof. In the two following cases, however, there is such a demonstrable connection:—

CASE 113. *Shoe-fetichism.* Mr. v. P., an old and honourable family, Pole, aged thirty-two, consulted me, in 1890, on account of "unnaturalness" of his sexual life. He gave the assurance that he came of a perfectly healthy family. He had been nervous from childhood, and had suffered from *chorea* since the age of eleven. For ten years he had suffered with sleeplessness and various neurasthenic ailments. From his fifteenth year he had recognized the difference of the sexes and been capable of sexual excitation. At the age of seventeen he had been seduced by a French governess, but coitus was not permitted; so that intense mutual sexual excitement (mutual masturbation) was all that was possible. In this situation his attention was attracted by her very elegant boots. They made a very deep impression. His intercourse with this lewd person lasted four months. During this association her shoes became a fetich for the unfortunate boy. He began to have an interest in ladies' shoes in general, and actually went about trying to catch sight of ladies wearing pretty boots. The shoe-fetichism gained great power over his mind. He had the governess touch his penis with her shoes, and thus ejaculation with great lustful feeling was immediately induced. After separation from the governess he went to girls, whom he made perform the same manipulation. This was usually sufficient for satisfaction. Only seldom did he resort to coitus as an auxiliary, and inclination for it grew less and less. His sexual life consisted of dream-pollutions, in which women's shoes played the exclusive *rôle*; and of gratification with women's shoes placed on his penis, but this had to be done by the girl. In the society of the opposite sex the only thing that interested him was the shoe, and that only when it was elegant, of the French style, with heels, and of a brilliant black, like the original.

In the course of time the following conditions were added: a prostitute's shoe that was elegant and *chic*; starched petticoats, and black hose, if possible. Nothing else in woman interested him. *He was absolutely indifferent to the naked foot.* Women have not the slightest psychic charm for him. He had never had masochistic desires in the sense of being trod upon. In the course of years his fetichism had gained such power over him that when he saw a lady in the street, of a certain appearance and with certain shoes, he was so intensely excited that he had to masturbate. Slight pressure on the penis sufficed to induce ejaculation in this state of severe neurasthenia. Shoes displayed in shops, and, of late, even advertisements of shoes, sufficed to excite him intensely. In states of intense *libido* he made use of onanism if shoes were not at his immediate command. The patient quite early recognized the pain and danger of his condition, and, even when he was free from neurasthenic ailments, he was morally very much depressed. He sought help of various physicians. Cold-water cures and hypnotism were unsuccessful. The most celebrated physicians advised him to marry, and assured him that, as soon as he once really loved a girl, he would be free from his fetichism. The patient had no confidence in his future, but he followed the advice of the physicians. He was cruelly disappointed in the hope which the authority of the physicians had aroused in him, though he led to the altar a lady distinguished by both mental and physical charms. The wedding night was terrible; he felt like a criminal, and did not approach his wife. The next day he saw a prostitute with the required equipment. He was weak enough to have intercourse with her in his way. Then he bought a pair of elegant ladies' boots and hid them in bed, and, by touching them, while in marital embrace, after a few days, he was able to perform his marital duty. He ejaculated tardily, for he had to force himself to coitus; and after a few weeks this artifice failed, because his imagination failed. He felt unspeakably miserable, and would have preferred to make an end of himself. He could no longer satisfy his wife, who was sensual, and much excited by their previous intercourse; and he saw her suffering severely, both mentally and morally. He could not, and would not, disclose his secret. He experienced disgust in marital intercourse; he felt afraid of his wife, and feared the coming of night and being alone with her. He could no longer induce erection.

He again made attempts with prostitutes, and satisfied himself by touching their shoes. Then the girl had to touch his penis, when he would have ejaculation; but, if this did not take place, he would attempt coitus with the lewd woman; without success, however, for ejaculation would occur immediately. In absolute despair, the patient came for consultation. He deeply regretted that, against his inner conviction, he had followed the unfortunate advice of the physicians, and made a virtuous wife unhappy, having deeply injured her, both mentally and morally. Could he answered to God for continuing such a marriage? Even if he were to discover himself to his wife, and she were to do everything for him, it would not help him; for the familiar perfume of the *demi-monde* was also necessary.

Aside from his mental pain, this unfortunate man presented no remarkable symptoms. Genitals perfectly normal. Prostate somewhat large. He complained that he was so under the domination of his boot-ideas that he would even blush when boots were talked about. His whole imagination was given up to such ideas. When he was on his estate, he often suddenly had to go a distance of ten miles to the city, to satisfy his fetichism at shoe-shops or with girls.

This pitiable man could not bring himself to take treatment; for his faith in physicians had been greatly shaken. An attempt to ascertain whether hypnosis and a removal of the fetichistic association by this means, were possible, proved abortive on account of the mental excitement of the unfortunate man, who was exclusively controlled by the thought that he had made his wife unhappy.

CASE 114. X., aged twenty-four, from a badly tainted family (mother's brother and grandfather insane, one sister epileptic, another sister subject to migraine, parents of excitable temperament). During dentition he had convulsions. At the age of seven he was taught to masturbate by a servant-girl. X. first experienced pleasure in these manipulations when the girl happened by chance to touch his penis with her slippered foot. Thus, in the predisposed boy, an association was established, as a result of which, from that time on, merely the sight of a woman's shoes, and, finally, merely the idea of them, sufficed to induce sexual excitement and erection. He now masturbated while looking at women's shoes, or while calling them up in imagination. The shoes of the schoolmistress excited him intensely, and in general he was affected by shoes that were partly concealed by female garments. One day he could not keep from grasping the teacher's shoes—an act that caused him great sexual excitement. In spite of punishment he could not keep from performing this act repeatedly. Finally, it was recognized that there must be an abnormal motive in play, and he was sent to a male teacher. He then revelled in the memory of shoe-scenes with his former school-mistress, and thus had erections, orgasms, and, after his fourteenth year, ejaculation. At the same time, he masturbated while thinking of a woman's shoe. One day the thought came to him to increase his pleasure by using such a shoe for masturbation. Thereafter he frequently took shoes secretly, and used them for that purpose.

Nothing else in a woman could excite him; the thought of coitus filled him with horror. Men did not interest him in any way. At the age of eighteen he opened a shop, and, among other things, dealt in ladies' shoes. He was excited sexually by fitting shoes for his female patrons, or by manipulating shoes that came for mending. One day while doing this he had an epileptic attack, and, soon after, another while practicing onanism in his customary way. Then he recognized for the first time the injury to health caused by his sexual practices. He tried to overcome his onanism, sold no more shoes, and attempted to free himself from the abnormal association between women's shoes and the sexual function. Then frequent pollutions, with erotic dreams about shoes, occurred, and the epileptic attacks continued. Though devoid of the slightest feeling for the female sex, he determined on marriage, which seemed to him to be the only remedy.

He married a pretty young lady. In spite of lively erections when he thought of his wife's shoes, in attempts at cohabitation he was absolutely impotent, because his distaste for coitus and for close intercourse in general was far more powerful than the influence of the shoe-idea, which induced sexual excitement. On account of his impotence, the patient applied to Dr. *Hammond,* who treated his epilepsy with bromides, and advised him to hang a shoe up over his bed, and look at it fixedly during coitus, at the same time imagining his wife to be a shoe. The patient became free from epileptic attacks, and potent so that he could have coitus about once a week. His sexual excitation by women's shoes also grew less and less (*Hammond,* "Sexual Impotence").

These two cases of shoe-fetichism,[77] which apparently depend upon subjective accidental associations, as is the case in fetichism generally, do not offer anything startling with reference to their objective cause, because, in the former case, it is only a matter of partial impression of the general appearance of woman, and in the latter, a partial impression of the exciting manipulation.

But there are cases—up till now only two have been closely observed —in which the determining association has decidedly not been brought about by any connection of the nature of the object with the otherwise normally exciting cause.

CASE 115. *Shoe-fetichism. Kurella,* in his "Naturgeschichte des Verbrechers," p. 213, tried to prove that this man was an impostor who invented an interesting nervous disease as a pretense for making a living by fraud. The author arrived at a different result.

O., born in 1865, student of theology, was tried before a magistrate as a fraud and mendicant. He came from a heavily tainted family, was afflicted with shoe-fetichism, had from his twenty-first year periodical episodes in which he was irresistibly forced to run away and give himself up to drinking-bouts, although by doing so he knowingly jeopardized his position and property. When in the army he repeatedly deserted and became a veritable degenerate, an enigma to his superiors, for at times his conduct was exemplary and beyond blemish.

Examined before a commission of army medical men, he was declared to suffer from "periodical insanity," inherited beyond doubt. In consequence this "congenital criminal" was dismissed from service. He sank deeper and deeper in the mire, became a tramp, lived by his wits, and was confined several times in an insane asylum.

The author found a pronounced asymmetry of the skull, and also the right foot much larger than the left, etc.

O. was able to trace his shoe-fetichism back to his eighth year. At that time he had frequently at school let things fall on the ground so that he might have a cause for coming near to the lady teacher's foot. Periodically the image of a woman's shoe impressed him so greatly that he could not resist the impulse to run away.

This same impulse had been the cause of his vagrancy. He held himself responsible for any punishable acts he was guilty of. The author tested him as to the existence of his shoe-fetichism and found definite proof that the same was not simulated. *Kurella* had assumed that the shoe-fetichism of the patient was a mere invention, and that, in fact, he had derived the idea from reading the author's book, "Psychopathia Sexualis," as other critics have done on similar occasions.

It became quite evident that O. had never seen or heard of the book. (*Cf.* the original report of *Kurella*, in which his reasons for stamping O. a criminal are given in detail.)

The scientific observations made by the author in this case were based upon the following points, viz.: hereditary taint, asymmetry of the skull and other signs of degeneration, sexual perversion with periodical psychical manifestations in which irresistible perverse impulses forced the patient to abnormal thoughts and acts.

Even during his lucid intervals, O. should not be held responsible for his actions, since nervous disturbances and other psychical anomalies in the shape of normal defects formed part of his degenerative psychopathic constitution.

O. suffered from an inherited degenerative mania, and was to be considered a danger to society (*Alzheimer*, Archiv. f. Psychiatrie, xxviii., 2).

CASE 116. L., aged thirty-seven, clerk, from tainted family, had his first erection at five years, when he saw his bed-fellow—an aged relative—put on his night-cap. The same thing occurred later, when he saw an old servant put on her night-cap. Later, simply the idea of an old, ugly woman's head, covered with a night-cap, was sufficient to cause an erection. The sight of a cap or of a naked woman or man only made no impression, but the mere touch of a night-cap induced erection, and sometimes even ejaculation. L. was not a masturbator, and had never been sexually active until his thirty-second year, when he married a young girl with whom he had fallen in love. On his marriage-night he remained cold until, from necessity he brought to his aid the memory-picture of an ugly woman's head with a night-cap. Coitus was immediately successful. Thereafter it was always necessary for him to use this means. Since childhood he had been subject to occasional attacks of depression, with tendency to suicide, and now and then to frightful hallucinations at night. When looking out of a window, he became dizzy and anxious. He was a perverse, peculiar, and easily embarrassed man, of bad mental constitution (*Charcot-Magnan*, "Arch. de neurol.," 1882, No. 12).

In this very peculiar case, the simultaneous coincidence of the first sexual citation and an absolutely heterogeneous impression seems to have determined the association.

Hammond (*op. cit.*) also mentions a case of accidental associative fetichism that is quite peculiar. A married man, aged thirty, who, in other respects, was healthy, physically and mentally, is said to have suddenly lost his sexual power after moving to another house, and to have regained it as soon as the furniture of the sleeping-room had been arranged as it was before.

(c) *The Fetich is Some Special Material.*

There is a third principal group of fetichists who have as a fetich neither a portion of the female body nor a part of female attire, but some *particular material* which is so used, not because it is a material for female garments, but because in itself it can arouse or increase sexual feelings. Such materials are *furs, velvets* and *silks*.

These cases differ from the foregoing instances of erotic dress-fetichism, in this, that these materials, unlike female linen, do not have any close relation to the female body; and, unlike shoes and gloves, they are not related to certain parts of the person which have peculiar symbolic significance. Moreover, this fetichism cannot be due to an accidental association, like that in the cases of the night-caps and the arrangement of the sleeping-room; for these cases form an entire group having the same object. It must be presumed that certain tactile sensations (a kind of tickling irritation which stands in some distant relation to lustful sensations?), in hyperaesthetic individuals, furnish the occasion for the origin of this fetichism.

The following is a personal observation of a man affected with this peculiar fetichism:

CASE 117. N. N., aged thirty-seven; of a neuropathic family; neuropathic constitution. He made the following statement: "From my earliest youth I have always had a deeply rooted partiality for furs and velvets, in so far that these materials cause me sexual excitement, and the sight and touch of them give me lustful pleasure. I can recall no event that caused this peculiarity (such as the simultaneous occurrence of the first sexual excitation and an impression of these materials—*i.e.*, first excitation by a woman dressed in them); in fact, I cannot remember when this enthusiasm began. However, by this I would not exclude the possibility of such an event—of an accidental connection in a first impression and consequent association; but I think it very improbable that such a thing took place, because I believe such an occurrence would have deeply impressed me. All I know is, that even when a small child, I had a lively desire to see and stroke furs, and thus had an obscure sexual pleasure. With the first occurrence of definite sexual ideas—*i.e.*, the direction of sexual thoughts to woman—the peculiar preference for women dressed in such materials was present. Since then, up to mature manhood, it has remained unchanged. A woman wearing furs or velvet, or, even better, both, excites me much more quickly and intensely than one devoid of these auxiliaries. To be sure, these materials are not an essential condition of excitation; the desire occurs also without them in response to the usual stimuli; but the sight and, particularly, the touch of these fetich-materials form for me a powerful aid to other normal stimuli and intensify erotic pleasure. Often merely the sight of only a passably pretty girl dressed in these materials causes me vivid excitement, and overcomes me completely. Even the sight of my fetich-materials gives me pleasure, but the touch of them much more. (To the penetrating odour of furs I am indifferent—rather, it is unpleasant— and it is endurable only by reason of the association with pleasing visual and tactile impressions.) I have an intense longing to touch these materials while on a woman's person, to stroke and kiss them, and bury my face in them. My greatest pleasure is, in the course of the act, to see and feel my fetich on the woman's shoulder.

"Fur, or velvet alone, exerts on me the effect described, the former much more intensely than the latter. The combination of the two has the most intense effect. Again, female garments made of velvet and fur, seen and touched when off the wearer, cause me sexual excitement; indeed, though to a less extent, the same effect is exerted by furs or robes having no relation to female attire, and also by the velvet and plush of furniture and drapery. Merely pictures of costumes of furs and velvet are objects of erotic interest to me; indeed, the very word "fur" has a magic charm, and immediately calls up erotic ideas.

"Fur is such an object of sexual interest to me that a man wearing fur that is effective (see below) makes a very unpleasant, repugnant, and disgusting impression on me, such as would be made on a normal person by a man in the costume and attitude of a ballet-dancer. Similarly repugnant to me is the sight of an old or ugly woman clad in beautiful furs, because contradiction feelings are thus aroused.
"This erotic delight in furs and velvet is something entirely different from simple aesthetic pleasure. I have a very lively appreciation of

beautiful female attire, and, at the same time, a particular partiality for point-lace; but this is purely of an aesthetic nature. A woman dressed in a point-lace *toilette* (or in other elegant, elaborate attire) is more *beautiful* than another; but one dressed in my fetich-material is more *charming*.

"Furs, however, exercise on me the effect described only when the fur has very thick, fine, smooth and rather long hair, that stands out like that of the so-called bearded furs. I have noticed that the effect depends upon this. I am entirely indifferent not only to the ordinary, coarse, bushy furs, but also to those that are commonly regarded as beautiful and precious, from which the long hair has been removed (seal, beaver), or of which the hair is naturally short (ermine); and likewise to those of which the hair is overlong and lies down (monkey, bear). The specific effect is exerted only by the standing long hair of the sable, marten, skunk, etc. Now, velvet is made of thick, fine, standing hairs (fibres); and its effect may be due to this. The effect seems to depend upon a very definite impression of the points of thick, fine hair upon the terminals of the sensory nerves.

"But how this peculiar impression on the tactile nerves is related to sexual instinct is a perfect enigma to me. The fact is, that this is the case with many men. I would also state expressly that beautiful female hair pleases me, but plays no more important part than the other charms; and that while touching fur I have no thought of female hair (the tactile sensation, also, has not the least resemblance to that imparted by female hair). There is never association of any other idea. Fur by itself arouses sensuality in me—how, I cannot explain.

"The mere aesthetic effect, the beauty of costly furs, to which every one is more or less susceptible, and which, since Raphael's Fornarina and Reubens' Helen Fourment, has been used as the foil and frame of female beauty by innumerable painters; which also plays so important a *rôle* in fashion—the art and science of female dress—this aesthetic effect, as has been remarked, explains nothing here. Beautiful furs have the same aesthetic effect on me as on normal individuals, and affect me in the same way that flowers, ribbons, precious stones, and other ornaments affect every one. Such things, when skilfully used enhance female beauty, and thus, under certain circumstances, may have an indirect sensual effect. They never have a direct, powerful, sensual effect on me, as do the fetich-materials mentioned.

"Though in me, and, in fact, in all 'fetichists,' the sensual and aesthetic effect must be strictly differentiated, nevertheless, that does not prevent me from demanding in my fetich a whole series of aesthetic qualities in form, style, color, etc. I could give a lengthy description of these qualities demanded by my tastes; but I omit it as not being essential to the real subject in hand. I would only call attention to the fact that erotic fetichism is complicated with purely aesthetic tastes.

"The specific erotic effect of my fetich-materials can be explained no better by the association with the idea of the person of the female wearing them, than by their aesthetic impression. For, in the first place, as has been said, these materials, as such, affect me when entirely isolated from the body; and, in the second place, articles of clothing of a much more private nature, and which undoubtedly call up associations, exert a much weaker influence over me. Thus the fetich-materials have an independent sensual value for me. Why, is an enigma to me.

"Feathers in women's hats, fans, etc., have the same erotic fetichistic effect on me as furs and velvet (similar tactile sensation of airy, peculiar tickling). Finally, the fetichistic effect, with much less intensity, is exerted by other smooth materials (satin and silk); but rough goods (cloth, flannel) have a repelling effect.

"In conclusion, I will mention that somewhere I read an article by *Carl Vogt* on microcephalic men, according to which these creatures, at the sight of furs, rushed for them and stroked them with every manifestation of delight. I am far from any thought, on this ground, to see in widespread fur-fetichism an atavistic retrogression to the taste of our hairy ancestors. Every cretin, with that simplicity belonging to its condition, touches anything that pleases him, and the act is not necessarily of a sexual nature; just as many normal men like to stroke a cat and the like, or even velvet furs, and are not thus excited sexually."

In the literature of this subject, there are a few cases belonging here:—

CASE 118. A boy, aged twelve, became powerfully excited sexually, when, by chance, he covered himself with a foxskin. From that time on there was masturbation with the employment of furs, or by means of taking a furry dog to bed. Ejaculation would result, sometimes followed by an hysterical attack. His nocturnal pollutions were induced by dreaming that he lay entirely covered up in a soft skin. He was absolutely insusceptible to stimuli coming from men or women. He was neurasthenic, suffered with delusions of being watched, and thought that every one noticed his sexual anomaly. He became bored with life on account of this, and finally became insane. He had marked taint; his genitals were imperfectly formed, and he presented other signs of degeneration (*Tarnowsky, op. cit.*, p. 22).

CASE 119. C. was an especial lover of velvet. He was attracted in a normal way by beautiful women, but it particularly excited him to have the person with whom he had sexual intercourse dressed in velvet. In this, it was remarkable that it was not so much the sight as the touch of the velvet that caused the excitation. C. told me that stroking a woman's velvet jacket would excite him sexually to an extent scarcely possible in any other way (Dr. *Moll, op. cit.*, p. 127).

A physician communicated to me the following case:—

In a brothel a man was known under the name of "Velvet." He would dress a sympathetic girl with a garment made of black velvet, and would excite and satisfy his sexual desires simply by stroking his face with a corner of her velvety dress, not touching any other part of the person at all.

Another authority assures me that this weakness for *furs, velvets* and *silks* and *feathers,* is quite common among masochists (*cf.* case 50).[78]

The following is a very peculiar case of material-fetichism. It is combined with the impulse to injure the fetich, which, in this case, represents an element of sadism toward the woman wearing the fetich, or impersonal sadism towards objects, which is of frequent occurrence in fetichists (*cf.* p. 253). This impulse to cause injury made this a remarkable criminal case:

CASE 120. In July, 1891, Alfred Bachman, aged twenty-five, locksmith, was brought before Judge N., in the second term of the criminal court, in Berlin. In April, 1891, the police had had numerous complaints, according to which some evil hand had cut women's dresses with a very sharp instrument. In the evening of 25th April, they were successful in arresting the perpetrator in the person of the accused. A policeman noticed how the accused pressed, in a remarkable manner, against a lady in the company of a gentleman, while they were going through a passage. The officer requested the lady to examine her dress, while he held the man under suspicion. It was ascertained that the dress had received quite a long slit. The accused was taken to the station, where he was examined. Besides a sharp knife, which he confessed he used for cutting dresses, two silk sashes, such as ladies wear on their dresses, were found on him; he also confessed that he had taken these from dresses in crowds. Finally, the examination of his person brought to light a lady's silken neck-scarf. The accused said he had found this. Since his statement in this case could not be refuted, complaint was therefore made to rest on the result of the search; in two instances in which complaint was made by the injured parties his acts were designated as injury to property, and in two other instances as theft. The accused, a man with a pale, expressionless face, who had often been punished before, gave the judge a strange explanation of his enigmatical action. A major's cook had once thrown him downstairs when he was entreating her, and since that time he had entertained great hatred of the whole female sex. There was a doubt about his responsibility, and he was therefore examined by a physician. The medical expert gave the opinion at the final trial that there was no reason to regard the accused as insane, though he was of low intelligence. The culprit defended himself in a peculiar manner. An irresistible impulse forced him to approach women wearing silk dresses. *The touch of silk material gave him a feeling of delight,* and this went so far that, in prison for examination, he had been excited if a silk thread happened to pass through his fingers while ravelling rags. Judge Müller considered the accused to be simply a dangerous, vicious man, who should be made harmless for a long time. He advised imprisonment for one year. The court sentenced him to six months' imprisonment, with loss of rights for a year.

A classical case of material-fetichism (silk) is the following related by Dr. *P. Garnier:*—

CASE 121. On 22nd September, 1881, V. was arrested in the streets of Paris whilst he interfered with the silk dresses of a lady in a manner which aroused the suspicion of his being a pickpocket. At first he was very much confused, but finally, after many vain excuses, made a clean confession of his "mania." He was twenty-nine years of age, an assistant in a bookseller's shop; his father was a drunkard and a religious zealot, his mother of abnormal character. She wished to make a priest of him. Since his early youth he felt an instinctive impulse—congenital as he believes—to touch silk. When at the age of twelve as a choir boy he was allowed to wear a silk sash, he could not often enough finger it. He could not describe the peculiar sensation which he experienced in doing so. Later on he became acquainted with a ten-year-old girl for whom he had a childish affection. When on Sundays he met this girl clad in a silk dress, he was impelled to lovingly put his arms around her and touch her silk dress. Later he found exceeding great pleasure in gazing at the silk gowns exposed in a dressmaker's shop and feeling them.

When they gave him remnants of silk material, he would hasten to put them next to his body, which act immediately produced erection, orgasm and even ejaculation. These lustful desires made him uneasy, so that he doubted his vocation to the priesthood and obtained his discharge from the seminary. In consequence of habitual masturbation he was at that time very neurasthenic. His silk-fetichism swayed him as ever. Only when a woman wore a silk gown could she charm him.

Even when a child, ladies with silk gowns played a prominent part in his dreams; later on the latter were accompanied by pollutions. On account of his natural shyness he did not resort to coitus until later in life, and then he could only succeed in it with a woman dressed in silk. He much preferred to mix with crowds in the street and there touch the silk gowns of ladies, which always produced ejaculation accompanied by powerful orgasms and intense lustful feelings. What gratified him more than being with the prettiest woman was to put on a silk petticoat when going to bed.

The forensic medical opinion declared him to be a heavily tainted subject who gave way to abnormal desires under the strain of morbid impulses. Pardon (Dr. *Garnier*, "Annales d'hygiène publique," 3ᵉ sérié, xxix., 5).

The following case of *kid-glove-fetichism* is peculiarly adapted to show the origin of fetichistic associations as well as the enormous influence permanently exercised by such an association, although itself based upon a psychico-physical and morbid predisposition.

CASE 122. Mr. Z., an American, thirty-three years of age, manufacturer, for eight years enjoying a happy married life, blessed with offspring; consulted me for a peculiar troublesome glove-fetichism. He despised himself on account of it, and said it brought him well nigh to the verge of despair and even insanity.

He claimed to come of thoroughly sound parents, but since infancy had been neuropathic and very excitable. By nature he was very sensual, whilst his wife was very frigid.

At the age of nine, he was seduced by schoolmates to practice masturbation, which gratified him immensely, and he yielded to it with passion.

One day when sexually excited he found a small bag of chamois skin. He placed it over his member and experienced thereby great sensual pleasure. After that he used it for onanistic manipulations, put it around his scrotum and carried it about with him day and night. This aroused in him an unusual interest for leather in general, but particularly for kid gloves.

With puberty this centered entirely in ladies' kid gloves, which simply fascinated him. If he touched his penis with one such glove it produced erection and even ejaculation.

Men's gloves did not excite him in the least, although he loved to wear them.

In consequence, nothing about woman attracted him but her kid gloves. These were his fetich. They must be long, with many buttons, and if worn out, dirty and saturated with perspiration at the finger-tips, they were preferable. Women wearing such, even if ugly and old, had a particular charm for him. Ladies with silk or cotton gloves did not attract him. He always looked at her gloves first when meeting a lady. As for the rest he took very little interest in the female sex.

When he could shake hands with a lady gloved with kid, the contact with the soft, warm leather would cause erection and orgasm in him.

Whenever he could get hold of such a glove he would at once retire to a lavatory, wrap it around his genitals and masturbate.

Later on when visiting brothels he would beg the girl to put on long gloves provided by himself for that purpose, which act alone would excite him so much that ejaculation ensued forthwith.

Z. became a collector of ladies' kid gloves. He would hide away hundreds of pairs in various places. These he would count and gloat over in his spare time, "as a miser would over his gold," place them over his genitals, bury his face in a pile of them, put one on his hand and then masturbate. This gave him more intense pleasure than coitus.

He made covers for his penis from them, or suspensories, wearing them for days. He preferred black, soft leather. He would fasten ladies' kid gloves around his waist in such a fashion that they would, apron-like, hang down over his genitals.

After marriage this fetichism grew worse. As a rule he was only virile when he put a pair of his wife's gloves by her head during coitus so that he could kiss them.

The acme of pleasure was when he could persuade his wife to put on kid gloves and thus touch his genitals previous to cohabitation.

Z. felt very unhappy on account of this fetichism, and made repeated but vain attempts to free himself of the curse.

Whenever he came across the word, or the picture of a glove in novels, fashion-plates, advertisements, etc., he was simply fascinated. At the theatre his eyes were riveted on the hands of the actresses. He could scarcely tear himself away from the show-windows of glove-dealers.

He often would stuff long gloves with wool or some such material to make them resemble arms and hands. Then he would make friction with artificial members between his limbs until he had achieved his object.

It was his habit to take ladies' kid gloves to bed with him and wrap them around his penis until he could feel them like a large leathern dildo between his legs.

In the larger towns he bought from the cleaners ladies' gloves which had not been called for, but preferred those most soiled and worn. Twice he admitted to have yielded to the temptation to steal such gloves, although in every other respect he was absolutely correct. When in a crowd he must touch ladies' hands whenever possible. At his office he allowed no opportunity to pass without shaking hands with ladies, in order to feel for "at least a second the soft, warm leather." His wife must wear as much as possible kid gloves or such made of chamois with which he provided her lavishly.

At his office he always had ladies' gloves lying on his desk. Not an hour passed in which he did not touch and stroke them. When especially excited (sexually) he put such a glove in his mouth and chewed it.

Other articles of the female toilet, likewise other parts of the female body besides the hand, did not attract him. Z. felt much depressed about this anomaly. He felt ashamed to look into the innocent eyes of his children, and prayed God to protect them from this curse of their father.

The object of fetichism may also be found in a thing which only by *sheer accident stands in relation to the body of woman*, as may be gathered from the following instance related by *Moll*. It proves, moreover, how by the merely accidental association of an apperception with a parallel sexual emotion—based, of course, upon a special psychic process—the object of such apperception may become a fetich which in its turn may some day disappear again.

The theory of association in connection with original perverse manifestations (based on organo-psychical motives) seems here quite acceptable. The same may be said of the data relating to masochism and sadism.

CASE 123. B., thirty years of age, apparently untainted, refined and sensitive; great lover of flowers; liked to kiss them, but without any sensual motive or sensual excitement; rather of frigid nature; did not before twenty-one practice onanism, and subsequently only at periods. When twenty-one he was introduced to a young lady who wore some large roses on her bosom. Ever since then large roses dominated over his sexual feelings. He incessantly bought roses; kissing them would produce erection. He took them to bed with him although he never touched his genitals with them. His pollutions henceforth were accompanied by dreams of roses. He would dream of roses of fairy-like beauty and, inhaling their fragrance, have ejaculation.

He became secretly engaged to his "lady of roses," but the platonic relations grew colder, and when the engagement was broken off the rose-fetichism suddenly and permanently disappeared. It never returned, even when he became again engaged after a long spell of melancholia (A. *Moll*, "Centralb. f. d. Krankheiten der Harn- und Sexual-organe," v., 3).

(d) *Beast-fetichism.*

In close relation to stuff-fetichism, certain cases must be considered in which beasts exercise an aphrodisical influence over human beings. One feels tempted to call it animal eroticism.

This perversion seems to be rooted in a fetichism the object of which is the skin of the beast.

The transmitting medium of this fetichism may, perhaps, be found in a peculiar idiosyncrasy of the tactile nerves which, by touching furs or animal skins, produces peculiar and lustful emotions (analogous to hair-, braid-, velvet-, and silk-fetichism). This may, perhaps, also explain that peculiar hobby for cats and dogs at times met with in sexually perverted persons (see especially case 118). The following case, coming under my personal observation, seems to favour this assumption.

CASE 124. *Zoophilia erotica*, animal eroticism, fetichism. Mr. N. N., twenty-one years of age, from a neuropathically tainted family, himself congenitally neuropathic. Even as a child he often felt impelled to perform at times quite indifferent actions for fear of encountering some untoward event. He learned easily, never had a severe illness, and early a great love for domestic animals, especially dogs and cats, because when petting them he experienced lustful emotions. For years he indulged in this play with animals, which sensually stimulated him, although in an innocent fashion, as it were. When he arrived at the age of puberty he recognized the immorality of his acts and tried to free himself from the habit. He succeeded in this, but henceforth he was troubled in his dreams by such situations which produced pollutions. He then began onanism. At first he practiced it by manipulation accompanied by the idea that he was petting and stroking animals. After some time he arrived at psychical onanism, produced by vividly imagining such situations, and accompanied by orgasm and ejaculation. This made him neurasthenic.

He claimed that sodomitic ideas never entered his mind, that the sex of the animals never influenced his fancies or actions, in fact he had given it no thought.

He never had homosexual instinct; but heterosexual desires were not foreign to him, though he had never indulged in coitus because of want of *libido* (from masturbation and neurasthenia!) and from fear of infection. He was drawn only to women of lithe figure and with a proud gait.

The usual symptoms of cerebro-spinal neurasthenia were present. Patient was of slight build and anaemic. He was greatly concerned to know whether his lost virility could be restored, as this would raise his waning self-esteem.

Suggestions how to avoid psychic onanism, to remove neurasthenia, to strengthen the sexual centres, to satisfy the sexual life in the normal way as soon as this should be possible and successful.

Epicrisis. No bestiality, but fetichism. Very likely the petting of domestic animals coupled with an abnormally premature sexual life coincided with a primary sexual emotion—probably originating from tactile sensations—and thus established an association between the two facts which by repetition became permanent ("Zeitschr. f. Psychiatrie," Bd. 50).

ANTIPATHIC SEXUALITY.

After the attainment of complete sexual development, among the most constant elements of self-consciousness in the individual are the knowledge of representing a definite sexual personality and the consciousness of desire, during the period of physiological activity of the reproductive organs (production of semen and ova), to perform sexual acts corresponding with that sexual personality—acts which, consciously or unconsciously, have a procreative purpose.

The sexual instinct and desire, save for indistinct feelings and impulses, remain latent until the period of development of the sexual organs. The child is of the neuter gender (*i.e.*, without pronounced male or female characteristics); and though, during this latent period—when sexuality has not yet risen into clear consciousness, is but virtually present, and unconnected with powerful organic sensations—abnormally early excitation of the genitals may occur, either spontaneously or as a result of external influence, and find satisfaction in masturbation; yet, notwithstanding this, the *psychical* relation to persons of the opposite sex is still absolutely wanting, and the sexual acts during this period exhibit more or less a reflex spinal character.

The existence of innocence, or of sexual neutrality, is the more remarkable, since very early in education, employment, dress, etc., the child undergoes a differentiation from children of the opposite sex. These impressions remain, however, devoid of psychical significance, because they apparently are stripped of sexual meaning; for the central organ (*cortex*) of sexual emotions and ideas is not yet capable of activity, owing to its undeveloped condition.

With the inception of anatomical and functional development of the generative organs, and the differentiation of form belonging to each sex, which goes hand in hand with it (in the boy as well as in the girl), rudiments of a mental feeling corresponding with the sex are developed; and in this, of course, education and external influences in general have a powerful effect upon the individual, who now begins to observe.

If the sexual development is normal and undisturbed, a definite character, corresponding with the sex, is developed. Certain well-defined inclinations and reactions in intercourse with persons of the opposite sex arise; and it is psychologically worthy of note with what relative rapidity each individual psychical type corresponding with the sex is evolved.

While modesty, for instance, during childhood, is essentially but an uncomprehended and incomprehensible exaction of education and imitation, expressed but imperfectly in the innocence and *naïveté* of the child; in the youth and maiden it becomes an imperative requirement of self-respect; and, if in any way it is offended, intense vaso-motor reaction (blushing) and psychical emotions are induced.

If the original constitution is favourable and normal, and factors injurious to the psycho-sexual development exercise no adverse influence, then a psycho-sexual personality is developed which is so unchangeable and corresponds so completely and harmoniously with the sex of the individual in question, that subsequent loss of the generative organs (as by castration) or the *climacterium* or senility, cannot essentially alter it.

This, however, must not be taken as a declaration that the castrated man or woman, the youth and the aged man, the maiden and the matron, the impotent and the potent man, do not differ essentially from each other in their psychical existence.

An interesting and important question for what follows is, whether the peripheral influences of the generative glands (testes and ovaries), or central cerebral conditions, are the determining factors in psycho-sexual development. The fact that congenital deficiency of the generative glands, or removal of them *before* puberty, have a great influence on physical and psycho-sexual development, so that the latter is stunted and assumes a type more closely resembling the opposite sex (eunuchs, certain viragoes, etc.), betokens their great importance in this respect.

That the physical processes taking place in the genital organs are only co-operative, and not the exclusive factors, in the process of development of the psycho-sexual character, is shown by the fact that, notwithstanding a normal anatomical and physiological state of these organs, a sexual instinct may be developed which is the exact opposite of that characteristic of the sex to which the individual belongs.

In this case, the cause is to be sought only in an anomaly of central conditions—in an abnormal psycho-sexual constitution. This constitution, as far as its anatomical and functional foundation is concerned, is as yet unknown. Since, in nearly all such cases, the individual tainted with antipathic sexual instinct displays a neuropathic predisposition in several directions, and the latter may be brought into relation with hereditary degenerate conditions, this anomaly of psycho-sexual feeling may be called, clinically, a functional sign of degeneration. This inverted sexuality appears spontaneously, without external cause, with the development of sexual life, as an individual manifestation of an abnormal form of the sexual life, having the force of a *congenital* phenomenon; or it develops upon a sexuality the beginning of which was normal, as a result of very definite injurious influences, and thus appears as an *acquired* anomaly. Upon what conditions this enigmatical phenomenon of acquired homosexual instinct depends, remains still unexplained, and is a mere matter of hypothesis. Careful examination of the so-called acquired cases makes it probable that the predisposition—also present here—consists of a latent homosexuality, or, at any rate, bi-sexuality, which, for its manifestation, requires the influence of accidental exciting causes to rouse it from its dormant state.

In so-called antipathic sexual instinct there are degrees of the phenomenon which quite correspond with the degrees of predisposition of the individuals. Thus, in the milder cases, there is simple hermaphroditism; in more pronounced cases, only homosexual feeling and instinct, but limited to the sexual life; in still more complete cases, the whole psychical personality, and even the bodily sensations, are transformed so as to correspond with the sexual inversion; and, in the complete cases, the physical form is correspondingly altered.

The following division of the various phenomena of this psycho-sexual anomaly is made, therefore, in accordance with these clinical facts.

A. HOMOSEXUAL FEELING AS AN ACQUIRED MANIFESTATION IN BOTH SEXES.

The determining factor here is the demonstration of perverse feeling for the same sex; not the proof of sexual acts with the same sex. These two phenomena must not be confounded with each other; *perversity* must not be taken for *perversion*.

Perverse sexual acts, without being dependent upon perversion, often come under observation. This is especially true with reference to sexual acts between persons of the same sex, particularly in pederasty. Here sexual parasthesia is not necessarily at work; but hyperaesthesia, with physical or psychical impossibility for natural sexual satisfaction.

Thus we find homosexual intercourse in impotent masturbators or debauchees, or for want of something better in sensual men and women under imprisonment, on ship-board, in garrisons, bagnios, boarding-schools, etc.

There is an immediate return to normal sexual intercourse as soon as the obstacles to it are removed. Very frequently the cause of such temporary aberration is *masturbation* and its results in youthful individuals.

Nothing is so prone to contaminate—under certain circumstances, even to exhaust—the source of all noble and ideal sentiments, which arise of themselves from a normally developing sexual instinct, as the practice of masturbation in early years. It despoils the unfolding bud of perfume and beauty, and leaves behind only the coarse, animal desire for sexual satisfaction. If an individual, thus depraved, reaches the age of maturity, there is wanting in him that aesthetic, ideal, pure and free impulse which draws the opposite sexes together. The glow of sensual sensibility wanes, and the inclination toward the opposite sex is weakened. This defect influences the morals, the character, fancy, feeling and instinct of the youthful masturbator, male or female, in an unfavorable manner, even causing, under certain circumstances, the desire for the opposite sex to sink to *nil*; so that masturbation is preferred to the natural mode of satisfaction.

Sometimes the development of the nobler sexual feelings toward the opposite sex suffers, on account of hypochondriacal fear of infection in sexual intercourse; or on account of an actual infection; or as a result of a faulty education which points out such dangers and exaggerates them. Again (especially in females), fear of the result of coitus (pregnancy), or abhorrence of men, by reason of physical or moral defects, may direct into perverse channels an instinct that makes itself felt with abnormal intensity. On the other hand, premature and perverse sexual satisfaction injures not merely the mind, but also the body; inasmuch as it induces neuroses of the sexual apparatus (irritable weakness of the centres governing erection and ejaculation; defective pleasurable feeling in coitus, etc.), while, at the same time, it maintains imagination and *libido* in continuous excitement.

Almost every masturbator at last reaches a point where, frightened on learning the results of the vice, or on experiencing them (neurasthenia), or led by example or seduction to the opposite sex, he wishes to free himself of the vice and re-instate his sexual life.

The moral and mental conditions are here the most favourable possible. The pure glow of sexual feeling is destroyed; the fire of sexual instinct is wanting, and self-confidence is lost; for every masturbator is more or less timid and cowardly. If the youthful sinner at last comes to make an attempt at coitus, he is either disappointed because enjoyment is wanting, on account of defective sensual feeling, or he is lacking in the physical strength necessary to accomplish the act. This fiasco has a fatal effect, and leads to absolute psychical impotence. A bad conscience and the memory of past failures prevent success in any further attempts. The ever present *libido sexualis*, however, demands satisfaction, and this moral and mental perversion separates further and further from woman.

For various reasons, however, (neurasthenic complaints, hypochondriacal fear of results, etc.), the individual is also kept from masturbation. At times, under such circumstances, bestiality is resorted to. Intercourse with the same sex is then near at hand,—as the result of seduction or of the feelings of friendship which, on the level of pathological sexuality, easily associate themselves with sexual feelings.

Passive and mutual onanism now become the equivalent of the avoided act. If there is a seducer,—which, unfortunately, often happens, —then the cultivated pederast is produced,—*i.e.*, a man who performs *quasi* acts of onanism with persons of his own sex, and, at the same time, feels and prefers himself in an active *rôle* corresponding with his real sex; who is mentally indifferent not only to persons of the opposite sex, but also to those of his own.

Sexual aberration reaches this degree in the *normally* constituted, *untainted*, mentally healthy individual. No case has yet been demonstrated in which perversity has been transformed into perversion—*i.e.*, into an inversion of the sexual instinct.[79]

With *tainted* individuals, the matter is quite different. The latent perverse sexuality is developed under the influence of neurasthenia induced by masturbation, abstinence, or otherwise.

Gradually, in contact with persons of the same sex, sexual excitation by them is induced. Related ideas are coloured with lustful feelings, and awaken corresponding desires. This decidedly degenerate reaction is the beginning of a process of physical and mental transformation, a description of which is attempted in what follows, and which is one of the most interesting psychological phenomena that have been observed. This metamorphosis presents different stages, or degrees.

1. *Degree: Simple Reversal of Sexual Feeling.*

This degree is attained when a person exercises an aphrodisiac effect over another person of the same sex who reciprocates the sexual feeling. Character and instinct, however, still correspond with the sex of the individual presenting the reversal of sexual feeling. He feels himself in the active *rôle*; he recognizes his impulse toward his own sex as an aberration and finally seeks aid.

With episodical improvement of the neurosis, at first even normal sexual feelings may reappear and assert themselves. The following case seems well suited to exemplify this stage of the psycho-sexual degeneration:—

CASE 125. *Acquired Antipathic Sexual Instinct.* "I am an official, and, as far as I know, come from an untainted family. My father died of an acute disease; my mother, still living, is *very nervous. A sister has been very intensely religious for some years.*

"I myself am tall, and, in speech, gait and manner, give a perfectly masculine impression. Measles is the only disease I have had; but since my thirteenth year I have suffered with so-called nervous headaches.

"My sexual life began in my thirteenth year, when I became acquainted with a boy somewhat older than myself, with whom I amused myself in mutual handling of the genitals. I had the first ejaculation in my fourteenth year. Seduced to onanism by two older school-mates, I practiced it partly with others and partly alone; in the latter case, however, always with the thought of persons of the female sex. My *libido sexualis* was very great, as it is today. Later, I tried to win a pretty, stout servant-girl who had very large breasts. I only did this so that she should lay bare the upper part of her body in my presence and let me kiss her mouth and breasts while she held my strongly erect penis in her hand and rubbed it. Even though I urgently asked her for coitus, she would only let me touch her genitals.

"After going to the university, I visited a brothel and succeeded without special effort.

"Then an event occurred which brought about a change in me. One evening I accompanied a friend home, and in a mild state of intoxication I grasped him by the genitals. He made but slight opposition. I then went up to his room with him, and we practiced mutual masturbation. From that time we indulged in it quite frequently; in fact, it came to placing the penis in the mouth with resultant ejaculations. But it is strange that I was not at all in love with this person, but passionately in love with another friend, near whom I never felt the slightest sexual excitement, and whom I never connected with sexual matters, even in thought. My visits to brothels, where I was gladly received, became more infrequent; in my friend I found a substitute, and did not desire sexual intercourse with women.

"We never practiced pederasty. That word was not even known between us. From the beginning of this relation with my friend, I again masturbated more frequently, and naturally the thought of females receded more and more into the background, and I thought more and more about young, handsome, strong men with the largest possible genitals. I preferred young fellows, from sixteen to twenty-five years old, without beards, but they had to be handsome and clean. Young labourers dressed in trousers of Manchester cloth or English leather, particularly masons, especially excited me.

"Persons in my own position had hardly any effect on me; but, at the sight of one of those strapping fellows of the lower class, I experienced marked sexual excitement. It seems to me that the touch of such trousers, the opening of them and the grasping of the penis, as well as kissing the fellow, would be the greatest delight. My sensibility to female charms is somewhat dulled; yet in sexual intercourse with a woman, particularly when she has well-developed breasts, I am always potent without the help of imagination. I have never attempted to make use of a young labourer, or the like, for the satisfaction of my evil desires, and never shall; but I often feel a longing to do it. I often impress on myself the mental image of such a man, and then masturbate at home.

"I am absolutely devoid of taste for female work. I rather like to move in female society, but dancing is repugnant to me. I have a lively interest in the fine arts. That my sexual sense is partly reversed is, I believe, in part due to greater convenience, which keeps me from entering into a relation with a girl; as the latter is a matter of too much trouble. To be constantly visiting houses of prostitution is, for aesthetic reasons, repugnant to me; and thus I am always returning to solitary onanism, which is very difficult for me to avoid.

"Hundreds of times I have said to myself that, in order to have a normal sexual feeling, it would be necessary for me, first of all, to overcome my irresistible passion for onanism,—a practice so repugnant to my aesthetic feeling. Again and again I have resolved with all my might to fight this passion; but I am still unsuccessful. When I felt the sexual impulse gaining strength, instead of seeking satisfaction in the natural manner, I preferred to masturbate, because I felt that I would thus have more enjoyment.

"And yet experience has taught me that I am always potent with girls, and that, too, without trouble and without the vision of masculine genitals. In one case, however, I did not attain ejaculation because the woman—it was in a brothel—was devoid of every charm. I cannot avoid the thought and severe self-accusation that, to a certain extent, my inverted sexuality is the result of excessive onanism; and this especially depresses me, because I am compelled to acknowledge that I scarcely feel strong enough to overcome this vice by the force of my own will.

"As a result of my relations for years with a fellow-student and pal, mentioned in this communication—which, however, began while we were at the university, and after we had been friends for seven years— the impulse to unnatural satisfaction of *libido* has grown much stronger. I trust you will permit the description of an incident which worried me for months:—

"In the summer of 1882, I made the acquaintance of a companion six years younger than myself, who, with several others, had been introduced to me and my acquaintances. I very soon felt a deep interest in this handsome man, who was unusually well-proportioned, slim, and full of health. After a few weeks of association, this liking ripened into friendship, and at last into passionate love, with feelings of the most intense jealousy. I very soon noticed that in this love sexual excitation was also very marked; and, notwithstanding my determination, aside from all others, to keep myself in check in relation to this man, whom I respected so highly for his superior character, one night, after free indulgence in beer, as we were enjoying a bottle of champagne in my room, and drinking to good, true and lasting friendship, I yielded to the irresistible impulse to embrace him, etc.

"When I saw him next day, I was so ashamed that I could not

look him in the face. I felt the deepest regret for my action, and accused myself bitterly for having thus sullied this friendship, which was to be and remain so pure and precious. In order to prove to him that I had lost control of myself only momentarily, at the end of the semester I urged him to make an excursion with me; and after some reluctance, the reason of which was only too clear to me, he consented. Several nights we slept in the same room without any attempt on my part to repeat my action. I wished to talk with him about the event of that night, but I could not bring myself to it; even when, during the next semester, we were separated, I could not induce myself to write to him on the subject; and when I visited him in March at X., it was the same. And yet I felt a great desire to clear up this dark point by an open statement. In October of the same year I was again in X., and this time found courage to speak without reserve; indeed, I asked him why he had not resisted me. He answered that, in part, it was because he wished to please me, and, in part, owing to the fact that he was somewhat apathetic as a result of being a little intoxicated. I explained to him my condition, and also gave him "Psychopathia Sexualis" to read, expressing the hope that by the force of my own will I should become fully and lastingly master of my unnatural impulse. Since this confession, the relation between this friend and me has been the most delightful and happy possible; there are the most friendly feelings on both sides, which are sincere and true; and it is to be hoped that they will endure.

"If I should not improve my abnormal condition, I am determined to put myself under your treatment; the more because, after a careful study of your work, I cannot count myself as belonging to the category of so-called homosexual males; and also because I have the firm conviction, or hope, at least, that a strong will, assisted and combined with skilful treatment, could transform me into a man of normal feeling."

CASE 126. Ilma S.,[80] aged twenty-nine; single, merchant's daughter; of a family having bad nervous taint. Father was a drinker and died by suicide, as also did the patient's brother and sister. A sister suffered with convulsive hysteria. Mother's father shot himself while insane. Mother was sickly, and paralyzed after apoplexy. The patient never had any severe illness. She was bright, enthusiastic and dreamy. Menses at the age of eighteen without difficulty; but thereafter they were very irregular. At fourteen, chlorosis and catalepsy from fright. Later, hysteria and an attack of hysterical insanity. At eighteen, relations with a young man which were not platonic. This man's love was passionately returned. From statements of the patient, it seemed that she was very sensual, and after separation from her lover practiced masturbation. After this she led a romantic life. In order to earn a living, she put on male clothing, and became a tutor; but she gave up her place because her mistress, not knowing her sex, fell in love with her and courted her. Then she

became a railway employee. In the company of her companions, in order
to conceal her sex, she was compelled to visit brothels with them, and
hear the most vulgar stories. This became so distasteful to her that she
gave up her place, resumed the garments of a female, and again sought
to earn her living. She was arrested for theft, and on account of severe
hystero-epilepsy was sent to the hospital. There inclination and impulse
toward the same sex were discovered. The patient became troublesome
on account of passionate love for female nurses and patients.

Her sexual inversion was considered congenital. With regard to this,
the patient made some interesting statements:—

"I am judged incorrectly, if it is thought that I feel myself a man
toward the female sex. In my whole thought and feeling I am much
more a woman. Did I not love my cousin as only a woman can love
a man?

"The change of my feelings originated in this, that, in Pesth, dressed
as a man, I had an opportunity to observe my cousin. I saw that I was
wholly deceived in him. That gave me terrible heart-pangs. I knew that
I could never love another man; that I belonged to those who love but
once. Of similar effect was the fact that, in the society of my companions at the railway, I was compelled to hear the most offensive language and visit the most disreputable houses. As a result of the insight
into men's motives, gained in this way, I took an unconquerable dislike
to them. However, since I am of a very passionate nature and need to
have some loving person on whom to depend, and to whom I can wholly
surrender myself, I felt myself more and more powerfully drawn towards
intelligent women and girls who were in sympathy with me."

The antipathic sexual instinct of this patient, which was clearly
acquired, expressed itself in a stormy and decidedly sensual way, and
was further augmented by masturbation; because constant control in
hospitals made sexual satisfaction with the same sex impossible. Character and occupation remained feminine. There were no manifestations
of viraginity. According to information lately received by the author, this
patient, after two years of treatment in an asylum, was entirely freed
of her neurosis and sexual inversion, and discharged cured.

CASE 127. Mr. X., aged thirty-five, single, civil servant; mother insane, brother hypochondriacal.

Patient was healthy, strong, of lively sensual temperament. He had
manifested powerful sexual instinct abnormally early, and masturbated
while yet a small boy. He had coitus the first time at the age of fourteen,
with enjoyment and complete power. When fifteen years old, a man
sought to seduce him, and performed manustupration on him. X. experienced a feeling of repulsion, and freed himself from this disgusting
situation. At maturity he committed excesses in *libido*, with coitus; in
1880 he became neurasthenic, being afflicted with weakness of erection

and premature ejaculation. He thus became less and less potent, and no longer experienced pleasure in the sexual act. At this period of sexual decadence, for a long time he still had what was previously foreign to him,—still incomprehensible to him,—an inclination for sexual intercourse with immature girls of the age of twelve or thirteen. His *libido* increased as virility diminished.

Gradually he developed inclination for boys of thirteen or fourteen. He was impelled to approach them.

Whenever he had the opportunity to touch boys who attracted him, he developed a strong erection, particularly when he was able to touch the boys' legs. From that time on he did not desire women. Sometimes he forced women to have coitus with him, but the erection was weak and ejaculation premature and devoid of pleasure.

Now only youths interested him. He dreamed about them and had pollutions. After 1882 he now and then had opportunity of lying with juveniles. This led to powerful sexual excitement, which he satisfied by masturbation. It was quite exceptional for him to venture touching his bed-fellow and indulging in mutual masturbation. He shunned pederasty. For the most part, he was compelled to satisfy his sexual needs by means of solitary masturbation. In the act he called up the vision of pleasing boys. After sexual intercourse with such boys, he always felt strengthened and refreshed, but morally depressed; because there was consciousness of having performed a perverse, indecent and punishable act. He found it painful that his disgusting impulse was more powerful than his will.

X. thought that his love for his own sex had resulted from great excess in natural sexual intercourse, and bemoaned his situation. On the occasion of a consultation, in December, 1889, he asked me whether there were any means to bring him back to a normal sexual condition, since he had no real horror of women, and would very gladly marry.

This intelligent patient, free from degenerative signs, presented no abnormal symptoms except those of sexual and spinal neurasthenia in a moderate degree.

II. Degree: Eviration and Defemination.

If, in cases of antipathic sexual instinct thus developed, no restoration occurs, then deep and lasting transformations of the *psychical* personality may occur. The process completing itself in this way may be briefly designated *eviration* (*defemination* in woman). The patient undergoes a deep change of character, particularly in his feelings and inclinations, which thus become those of a female. After this, he also feels himself to be a woman during the sexual act, has desire only for passive sexual indulgence, and, under certain circumstances, sinks to the level of a prostitute. In this condition of deep and more lasting psycho-sexual transformation, the individual is like unto the (congenital) homo-sexual of high grade. The possibility of a restoration of the previous mental and sexual personality seems in such a case, precluded.

The following case is a classical example of this variety of lasting acquired antipathic sexual instinct:—

CASE 128. Sch., aged thirty, physician, one day told me the story of his life and malady, asking for explanation and advice concerning certain anomalies of his sexual life. The following description gives, for the most part verbatim, the details of the autobiography; only in some portions it is shortened:—

"My parents were healthy. As a child I was sickly; but with good care I thrived, and got on well in school. When eleven years old, I was taught to masturbate by my playmates, and gave myself up to it passion-ately. Until I was fifteen, I learned easily. On account of frequent pollu-tions, I became less capable, and did not get on well in school, and was uncertain and embarrassed when called on by the teacher. Fright-ened by my loss of capability, and recognizing that the loss of semen was responsible for it, I gave up masturbation; but the pollutions be-came even more frequent, so that I often had two or three in a night. In despair, I now consulted one physician after another. None were able to help me.

"Since I grew weaker and weaker, by reason of the loss of semen, with the sexual appetite growing more and more powerful, I sought houses of prostitution. But I was there unable to find satisfac-tion; for, even though the sight of a naked female pleased me, neither orgasm nor erection occurred; and even manustupration by the girl was not capable of inducing erection. Scarcely would I leave the house, when the impulse would seize me again, and I would have violent erections. I grew ashamed before the girls, and ceased to visit such houses. Thus a couple of years passed. My sexual life consisted of pollutions. My inclination towards the opposite sex grew less and less. At nineteen I went to the university. The theatre had more attractions for me: I wished to become an actor. My parents were not willing. At the metropolis I was compelled now and then to visit girls with my comrades. I feared such a situation; because I knew that coitus was impossible for me, and because my friends might discover my impotence. Therefore, I avoided, as far as possible, the danger of becoming the butt of their jokes and ridicule.

"One evening, in the opera-house, an old gentleman sat near me. He courted me. I laughed heartily at the foolish old man, and entered into his joke. Unexpectedly he caught hold of my genitals, which imme-diately caused my penis to become erect. Frightened, I demanded of him what he meant. He said that he was in love with me. Having heard of hermaphrodites in the clinics, I thought I had one before me, and became curious to see his genitals. The old man was very willing, and went with me to the water closet. When I saw his penis erect to the maximum extent, I became frightened and fled.

"This man followed me, and made strange proposals which I did not understand, and repelled. He did not give me any rest. I learned the secrets of male love for males, and felt that my sexuality was excited by it. But I resisted the shameful passion (as I then regarded it) and, for the next three years, I remained free from it. During this time I repeatedly attempted coitus with girls in vain. My attempts to free myself of my impotence by means of medical treatment were also in vain. Once, when my sexual life was troubling me again, I recalled what the old man had told me: that male-loving men were accustomed to meet on the E. Promenade.

After a hard struggle, and with beating heart, I went there, made the acquaintance of a blonde man, and allowed myself to be seduced. The first step was taken. This kind of sexual love was satisfactory to me. I always preferred to be in the arms of a strong man. The satisfaction consisted of mutual masturbation; occasionally in kissing the penis of the other person. I was then twenty-three years old. Sitting, together with my comrades, on the beds of patients in the clinic during the lectures, excited me so intensely that I could scarcely listen to the lectures. In the same year I entered into a formal love-relation with a merchant of thirty-four. We lived as man and wife. X. played the man, and fell more and more in love. I gave up to him, but now and then I had to play the man. After a time I grew tired of him, became unfaithful and he grew jealous. There were terrible scenes, which led to temporary separation, and finally to actual rupture. (The merchant afterwards became insane, and died by suicide.)

"I made many acquaintances, and loved the most ordinary people. I preferred those having a full beard, who were tall and of middle age, and able to play the active *rôle* well. I developed rectal inflammation. The professor thought it was the result of sitting too much while preparing for examinations. I developed a fistula, and had to undergo an operation; but this did not cure me of my desire to let myself be used passively. I became a physician and went to a provincial town, where I had to live like a nun. I developed a desire to move in ladies' society, and was gladly welcomed there; because it was found that I was not so one-sided as most men, and was interested in toilettes and such feminine things. However, I felt very unhappy and lonesome. Fortunately, in this town, I made the acquaintance of a man, a 'sister,' who felt like me. For some time I was taken care of by him. When he had to leave I had an attack of despair, with depression, which was accompanied by thoughts of suicide.

"When it became impossible for me to longer endure the town,

I became a military surgeon in the capital. There I began to live again, and often made two or three acquaintances in one day. I had never loved boys or young people; only fully developed men. The thought of falling into the hands of the police was frightful. Thus far I have escaped the clutches of the blackmailer. At the same time, I could not keep myself from the gratification of my impulse. After some months I fell in love with an official of forty. I remained true to him for a year, and we lived like a pair of lovers. I was the wife and was formally courted by the lover. One day I was transferred to a small town. We were in despair. The last night was spent in continually kissing and caressing one another.

"In T. I was unspeakably unhappy, in spite of some 'sisters' whom I found. I could not forget my lover. In order to satisfy my sexual desire, which cried for satisfaction, I chose soldiers. Money obtained men; but they remained cold, and I had no enjoyment with them. I was successful in being retransferred to the capital, where there was a new love relation, but much jealousy; because my lover liked to go into the society of 'sisters,' and was proud and coquettish. There was a rupture. I was very unhappy and very glad to be transferred from the capital. I now stayed in C., alone and in despair. Two infantry privates were brought into service, but with the same unsatisfactory results. When shall I ever find true love again?

"I am over medium height, well developed, and look somewhat aged; and, therefore, when I wish to make conquests I use the arts of the toilet. My manner, movements and face are masculine. Physically I feel as youthful as a boy of twenty. I love the theatre, and especially art. My interest in the stage is in the actresses, whose every movement and gesture I notice and criticize.

"In the society of gentlemen I am silent and embarrassed, while in the society of those like myself I am free, witty, and as fawning as a cat if a man is sympathetic. If I am without love, I become deeply melancholic; but the favors of the first handsome man dispel my depression. In other ways I am frivolous and very ambitious. My profession is nothing to me. Masculine pursuits do not interest me. I prefer novels and going to the theatre. I am effeminate, sensitive, easily moved, easily injured and nervous. A sudden noise makes my whole body tremble, and I have to collect myself in order to keep from crying out."

Remarks: The case under review is certainly one of acquired sexual perversion, since sexual feeling was originally directed towards the female sex. Sch. became neurasthenic through masturbation.

A reduced ability to respond on the part of the erection-centre develops, partly as a manifestation of a neurasthenic neurosis, and with it relative impotence. In this way, feeling towards the opposite sex cools off, although *sexual desire* persists. The acquired perverted sexual feeling must have been a pathological one, for the very first touch by a person of the same sex supplied sufficient stimulus for the erection-centre. The perversion of the sexual feeling then became ever more pronounced. To start with, Sch. still felt himself to be performing the role of the man during the sex act, but with time this develops more and more into a feeling and urge for satisfaction, as is the rule with the (congenital) homosexual.

The result of this emasculation is that the passive role and even more passive pederasty become desirable. And this urge extends its influence to the character, which becomes feminine to the extent that Sch. prefers to associate with real *women*, is more and more interested in feminine pastimes, and even resorts to make-up and other titivation in order to revive his fading charms and make "conquests."

The foregoing facts concerning acquired antipathic sexual instinct and effemination find an interesting confirmation in the following ethnological data:—

Herodotus already describes a peculiar disease which frequently affected the Scythians. The disease consisted in this: that men became effeminate in character, put on female garments, did the work of women, and even became effeminate in appearance. As an explanation of this insanity of the Scythians,[81] *Herodotus* relates the myth that the goddess Venus, angered by the plundering of the temple at Ascalon by the Scythians, had made women of these plunderers and their posterity.

Hippocrates, not believing in supernatural diseases, recognized that impotence was here a causative factor, and explained it, though incorrectly, as due to the custom of the Scythians to have themselves bled behind the ears in order to curse disease superinduced by constant horseback riding. He thought that these veins were of great importance in the preservation of the sexual powers, and that when they were severed, impotence was induced. Since the Scythians considered their impotence due to divine punishment and incurable, they put on the clothing of females, and lived as women among women.

It is worthy of note that, according to *Klaproth* ("Reise in dem Kaukasus," Berlin, 1812, v., p. 285) and *Chotomski*, even at the present time impotence is very frequent among the Tartars, as a result of riding unsaddled horses. The same is observed among the Apaches and Navajos of the western continent who ride excessively, scarcely ever going on foot, and are remarkable for small genitals and mild *libido* and virility. *Sprengel*, *Lallemand* and *Nysten* recognize the fact that excessive riding may be injurious to the sexual organs.

Hammond reports analogous observations of great interest concerning the Pueblo Indians of New Mexico. These descendants of the Aztecs cultivate so-called "mujerados," of which every Pueblo tribe requires one in the religious ceremonies (actual orgies in the spring), in which pederasty plays an important part. In order to cultivate a "mujerado," a very powerful man is chosen, and he is made to masturbate excessively and ride constantly. Gradually such irritable weakness of the genital organs is engendered that, in riding, great loss of semen is induced. This condition of irritability passes into paralytic impotence. Then atrophy of the testicles and penis sets in, the hair of the beard falls out, the voice loses its depth and compass, and physical strength and energy decrease. Inclinations and disposition become feminine. The "mujerado" loses his position in society as a man. He takes on feminine manners and customs, and associates with women. Yet, for religious reasons, he is held in honour. It is probable that, at other times than during the festivals, he is used by the chiefs for pederasty. *Hammond* had an opportunity to examine two "mujerados." One had become such seven years before, and was thirty-five years old at the time. Seven years previous, he was entirely masculine and potent. He had noticed gradual atrophy of the testicles and penis. At the same time he lost *libido* and the power of erection. He differed in nowise, in dress and manner, from the women among whom *Hammond* found him. The genital hair was wanting, the penis was shrunken, the scrotum lax and pendulous, and the testicles were very much atrophied and no longer sensitive to pressure. The "mujerado" had large breasts like a pregnant woman, and asserted that he had nursed several children whose mothers had died. A second "mujerado," aged thirty-six, after he had been ten years in the condition, presented the same peculiarities, though with less development of breasts. Like the first, the voice was high and thin. The body was plump.

III. Degree: Stage of Transition to Change of Sex Delusion.

A further degree of development is represented by those cases in which *physical* sensation is also transformed in the sense of a change of sex. In this respect the following case is unique:—

CASE 129. *Autobiography.* "Born in Hungary in 1844, for many years I was the only child of my parents; for the other children died for the most part of general weakness: A brother of later birth is still living.

"I come of a family in which nervous and mental diseases have been numerous. It is said that I was very pretty as a little child, with blonde locks and transparent skin; very obedient, quiet and modest, so that I was taken everywhere in the society of ladies without any offense on my part.

"With a very active imagination—my enemy through life—my talents developed rapidly. I could read and write at the age of four; my memory reaches back to my third year. I played with everything that fell into my hands,—with leaden soldiers, or stones, or ribbons from a toy-shop; but a machine for working in wood, that was given to me as a present, I did not like. I liked best to be at home with my mother, who was everything to me. I had two or three friends with whom I got on good-naturedly; but I liked to play with her sisters quite as well, who always treated me like a girl, which at first did not embarrass me. I must have already been on the road to become just like a girl; at least, I can still well remember how it was always said: 'He is not intended for a boy.' At this I tried to play the boy,— imitated my companions in everything, and tried to surpass them in wildness. In this I succeeded. There was no tree or building too high for me to reach its top. I took great delight in soldiers. I avoided girls more, because I did not wish to play with their playthings; and it always annoyed me that they treated me so much like one of themselves.

"In the society of mature people, however, I was always modest, and, always regarded with favor. Fantastic dreams about wild animals— which once drove me out of bed without waking me—frequently troubled me. I was always very simply but very elegantly dressed, and thus developed a taste for beautiful clothing. It seems peculiar to me that, from the time of my school-days, I had a partiality for ladies' gloves, which I put on secretly as often as I could. Thus, when once my mother was about to give away a pair of gloves, I made great opposition to it, and told her, when she asked why I acted so, that I wanted them myself. I was laughed at; and from that time I took good care not to display my preference for female things. Yet my delight in them was very great. I took especial pleasure in masquerade costumes—*i.e.*, only in female attire. If I saw them, I envied their owners. What seemed to me the prettiest sight was: two young men, beautifully dressed as white ladies, with masks on; and yet I would not have shown myself to others as a girl for anything; I was so afraid of being ridiculed. At school I worked very hard, and was always among the first. From childhood my parents taught me that duty came first; and they always set me an example. It was also a pleasure for me to attend school; for the teachers were kind, and the elder pupils did not plague the younger ones. We left my first home; for my father was compelled, on account of his business,—which was dear to him,—to separate from his family for a year. We moved to Germany. Here there was a stricter, rougher manner, partly in teachers and partly in pupils; and I was again ridiculed on account of my girlishness. My schoolmates went so far as to give a girl, who had exactly my features, my name, and me hers; so that I hated the girl. But I later came to be on terms of friendship with her after her marriage. My mother tried to dress me elegantly; but this was repugnant to me, because it made me the object of taunting. So, finally, I was delighted when I had correct trousers and coats. But with these came a new annoyance. They irritated my genitals, particularly when the cloth was rough; and the touch of tailors while measuring me, on account of their tickling, which almost convulsed me, was unen-durable, particularly about the genitals. Then I had to practice gym-nastics; and I simply could do nothing at all, or only indifferently the things that even girls can do easily. While bathing I was troubled by feeling ashamed to undress; but I liked to bathe. Until my twelfth year I had a great weakness in my back. I learned to swim late, but ulti-mately so well that I took long swims. At thirteen I had pubic hair, and was about six feet tall; but my face was feminine until my eighteenth year, when my beard came in abundance and gave me rest from resemblance to woman. An inguinal hernia that was acquired in my twelfth year, and cured when I was twenty, gave me much trouble, particularly in gymnastics. Besides, from my twelfth year on, I had, after sitting long, and particularly while working at night, an itching, burning and twitching, extending from the penis to my back, which the acts of sitting and standing increased, and which was made worse by catching cold. But I had no suspicion whatever that this could be connected with the genitals. Since none of my friends suffered in this way, it seemed strange to me; and it required the greatest patience to endure it; the more owing to the fact that my abdomen troubled me.

"In sexual matters I was still perfectly innocent; but now, as at the age of twelve or thirteen, I had a definite feeling of preferring to be a young lady. A young lady's form was more pleasing to me; her quiet manner, her deportment, but particularly her attire, attracted me. But I was careful not to allow this to be noticed; and yet I am sure that I should not have shrunk from the castration-knife, could I have thus attained my desire. If I had been asked to say why I preferred female attire, I could have said nothing more than that it attracted me power-fully; perhaps, also, I seemed to myself, on account of my uncommonly white skin, more like a girl. The skin of my face and hands, par-ticularly, was very sensitive. Girls liked my society; and, though I should have preferred to have been with them constantly, I avoided them when I could; for I had to exaggerate in order not to appear feminine. In my heart I always envied them. I was particularly envious when one of my young girl friends got long dresses and wore gloves and veils. When, at the age of fifteen, I was on a journey, a young lady, with whom I was boarding, proposed that I should mask as a lady and go out with her; but, owing to the fact that she was not alone, I did not acquiesce, much as I should have liked it. While on this journey, I was pleased at seeing boys in one city wearing blouses with short sleeves, and the arms bare. A lady elaborately dressed was like a goddess to me; and if even her hand touched me coldly I was happy and envious, and only too gladly would have put myself in her place in the beautiful garments and lovely form. Nevertheless, I studied assiduously, and passed through the Realschule and the Gymnasium in nine years, passing a good final examination. I remember, when fifteen, to have first expressed to a friend the wish to be a girl. In answer to his question, I could not give the reason why. At seventeen I got intó fast society; I drank beer, smoked, and tried to joke with waiter-girls. The latter liked my society, but they always treated me as if I wore petticoats. I could not take dancing lessons, they repelled me so; but if I could have gone as a mask, it would have been different. My friends loved me dearly; I hated only one, who seduced me into onanism. Shame on those days, which injured me for life! I practiced it quite frequently, but in it seemed to myself like a double man. I cannot describe the feeling; I think it was masculine, but mixed with feminine elements. I could not approach girls; I feared them, but they were not strange to me. They impressed me as being more like myself; I envied them. I would have denied myself all pleasures if, after my classes, at home I could have been a girl and thus have gone out. Crinoline and a smoothly-fitting glove were my ideals. With every lady's gown I saw I fancied how I should feel in it,—*i.e.*, as a lady. I had no inclination toward men. But I remember that I was somewhat lovingly attached to a very handsome friend with a girl's face and dark hair, though I think I had no other wish than that we both might be girls.

"At the high-school I finally once had coitus; I felt as though I should prefer to be lying under the girl and exchange my penis for her vagina. To her astonishment, the girl had to treat me as a girl, and did it willingly; but she treated me as if I were she (she was still quite inexperienced, and, therefore, did not laugh at me).

"As a student, at times I was wild, but I always felt that I assumed this wildness as a mask. I drank and duelled, but I could not take lessons in dancing, because I was afraid of betraying myself. My friendships were close, but without other thoughts. It pleased me most to have a friend masked as a lady, or to study the ladies' costumes at a ball. I understood such things perfectly. Gradually I began to feel like a girl.

"On account of unhappy circumstances, I twice attempted suicide. Without any cause I once did not sleep for fourteen days, had many hallucinations (visual and auditory at the same time), and was with both the living and the dead. The latter habit of thought remains. I also had a friend (a lady) who knew my hobby and put on my gloves for me; but she always looked upon me as a girl. Thus I understood women better than other men did, and in what they differed from men; so I was always treated according to the custom of women—as if they had found in me a female friend. On the whole, I could not endure obscenity, and indulged in it myself only out of bragging when it was necessary. I soon overcame my aversion to foul odors and blood, and even liked them. Only some things I could not look at without nausea. I was wanting in only one respect: I could not understand my own condition. I knew that I had feminine inclinations, but believed that

I was a man. Yet I doubt whether, with the exception of the attempts of coitus, which never gave me pleasure (which I ascribe to onanism), I ever admired a woman without wishing I were she; or without asking myself whether I should not like to be the woman, or be in her attire. Obstetrics I learned with difficulty (I was ashamed for the exposed girls, and had a feeling of pity for them); and even now I have to overcome a feeling of fright in obstetrical cases; indeed, it has happened that I thought I felt the traction myself. After filling several positions successfully as a physician, I went through a military campaign as a volunteer surgeon. Riding, which, while a student, was painful to me, because in it the genitals had more of a feminine feeling, was difficult for me (it would have been easier in the female style).

"Still, I always thought I was a man with obscure masculine feeling; and whenever I associated with ladies, I was still soon treated as an inexperienced lady. When I wore a uniform for the first time, I should have much preferred to have slipped into a lady's costume, with a veil; I was disturbed when the stately uniform attracted attention. In private practice I was successful in the three principal branches. Then I made another military campaign; and during this I came to understand my nature; for I think that, since the first ass ever made, no beast of burden has ever had to endure with so much patience as I have. Decorations were not wanting, but I was indifferent to them.

"Thus I went through life, such as it was, never satisfied with myself, full of dissatisfaction with the world, and vacillating between sentimentality and a wildness that was for the most part affected.

"My experience as a candidate for matrimony was very peculiar. I should have preferred not to marry, but family circumstances and practice forced me to it. I married an energetic, amiable lady, of a family in which female government was rampant. I was in love with her as much as one of us can be in love—*i.e.*, what we love we love with our whole hearts, and live in it, even though we do not show it as much as a genuine man does. We love our brides with all the love of a woman, almost as a woman might love her bridegroom. But I cannot say this for myself; for I still believed that I was but a depressed man, who would come to himself, and find himself out by marriage. But, even on my marriage night, I felt that I was only a woman in man's form; it seemed to me that my place was under the woman. On the whole, we lived contented and happy, and for two years were childless. After a difficult pregnancy, during which time I lay at the point of death in the enemy's own country, my wife gave birth to our first boy in a difficult labor,—a boy still afflicted with a melancholy nature. Then came a second, who is very quiet; a third, full of peculiarities; a fourth, a fifth; and all have the predisposition to neurasthenia. Since I always felt out of my own place, I went much in gay society; but I always worked as much as human strength would endure. I studied and operated;

and I experimented with many drugs and methods of cure, always on myself. I left the regulation of the house to my wife, as she understood housekeeping very well. My marital duties I performed as well as I could, but without personal satisfaction. Since the first coitus, the masculine position in it has been repugnant, and also difficult for me. I should have much preferred to have the other *rôle*. When I had to deliver my wife, it almost broke my heart; for I knew how to appreciate her pain. Thus we lived long together, until severe gout drove me to various baths, and made me neurasthenic. At the same time, I became so anaemic that every few months I had to take iron for some time; otherwise I would be almost chlorotic or hysterical, or both. Angina pectoris often troubled me; then came unilateral cramps of chin, nose, neck and larynx; hemicrania and cramps of the diaphragm and chest muscles. For about three years I had a feeling as if the prostate were enlarged,—a bearing-down feeling, as if giving birth to something; and also pain in the hips, constant pain in the back, and the like. Yet, with the strength of despair, I fought against these complaints, which impressed me as being female or effeminate, until three years ago, when a severe attack of arthritis completely broke me down.

"But before this terrible attack of gout occurred, in despair, to lessen the pain of gout, I had taken hot baths, as near the temperature of the body as possible. On one of these occasions it happened that I suddenly changed, and seemed to be near death. I sprang with all my remaining strength out of the bath; I had felt exactly like a woman with *libido*. This happened when the extract of Indian hemp came into vogue, and was highly prized. In a state of fear of a threatened attack of gout (feeling perfectly indifferent about life), I took three or four times the usual dose of it, and almost died of hashish poisoning. Convulsive laughter, a feeling of unheard of strength and swiftness, a peculiar feeling in brain and eyes, millions of sparks streaming from the brain through the skin,—all these feelings occurred. But I could not force myself to speak. All at once I saw myself a woman from my toes to my breast; I felt, as before while in the bath, that the genitals had shrunken, the pelvis broadened, the breasts swollen out; a feeling of unspeakable delight came over me. I closed my eyes, so that at least I did not see the face changed. My physician looked as if he had a gigantic potato instead of a head; my wife had the full moon on her thorax. And yet, I was strong enough to briefly record my will in my note-book when both left the room for a short time.

"But who could describe my fright when, on the next morning, I awoke and found myself feeling as if completely changed into a woman; and when, on standing and walking, I felt female genitals and breasts! When at last I raised myself out of bed, I felt that a complete transformation had taken place in me. During my illness a visitor said: 'He is too patient for a man.' And the visitor gave me a plant in bloom, which seemed strange, but pleased me. From that time I was patient, and would do nothing in a hurry; but I became tenacious, like a cat, though, at the same time, mild, forgiving and no longer bearing enmity, —in short, I had a woman's disposition. During the last sickness I had many visual and auditory hallucinations,—spoke with the dead, etc.; saw and heard familiar spirits; felt like a double person; but, while lying ill, I did not notice that the man in me had been extinguished. The change in my disposition was a piece of good fortune, for I had a stroke of paralysis which would certainly have killed me had I been of my former disposition; but now I was reconciled, for I no longer recognized myself. Owing to the fact that I still often confounded neurasthenic symptoms with the gout, I took many baths, until an itching of the skin, with the feeling of scabies, instead of being diminished, was so increased that I gave up all external treatment (I was made more and more anaemic by the baths), and hardened myself as best I could. But the imperative female feeling remained, and became so strong that I wear only the mask of a man, and in everything else feel like a woman; and gradually I have lost memory of the former individuality. What was left of me by the gout, influenza ruined entirely.

"*Present condition:* I am tall, slightly bald, and the beard is growing gray. I begin to stoop. Since having influenza I have lost about one-fourth of my strength. Owing to a valvular lesion, my face looks somewhat red; full beard; chronic conjunctivitis; more muscular than fat. The left foot seems to be developing varicose veins, and it often goes to sleep; but it is not really thickened, though it seems to be.

"The mammary region, though small, swells out perceptibly. The abdomen is feminine in form; the feet are placed like a woman's, and the calves, etc., are feminine; and it is the same with arms and hands. I can wear ladies' hose and gloves 7½ to 7¾ in size. I also wear a corset without annoyance. My weight varies between 168 and 184 pounds. Urine without albumen or sugar, but it contains an excess of uric acid. But when there is not too much uric acid in it, it is clear, and almost as clear as water after any excitement. Bowels usually regular, but should they not be, then come all the symptoms of female constipation. Sleep is poor,—for weeks at a time only of two or three hours' duration. Appetite quite good; but, on the whole, my stomach will not bear more than that of a strong woman, and reacts to irritating food with cutaneous eruption and burning in the urethra. The skin is white, and, for the most part, feels quite smooth; there has been unbearable cutaneous itching for the last two years; but during the last few weeks this has diminished, and is now present only in the popliteal spaces and on the scrotum.

"Tendency to perspire. Perspiration was previously as good as wanting, but now there are all the odious peculiarities of the female perspiration, particularly about the lower part of the body; so that I have to keep myself cleaner than a woman (I perfume my handkerchief, and use perfumed soap and *eau-de-Cologne*).

"*General feeling:* I feel like a woman in a man's form; and even though I often am sensible of the man's form, yet it is always in a feminine sense. Thus, for example, I feel the penis as clitoris; the urethra and vaginal orifice, which always feels a little wet, even when it is actually dry; the scrotum as *labia majora*; in short, I always feel the vulva. And all that that means one alone can know who feels or has felt so. But the skin all over my body feels feminine; it receives all impressions, whether of touch, of warmth, or whether unfriendly, as feminine, and I have the sensations of a woman. I cannot go with bare hands, as both heat and cold trouble me. When the time is past when we men are permitted to carry sun-umbrellas, I have to endure great sensitiveness of the skin of my face, until sun-umbrellas can again be used. On awakening in the morning, I am confused for a few moments, as if I were seeking for myself; then the imperative feeling of being a woman awakens. I feel the sense of the vulva (that one is there), and always greet the day with a soft or loud sigh; for I have fear again of the play that must be carried on throughout the day. I had to learn everything anew; the knife—apparatus, everything—has felt different for the last three years; and with the change of muscular sense I had to learn everything over again. I have been successful, and only the use of the saw and bone-chisel are difficult; it is almost as if my strength were not quite sufficient. On the other hand, I have a keener sense of touch in working with the curette in the soft parts. It is unpleasant that, in examining ladies, I often feel their sensations; but this, indeed, does not repel them. The most unpleasant thing I experience is foetal movement. For a long time—several months—I was troubled by reading the thoughts of both sexes, and I still have to fight against it. I can endure it better with women; with men it is repugnant. Three years ago I had not yet consciously seen the world with a woman's eyes; this change in the relation of the eyes to the brain came almost suddenly, with violent headache. I was with a lady whose sexual feeling was reversed, when suddenly I saw her changed in the sense I now feel myself,— *viz.*, she as man,—and I felt myself a woman in contrast, with her; so that I left her with ill-concealed vexation. At that time she had not yet come to understand her own condition perfectly.

"Since then, all my sensory impressions are as if they were feminine in form and relation. The cerebral system almost immediately adjusted itself to the vegetative; so that all my ailments were manifested in a feminine way. The sensitiveness of all nerves, particularly that of the auditory and olfactory and trigeminal, increased to a condition of nervousness. If only a window slammed, I was frightened inwardly; for a man dare not tremble at such things. If food is not absolutely fresh, I perceive a cadaverous odour. I could never depend on the trigeminus;

for the pain would jump whimsically from one branch of it to another; from a tooth to an eye. But, since my transformation, I bear toothache and migraine more easily, and have less feeling of fear with angina pectoris. It seems to me a strange fact that I feel myself to be a fearful, weak being, and yet, when danger threatens, I am rather cool and collected, and this is true in dangerous operations. The stomach rebels against the slightest indiscretion (in female diet) that is committed without thought of the female nature, either by ructus or other symptoms; but particularly against abuse of alcoholics. The indisposition after intoxication that a man who feels like a woman experiences is much worse than any a student could get up. It seems to me almost as if one feeling like a woman were entirely controlled by the vegetative system.

"Small as my nipples are, they demand room, and as at puberty the nipples are swollen and painful. On this account, the white shirt, the waistcoat and the coat trouble me. I feel as though the pelvis were female; and it is the same with the anus and nates. At first the sense of a female abdomen was troublesome to me; for it cannot bear trousers, and it always possesses or induces the feminine feeling. I also have the imperative feeling of a waist. It is as I were robbed of my own skin, and put in a woman's skin that fitted me perfectly, but which felt everything as if it covered a woman; and whose sensations passed through the man's body, and exterminated the masculine element. The testes, even though not atrophied or degenerated, are still no longer testes, and often cause me pain, with the feeling that they belong in the abdomen, and should be fastened there; and their mobility often bothers me.

"Every four weeks, at the time of the full moon, I have the menstrual discomfort of a woman for five days, physically and mentally, only I do not bleed; but I have the feeling of a loss of fluid; a feeling that the genitals and abdomen are (internally) swollen. A very pleasant period comes when, afterward and later in the interval of a day or two, the physiological desire for procreation comes, which with all power permeates the woman. My whole body is then filled with this sensation, as an immersed piece of sugar is filled with water, or as full as a soaked sponge. It is like this: first, a woman longing for love, and then, for a man; and, in fact, the desire, as it seems to me, is more a longing to be possessed than a wish for coitus. The intense natural instinct or the feminine concupiscence overcomes the feeling of modesty, so that indirectly coitus is desired. I have never felt coitus in a masculine way more than three times in my life; and even if it were so in general, I was always indifferent about it. But, during the last three years, I have experienced it passively, like a woman; in fact, oftentimes with the feeling of feminine ejaculation; and I always feel that I am impregnated. I am always fatigued as a woman is after it, and often feel ill, as a man never does. Sometimes it caused me such great pleasure that there is nothing with which I can compare it; it is the most blissful and powerful feeling in the world; at that moment the woman is simply a vulva that has devoured the whole person.

"During the last three years I have never lost for an instant the feeling of being a woman, and now, owing to habit, this is no longer annoying to me, though during this period I have felt debased; for a man could endure to feel like a woman without a desire for enjoyment; but when desires come, the happiness ceases! Then come the burning, the heat, the feeling of turgor of the genitals (when the penis is not in a state of erection the genitals do not play any part). In case of intense desire, the feeling of sucking in the vagina and vulva is really terrible—a hellish pain of lust hardly to be endured. If I then have opportunity to perform coitus, it is better; but, owing to defective sense of being possessed by the other, it does not afford complete satisfaction; the feeling of sterility comes with its weight of shame, added to the feeling of passive copulation and injured modesty. I seem almost like a prostitute. Reason does not give any help; the imperative feeling of femininity dominates and rules everything. The difficulty in carrying on one's occupation, under such circumstances, is easily appreciated; but it is possible to force one's self to it. Of course, it is almost impossible to sit, walk, or lie down; at least, any one of these cannot be endured long; and with the constant touch of the trousers, etc., it is unendurable.

"Marriage then, except during coitus, where the man has to feel himself a woman, is like two women living together, one of whom regards herself as in the mask of a man. If the periodical menstruation fails to occur, then come the feelings of pregnancy or of sexual satiety, which a man never experiences, but which take possession of the whole being, just as the feeling of femininity does, and are repugnant in themselves; and, therefore, I gladly welcome the regular menstrual periods again. When erotic dreams or ideas occur, I see myself in the form I have as a woman, and see erected organs presenting. Since the anus feels feminine, it would not be hard to become a passive pederast; only positive religious command prevents it, as all other deterrent ideas would be overcome. Since such conditions are repugnant, as they would be to any one, I have a desire to be sexless, or to make myself sexless. If I had been single, I should long ago have taken leave of testes, scrotum and penis.

"Of what use is female pleasure, when one does not conceive? What good comes from excitation of female love, when one has only a wife for gratification, even though copulation is felt as though it were with a man? What a terrible feeling of shame is caused by the feminine perspiration! How the feeling for dress and ornament lowers a man! Even in his changed form, even when he can no longer recall the masculine sexual feeling, he would not wish to be forced to feel like a woman. He still knows very well that, heretofore, he did not constantly feel sexually; that he was merely a human being uninfluenced by sex. Now, suddenly, he has to regard his former individuality as a mask, and constantly feel like a woman, only having a change when, every four weeks, he has his periodical sickness, and in the intervals his insatiable female desire. If he could but awake without immediately being forced to feel like a woman! At last he longs for a moment in which he might raise his mask; but that moment does not come. He can only find amelioration of his misery when he can put on some bit of female attire or finery, an under-garment, etc.; for he dare not go about as a woman. To be compelled to fulfil all the duties of a calling with the feeling of being a woman costumed as a man, and to see no end of it, is no trifle. Religion alone saves from a great lapse; but it does not prevent the pain when temptation affects the man who feels as a woman; and so it must be felt and endured! When a respectable man who enjoys an unusual degree of public confidence, and possesses authority, must go about with his vulva—imaginary though it be; when one, leaving his arduous daily task, is compelled to examine the *toilette* of the first lady he meets, and criticize her with feminine eyes, and to read her thoughts in her face; when a journal of fashions possesses an interest equal to that of a scientific work (I felt this as a child); when one must conceal his condition from his wife, whose thoughts, the moment he feels like a woman, he can read in her face, while it becomes perfectly clear to her that he has changed in body and soul—what must all this be? The misery caused by the feminine gentleness that must be overcome? Oftentimes, of course, when I am away alone, it is possible to live for a time more like a woman; for example, to wear female attire, especially at night, to keep gloves on, or to wear a veil or a mask in my room; so that thus there is rest from excessive *libido*. But when the feminine feeling has once gained an entrance, it imperatively demands recognition. It is often satisfied with a moderate concession, such as the wearing of a bracelet above the cuff; but it imperatively demands some concession. My only happiness is to see myself dressed as a woman without a feeling of shame; indeed, when my face is veiled or masked, I prefer it so, and thus think of myself. Like every one of Fashion's fools, I have a taste for the prevailing mode, so greatly am I transformed. To become accustomed to the thought of feeling only like a woman, and only to remember the previous manner of thought to a certain extent in contrast with it, and, at the same time, to express one's self as a man, requires a long time and an infinite amount of persistence.

"Nevertheless, in spite of everything, it will happen that I betray myself by some expression of feminine feeling, either in sexual matters, when I say that I feel so and so, expressing what a man without the female feeling cannot know; or when I accidentally betray that female attire is my talent. Before women, of course, this does not amount to anything; for a woman is greatly flattered when a man understands something of her matters; but this must not be displayed to my own wife. How frightened I once was when my wife said to a friend that I had great taste in ladies' dress! How a haughty, stylish lady was astonished when, as she was about to make a great error in the education of her little daughter, I described to her in writing and verbally all the feminine feelings! To be sure, I lied to her, saying that my knowledge had been gleaned from letters. But her confidence in me is as great as ever; and the child, who was on the road to insanity, is rational and happy. She had confessed all the feminine inclinations as sins; now she knows what, as a girl, she must bear and control by will and religion; and she feels that she is human. Both ladies would laugh heartily if they knew that I had only drawn on my own sad experience. I must also add that I now have a finer sense of temperature, and, besides, a sense of the elasticity of the skin and tension of the intestines, etc., in patients, that was unknown to me before; that in operations and autopsies, poisonous fluids more readily penetrate my (uninjured) skin. Every autopsy causes me pain; examination of a prostitute, or a woman having a discharge, a cancerous odor, or the like, is actually repugnant to me. In all respects I am now under the influence of antipathy and sympathy, from the sense of colour to my judgment of a person. Women usually see in each other the periodical sexual disposition; and, therefore, a lady wears a veil, if she is not always accustomed to wear one, and usually she perfumes herself, even though it be only with handkerchief or gloves; for her olfactory sense in relation to her own sex is intense. Odours have an incredible effect on the female organism; thus, for example, the odours of violets and roses quiet me, while others disgust me; and with Ylang-Ylang I cannot contain myself for sexual excitement. Contact with a woman seems homogeneous to me; coitus with my wife seems possible to me because she is somewhat masculine, and has a firm skin; and yet it is more an *amor lesbicus.*

"Besides, I always feel passive. Often at night, when I cannot sleep for excitement, it is finally accomplished, if I have my thighs apart, like a woman having intercourse with a man (i.e., he can sleep in that position) or if I lie on my side; but an arm or the bedclothing must not touch the breasts, or there is no sleep; and there must be no pressure on the abdomen. I sleep best in a chemise and night-robe, and with gloves on; for my hands easily get cold. I am also comfortable in female drawers and petticoats, because they do not touch the genitals. I liked female dresses best when crinolines were worn. Female dresses do not annoy the feminine-feeling man; for he, like every woman, feels them as belonging to his person, and not as something foreign.

"My dearest associate is a lady suffering with neurasthenia, who, since her last confinement, feels like a man, but who, since I explained these feelings to her, abstains from intercourse as much as possible, a thing I, as a husband, dare not do. She, by her example, helps me to endure my condition. She has a most perfect memory of the female feelings, and has often given me good advice. Were she a man and I a young girl I should seek to win her; for her I should be glad to endure the fate of a woman. But her present appearance is quite different from what it formerly was. She is a very elegantly dressed gentleman, notwithstanding bosom and hair; she also speaks quickly and concisely, and no longer takes pleasure in the things that please me. She has a kind of melancholy dissatisfaction with the world, but she bears her fate worthily and with resignation, finding her comfort only in religion and the fulfilment of her duty. At the time of the menses, she almost dies. She no longer likes female society and conversation, and has no liking for delicacies.

"A youthful friend felt like a girl from the very first, and had inclinations towards the male sex. His sister had the opposite condition; and when the uterus demanded its right, and she saw herself as a loving woman in spite of her masculinity, she cut the matter short, and committed suicide by drowning.

"Since complete effemination, the principal changes I have observed in myself are:—

"1. The constant feeling of being a woman from top to toe.

"2. The constant feeling of having female genitals.

"3. The periodicity of the monthly menstruation.

"4. The regular occurrence of female desire, though not directed to any particular man.

"5. The passive female feeling in coitus.

"6. After that, the feeling of impregnation.

"7. The female feeling in thought of coitus.

"8. At the sight of women, the feeling of being of their kind, and the feminine interest in them.

"9. At the sight of men, the feminine interest in them.

"10. At the sight of children, the same feeling.

"11. The changed disposition and much greater patience.

"12. The final resignation to my fate, for which I have nothing to thank but positive religion; without it I should have long ago committed suicide.

"To be a man and to be compelled to feel that every woman either has intercourse or desires it. This is hard to endure."

The foregoing autobiography, scientifically so important, was accompanied by the following no less interesting letter:—

"SIR,—I must next beg your indulgence for troubling you with my communication. I lost all control, and thought of myself only as a monster before which I myself shuddered. Then your work gave me courage again; and I determined to go to the bottom of the matter, and examine my past life, let the result be what it might. It seemed a duty of gratitude to you to tell you the result of my recollection and observation, since I had not seen any description by you of an analogous case; and, finally, I also thought it might perhaps interest you to learn, from the pen of a physician, how such a worthless human, or masculine, being thinks and feels under the weight of the imperative idea of being a woman.

"It is not perfect; but I no longer have the strength to reflect more upon it, and have no desire to go into the matter more deeply. Much is repeated; but I beg you to remember that any mask may be allowed to fall off, particularly when it is not voluntarily worn, but enforced.

"After reading your work, I hope that, if I fulfil my duties as physician, citizen, father and husband, I may still count myself among human beings who do not deserve merely to be despised.

"Finally, I wished to lay the result of my recollection and reflection before you, in order to show that one thinking and feeling like a woman can still be a physician. I consider it a great injustice to debar woman from Medicine. A woman, through her feeling, is prone to many ailments which, in spite of all skill in diagnosis, remain obscure to a man; at least, in the diseases of women and children. If I could have my way, I should have every physician live the life of a woman for three months; then he would have a better understanding and more consideration in matters affecting the half of humanity from which he comes; then he would learn to value the greatness of woman, and appreciate the difficulty of her lot."

Remarks: The badly tainted patient was originally psycho-sexually abnormal, in that, in character and in the sexual act, he felt as a female. The abnormal feeling remained purely a psychical anomaly until three years ago, when, owing to severe neurasthenia, it received overmastering support in imperative bodily sensations of a sexual change, which now dominate consciousness. Then, to the patient's horror, he felt bodily like a woman; and, under the impulse of his imperative feminine sensations, he experienced a complete transformation of his former masculine feeling, thought and will; in fact, of his whole sexual life, in the sense of eviration. At the same time, his "ego" was able to control these abnormal psycho-physical manifestations, and prevent descent to *paranoia,*—a remarkable example of imperative feelings and ideas on the basis of neurotic taint, which is of great value for a comprehension of the manner in which the psycho-sexual transformation may be accomplished. In 1893, three years later, this unhappy colleague sent me a new account of his present state. This corresponded essentially with the former. His physical and psychical feelings were absolutely those of a woman; but his intellectual powers were intact, and he was thus saved from *paranoia*.

A counterpart to this case, which is of clinical and psychological moment, is that of a lady as given in:—

CASE 130. Mrs. X., daughter of a high official. Her mother died of nervous disease. The father was untainted, and died from pneumonia at a good old age. Her brothers and sisters had inferior psychopathic dispositions; one brother was of abnormal character, and very neurasthenic.

As a girl Mrs. X. had decided inclinations for boys' sports. So long as she wore short dresses she used to rove about the fields and woods in the freest manner, and climbed the most dangerous rocks and cliffs. She had no taste for dresses and finery. Once, when they gave her a dress made in boys' fashion, she was highly delighted; and when at school they dressed her up in boys' clothes on the occasion of some theatrical performance, she was filled with bliss.

Otherwise nothing betrayed her homosexual inclinations. Up to her marriage (at the age of twenty-one) she could not recall to mind a single instance in which she felt herself drawn to persons of her own sex. Men were equally indifferent to her. When matured she had many admirers. This flattered her greatly. However, she claimed that the difference of the sexes never entered her mind; she was only influenced by the difference in the dress.

When attending the first and only ball she felt interest only in intellectual conversation, but not in dancing or the dancers.

At the age of eighteen the menses set in without difficulty. She always looked upon menstruation as an unnecessary and bothersome function. Her engagement with a man who, though good and rich, yet possessed not the slightest knowledge of woman's nature, was a matter of utter indifference to her. She had neither sympathy for nor antipathy against matrimony. Her connubial duties were at first painful to her, later on simply loathsome. She never experienced sexual pleasure, but became the mother of six children. When her husband began to observe *coitus interruptus*, on account of the prolific consequences, her religious and moral sentiments were hurt. Mrs. X. grew more and more neurasthenic, peevish and unhappy.

She suffered from prolapsed uterus and vaginal erosions and became anaemic. Gynecological treatment and visits to watering-places procured but slight improvements.

At the age of thirty-six she had an apoplectic stroke, which confined her to bed for two years, with heavy neurasthenic ailments (insomnia, pressure in the head, palpitation of the heart, psychical depression, feelings of lost physical and mental power, bordering even on insanity, etc.). During this long illness a peculiar change of her psychical and physical feelings took place.

The small talk of the ladies visiting her about love, toilet, finery, fashions, domestic and servants' affairs disgusted her. She felt mortified at being a woman. She could not even make up her mind again to look in the mirror. She loathed combing her hair and making her toilet. Much to the surprise of her own people her hitherto soft and decidedly feminine features assumed a strongly masculine character, so much so that she gave the impression of being a man clad in female garb. She complained to her trusted physician that her periods had stopped,— in fact, she had nothing to do with such functions. When they recurred again she felt ill-tempered, and found the odor of the menstrual flow most nauseating, but definitely refused the use of perfumes, which affected her in a similar unpleasant manner.

But in other ways she felt that a peculiar change had come over her entire being. She had athletic spells, and great desire for gymnastic exercises. At times she felt as if she were just twenty. She was startled,— when her neurasthenic brain allowed of thought at all,—at the flight and novelty of her thoughts, at her quick and precise method of arriving at conclusions and forming opinions, at the curt and short way of expressing herself, and her novel choice of words not always becoming to a lady. Even an inclination to use curse words and oaths was noticeable in this otherwise so pious and correct woman.

She reproached herself bitterly, and grieved because she had lost her femininity, and scandalized her friends by her thoughts, sentiments, and actions.

She also perceived a change in her body. She was horrified to notice her breasts disappearing, that her pelvis grew smaller and narrower, the bones became more massive, and her skin rougher and harder.

She refused to wear any more a lady's night-dress or a lady's cap, and put away her bracelets, earrings and fans. Her maid and her dress-maker noticed a different odour coming from her person; her voice also grew deeper, rougher, and quite masculine.

When the patient was finally able to leave her bed, the female gait had altered, feminine gestures and movments in her female attire were forced, and she could no longer bear to wear a veil over her face. Her former period of life spent as a woman seemed strange to her, as if it did not belong to her existence at all; she could play no longer the *rôle* of woman. She assumed more and more the character of a man. She experienced strange feelings in her abdomen; and complained to the physician attending her that she could feel no longer the internal organs of generation, that her body was closed up, the region of her genitals enlarged, and often had the sensation of possessing a penis and scrotum. She showed, also, unmistakable symptoms of male *libido*.

All these observations affected her deeply, filled her with horror, and depressed her so much that an attack of insanity was apprehended. But by incessant efforts and kind advice the family physician finally succeeded in calming the patient and piloting her safely over this dangerous point. Little by little she gained her equilibrium in this novel, strange and morbid physico-psychical form. She took pains in performing her duties as housewife and mother. It was interesting to observe the truly manly firmness of will which she developed, but her former softness of character had vanished. She assumed the *rôle* of the man in her house, a circumstance which led to many dissensions and misunderstandings. She became an enigma which her husband was unable to solve.

She complained to her physician that at times a "bestial masculine *libido*" threatened to overcome her, which made her despondent. Marital intercourse with the husband appeared to her most repulsive—in fact, impossible. Periodically the patient experienced feminine emotions, but they became scarcer and weaker as time went by. At such periods she became conscious again of her female genitals and breasts, but these episodes affected her painfully, and she felt that such a "second transmutation" would be unbearable, and would drive her to insanity.

She now became reconciled to her change of sex, brought about by her severe illness, and bore her fate with resignation, finding much support in her religious convictions.

What affected her most keenly was the fact that, like an actress, she must move in a strange sphere—*i.e.*, in that of a woman (Status Praesens," Sept., 1892).

IV. *Degree: Delusion of Sexual Change.*

A final possible stage in this disease-process is the delusion of a transformation of sex. It arises from sexual neurasthenia that has developed into general depression, resulting in a mental disease,—*paranoia*.

The following cases show the development of the interesting neuro-psychological process to its height:—

CASE 131. K., aged thirty-six, male, single, servant, received at the clinic on 26th February, 1889, typical case of persecutory delusion, resulting from *neurasthenia*, with olfactory hallucinations, sensations, etc.

He came of a predisposed family. Several brothers and sisters were psychopathic. Patient had a hydrocephalic skull, depressed in the region of the right fontanelle; eyes neuropathic. He had always been very sensual; began to masturbate at nineteen; had coitus at twenty-three; begat three illegitimate children. He gave up further sexual intercourse on account of fear of begetting more children, and of being unable to provide for them. Abstinence proved very painful to him. He also gave up masturbation, and was then troubled with pollutions. A year and a half ago he became sexually neurasthenic, had diurnal pollutions, became thereafter ill and miserable, and, after a time, generally neurasthenic, finally developing *paranoia*.

A year ago he began to have paraesthetic sensations,—as if there were a great coil in the place of his genitals; and then he felt that his scrotum and penis were gone, and that his genitals were changed into those of a female.

He felt the growth of his breasts; that his hair was that of a woman; and that feminine garments were on his body. He thought himself a woman. The people in the street gave utterance to corresponding remarks: "Look at the woman! The old blowhard!" In a half-dreamy state, he had the feeling as if he played the part of a woman in coitus with a man, which caused him the most lively feelings of pleasure. During his stay at the clinic, a remission of the *paranoia* occurred, and, at the same time, a marked improvement of the neurasthenia. Then the feelings and ideas due to a developing sexual change disappeared.

A more advanced case of eviration, on the way to a delusion of sexual change is the following:—

CASE 132. Franz St., aged thirty-three; schoolteacher, single; probably of tainted family; always neuropathic, emotional, timid, intolerant of alcohol; began to masturbate at eighteen. At thirty there were manifestations of *neurasthenia* (pollutions with consequent fatigue, soon beginning to occur during the day; pain in the region of the *sacral plexus*, etc.). Gradually, spinal irritation, pressure in the head, and cerebral neurasthenia were added. Since the beginning of 1885 the patient had given up coitus, in which he no longer experienced pleasurable feeling. He masturbated frequently.

In 1888 he began to have delusions of suspicion. He noticed that he was avoided, and that he had unpleasant odours about him (olfactory hallucinations). In this way he explained the altered attitude of people, and their sneezing, coughing, etc.

He could smell corpses and foul urine. He recognized the cause of his bad smells in inward pollutions. He recognized these in a feeling he had as if a fluid flowed up from the symphysis towards the breasts. Patient soon left the clinic.

In 1889 he was again received in an advanced stage of persecutory masturbation delusions (delusions of physical persecution).

In the beginning of May, 1889, the patient attracted notice, in that he was cross when he was addressed as "mister." He protested against it because he was a woman. Voices told him this. He noticed that his breasts were growing. Some weeks before, others had touched him in a sensual manner. He heard it said that he was a whore. Of late, dreams of pregnancy. He dreamed that, as a woman, he indulged in coitus. He felt the insertion of the penis, and, during the hallucinatory act, also a feeling of ejaculation.

Head straight; facial form long and narrow; parietal eminences prominent; genitals normally developed.

The following case, observed in the asylum at Illenau, is a pertinent example of lasting delusional alteration of sexual consciousness:

CASE 133. Delusion of sexual change. N., aged twenty-three, single, pianist, was received in the asylum at Illenau in the last part of October, 1865. He came of a family in which there was said to be no hereditary taint! but there was phthisis (father and brother died of pulmonary tuberculosis). Patient, as a child, was weakly and dull, though especially talented in music. He was always of abnormal character; silent, retiring, unsocial, and sullen. He practiced masturbation after fifteen. After a few years neurasthenic symptoms (palpitation of the heart, lassitude, occasional pressure in the head, etc.) and also hypochondriacal symptoms were manifested. During the last year he had worked with great difficulty. For about six months neurasthenia had increased. He complained of palpitation of the heart, pressure in the head, and sleeplessness; was very irritable, and seemed to be sexually excited. He declared that he must marry for his health. He fell in love with an artiste, but almost at the same time (September, 1865), fell ill with persecutory delusions (ideas of enemies, derision in the street, poison in food; obstacles were placed on the bridge to keep him from going to his beloved). On account of increasing excitement and conflicts with those about him that he considered inimical to him, he was taken to the asylum. At first he presented the picture of a typical paranoid delusions with symptoms of sexual, and later general, neurasthenia, though the delusions of persecution did not rest upon this neurotic foundation. It was only occasionally that the patient heard such sentences as this: "Now the semen will be drawn from him. Now the bladder will be cut out."

In the course of the years 1866-68, the delusions of persecution became less and less apparent, and were for the most part replaced by erotic ideas. The somatic and mental basis was a lasting and powerful excitation of the sexual sphere. The patient fell in love with every woman he saw, heard voices which told him to approach her, and beg to be allowed to marry, declaring that, if he were not given a wife, he would waste away. With continuance of masturbation, in 1869, signs of future effemination made themselves manifest. "He would, if he should get a wife, love her only platonically." The patient grew more and more peculiar, lived in a circle of erotic ideas, saw prostitution practiced in the asylum, and now and then heard voices which imputed immoral conduct with women to him. For this reason he avoided the society of women, and only associated with them for the sake of music when two witnesses were with him.

In the course of the year 1872, the neurasthenic condition became markedly increased. Now persecutory delusions again came into the foreground, and took on a clinical colouring from the neurotic basis. Olfactory hallucinations occurred. Magnetic influences were at work on him—"magnetic waves produced by striking an anvil" (false interpretation of sensations due to spinal asthenia). With continued and intense sexual excitement and excess in masturbation, the process of effemination constantly progressed. Only episodically was he a man and inclined towards a woman, complaining that the shameless prostitution of the men in the house made it impossible for a lady to come to him. He was dying of magnetically poisoned air and unsatisfied love. Without love he could not live. He was poisoned by lewd poison that affected his sexual desire. The lady whom he loved was surrounded here by the lowest vice. The prostitutes in the house had fortune-chains; that is, chains in which, without moving, a man can indulge in lustful pleasure. He was ready now to satisfy himself with prostitutes. He was possessed of a wonderful ray of thought that emanated from his eyes, which were worth 20,000,000. His compositions were worth 500,000 francs. With these indications of delusions of grandeur, there were also those of persecution—the food was poisoned by venereal excrements; he tasted and smelled poison, heard infamous accusations, and asked for appliances to close his ears.

From August, 1872, however, the signs of effemination became more and more frequent. He acted somewhat affectedly, declaring that he could no longer live among men that drink and smoke. He thought and felt like a woman. He must thenceforth be treated like a woman and transferred to a female ward. He asked for confections and delicate desserts. Occasionally, on account of tenesmus and cystospasm, he asked to be transferred to a lying-in hospital and treated as a woman very ill in pregnancy. The abnormal magnetism of masculine attendants had an unfavourable effect on him.

At times he still felt himself to be a man, but in a way which indicated his abnormally altered sexual feeling. He pleaded only for satisfaction by means of masturbation, or for marriage without coitus. Marriage was a sensual institution. The girl that he would take for a wife must be a masturbator.

About the end of December, 1872, his personality became completely feminine. From that time he remained a woman. He had always been a woman, but in his babyhood a French Quaker, an artist, had put masculine genitals on him, and by rubbing and distorting his thorax had prevented the development of his breasts.

After this he demanded to be transferred to the female department, as protection from men that wished to violate him, and asked for female clothing. Eventually he also desired to be given employment in a toy-shop, with crocheting and embroidery work to do, or a place in a dress-making establishment with female work. From the time of the change of sex, the patient began a new reckoning of time. He conceived his previous personality in memory as that of a cousin.

He always spoke of himself in the third person, and called himself the Countess V., the dearest friend of the Empress Eugenie; asked for perfumes, corsets, etc. He took the other men of the ward for girls, tried to raise a head of hair, and demanded "Oriental Hair-Remover," in order that no one may doubt his gender. He took delight in praising onanism, for "she had been an onanist from fifteen, and had never desired any other kind of sexual satisfaction." Occasionally neurasthenic symptoms, olfactory hallucinations, and persecutory delusions were observed. All the events up to the time of December, 1872, belonged to the personality of the cousin.

The patient's delusion that he was the Countess V. could no longer be corrected. She proved her identity by the fact that the nurse had examined her, and found her to be a lady. The countess would not marry, because she hated men. Since he was not provided with female clothing and shoes, he spent the greatest part of the day in bed, acted like an invalid lady of position, affectedly and modestly, and asked for bon-bons and the like. His hair was done up in a knot as well as it allowed, and the beard was pulled out. Breasts were made of rolls of bread.

In 1874 caries began in the left knee-joint, to which pulmonary tuberculosis was soon added. Death on 2nd December, 1874. Skull normal. Frontal lobes atrophic. Brain anaemic. Microscopical (Dr. *Schüle*). In the superior layer of the frontal lobe, ganglion cells somewhat shrunken; in the *adventitia* of the vessel, numerous fat-corpuscles; *ganglia* unchanged; isolated pigment particles and colloid bodies. The lower layers of the *cortex* normal. Genitals very large; testicles small, lax, and showed no change microscopically on section.

The delusion of sexual transformation, displayed in its conditions and phases of development in the foregoing case, is a manifestation remarkably infrequent in the pathology of the human mind. Besides the foregoing cases, personally observed, I have seen such a case, as an episodical phenomenon, in a lady having sexual inversion (case 118, of the seventh edition of this work), one in a girl affected with original *paranoia*, and another in a lady suffering with original *paranoia*.

Save for a case briefly reported by *Arndt* [82] in his textbook, and one quite superficially described by *Sérieux* ("Recherches Clinique," p. 33), and the two cases known to *Esquirol*,[83] I cannot recall any cases of delusion of sexual transformation in literature.

I have already mentioned the interesting relations existing between the facts of delusional transformation of sex and the so-called insanity of the Scythians.

Marandon ("Annales médico-psychologiques," 1877, p. 161), like others, has erroneously presumed that with the ancient Scythians there was an actual delusion, and that the condition was not merely that of eviration. According to the law of empirical actuality, the delusion, so infrequent today, must also have been very infrequent in ancient times. Since it can only be conceived as arising on the basis of *paranoia*, there can be no thought of its endemic occurrence; it can only be regarded as a superstitious manifestation of eviration (the result of anger of the goddess), as is also evident from the statements of Hippocrates.

The facts of the so-called Scythian insanity, as well as the facts lately learned about the Pueblo Indians, are also worthy of note anthropologically, in so far as atrophy of the testes and genitals in general, and approximation to the female type, physically and mentally, were observed. This is the more remarkable, since, in men who have lost their procreative organs, such a reversal of instinct is quite as unusual as in women, with due alteration of details (in comparing cases), after the natural or artificial *climacteric*.

B. HOMOSEXUAL FEELING AS AN ABNORMAL CONGENITAL MANIFESTATION.[84]

The essential feature of this strange manifestation of the sexual life is the want of sexual sensibility for the opposite sex, even to the extent of horror, while sexual inclination and impulse toward the same sex are present. At the same time, the genitals are normally developed, the sexual glands perform their functions properly, and the sexual type is completely differentiated.

Feeling, thought, will, and the whole character, in cases of the complete development of the anomaly, correspond with the peculiar sexual instinct, but not with the sex which the individual represents anatomically and physiologically. This abnormal mode of feeling may not infrequently be recognized in the manner, dress and calling of the individuals, who may go so far as to yield to an impulse to put on the distinctive clothing corresponding with the sexual *rôle* in which they feel themselves to be.

Anthropologically and clinically, this abnormal manifestation presents various degrees of development:—

1. Traces of heterosexual, with predominating homosexual, instinct (psycho-sexual hermaphroditism).

2. There exists inclination only towards the same sex (homosexuality).

3. The entire mental existence is altered to correspond with the abnormal sexual instinct (effemination and viraginity).

4. The form of the body approaches that which corresponds to the abnormal sexual instinct. However actual transitions to hermaphrodites never occur, but, on the contrary, completely differentiated genitals; so that, just as in all pathological perversions of the sexual life, the cause must be sought in the brain (hermaphroditism and pseudo-hermaphroditism).

The first definite communications [85] concerning this enigmatical phenomenon of Nature are made by *Casper* ("Ueber Nothzucht und Päderastie," *Casper's* "Vierteljahrsschrift," 1852, i.), who, it is true, classes it with pederasty, but makes the pertinent remark that this anomaly is, in most cases, congenital, and, at the same time, to be regarded as a mental hermaphroditism. There exists here an actual disgust of sexual contact with women, while the imagination is filled with beautiful young men, and with statues and pictures of them. It did not escape *Casper* that in such cases placing of the penis in the anus (pederasty) is not the rule, but that, by means of other sexual acts (mutual onanism), sexual satisfaction is sought and obtained.

In his "Clinical Novels" (1863, p. 33) *Casper* gives the interesting confession of a man showing this perversion of the sexual instinct, and does not hesitate to assert that, aside from vicious imagination and vice, as a result of over-indulgence in normal sexual intercourse, there are numerous cases in which "pederasty" has its origin in a remarkable, obscure impulse, which is congenital and inexplicable. About the middle of the "sixties" a certain assessor, *Ulrichs*, himself subject to this perverse instinct, declared, in numerous articles, under the *nom-de-plume* "Numa Numantius," [86] that the sexual mental life was not connected with the bodily sex; that there were male individuals that felt like women toward men (the mind of a woman in a man's body). He called these people *"urnings,"* and demanded nothing less than the legal and social recognition of this sexual love of the urnings as congenital and, therefore, as right; and the permission of marriage among them. *Ulrichs* failed, however, to prove that this certainly congenital and paradoxical sexual feeling was physiological, and not pathological.

Griesinger ("Archiv f. Psychiatrie," i., p. 651) threw the first ray of light on these facts, anthropologically and clinically, by pointing out the marked hereditary taint of the individual in a case which came under his own observation.

We owe thanks to *Westphal* ("Archiv f. Psychiatrie," ii., p. 73) for the first systematic consideration of the manifestation in question, which he defined as "congenital reversal of the sexual feeling, with consciousness of the abnormality of the manifestation," and designated with the name, since generally accepted, of *antipathic sexual instinct.* At the same time, he began a series of cases, which up to this time has numbered about 200, those reported in this monograph not being included.

Westphal leaves it undecided as to whether antipathic sexual feeling is a symptom of a neuropathic or of a psychopathic condition, or whether it may occur as an isolated manifestation. He holds fast to the opinion that the condition is congenital.

From the cases published up to 1877 I have designated this peculiar sexual feeling as a functional sign of degeneration, and as a partial manifestation of a neuro- (psycho-) pathic state, in most cases hereditary—a supposition which has found renewed confirmation in a consideration of additional cases. The following peculiarities may be given as the signs of this neuro- (psycho-) pathic taint:—

1. The sexual life of individuals thus organized manifests itself, as a rule, abnormally early, and thereafter with abnormal power. Not infrequently still other perverse manifestations are presented besides the abnormal method of sexual satisfaction, which in itself is conditioned by the peculiar sexual feeling.

2. The psychical love manifest in these men is, for the most part, exaggerated and exalted in the same way as their sexual instinct is manifested in consciousness, with a strange and even compelling force.

3. By the side of the functional signs of degeneration attending antipathic sexual feeling are found other functional, and in many cases anatomical, evidences of degeneration.

4. Neuroses (hysteria, neurasthenic, epileptoid states, etc.) co-exist. Almost invariably the existence of temporary or lasting neurasthenia may be proved. As a rule, this is constitutional, having its root in congenital conditions. It is awakened and maintained by masturbation or enforced abstinence.

In male individuals, owing to these practices or to congenital disposition, there is finally *neurasthenia* which manifests itself essentially in irritable weakness of the ejaculation centre. Thus it is explained that, in most of the cases, simply embracing and kissing, or even only the sight of the loved person, induce the act of ejaculation. Frequently this is accompanied by an abnormally powerful feeling of lustful pleasure, which may be so intense as to suggest a feeling of "magnetic" currents passing through the body.

5. In the majority of cases, psychical anomalies (brilliant endowment in art, especially music, poetry, etc., by the side of bad intellectual powers or original eccentricity) are present, which may extend to pronounced conditions of mental degeneration (imbecility, moral insanity).

In many homosexuals, either temporarily or permanently, insanity of a degenerative character (pathological emotional states, periodical insanity, *paranoia*, etc.) makes its appearance.

6. In almost all cases where an examination of the physical and mental peculiarities of the ancestors and blood relations has been pos-

sible, neurosis, psychoses, degenerative signs, etc., have been found in the families.[87]

The depth of congenital antipathic sexual feeling is shown by the fact that the lustful dream of the male-loving homosexual has for its content only male individuals; that of the female-loving woman, only female individuals, with corresponding situations.

The observation of *Westphal*, that the consciousness of one congenitally defective in sexual desires towards the opposite sex is painfully affected by the impulse toward the same sex, is true in only a number of cases. Indeed, in many instances, the consciousness of the abnormality of the condition is wanting. The majority of homosexuals are happy in their perverse sexual feeling and impulse, and unhappy only in so far as social and legal barriers stand in the way of the satisfaction of their instinct towards their own sex.

The study of antipathic sexual feeling points directly to anomalies of the cerebral organization of the affected individuals. The very fact that in these cases, with few exceptions, the sexual glands are found quite normal, anatomically and functionally seems to favor this assumption.

This enigmatical manifestation in the nature of man has led to many attempts of explanation.

Among *lay* persons, it is called vice; in the language of the *law*, crime. Those tainted with it, although recognizing it as an abnormality, claim for it the same rights and privileges that are accorded to normal (hetero-sexual) love, on account of its being based upon a freak of nature. From *Plato* down to *Ulrichs*, in antipathic sexual circles, this standpoint is maintained. *Plato's* "Banquet," chapters viii. and ix., are quoted for that purpose, *viz.:* "There is no Aphrodites without an Eros. But there are two goddesses. The older Aphrodites came into existence without a mother; being the daughter of Uranos she is called Urania. The younger Aphrodites is the daughter of Zeus and Diana and is called Pandemos. The Eros of the former must, therefore, be Uranos, that of the latter Pandemos. With the love of Eros Pandemos the ordinary human beings love; Eros Uranos did not choose a female but a male; this is the love for boys. Whoever is inspired with this love turns to the male sex." From many other places in the classics the impression may be won that Uranic love attained a higher position even than her sister. More recent explanations of the homosexual instinct have emanated from philosophers, psychologists and natural scientists.

One of the most peculiar explanations is advanced by *Schopenhauer* ("Die Welt als Wille und Vorstellung"), who seriously contends that nature seeks to prevent old men (*i.e.*, over fifty years of age) from begetting children, since experience teaches that these never turn out good. For this purpose nature in her wisdom has turned the sexual instinct in old men towards their own sex! The great philosopher and thinker evidently was not aware that sexual inversion, as a rule, exists from the beginning, and that pederasty, occurring in the *senium*, is only sexual perversity, but by no means proves the presence of perversion.

Binet attempts to explain these peculiar manifestations from a *psychological* standpoint, thinking (with *Condillac*) to reduce them—together with other *bizarre* psychical phenomena—to the law of association of ideas, *i.e.*, association of ideas with sentiments in the state of being born, at the beginning. This clever psychologist assumes that the instinct not as yet sexually differentiated is determined by the coincidence of a vivid sexual emotion with the simultaneous sight or contact of a person of the opposite sex. In this manner a mighty association is created, which takes root by repeating itself, whilst the original associative process is forgotten or becomes latent. Even today *v. Schrenck-Notzing* and others lean to this opinion, in their efforts to explain the inverted sexual instinct (chiefly when acquired); but it cannot withstand serious criticism. Psychological forces are insufficient to explain manifestations of so thoroughly degenerated a character (see below).

Chevalier ("Inversion Sexuelle," Paris, 1893) rightly demurs against *Binet* that these attempts at psychological explanations explain neither the precocity of homosexual impulses, *i.e.*, such as have existed long before sexual feelings were associated with imagination, nor the aversion towards the opposite sex, nor early appearance of secondary psychico-sexual manifestations. Nevertheless, *Binet's* subtle remark that the lasting presence of such associations is only possible in predisposed (tainted) individuals is worthy of note.

Neither do the explanations attempted by physicians and naturalists prove anything to satisfaction. *Gley* ("Revue philosophique," January, 1884) maintains that those afflicted with inverted sexual instinct have a female brain (!) but masculine sexual glands, and that an existing morbid condition of the brain determines the sexual life, whilst normally the sexual glands influence the sexual cerebral functions. *Magnan* ("Annales méd. psychol.," 1885, p. 458) also speaks of a female brain in the body of a man and *vice versa*. *Ulrichs* ("Memnon," 1868) comes closer to the point when he speaks of the mind of a woman in an innately male body, and thus seeks to explain congenital effemination. According to *Mantegazza* (*op. cit.* 1886, p. 106), anatomical anomalies exist in such persons in so far as the natural *plexus* of the genital nerves terminates in the rectum, thus misdirecting thither all lustful desires. But surely nature never is guilty of such errors or mutations. Neither does she burden a masculine body with a female brain. The author of this hypothesis, otherwise so acute, quite overlooks the fact that the individuals given to sexual inversion, as a rule, abhor the use of the anus—*viz.*, pederasty. *Mantegazza* reverts, as a support for his hypothesis, to the communications which he received from a well-known prominent author, who assured him that he was not as yet satisfied in his own mind whether he derived greater pleasure from coitus than from defecation. Even if we admit the correctness of this statement, it would only prove that its author was sexually abnormal, and that he derived but a minimum of pleasure from coitus. Moreover, one would come to the conclusion that the mucous membrane of his rectum was, in some abnormal manner, erogenous.

Bernhardi ("Der Uranismus," Berlin, 1882) casually found in five hermaphrodites (*"Pathici"*) absence of *spermatozoa*, in four cases not even sperm crystals, and thought to find the solution of this "enigma of many thousand years" in the assumption that the hermaphrodite was a "monster of the feminine sex, having nothing else in common with the male than the male genitals, which in some cases are even only imperfectly developed." This author could not even base his contention upon an autopsy, which, no doubt, would have eventually established a case of hermaphroditism.

Those practicing active viraginity and hermaphroditism he styles as "monsters of masculine gender in opposition to which the passive tribade is as perfect a woman as the active paedicator is a perfect man."

The author of this book has made an attempt to utilize facts of heredity for an explanation of this anomaly. Proceeding from the experience that manifestations of sexual perversion are frequently found in the parents, he suspects that the various grades of congenital sexual inversion represent various grades of sexual anomaly inherited by birth, acquired by ascendency, or otherwise developed. In this connection, the law of progressive heredity must also be considered.

All attempts at explanation made hitherto on the ground of natural philosophy or psychology, or those of a merely speculative character are insufficient.

Later researches, however, proceeding on embryological (onto- and phylogenetic) and anthropological lines seem to promise good results.

Emanating from *Frank Lydston* ("Philadelphia Med. and Surg. Recorder," September, 1888) and *Kiernan* ("Medical Standard," November, 1888), they are based (1) on the fact that bisexual organization is still found in the lower animal kingdom, and (2) on the supposition that mono-sexuality gradually developed from bisexuality. *Kiernan* assumes in trying to subordinate sexual inversion to the category of hermaphroditism that in individuals thus affected retrogression into the earlier hermaphrodisic forms of the animal kingdom may take place at least functionally. These are his own words: "The original bisexuality of the ancestors of the race, shown in the rudimentary female organs of the male, could not fail to occasion functional, if not organic reversions, when mental or physical manifestations were interfered with by disease or congenital defect. It seems certain that a feminely functionating brain can occupy a male body and *vice versa*.

Chevalier (*op. cit.*, p. 408) proceeds from the original bisexual life in the animal kingdom, and the original bisexual predisposition in the human foetus.

According to him the difference in the gender, with marked physical and psychical sexual character, is only the result of endless processes of evolution. The psycho-physical sexual difference runs parallel with the high level of the evolving process. The individual being must also itself pass through these grades of evolution; it is originally bisexual, but in the struggle between the male and female elements either one or the other is conquered, and a monosexual being is evolved which corresponds with the type of the present stage of evolution. But traces of the conquered sexuality remain. Under certain circumstances, these latent sexual characteristics may gain Darwin's signification, *i.e.*, they may provoke manifestations of inverted sexuality. *Chevalier* does not, however, look upon such processes as a retrogression (atavism), in the sense of *Lombroso's* opinion and that of others, but rather considers them with *Lacassagne* as disturbances in the present stage of evolution.

If the structure of this opinion is continued, the following anthropological and historical facts may be evolved:

1. The sexual apparatus consists of (*a*) the sexual glands and the organs of reproduction; (*b*) the spinal centres, which act either as a check or a stimulus upon (*a*); (*c*) the cerebral regions, in which the psychical processes of the sexual life are enacted.

Since the original predisposition of (*a*) is of a bisexual character, the same must be claimed for (*b*) and (*c*).

2. The tendency of nature in the present stage of evolution is the reproduction of monosexual individuals, and the law of experience teaches that that cerebral centre is normally developed which corresponds with the sexual glands ("Law of the Sexual Homologous Development").

3. This destruction of antipathic sexuality is at present not yet completed. In the same manner in which the appendix in the intestinal tube points to former stages of organization, so may also be found in the sexual apparatus—in the male as well as in the female—residua, which point to the original onto- and phylogenetic bisexuality, not to speak of hermaphrodisic malformations, which may be looked upon merely as partial excesses of development, or disturbances in the formation of the sexual organization, and especially of the *external* genitals.

The residua referred to are, in the male, the prostatic utricle (remnants of the "Müllersche Gänge") and the nipple, in woman the paroophoron (remnants of the original renal portions of the Wolffian bodies), and the epoophoron (remnants of Wolff's ganglia, and analogous with the epididymis in the male). *Beigel, Klebs, Fürst* and others have found in the human female suggestions of the Wolffian bodies in the shape of the so-called Gartnerian canals, which in the female ruminants are regularly present in the lateral wall of the uterus.

4. Besides, a long line of clinical and anthropological facts favor this assumption.

I will only call attention to the not infrequent cases of individuals with characters of mixed or (in the sense of sexual inversion) predominating physical and psychical sexuality ("female men and male women"), to the appearance of the female character (psychically and physically) in men, consequent upon castration (*eunuchs*), and of the male character in woman after the removal of the ovaries in early youth, also to the manifestations of viraginity in insanity at the climacteric, and even to the development of a second gender.

Professor *Kaltenbach* gives a remarkable instance of such a second (antipathic) sexual life, developed upon *climax praecox*.

On the 17th of February, 1892, he consulted me about "a woman, thirty years of age, married two years, who formerly had irregular menstruations."

Since June, 1891, a sudden series of manifestations which corresponded with the process of masculine puberty, *viz.*, full beard, hair of the head much darker, eyebrows and pubis strongly developed, chest and abdomen covered with hair as in a man.

Increased activity of the sudoriparous and sebaceous glands. Upon chest, back and face strong miliary and acne developments, whilst formerly the tint was classically white and smooth. Change of voice—formerly rich soprano, now a "lieutenant's voice." The entire facial expression changed. Complete change of carriage: chest broad, waist gone, abdomen prominent with adipose tissue, short thick-set neck, masculine all over. Lower part of face broad, breasts flat and masculine. Psychical changes: formerly mild and tractable, now energetic, hard to control, even aggressive. From the beginning of marriage no adequate sexual desire, but no traces of inversion.

In the sexual organs also highly interesting changes may be found. "Thus this young woman has changed into a man, to all intents and purposes."

My explanation of the case:—

"Premature ejaculation, loss of former feminine sexuality. Physical and psychical development of male sexuality, hitherto latent. Interesting illustration of the bi-sexual predisposition, and of the possibility of continued existence of a second sexuality in a latent state, under conditions hitherto unknown."

Unfortunately, I could obtain no further information about the subsequent metamorphosis of this case, or the presence of probable hereditary taint.

See also cases 129 and 130. In these severe neurasthenia was the causating element of change of sex, based upon heavy taint; the change, however, being only psychical, and not affecting the physical sexual character.

5. These manifestations of inverted sexuality are evidently found

only in persons with *organic taint*.[88] In normal constitutions the law of mono-sexual development, homologous with the sexual glands, remains intact. That the cerebral centre is developed under other conditions, quite independent from the peripheral sexual organs (including the sexual glands), is evident from the cases of hermaphroditism (at least, so far as pseudo-hermaphroditism is concerned), in which the law referred to above remains intact in the sense of mono-sexual development, analogous to the sexual glands. In true hermaphroditism, however, physically as well as psychically, a mutual influence of both centres prevails, and thus also a neutralization of the love life, assuming even a state of asexuality, and a tendency to physically and psychically combine and put into operation both these sexual characters.

But hermaphroditism and sexual inversion stand in no relation to each other. This is clear from the fact that the hermaphrodite (or, praccally speaking, the pseudo-hermaphrodite) follows the law of evolution quoted above, and does not offer inverted sexuality, whilst, on the other hand, hermaphroditism has never been anatomically observed in cases of antipathic sexual instinct. This follows, without further argument, from the difference of the conditions under which they originate, for in sexual inversion we must look for the cause in central (cerebral) defects, and in hermaphroditism in the anomalies affecting the peripheral sexual apparatus.

The facts quoted seem to support an attempt of an historical and anthropological explanation of sexual inversion.

It is a disturbance of the law of the development of the cerebral centre, homologous to the sexual glands (homosexuality), and eventually also of the law of the mono-sexual formation of the individual (psychical "hermaphroditism"). In the former case it is the centre of bi-sexual predisposition, antagonistic to the gender represented by the sexual gland, which in a paradoxical manner conquers that originally intended to be superior; yet the law of mono-sexual development obtains.[89]

In the other case victory lies with neither centre; yet an indication of the tendency of mono-sexual development remains, in so far that one is predominant, as a rule the opposite. This is the more remarkable since it has not the support of a corresponding sexual gland—in fact, not even a peripheral sexual apparatus, another proof that the cerebral centre is autonomous, and in its development independent of the sexual glands.

In the first case it must be assumed that the centre which by right should have conquered was too weak. This fact may be recognized in the subsequently weak *libido* in the sexual character, but feebly marked in the physical and psychical conditions.

In the second case both centres were too weak to obtain victory and superiority.

This defect of the natural laws must, from the anthropological and clinical standpoint, be considered as a manifestation of degeneration. In fact, in all cases of sexual inversion a taint of a hereditary character may be established. What causes produce this factor of taint and its activity is a question which cannot be well answered by science in its present stage.[90]

There are plenty of analogous cases to be found in tainted individuals. For the symptoms of influences disturbing physical and psychical evolution, and plainly to be found in the germ of procreation, exhibit themselves in many other manifestations of a defective or perverse character (signs of anatomical, functional, somatic and psychical degeneration).

The antipathic sexual instinct is only the strongest mark left by a whole series of exhibitions of the partial development of psychical and physical inverted sexual characters (see above), and one may be easily permitted to say: The more indistinct the psychical and physical sexual characters appear in the individual, the deeper it is below the present level of perfect homologous mono-sexuality obtained in the evolution of manifold thousands of years.

The cerebral centre mediates the psychical and, indirectly, also the physical sexual characters. The various grades of congenital antipathic sexuality will be found to correspond with the intensity of various grades of taint.

The same holds good with regard to "acquired" sexual inversion, which exhibits itself only later in life. Untainted man will never become sexually inverted through onanism or seduction by persons of the same sex; for, as soon as the extrinsic influences cease, he returns to normal sexual functions. The tainted individual, however, whose psycho-sexual centre is originally weak, is in a different position. All possible psychical and physical deficiences, especially neurasthenic, are able to impair his weakened sexuality, homologous though it may have been hitherto to the sexual glands. These evil influences may render him furthermost psychically bi-sexual, then invertedly mono-sexual, and eventually may effect even castration, by way of producing physical and psychical characters of sexuality, in the sense of predominating antipathic, or the destruction of original, centres. On pages 188, etc., I have tried to show in how far neurasthenia may give the impulse for the development of antipathic sexuality.

CONGENITAL ANTIPATHIC SEXUAL INSTINCT IN MAN.

The sexual acts by means of which male homosexuals seek and find satisfaction are multifarious. There are individuals of fine feeling and strength of will who sometimes satisfy themselves with platonic love, with the risk however, of becoming nervous (neurasthenic) and insane as a result of this enforced abstinence. In other instances, for the same reasons which may lead normal individuals to avoid coitus, onanism for want of something better is indulged in.

In homosexuals with nervous systems congenitally irritable, or injured by onanism (irritable weakness of the ejaculation centre), simple embraces or caresses, with or without contact of the genitals, are sufficient to induce ejaculation and consequent satisfaction. In less irritable individuals, the sexual act consists of manustupration by the loved person, or mutual onanism, or imitation of coitus between the thighs. In homosexuals morally perverse and potent, in regard to erections, the sexual desire is satisfied by pederasty—an act, however, which is repugnant to perverted individuals that are not defective morally, much in the same way as it is to normal men. The statement of homosexuals is remarkable, that the adequate sexual act with persons of the same sex gives them a feeling of great satisfaction and accession of strength, while satisfaction by solitary onanism, or by enforced coitus with a woman, affects them in an unfavorable way, making them miserable and increasing their neurasthenic symptoms.

As to the frequency [91] of the occurrence of the anomaly, it is difficult to reach a just conclusion, since those affected with it not often break from their reserve; and in criminal cases the homosexual with perversion of sexual instinct is usually classed with the person given to pederasty for simply vicious reasons. According to *Casper's* and *Tardieu's*, as well as my own, experience, this anomaly is much more frequent than reported cases would lead us to presume.

Ulrichs ("Kritische Pfeile," p. 2, 1880) declares that, on an average, there is one person affected with antipathic sexual instinct to every 200 mature men, or to every 800 of the population; and that the percentage among the Magyars and South Slavs is still greater,—statements which may be regarded as untrustworthy. The subject of one of my cases knows personally, at his home (13,000 inhabitants), fourteen homosexuals. He further declares that he is acquainted with at least eighty in a city of 60,000 inhabitants. It is to be presumed that this man, otherwise worthy of belief, makes no distinction between the congenital and the acquired anomaly.

1. *Psychical Hermaphroditism.*[92]

The characteristic mark of this degree of inversion of the sexual instinct is that, by the side of the pronounced sexual instinct and desire for the same sex, a desire toward the opposite sex is present; but the latter is much weaker and is manifested episodically only, while homosexuality is primary, and, in time and intensity, forms the most striking feature of the sexual life.

The hetero-sexual instinct may be but rudimentary, manifesting itself simply in unconscious (dream) life; or (episodically, at least) it may be powerfully exhibited.

The sexual instinct toward the opposite sex may be strengthened by the exercise of will and self-control; by moral treatment, and possibly by hypnotic suggestion; by improvement of the constitution and the removal of *neuroses* (neurasthenia); but especially by abstinence from masturbation.

However, there is always the danger that homosexual feelings, in that they are the most powerful, may become permanent, and lead to enduring and exclusive antipathic sexual instinct. This is especially to be feared as a result of the influences of masturbation (just as in acquired inversion of the sexual instinct) and its neurasthenia and consequent exacerbations; and, further, it is to be found as a consequence of unfavourable experiences in sexual intercourse with persons of the opposite sex (defective feeling of pleasure in coitus, failure in coitus on account of weakness of erection and premature ejaculation, infection).

On the other hand, it is possible that aesthetic and ethical sympathy with persons of the opposite sex may favour the development of heterosexual desires. Thus it happens that the individual, according to the predominance of favourable or unfavourable influences, experiences now hetero-sexual, now homosexual, feeling.

It seems to me probable that such hermaphrodites from constitutional taint are rather numerous.[93] Since they attract very little attention socially, and since such secrets of married life are only exceptionally brought to the knowledge of the physician, it is at once apparent why this interesting and practically important transitional group to the group of absolute inverted sexuality has thus far escaped scientific investigation.

Many cases of frigidity of wives and husbands may possibly depend upon this anomaly. Sexual intercourse with the opposite sex is, in itself, possible. At any rate, in cases of this degree, no horror of the other sex exists. Here is a fertile field for the application of medical and moral therapeutics (see below).

The differential diagnosis from acquired antipathic sexual instinct may present difficulties; for, in such cases, so long as the vestiges of a normal sexual instinct are not absolutely lost, the actual symptoms are the same (see below).

In the first degree, the sexual satisfaction of homosexual impulses consists in passive and mutual onanism and coitus between the thighs.

CASE 134. *Antipathic sexual instinct with sexual satisfaction in hetero-sexual intercourse.* Mr. Z., aged thirty-six, consulted me on account of an anomaly of his sexual feelings, which had become a matter of anxiety to him in connection with an intended marriage. Patient's father was neuropathic, and suffered with nightmare and night-terrors. Grandfather was also neuropathic; father's brother an idiot. Patient's mother and her family were healthy and normal mentally. The patient had three sisters and one brother, the latter being subject to moral insanity. Two sisters were healthy, and enjoying happy married lives.

As a child, the patient was weak, nervous, and subject to night-terrors, like his father; but he never had any severe illness, except *coxitis*, as a result of which he limped slightly. Sexual impulses were manifested early. At eight, without any teaching, he began to masturbate. From his fourteenth year, ejaculation. He was mentally well endowed, and his principal interest was in art and literature. He was always weak muscularly, and had no inclination for boyish sports and later for manly occupations. He had a certain interest for female toilettes, ornaments, and occupations. From the time of puberty the patient noticed in himself an inexplicable inclination towards male persons. Youths of the lowest classes were most attractive to him. Cavalry men especially excited his interest. He experienced a lustful desire to press himself against such individuals from behind. Occasionally, in crowds, it was possible for him to do this; and in such an event an intense feeling of pleasure passed over him. After his twenty-second year, on such occasions, he now and then had an ejaculation. From that time ejaculation occurred when a sympathetic man laid his hand on the patient's thigh. He was now in great anxiety lest he might sometime assault a man sexually. People of the lower classes, wearing tight, brown trousers, were especially dangerous for him. His greatest pleasure would be to embrace such a man and press himself to him; but, unfortunately, the morality of his country did not allow such a thing. Pederasty seemed disgusting to him.

It gave him great pleasure to gain a sight of the genitals of males. He was always compelled to look at the genitals of every man he met. In circuses, theatres, etc., only male performers interested him. Patient had never noticed any inclination for women. He did not avoid them, even danced with them on occasion, but he never felt the slightest sensual excitation under such circumstances.

At the age of twenty-eight the patient was neurasthenic as a result of his excessive masturbation.

Then frequent pollutions in sleep occurred, which weakened him very much. It was only occasionally that he dreamed of men when he had pollutions; and never of women. A lascivious dream-picture (pederasty) had occurred but once. He dreamed of death-scenes, of being attacked by dogs, etc. After these, as before, he suffered with great *libido*. Often there came up before him such lascivious thoughts as gloating over the death of animals in the slaughter-house, or allowing himself to be whipped by boys; but he always overcame such desires, and also the impulse to dress in a military uniform.

In order to cure himself of masturbation, and to thoroughly satisfy his *libido*, he determined to frequent brothels. He first attempted sexual intercourse with a woman when twenty-one, after over-indulgence in wine. The beauty of the female form, and female nudity in general, made no impression on him. However, he was able to enjoy the act of coitus, and thereafter he visited brothels regularly for "purposes of health."

From this time he took great pleasure in hearing men tell stories of their sexual relations with the opposite sex.

Ideas of flagellation would also come to him while in a brothel, but the retention of such fancies was not essential for the performance of coitus. He considered sexual intercourse with prostitutes only a remedy against the desire for masturbation and men—a kind of safety-valve to prevent compromising himself with some man.

The patient wished to marry, but feared not only that he could have no love for a decent woman, but also that he might be impotent for intercourse with her. Hence his thought and need of medical advice.

The patient was very intelligent, and, in all respects, was of masculine appearance. In dress and manner he presented nothing that would attract attention. Gait, voice and frame—the pelvis especially—masculine in character. Genitals of normal development. The normal growth of hair for a male was abundant. The patient's relatives and friends had not the slightest suspicion of his sexual anomalies. In his inverted sexual fantasies he had never felt himself in the rôle of a woman towards a man. For some years he had been entirely free from neurasthenic troubles.

The question as to whether he considered himself a subject of congenital sexual inversion he could not answer. It seems probable that there was a congenital weak inclination for the opposite sex, with a greater one for the same sex, which, as a result of early masturbation in consequence of the homosexual instinct, was still more weakened, but not reduced to nil. With the cessation of masturbation, the feeling for women became in a measure more natural, but only in a coarsely sensual way.

Since the patient explained that, for reasons of family and business, it was necessary for him to marry, it was impossible to eliminate this delicate point.

Fortunately, the patient confined himself to the question as to his virility as a husband; and it was necessary to reply that he was virile, and that he would probably be so in conjugal intercourse with the wife of his choice—at least, if she were to be in mental sympathy with him; moreover that he could at all times improve his power by exercising his imagination in the right direction.

The main object was to strengthen the sexual inclination for the opposite sex, which was defective, but not absolutely wanting. This could be done by avoiding and opposing all homosexual feelings and impulses, possibly with the help of the artificial inhibitory influences of hypnotic suggestion (removal of homosexual desires by suggestion); by the excitation and exercise of normal sexual desires and impulses;

by complete abstinence from masturbation, and eradication of the remnants of the neurasthenic condition of the nervous system by means of hydrotherapy, and possibly general faradization.

CASE 135. V., age twenty-nine, official; father hypochondriac, mother neuropathic; four other children normal; one sister homo-sexual.

V. was very talented, learned easily and had a most excellent religious education. Very nervous and emotional. At the age of nine he began to masturbate of his own accord. When fourteen he recognized the danger of this practice and fought with some success against it; but he began to rave about male statuary, also about young men. When puberty set in, he took slight interest in women. At twenty, first intercourse with a woman, but though potent, he derived no satisfaction from it. Afterwards only for want of something better (about six times) hetero-sexual intercourse.

He admitted to have had very frequently intercourse with men (mutual masturbation, coitus between the thighs, fellatio). He took either the active or passive *rôle*.

At the consultation he was in despair and wept bitterly. He abhorred his sexual anomaly, and said that he had desperately battled against it, but without success. In woman he found only moderate animal satisfaction, psychical gratification being totally absent. Yet he craved for the happiness of family life.

Excepting an abnormally broad pelvis (100 cm.) there was nothing in his character or personal appearance that lacked the qualities of the masculine type.

CASE 136. K., age thirty; in the family on his mother's side there were several cases of insanity.

Both parents were neurasthenic, irritable and excitable, and lived unhappily together.

K. had from his early childhood sympathy only for men, chiefly for male servants.

Pollutions at the age of fourteen, often coupled with homosexual dreams.

Descriptions of bullfights and tortures of animals greatly excited him sexually.

When fifteen he began, of his own accord, auto-masturbation. At the age of twenty-one, homo-sexual intercourse with men (only mutual masturbation). Off and on psychical onanism associated with thoughts of men.

His inclinations to women were of a transient nature. When pressed to enter wedlock he could not decide in its favour.

He never had intercourse with a woman, partly because he had no confidence in his virility, and partly from fear of infection.

For years he was highly neurasthenic, which rendered him for whole periods psychically unfit for any kind of work. He was listless and devoid of energy, but in structure and personal appearance masculine. Genitals normal.

Advice: Treatment for neurasthenia, energetic combat with homosexual desires, society of ladies, eventually coitus condomatus. Wedlock, when suited, as his station in life demanded it.

After four months K. returned. He had conscientiously acted upon the medical advice, was successful in coitus, dreamed of women, disdained the idea of sexual relations with men, but during the heated season still experienced homosexual impulses (due to exacerbation of neurasthenia, superinduced by the hot weather).

He hoped to marry at an early date, and anticipated much happiness from the married state.

CASE 137. *Psychical hermaphroditism.* Hetero-sexual feeling early interfered with by masturbation, but episodically very intense. Homosexual feeling from the beginning perverse (sexual excitation by men's boots).

Mr. X., of high social position, aged twenty-eight, came to me in September, 1887, in a despairing mood, to consult me on account of a perversion of his sexual life which made life seem almost unbearable to him, and which had repeatedly brought him near to suicide. The patient came of a family in which neuroses and psychoses had been of frequent occurrence. In the father's family there had been marriage between first cousins for three generations. The father was said to have been a healthy man, and to have lived morally in marriage. However, his father's preference for fine-looking servants seemed remarkable to the son. The mother's family was described as eccentric. The mother's grandfather and great-grandfather died melancholic; her sister was insane; a daughter of the grandfather's brother was hysterical, and had nymphomania. Only three of the mother's twelve brothers and sisters married. Of these, one brother was homosexual, and always nervous as a result of excessive masturbation. The patient's mother was said to have been a bigot of small mental endowment, nervous, irritable, and inclined to melancholia.

Patient had a sister and a brother. The brother was neuropathic and frequently melancholic; and, though mature had never shown the slightest trace of sexual inclinations. The sister was an acknowledged beauty, and much sought by gentlemen. This lady was married, but childless, as reported, owing to the impotence of her husband. She had always been indifferent to the attentions shown her by men, but was charmed by female beauty, and actually in love with some of her female friends.

With respect to himself, the patient asserted that when he was four years old he dreamed of handsome jockeys wearing shining boots.

He never dreamed of women when he grew older. His nightly pollutions were always induced by "boot-dreams." From his fourth year he had a peculiar partiality for men, or, more correctly, for lackeys wearing shining boots. At first they only excited his interest, but with development of his sexual functions, the sight of them caused powerful erections and lustful pleaure. It was only servants' boots that affected him; the same kind of boots on persons of like social station were without effect on him. In a homo-sexual sense, there was no sexual impulse connected with these situations. Even the thought of such a possibility was disgusting to him. At times, however, he had sensually coloured ideas—such as being his servant's servant, and drawing off his boots; the idea of being stepped on by him, or of having to blacken his boots, was most pleasing. The pride of the aristocrat rose up against such thoughts. In general, these notions about boots were disgusting and painful to him.

Sexual instinct was early and powerfully developed. It first found expression in indulgence in sensual thoughts about boots, and, after puberty, in dreams accompanied by pollutions; otherwise, mental and physical development was undisturbed. Patient was well endowed mentally—learned easily, finished his studies, and became an officer. On account of his distinguished, manly appearance and his high position, he was much sought in society.

He characterized himself as a clever, quiet, strong-willed, but superficial man. He asserted that he was a passionate hunter and rider, and that he had never had any inclination for feminine pursuits. In the society of ladies he had always been reserved; dancing always tired him. He never had an interest in any lady of high social position. As for women, only the buxom peasant girls, such as are the models of painters in Rome, had taken his fancy. He had, however, never felt any sexual interest even in such representatives of the female sex. At the theatre and circus only male performers had attracted him; but, at the same time, they caused him no sensual feelings. As for men, only their boots excited him, and, indeed, only when the wearers belonged to the servant class and were handsome men. Men of his own position, wearing ever so fine boots, were absolutely indifferent to him.

With reference to his sexual inclinations, the patient was still uncertain whether he felt these more towards the opposite sex or his own. He was inclined to think that originally he had more inclination for women, but that this sympathy was, in any case, very weak. He stated with certainty that the sight of a naked man made no impression on him, and that the sight of male genitals was even repugnant to him. As for woman, this was not exactly the case; but even the most beautiful feminine form did not excite him sexually. When a young officer, he was now and then compelled to accompany his comrades to brothels. He was the more easily persuaded to this, since he hoped by this means to get rid of his vile partiality for boots; but he was impotent unless he brought the thought of boots to his aid. Under such circumstances, the act of cohabitation was normally performed, but without pleasurable feeling. Patient felt no impulse to intercourse with women, always requiring some external cause—*i.e.*, persuasion. Left to himself his sexual life consisted in revelling in ideas about boots, and in corresponding dreams coupled with pollutions. As the impulse to kiss his servant's boots, to draw them off, etc., became more and more connected with these dreams and ideas the patient determined to use every means to rid himself of this disgusting desire, which deeply wounded his pride. At that time, being in his twentieth year, and in Paris, he recalled a very beautiful peasant girl, who lived in his distant home. He hoped, with her assistance, to free himself of his sexual perversion. He went home, and tried to win the girl's favor. He asserted that at that time he was deeply in love with this person, and that the sight of her, or the touch of her dress, gave him sensual pleasure; and, when she once kissed him, he had a powerful erection. After about a year and a half, the patient succeeded in gaining his desires with this person.

He was potent, but ejaculated tardily (ten to twenty minutes), and never had a pleasurable feeling in the act.

After about a year and a half of sexual intercourse with this girl, his love for her grew cold, because he did not find her so "fine and pure" as he wished. From this time it was necessary for him to call upon ideas about boots for help, which had been latent, in order to be potent in sexual intercourse with her. In proportion as his power failed, these ideas arose spontaneously. Thereafter he had coitus with other women. Now and then, especially when the woman was in sympathy with him, the act took place without any assistance of imagination.

It once happened that the patient committed rape. It is remarkable that on this single occasion he had a pleasurable feeling in the (forced) act. Immediately after the deed he had a feeling of disgust. When, an hour after the forced indulgence, he had coitus with the same woman, with her consent, he experienced no feeling of pleasure.

With the decline of virility—*i.e.*, when it was maintained only with ideas about boots—*libido* for the opposite sex decreased. The patient's slight *libido* and weak inclination for women were evidenced by the fact that, while he still sustained sexual relations with the peasant girl, he began to masturbate. He learned the vice from "Rousseau's Confessions," the book accidentally falling into his hands. The boot-fancies immediately linked themselves with corresponding impulses. He then had violent erections, masturbated, and ejaculation afforded him a lively feeling of pleasure, which was denied to him in coitus; and at first he felt himself mentally brighter and fresher, as a result of masturbation.

In time, however, symptoms of sexual, and later on of general neurasthenia, with spinal irritation, appeared. He then temporarily gave up masturbation, and sought his first love; but she was now more than ever indifferent to him. Since he finally became impotent, even when he called ideas of boots to his assistance, he gave up women entirely, and again practiced masturbation, which protected him from the impulse to kiss and blacken, etc., servants' boots. At the same time, he felt his sexual position keenly. He again occasionally attempted coitus, and was successful in it as soon as he thought of blackened boots. After continued abstinence from masturbation, he was at times successful in coitus without any artificial aid.

The patient said that his sexual needs were intense. If no ejaculation had taken place for a long time, he became congestive, psychically much excited, and tormented by repugnant images of boots, so that he was forced to have coitus, or, preferably, to masturbate.

During the past year his moral position became most painfully complicated by the fact that, as the last of a wealthy line of high position, and at the importunate desire of his parents, he must marry. The bride was of rare beauty, and mentally in perfect sympathy with him; but, as a woman, she was as indifferent to him as any other. Aesthetically she satisfied him "as any work of art would"; in his eyes, she was simply ideal. To honor her in a platonic way would be happiness worth striving for; but to possess her as a wife was a painful thought. He was certain beforehand that with her he would be impotent, save with the help of ideas of boots. To use such means, however, was in opposition to his respect and his moral and aesthetic feelings for the lady. Were he to soil her with such thoughts, she would lose, in his eyes, all her aesthetic value; and then he would become impotent for her, and she would become repugnant to him. The patient considered his position one of despair, and confessed that he had of late been repeatedly near suicide.

He was a man of much intelligence, and decidedly of masculine appearance, with abundant growth of beard, deep voice, and normal genitals. The eye had a neuropathic expression. No signs of degeneration. Symptoms of spinal neurasthenia. It was possible to reassure the patient, and give him hope of his future.

The medical advice consisted in means for combating the neurasthenia, and the interdiction of masturbation and indulgence of the fancy in images of boots, in the hope that, with the removal of the neurasthenia, cohabitation without ideas of boots would become possible; and that, in time, the patient would become morally and physically capable of marriage.

In the latter part of October, 1888, the patient wrote to me that he had resolutely resisted masturbation and his imagination. In the interval he had had but one dream about boots, and scarcely a pollution. He had been free from homosexual inclinations, but, in spite of this, there was often considerable sexual excitement, without anything like adequate *libido* for woman. In this deplorable situation, he was now compelled by circumstances to marry in three months.

2. HOMOSEXUAL INDIVIDUALS, OR URNINGS.

In contradistinction from the preceding group of psycho-sexual heraphrodites, there are here predominant, from the beginning, sexual desires and inclinations for persons of the same sex exclusively; but, in contrast with the following group, the anomaly is limited to the sexual life, and does not more deeply and seriously affect character and mental personality.

The sexual life of these homosexuals, with due alteration of details, is entirely like that in normal hetero-sexual love; but, since it is the exact opposite of the natural feeling, it becomes a caricature, and the more so as these individuals, at the same time, and as a rule, are subject to excessive sexual desire: for which reason, their love for their own sex is emotional and passionate.

The homosexual loves and deifies the male object of his affections, just as the normal man idealizes the woman he loves. He is capable of the greatest sacrifice for him, and experiences the pangs of unhappy, often unrequited, love; he suffers from the disloyalty of the beloved object, and is subject to jealousy, etc.

The attention of the male-loving man is given only to male dancers, actors, athletes, statues, etc. The sight of female charms is indifferent to him, if not repulsive. A naked woman is disgusting to him, while the sight of male genitals, hips, etc., affords him infinite pleasure.

Bodily contact with a sympathetic man induces a thrill of delight; and, since such individuals are in most cases sexually neurasthenic (congenitally or from onanism or enforced abstinence from sexual intercourse), under such circumstances ejaculation is very easily induced, which even in the most intimate intercourse with women cannot be induced at all, or only by mechanical means. The sexual act with a man, in many instances, affords pleasure, and leaves behind a feeling of comfort. Should the homosexual be able to force himself to coitus, in which, as a rule, disgust has the effect of an inhibitory character, and makes the act possible, then his feeling is something like that of a man compelled to take disgusting food or drink. However, experience teaches that not infrequently urnings belonging to this group marry, either from ethical or social considerations.

Such unfortunates are relatively potent, in so far that in marital intercourse they incite their imagination, and, instead of thinking of their wives, they call up the image of some loved male person. But for them coitus is a great sacrifice, and no pleasure. It makes them, for days after, nervous and miserable. If such homosexuals, by means of powerful stimulation of their fancy, or under the influence of alcoholic drink, or by erections induced by an overfilled bladder, etc., are not enabled to overcome the inhibitory feelings and ideas, then they are entirely impotent; while the mere touch of a man may induce intense erection, and even ejaculation.

Dancing with a woman is unpleasant to a homosexual, but to dance with a man, especially one with an attractive form, is to him the greatest of pleasures.

The male homosexual, if he possess higher culture, is not opposed to non-sexual intercourse with woman, when by mind and refinement they make conversation charming. It is only woman in her sexual *rôle* that he abhors.

In this degree of sexual degeneration, character and occupation correspond with the sex which the individual represents. Sexual perversion remains an isolated anomaly of the mental being of the individual, deeply affecting the social existence. In accordance with this, these individuals feel themselves during the sexual act in the same *rôle* which would naturally be theirs in hetero-sexual intercourse.

However, transitions to group 3 occur, inasmuch as sometimes the passive *rôle* which corresponds with homosexual feeling is thought of or desired, or at least forms the subject of dreams. Moreover, leanings to occupations and tendencies of taste are manifested which do not correspond with the sex of the individual. In many cases one gets the impression that such symptoms are artificial, the result of educational influences; in other cases, that they represent deeper acquired degenerations of the original anomaly, superinduced by perverse sexual activity (masturbation), and analogous to the signs of progressive degeneration observed in acquired sexual inversion.

Regarding the manner of sexual satisfaction, it must be stated that with many male homosexuals, the mere embrace is sufficient to induce ejaculation, subject as they are to irritable weakness of the sexual apparatus. In cases of sexual hyperaesthesia, and of paraesthesia of the moral sense, great pleasure is afforded by intercourse with persons of the lowest condition.

On the same basis, desire to commit pederasty (active, of course) and other similar aberrations occur, though it is but seldom, and apparently only in cases of moral defect and by reason of excessive desire in especially passionate individuals, that active pederasty is indulged in.

The sexual desire of mature homosexuals, *in contradistinction to old and decrepit debauchees, who prefer boys (and indulge in pederasty by preference*), *seems never to be directed to immature males.* Only for want of better material, and in case of violent passion, does the urning become dangerous to boys.

CASE 138. Z., age thirty-six, wholesale merchant; parents were said to have been healthy; physical and mental development normal; irrelevant children's diseases; at fourteen onanism of his own accord; began to rave about boys of his own age when fifteen. Never took the slightest notice of the opposite sex.

At twenty-four he went for the first time to a brothel, but took to flight when he saw the nude female figure.

At twenty-five sexual intercourse with men of his own stamp (fervent embraces with ejaculation, at times mutual masturbation).

For business reasons, and with a view to curing his abnormal passion, he married at the age of twenty-eight a lady endowed with many physical and mental charms. By the aid of imagination (thinking of intercourse with a handsome young man), Z. succeeded in being potent with his wife, whom at heart he loved passionately. This strain, however, superinduced neurasthenia. When a child was born he gradually withdrew from his wife, who was anyhow endowed with a frigid nature, chiefly because he was haunted by the fear of procreating offspring afflicted with his own anomaly.

Homosexual feelings and thoughts began to sway him again, which he sought to eradicate by means of masturbation.

He fell in love with a handsome young man, but overcame the weakness at the cost of his own health as the severe struggle brought on a pronounced attack of cerebral neurasthenia. He came to me for advice, as his homosexual tendency had become too powerful to be resisted any longer. He was afraid that his secret affliction might be discovered, thus rendering his position in society impossible. Like many of his fellow-sufferers he had taken to drink. Although he found that alcohol relieved his nervous disorders (physical weakness, psychical inertness and depression) his *libido* was increased.

Z. was a man of refined thought, mentally well endowed, in appearance masculine and normal. He deeply deplored his position and loathed his weakness to automasturbation (at times also mutual).

Mutual kisses and embraces satisfied him. Morally, he said, he had sunk so low that he would feign abandon himself to this perverse passion were it not for the consideration he had for his wife and child.

My advice was to strenuously combat these homosexual impulses, perform his marital duties whenever possible, eschew alcohol and masturbation, which increases homosexual feelings and kills the love for woman, and undergo treatment for neurasthenia. If he could not find relief and the situation became unbearable he must confine himself to kisses and embraces with the male.

CASE 139. V., aged thirty-six, merchant; mother psychopathic; sister healthy; brother neuropsychopathic.

V. was early drawn to persons of his own sex, at first to school- and playmates; with the advent of puberty to adults; never to persons of the opposite sex whose charms had no interest for him. At the age of six he felt annoyed at not being a girl. Dolls and girls' games he always preferred.

At twelve a schoolmate seduced him to masturbate. His dreams (with pollutions when virile) were exclusively of an homosexual character. He practiced mutual masturbation with men, coitus between the thighs, exceptionally sucking the other person's member. He had felt a pronounced position as to the active or passive *rôle* in the act. Rarely and only for want of something better, coitus with a woman. He was potent when he thought during the act of a man, but never experienced real pleasure. The sexual act with a woman appeared to him as a miserable substitute for the homosexual act. During recent years intimate relations with a young man.

V. acknowledged the abnormality of his sexual life.

Genitals normal. Secondary physical and psychical sexual characteristics thoroughly masculine. No pathological conditions. Arrested for having committed mutual masturbation, he was tried, found guilty and sent to prison. He felt his sentence keenly, but only because it brought dishonour to him and his family. He could not help feeling and acting in his abnormal manner.

CASE 140. H., age thirty, member of high society; mother neuropathic.

When a boy he felt drawn to his schoolmates. At the age of four-teen a playmate older than himself committed pederasty on him. He liked it, but nevertheless felt pangs of conscience and never allowed the act to be repeated again. Later on he practiced mutual masturbation. As neurasthenia increased it sufficed when he embraced and pressed a companion to himself to produce ejaculation. He confined himself to this method when seeking satisfaction. He never had a liking for persons of the other sex and was unconscious of his anomaly. At twenty he made some attempts, among girls, in order to cure his sexual life. Up to that time he had looked upon his abnormal practices merely as a youthful aberration. He was potent in coitus, but derived no gratification from it, for which reason he turned to man again. His weakness was for young men eighteen to twenty years of age. He had no sympathy for men older than that. He never played a well defined *rôle* in his relations with other men, but his social situation affected him keenly. He was forever haunted by the fear of detection, and said he could never survive the shame of it. There was nothing in habits or behaviour which betrayed antipathic sexual instinct. Genitals normal. No signs of degeneration. He had no faith in ever changing his abnormal sexuality. For women he had no taste whatsoever.

CASE 141. Y., age forty, manufacturer; father neuropathic; died of cerebral apoplexy; mother's family with taint of insanity; two other children of the family, though sexually normal, were constitutionally neuropathic. At eight masturbation of his own accord. At fifteen he felt drawn to other handsome boys of his own age, of whom he seduced several to masturbation. With puberty he was attracted by youths seventeen to twenty years of age, but they must be beardless and have pretty, soft and girl-like features. Girls had no charm for him.

He soon recognized the pathological character of his sexual life; but he considered his method of satisfying his abnormal needs as in accordance with nature and felt no remorse. To touch a woman was loathsome to him. He had twice attempted coitus, but without success. In like manner, he looked upon auto-masturbation as a filthy act. He averred that he had honestly striven to strip off this dreadful impulse, which made an outcast of him before the whole world. But all his efforts were in vain, for he felt forced by nature to seek satisfaction in his own manner. He always played the active *rôle* and confined himself entirely to acts not proscribed by the law of the land. Yet he became involved in some affair, lost his position, which was one of confidence and good remuneration, became a vagabond until he decided to cross the ocean and begin a new life. Being clever and honourable he succeeded.

When first I met Y., he was in despair and firmly contemplated suicide, especially since a medical man had failed with hypnotic treatment, on account of Y. not reacting to suggestion.

He was inclined to neurasthenia. Penis small. No pathological symptoms. Masculine in every respect.

CASE 142. T., age thirty-four; merchant; mother neuropathic and weakly; father healthy. At the age of nine a schoolmate taught him how to masturbate. He practiced mutual masturbation with his brother, who slept with him in the same bed; once taking the penis into the mouth. On one occasion, when yet a boy, it happened he licked the place where previously a soldier had urinated. At fourteen first love for a schoolmate of ten. At the age of seventeen he took a dislike to handsome young men, and centered his affection in decrepit old men.

One night he heard his aged father "give a groan of sexual satisfaction." This excited him immensely as he imagined his father performing the marital act. Since that time the picture of old men performing the homosexual act enlivened his dreams (with pollution), and was present in his mind during masturbation. The older, the more decrepit and feeble the old man was, when he saw such, the stronger his sexual excitement would be even unto ejaculation. At twenty-three he sought a cure with a prostitute; but erection failed him, and he made no other attempts. Young men and boys left him callous.

At twenty-nine he conceived a violent love for an old man whom he accompanied for years on his daily walks. Intimate relations were, however, precluded. But he often had ejaculations on these walks. To free himself of this humiliating situation he once more went to a prostitute, but it proved a fiasco. He now fell upon the idea to hire a decrepit old man, take him along and make him have coitus whilst he looked on. This caused erection in him, and he was able to have coitus himself. The act, however, gave him no pleasure, but he felt psychically relieved, especially when he was potent in the absence of the old man. But this did not last long. He became sexually and generally neurasthenic, depressed, shy and impotent, and gave himself up to psychical onanism coupled with thoughts of old men in homosexual situations.

T. was masculine in appearance, and presented no special marks beyond his heavy sexual neurasthenia.

CASE 143. Z., age twenty-eight, merchant; father very nervous and irritable; mother hysteropathic. He was himself constitutionally nervous, suffered from enuresis to his eighteenth year, and was a frail boy. Proper physical development really began only when he was twenty years of age. The first sexual emotions he experienced when, a boy of eight, he witnessed other boys being caned on the buttocks. Although he felt compassion for the boys, he yet had a feeling of lustful pleasure pervading his whole body. Some time afterwards he was late for school and on the way the anticipation of a caning on the buttocks excited him so much that for a short time he could not move and had violent erection.

At eleven he fell in love with a "beautiful, blond boy who had wondrously lovely, intelligent and lustrous eyes."

It gave him immense pleasure to see this boy home, and he often craved for kisses and caresses from him. But he recognized the unbecoming nature of this desire, and did not allow the boy to have an inkling of them.

At that time he met a girl once, two years his junior, who pleased him so much that he covered her with kisses. This, however, remained a solitary episode.

At thirteen he was seduced to onanism. But he did not cultivate the habit, as he found protection in his "more refined feelings for young men" and disdained to "drag his pure, divine love" in the gutter.

At seventeen he became desperately enamored with a companion "with lovely brown eyes, noble features and dark complexion." He suffered untold tortures through this unhappy love for two and one-half years, when he was separated from his companion. If ever he were to meet him again, the old fire would be certain to flare up anew. On two other occasions he fell in love with comrades, but not so violently as in the first instance. At twenty he had coitus, but derived no pleasure from the act. He continued his relations with women for the purpose of avoiding masturbation, to appear potent and to mask his homosexual tendency.

Although he had no horror of a woman, women did not excite him. "A woman is a work of art, a statue."

Endowed with a strong will power he was able to master his abnormal inclination. But his sexual position appeared to him unsatisfactory, especially as he looked upon coitus as a coarsely sensual enjoyment, and erection became difficult.

In the consultation no abnormal signs could be detected. He appeared to be virile and mentally sound.

CASE 144. P., age thirty-seven; mother very nervous, suffered from migraine. As a boy he was subject to attacks of hysteria gravis. Was always drawn to handsome young men and became highly excited when he could see their genitals. With puberty he practiced mutual masturbation with men; but they must be about twenty-five to thirty years old. He played the female rôle in the sexual act. He loved with the whole intensity of woman, and only posed as a man like an actor on the stage. Other boys sneered at him on account of his girlish ways and habits. In the hope of correcting his sexual life he married. He forced himself to coitus with the wife and produced potency by imagining her to be a young man. They had one child. But he himself became neurasthenic, his imagination waned and he became impotent. For two years he avoided coitus, resumed his homosexual practices and was apprehended by the police in the act of mutual masturbation with a young man.

He pleaded that prolonged sexual abstinence had unduly excited him when he saw the genitals of a man and in his confusion he had yielded to the impulse.

There was no amnesia. Thoroughly virile. Decent appearance. Genitals normal. Short imprisonment.

CASE 145. N., aged forty-one, unmarried. Father and mother near relatives, but both psychically normal. An uncle on the father's side was insane. N.'s brothers were hyper- and hetero-sexual. At the age of nine he felt strong inclinations to other boys. At fifteen mutual masturbation and coitus between the thighs.

At sixteen a love affair with a young man. His homosexual love developed, so he claimed, just as the love affairs between man and woman do in novels.

Only handsome young men of the age of twenty to twenty-four

attracted him. His erotic dreams were solely homo-sexual. He played the female *rôle*, also in actual intercourse with men.

His soul was of feminine character, so he said. He never cared for boys' games, only for cooking and girls' work. Manly sports and smoking and drinking he disdained. He led a varied life, served as a cook in a foreign country and gave great satisfaction; but he lost his place because he entered upon a love-affair with the son of his employer.

At twenty-two he recognized the abnormality of his sexual position. He became alarmed and began to frequent brothels to cure himself of his perverse habits, but erection absolutely failed him.

When his family discovered the true state of affairs he became confused with shame and made an attempt on his own life. But he recovered, went abroad (cast out by his family), disgusted with himself and his unhappy life. His only hope was that with old age relief would come. He came for medical advice to find "honour and rest." The secondary physical sexual characteristics were quite normal and of the masculine type. Genitals normal. He thought of castration or entering a monastery.

Advice: Suggestive treatment.

CASE 146. Once summer's evening, at twilight, X.Y., a doctor of medicine in a North German city, was trodden on by a watchman as he (the doctor) was committing an immoral act with a tramp on a path in a field. He was practicing masturbation on him and thereupon putting the tramp's penis into his mouth. X. escaped legal prosecution by flight. The state prosecutor's office decided not to institute proceedings, since there had been no public scandal and insertion of the penis in the (other party's) anus had not taken place. Extensive correspondence of a homosexual nature was found among X.'s possessions, which proved that for years he had been having homosexual relations of some intensity with all classes of people.

X. comes of a diseased family. His paternal grandfather died by suicide while insane. His father was a weak, peculiar man. One of the patient's brothers masturbated at the age of two. A cousin was sexually perverted and practiced the same immoral acts as X. when only a boy, became mentally unstable and died of a spinal disease. A paternal great-uncle was an hermaphrodite. His mother's sister was insane. His mother is said to be healthy. But X.'s brother is nervous and given to sudden and violent anger.

X. himself was also a nervous child. The miaowing of a cat would fill him with the greatest fear, and even if someone only imitated a cat, he would cry bitterly and run and cling to others for protection. Minor illnesses caused him to run a high temperature. He was a quiet, dreamy child, of excitable imagination, but of slight intellectual talent.

He did not indulge much in boyish games, put preferred girlish pastimes. It gave him special pleasure to curl the hair of the housemaid or of his brother.

At the age of 13, X. went to an institute. There he practiced mutual masturbation, seduced his comrades, and his cynical behavior made him so unmanageable that he had to be sent home. In those days his parents already found love-letters of lascivious and perverted sexual content belonging to him. From the age of 17 onwards he studied under the strict supervision of a high-school teacher. However, the progress he made in his work was pitifully slow. He only had talent for music. After completing his studies, the patient, now aged 19, went to a university. Here he attracted attention because of his cynical character and the fact that he went about with young men about whom rumors concerning homosexual habits were rife. He began to be dandified, showed a liking for spectacular ties, wore low-cut shirts, forced his feet into narrow boots, and curled his hair in an ostentatious way. These peculiarities disappeared, however, when he finished at the university and returned home.

At the age of 24 he began to pass through a long period of neurasthenia. From then until he was 29, he appeared to be serious-minded, and showed himself efficient in his profession; but his constant companions were always gentry of doubtful reputation and he avoided associating with the fair sex.

The patient would not allow a personal examination to be carried out on him, but excused himself in writing, saying that this would be no good, since his predilection for his own sex had existed since childhood and was congenital. He had always had a horror of women, and had never managed to bring himself to savour their charms. Towards men he felt himself in the role of a man. He acknowledged that his attraction towards his own sex was abnormal, but excused his sexual indulgence on the grounds that it was a naturally pathological condition.

Since his flight, X. has been living outside Germany, in the south of Italy, and, to judge from his letters, he still professes homosexuality. X. is a dignified, stately man of entirely masculine appearance; he has a thick beard and normally formed genitals. A short time ago, Dr. X. placed his autobiography at my disposal, and I have taken from it the following information which merits being passed on.

"When, at the age of seven, I began to attend a private school, I felt very ill at ease and found that my schoolmates were very uncongenial to me. I only felt myself drawn towards one of them, who was a very attractive child, and I loved him almost passionately. In our childish games, I always knew how to arrange it so that I could appear in girl's clothes, and I derived the greatest pleasure from making complicated hairstyles for our servant-girls. I often regretted not being a girl.

"My sexual instinct awakened when I was 13, and from the very beginning I sought out powerful-looking young men. At first, I wasn't quite sure as to whether this was abnormal; but I soon realized that it was when I saw and heard how my contemporaries were constituted sexually. I began to masturbate at the age of 13. When I was 17, I left home and went to a high-school in a larger city, where I was a boarder under the supervision of a high-school teacher, with whose son I subsequently had sexual intercourse. This was the first time that I experienced sexual satisfaction. Later on, I got to know a young artist there, who very soon noticed that I was abnormal and admitted to me that the same was true of himself. From him I learned that such abnormality was a common occurrence, and this information disposed of the idea, that often depressed me, that I was alone in my abnormality. This young man had a wide circle of similarly constituted acquaintances, to whom he introduced me. In this circle I attracted much attention, since it was asserted on all sides that I was very attractive physically. Soon I was the object of passionate love by an older man, but, not finding him to my taste, I only put up with him for a short time before responding to the overtures of a younger, most handsome officer, who swore he was my slave. Actually, this was my first love.

"After passing my final school examination, at the age of 19, I was free from school discipline and was able to make the acquaintance of a large number of people similar to, or just like, myself, among them Karl Ulrichs (Numa Numantius).

"Later, when I began my medical studies and associated with many normal young people, I was often in the position of having to accept a proposal to visit public prostitutes. Since I made myself look a complete fool with a number of these women who were very beautiful, the opinion began to gain ground among my acquaintances that I was impotent, and I lent substance to these rumours by alleging previous excesses with women. At that time, I knew a large number of people outside my immediate circle, and these were so full of my physical attraction that I was known far and wide as extraordinarily handsome. The result was that someone was always travelling to visit me, and I received such a quantity of love-letters that this often created embarrassment for me. The situation reached its climax somewhat later, when I was living at the hospital as a physician of one year's standing. There I moved about like a celebrity, and the jealous scenes of which I was the centre very nearly led to the exposure of the whole business. Shortly afterwards, I became ill through inflammation of a shoulder-joint, and only recovered after three months. During my indisposition I had been receiving several sub-cutaneous injections of morphium, which were then discontinued, but which I continued to give myself in secret during my convalescence. Next, I spent a few months in Vienna for purposes of special studies before my entry into independent practice. Here, recommendations from various people had gained me access to circles of persons similar to me, and I was able to observe that the abnormality in question is just as widespread, in its very varied manifestations, among the lower classes as in the higher; I also found that those who practice commercially, i.e., who are to be had for money, are not infrequently to be found among the upper classes as well.

"When I settled down as a doctor in the country, I had hoped to be able to rid myself of my addiction to morphium by means of cocaine, and thus fell a prey to the latter, whose hold I only succeeded in shaking off completely after three relapses (this was 1 year and 9 months ago). In my position, it was impossible for me to obtain sexual satisfaction, and it was therefore with pleasure that I discovered that cocaine resulted in the extinguishing of desire. The first time I succeeded in freeing myself from cocaine under the energetic care of my aunt, I went away for a few weeks to recover from the strain. But my perverted desires were again aroused in all their violence, and when one evening I had been amusing myself with a man in the open country just outside the town, I was informed the next day by the state prosecutor's office that I had been seen and denounced, but that the offense of which I was accused was not punishable, in accordance with a decision of the German High Court. Meanwhile I should watch my behavior, since the story of the occurrence had already become widely known. I therefore felt obliged to leave Germany after this episode and to seek myself a new home, where neither the law nor public opinion would be opposed to what, like all abnormal urges probably, could not be suppressed by mere strength of will. Since I did not doubt for one moment that my tendencies were contrary to current social concepts, I repeatedly tried to master my desire; but the only result was to intensify them, which impression has been confirmed to me by acquaintances. As I felt myself drawn exclusively towards powerful, youthful and entirely masculine individuals, that is, to a type that very seldom felt inclined to accede to my wishes, it often happened that I was forced to buy their favours. Since my desires are limited to persons of the lower social order, I could always find someone who could be had for money. I hope that the following revelations will not excite your repugnance; originally, I wanted to omit them, but I have to include them for the sake of the completeness of this information, since they should add important material to the case history. I experience the need to perform the sex act in the following manner:

"I take the penis of the young man in my mouth and move it with my mouth in such a way that he whom I desire ejaculates semen; I then spit out the sperms into his perinaeum, tell him to compress his thighs, and I insert my penis opposite and between his compressed thighs. While this is being done, it is necessary that the young man should embrace me as strongly as possible. These things that I have just told of having done give me the same pleasure as though I myself ejaculated. To obtain ejaculation by inserting the penis in the anus or by friction with the hand is in no way pleasant to me.

"On the other hand, I have found that those who received my penis and did what I have described above gave my desires complete satisfaction.

"With regard to my person, I must add the following: I am 186 cm tall, of entirely masculine appearance, and, apart from an abnormal irritability of the skin, in good health. I have very thick fair hair on my head, and my beard is also thick and fair. My genitals are of medium size and normally formed. I am able, without feeling tired, to perform the sex act I have described four to six times within twenty-four hours. My way of life is very moderate and regular. I consume only moderate quantities of alcohol and tobacco. I play the piano fairly well, and some of my compositions have been acclaimed with much enthusiasm. A short time ago I completed a novel, my first work, which has been favorably criticized by my friends. The subject of the novel concerns various problems in the lives of sexual perverts.

"Since a large number of my fellow-sufferers were known to me personally, I was naturally often in a position to make observations on the various kinds of abnormality. Perhaps it will be of use to you if I give you the following information.

"The most abnormal thing I ever knew of was the habit of a gentleman who lived near Berlin. He preferred young men with dirty feet to all others and would lick their feet like one possessed. A similar case was a gentleman in Leipzig, who is said to have derived very great pleasure from placing his tongue in an extremely dirty anus. There is a man in Paris who compelled one of my friends to urinate into his mouth. I am assured that there are various others who feel such ecstasy at the sight of riding boots or of military uniforms that they ejaculate spontaneously.

"There are two persons in Vienna who afford a particular example of the degree to which many feel like women—which is not so in my case. These individuals use women's names; one is a barber, who calls himself 'French Laura,' while the other, a former butcher, is called 'Selcher-Fanny.' Both of them lose no opportunity at carnival-time of appearing in female dress, and always in the most fantastic disguises. In Hamburg there is a person whom many believe to be a woman, because she is always dressed as such in her house, which she only leaves occasionally, and then also in female attire. This individual even wanted to pose as a godmother at a christening, which caused a great scandal.

"Feminine vices, such as love of gossip, unreliability and weakness of character, are the rule with such persons.

"I am acquainted with several cases of sexual perversion in whom epilepsy and psychoses are present. Hernias are quite frequent. In my practice, many persons come to me because of recommendations from friends to be treated for diseases of the anus. I saw two syphilitic and one local chancre, and several fissures; and at present I am treating a gentleman for condylomata of the anus, which form a rounded tumor as large as a fist and of similar shape to a cauliflower.

"In Vienna, I once saw a case of primary affection of the soft palate in a young man, who used to frequent fancy-dress balls dressed as a girl and entice young men; he would then pretend that he was menstruating, and thus induce the others to use him through the mouth. It was alleged that in this way he had once deceived fourteen men in one evening. Since, in none of the publications concerning sexual perversion, that I have seen, have I found anything concerning the intercourse of homosexuals among themselves, I should like, in conclusion, to add something more on the subject.

"As soon as sexual perverts make each other's acquaintance, there is a detailed exchange of information on their experiences to date, their love-affairs and conquests, provided such a conversation is not ruled out by social differences. Only in very few cases was there no such exchange with my new acquaintances. Among themselves perverts describe themselves as 'aunts,' in Vienna as 'sisters,' while two very manly looking public prostitutes in Vienna, whom I happened to meet and who had a homosexual relationship with each other, told me that the corresponding type in women goes by the name of 'uncle.' Since I have been aware of my own abnormal urge, I have met more than a thousand individuals similar to myself. Nearly every larger town has some sort of meeting place, as well as a so-called promenade. In smaller towns there are relatively few 'aunts'; however, in a small town of 2300 inhabitants, I found 8, in a town of 7000 inhabitants, 18, of whom I was absolutely sure—to say nothing of those whom I suspected. In my own native town of 30,000 inhabitants, I know about 120 'aunts' personally. Most of them—particularly myself, who possess the instinct to a very high degree—have the ability of being able to tell immediately whether another is also a pervert, or in the language of the 'aunts,' whether he is 'reasonable' or 'unreasonable.' My acquaintances are often surprised at the sureness of my judgments. Individuals who are apparently entirely masculine have been recognized by me as 'aunts' at first sight. On the other hand, I have the ability to behave in such a masculine way that people to whom I was recommended have expressed doubts as to my 'genuineness.' If I am in the mood, I can behave exactly like a woman.

"Since the majority of 'aunts,' including myself, do not regard their abnormality as a misfortune in any way, but would regret it if their condition should change, and since, furthermore, it is my opinion and that of all the others this congenital condition cannot be influenced, we all hope that an amendment may be introduced in the appropriate paragraph of the Criminal Law Code, so that only rape or the causing of a public scandal, when these can be proved at one and the same time, shall be deemed punishable."

3. EFFEMINATION.

There are various transitions from the foregoing cases to those making up this category, characterized by the degree in which the psychical personality, especially in general manner of feeling and inclinations, is influenced by the abnormal sexual feeling. In this group are fully developed cases in which males are females in feeling; and *vice versa* women, males. This abnormality of feeling and of development of the character is often apparent in childhood. The boy likes to spend his time with girls, play with dolls, and help his mother about the house; he likes to cook, sew, knit; he develops tastes in female *toilettes*, and even becomes the adviser of his sisters. As he grows older he eschews smoking, drinking and manly sports, and, on the contrary, finds pleasure in adornment of persons, art, *belle-lettres*, etc., even to the extent of giving himself entirely to the cultivation of the beautiful. Since woman possesses parallel inclinations, he prefers to move in the society of women.

If he can assume the role of a female at a masquerade it is his greatest delight. He seeks to please his lover, so to speak, by studiously trying to represent what pleases the female-loving man in the opposite sex—modesty, sweetness, taste for aesthetics, poetry, etc. Efforts to approach the female appearance in gait, attitude and attire are frequently seen.

With reference to the sexual feeling and instinct of these urnings, thoroughly permeated in all their mental being, the men, without exception, feel themselves to be females. Thus they feel themselves to be antagonistic to persons of their own sex constituted like themselves, as of course, they are like them in form. But, on the other hand, they are drawn towards those of their own sex that are homosexual or sexually normal. The same jealousy which occurs in normal sexual life also occurs here, when rivalry is threatened; and, indeed, since they are, as a rule, hyperaesthetic sexually, this jealousy is often boundless.

In cases of completely developed inverted sexuality, hetero-sexual love is looked upon as a thing absolutely incomprehensible; sexual intercourse with a person of the opposite sex is unthinkable, impossible. Such an attempt brings on the inhibitory concept of disgust or even horror, which makes erection impossible. Only two of my cases transitional to the third category were able, with the aid of imagination which made the female in question assume the *rôle* of man, to have coitus for the time being; but the act, which yielded no gratification, was a great sacrifice, and afforded no pleasure.

In homosexual intercourse effeminated man feels himself in the act always as a woman. The means of indulgence, where there is irritable weakness of the ejaculation centre, are simply lying underneath, or passive coitus between the thigh; in other cases, passive masturbation, or ejaculation into the mouth of the man desired. Some have a desire for passive pederasty; occasionally a desire for active pederasty occurs. In one attempt of this kind, the man desisted because of the disgust which seized him when the act reminded him of coitus.

There was never inclination for immature persons (boy-love.) Not infrequently there were only platonic desires.

CASE 147. E., aged thirty-one, son of an inveterate drunkard. No other taint in the family. Grew up in a village. At the age of six he began to feel happy when in the company of men with beards. At the age of eleven he began to blush whenever he met a handsome man, and dared not look at them. He was at ease when in the company of women. He wore girl's garments up to his seventh year, and was very unhappy when he was deprived of them. Occupation in the kitchen and about the house he liked best. His school time passed without events. Now and then he had intimate liking for a certain schoolmate, but this wore off.

Dreams of men with beards clad in blue clothes became more frequent.

He joined an athletic society that he might converse with men, liked to go to balls, not on account of the girls, who were a matter of indifference to him, but to see the fine men, thinking all the time that he was in the embrace of one of them. He felt lonely, however, and dissatisfied, and gradually became conscious of being quite unlike the other young fellows. All his thoughts and aims were to find a man who could love him.

At seventeen he was seduced by another man to mutual masturbation. Delight, shame and fear were the reaction. He recognized the abnormality of his sexual feelings, became depressed, came near committing suicide. He finally became reconciled with his abnormal position and craved for men, but being shy by nature he found but little opportunity. He felt uneasy when girls sought his company. When twenty-six he went to live in a large city and now found plenty of opportunities for homo-sexual intercourse. For some time he lived with another man of his own age as husband and wife. He felt happy in the rôle of woman. Sexual gratification was obtained by mutual masturbation and coitus between the thighs.

He was a skilful workman, well liked, and in appearance and behavior masculine. Genitals normal. No signs of degeneration.

His younger brother was also homosexual.

Two sisters, who both died young, avoided men, never cared for work in the kitchen, but preferred that in the stable, and were skilful in all handicrafts of men.

CASE 148. C., age twenty-eight, gentleman of leisure; father neuropathic; mother very nervous. One brother suffered from paranoia, another was psychically degenerated. Three younger members of the family were normal.

C. was neuropathically tainted; slight convulsive tic. As long as he can remember he felt drawn to male persons, at first only to his schoolmates. When puberty set in he fell in love with male teachers, who used to visit at the house of his parents. He felt himself in the female *rôle*. His dreams, with pollutions, were always about men. He was gifted in music and poetry and loved the theatre. For science, especially mathematics, he had no talents and passed his final examinations only with difficulty. Psychically, he declared, he was a woman. Loved to play with dolls and concerned himself by preference with woman's affairs, disdaining all the pursuits of men. He liked best the society of young girls, because they were sympathetic and had an affinity of soul. When in the company of men he was shy and confused like a maiden. He never smoked, and disliked alcoholic drinks. He feign would have liked to spend his time in cooking, knitting and embroidering. He had no libido. Sexual intercourse with men only a few times, although his ideal was to play the *rôle* of the woman on such occasions. Coitus with a woman he abhorred. After reading "Psychopathia Sexualis," he became alarmed, was afraid of coming in conflict with the police and avoided sexual relations with men. But pollutions became very frequent, and neurasthenia supervened. He came for medical advice.

C. had an abundant beard, and was of a decidedly masculine type, excepting soft features and a remarkably fine skin. Genitals normal, except a deficient descent of one of the testicles. In his behaviour, gait, and appearance nothing unusual, though he had the illusion that everybody noticed his abnormal sexual proclivity. He shunned society for that reason. Lascivious talk made him blush like a maiden. Once when someone turned the topic of conversation on antipathic sexual instinct, he fainted. Music brought on a heavy perspiration all over his body. Upon closer acquaintance he showed psychical femininity; he was as timid as a girl, and without a vestige of independence. Nervous restlessness, convulsive tic, numerous neurasthenic complications put on him the stamp of a constitutionally tainted neuropathic individual.

CASE 149. B., waiter, forty-two years of age, unmarried, was sent to me by his own physician (with whom he had fallen in love), as a case of sexual inversion. B. gave readily in modest language an account of his previous life and especially his sexual life. He seemed pleased to obtain at last an authentic explanation of his abnormal state which he had always considered a disease.

B. possessed no knowledge of his grandparents. The father was of an irascible, excitable nature, a drinker, and of strong sexual wants. After begetting twenty-four children with the same woman, he obtained a divorce, and after that had three children by his housekeeper. The mother was a healthy woman. Of the twenty-four children only six are now among the living, several of whom suffer from nervous affections, but are sexually normal, except one sister who for ever runs after the men.

B. claimed to have always been delicate and sickly. His sexual life awoke at the age of eight. He began to masturbate and derived much pleasure from stimulating the penis of other boys in his mouth. At the age of twelve he began to fall in love with men, preferring those in the thirties and with moustaches. His sexual needs at that period were extraordinary and erections and pollutions were frequent. He masturbated daily, thinking of some man whom he loved. His ambition was always to stimulate the penis of a man in his mouth, which thought caused ejaculation accompanied by the utmost lust. But only twelve times thus far had he been successful in this. He never felt nausea at the penis of others if they were sympathetic; on the contrary. Active as well as passive pederasty disgusted him thoroughly and he never accepted such offers. During the perverse act he played the *rôle* of woman. His love for sympathetic men was boundless. He could do anything for the man whom he thus loved, and when beholding him he trembled with excitement and lustful feelings.

When nineteen he was several times lured by his companions to a brothel, but coitus did not please him and only at the moment of ejaculation did he experience a sort of gratification. He could only be virile with woman when he thought of her during the act as the man whom he loved. He much rather would have preferred the woman to allow him fellatio; but she refused. For want of something better he indulged in coitus; twice even he was a father. The younger of the two children, now a girl of eight, has already begun masturbation and mutual onanism, which fact troubled him very much. Was there no remedy for this?

Patient said that towards men he always felt himself to be of feminine type (this also during sexual intercourse). His idea was that this sexual perversion originated from the fact that his father when begetting him wished to beget a girl. The other children of the family always teased him on account of his girlish ways and manners. To sweep the rooms and wash the dishes were ever pleasant occupations for him. His housework was always much admired and praised because he was cleverer than the girls. Whenever he could he would don girl's attire. At the *Mardi-gras* balls he always wore the female mask. He made a capital coquette on account of his female nature.

Drinking, smoking, manly sports and occupations never suited him, but he was passionately fond of sewing and was often upbraided on account of his weakness for dolls when a boy. When at the circus or the theatre his attention was only drawn to the male performers. He had an irresistible desire to loiter about W.C.'s. in order to get a look at the men's genitals.

Female charms never attracted him. Coitus was only possible when aided by the thought of a beloved man. Nocturnal pollutions were always produced by lascivious dreams about men.

Despite numerous sexual excesses B. had never suffered from *neurasthenia sexualis*; neither were there symptoms of neurasthenia of any kind.

Features delicate; sparse side whiskers and moustache, which began to grow only when he was twenty-eight. His external appearance, excepting a light, swinging gait, did not indicate female nature. He observed that he was often teased on account of his womanish carriage. His manners were highly modest. Genitals large, well developed, quite normal, with abundance of hair; pelvis masculine. Cranium affected by rickets, slightly hydrocephalic; parietal bones rather bulging. Countenance exceptionally small. Patient said he was easily provoked to wrath.

CASE 150. *Taylor* had occasion to examine a certain Eliza Edwards, aged twenty-four. It was discovered that she was of masculine sex. E. had worn female clothing from her fourteenth year, and had also been an actress. The hair was worn long, after the manner of females, and parted in the middle. The form of the face was feminine, but otherwise the body was masculine. The beard was carefully pulled out. The masculine, well-developed genitals were fixed in an upward position by an artful bandage. The condition of the anus indicated passive pederasty (Taylor, "Med. Jurisp." 1873, ii., p. 473).

CASE 151. An official of middle age, who for some years had been happy in family life, and was married to a virtuous woman, presented a peculiar manifestation of antipathic sexual feeling.

One day, through the indiscretion of a prostitute, the following scandal became public: About once a week X. would appear in a house of prostitution, and there dress himself up as a woman, always requiring, as a part of his costume, a *coiffure*. When his toilet was completed, he would lie down on the bed, and have the prostitute perform manustupration. But he very much preferred to have a male person (a servant of the house). This man's father was hereditarily tainted, had been insane several times, and was afflicted with excessive and lessened sexual desire.

4. HERMAPHRODITISM.

Forming direct transitions from the foregoing groups are those individuals of antipathic sexuality in whom not only the character and all the feelings are in accord with the abnormal sexual instinct, but also the frame, the features, voice, etc.; so that the individual approaches the opposite sex anthropologically, and in more than a psychical and psychosexual way. This anthropological form of the cerebral anomaly apparently represents a very high degree of degeneration; but that this variation is based on an entirely different ground than the teratological manifestation of hermaphroditism, in an anatomical sense, is clearly shown by the fact that thus far, in the domain of inverted sexuality, no transitions to hermaphroditic malformation of the genitals have been observed. The genitals of these persons always prove to be fully differentiated sexually, though not infrequently there are present anatomical signs of degeneration (*epispadiasis*, etc.), in the sense of arrests of development in organs that are otherwise well marked.

There is yet wanting a sufficient record of cases belonging to this interesting group of women in masculine attire with masculine genitals. Every experienced observer of his fellow-men remembers masculine persons that were very remarkable for their womanish character and type (wide hips, form rounded by abundant development of adipose tissue, absense or insufficient development of beard, feminine features, delicate complexion, falsetto voice, etc.).

In persons belonging to the fourth group, and in certain ones in the third, forming transitions to the fourth, there seems to be a feeling of shame (sexual) towards persons of the same sex, and not towards those of the opposite sex.

CASE 152. (Hermaphroditism). Mr. v. H., aged thirty, single; of neuropathic mother. Nervous and mental diseases were said not to have occurred in the patient's family, and his only brother was said to be mentally and physically completely normal. The pattient developed tardily physically, and, therefore, spent much of his time at the seashore and climatic resorts. From childhood he was of neuropathic constitution, and, according to the statements of his relatives, unlike other boys. His disinclination for masculine pursuits and his preference for feminine amusements were early remarked. Thus he avoided all boyish games and gymnastic exercises, while doll-play and feminine occupations were particularly pleasing to him. Subsequently he developed well physically, and escaped severe illnesses, but he remained mentally abnormal, incapable of an earnest aim in life, and decidedly feminine in thought and feeling.

In his seventeenth year pollution occurred, became more frequent, and finally took place during the day; so that the patient grew weak, and manifested various nervous disturbances. Symptoms of *neurasthenia* made their appearance, and lasted for some years, but they became milder with the decrease in the number of pollutions. Onanism was denied, but was very probable. An indolent, effeminate, dreamy habit of thought had become more and more noticeable ever since puberty. All efforts to induce the patient to take up an earnest pursuit in life were in vain. His intellectual functions, though formally quite undisturbed, were never equal to the motive of an independent character, and the higher ideals of life. He remained dependent, an overgrown child; and nothing more clearly indicated his original abnormal condition than an actual incapability to take care of money, and his own confession that he had no ability to use money reasonably; that as soon as he had money he wasted it for curios, toilet-articles, and the like.

Incapable as he was of a reasonable use of money, the patient was no more capable of leading a social existence, indeed, he was incapable of gaining an insight into its significance and value.

He learned very poorly, spending his time in *toilettes* and artistic nothings, particularly in painting, for which he evinced a certain capability; but in this direction he accomplished nothing, since he was wanting in perseverance. He could not be brought to take up any earnest thought; he had a mind only for externals, was always distracted, and serious things quickly wearied him. Preposterous acts, senseless journeys, waste of money and debts repeatedly occurred throughout the course of his later life; and even for these positive faults in his life he was wanting in understanding. He was self-willed and intractable, and never did well when an attempt was made to put him on his feet and point out to him his own interests.

With these manifestations of an original abnormal and defective mind, there were notable indications of perverse sexual feeling, which were also indicated in the somatic condition of the patient. Sexually, the patient felt like a woman towards men, and had inclinations towards people of his own sex, with indifference, if not actual disinclination, for females.

In his twenty-second year it was asserted that he had sexual intercourse with women, and was able to perform the act of coitus normally; but, partly on account of increase of neurasthenic symptoms which was occasional after coitus, and partly on account of fear of infection— but really by reason of a want of satisfaction—he seen ceased to indulge in such intercourse. Concerning his abnormal sexual condition, he was not quite clear; he was conscious of an inclination towards the male sex, but confessed, only in a shame-faced way, that he had certain pleasurable feelings of friendship for masculine individuals, which, however, were not accompanied by any sensual feelings. The female sex he did not exactly abhor; he could even bring himself to marry a woman who could have an attraction for him, by means of similarity in artistic tastes, if he could but be freed from conjugal duties, which were unpleasant to him, and the performance of which made him tired and weak. He denied having had sexual intercourse with men, but his blushing and embarrassment, and, still more, an occurrence in N., where the patient some time before provoked a scandal by attempting to have sexual intercourse with youths, showed him to speak falsely.

His external appearance also, condition, form, gestures, manners and dress were remarkable, and decidedly recalled the feminine form and characteristics. The patient, however, was over middle height, *but thorax and pelvis were decidedly of feminine form. The body was rich in fat; the skin was well groomed, delicate and soft.* This impression of a woman in masculine dress was further increased by *a thin growth of hair on the face*, which was shaven, with the exception of a small moustache; by the mincing gait; the shy, effeminate manner; the feminine features; the swimming, neuropathic expression of the eyes; the traces of powder and paint; the curtailed cut of the clothing, with the bosom-like prominence of the upper garments; the fringed feminine cravat; and the hair brushed down smoothly from the brow to the temples. The physical examination made undoubted the feminine form of the body. The external genitals were well developed, though the left testicle had remained in the canal; *the growth of hair on the mons veneris was thin, and the latter was unusually rich in fat and prominent. The voice was high, and without masculine timbre.*

The occupation and manner of thought of v. H. were decidedly feminine. He had a *boudoir* and a well-supplied toilet-table, at which he spent many hours in all kinds of arts for beautifying himself. He abhorred the chase, practice with arms, and such masculine pursuits, and called himself an *aesthete*; spoke with preference of his paintings and attempts at poetry. He was interested in feminine occupations, in which —*e.g.*, embroidery—he engaged, and called his greatest pleasure. He could spend his life in an artistic and aesthetic circle of ladies and gentlemen, in conversation, music and aesthetics. His conversation was preferably about feminine things,—fashions, needlework, cooking and household work.

The patient was well nourished, but anaemic. He was of neuropathic constitution, and presented symptoms of neurasthenia, which were maintained by a bad manner of life, lying abed, living in-doors, and effeminateness.

He complained of occasional pain and pressure in the head, and had habitual constipation. He was easily frightened; complained of occasional lassitude and fatigue, and drawing pains in the extremities, in the direction of the lumbo-abdominal nerves. After pollutions, and regularly after eating, he felt tired and relaxed; he was sensitive to pressure over the spinous processes of the dorsal vertebrae, as also to pressure along accessible nerves. He felt peculiar sympathies and antipathies towards certain persons, and, when he met people for whom he had an antipathy, he fell into a condition of peculiar fear and confusion. His pollutions, though later on they occurred but seldom, were pathological, in that they occurred by day, and were unaccompanied by any sensual excitement.

Opinion.

1. Mr. v. H., according to all observations and reports, was mentally an abnormal and defective person, and that, in fact, from the beginning. His antipathic sexual instinct represented a part of his abnormal physical and mental condition.

2. This condition, in that it was congenital, was incurable. There existed defective organization of the highest cerebral centres, which rendered him incapable of leading an independent life, and of obtaining a position in life. His perverse sexual instinct prevented him from exercising normal sexual functions; and this was attended by all the social consequences of such an anomaly, and the danger of satisfaction of perverse impulses arising out of his abnormal organization, with consequent social and legal conflicts. Fear of the latter, however, could not be great, since the (perverse) sexual impulse of the patient was weak.

3. Mr. v. H., in the legal sense of the word, was not irresponsible, and neither fit for, or in need of, treatment in a hospital for the insane.

It was possible for him—though but an overgrown child, and incapable of personal independence—to live in society, even under the care and guidance of normal individuals. To a certain extent, it was possible for him to respect the laws and restrictions of society, and to judge his own acts; but, with respect to possible sexual errors and conflicts with criminal laws, it must be emphasized that his sexual instinct was abnormal, having its origin in organic pathological conditions; and the circumstance should have been eventually used in his favour. On account of his notorious lack of independence, he could not be discharged from parental care or guardianship, inasmuch as otherwise he would be ruined financially.

4. Mr. v. H. was also physically ill. He presented signs of slight anaemia and of *neurasthenia*.

A rational regulation of his manner of life and a tonic regimen, and, if possible, hydro-therapeutic treatment, seemed necessary. The suspicion that this trouble had its origin in early masturbation should be entertained, and the possibility of the existence of spermatorrhoea, that is of importance etiologically and therapeutically, was probable. (Personal case. *Zeitschr. f. Psychiatrie.*)

CONGENITAL SEXUAL INVERSION IN WOMAN.[94]

Science in its present stage has but few data to fall back on, so far as the occurrence [95] of homosexual instinct in woman is concerned as compared with man.

It would not be fair to draw from this the conclusion that sexual inversion in woman is rare, for if this anomaly is really a manifestation of functional degeneration, then degenerative influences will prevail alike in the female as well as in the male.

The causes of apparent infrequency in woman may be found in the following facts: (1) It is more difficult to gain the confidence of the sexually perverse woman; (2) this anomaly, in so far as it leads to sexual intercourse, among women, does not fall (in Germany at any rate) under the criminal code, and therefore remains hidden from public knowledge; (3) sexual inversion does not affect woman in the same manner as it does man, for it does not render woman impotent; (4) because woman (whether sexually inverted or not) is by nature not as sensual and certainly not as aggressive in the pursuit of sexual needs as man, for which reason the inverted sexual intercourse among women is less noticeable, and by outsiders is considered mere friendship. Indeed, there are cases on record (psychical hermaphroditism, even homosexuality) in which the causes of female frigidity remain unknown even to the husband.

Certain passages in the Bible,[96] the history of Greece ("Sapphic Love"), the moral history of ancient Rome and of the Middle Ages,[97] offer proofs that sexual meeting of women took place at all times, the same as it is practiced now-a-days in the harem, in female prisons, brothels and young ladies' seminaries (see below, Lesbian love).

Still it must be admitted that many of these cases are to be reduced to causes of perversity and not perversion.[98]

The chief reason why inverted sexuality in woman is still covered with the veil of mystery is that the homosexual act so far as woman is concerned, does not fall under the law.

I cannot lay sufficient stress upon the fact that sexual acts between persons of the same sex do not necessarily constitute antipathic sexual instinct. The latter exists only when the physical and psychical secondary sexual characteristics of the same sex exert an attracting influence over the individual and provoke in him or her the impulse to sexual acts.

I have through long experience gained the impression that inverted sexuality occurs in woman as frequently as in man. But the chaster education of the girl deprives the sexual instinct of its predominant character; seduction to mutual masturbation is less frequent; the sexual instinct in the girl begins to develop only when she is, with the advent of puberty, introduced to the society of the other sex, and is thus naturally led primarily into hetero-sexual channels. All these circumstances work in her favour, often serve to correct abnormal inclinations and tastes, and force her into the ways of normal sexual intercourse. We may, however, safely assume that many cases of frigidity or anaphrodisia in married women are rooted in undeveloped or suppressed antipathic sexual instinct.

The situation changes when the predisposed female is also tainted with other anomalies of an hypersexual character and is led through it or seduced by other females to masturbation or homosexual acts.

In these cases we find situations analogous to those which have been described as existing in men afflicted with "acquired" antipathic sexual instinct.

As possible sources from which homosexual love in woman may spring, the following may be mentioned:

1. Constitutional hypersexuality impelling to automasturbation. This leads to neurasthenia and its evil consequences, to anaphrodisia in the normal sexual intercourse so long as *libido* remains active.

2. Hypersexuality also leads for want of something better to homosexual intercourse (inmates of prisons, daughters of the high classes of society who are guarded so very carefully in their relations with men, or are afraid of impregnation,—this latter group is very numerous). Frequently female servants are the seducers, or lady friends with perverse sexual inclinations, and lady teachers in seminaries.

3. Wives of impotent husbands who can only sexually excite, but not satisfy, woman, thus producing in her unsatisfied desire, recourse to masturbation, pollutions of a woman, neurasthenia, nausea for coitus and ultimately disgust with the male sex in general.

4. Prostitutes of gross sensuality who, disgusted with the intercourse with perverse and impotent men by whom they are used for the performance of the most revolting sexual acts, seek compensation in the sympathetic embrace of persons of their own sex. These cases are of very frequent occurrence.

Careful observation among the ladies of large cities soon convinces one that homosexuality is by no means a rarity. Uranism may nearly always be suspected in females wearing their hair short, or who dress in the fashion of men, or pursue the sports and pastimes of their male acquaintances; also in opera singers and actresses, who appear in male attire on the stage by preference.

So far as the clinical aspect is concerned I may be brief, for this anomaly shows the same qualifications alike in man and woman, with one alteration of details, and runs through the same grades. *Psychico-hermaphrodisic* and many homosexual women do not betray their anomaly by external appearances nor by mental (masculine) sexual characteristics.

Remarkable, however, it is that Dr. *Flatau* (*Moll, op. cit.*, p. 334) in examining the larynx of twenty-three homosexual women found in several of them a decidedly masculine formation.

In the transition to the subsequent grade, *i.e.*, that of masculinity (analogous to effeminacy in the male) strong preference for male garments will be found. In dreams, but also in the ideal or real homosexual function, the individual in question plays an indifferent sexual *rôle*.

Where viraginity is fully developed, the woman so acting assumes definitely the masculine *rôle*.

In this grade modesty finds expression only towards the same but not the opposite sex.

In such cases the sexual anomaly often manifests itself by strongly marked characteristics of male sexuality.

The female homosexual may chiefly be found in the haunts of boys. She is the rival in their play, preferring the rocking-horse, playing at soldiers, etc., to dolls and other girlish occupations. The toilet is neglected, and rough boyish manners are affected. Love for art finds a substitute in the pursuits of the sciences. At times smoking and drinking are cultivated even with passion.

Perfumes and sweetmeats are disdained. The consciousness of being a woman and thus to be deprived of the gay college life, or to be barred out from the military career, produces painful reflections.

The masculine soul, heaving in the female bosom, finds pleasure in the pursuit of manly sports, and in manifestations of courage and bravado. There is a strong desire to imitate the male fashion in dressing the hair and in general attire, under favourable circumstances even to don male attire and impose in it. Arrests of women in men's clothing are by no means of rare occurrence. A case of a woman who for years successfully posed as a man (hunter, soldier, etc.,) is related by *Müller* in *Friedreich's* "Blätter"; another by *Wise* (*op. cit.*) and others.

The ideals of such *viragines* are certain female characters who in the past or the present have excelled by virtue of genius and brave and noble deeds.

Hermaphroditism represents the extreme grade of degenerative homosexuality. The woman of this type possesses of the feminine qualities only the genital organs; thought, sentiment, action, even external appearance are those of the man.

Often enough does one come across in life such characters, whose frame, pelvis, gait, appearance, coarse masculine features, rough deep voice, etc., betray rather the man than the woman. *Moll* (*op. cit.*, p. 331) has given many interesting items about the mode of life led by these men-women, and about the way in which they satisfy their sexual needs.

With due alteration of details, the situation is the same as with the man-loving man. These creatures seek, find, recognize, love one another, often live together as "father" and "mother" in pseudo marriage. Suspicion may always be turned towards homosexuality when one reads in the advertisement columns of the daily papers: "Wanted, by a lady, a lady friend and companion."

Numerous psychical hermaphrodites of the female gender, and even homosexualists, enter upon matrimony with men partly on account of being ignorant of their own anomaly, and partly because they wish to be provided for. Some of these marriages linger on in a way, the husband, perhaps, being psychically sympathetic, thus rendering the marital act possible to the unhappy wife. But in most cases, when one or two children have been born, she seeks under all kinds of pretexts to avoid the connubial duty.

More frequently, however, incompatibility wrecks these unions. Homosexual intercourse continues after marriage just the same as with the homosexual man.

When viraginity prevails marriage is impossible, for the very thought of coitus with a man arouses disgust and horror.

The intersexual gratification among these women seems to be reduced to kissing and embraces, which seems to satisfy those of weak sexual instinct, but produces in sexually neurasthenic females ejaculation.

Automasturbation, for want of something better, seems to occur in all grades of the anomaly the same as in men.

Strongly sensual individuals may resort to cunnilingus or mutual masturbation.

In grades 3 and 4 the desire to adopt the active *rôle* towards the beloved person of the same sex seems to invite the use of the priapus.

CASE 153. *Psychical hermaphroditism.* Mrs. X., twenty-six years of age, suffered from neurasthenia. She was hereditarily tainted, suffered periodically from delusions. She had been married seven years, had two healthy children, a boy of six and a girl of four years. Success in gaining the confidence of the patient. She confessed that she always inclined more to persons of her own sex, and that, although she esteemed and liked her husband, sexual intercourse disgusted her. Since the birth of the younger of the two children she had prevailed upon him to give it up altogether. When at the seminary she interested herself in other young ladies in a manner which she could only describe as love. At times, however, she also found herself drawn to certain gentlemen, and especially of late her virtue had been sorely tried by an admirer to whose advances she was afraid she might succumb, for which reason she avoided being alone with him. But such episodes were only of a quite transient character as compared with her passionate liking for persons of her own sex. Her whole desire was to be kissed and embraced by them and have the most intimate intercourse with them. She suffered much from nervousness because she could not always realize these desires. The patient is not aware of this inclination to persons of the same sex being of a sexual character, for beyond kissing, embracing, or fondling them she would not know what to do with them. Patient thought herself to be of a sensual nature. It was likely that she was addicted to masturbation.

She considered her sexual perversion as "unnatural, morbid."

There was nothing in the behaviour or the manners or the external appearance of this lady which in the least betrayed her anomaly.

CASE 154. *Psychical hermaphroditism.* Mrs. M., forty-four years of age, claimed to be an instance illustrating the fact that in *one* and *the same* human being, be it man or woman, the inverted as well as the normal direction of sexual life may be combined. The father of this lady was very musical, generally possessed considerable talents for art, was a great admirer of the gentle sex, and himself of exceptional beauty. He died of dementia in an asylum after repeated apoplectic attacks. His brother was neuropsychopathic, as a child was afflicted with somnambulism, and later on with excessive sexual desire. Although married and father of several married sons, he fell desperately in love with Mrs. M., then eighteen years of age, and attempted to abduct her.

Her grandfather (on the paternal side) was very eccentric and a well known artist, who had originally studied theology, but for love of the dramatic art became a mimic and singer. He was given to heavy drinking and sexual excess, extravagant and fond of splendour, and died at the age of forty-nine from apoplexy. Her mother's father and her mother both died of pulmonary tuberculosis.

She had eleven brothers and sisters, but only six survived. Two brothers died at the age of sixteen and twenty of tuberculosis. One brother was suffering from laryngeal tuberculosis. Four living sisters the same as Mrs. M. were physically like unto the father, very nervous and shy. Two younger sisters were married and in good health, and both had healthy children. Another one, a maiden, was suffering from nervous affection.

Mrs. M. was the mother of four children, mostly delicate and neuropathic.

There was nothing of importance in the history of the patient's childhood. She learned easily, had gifts for poetry and aesthetics, was somewhat affected, loved to read novels and sentimental literature, was of neuropathic constitution and very sensitive to changes of temperature, the slightest draught would make her flesh creep. It is noteworthy, however, that one day when ten years of age she fancied her mother did not love her. Thereupon she put a lot of sulphur matches in her coffee and drank it to make herself ill, in order to draw her mother's love to herself.

Puberty began without difficulty at the age of eleven, with subsequent regular menses. Even previous to that period sexual life had awakened, which ever since was very potent. The first sentiments and emotions lay in the homosexual direction. She conceived a passionate, though platonic, affection for a young lady, wrote love-songs and sonnets to her, and never was happier than when, upon one occasion, she could admire the "charms of her beloved" in the bath, or when she could gaze upon the neck, shoulders and breasts of this lady whilst dressing. She could resist only with difficulty the desire to touch these physical charms. When a girl she was deeply in love with Raphael's and Guido Reni's Madonnas. She was irresistibly impelled to follow pretty girls and ladies by the hour, no matter how inclement the weather might be, admiring their air of refinement and watching for a chance of showing them a favour, giving them flowers, etc. The patient asserted that up to her nineteenth year she had not the slightest knowledge of the difference of sexes, since she had been brought up by a prudish old maiden aunt like a nun in a cloister. In consequence of this complete ignorance she fell a victim to a man who loved her passionately and insidiously betrayed her virtue. She became the wife of this man, gave birth to a child, and led an "eccentrically" sexual life with him, but felt satisfied with the sexual intercourse. A few years later she became a widow. Since then her affections again turned to persons of her own sex, the principal reason for which was, the patient averred, the fear of the results of sexual intercourse with man.

At the age of twenty-seven she entered upon a second marriage with a man of infirm constitution. It was not a love match. Thrice she became a mother, and fulfilled all the conditions of maternity; but her health ran down, and during the latter years her dislike for coitus ever increased, chiefly on account of her husband's infirmity, although her desire for sexual gratification remained strong.

Three years after her second husband's death, she discovered that her daughter by the first husband, now nine years of age, was given to masturbation and going into decline. She read an article about this vice in the *Enclopaedia*, and now could not resist the temptation to try it herself and thus became an onanist. She hesitated to give a full account of this period of her life. She stated, however, that she became sexually so excited that she had to send her two daughters away from home in order to preserve them from something "terrible." The two boys could remain at home.

Patient became neurasthenic because of masturbation (spinal irritation, pressure in the head, languor, mental constipation, etc.) at times even dysthymic, with worrying boredom.

Her sexual inclinations turned now to woman, now to man. But she controlled herself, suffered much from her abstinence, especially since she resorted to masturbation on account of her neurasthenic afflictions only at the last instance. At the age of forty-four—still having regular periods—the patient suffered from a violent passion for a young man with whom, on account of her avocation, she was bound to be in constant contact.

The patient did not offer anything extraordinary in her external appearance; though graceful of build, she was slight of form. Pelvis decidedly feminine, but arms and legs large, and of pronounced masculine type. Female boots did not really fit her, and she had quite crippled and malformed her feet by forcing them into narrow shoes. Genitals quite normal. Excepting a dropped womb with hypertrophy of the vaginal portion, no changes were noticeable. She still claimed to be essentially homosexual, and declared that her inclination and desire for the opposite sex were only periodical and grossly sensual. Although she had strong sexual feelings towards the man aforementioned, yet her greatest and noblest pleasure she found in pressing a kiss upon the soft cheek of a sweet girl. This pleasure she enjoyed often, for she was the "favorite aunt" among these "dear creatures," to whom she rendered the services of the "cavalier" unstintingly, always feeling herself in the *rôle* of the man.

CASE 155. *Homosexuality*. Miss L., fifty-five years of age. No information about her father's family. The parents of her mother were described as irascible, capricious and nervous. One brother of her mother was an epileptic, another eccentric and mentally abnormal.

Mother was sexually hyperaesthetic, and for a long time a nymphomaniac. She was considered to be psychopathic and died at the age of sixty-nine of cerebral disease.

Miss L. developed normally, had only slight illnesses in childhood, and was mentally well endowed, but of a neuropathic constitution, emotional, and troubled with numerous fads.

At the age of thirteen, two years previous to her first menstruation, she fell in love with a girl-friend ("a dreamy feeling, quite pure of sensuality").

Her second love was for a girl older than herself who was a bride; this was accompanied by tantalizing sensual desires, jealousy, and an "undefined consciousness of mystical impropriety." She was refused by this lady and now fell in love with a married woman, who was a mother and twenty years her senior. As she controlled her sensual emotions, this lady never even divined the true reason of this enthusiastic friendship which lasted for twelve years. Patient described this period as a veritable martyrdom.

Since she was twenty-five she had begun to masturbate. Patient seriously thought that, perhaps, by marriage she might save herself, but her conscience objected, for her children might inherit her weakness, or she might make a sincere husband unhappy.

At the age of twenty-seven she was approached with direct proposals by a girl who denounced abstinence as absurd, and plainly described the homosexual instinct which ruled her and was very impetuous in her demands. She suffered the caresses of the girl, but would not consent to sexual intercourse, as sensuality without love disgusted her.

Mentally and bodily dissatisfied she found the years pass by, leaving the consciousness of a spoiled life. Now and then she became enthusiastic about ladies of her acquaintance, but controlled herself. She also rid herself from masturbation.

When she was thirty-eight years of age she became acquainted with a girl nineteen years her junior, of exceptional beauty, who came from a demoralized family, and had been at an early age seduced by her cousins to mutual masturbation. It could not be ascertained whether this girl A. was a case of psychical hermaphrodism or of acquired sexual inversion. The former hypothesis seems the likelier of the two.

The following is taken from an autobiography of Miss L.:—

"Miss A., my pupil, began to show me her idolatrous love. She was sympathetic to the highest degree. Since I knew that she was entangled in a hopeless love affair with a dissolute fellow and continued intimate intercourse with demoralized female cousins, I decided not to repulse her. Compassion and the conviction that she was surely drifting into moral decay determined me to suffer her advances.

"I did not consider her affection as dangerous, as I did not think it possible that (considering her love affair) in ONE soul *two* passions (one for a man and another for a woman) could exist simultaneously. Moreover, I was certain of my power of resistance. I kept, therefore, Miss A. about me, renewed my moral resolutions, and considered it to be my duty to use her love for me for ennobling her character. The folly of this I soon found out. One day whilst I lay asleep Miss A. took occasion to satisfy her lust on me. Although I woke up just in time, I did not have the moral strength to resist her. I was highly excited, intoxicated as it were—and she prevailed.

"What I suffered immediately after this occurrence beggars description. Worry over the broken resolutions, which to keep I had made such strenuous efforts, fear of detection and subsequent contempt, exuberant joy at last to be rid of the torturing watchings and longings of the single state, unspeakable sensual pleasure, wrath against the evil companion, mingled with feelings of the deepest tenderness towards her. Miss A. calmly smiled at my excitement, and with caresses soothed my anger.

"I accepted the situation. Our intimacy lasted for years. We practiced mutual masturbation, but never to excess or in a cynical fashion.

"Little by little this sensual companionship ceased. Miss A's tenderness weakened; mine, however, remained as before, although I felt no longer the same sensual cravings. Miss A. thought of marriage, partly in order to find a home, but especially because her sensual desires had turned into the normal paths. She succeeded in finding a husband. I sincerely hope she will make him happy, but I doubt it. Thus I have the prospect before me of lingering on with the same joyless, peaceless life as in youthful days.

"It is with sadness that I remember the years of our loving union. It does not disturb my conscience to have had sexual intercourse with Miss A., for I succumbed to her seduction, having honestly endeavoured to save her from moral ruin and to bring her up an educated and moral being. In this I honestly think I have succeeded after all. Besides, I rest in the thought that the moral code is established only for normal humans, but is not binding for anomalies. Of course, the human being who is endowed by nature with sentiments of refinement, but whose constitution is abnormal and outside the conventionalities of society, can never be truly happy. But I experienced a sad tranquillity and felt happy when I thought Miss A. to be so too.

"This is the history of an unhappy woman who, by the fatal caprice of nature, is deprived of all joy of life and made a victim of sorrow."

The author of this woeful story was a lady of great refinement. But she had coarse features, a powerful but throughout feminine frame. She passed through the menopause without trouble, and since then had been entirely free from sensual worry. Sexually she had never played a defined *rôle* towards the woman she loved; for men she never felt the slightest inclination.

Her statements about the family relations and the health of her paramour, Miss A., established a heavy taint beyond doubt. The father died in an insane asylum, the mother was deranged during the period of her menopause, neuroses were of frequent occurrence in the family, and Miss A. herself suffered at times heavily from hysteropathy, with hallucinations and delirium.

CASE 156. *Homosexuality*. S. J., age thirty-eight, governess. Came to me for medical advice on account of nervous trouble. Father was periodically insane, and died from cerebral disease. Patient was an only child. She suffered early from anxiety and alarming fancies, *e.g.*, that she would wake up in a coffin after it had been fastened down; that she would forget something when going to confession, and thus receive holy communion unworthily. Was often troubled with headaches, very excitable, easily startled, but notwithstanding had a great desire to see exciting things such as funerals, etc.

From the earliest youth she was subject to sexual excitement, and spontaneously practiced masturbation. At the age of fourteen she began to menstruate. Her periods were often accompanied by colicky pains, intense sexual excitement, neuralgia and mental depression. With the age of eighteen she gave up masturbation successfully.

The patient never experienced an inclination towards a person of the opposite sex. Marriage to her only meant to find a home. But she was mightily drawn to girls. At first she considered this affection merely as friendship, but she soon recognized from the intensity of her love for girl friends and her deep longings for their constant society that it meant more than mere friendship.

To her it is inconceivable that a girl could love a man, although she can comprehend the feeling of man towards woman. She always took the deepest interest in pretty girls and ladies, the sight of whom caused her intense excitement. Her desire was ever to embrace and kiss these dear creatures. She never dreamed of men, always of girls only. To revel in looking at them was the acme of pleasure. Whenever she lost a "girl friend" she felt in despair.

Patient claimed that she never felt in a defined *rôle*, even in her dreams, towards her girl friends. In appearance she was thoroughly feminine and modest. Feminine pelvis, large mammae, no indication of beard.

CASE 157. *Homosexuality*. Mrs. R., aged thirty-five, of high social position, was brought to me in 1886 by her husband for advice.

Father was a physician; very neuropathic. Paternal grandfather was healthy and normal, and reached the age of ninety-six. Facts concerning paternal grandmother are wanting. All the children of father's family were said to have been nervous. The patient's mother was nervous, and suffered with asthma. The mother's parents were healthy. One of the mother's sisters had melancholia.

From her tenth year patient had been subject to habitual headache. With the exception of measles, she had no illness. She was gifted, and enjoyed the best of training, having especial talent for music and languages. It became necessary for her to prepare herself for the work of a governess, and during her earlier years she was mentally overworked. She passed through an attack of melancholia without delirium, of some months' duration, at seventeen. The patient asserted that she had always had sympathy only for her own sex, and found only an aesthetic interest in men. She never had any taste for female work. As a little girl, she preferred to play with boys.

She said she remained well until her twenty-seventh year. Then, without external cause, she became depressed and considered herself a bad, sinful person, had no pleasure in anything, and was sleepless. During this time of illness she was also troubled with delusions: she must think of her death and that of her relatives. Recovery after about five months. She then became a governess, was overworked, but remained well, except for occasional neurasthenic symptoms and spinal irritation.

At twenty-eight she made the acquaintance of a lady five years younger than herself. She fell in love with her, and her love was returned. The love was very sensual, and satisfied by mutual masturbation. "I loved her as a god; hers is a noble soul," she said, when she mentioned this love-bond. It lasted four years and was ended by the (unfortunate) marriage of her friend.

In 1885, after much emotional strain, the patient became ill with symptoms of hystero-neurasthenia (dyspepsia, spinal irritation, and tonic spasmodic attacks; attacks of hemiopia with migraine and transitory aphasia; itching of the sexual organs and anus). In February, 1886, these symptoms disappeared.

In March she became acquainted with her present husband, whom she married without taking much time for reflection; for he was rich, much in love with her, and his character was in sympathy with her own.

On 6th April, she read the sentence, "Death misses no one." Like a flash of lightning in a clear sky, the former delusions of death returned. She was forced to meditate on the most horrible manner of death for herself and those about her, and constantly imagined death-scenes. She lost rest and sleep, and took no pleasure in anything. Her condition improved. Late in May, 1886, she was married, but was still troubled by painful thoughts at that time: that she would bring misfortune on her husband and those about her.

First coitus on 6th June, 1886. She was deeply depressed morally by it. She had no such conception of matrimony. The husband, who really loved his wife, did all he could to quiet her. He consulted physicians, who thought all would be well after pregnancy. The husband was unable to explain the peculiar behaviour of his wife. She was friendly towards him, and tolerated his caresses. In coitus, which was actually carried out, she was entirely passive, and after the act she was tired, exhausted all day long, nervous, and troubled with spinal irritation.

A bridal tour brought about a meeting with her old friend, who had lived in an unhappy marriage for three years. The two ladies trembled with joy and excitement as they sank into each other's arms, and became inseparable. The husband saw that this friendly relation was a peculiar one, and hastened their departure. He had an opportunity of ascertaining, through the correspondence of his wife with this friend, that the letters interchanged were like those of two lovers.

Mrs. R. became pregnant. During pregnancy the remains of depression and delusions disappeared. In September, during about the ninth week of pregnancy, abortion took place. After that, renewed symptoms of hystero-neurasthenia. In addition to this, there were forward inclination and sideways position of the right side of the uterus, anemia and low tone of the ventricle.

At the consultation the patient gave the impression of a very neuropathic, tainted person. The neuropathic expression of the eyes cannot be described. Appearance entirely feminine. With the exception of a very narrow arched palate, there was no skeletal abnormality. With difficulty the patient could be brought to give the details of her sexual abnormality. She complained that she had married without knowing what marriage between men and women was. She loved her husband dearly for his mental qualities, but marital intercourse was a pain to her; she did it unwillingly, without ever finding any satisfaction in it. After the act, all day long she was weary and exhausted. Since the abortion and the interdiction of sexual intercourse by the physicians, she had been better; but she thought of the future with horror. She esteemed her husband, and loved him mentally; but she would do anything for him, if he would but avoid her sexually in the future. She hoped to have sexual feeling for him in time. When he played the violin, she seemed to feel the beginning of an inclination for him that was something more than friendship; but it was only transitory, and she could get no assurance for the future in it. Her greatest happiness was in correspondence with her former lover. She felt that this was wrong, but she could not give it up; for to do so made her miserable.

CASE 158. *Homosexuality.* Miss X., of the middle class in a large city. At the end of my observations she was twenty-two years of age.

She was considered a beauty; much admired by men; decidedly sensual; a born Aspasia; refused all proposals of marriage. She reciprocated, however, the advances of one admirer, a youthful scholar, entertained relations with him, that is to say, she allowed him to kiss her, but not as a lover. When on one occasion, Mr. T. thought he had obtained the aim of his attentions, she begged him under tears to desist, alleging that her refusal was not based upon moral principles, but rooted in deeper psychical reasons. Subsequently epistolary correspondence between the two disclosed the existence of sexual inversion.

Her father was given to drink, her mother hystero-pathic. She herself was of neuropathic constitution, had a large bust and the appearance of an exceptionally handsome woman, but was strikingly mannish in her manners, had masculine tastes, loved gymnastics and horseback exercise, smoked, and had masculine carriage and gait. She would like to go on the stage.

Recently she caused much talk on account of her enthusiastic friendships with young ladies. One young lady lived with her. They slept in the same bed.

Up to her puberty Miss X. claimed to have been sexually indifferent.

At the age of seventeen, while at a spa, she made the acquaintance of a young foreigner whose "royal" appearance fascinated her. She was happy when, on a certain occasion, she could dance with him the whole evening. The next evening at twilight she happened to witness a revolting scene. This charming young man was opposite her window in the shrubbery of the gardens having coitus with a woman during menstruation after the manner of the beasts. The sight of the flowing blood aroused the bestiality of the man. Miss X. was horrified, almost annihilated, and felt it difficult to recover her mental balance. For a long time she lost sleep and her appetite, and from that time she saw in man only the embodiment of coarse vulgarity.

Two years later, in a public park, she was approached by a young lady who smiled and looked upon her in such a peculiar fashion that she felt a thrill through her soul.

The day after, Miss X. was irresistibly impelled to go to the park again. The young lady was already there, and seemed to be waiting for her. They greeted each other like old acquaintances; talked and joked together, made fresh appointments, and when the weather became too inclement they met at the *boudoir* of the young lady.

"One day," Miss X. relates in her confidential revelation, "she led me to her divan, and whilst she was seated I knelt down at her feet. She fastened her timid eyes upon me, stroked away the hair from my forehead, and said, 'Ah! if I only could love you once really! May I?' I consented, and whilst we thus sat together, gazing into each other's eyes, we drifted into that current which allows of no retreat. . . . She was enchantingly beautiful. All I wished was to possess the power of the artist to immortalize that form upon the canvas. To me it was a novel experience. I was intoxicated. We abandoned ourselves to each other without restriction, drunk with the ravages of sensual feminine pleasure. I do not believe that man can ever grasp the exuberance of such piquant tenderness; man is not sufficiently refined; he is much too coarse. . . . Our wild orgy lasted until I sank down exhausted, powerless, unnerved. I fell asleep on her bed. Suddenly I awoke with an unspeakable thrill, hitherto unknown to me, running through my whole being. She was upon me—carrying out cunnilingus—the highest pleasure for her, whilst this continued she did not allow me to do anything except kiss her breasts, which caused her to quiver convulsively.

"This intercourse lasted for a whole year, when the removal of her father to another city separated us."

Miss X. admitted that in this homosexual intercourse she always felt in the *rôle* of man towards the woman, and that on one occasion, for want of something better, she granted *cunnilingus* to one of her male admirers.

CASE 159. *Homosexuality.* Mrs. C., aged thirty-two, wife of an official, a large, not uncomely woman, feminine in appearance, came of a neuropathic and emotional mother. A brother was psychopathic, and died of drink. Patient was always peculiar, obstinate, silent, quick-tempered, and eccentric. The brothers and sisters were excitable people. Pulmonary tuberculosis had been frequent in the family. When only a girl of thirteen, with signs of great sexual excitement, she attracted attention by enthusiastic love for a female friend of her own age. Her education was strict, though the patient secretly read many novels, and wrote innumerable poems. She married at eighteen to free herself from unpleasant circumstances at home.

She said she had always been indifferent towards men. In fact, she avoided balls. Female statues pleased her. Her greatest happiness was to think of marriage with a beloved woman. She was not aware of her sexual peculiarity until marriage, and the thing had remained inexplicable to her. Patient did her marital duty, and bore three children, two of whom were subject to convulsions. She lived pleasantly with her husband, but she esteemed him only for his moral qualities. She gladly avoided coitus. "I should have preferred intercourse with a woman."

Until 1878 she had been neurasthenic. On the occasion of a sojourn at a watering-place she made the acquaintance of a female urning, whose history I have reported as case 6, in the "Irrenfreund," No. 1, 1884.

The patient came home a changed person. Her husband said: "She was no longer a woman, no longer had any love for me and the children, and would have no more of marital approaches. She was inflamed with passionate love for her female friend, and had taste for nothing else." After the husband forbade her lover the house, there was interchange of letters with such expressions in them as "My dove! I live only for you, my soul." There were meetings and frightful excitement when an expected letter did not come. The relation was in no way platonic. From certain indications it was presumable that mutual masturbation was the means of sexual satisfaction. This relation lasted until 1882, and made the patient decidedly neurasthenic.

She absolutely neglected the house, and her husband hired a woman of sixty years as a housekeeper, and also a governess for the children. The patient fell in love with both, who, at least, allowed caresses, and profited materially through the love of their mistress.

In the latter part of 1883, on account of developing pulmonary tuberculosis, she had to go south. There she became acquainted with a Russian lady of forty years, and fell passionately in love with her; but she did not meet with a return of love in her sense. One day insanity became manifest. She thought the Russian lady a nihilist; that she was magnetized by her; and she presented formal persecutory delusions. She fled, was caught in an Italian city, and placed in a hospital, where she soon became quiet. Again she worried the lady with her love, felt herself very unhappy, and planned suicide.

When she returned home she was greatly depressed because she did not have the lady, and was harsh towards her family. A delusive, erotic state of excitement came on about the end of May, 1884. She danced, shouted, and called herself a man; demanded her former lover, and said she was of royal blood. She escaped from the house in male attire, and was taken to the asylum in a state of eroto-maniacal excitement. After a few days the exaltation disappeared. The patient became quiet, and made a desperate attempt at suicide; after it she was in great anguish of mind with weariness of life. The perverse sexual feeling grew less and less noticeable as tuberculosis progressed. The patient died of tuberculosis in the beginning of 1885.

The examination of the brain presented nothing unusual so far as architecture and arrangement of convolutions were concerned. Weight of brain 1150 grammes. Skull slightly asymmetrical. No anatomical signs of degeneration. External and internal genitals without anomaly.

CASE 160. (*Homosexuality in Transition to Viraginity.*) Mrs. v. T., wife of a manufacturer; age twenty-six; married only a few months; was brought by her husband for consultation because after a banquet she had fallen upon the neck of a lady guest, covered her profusely with kisses and caressed her like a lover, thus causing a scandal.

Mrs. T. said that she had before their marriage explained to her husband her antipathic sexual feelings, and had told him that she esteemed him solely for his mental qualities. She accepted her conjugal duties merely as a matter of unavoidable necessity. Her only condition was that she should be on top during coitus. In this position she obtained a sort of gratification, for she imagined his body to be that of a beloved woman beneath her.

Her brother was neuropathic, of feminine type, suffered from hysteria, and was very weak in his sexual needs; one of his sisters, it was said, bought her conjugal rights from her husband for a sum of money, giving him full liberty to find sexual satisfaction elsewhere. The mother was hyper-sexual, and known as a nymphomaniac. She made her daughter sleep in the same bed with her till she reached the age of fourteen. At fifteen v. T. was sent to a girl's school. Being extraordinarily bright, she learned quickly and soon dominated over all the other girls in her form.

At the age of seven she had a psychical trauma when a friend of the family exhibited himself before her.

Menses began at twelve, were regular and without nervous concomitants. At that age she began already to be powerfully drawn to other girls. Although for several years she never associated these yearnings with sexual feelings, she yet looked upon them as an anomaly. She only felt bashful when undressing in the presence of persons of her own sex. At twenty the sexual instinct awoke. At once she turned to girls for gratification, avoiding men entirely. She had sensual love affairs with girls by the scores. When she returned home from school, having no supervision and plenty of money, she found it easy to give her passion full sway. She always felt like a man towards woman. Masturbation with a desirable woman was the common occurrence in her orgies, until a female cousin taught her the mysteries of Lesbian love. She now coupled the act with cunnilingus. She always played the active *rôle*, and never allowed others to satisfy themselves on her own body. Homosexual women she disdained. She gave preference to unmarried women of high standing endowed with mental gifts, of voluptuous, Diana-like figure, but of modest and retiring disposition. (Sensual women she did not care for.) Whenever she met such a woman, she would become erotically so excited that she fell upon her person like a hungry wild beast. She said that at such moments everything appeared to her in a reddish gleam, and consciousness was obliterated for the time being. Her nerves were easily unstrung, and she could not master her feelings.

At the age of twenty-three she became acquainted with a young woman who, to all appearances, was not homosexual, but very hyper-sexual, and could not find sexual satisfaction on account of impotence in her husband. The relations with this woman stimulated T.'s homosexuality to a very high pitch and increased her sexual needs. She furnished an apartment away from home, where she had regular orgies with the finger and the tongue, sometimes for hours, until she herself collapsed in a state of exhaustion. She had a love affair with a dressmaker's model with whom she had herself photographed in man's attire, visited, in the same costume, with her places of amusement and was finally arrested on one of these occasions. She escaped with a warning and gave up male attire out-of-doors.

A year before her marriage she had a period of melancholia. At that time she contemplated suicide, and wrote a farewell letter to an intimate lady friend, a sort of confession, from which a few passages are given:

"I was born a girl, but a misdirected education forced my fiery imagination early into the wrong direction. At twelve I had a mania to pose as a boy and court the attention of ladies. I recognized this abnormal impulse as a mania, but, like fate, it grew with the years. The power to rid myself of it was lost. It was my hashish, my happiness, and grew into an overpowering passion. I felt like a man, forced to play the active *rôle*. My exuberant disposition, fierce sensuousness and deep-rooted perverse instinct gradually forged me into the chains of Lesbian love. I took a certain interest in man, but a single touch by a woman made my whole nervous system tremble. I have suffered untold tortures in the bane of this passion.

"The reading of French novels and lascivious companions taught me all the tricks of perverse erotics, and the latent impulse became a conscious perversity. Nature has made a mistake in the choice of my sexuality and I must do a life-long penance for it, for the moral power to suffer the unavoidable with dignity is lost. Irresistibly I have been drawn into the maelstrom of passion and shall be swallowed up by it. . . .

"I languished for your sweet body. I was jealous of your Victor as one rival is of the other. In my jealousy I suffered the tortures of hell. I hated that man unto death. I cursed my fate that made me a woman. I was satisfied to play a stupid comedy before you, to endow you with an artificial member. It only increased the heat of my passion. Courage failed me to tell you the truth, because it would have been so miserable and ludicrous. Now you know all. You will not despise me, though; you will only feel what I have suffered. All my joys resemble more a momentary intoxication than the real gold of happiness. It was all but an illusion. I have fooled life and life has fooled me. We are quits. I say good-bye. Think sometimes in the hour of happiness of your poor, comical fool who loved you truly and so well. . . ."

The sexual life of this woman contained also traces of masochism and sadism. If the woman whom she worshipped had chided or even struck her, it would have been a delight—so she claimed—and at the time of sexual excitement she felt more like biting than kissing the object of her love.

She was highly cultured and intellectual, felt her false position painfully, but rather on account of her family than her own self. She looked upon it all as fate, over which she had no control. She bewailed it and declared herself ready to do anything to get rid of this perversion and become a true wife and good mother, for she would take good care that her child were brought up in the right way. She would do everything to reconcile her husband and perform her marital duties, but she could not bear his moustache, and she must first rid herself of her unfortunate impulsive passion.

The physical and psychical secondary sexual characteristics were partly masculine, partly feminine. Her love for sport, smoking and drinking, her preference for clothes cut in the fashion of men, her lack of skill in and liking for female occupations, her love for the study of obtuse and philosophical subjects, her gait and carriage, severe features, deep voice, robust skeleton, powerful muscles and absence of adipose layers bore the stamp of the masculine character. The pelvis also (small hips), distance of the spine 22 cm, of the cristae 26 cm, and of the torchanteres (ball of the hip-bones) 31 cm, approached the masculine figure. Vagina, uterus, ovaries normal, clitoris rather large. Breasts well developed, hair on mons veneris female.

I sent her to an hydropathic establishment, where an experienced colleague succeeded in a few months to free this patient by means of hydro- and suggestive treatment, from her homosexual affliction. She became a decent, sexually at least, neutral person. The relatives with whom she lived afterwards for a considerable time found her behaviour absolutely correct.

CASE 161. *Masculinity*. Miss N., twenty-five years of age. Parents supposed to be healthy. Her brothers and sisters were all neuropathic. Three of her sisters were married. She was very talented, especially in the fine arts. Even in her earliest childhood she preferred playing at soldiers and other boys' games; she was bold and tomboyish, and tried even to excel her little companions of the other sex. She never had a liking for dolls, needlework or domestic duties. Puberty at fifteen. She soon fell in love with young ladies, but only in a platonic fashion, for she was a "respectable girl." For several years since then her *libido* was very strong. She could hardly restrain herself. Her dreams were of a lascivious nature, only about females, with herself in the *rôle* of man. She was desperately in love with a woman of forty, whom she tormented with her jealous conduct.

Miss N. was indifferent to men. She could safely live with a man in the same room, whilst towards persons of her own sex she was most bashful.

She was quite conscious of her pathological condition.

Masculine features, deep voice, manly gait, without beard, small breasts; cropped her hair short, and made the impression of a man in woman's clothes.

CASE 162. *Masculinity.* C. R., maid-servant, aged twenty-six, suffered from the time of her development with original paranoia and hysteria. As a result of her delusions, her life had been somewhat romantic, and in 1884, in Switzerland, where she had gone on account of delusions of persecution, she came under the observation of the authorities. On this occasion it was ascertained that R. was affected with sexual inversion.

Concerning her parents and relatives, there was no information at hand. R. asserted that, with the exception of an inflammation of the lungs at the age of sixteen, she had never been severely ill.

First menstruation at fifteen, without any difficulties; thereafter it was very often irregular and abnormally excessive. The patient declared that she never had had inclinations towards the opposite sex, and had never allowed the approach of a man. She never could understand how her friends could describe the beauty and amiability of men. But it was charming and inspiring for her to imprint a kiss on the lips of a beloved female friend. She had a love for girls that was incomprehensible to her. She had passionately loved and kissed some of her female friends, and she would have given up her life for them. Her greatest delight would have been to have constantly lived with such a friend and absolutely possessed her.

In this she felt towards the beloved girl like a man. Even as a little child she had an inclination only for the play of boys, and she loved to hear shooting and military music, was always much excited by them, and would gladly have gone as a soldier. The chase and war have been her ideals. In the theatre only feminine performers interested her. She knew very well that all of this inclination was unwomanly, but she could not help it. It had always been a great pleasure for her to go about in male clothing, and in the same way she had always preferred masculine work, and had shown unusual skill in it; while with reference to feminine occupations, especially handiwork, she had to say the contrary. The patient had also a weakness for smoking and spirits. On account of persecutory delusions, in order to rid herself of her persecutions, the patient had often gone about in male attire and played the part of a man. She did this with such (natural) skill that, as a rule, she was able to deceive people concerning her sex.

It is authoritatively established that in 1884 for a long time the patient went about in male attire, now in the garments of a civilian, now in the uniform of a lieutenant; and in August of the same year, dressed as a male servant, she fled to Switzerland through delusions of persecution. There she found service in a merchant's family and fell in love with the daughter of the house, "the beautiful Anna," who, on her side, not recognizing the sex of R., fell in love with the handsome young man.

Concerning this episode the patient made the following characteristic statement: "I was madly in love with Anna. I don't know how it came about, and I cannot put myself right concerning this impulse. In this fatal love lies the reason why I played the *rôle* of a man so long. I have never yet felt any love for a man, and I believe that my love is for the female and not the male sex. I can in nowise understand my condition."

From Switzerland R. wrote letters home to her friend Amelia, which were produced at the examination. They are letters showing passionate love, which goes beyond the bounds of friendship. She apostrophizes her friend: "My flower, sun of my heart, longing of my soul." She was her greatest happiness on earth; her heart was hers. And in her letters to her friends' parents she wrote: "You, too, should watch my 'flower,' for if she should die I also would be unable to endure life."

For the purpose of investigating her mental condition, R. remained for some time in an asylum. On one occasion, when Anna was allowed to pay R. a visit, there was no end of passionate embraces and kisses. The visitor acknowledged freely that they had before secretly embraced and kissed in the same way.

R. was a tall, slim, stately person, of feminine form in all respects, but masculine features. Cranium regular; no anatomical signs of degeneration. Genitals normal and indicative of virginity. R. made the impression of a morally pure and modest person. All the circumstances indicated that she had only indulged in platonic love. Eye and appearance were indicative of a neurasthenic person. Severe hysteria, occasional cataleptoid attacks, with visionary and delirious states. The patient was very easily brought into a state of somnambulism by hypnotic influence, and in this condition was susceptible to all possible suggestions. (Personal case. "*Friedreich's* Blätter," 1881, Heft i.)

CASE 163. *Masculinity*. Miss O., twenty-three years of age. Mother constitutionally and heavily hysteropathic. Mother's father insane. Father's family untainted.

Father died early of pneumonia. Patient was brought to me by her trustee because she ran away recently from home in male attire in order to rove through the world and become an "artiste." Very gifted in music.

For several years she attracted much attention by her bold, mannish behaviour, and by wearing her hair and attire in male fashion. Since she was thirteen she was demonstrative in her love for girl friends, whom she often wearied with fervent embraces.

She did not seek to conceal her passionate fondness for persons of her own sex. Claimed that since her thirteenth year she was fully conscious of the fact that she could love only women. She felt as a man towards woman; though she looked like a man, and would much rather wear men's clothes.

A short time ago she seriously asked a relative who was in the police department to obtain permission for her to go about in male attire.

Her erotic dreams dealt only with intimate intercourse with female friends. She never took the slightest interest in men, and never thought of marriage.

She felt quite happy in her abnormal sexual condition, and did not recognize it as pathological. She could not comprehend that her sexual instinct differed from that of other women.

The circumference of the head was 51 cm. Frame quite feminine; but the feet were exceptionally large and more of masculine type. Carriage, attitude and gait quite masculine. Feminine voice. Monthly periods regular since her thirteenth year.

CASE 164. (*Masculinity*.) On the 5th of October, 1898, the police brought to my clinic W., age thirty-six, a charwoman, for examination as to her sanity. She had engaged herself to a young girl under the pretext that she was a man and belonged to an aristocratic family. Examination proved this to be a classical case of original paranoia. When she was five she imagined that the couple with whom she lived were only her foster parents, at eighteen that she came from a distinguished family, at twenty-nine that her father was a king, her mother a countess. Circumference of cranium 53 cm., parietal bones slightly bulging. Ears abnormally small, of uneven size, misformed, the right lobe joined groin-like to the cheek, the left properly developed. Palate very narrow and steep. Teeth carious, many missing (Rachitis). Stature medium size, willowy. Chest strongly arched. Waist and region of hips smaller than in the normal. A prominent gynecologist examined the pelvic regions and found a small pelvis, narrow at the inferior outlet, in form almost typically masculine. Ilium less inclined than in the normal.

The rather hard lines and severe features of the face gave it a rather masculine appearance. Her hair was cut short. Gait and bearing masculine. Skin very rough, adipose layers sparse, breasts stunted. Genitals normal, hymen intact. She was loath to speak of her sexual life, but wanted an explanation why she had no desire for men and only for persons of her own sex. "Her genitals could not be right." Menses from the age of sixteen, but the flow of blood came but seldom, and even then very sparsely. With the advent of puberty inclinations to persons of her own sex. She never was sensual. Her sexual ideas were always about the female sex in general, never concentratd on an individual. In this wise she had lived with another girl of her own age; but their relations had been those of sisters; sexual acts had never taken place between them. She felt towards other women as a man does; she loathed the idea of sexual intercourse with a man. When a child she preferred playing with boys. When playing at "robbers" she would be the captain and chose a girl for her wife, but without any sexual moment. At sixteen she thought she possessed the qualities of a man. She was then in a convent and there learned from a woman masturbation. The thought of this woman was always present when she masturbated, and acted as a sexual stimulus. Later on she thought of other females during the act, but without decided individuality.

At thirty-three she became neurasthenic, gave up the practice successfully. She bewailed the fact that she was not born a man, as she hated feminine things and dress generally. Would much rather have been a soldier. Sweetmeats she disdained, preferring a cigar. She was a bright, intelligent person. Larynx and voice feminine. She became convinced that she could not marry a woman and upon promise to conquer her perverse sexual inclinations she was dismissed.

CASE 165. Miss X., aged thirty-eight, consulted me late in the fall of 1881, on account of severe spinal irritation and obstinate sleeplessness, in combating which she had become addicted to morphine and chloral. Her mother and sister were nervous sufferers, but the rest of the family were healthy. The trouble dated from a fall on her back in 1872, at which time the patient was terribly frightened, though, when a girl, she had been subject to muscular cramps and hysterical symptoms. Following this shock, a neurasthenic and hysterical neurosis developed, with predominating spinal irritation and sleeplessness. Episodically, hysterical paraplegia, lasting as long as eight months, and hysterical hallucinatory delirium, with convulsive attacks, occurred. In the course of this, symptoms of morphinism were added. A stay of some months in the hospital relieved the latter, and considerably improved the neurasthenic neurosis, in the treatment of which general faradization exerted a remarkably favourable influence.

Even at the first meeting, the patient produced a remarkable impression by reason of her attire, features and conduct. She wore a gentleman's hat, her hair closely cut, eye-glasses, a gentleman's cravat, a coat-like outer garment of masculine cut that reached well down over her gown, and boots with high heels. She had coarse, somewhat masculine features; a harsh, deep voice; and made rather the impression of a man in female attire than that of a lady, if one but overlooked the bosom and the decidedly feminine form of the pelvis. During the long time that she was observed, there were never signs of eroticism. When questioned concerning her attire, she would only respond that the style she chose suited her better. Gradually it was ascertained from her that, even when she was a small girl, she had had a preference for horses and masculine pursuits, and never any interest in feminine occupations. Later she developed a particular pleasure in reading, and prepared herself to be a teacher. Dancing had never pleased her; it had always seemed silly to her. The *ballet* had never interested her. Her greatest pleasure had always been in the circus. Until her sickness, in 1872, she had neither had inclination for persons of the opposite nor of those of her own sex. From that time she had, what was remarkable to herself, a peculiar friendship for females, particularly for young ladies; and she had a desire, and satisfied it, to wear hats and coats of masculine style. Since 1869, she had worn her hair short, and parted it on the side, as men do. She asserted that she was never sexually excited in the company of men, but that her friendship and self-sacrifice for sympathetic ladies was unbounded; while from that time she also experienced repugnance for gentlemen and their society.

Her relatives reported that, before 1872, the patient had a proposal of marriage, which she refused; and that when she returned from a sojourn at a watering place, in 1874, she was sexually changed, and occasionally showed that she did not regard herself as a female.

Since that time she would associate only with ladies, had a kind of love-relation with one or another, and made remarks which indicated that she looked upon herself as a man. This predilection for women was decidedly more than mere friendship, since it expressed itself in tears, jealousy, etc.

When, in 1874, she was stopping at a watering place, a young lady, who took her for a man in disguise, fell in love with her. When this lady married, later, the patient was for a long time depressed, and spoke of unfaithfulness. Moreover, since her illness, her relatives were struck by her desire for masculine attire, her masculine conduct, and disinclination for feminine pursuits; while, previously, at least sexually, she had presented nothing unusual.

Further investigation showed that the patient had a love-relation, which was not purely platonic, with the lady described in case 159; and that she wrote her affectionate letters like those of a lover to his beloved. In 1887 I again saw the patient in a sanatorium, where she had been placed on account of hystero-epileptic attacks, spinal irritation, and morphinism. The inverted sexual feeling existed unchanged, and only by the most careful watching was the patient kept from improper advances towards her fellow-patients.

Her condition remained quite unchanged until 1889. Then the patient began to fail, and she died of "exhaustion," in August, 1889. The autopsy showed, in the vegetative organs, amyloid degeneration of the kidneys, fibroma of the uterus, and cyst of the left ovary. The frontal bone was much thickened, uneven on the inner surface, with numerous exostoses; dura adherent to vault of cranium. Long diameter of skull, 175 millimetres; lateral diameter, 148 millimetres; weight of the edematous, but not atrophied brain, 1175 grammes. The meninges delicate, easily removed. Cortex pale. Convolutions broad, not numerous, regularly arranged. Nothing abnormal in cerebellum and great ganglia.

CASE 166. *Hermaphroditism.*[99] History: On 4th November, 1889, the father-in-law of a certain Countess V., complained that the latter had swindled him out of 800f., under the pretense of requiring a bond as secretary of a stock company. It was ascertained that Sandor had entered into matrimonial contracts and escaped from the nuptials in the spring of 1889; and, more than this, that this ostensible Count Sandor was no man at all, but a woman in male attire—Sarolta (Charlotte), Countess V.

S. was arrested, and, on account of deception and forgery of public documents, brought to examination. At the first hearing S. confessed that she was born on the 6th Sept., 1866; that she was a female, Catholic, single, and worked as an authoress under the name of Count Sandor V.

From the autobiography of this man-woman I have gleaned the following remarkable facts that have been independently confirmed:—

S. came of an ancient, noble and highly respected family of Hungary, in which there had been eccentricity and family peculiarities. A sister of the maternal grandmother was hysterical, a somnambulist, and lay seventeen years in bed, on account of fancied paralysis. A second great-aunt spent seven years in bed, on account of a fancied fatal illness, and at the same time gave balls. A third had the whim that a certain table in her *salon* was bewitched. When anything was laid on this table, she would become greatly excited and cry, "Bewitched! bewitched!" and run with the object into a room which she called the "Black Chamber," and the key of which she never let out of her hands. After the death of this lady, there were found in this chamber a number of shawls, ornaments, bank-notes, etc. A fourth great-aunt during two years did not leave her room, and neither washed herself nor combed her hair; then she again made her appearance. All these ladies were, nevertheless, intellectual, finely educated and amiable.

S.'s mother was nervous, and could not bear the light of the moon.

She inherited many of the peculiarities of her father's family. One line of the family gave itself up almost entirely to spiritualism. Two blood relations on the father's side shot themselves. The majority of her male relatives were unusually talented; the females were decidedly narrow-minded and domesticated. S.'s father had a high position, which, however, on account of his eccentricity and extravagance (he wasted over a million and a half), he lost.

Among many foolish things that her father encouraged in her was the fact that he brought her up as a boy, called her Sandor, allowed her to ride, drive and hunt, admiring her muscular energy.

On the other hand, this foolish father allowed his second son to go about in female attire, and had him brought up as a girl. This farce ceased when the son was sent to a higher school at the age of fifteen.

Sarolta-Sandor remained under her father's influence till her twelfth year, and then came under the care of her eccentric maternal grandmother in Dresden, by whom, when the masculine play became too obvious, she was placed in an institute and made to wear female attire.

At thirteen she had a love-relation with an English girl, to whom she represented herself as a boy, and ran away with her.

Sarolta returned to her mother, who, however, could do nothing, and was compelled to allow her daughter to again become Sandor, wear male clothes, and, at least once a year, to fall in love with persons of her own sex.

At the same time S. received a careful education and made long journeys with her father, of course always as a young gentleman. She early became independent and visited *cafés*, even those of doubtful character, and, indeed, boasted one day that in a brothel she had had a girl sitting on each knee. S. was often intoxicated, had a passion for masculine sports and was a very skillful fencer.

She felt herself drawn particularly towards actresses, or others of similar position, and, if possible, towards those who were not very young. She asserted that she never had any inclination for a young man, and that she had felt, from year to year, an increasing dislike for young men.

"I preferred to go into the society of ladies with ugly, ill-favoured men, so that none of them could put me in the shade. If I noticed that any of the men awakened the sympathies of the ladies, I felt jealous. I preferred ladies who were bright and pretty; I could not endure them if they were fat or much inclined towards men. It delighted me if the passion of a lady was disclosed under a poetic veil. All immodesty in a woman was disgusting to me. I had an indescribable aversion for female attire—indeed, for everything feminine, but only in as far as it concerned me; for, on the other hand, I was all enthusiasm for the beautiful sex."

During the last ten years S. had lived almost constantly away from her relatives, in the guise of a man. She had had many *liaisons* with ladies, travelled much, spent much, and made debts.

At the same time she carried on literary work, and was a valued collaborator on two noted journals of the capital.

Her passion for ladies was very changeable; constancy in love was entirely wanting.

Only once did such a *liaison* last three years. It was years before that S., at Castle G., made the acquaintance of Emma E., who was ten years older than herself. She fell in love with her, made a marriage contract with her, and they lived together as man and wife for three years at the capital.

A new love, which proved fatal to S., caused her to sever her matrimonial relations with E. The latter would not have it so. Only with the greatest sacrifice was S. able to purchase her freedom from E., who still looked upon herself as a divorced wife, and regarded herself as the Countess V.! That S. also had the power to excite passion in other women was shown by the fact that when she (before her marriage with E.) had grown tired of a Miss D., after having spent thousands of guldens on her, she was threatened with shooting by D. if she should become untrue.

It was in the summer of 1887, while at a watering-place, that S. made the acquaintance of a distinguished official's family. Immediately she fell in love with the daughter, Marie, and her love was returned.

Her mother and cousin tried in vain to break up this affair. During the winter the lovers corresponded zealously. In April, 1888, Count S. paid her a visit, and in May, 1889, attained her wish; in that Marie—who, in the meantime, had given up a position as teacher—became her bride in the presence of a friend of her lover, the ceremony being performed in an arbor, by a pseudo-priest, in Hungary. S., with her friend, forged the marriage certificate. The pair lived happily, and, without the interference of the father-in-law, this false marriage, probably, would have lasted much longer. It is remarkable that, during the comparatively long existence of the relation, S. was able to deceive completely the family of her bride with regard to her true sex.

S. was a passionate smoker, and in all respects her tastes and passions were masculine. Her letters and even legal documents reached her under the address of "Count S." She often spoke of having to drill. From remarks of the father-in-law it seems that S. (and she afterwards confessed it) knew how to imitate a scrotum with handkerchiefs or gloves stuffed in the trousers. The father-in-law also, on one occasion, noticed something like an erected member on his future son-in-law (probably a priapus). She also occasionally remarked that she was obliged to wear a suspensory bandage while riding. The fact is, S. wore a bandage around the body possibly as a means of retaining a priapus.

Though S. often had herself shaved like a man, the servants in the hotel where she lived were convinced that she was a woman, because the chambermaids found traces of menstrual blood on her linen (which S. explained, however, as haemorrhoidal); and, on the occasion of a bath which S. was accustomed to take, they claimed to have convinced themselves of her real sex by looking through the key-hole.

The family of Marie make it seem probable that she for a long time was deceived with regard to the true sex of her false bridegroom. The following passage in a letter from Marie to S., 26th August, 1889, speaks in favour of the incredible simplicity and innocence of this unfortunate girl: "I don't like children any more, but if I had a little Bezerl or Patscherl by my Sandi—ah, what happiness, Sandi mine!"

A large number of manuscripts allow conclusions to be drawn concerning S.'s mental individuality. The chirography possesses the character of firmness and certainty. The characters are genuinely masculine. The same peculiarities repeat themselves everywhere in their contents—wild, unbridled passion; hatred and resistance to all that opposes the heart thirsting for love; poetical love, which is not marred by one ignoble blot, enthusiasm for the beautiful and noble; appreciation of science and the arts.

Her writings betray a wonderfully wide range of reading in classics of all languages, in citations from poets and prose writers of all lands. The evidence of those qualified to judge literary work shows that S.'s poetical and literary ability was by no means small. The letters and writings concerning the relation with Marie are psychologically worthy of notice.

S. speaks of the happiness there was for her when by M.'s side, and expresses boundless longing to see her beloved, if only for a moment. After such a happiness she could have but one wish—to exchange her cell for the grave. The bitterest thing was the knowledge that now Marie, too, hated her. Hot tears, enough to drown herself in, she had shed over her lost happiness. Whole quires of paper are given up to the apotheosis of this love, and reminiscences of the time of the first love and acquaintance.

S. complained of her heart, that would allow no reason to direct it; she expressed emotions which were such as only could be felt—not simulated. Then, again, there were outbreaks of most silly passion, with the declaration that she could not live without Marie. "Thy dear, sweet voice; the voice whose tone perchance would raise me from the dead; that has been for me like the warm breath of Paradise! Thy presence alone were enough to alleviate my mental and moral anguish. It was a magnetic stream; it was a peculiar power your being exercised over mine, which I cannot quite define; and, therefore, I cling to that ever-true definition: I love you because I love you. In the night of sorrow I had but one star—the star of Marie's love. That star has lost its light;

now there remains but its shimmer—the sweet, sad memory which even lights with its soft ray the deepening night of death, a ray of hope."

This writing ends with the apostrophe: "Gentlemen, you learned in the law, psychologists and pathologists, do me justice; Love led me to take the step I took; all my deeds were conditioned by it. God put it in my heart.

"If he created me so, and not otherwise, am I then guilty; or is it the eternal, incomprehensible way of fate? I relied on God, that one day my emancipation would come; for my thought was only love itself, which is the foundation, the guiding principle, of His teaching and His kingdom.

"O God, Thou All-pitying, Almighty One! Thou seest my distress; Thou knowest how I suffer. Incline Thyself to me; extend Thy helping hand to me, deserted by all the world. Only God is just. How beautifully does Victor Hugo describe this in his 'Legendes du Siècle'! How sad do Mendelssohn's words sound to me: 'Nightly in dreams I see thee'!"

Though S. knew that none of her writings reached her lover, she did not grow tired of writing of her pain and delight in love, in page after page of deification of Marie. And to induce one more pure flood of tears, on one still, clear summer evening, when the lake was aglow with the setting sun like molten gold, and the bells of St. Anna and Maria-Wörth, blending in harmonious melancholy, gave tidings of rest and peace, she wrote: "For that poor soul, for this poor heart that beats for thee till the last breath."

Personal examination: The first meeting which the experts had with S. was in a measure, a time of embarrassment to both sides; for them, because perhaps S.'s somewhat dazzling and forced masculine carriage impressed them; for her, because she thought she was to be marked with the stigma of moral insanity. She had a pleasant and intelligent face, which, in spite of a certain delicacy of features and diminutiveness of all its parts, gave a decidedly masculine impression, had it not been for the absence of a moustache. It was even difficult for the experts to realize that they were concerned with a woman, despite the fact of female attire and constant association; while, on the other hand, intercourse with the man Sandor was much more free, natural, and apparently correct. The accused also felt this. She immediately became more open, more communicative, more free, as soon as she was treated like a man.

In spite of her inclination for the female sex, which had been present from her earliest years, she asserted that in her thirteenth year she first felt a trace of sexual feeling, which expressed itself in kisses, embraces, and caresses, with sexual pleasure, and this on the occasion of her elopement with the red-haired English girl from the Dresden institute. At that time feminine forms exclusively appeared to her in dream-pictures, and ever since, in sensual dreams, she felt herself in the situation of a man, and occasionally, also, at such times, experienced ejaculation.

She knew nothing of solitary or mutual onanism. Such a thing seemed very disgusting to her, and not conducive to manliness. She had, also, never allowed herself to be touched on the genitals by others, because it would have revealed her great secret. The menses began at seventeen, but were always scanty and without pain. It was plain to be seen that S. had a horror of speaking of menstruation; that it was a thing repugnant to her masculine consciousness and feeling. She recognized the abnormality of her sexual inclinations, but had no desire to have them changed, since in this perverse feeling she felt both well and happy. The idea of sexual intercourse with men disgusted her, and she also thought it would be impossible.

Her modesty was so great that she would prefer to sleep among men rather than among women. Thus, when it was necessary for her to answer the calls of nature or to change her linen, it was necessary for her to ask her companion in the cell to turn her face to the window, that she might not see her.

When occasionally S. came in contact with this companion—a woman from the lower walks of life—she experienced a sexual excitement that made her blush. Indeed, without being asked, S. related that she was overcome with actual fear when, in her cell, she was compelled to force herself into the unusual female attire. Her only comfort was that she was at least allowed to keep a shirt. Remarkable, and what also speaks for the significance of olfactory sensations in her sexual life, is her statement that, on the occasions of Marie's absence, she had sought those places on which Marie's head was accustomed to repose, and smelled them, in order to experience the delight of inhaling the odour of her hair. Among women, those who were beautiful, or voluptuous, or quite young, did not particularly interest her. The physical charms of women she made subordinate. As by magnetic attraction, she felt herself drawn to those between twenty-four and thirty. She found her sexual satisfaction exclusively in the body of a woman (never in her own person), in the form of manustupration of the beloved woman, or cunnilingus. Occasionally she availed herself of a stocking stuffed with oakum as a priapus. These admissions were made only unwillingly by S., and with apparent shame; just as in her writings immodesty or cynicism are never found.

She was religious, had a lively interest in all that is noble and beautiful—men excepted—and was very sensitive to the opinion others entertained of her morality.

She deeply regretted that in her passion she made Marie unhappy, and regarded her sexual feelings as perverse, and such a love of one woman for another, among normal individuals, as morally reprehensible. She had great literary talent and an extraordinary memory. Her only weakness was her great frivolity and her incapability to manage money and property reasonably. But she was conscious of this weakness, and did not care to talk about it.

She was 153 centimetres tall, of delicate build, thin, but remarkably muscular on the breast and thighs. Her gait in female attire was awkward. Her movements were powerful, not unpleasing, though they were somewhat masculine and lacking in grace. She greeted one with a firm pressure of the hand. Her whole carriage was decided, firm and somewhat self-conscious. Her glance was intelligent; mien somewhat diffident. Feet and hands remarkably small, having remained in an infantile stage of development. Extensor surfaces of the extremities remarkably well covered with hair, while there was not the slightest trace of beard, in spite of all shaving experiments. The hips did not correspond in any way with those of a female. Waist wanting. Pelvis so slim and so little prominent, that a line drawn from the axilla to the corresponding knee was straight—not curved inward by a waist or outward by the pelvis. The skull slightly oxycephalic, and in all its measurements below the average of the female skull by at least one centimetre.

Circumference of the head 52 centimetres; occipital half circumference, 24 centimetres; line from ear to ear, over the vertex, 23 centimetres; anterior half-circumference, 28.5 centimetres; line from glabella to occiput, 30 centimetres; ear-chin line, 26.5 centimetres; long diameter, 17 centimetres; greatest lateral diameter, 13 centimetres; diameter at auditory meati, 12 centimetres; zygomatic diameter, 11.2 centimetres. Upper jaw strikingly projecting, its alveolar process projecting beyond the under jaw about 0.5 centimetre. Position of the teeth not fully normal; right upper canine not developed. Mouth remarkably small; ears prominent; lobes not differentiated, passing over into the skin of the cheek. Hard palate, narrow and high; voice rough and deep; breasts fairly well developed, soft and without secretion. Mons veneris covered with thick, dark hair. Genitals completely feminine, without trace of hermaphroditic appearance, but at the stage of development of those of a ten-year-old girl. The labia majora touching each other almost completely; labia minora having a cock's-comb-like form, and projecting under the labia majora. Clitoris small and very sensitive. Frenulum delicate; perineum very narrow; introitus vaginae narrow; mucous membrane normal. Hymen wanting (probably congenitally); likewise the carunculae myrtiformes. Vagina so narrow that the insertion of an erect male member would be impossible; also very sensitive; certain coitus had not taken place. Uterus felt, through the rectum, to be about the size of a walnut, immovable and retroflected.

Pelvis generally narrowed (dwarf-pelvis), and of decidedly masculine type. Distance between anterior superior spines 22.5 centimetres (instead of 26.3 centimetres). Distance between the crests of the ilii,

26.5 centimetres (instead of 29.3 centimetres); between the trochanters, 27.7 centrimetres (31); the external conjugate diameter, 17.2 centimetres (19 to 20); therefore, the internal conjugate, presumably, 7.7 centimetres (10.8). On account of narrowness of the pelvis, the direction of the thighs not convergent, as in a woman, but straight.

The opinion given showed that in S. there was a congenitally abnormal inversion of the sexual instinct, which, indeed, expressed itself, anthropologically, in anomalies of development of the body, depending upon great hereditary taint; further, that the criminal acts of S. had their foundation in her abnormal and irresistible sexuality.

S.'s characteristic expressions—"God put love in my heart. If He created me so, and not otherwise, am I, then, guilty; or is it the eternal, incomprehensible way of fate?"—are really justified.

The court granted pardon. The "countess in male attire," as she was called in the newspapers, returned to her home, and again gave herself out as Count Sandor. Her only distress was her lost happiness with her beloved Marie.

A married woman, in Brandon, Wisconsin, whose case is reported by *Dr. Kiernan* ("The Medical Standard," 1888, November and December), was more fortunate. She eloped, in 1883, with a young girl, married her, and lived with her as husband undisturbed.

An interesting "historical" example of hermaphroditism is a case reported by *Spitzka* ("Chicago Medical Review," 20th August, 1881). The gentleman in question was Governor of New York and lived in the reign of Queen Anne. He was apparently affected with moral insanity; was terribly licentious, and, in spite of his high position, could not keep himself from going about in the streets in female attire, coquetting with all the allurements of a prostitute.

In a picture of him that has been preserved, his narrow brow, asymmetrical face, feminine features, and sensual mouth at once attract attention. It is certain that he never actually regarded himself as a woman.

Complications of Antipathic Sexual Instinct.

Moreover, in individuals afflicted with sexual inversion, in themselves, the perverse sexual feeling and inclination may be complicated with other perverse manifestations. Thus here, with reference to the activity of the instinct, there may be acts quite analogous to acts indulged in by individuals in perverse satisfaction of the instinct, but who, at the same time, have a natural inclination towards persons of the opposite sex.

Owing to the circumstance that abnormally increased sexuality is almost a regular accompaniment of antipathic sexual feeling, acts of lustful sadistic cruelty in the satisfaction of *libido* are easily possible. A remarkable example of this is the case of *Zastrow* (*Casper-Liman*, 7. Auflage, Bd. i., p. 160; ii., p. 487), who bit one of his victims (a boy), tore his prepuce, slit the anus, and strangled the child.

Z. came of a psychopathic grandfather and melancholic mother. His brother indulged in abnormal sexual pleasures, and committed suicide.

Z. was a congenital homosexual, and in habits and occupation masculine. There was phimosis. Mentally, he was a weak, perverse, socially useless man. He had a horror of women and, in his dreams, he felt himself like a woman towards a man. He was painfully conscious of his want of normal sexual feeling and of his perverse instinct, and sought satisfaction in mutual onanism, with frequent desire for pederasty.

Similar sadistic feelings of this kind, in those afflicted with antipathic sexual instinct, are found in some of the foregoing histories (*cf.* cases 128 and 129 of this edition, and case 96 of the sixth edition; also *Moll*, "Contr. Sexualempfindung," second edition, p. 189; v. *Krafft*, "Jahrb. f. Psychiatrie," xii., pp. 357 and 89; *Moll*, "Untersuchungen über Libido sexualis," cases 26 and 27).

As examples of perverse sexual satisfaction dependent on antipathic sexual instinct, may be mentioned the Greek, who, as *Athenäus* reports, was in love with a statue of Cupid, and defiled it, in the temple of Delphi; and besides the monstrous cases reported by *Tardieu* ("Attentats," p. 272), the terrible one reported by *Lombroso* ("L'uomo delinquente," p. 200), of a certain Artusio, who wounded a boy in the abdomen, and abused him sexually *by means of the incision.*

Cases 92, 110 and 115 (eighth edition) show that fetichism may may also occur with antipathic sexual instinct; moreover a case of shoe-fetichism related by me in "Jahrbücher f. Psychiatrie," xii., 1; *Moll, op. cit.,* second edition, p. 179; *Garnier*, "Les Fetichistes," p. 98.

The following case, taken from *Garnier*, is a classical example of boot-fetichism. At times masochism forms a complication of sexual inversion. *Cf. Moll*, second edition, p. 172 (case 12) and p. 190; *Hem*, "Internat. Centralbl. f. d. Physiol. and Pathol. der Harn- und Sexualorgane," iv., Heft 5 (homosexuality in a woman with passive flagellantism and coprophagia); v. *Krafft*, case 43 in sixth edition of this book, also case 137 of this edition and 114 of eighth edition; ditto "Jahrbücher für Psychiatrie," xii., p. 339 (homosexuality, abortive masochism), p. 351 (psych. hermaphrod. masochism).

CASE 167. *Homosexuality.* X., twenty-six years of age, of the upper class, was arrested for having practiced masturbation in a public park. By heredity heavily tainted; skull abnormal; was peculiar from earliest youth; psychically abnormal; at the age of ten he began to show a peculiar interest in patent leather shoes; began to masturbate at thirteen, but in order to procure ejaculation he had to fasten his eyes upon patent leather shoes. He never felt any inclination towards women, and when, at the age of twenty-one, he once attempted coitus at a brothel derived no satisfaction from the act. With the tweny-fourth year his homosexual instinct began to assert itself more and more. But he felt himself drawn only to young men who wore elegant clothes and patent leather boots. Thinking of such men, he masturbated. His ideal was to live with such a man and practice mutual masturbation. Unable to realize his wishes, he would introduce a ball into his anus, and moving it in and out fancy himself to have coitus with his ideal young man wearing patent leather boots. Simultaneously he would masturbate. During this imitation of passive pederasty he would wear drawers made of red silk. For some time he was wont to stick notices on public buildings to this effect: "My buttocks are at the disposal of handsome gentlemen who wear patent leather boots." Whilst writing such notices and looking at his own patent leather shoes, he would have an erection. Since his sixteenth year, when young men began to interest him, he had eyes only for their patent leather boots. He loved to loiter about the show-windows of boot shops and the drilling-grounds of the military school, where he had opportunity for admiring the officers in their patent leather boots. One day he bought a pair for himself and became quite intoxicated by gazing at them. The very smell of them was sufficient to excite him very much sexually. He finally put them on, that in them he might make conquests; but he was not successful. Now he used them for another purpose. He would, while masturbating, ejaculate into them. The most intense lustful pleasure he derived when he put, during this act, one of the shoes to his anus or between the thighs, rubbing it about there. When one day X. found a defect on the uppers of one of these shoes, which he always saved most carefully, he was very dejected. He looked upon himself as a person who has just discovered the first wrinkle in the face of his beloved. One day when in the park he thought that a young man made advances to him according to his own desire; he was highly elated, and could not resist exposing his person. He was arrested, but not sentenced. He was sent to an insane asylum (*Garnier*, "Les Fetichistes," p. 114).

In general, the *acquired* cases are characterized in that:—

1. The homosexual instinct appears as a secondary factor, and always may be referred to influences (masturbatic neurasthenia, mental) which disturbed normal sexual satisfaction. It is, however, probable that here, in spite of powerful sensual libido, the feeling and inclination for the opposite sex are weak from the beginning, especially in a spiritual and aesthetic sense.

2. The homosexual instinct, so long as sexual inversion has not yet taken place, is looked upon, by the individual affected, as vicious and abnormal, and yielded to only for want of something better.

3. The heterosexual instinct long remains predominant, and the impossibility to satisfy it gives pain. It weakens in proportion as the homosexual feeling gains in strength.

On the other hand, in *congenital* cases:—

(*a*) The homosexual instinct is the one that occurs primarily, and becomes dominant in the sexual life. It appears as the natural manner of satisfaction, and also dominates the dream-life of the individual.

(*b*) The heterosexual instinct fails completely, or, if it should make its appearance in the history of the individual (psycho-sexual hermaphroditism), it is still but an episodical phenomenon which has no root in the mental constitution, and is essentially but a means to satisfaction of sexual desire.

The differentiation of the above groups of congenital inverted sexuality from one another, and from the cases in which the anomaly is acquired, will, after the foregoing, present no difficulties.

The prognosis of the cases of acquired antipathic sexual instinct is, at all events, much more favourable than that of the congenital cases. In the former, the occurrence of effemination—the mental inversion of the individual, in the sense of perverse sexual feeling—is the limit beyond which there is no longer hope of benefit from therapy. In the congenital cases, the various categories established in this book form as many stages of psycho-sexual taint, and benefit is *probable* only within the category of the psychical hermaphrodites, though *possible* (see the case of *Schrenck-Notzing*) in that of homosexuals.

The *prophylaxis* of these conditions becomes thus the more important—for the congenital cases, prohibition of the reproduction of such unfortunates; for the acquired cases, protection from the injurious influences which experience teaches may lead to the fatal inversion of the sexual instinct.

Numerous *predisposed* individuals meet this sad fate, because parents and teachers have no suspicion of the danger which masturbation brings in its train to children.

In many schools and academies masturbation and vice are actually cultivated. At present much too little attention is given to the mental and moral peculiarities of the pupils.

If only the tasks are done, nothing more is asked. That many pupils are thus ruined in body and soul is never considered.

In obedience to affected prudery, the sexual life is made a mystery to the developing youth, and not the slightest attention given to the excitations of his sexual instinct. How few family physicians are ever called in, during the years of development of children, to give advice to their patients that are often so greatly predisposed!

It is thought that all must be left to Nature; in the meantime, Nature rises in her power, and leads the helpless, unprotected innocent into dangerous by-paths.

DIAGNOSIS, PROGNOSIS AND THERAPY OF ANTIPATHIC SEXUAL INSTINCT

The diagnosis of antipathic sexual instinct is of great clinical and, particularly, forensic import. At the first glance, it opens some difficulties, since the symptoms are rather of a subjective nature and the perverse acts offer so many aspects which may mean perversion as well as perversity. Much depends on the veracity of the patient, and that leaves in many cases much to be desired. Autobiographies are to be taken with a grain of salt, and should be discounted. Nevertheless the expert will soon be able to weed out exaggeration and untruth. Antipathic sexual instinct is such a complicated psychical anomaly that only the experienced specialist can quickly distinguish between truth and fiction.

True knowledge is easiest ascertained from those who despair of their existence, meditate suicide (which frequently is found in those who have cultured minds and realize the anomaly of their position), but as a last resort come to the medical man for advice; also from those who are confronted with legal proceedings, or who through circumstances are forced into marriage and doubt their virility. These patients have an urgent need for help, and will tell the truth. In strong contrast to these really unfortunate beings stand those, generally of but little ethical and intellectual value, who seek to enrich medical knowledge by fatuous gossip about their disease. Every case of genuine homosexuality has its etiology, its concomitant physical and psychical symptoms, its reactions upon the whole psychical being, and must be reduced to an abnormal sexual instinct which is diametrically opposed to the physical sex of the affected individual, as it can be explained upon that basis only. The diagnosis is to be found in the history, the causes and development, the previous life, the psycho-sexual development of the case. To form a clear opinion it behooves judging the case from the standpoint of the anthropological clinical history of its development, and to collect synthetically all the various details.

The opinion will then be as definitely established as in any other clinical case.

The first important point based upon ripe experience is the fact that antipathic sexual instinct as an anomaly of sexual life is only found in individuals who are tainted, as a rule, hereditarily. Initially particular stress should be laid upon this point. In all cases in which anamnesis has been proved, this taint will be readily found. In itself, this proof is of no value, for perversity also grows in this soil. But it assumes importance when the same frailty is found to exist in several members of the same family or appears in the form of other perversions of the sexual life either in the individual himself under consideration, or in other members of his family. Often enough the patient presents other psychical or neurotic anomalies, even psychical diseases, defects or such like. They are so frequent and numerous that one is often led to doubt whether the manifestation under observation belongs to the sphere of neuropathia or that of psychopathia.

These neurotic and psychopathic manifestations demand a most careful scrutiny as to their meaning. Not uncommonly they are signs of taint or degeneration of equivalent value with antipathic sexual instinct, or they may be reactions emanating from external defects to which tainted individuals are more subject than normal man is, often indirectly depending on antipathic sexual instinct on the ground of psychical conflicts in which these unfortunates are frequently implicated by virtue of their sexual perversions; or they may be found to spring from the imperfect or perverse gratification of their sexual needs (onanism).

Certain it is that these persons are, as a rule, also abnormal so far as character is concerned. They are neither man nor woman, a mixture of both, with secondary psychical and physical characteristics of the one as well as the other sex, which grow out of the interfering influences of a bisexual predisposition and disturb the development of a well defined and complete being. But this peculiarity is only found in fully developed cases. A psychical disease in itself is not a necessary adjunct to antipathic sexual instinct. All nations and all eras have produced perverse men, whose renown and greatness adorn the history of their mother country or that of the world.

This abnormality must not be looked upon as a pathological condition or as a crime, but the development of the sexual life with its reacting effects upon the mind and the moral sense; it may proceed with the same harmony and satisfying influence as in the normally disposed, a further argument in favor of the assumption that antipathic sexual instinct is an equivalent for heterosexuality. If ethical and intellectual defects are present, they may be looked upon merely as complicated anomalies resulting from the taint.

An important factor is precocity in sexual life, which together with its antithesis, i.e., retarded puberty, is the distinguishing mark of a degenerated constitution. It is quite another thing when the sexual life takes an inverted course at an early period, particularly at a time when evil influences or bad examples cannot be at work. For instance, when little boys prefer male adults to their female relations, or show a predilection for girls' games and occupations or particular skill in sewing, knitting, embroidering, etc., or inclination for female toilet, find pleasure in wearing girls' clothing, choose girls' characters in private theatricals or in masquerades and betray great cleverness in impersonating the female character, etc.

Homosexual acts (mutual masturbation, etc.) previous to puberty are no proof of antipathic sexuality. They may spring from hypersexuality, precocity or some external influences. They do not necessarily lead to inverted sexuality, only then when the individual is predisposed. It is at the time of puberty that the sexual life is developed and receives its direction for the rest of life. An unconscious desire for sexual union, often enough stimulated by individuals of the same sex, brings the playmates together, tickling and other tactile irritations—quite apart from the genuine sexual instinct—lead to acts of masturbation, but they are not coupled with psychical feelings in the sense of homosexual acts. The same analogous manifestations may be observed in young animals.

But rarely antipathic sexuality develops from these horseplays. Puberty teaches the youthful sinner to know his true sex soon enough. From the sexual instinct, based upon a series of physical and psychical attractions, emanates the sexual leaning to persons of the opposite gender, and the earlier homosexual encounters are remembered with shame and confusion. But the homosexual act committed *after* puberty has set in, is *the decisive* step in the wrong direction. The stadium of sexual differentiation covers sometimes a long period and often reaches far beyond that of physical sexual development.

Of great value in diagnosing a case is to ascertain the dream-life and that of sleep in the patient. The true status of the sexual instinct is here often pitifully portrayed. Nocturnal pollutions are found to be coloured (a) in cases of psychical hermaphroditism predominantly, (b) in all the other grades of the anomaly exclusively in the sense of homosexuality. In cases of effeminatio (viraginity) they are accompanied by dream-pictures delineating the passive (in man) or the active (in woman) *rôle* in the sexual act.

The presence of physical or psychical abnormal characteristics may aid diagnosis if they are coupled with other more distinctive signs. By themselves they prove nothing, as they are also found in individuals not tainted, for instance, in gynaecomasts, bearded women, etc., etc.

In the well-pronounced cases of antipathic sexual instinct (effeminatio and viraginity) the physical and psychical characteristics of inverted sexuality are so plentiful that a mistake cannot occur. They are simply men in women's garb, and women in men's attire, especially if they have full freedom of action. Psychically they consider themselves to belong to the opposite sex. We have seen female homosexuals in the army, and male homosexuals among the waitresses in restaurants. They act, walk, gesticulate and behave in every way exactly as if they were persons of the sex which they simulate. I have known male homosexuals who excelled woman in wiles, loquacity, coquetry, etc., etc.

In pronounced cases bashfulness and timidity in the presence of persons of his own sex will be observed in the homosexual individual.

That homosexuals know each other instinctively is a fable. They recognize one another by their gait, natural shyness and by signs just the same as normal persons of opposite sexes do if they go adventure hunting.

The higher grades of homosexuality show a horror of women to the extent of absolute impotence. Imagination sometimes assists in producing erection and rendering coitus possible. Diagnosis is definitely established when absolute proof is at hand that a homosexual person is permanently attracted by a person of the same sex and led to a sexual act with that person, the act granting full satisfaction to the sexual instinct, whilst similar attractions do not exist in persons of the opposite sex, and if the disgust for persons of the opposite sex is insuperable.

The distinction between congenital and acquired (or rather retarded) homosexuality is considered to be of theoretical and therapeutical value.

Some authors claim that congenital homosexuality does not exist, but that this anomaly is acquired from others. But I cannot accept their arguments, for they do not explain the presence of the distinguishing symptoms so often found in the earliest years of the individuals afflicted, i.e., at a period in which external influences may be considered to be absolutely excluded.

CASE 168. Taken from *Moll*, "Libido Sexualis," case 69, p. 726. A young man, thirty-four years of age, was from age seventeen drawn to young men, and had no liking for girls. He was an effeminate character, had a girl's nickname, and played with dolls. When drunk he allowed men to masturbate him. When sober, however, he would not permit it, because he thought it stupid.

To parents and teachers, the experiences detailed in this and numerous other scientific works on masturbation, present valuable suggestions.

Educators are often too "naïve" in their views, and their power of observation is too limited to notice the sexual abuses rampant among the boys entrusted to their care and practiced even during lesson time. In a few exceptional cases they have even become seducers of boys. Everything that is calculated to unduly further the development of the sexual life—such as prolonged sitting on the form, the use of alcoholic drinks, etc.—should be strictly avoided. A boy with inverted sexuality should be rigidly excluded from all public educational institutions for boys and sent to a hospital for nervous disorders. Boys should not be permitted to sleep together at home. Swimming lessons and bathing *en masse* should be under the careful and strict supervision of a competent person.

Neither should a child with antipathic sexual instinct be placed under the isolated tuition of a tutor or private master, for frequently the first object of homosexual love is the instructor at home. Care should be taken that tainted children are not caressed and fondled by persons of the same sex. Beating on the buttocks should never be permitted.

The best place for children that are perversely (sexually) inclined is the public school where co-education of the sexes prevails. An early preference for games, occupations and pastimes of the opposite sex should be strongly discountenanced and interdicted. Masturbation should be carefully watched in both sexes. Early signs of antipathic sexual instinct should at once be noticed, and hypnotic and suggestive treatment applied, for there is more hope for eradicating the evil in its earlier stages than when the individual so tainted has already been lost in the quagmire of sexual perversion.

The lines of *treatment*, when antipathic sexual instinct exists, are the following:

1. Prevention of onanism and removal of other influences injurious to the sexual life.

2. Cure of the neurosis (*neurasthenia*) arising out of the unhygienic conditions of the sexual life.

3. Mental treatment, in the sense of combating homosexual, and encouraging heterosexual, feelings and impulses.

The momentum of the treatment lies in fulfilling the third indication, particularly with reference to onanism.

Only in very few cases, where acquired antipathic sexual instinct has not progressed far, can the fulfilment of 1 and 2 be sufficient, as a case fully reported by the author in the "Irrenfreund," 1885, No. 1, proves. *Cf.* case 128, ninth edition of this book.

As a rule, physical treatment, even though it be reinforced mentally by good advice with reference to the avoidance of masturbation, the repression of homosexual feelings and impulses, and the encouragement of heterosexual desires, will not prove sufficient, even in cases of acquired sexual inversion.

Here a method of mental treatment—hypnotic suggestion—is all that can really benefit the patient.

I know of but one case in which auto-suggestion proved successful, *cf.* case 129, ninth edition.

As a rule, only *suggestion coming from a second person*, and that by means of *hypnosis*, promises success.

In such cases, the object of post hypnotic suggestion is to remove the impulse to masturbation and homosexual feelings, and to encourage heterosexual emotions with a sense of virility.

A prerequisite is, of course, the possibility to induce hypnosis of

sufficient intensity. It is, unfortunately, in these very cases of neurasthenia that this proves impossible, since the subject is often excited,
embarrassed, and in no condition to concentrate the thoughts.

By reason of the great benefit that can be given to such unfortunates, and with *Ladame's* case in view (see below), in all such cases,
everything should be done to force hypnosis—the only means of salvation.
The result, in the three following cases, was satisfactory:

CASE 169. *Antipathic sexual instinct acquired through masturbation.* Mr. X., merchant, aged twenty-nine. Father's parents healthy.
Nothing nervous in father's family.

Father was an irritable, peevish old man. One brother of the father
was a man-about-town, and died unmarried.

Mother died in third confinement, when the patient was six years
old; she had a deep, rough, masculine voice, and coarse appearance. Of
the children, one brother is irritable, "melancholic," and indifferent to
women.

When a child, patient had scarlet fever with delirium. Up to his
fourteenth year he was light-hearted and social, but, after that, quiet,
solitary, and "melancholic." The first trace of sexual feeling appeared in
his tenth or eleventh year, and at that time he learned masturbation
from other boys, and practiced mutual onanism with them.

At the age of thirteen or fourteen, ejaculation for the first time.
Patient had felt no evil results of onanism until the last three months.

At school he learned easily, but was troubled with headaches. After
the age of twenty, pollutions, in spite of daily practice of onanism. With
pollutions occurred "procreative" dreams, as man and wife might perform the act. In his seventeenth year he was seduced into mutual onanism by a man having a love for men. He found satisfaction in this, inasmuch as he was always very passionate sexually. It was a long time
before the patient again sought new opportunities for intercourse with
males. He did it simply to rid himself of semen.

He felt no friendship or love for the person with whom he had
intercourse. He felt satisfaction only when he played the passive *rôle*—
when manustupration was practiced on him. When the act was once
completed, he had no respect for the individual. If it happened that,
later, he came to respect the man, then he ceased to indulge in the act
with him. Later it became indifferent to him whether he masturbated
or had masturbation practiced on him. When he himself practiced onanism, he always thought of pleasing men practicing onanism on him
during the act. He preferred a hard, rough hand.

The patient thought that, had he not been led astray, he would
have arrived at a natural mode of satisfaction of his sexual desires. He
never felt love for his own sex, though he had pleased himself with

the thought of loving men. At first he had had sensual inclinations towards the opposite sex. He had taken pleasure in dancing, and he had been pleased with women, but he had taken more pleasure in the figure than the face. He had had erections at the sight of women that pleased him. He had never attempted coitus, for fear of infection; whether he was potent or not with women, he did not know. He thought he could be so no longer, because his feeling for women had grown cold, especially during late years.

While previously, in his sensual dreams, he had had ideas of both men and women, of late years he had dreamed only of approaches to men; he could not remember that he had dreamed, in late years, of sexual relations with a woman. At the theatre, as well as in the circus and ballet, the feminine figure had always interested him. In museums, masculine and feminine statues had affected him equally.

Patient was a great smoker, a beer-drinker, loved male society, and was an athlete and skater. Anything dandified was repugnant to him, and he had never felt any desire to please men; he would even have preferred to please women.

He now felt his position to be painful, because onanism had obtained the upper hand. Masturbation, that had previously been practiced without evil effects, now began to disclose its bad results.

Since July, 1889, he had suffered with neuralgia of the testicles. The pain occurred particularly at night; and at night there was also trembling (increased reflex excitability).

Sleep was not refreshing, and he would wake up with pain in the testicles. He was inclined, now, to indulge more frequently in onanism. He was afraid of the consequences of the habit. He hoped that his sexual life might still be turned into normal channels. Now, he thought of the future; he had a relation with a girl, who was attractive to him, and the thought of possessing her as a wife was pleasing.

For five days he had abstained from onanism, but he could scarcely believe that he would be able, with his own strength, to overcome the habit. Of late he had been very much depressed, having lost all desire for work, and become tired of life.

Patient was tall, powerful, well nourished, and had a thick growth of beard. Skull and skeleton normal. Knee-jerks very prompt; deep reflexes in upper extremities much increased. Pupils dilated, equal, and acted promptly. Carotids of equal calibre; hyperaesthesia urethrae; cords and testicles not sensitive; genitals normal.

The patient was calmed, and given hope for the future, provided that he gave up onanism and attempted to transfer his sexual desires from persons of his own sex to females.

Hip-baths (24° to 20° R.); extr. Secal. cornut. aquos., 0.5; antipyrin, 1.0 (*pro die*); pot. brom. 4.0 (evenings), were ordered.

13th December. Today the patient came, in a disturbed condition of mind, complaining that, unaided, he was unable to resist the impulse to masturbate, and he asked for help.

A trial of hypnosis induced a condition of deep lethargy in the patient.

He was given the following suggestions:

1. I can not, must not, and will not masturbate again.

2. I abhor the love of my own sex, and shall never again think men handsome.

3. I shall and will become well again, fall in love with a virtuous woman, be happy, and make her happy.

14th December. While out walking today, patient saw a handsome man, and felt himself powerfully drawn towards him.

From this time there were hypnotic sittings every second day, with the above suggestions.

18th December (fourth sitting), somnambulism occurred; the impulse to onanism and interest in men disappeared.

At the eighth sitting "complete virility" was added to the above suggestions. The patient felt himself morally elevated and physically strengthened. The neuralgia of the testicles had disappeared. He now found that he was without sexual feeling.

He now believed himself free from masturbation and inverted sexual inclination.

After the eleventh sitting he thought further help was unnecessary. He wished to go home, and marry. He felt well and potent. Early in January, 1890, treatment ceased.

In March, 1890, the patient wrote: "I have since had several occasions on which it has been necessary for me to use all my moral strength in order to overcome my habit, and, thank God, I have been successful in freeing myself from this vice. Several times I have had opportunity for sexual intercourse, and I have found pleasure in it. I look calmly on my happy future."

Other cases successfully treated by suggestion may be found in *Wetterstrand*, Der Hypnotismus und seine Anwendung in der praktischen Medicin, 1891, p. 52 u. ff.;—*Bernheim*, "Hypnotisme," Paris, 1891, etc., p. 38.

The foregoing details of the successful results of hypnotic suggestion, in cases of acquired sexual inversion, make it seem possible that those unfortunates who are afflicted with congenital perversion may be helped in some degree by the same means.

Of course the proposition is different as regards cases of a congenital anomaly. To correct a morbid psychosexual existence is a most difficult problem.

The most favourable cases are those of *psychosexual hermaphroditism* in which at least rudimentary heterosexual feelings may be strengthened by suggestion and brought into active practice.

CASE 170. Mr. von X., aged twenty-five, landed proprietor. He came of a neuropathic, irascible father, who was said to have been sexually normal. His mother was nervous, as were her two sisters. Maternal grandmother was nervous, and maternal grandfather a *roué*, much given to venery. Patient was like his mother, and an only child. From birth he was weak, suffered much with migraine, and was nervous. He passed through several illnesses. At fifteen he began masturbation, without having been taught.

Until his seventeenth year he never had feeling for men, or, in fact, any sexual inclination; but at this time desire for men arose. He fell in love with a comrade. His friend returned his love. They embraced and kissed and indulged in mutual onanism. Occasionally patient practiced coitus between the thighs of a man. He abhorred pederasty. Lascivious dreams were concerned only with men. In circus and theatre males alone interested him. The inclination was for those of about twenty years. Handsome, tall forms were enticing to him. Given these conditions, he was quite indifferent to other characteristics of the men. In his sexual affairs with men his part was always that of a man.

After his eighteenth year the patient was always a source of anxiety to his highly respected parents, for he then began a love-affair with a male waiter, who fleeced him and made him an object of remark and ridicule. He was taken home. He consorted with servants and hostlers. He caused a scandal. He was sent away to travel about. In London he got into a "blackmailing scrape," but succeeded in escaping to his home.

He profited in no way by this bitter experience, and again showed disgraceful inclinations towards men. Patient was sent to me to be cured of his fatal peculiarity (December, 1888). Tall, stately, robust, well-nourished, of masculine build; large, well-formed genitals. Gait, voice, and attitude masculine. Pronounced masculine passions. He smoked but little, and only cigarettes; drank little, and was fond of confectionery. He loved music, arts, aesthetics, flowers, and moved in ladies' society by preference. He wore a moustache, the face being otherwise cleanly shaved. His garments were in nowise remarkable. He was a soft, *blasé* fellow, and a do-nothing. He would lie in bed mornings, and could scarcely be made to rise before noon. He said he had never regarded his inclination towards his own sex as abnormal. He looked upon it as congenital; but, taught by his evil experiences, he wished to be cured of his perversion. He had little faith in his own will. He had tried to reform, but always lapsed into masturbation, which he found injurious, inasmuch as it caused (slight) neurasthenic symptoms. There was no moral defect. Intelligence was a little below the average. Careful education and aristocratic manners were apparent. The exquisite neuropathic eye betrayed a nervous constitution. The patient was not a complete and hopeless homesexual. *He had heterosexual feelings, his sensual inclinations towards the opposite sex, however, were manifested but weakly and infrequently.* When nineteen, he was first taken to a brothel by friends. He experienced no horror of a woman, had efficient erections, and some pleasure in coitus, but not the instinctive delight he experienced while embracing men.

Since then, patient asserted that he had had coitus six times, twice of his own accord. He gave the assurance that he was always capable of it, but he did it only for want of something better, as he did masturbation, when the sexual impulse troubled him, as a substitute for intercourse with men. He had thought of the possibility of finding a sympathetic lady and marrying her. He would regard marital cohabitation and abstinence from intercourse with men as hard duties.

Since there were rudiments of heterosexual feelings present, and the case could not be looked upon as hopeless, it seemed that treatment was indicated. The indications were clear enough, but there was no support for them in the will of the indolent patient, so unconscious of his own position. It seemed desirable to seek support for the moral influence in hypnosis. The fulfilment of this hope seemed doubtful, because the famous *Hansen* had tried several times, in vain, to hypnotize him.

At the same time, by reason of the most important social interests of the patient, it was necessary to make another attempt. To my great surprise, *Bernheim's* procedure induced immediately a condition of deep lethargy, with possibility of post-hypnotic suggestion.

At the second sitting somnambulism was induced by merely looking at him. The patient easily yielded to suggestions of all kinds; indeed, contractures were induced by stroking him. He was awakened by counting three. Awakened, patient had amnesia for all the events of the hypnotic state. Hypnosis was induced every second or third day for the communication of hypnotic suggestions. At the same time, moral and hydrotherapeutic measures were employed.

The hypnotic suggestions were as follows:

1. I abhor onanism, because it makes me weak and miserable.

2. I no longer have inclination towards men; for love for men is against religion, nature and law.

3. I feel an inclination towards woman; for woman is lovely and desirable, and created for man.

During the sittings the patient always repeated *verbatim* these suggestions. After the fourth sitting it was noticeable, that, when taken into society, he paid court to ladies. Shortly after that, when a famous primadonna sang, he was all enthusiasm for her. Some days later the patient sought the address of a brothel.

Yet he preferred the society of young gentlemen; but the most careful watching failed to reveal anything suspicious.

17th February. Patient asked to be allowed to indulge in coitus, and was very well satisfied with his experience with one of the *demi-mondes*.

16th March. Up to this time, hypnosis twice a week. The patient always passed into deep somnambulism by simply being looked at, and, at request, repeated the suggestions. He was susceptible to all kinds of post-hypnotic suggestion, and, in the waking state, knew not the least of the influences exerted on him in the hypnotic state. In the hypnotic condition he always gave the assurance that he was free from onanism and sexual feeling for men. Since he gave the same answers in hypnosis—e.g., that on such and such a date he practiced onanism for the last time, and that he was too much under the will of the physician to be able to lie—his assertions deserved belief; the more, since he looked well and was free from all neurasthenic symptoms, and, in the society of men, not the slightest suspicion rested on him. An open, free, and manly bearing was developed.

Moreover, since, of his own will, he now and then indulged in coitus with pleasure, and occasional pollutions were induced by lascivious dreams which concerned women, there could be no doubt of the favourable change of his sexual life; and it was presumable that the hypnotic suggestions had developed into auto-suggestive inclinations, which directed his feelings, thoughts and will. Probably the patient will always remain of frigid nature; but he more often spoke of marriage, and of his intention to win a wife as soon as he had become acquainted with a sympathetic lady. Treatment was stopped. (Author's own case, "Internat. Centralbl. für die Physiol. und Pathol. der Harn- und Sexualorgane" Band i.)

In July, 1889, I received a letter from his father, telling me of his son's good health and conduct.

On 24th May, 1890, by chance, I met my former patient, while on a journey. His bright, healthful appearance allowed the most favourable opinion of his condition. He told me that he still had sympathetic feeling for some men, but never anything like love. He occasionally had pleasurable coitus with women, and now thought of marriage.

I hypnotized him, in the former manner, to try him, and asked for the commands I had given him. In a deep condition of somnambulism, and in the same tone of voice as formerly, the patient repeated the suggestions he had received in December, 1888—an excellent example of the possible duration and power of post-hypnotic suggestion.

Other cases may be found in the eighth edition, cases 137, 138, 140, 141; and ninth edition, case 133, of this book.

The cases quoted by the author, as well as those given by *Ladame*, in which suggestion removed the homosexual instinct, or, at least, neutralized it (as a protection from shame and law), seem to afford a proof that even the gravest cases of congenital sexual inversion may be benefited by the application of hypnotism.

Wetterstrand (*cf. Schrenck, op. cit.*, case 49), *Bernheim* (*cf. Schrenck,* case 51), *Müller* (*cf. Schrenck*, case 53), *Schrenck* (*op. cit.*, cases 66, 67), report even complete success in displacing the homosexual by the heterosexual instinct coupled with virility. *Schrenck* (*op. cit.*, cases 62, 63) succeeded also in cases of effeminate men.

But only when hypnotism produces deep somnambulism, decided and lasting results may be hoped for, which, after all, are nothing more than suggestive training, not a real cure. They are marvellous artifacts of hypnotic science practiced on abnormal human beings, but by no means *"transformations"* (*cf. Schrenck*) of a psychosexual existence.

Very instructive in this respect is a case related by *Schrenck*, the representative of which after a cure was effected says of himself: "I am ever conscious of a certain insuperable coercion which does not rest upon moral principles, but must, as I believe, be referable directly to treatment." At any rate such "cures" afford no proof whatsoever against the assumption of original cause of sexual inversion.

It is necessary here to warn the reader against illusions about the true value of hypnotic therapy.

Attempts have been repeatedly made to question the right of the medical adviser to treat cases of antipathic sexuality. The advice given to the unfortunates so afflicted was to become reconciled with their anomaly and to eschew homosexual intercourse. In some cases in which the libido was weak or the sense of morality was not entirely blunted, success has been achieved. It was pointed out to these unfortunate beings that there are many other dreadful afflictions, such as trigeminal neuralgia or malignant tumors, which man must bear with resignation. This view involves, however, a defective knowledge of the meaning and bearing of antipathic sexual instinct, in so far as this affliction means nothing more or less than a hopeless existence, a life without love, an undignified comedy before human society, and moral and psychical marasmus if the advice is adopted; on the other hand, eventual loss of social position, civic honour and liberty are involved.

Castration is out of the question, because it is difficult to justify such an operation, for the antipathic sexual instinct with its psychical tortures, cannot be extirpated by this process even though the libido be diminished.

To confine such people in an insant asylum is a monstrous idea. Justification for it can only exist if the perverse individual suffers also from a psychosis which renders confinement imperative.

Another objection which has been made against treatment is that the welfare of society is jeopardized in so far as an opportunity is given to tainted individuals to propagate their perversions.

This objection appears ludicrous because no one has yet thought of prohibiting the marriage of the congenital libertine or habitual drunkard. My experience teaches me that the sexual perverts in general by no means constitute the worst type of degeneration. The progeny of individuals thus tainted, which I have had occasion to observe, has offered no pronounced manifestations of neuropathic constitution or taint.

Psychopathia sexualis is not often met with as a family failing or a mark of heredity.

The number of cases which have actually been cured of this anomaly will always be limited, because many of these unfortunates refrain from taking into their confidence even the medical man. Others despair beforehand of the efficacy of treatment, while some who practice homosexual intercourse and find satisfaction in it, hesitate to exchange their method for something uncertain. Again others demur for fear of becoming potent, and thus transmitting their own weakness to the offspring. Others present psychical impediments which seem insurmountable, or they do not react to hypnotic influence or suggestion, thus rendering treatment futile.

If an individual afflicted with antipathic sexual instinct, for ethical, social or any other reasons, demands treatment, surely it cannot be denied him. It is the sacred duty of every medical man to give advice and aid to the best of his ability and knowledge whenever it is asked for. The health and welfare of the patient must ever be paramount to that of society at large. Hygiene and prophylaxis enable him at all times to recompense the community for any damage he may have done in an isolated case.

Moreover, in the majority of cases the patient is quite satisfied when he becomes sexually neutral, and under these circumstances medical skill has rendered a great service to both society and the individual himself.

V. SPECIAL PATHOLOGY

THE MANIFESTATIONS OF ABNORMAL SEXUAL LIFE IN THE VARIOUS FORMS AND STATES OF MENTAL DISTURBANCE.

ARREST OF MENTAL DEVELOPMENT.

SEXUAL life in idiots is, generally speaking, but slightly developed. It is wanting entirely in idiots of high grade. In such instances the genitals are frequently small and deformed, and menstruation is late or does not occur at all. There is either impotence or sterility. Even in idiots of low grade, sexuality is not prominent. In rare cases it is manifested with a certain periodicity, and then with greater intensity. It may then find expression in sudden impulses, and be violently satisfied. Perversions of the sexual instinct do not seem to occur at the lowest levels of mental development.

When the desire for sexual satisfaction is opposed in these cases, great passion is excited, with danger of murderous assault on the person attacked. It is to be expected that idiots should not exercise choice, and even attempt to satisfy the sexual instinct on their nearest relatives.

Thus *Marc-Ideler* reports the case of an idiot who attempted to rape his sister, and had almost strangled her when he was discovered.

Friedreich reports an analogous case (*"Friedreich's* Blätter," 1858, p. 50).

I have repeatedly had occasion to give opinions in cases of attempts to rape little girls.

Giraud ("Annal. méd. psych.," 1885, No. 7) also reports a case of this kind. Consciousness of the significance of the act is always wanting; but an instinctive knowledge that such obscene acts are not publicly permitted is often present, and causes the act to be undertaken in a deserted place.

In imbeciles the sexual instinct is usually developed as in normal individuals. The moral inhibitory ideas are cloudy, and, therefore, the sexual impulse is more or less openly manifested. For this reason imbeciles are sources of disturbance in society. Abnormal intensity and perversion of the sexual instinct are infrequent.

The most frequent manner of satisfying the sexual desire is onanism. The weak-minded seldom make sexual attacks on adults of the opposite sex.

Sexual satisfaction with animals is frequently attempted. The great majority of cases of injury (sexual) to animals must be attributed to imbeciles. Children are quite often their victims.

Emminghaus ("*Maschka's* Hanb.," iv., p. 234) draws attention to the frequency of unrestricted manifestation of sexual instinct, which comprises open masturbation, exhibition of the genitals, attacks on children and those of the same sex, and sodomy.

Giraud ("Annal. méd. psychol.," 1855, No. 1) has reported a whole series of immoral attacks on children [1]:—

1. H., aged seventeen, imbecile, enticed a little girl into a barn, by giving her nuts. There he exposed her genitals and showed his own, making movements of coitus on the child's abdomen. He had no idea of the moral significance of the act.

2. L., aged twenty-one; imbecile; degenerate. While he was watching cattle, his sister of eleven years, with a playmate of eight years, came and told him how some unknown man had attempted to do them violence. L. led the children to a deserted house and attempted coitus with the younger child, but let her go because immission was unsuccessful, and because the child cried out. On the way home he promised to marry her if she would not say anything. At the trial he thought that by marriage he could right the wrong he had done.

3. G., aged twenty-one, microcephalic, imbecile, had masturbated since his sixth year, and practiced active and passive pederasty. He had repeatedly tried to perform pederasty with boys, and attacked little girls. He was absolutely without an understanding of his acts. His sexual desires were manifested periodically and intensely, as in animals.[2]

4. B., aged twenty-one; imbecile. While alone in a forest with his sister of nineteen, he demanded that she allow coitus. She refused. He threatened to strangle her, and stabbed her with a knife. The frightened girl wrenched his penis, and he then left her and quietly went on with his work. B. had a deformed, microcephalic skull, and had no sense of the significance of his act.

Emminghaus (*op. cit.*, p. 234) reports the case of an exhibitionist:—

CASE 171. A man, aged forty, married, had for sixteen years been accustomed to exhibit himself in parks, at dusk, to little girls and servants, and drew their attention to himself by whistling. After having been frequently punished for it, he avoided the places, but he carried on his practice elsewhere. Hydrocephalus. Mental weakness of slight degree. Mild sentence passed.

CASE 172. X., of tainted family; imbecile; defective and perverted in intellect, feeling and will. For help and protection he was brought before an officer. It was complained that he had repeatedly exposed his genitals to servant-girls, and had shown himself at windows with the upper portion of his body naked. No other manifestations of inverted sexual instinct. No onanism reported (*Sander*, "Archiv f. Psych.," p. 655).

CASE 173. *Pederasty with a child.* On 8th April, 1884, at ten o'clock, A.M., while X. was sitting in the street, holding a boy of eighteen months on her lap, a certain Vallario approached and took the child from X., saying he was going to take it for a walk. He went the distance of half a kilometre, and returned, saying that the child had fallen from his arms, and thus injured its anus. The anus was torn, and blood was pouring from it. At the place where the deed was done, traces of semen were found. V. confessed his horrible crime, and, at his final trial, he acted so strangely that an examination of his mental condition was made. He had impressed the prison attendants as being an imbecile. V., aged forty-five, mason, defective morally and intellectually; narrow, deformed facial bones; the halves of the face and the ears asymmetrical; brow low and retreating; genitals normal. V. showed general diminution of cutaneous sensibility, was imbecile, and had no ideas. He lived in the present, had no ambition, and did nothing of his own will. He had no desires and no emotional feeling. He had never had coitus. Nothing more could be ascertained about his sexual life. Proofs of intellectual and moral idiocy, due to microcephaly; the crime was ascribed to a perverse, uncontrollable sexual impulse. Sent to an asylum (*Virgilio*, "Il Manicomio," v: year, No. 3).

A case mentioned by *L. Meyer* ("Arch. f. Psych.," Bd. i., p. 103) shows how female imbeciles may indulge in shameless prostitution and immorality.[3]

STATES OF ACQUIRED MENTAL WEAKNESS.

The numerous anomalies of the sexual life in senile dementia have been described in the section on "General Pathology." In other conditions of acquired mental weakness—those due to apoplexy; head injury; to the secondary stages of psychoses; or to inflammatory processes in the cortex (syphilis, syphilitic dementia),—perversions of the sexual instinct seem to be infrequent; and here the immoral sexual acts seem to depend on abnormally increased or uninhibited sexual feeling, which, in itself, is not abnormal.

1. DEMENTIA CONSECUTIVE TO PSYCHOSES.

Casper ("Klin. Novellen," Fall 31) reports a case that belongs here. It is that of a physician, aged thirty-three, who attempted rape on a child. He was weakened mentally, as a result of hypochondriacal melancholia. He excused his deed in a very silly way, and had no appreciation of the moral and criminal meaning of the act, which was apparently the result of a sexual impulse that could not be controlled on account of his mental weakness.

Case 21, in *Limun's*, "Zweifelhafte Geisteszustände," is an analogous case (dementia after melancholia; offense against morals by exhibition).

2. DEMENTIA AFTER APOPLEXY.

CASE 174. B., aged fifty-two. He passed through a cerebral attack, and was no longer able to carry on his business as a merchant.

One day, in the absence of his wife, he locked two girls in the house, gave them liquors to drink, and then carried out sexual acts with the children. He commanded them to say nothing, and went to his business. The medical expert established mental weakness, resulting from repeated apoplexies. B., who, up to this time, had been well-behaved, says he committed the criminal act because of an uncontrollable and incomprehensible impulse; and that, when he came to himself, he was ashamed, and sent the girls away. Since his apoplectic attack, B. had been weak-minded, incapable of business, and hemiplegic; but, soon after arrest, he made an unskilful attempt at suicide. He often cried childishly. His moral and intellectual energy in opposing his sexual impulses was certainly much weakened. No sentence (*Giraud*, "Ann. méd. Psychol.," March, 1881).

3. DEMENTIA AFTER APOPLEXY OF HEAD.

CASE 175. K., when fourteen years old, was injured on the head by a horse. The skull was fractured in several places, and several pieces of bone required removal.

From that time K. was weak mentally, irascible, and ill-tempered. Gradually he developed an inordinate and truly beastly sensuality, which drove him to the most immoral acts. One day he raped a girl of twelve, and strangled her for fear of discovery. Arrested, he confessed. The medical experts declared him responsible, and he was executed.

The autopsy revealed ossification of almost all the sutures, remarkable asymmetry of the halves of the skull, and evidences of healed fractures. The affected hemisphere had bands of cicatricial tissue running through it, and was one-third smaller than the other (*Friedreich's* "Blätter," 1885, Heft 6).

4. ACQUIRED MENTAL WEAKNESS, PROBABLY RESULTING FROM SYPHILIS.

CASE 176. X., officer, had repeatedly committed immoral acts with little girls; among other things, he had induced them to perform masturbation on him, had exposed his genitals, and handled theirs.

X., formerly healthy, and of blameless life, was infected with syphilis in 1867. In 1879 paralysis of the left abducens occurred. Thereafter mental weakness was noticed, with a change of his disposition and character. Headache, occasional incoherence of speech, failure of power of thought and logic, occasional inequality of pupils, and paresis of the right facial muscles, were observed.

X., aged thirty-seven, showed no trace of syphilis when examined. The paralysis of the left abducens was still present. The left eye was amblyopic. He was mentally weak. Concerning the trial that was before him, he said it was nothing but a harmless misunderstanding. Indications of aphasia. Weakness of memory, particularly for recent events. Superficial emotional reaction; rapid exhaustion of memory and ability to speak. Proved: that the ethical defect and the perverse sexual impulse are the symptoms of an abnormal condition of brain induced by syphilis.

Suspension of criminal proceedings (personal case, "Jahrbücher für Psychiatrie").

5. GENERAL PARESIS.

Here the sexual life is usually abnormally affected; in the incipient stages of the disease, as well as in episodical states of excitement, it is intensified, and sometimes perverse. In the final stages *libido* and sexual power usually become *nil*.

Just as in the prodromal stage of the senile forms, one sees here, in connection with more or less evident losses in the moral and intellectual spheres, expressions of an apparently intensified sexual instinct (obscene talk, lasciviousness in intercourse with the opposite sex, thoughts of marriage, frequenting of brothels, etc.), which is characteristic of the clouding of consciousness.

Seduction, abduction and public scandal are here the order of the day. At first there is still some appreciation of the circumstances, though the cynicism of the acts is striking enough. As the mental weakness increases, such patients become criminal by reason of exhibition, masturbation in the streets and attempts at immoral acts with children.

If conditions of mental excitement come on, attempts at rape are committed, or at least, grossly immoral acts,—the patient attacks women on the street, appears in public in very imperfect dress; or, half-clothed, tries to force his way into strange houses, to cohabit with the wife of an acquaintance, or to marry the daughter on the spot.

Numerous cases belonging to this category are cited by *Tardieu* ("Attentats aux moeurs"); *Mendel* ("Progressive Paralyse der Irren," 1880, p. 123); *Westphal* ("Arch. f. Psych., vii., p. 622); and a case by *Petrucci* ("Annal. méd. Psychol.," 1875) shows that bigamy may also occur here.

The brutal disregard of consequences with which the patients in the advanced stages attempt to satisfy their sexual needs is characteristic.

In a case reported by *Legrand* ("La folie," p. 519), the father of a family was found masturbating in the open street. After the act he consumed his semen.

A patient seen by me, an officer, of a prominent family, in broad daylight, made attacks on little girls at a watering-place.

A similar case is reported by Dr. *Régis* ("De la dynamic ou exaltation fonctionnelle au début de la paral. gén.," 1878).

Cases reported by *Tarnowsky* (*op. cit.*, p. 82) show that also pederasty and bestiality may occur in the prodromal stages and course of this malady.

EPILEPSY.

Epilepsy is allied to the acquired states of mental weakness because it often leads to them, and then all the possibilities of reckless satisfaction of the sexual impulse that have been mentioned may occur. Moreover, in many epileptics the sexual instinct is very intense. For the most part it is satisfied by masturbation, now and then by attacks on children, and by pederasty. Perversion of the instinct with perverse sexual acts seems to be infrequent.

Much more important are the numerous cases in literature in which epileptics, who, during intervals, present no signs of active sexual impulse, but manifest it in connection with epileptic attacks, or during the time of equivalent or post-epileptic exceptional mental states. These cases have scarcely yet been studied clinically, and forensically not at all; but they deserve careful study. In this way certain cases of violence and rape would be understood, and legal murders prevented.

From the following facts it will certainly be clear that the cerebral changes which accompany the epileptic outbreak may induce an abnormal excitation of the sexual instinct.[4] Besides, in the exceptional mental states of epileptics, they are unable to resist their impulses, by reason of the disturbance of consciousness.

For years I have known a young epileptic, of bad heredity, who, always after frequent epileptic seizures, attacks his mother and tries to violate her. After a time he comes to himself, and has no recollection of his acts. In the intervals he is very strict in morals, and has but slight sexual inclination.

Some years ago I became acquainted with a young peasant, who, during epileptic attacks, masturbated shamelessly, but during the intervals was above reproach.

Simon ("Crimes et délits," p. 220) mentions an epileptic girl of twenty-three, well educated, and of the best morals, who, in attacks of vertigo, would shout out obscene words, then raise her dress, make lascivious movements, and try to tear open her undergarments.

Kiernan ("Alienist and Neurologist," January, 1884) reports the case of an epileptic who always had, as an aura, the vision of a beautiful woman in lascivious attitudes, which induced ejaculation. After some years, with treatment with potassium bromide, the vision was changed to that of a devil attacking him with a pitchfork. The instant this reached him, he became unconscious.

The same author speaks of a very respectable man who had, two or three times a year, epileptic attacks of furor and melancholy, with impulses to pederasty, which lasted a week or two; and of a lady who, with epilepsy that came on during the climacteric, had sexual desire for boys.

CASE 177. W., of good heredity, previously healthy; before and after the attack, sound mentally, quiet, kind, temperate. On 13th April, 1877, he had no appetite. On the 14th, in the presence of his wife and children, he demanded coitus, first of his wife's friend, who was present, then of his wife. Taken away, he had an epileptoid attack; after this he became wildly maniacal and destructive, threw hot water on those that tried to approach him, and threw a child in the stove. Then he soon became quiet, but for some days remained confused, and finally came to himself with no recollection of the events of his attack (*Kowalewsky*, "Jahrbücher f. Psych.," 1879).

Another case, examined by *Caspar* ("Klin. Novellen," p. 267), may be attributed to epilepsy (latent). A respectable man attacked four women, one after another, in the open street (one before two witnesses), and violated one of them, "notwithstanding that his young, pretty and healthy wife" lived hard by.

The epileptic significance of the sexual acts in the following cases is unequivocal:—

CASE 178. L., an official, aged forty; a kind husband and father. During four years he had offended public morals twenty-five times, for which he had to endure long imprisonment.

In the first seven complaints he was accused of exposing his genitals to girls from eleven to thirteen years old, while passing them on horseback, and calling their attention by obscene words. While in confinement, he had exposed his genitals at a window which opened on a popular street.

L.'s father was insane; his brother was once met on the street wearing only a shirt. During his military service L. had had two attacks of severe fainting. Since 1859 he had suffered with peculiar attacks of vertigo, at such times becoming weak, tremulous, and deathly pale; it grew dark before his eyes, he saw bright stars, and was forced to get support in order to keep upright. After violent attacks, great weakness, profuse sweating.

Since 1861 he had been very irritable, which, respected though he was as an official, caused him much trouble in his work. His wife noticed the change in him. He had days when he would run about the house as if insane, holding his head between his hands, striking the wall, and complaining of headache. In 1864 he fell to the ground four times, lying there stiff, with eyes open. Confused states of consciousness were also proved to have occurred.

L. declared that he had not the slightest remembrance of the crime of which he was accused. Observation showed further and more violent attacks of epileptic vertigo. L. was not sentenced. In 1875 paretic dementia developed with rapidly fatal results (*Westphal*, "Arch. f. Psych.," vii., p. 113).

CASE 179. A rich man of twenty-six had lived for a year with a girl with whom he was very much in love. He cohabited but rarely, but was never perverse.

Twice during the year, after excessive indulgence in alcohol, he had had epileptic attacks. One evening after dinner, at which he had taken much wine, he hurried to the house of his mistress, and into her sleeping-apartment, although the servant told him she was not at home. From there he hastened into a room where a boy of fourteen was sleeping, and began to violate him. At the cry of the child, whose prepuce and hand he had injured, the servant hurried to them. He left the boy and raped the maid; after that he went to bed and slept twelve hours. When he awoke, he had an indistinct remembrance of intoxication and coitus. Thereafter there were repeated epileptic attacks (*Tarnowsky, op. cit.*, p. 52).

CASE 180. X., of high social position, led a dissolute life for some time, and had epileptic attacks. He became engaged. On his wedding day, shortly before the ceremony, he appeared on his brother's arm before the assembled guests. When he came before his bride, he exposed his genitals and began to masturbate. He was at once taken to an expert in mental disease. On the way he constantly masturbated, and for some days was actuated by this impulse, which gradually decreased in intensity. After this paroxysm the patient had only a confused remembrance of the events, and could give no explanation of his acts (*Tarnowsky, op. cit.*, p. 53).

CASE 181. Z., aged twenty-seven; very bad heredity; epileptic. He violated a girl of eleven, and then killed her. He lied about the deed. Absence of memory, *i.e.*, mental confusion at the time of the crime, was not proved. *Pugliese*, "Arch. di Psich," viii., p. 622).

CASE 182. V., aged sixty; physician; violated children. Sentenced to imprisonment for two years. Dr. *Marandon* later on proved the existence of epileptoid attacks of apprehensiveness, demential, erotic and hypochondriacal delusions and occasional attacks of fear (*Lacassagne*, "Lyon. méd.," 1887, No. 51).

CASE 183. On 4th August, 1878, H., aged about fifteen, was picking gooseberries with several little girls and boys as her companions. Suddenly she threw L., aged ten, to the ground and exposed her, and ordered A., aged eight, and O., aged five, to bring about a joining of members with the girl, and they obeyed.

H. had a good character. For five years she had been subject to irritability, headache, vertigo and epileptic attacks. Her mental and physical development had been arrested. She had not menstruated, but she manifested menstrual symptoms. Her mother was suspected to be epileptic. For three months H., after seizures, had frequently done strange things, and afterward had no remembrance of them.

H. seemed to have been deflowered. Mental defect was not apparent. She said she had no remembrance of the act of which she was accused. According to her mother's testimony, she had an epileptic attack on the morning of 4th August, and she had been, on that account, told by her mother not to leave the house (*Pürkhauer*, "Friedreich's Blätter f. ger. Med.," 1879, H. 5).

CASE 184. *Immoral acts of an epileptic in states of abnormal unconsciousness.*—T., revenue collector; aged fifty-two; married. He was charged of being guilty of immorality with boys for the past seventeen years, by practicing masturbation on them, and by inducing them to carry out the act on himself. The accused, a respected officer, was overcome by the terrible crime attributed to him, and declared that he knew nothing of the deeds of which he was accused. His mental integrity was questionable. His family physician, who had known him twenty years, emphasized his peculiar, retiring disposition and his mercurial moods. His wife asserted that T. once tried to throw her in the water, and that he sometimes had outbreaks in which he tore off his clothing, and tried to throw himself out of window. T. knew nothing of these attacks. Other witnesses testified to strange changes of mood and peculiarities of character. A physician reported the observation of occasional attacks of vertigo and convulsions in him.

T.'s grandfather was insane; his father was affected with chronic alcoholism, and of late years had had epileptiform attacks. The father's brother was insane, and had killed a relative while in a delirious state. Another uncle of T. had killed himself. Of T.'s three children, one was weak-minded, another cross-eyed, and the third was subject to convulsions. The accused asserted that he had occasional attacks in which consciousness was so reduced that he did not know what he was about. These attacks were ushered in by an auro-like pain in the back of his neck. He was then impelled to go out in the air. He did not know where he went. His wife had perfectly satisfied him sexually. For eighteen years he had had chronic eczema of the scrotum, which had often caused him to have extraordinary sexual excitement. The opinions of the six experts were contradictory (sane,—attacks of latent epilepsy); the jury disagreed, and he was dismissed. Dr. *Legrand du Saulle*, who was called as an expert witness, found that, until his twenty-second year, T. had urinated in bed from ten to eighteen times a year. After that time nocturnal bedwetting had ceased; but, from that time, states of mental confusion, lasting from an hour to a day, had occurred occasionally, and they left the patient without any remembrance of them. Soon T. was arrested again for public immorality, and sentenced to imprisonment for fifteen months. In prison he grew sick, and apparently much weaker mentally. For this reason he was pardoned, but the mental weakness increased. T. was noticed to have repeated epileptoid convulsions (tonic convulsion with tremor and loss of consciousness) (*Auzouy*, "Annal. méd. psychol.," 1874, Nov.; *Legrand du Saulle*, "Etude méd. légale," etc., p. 99).

The following cases of immoral acts with children, observed by the author and reported in "*Friedreich's* Blätter," will serve to conclude this group,[5] so important in its legal bearings. It is the more important, in that a state of unconsciousness was established at the time of the act, and because, for allied reasons, the facts related show how a complicated and refined act becomes possible in such a state of unconsciousness.

CASE 185. P., aged forty-nine; married, hospital beneficiary. He was accused of having committed the following terrible acts with two girls,—D., aged ten, and G., aged nine,—whom he had taken to his work-shop on 25th May, 1883.

D. testified: "I was in the meadow with G. and my sister J., aged three. P. called us into his shop and fastened the door. Then he kissed us, tried to put his tongue in my mouth and licked my face; he held me on his knees, opened his trousers, lifted up my skirt, tickled my genitals with his finger, and rubbed my vulva with his member until I became moist. When I cried, he gave me twelve kreuzers, and threatened to shoot me if I exposed him. At last he tried to persuade me to come again the next day."

G. testified: "P. kissed D.'s buttocks and genitals and assaulted me with attempts to do the same. He then took the little boy, who was only three years old, in his arms, kissed him, and held his own naked sexual parts against him. Afterwards he asked us our names and opined that D.'s genitals were much bigger than mine. He tried to force us to take his member, hold it in our hands, and see how it became erect."

At his examination, 29th May, P. said he had but an indistinct recollection of having fondled, caressed and made presents to a little girl a short time before. If he had done anything more, it must have been in an irresponsible condition. Besides, he had suffered for years with weakness in his head as result of an injury. On 22nd June he knew nothing of the events of 25th May, and nothing of his examination on 29th May. This amnesia was shown also on cross-examination.

P. came of a family affected with cerebral disease; a brother was epileptic. P. was formerly a drinker. Years before he had actually received an injury to his head. Since then, from time to time, he had attacks of mental disturbance, introduced by moroseness, irritability, tendency to alcoholic excesses, apprehension, and delusions of persecution sufficient to induce threats and deeds of violence. At the same time he would have auditory hyperaesthesia, vertigo, headache and cerebral congestion,—all this, with great mental confusion and amnesia for the whole period of the attack, which sometimes lasted for weeks.

During the intervals he was subject to headache, which started from the seat of injury on the head (a small scar in the skin over the right temple), which was painful on pressure. With exacerbation of the headache he became very irritable, morose to an extent that inclined him to suicide, and mentally like one drunk. In 1879, while in such a state, he made an impulsive attempt at suicide, of which he afterward had no remembrance. Soon after this, being sent to a hospital, he gave the impression of being epileptic, and for a long time was treated with pot. bromide. At the end of 1879 he was taken to the infirmary, no actual epileptic attack having been observed.

During his lucid intervals he was a virtuous, industrious, good-natured man, and had never shown any sexual excitement; and, until this time, never sexual inclinations, even during his mental confusion. Moreover, until lately he had lived with his wife. At the time of the criminal act he had shown signs of an approaching attack, and had asked the physician to prescribe pot. bromide.

P. asserted that, since the injury to his head, he had been intolerant of heat and alcohol, which immediately brought on headache and confusion. The medical examination proved the truth of his assertions about mental weakness, irritability and poor sleep.

If pressure were made at the seat of the trauma, P. became congested, irritable, confused and trembled all over; he appeared excited; consciousness was disturbed, and remained so for hours.

At times, when he was free from the sensations that started from the scar, he seemed kind, free, willing and open, though he was mentally weak and cloudy. P. was not sentenced (*see* "*Friedreich's* Blätter" for full report).

PERIODICAL INSANITY.

Just as in cases of non-periodical mania, an abnormal intensity or a noticeable prominence of the sexual sphere is very often manifested in the periodical attacks (see below "Mania").

The following case, reported by *Servaes* ("Arch. f. Psych."), shows that it then may also be perverted:

CASE 186. Catherine W., aged sixteen; she had not yet menstruated; previously healthy. Father very irascible.

Seven weeks before admission (3rd December, 1872), melancholic depression and irritability. 27th November, maniacal outbreak, lasting two days; thereafter, melancholic. 6th December, normal condition.

24th December (twenty-eight days after the first maniacal attack), silent, shy, depressed. 27th December, exaltation (jolly, laughing, etc.), with violent love for an attendant (female). 31st December, suddenly melancholic catalepsy, which disappeared after two hours. 20th January, 1873, new attack like the previous one. A similar one on 18th February, with traces of menses. The patient had no recollection whatever of what had occurred in the paroxysms, and blushed scarlet with astonishment and shame when told about them.

Thereafter there were abortive attacks, which entirely disappeared, to give place to the normal mental condition in June.

In a case reported by *Gock* ("Arch. f. Psych." v.), which was probably circular insanity, in a man of very bad heredity, during the state of exaltation there was manifestation of sexual feeling for men. In this case, however, the patient thought himself a girl, and it is questionable whether the sexual inclination was induced by the delusion or by an antipathic sexual instinct.

In connection with these cases of abnormal manifestation of the sexual instinct are those which, as a symptom of mania, manifest an abnormal and frequently a perverse sexual instinct in an impulsive way, analogous to dipsomania, while in the intervals the sexual instinct is neither intense nor perverse.

Quite a genuine case of such *periodical psychopathia sexualis*, connected with the process of menstruation, is the following reported by *Anjél* ("Arch. f. Psych." xv., Heft 2):—

CASE 187. A quiet lady, near the menopause. Very bad heredity. In her youth attacks of *petit mal*. Always eccentric, quick-tempered; very moral; childless marriage.

Several years ago, after a violent emotional disturbance, a hystero-epileptic attack, with post-epileptic insanity of several weeks' duration. Thereafter there was sleeplessness for several months. Following this, there was always menstrual insomnia, and the impulse to embrace and kiss boys of ten, and fondle their genitals. During this excitement there was no desire for coitus; certainly not for intercourse with adults.

The patient often spoke openly of this impulse, and asked to be watched, as she was not to be trusted. In the intervals she anxiously avoided all talk of it, was very modest, and in no way passionate sexually.

With reference to the still imperfectly known cases of periodical *psychopathia sexualis* of this kind *Tarnowsky* (*op. cit.*, p. 38) has made valuable contributions, though his cases were not all of a periodic nature.

Tarnowsky reports cases where married, cultured men, the fathers of families, were, from time to time, compelled to perform the most terrible sexual acts, while during the intervals they were sexually normal, abhorred their paroxysmal sexual acts, and shuddered before the expectation of their repetition.

If a new paroxysm came on, the normal sexual instinct disappeared; a state of mental excitement arose with insomnia, and thoughts and impulses to commit the perverse sexual acts, with anxious confusion and an increasing impulse to the abhorred indulgence. In this state the act was a relief, because it ended the condition. The analogy with periodic alcoholism is complete.

For other cases (of periodical pederasty, *see Tarnowsky, op. cit.*, p. 41. The case there reported, on page 46 belongs in the category of epilepsy.

The following case, reported by *Anjél* ("Arch. f. Psych.," xv., Heft 2), is one of the most typical of the convulsive-like occurrence of sexual excitement:—

CASE 188. A gentleman of high social position, aged forty-five; generally respected and beloved; heredity good; very moral; married fifteen years. Previously sexually normal, the father of several healthy children, and living in happy matrimony. Eight years ago he had a sudden fright. For some weeks thereafter he had a feeling of apprehension of cardiac attacks. Then came attacks, at intervals of several months or a year, of what the patient called his "moral catarrh." He became sleepless. After three days, loss of appetite, increasing irritability, strange appearance; fixed stare, staring into space; paleness, changing with redness; tremor of the fingers; red, shining eyes, with peculiar glassy expression; and violent, quick manner of speech. There was a desire for girls of from five to ten years, even for his own daughters. He would beg his wife to guard the children. For days at a time, while in this state, he would shut himself in his room. Previously he was compelled to pass school-girls on the street, and he found a peculiar pleasure in exposing his genitals before them, by acting as if about to urinate.

For fear of exposure, he shut himself in his room, morose, incapable of movement, and torn by feelings of fear. Consciousness seemed to be undisturbed. The attacks lasted from eight to fourteen days. The cause of their return was not clear. Improvement was sudden; there was great desire for sleep, and, after this was satisfied, he was well again. In the interval there was nothing abnormal. *Anjél* assumed an epileptic foundation, and considered the attacks to be the psychical equivalents of epileptic convulsions.

MANIA.

With the general excitation that here exists in the psychical organ, the sexual sphere is likewise often implicated. In maniacal individuals of the female sex, this is the rule. In certain cases, it may be questionable whether the instinct, which, in itself, is not intensified, is simply recklessly manifested, or whether it is present in actual abnormal intensity. For the most part, the latter is the true assumption—certainly so where sexual delusions and their religious equivalents are constantly expressed. In accordance with the degrees of intensity of the disease, the intensified instinct is expressed in different forms.

In simple maniacal exaltation in men, courting, frivolity, and lasciviousness in speech, and frequenting of brothels, are observed; in women, inclination for the society of men, personal adornment, perfumes, talk of marriage and scandals, suspicion of the virtue of other women; or there is manifested the religious equivalent—pilgrimages, missionary work, desire to become a monk or the servant of a priest; and in this case there is much talk about innocence and virginity.

At the height of mania there may be seen invitations to coitus, exhibition, obscenity, great excitation at sight of women, tendency to smear the person with saliva, urine, and even faeces; religio-sexual delusions,—to be under the protection of the Holy Ghost, to have given birth to Christ, etc.; open onanism and pelvic movements of coitus.

In maniacal men care must be taken to prevent shameless masturbation and sexual attacks on women.

NYMPHOMANIA AND SATYRIASIS.[6]

The description of these conditions is simply an annex to the attempt made on page 46 to explain excessive sexual desire, in so far as we take into consideration temporary sexual affects emanating therefrom, no matter whether they are occasioned by abstinence or are of a permanent character. They may become so predominant that they completely sway the field of imagination and desire, and imperatively demand the relief of the affect in the corresponding sexual act. In acute and severe cases, ethics and will-power lose their controlling influence entirely, while in chronic and milder cases restraint is still possible to a certain degree. At the acme of paroxysm hallucinations, delirium and benumbed consciousness make their appearance, and often continue during a prolonged period.

Such cases have led to the classification of nymphomania as a proper psychical disease. But this is an error, for nymphomania is only a syndrome within the sphere of psychical degeneration. As such it may manifest itself as an *acute paroxysmic* condition, analogous to dipsomania, frequently coinciding with menstrual phases, recurring either in stated periodical cycles, or at irregular intervals. Or it may be a complication or combination of other conditions and appear episodically in senile dementia, involutional psychosis, mania in degenerates, and delirium acutum ("acute deadly nymphomania").

Moreau (*op. cit.*) reports an interesting case. A young girl became suddenly a nymphomaniac when forsaken by her betrothed; she revelled in cynical songs and expressions, and lascivious attitudes and gestures. She refused to put on her garments, had to be held down in bed by muscular men (!) and furiously demanded coitus. Insomnia, congestion of the facial nerves, a dry tongue, and rapid pulse. Within a few days lethal collapse.

Louyer-Villermay (*op. cit.*): Miss X., aged thirty; modest and decent, was suddenly seized with an attack of nymphomania, unlimited desire for sexual gratification, obscene delirium. Death from exhaustion within a few days. *Cf.* three other cases with deadly result by *Maresch*, Psychiatr. Centralblatt, 1871.

Chronic Nymphomania is more frequently met with, but seems to occur only in individuals psychically degenerated. It is the result of sexual hyperaesthesia and exacerbations thereof reaching even to the state of sexual affects which manifest themselves in impulsive acts, or, in milder cases, are complicated with delusions. These, however, need not by necessity lead to involuntary acts, in as much as ethical considerations may counterbalance the milder forms of sexual excitement and, moreover, recourse to solitary masturbation as a means of temporary relief is here always possible.

These milder cases of nymphomania claim our sympathy not less than those unfortunate women who by irresistible impulses are forced to sacrifice feminine honour and dignity, for they are fully conscious of their painful situation, they are a toy in the grip of a morbid imagination which revolves solely around sexual ideas and grasps even the most distant points in the sense of an aphrodisiac. Even in their sleep they are pursued by lascivious dreams. In the daytime the slightest cause will produce a crisis in which a veritable abnormal mental and sexual excitement, coupled with painful sensations (pressure, vibration, pulsation, etc.,) in the genitals torments them. Temporary relief comes in time in the shape of neurasthenia of the genitals (neurasthenia = nervous debility), which reacts promptly on the centre of ejaculation and readily causes pollutions in lascivious dreams, or some erotic crisis when awake. Full gratification, however, they cannot find any more than those of their unfortunate fellow-sufferers who abandon themselves to men. This *anaphrodisia* explains to a large extent the persistence of the sexual affect, *i.e.*, that nymphomania which heaps crisis up on crisis.

Neurasthenia which inhibits orgasm and sensual gratification, no doubt, fully explains this anaphrodisia which restrains the beneficient assuagement of sexual emotions, yet maintaining an incessant craving (excessive *libido*), forces the woman, morally devoid of all power of resistance, to auto-masturbation or psychical onanism, and eventually as a nymphomaniac to prostitution in which to find satisfaction and relief with one man after another.

This neurasthenia is often caused by an abnormally early and powerful sexual instinct, which prescribes onanism; or it may be reduced to enforced continence with strong coexisting sexual appetite.

CASE 189. Mrs. V., from earliest youth mania for men. Of good ancestors, highly cultured, good-natured, very modest, blushed easily, but always the terror of the family. Indeed when she was alone with a member of the opposite sex, irrespective of whether he was a child, in the prime of life or an old man, or whether he was handsome or ugly, she would immediately remove her clothes and urgently request that he satisfy her desire by inserting either his penis or his hand. Marriage was resorted to as a cure. She loved her husband most ardently, but nevertheless was unable to restrain herself from demanding intercourse from any man, if she happened to catch him alone, whether he was a friend, a paid gigolo or a schoolboy.

Nothing could cure her of this failing. Even when she was a grandmother, she even wished to rape her twelve year old son as he lay in bed. He tore himself away and fled, and his brother gave her a severe punishment. But it was all in vain. When sent to a convent she was a model of good conduct and committed not the slightest act of indiscretion. But the moment she returned home, she resumed her perverse practices. The family sent her away, giving her a small allowance. She worked hard to earn the money she needed for "buying her lovers." In looking at the trim, neat matron of sixty-five years of age, with her modest manners and a most amiable disposition, no one could ever suspect how shamelessly needy in her sexual life she was even then.

At last she was sent to an insane asylum, where she lived till May, 1858, when in her seventy-third year, she succumbed to a stroke of cerebral apoplexy. Her behavior at the asylum when under surveillance, was beyond reproach; but if left to herself she utilized every opportunity in the same old fashion even to within a few days before her death. No other signs of mental anomaly could be detected in her. (*Trelat*, "folie lucide.")

CASE 190. *Chronic nymphomania.* Mrs. E., age forty-seven. An uncle on father's side insane. Father suffered from self-conceit and was given to sexual excess. A brother of the patient died from acute cerebral inflammation. Always nervous, eccentric, erotic, began coitus at the age of ten. Married at nineteen. Although her husband was virile, she maintained a number of male friends. Fully conscious of the abominable nature of her conduct, she was powerless in restraining her insatiable appetite. She kept up appearances, however. Later on she claimed that she had suffered from a "monomania for men."

She had six confinements. One day she was thrown from a carriage and sustained concussion of the brain. This caused melancholia and delusions of persecution. With approaching menopause the menses became frequent and very profuse, but the libido gradually disappeared. Slight degree of dropped uterus and prolapsed anus.

Chronic conditions of nymphomania are apt to weaken public morality and lead to offenses against decency. Woe unto the man who falls into the meshes of such an insatiable nymphomaniac, whose sexual appetite is never appeased. Heavy neurasthenia and impotence are the inevitable consequences. These unfortunate women disseminate the spirit of lewdness, demoralize their surroundings, become a danger to boys, and are liable to corrupt girls also, for there are homosexual nymphomaniacs as well.[7] By exposing their feminine charms, even by exhibition, they lure men. Nymphomaniacs endowed with the world's riches purchase lovers. In many instances they resort to prostitution.

The conditions of *Satyriasis* in men are analogous to nymphomania. It is a central disturbance, either of an acute character or chronic. In the acute stage it may lead to hallucinations of erotic content, and where compensation of the sexual affect is rendered impossible, to furious mania, delirium acutum.

This pathological sexual affect, stigmatised by abnormal intensity and duration, fills the whole psychical life. Occurrences of the commonest and most indifferent nature are taken as sensual hints or suggestions. The lustful colouring of thoughts, ideas or natural perceptions by the senses is strongly exaggerated. At the acme of the crisis the patient is in a "rut-like" condition, in which consciousness is clouded and a general physical excitement, similar to that during coitus (*cf.* p. 26) pervades the whole frame. Ejaculation may be concatenated with a renewed phase of orgasm in which the genital organs retain a permanent turgescence (priapism). The individual afflicted with satyriasis is forever exposed to the peril of commiting rape, thus becoming a common danger to all persons of the opposite sex. For want of something better he resorts to masturbation and sodomy. Luckily satyriasis is a rare disease. It is not due to poisoning with cantharides, as some claim, which only produces priapism, that is to say, though at first causing erotic sensations and erection, after repeated doses it produces the opposite effect.

Analogous with chronic nymphomania a mild satyriasis exists in men (chiefly after Abusus Veneris) who suffer from neurasthenia due to masturbation and subsequent impotence, yet are the slaves of an insatiable libido. The imagination—the same as in acute cases—is highly excited and consciousness is completely filled with obscene pictures and situations. The whole train of thought, the entire realm of desire in these men is directed to sexual matters. Impotence and anaphrodisia assisted by perverse fantasies lead them to the worst perversities possible in the sexual act and render them particularly dangerous to children. They give offense by exhibition, by masturbation and by sexual acts with persons of the other sex in public. They are lascivious in speech and revel in filthy language, etc.

Satyriasis is often observed in the incipient stages of senile and paralytic dementia.

CASE 191. *Satyriasis.* Acute delirium because of abstinence. On the 29th of May, 1882, F., age twenty-three, unmarried, cobbler, was received at the psychiatric clinic at Graz. Father irascible, mother neuropathic, uncle on mother's side insane.

Patient never had a severe illness, was not addicted to drink, but sexually very needy. Five days previously he was attacked with an acute psychical disease. In broad daylight, and in the presence of two witnesses, he made two separate attempts at rape, went into a fit of delirium, raving about obscene matters when arrested, constantly masturbated, and became a raving maniac with violent motoric irritability and fever. Treatment with ergotine brought relief.

On January 5th, 1888, he was again arrested in a fit of raving mania. On the 4th, he had been morose, irritable, squeamish, sleepless. He became furious when he was foiled in two assaults on women. On the 6th his condition became very much aggravated, heavy delirium acutum (disturbance of consciousness, jactation, grinding of teeth, facial contortions and other motoric manifestations, temperature 40.7°). Masturbation as if by instinct. Recovery under treatment with ergotine till the 11th of January.

When restored to health again he gave some interesting details about his illness.

His sexual needs were always very great. Coitus at sixteen. Continence caused headaches, great psychical irritability, dislike for work, laziness, sleeplessness. Having no opportunity for coitus he resorted to masturbation, once or twice daily.

For two months he had had no sexual intercourse. As sexual excitement increased, masturbation failed as a means of compensation, but the desire for coitus became more vehement than ever. At the acme of the attack his memory failed him. In his normal state he was a decent man and looked upon his state as a pathological condition which filled him with alarm for the future.

CASE 192. On the afternoon of 7th July, 1874, Clemens, engineer, being on his way, on business, from Trieste to Vienna, left the train at the town of Bruck, and, passing through the town to the neighbouring village of St. Ruprecht, attempted a rape on an old woman, aged seventy, whom he found alone in a house. He was seized by the neighbours and arrested by the local police. At his hearing he declared that he had tried to find the pound, in order to satisfy his sexual desire with a bitch. He said that he often suffered with such sexual excitement. He did not deny his act, but excused it as the result of disease. The heat, the motion of the cars, and anxiety about his family, to whom he wished to go, had confused him and made him ill. Shame and remorse were not shown. His conduct was open, his mien gay; eyes red and bright, head hot, tongue coated; pulse full, soft, beating over 100; fingers somewhat tremulous. The statements of the accused were precise but hurried; his glance uncertain, and with an unmistakable expression of lasciviousness. To the medical expert summoned to examine him he gave the impression of one suffering with disease—as if he were in the beginning of alcoholic insanity.

C. was forty-five years old, married, father of one child. He did not know what diseases his parents or other members of his family had. In childhood he was weak and neuropathic. At the age of five his head was injured by a blow with a hoe. A scar one-half cm. broad by one cm. long, situated on the right parietal and frontal bones, dated from that injury. The bone was here somewhat depressed. The overlying skin was united to the bone. Pressure at this point caused pain, which radiated along the lower branch of the trigeminal nerve. This spot was also at times spontaneously painful. In his youth he suffered "fainting spells"; before puberty, pneumonia, rheumatism and intestinal catarrh. At the age of seven he experienced a peculiar inclination for men—*i.e.*, for a certain superior. Whenever he saw this man, he had a peculiar feeling in his heart and kissed the ground he walked on. At ten he fell in love with a certain deputy. Later he had an enthusiasm for men, though it was entirely platonic. He began to masturbate at the age of fourteen; first intercourse at seventeen. Then the earlier manifestations of inverted sexual feeling disappeared entirely. At that time he passed through a peculiar acute psychopathic condition, which he described as a kind of clairvoyance. From fifteen, haemorrhoids, with symptoms of abdominal plethora. When he had profuse haemorrhoidal haemorrhage, which occurred usually every three or four weeks, he was better. At other times he was constantly in a condition of painful sexual excitement, which he satisfied partly by means of onanism and partly by coitus. Every woman he met excited him; even when he was among female relatives he was impelled to make indecent proposals. Sometimes it was possible for him to master his desire; sometimes he was driven to indecent acts. If, after these, he was ejected from the house, it seemed perfectly right to him; for he thought that he needed such correction and support against his powerful impulse, which was a burden to him. No periodicity in this sexual excitement was recognizable.

Until 1861 he committed venereal excesses and was several times infected with gonorrhoea and chancres. In 1861, marriage. He was sexually satisfied, but became a burden to his wife on account of his great sensuality. In 1864 he passed through an attack of mania in the hospital at Fiume, and in the same year he again fell ill, and was taken to the insane asylum at Ybbs, where he remained until 1867. There he suffered with recurrent mania, accompanied by great sexual excitement. He said that intestinal catarrh and anxiety were the cause of his illness at that time.

Thereafter he was well, but he suffered much on account of his excessive sexual desire. If he were absent from his wife but a short time the impulse became so powerful that man or animal was indifferent to him for the satisfaction of his lust. In summer these impulses were much stronger, and were always accompanied by abdominal plethora. Something that he remembered in medical reading made him think in his case the ganglionic system was more powerful than the cerebral. In October, 1873, on account of business, he had to leave his wife. From that time until Easter, with the exception of occasional masturbation, there was no sexual indulgence. After that he made use of women as well as bitches. From the middle of June until 7th of July, he had no opportunity for sexual indulgence. He felt nervously excited, relaxed, and as if he were going crazy. Of late he had slept badly. A longing for his wife, who lived in Vienna, drove him to leave his business. He obtained leave of absence. The heat and the noise of the train confused him, and he could no longer hold out against his sexual excitement and the pressure of blood in his abdomen. Everything danced before his eyes. He left the car at Bruck, and was absolutely confused, not knowing where he went; and for a moment the thought came to him to throw himself in the water; everything appeared as in a mist before his eyes. Then he saw a woman, exposed his genitals, and tried to embrace her. She cried for help, and thus he was arrested.

After the attempt it suddenly became clear to him what he had done. He openly confessed his crime, which he remembered in all its details, but which seemed to him to be something abnormal. He could not help it. For some days after this C. suffered with headache and congestions, and was now and then excited and restless, and slept badly. His mental functions were undisturbed, but he was, nevertheless, a congenitally peculiar man, with a character weak and devoid of energy. The facial expression had something lascivious and peculiar about it. He suffered with haemorrhoids. The genitals presented nothing abnormal. The cranium was narrow and retreating at the forehead. Body large and well nourished. With the exception of diarrhoea, there was no disturbance of the vegetative functions.

CASE 193. For three years farmer D., universally respected, married, aged thirty-five, had manifested states of sexual excitement with increasing frequency and severity, which during the past year had become true paroxysms of satyriasis. It was impossible to discover hereditary or other organic causes. D. was compelled at times, when his sexual excitement was excessive, to perform the sexual act from ten to fifteen times in twenty-four hours, without deriving any feeling of satisfaction. Gradually he developed a condition of general nervous hyper-irritability with increased emotional irritability to the extent of pathological outbreaks of anger, and impulse to over indulgence in alcohol, which induced symptoms of alcoholism. His attacks of satyriasis became so violent that consciousness was interfered with, and the patient raged about in blind impulse to sexual acts. He demanded that his wife give herself to other men or to animals in his presence; that she allow copulation with him, in the presence of the daughter, because this would afford him greater enjoyment. Memory for the events of these attacks, in which the extreme irritability even led to outbreaks of maniacal rage, was entirely wanting. D. himself thought that he must have had moments in which he no longer had control of his senses, and without satisfaction from his wife would have been compelled to seize the next best female. After an attack of violent emotion these attacks of sexual excitement suddenly disappeared (*Lentz*, Bulletin de la société de méd. mentale de Belgique, No. 21).

MELANCHOLIA.

The thoughts and feelings of melancholiacs are not favourable for the excitation of sexual desires. At the same time, these patients sometimes masturbate. In my experience such cases have always been hereditarily predisposed and previously given to onanism. The act did not seem to be so much due to a lustful desire as to be induced by habit, *ennui*, anxiety and the impulse to change temporarily the painful mental condition.

HYSTERIA.

In this neurosis the sexual life is very frequently abnormal; indeed, always in predisposed individuals. All the possible anomalies of the sexual function may occur here, with sudden changes and peculiar activity; and, on an hereditary degenerate basis and in moral imbecility, they may appear in the most perverse forms. The abnormal change and inversion of the sexual feeling are never without effect upon the patient's disposition.

The following case, reported by *Giraud*, is one of this nature worthy of repetition:—

CASE 194. Marianne L., of Bordeaux. At night, while the household was asleep under the influence of narcotics which she had administered, she had given the children of the house to her lover for sexual enjoyment, and made them witness immoral acts. It was found that L. was hysterical (hemianaesthesia and convulsive attacks), but before her illness she had been a moral, trustworthy person. Since her illness she had become a shameless prostitute, and lost all moral sense.

In the hysterical the sexual sphere is often abnormally excited. This excitement may be intermittent (menstrual?). Shameless prostitution, even in married women, may result. In a milder form the sexual impulse expresses itself in onanism, going about in a room naked, smearing the person with urine and other filthy things, or wearing male attire, etc.

Schüle ("Klin. Psychiatrie," 1886, p. 237), finds very frequently an abnormally intense sexual impulse "which disposes girls, and even women living in happy marriage, to become nymphomaniacs."

The author cites known cases in which, on the wedding-journey, attempts at flight with men who had been accidentally met were made; and respected wives who enter into liaisons, and sacrificed everything to their insatiable impulse.

In hysterical insanity the abnormally intense sexual impulse may express itself in delusions of jealousy, unfounded accusations against men for immoral acts,[8] hallucinations of coitus,[9] etc.

Occasionally frigidity may occur, with absence of lustful feeling—due, for the most part, to genital anaesthesia.

PARANOIA.

Abnormal manifestations in the sexual sphere, in the various forms of paranoia, are not infrequent. Many of these cases are developed on sexual abuse (masturbatic paranoia) or sexual excitement; and, according to experience, in individuals psychically degenerate, with other functional signs of degeneracy, the sexual sphere is, for the most part, deeply implicated.

In religious paranoia and erotica the abnormally intense and, under certain circumstances, perverse sexual instinct is most clearly manifested. In the first variety, however, the condition of sexual excitation is expressed not so much in a direct method of satisfaction of the sexual desires as (there are exceptions) in platonic love—in enthusiastic admiration of a person of the opposite sex who is pleasing aesthetically. Under certain circumstances, the enthusiasm is for an imaginary person, a portrait, or a statue.

A love for the opposite sex that is weak and purely mental also, often has its basis in weakness of the genitals due to long-continued masturbation; and, under the guise of virtuous admiration for a beloved person, great lasciviousness and sexual perversion are often concealed. Episodically, especially in women, violent sexual excitement may occur as a nymphomania.

For the most part, religious paranoia rests upon sexuality which manifests itself in a sexual impulse abnormally early and intense. The libido finds satisfaction in masturbation or religious enthusiasm, the object of which may be a certain minister, saint, etc.

The psycho-pathological relations between the sexual and religious domains have been described in detail on p. 6 and following.

Apart from masturbation, sexual crimes are relatively frequent in religious paranoia.

Marc's work (p. 160) contains a remarkable example of religious insanity.

Giraud ("Annal. méd. psychol.") has reported a case of immorality with a little girl by a religious paranoiac, aged forty-three, who was temporarily erotic. Here, also, belongs a case of incest (*Liman*, "Vierteljahrsschr. f. ger. Med.").

CASE 195. M. impregnated his daughter. His wife, mother of eighteen children, and herself pregnant by her husband, lodged the complaint. M. had had religious paranoia for two years. "It was revealed to me that I should beget the Eternal Son with my daughter. Then a man of flesh and blood would arise by my faith, who would be 1800 years old. He would be a bridge between the Old and the New Testament." This command, which he deemed divine, was the cause of his insane act.

Sexual acts that have a pathological motive sometimes occur in persecutory paranoia.

CASE 196. A woman of thirty had, under promise of money and food, enticed a boy of five, who played near her, handled his genitals, and then attempted coitus. She was a teacher who had been betrayed and then cast off. Previously moral, for some time she had given herself to prostitution. The explanation of her immoral change was given, when it was found that she had various delusions of persecution, and thought she was under the secret influence of her seducer, who impelled her to sexual acts. She also believed that the boy had been put in her way by her seducer. Coarse sensuality as a motive for her crime came less into consideration, as it would have been easy for her to satisfy sexual desire in a natural way (*Küssner*, "Berl. klin. Wochenschrift").

CASE 197. *Immoral Acts With Children—Paranoia.* On the 26th of May, X., aged forty-six, railway official, was arrested in the act of sucking the penis of a boy eight years of age in the public highway. On the way to prison he committed the same offense on a fellow prisoner, who was riding in the same vehicle with him; and again on another prisoner. He was sent to the psychiatric ward of the hospital, where he made similar attempts. He was then isolated.

The medical examination proved persecutory delusions, developed from constitutional neurasthenia. X. was heavily tainted by heredity. His illusion was that the administration under which he had served were persecuting him and tried to force him to resume his former duties. He had noticed that persons who were friendly to him, especially his superiors, tried to show him a way in which he could rid himself of this fear of persecution. They did so by putting a finger in their mouth and sucking it. Still plainer were the suggestions of his chums who, pointing to a dog, *i.e.*, meaning himself, would speak of "licking." This started the idea in him that if he could be apprehended in the act of licking somebody's genitals, his superiors would become disgusted with him and dismiss him from service, in which way he would regain his freedom.

For a long time he could not muster up courage enough to commit such an act, but the idea became so strong that at first he resorted to *cunnilingus* with prostitutes, who invited him with cunning looks to this delectable feast. As these women, however, refused to denounce him to the authorities, he attacked boys and girls—the sex was immaterial—who, he fancied, invited him by gestures to the act. He could not understand, however, why he should come in conflict with the police by committing an act which was suggested to him by his superiors in office, —and all this in spite of the continued persecution of the railway administration.

It is strange that X. should have had recourse to such an abominable and nauseating sexual act and not to theft or some other act of dishonesty, unless it is explained on the ground of an increasing neurasthenia, coupled with a perversion of the sexual instinct and subsequent impotence. He was always hypersexual, with an heterosexual predisposition, suffered for years from *neurasthenia*, and derived no satisfaction from coitus. As in time erection became difficult, he had consulted several physicians, who advised abstinence. His excessive *libido* rendered it difficult to follow this advice, and impotence prevented coitus. This suggested *cunnilingus*, which granted a certain amount of sexual gratification and at times even produced ejaculation. This also compensated him for the nausea he experienced during the act and paved the way to his folly on children.

He claimed that in this act he found sexual satisfaction, but the chief object for it always was to rid himself of persecution by his superiors. This passion calmed down under treatment at the hospital, and he became a decent man when put under domestic supervision.

Cullerre ("Perversions sexuelles chez les persécutés," in "Annal. médico-psychol.," March, 1886) has reported similar cases,—the case of a patient who, suffering with delusions of sexual persecution, tried to violate his sister, giving as a reason that the impulse was given him by Bonapartists.

In another case a captain, suffering with delusions of persecution by electro-magnetism, was driven to pederasty,—a thing he abhorred. In a similar case the persecutor impelled to onanism and pederasty.

VI. PATHOLOGICAL SEXUALITY IN ITS LEGAL ASPECTS [1]

THE laws of all civilized nations punish those who commit perverse sexual acts. Inasmuch as the preservation of chastity and morals is one of the most important reasons for the existence of the commonwealth, the state cannot be too careful, as a protector of morality, in the struggle against sensuality. This contest is unequal; because only a certain number of the sexual crimes can be legally combatted, and the infractions of the laws by so powerful a natural instinct can be but little influenced by punishment. It also lies in the nature of the sexual crimes that but a part of them ever reach the knowledge of the authorities. Public sentiment, in that it looks upon them as disgraceful, lends much aid.

Criminal statistics prove the sad fact that sexual crimes are progressively increasing in our modern civilization.[2] This is particularly the case with immoral acts with children under the age of fourteen.

Casper (Clinical novels), drew attention to this deplorable fact early in the sixties of the 19th century. As a criminal physician (Berlin) he had fifty-two cases of crimes against morality under observation from 1842-57, but during the decade of 1852-1861 the number rose to 138.

According to the *"Comptes rendus de la justice criminelle en France,"* during the period of 1826-1840, *"attentats aux moeurs"* formed only 20 per cent. of the criminal proceedings, whilst from 1856-60 the average rose to 53 per cent. Sexual atrocities on children were but 1-13 of all cases tried before the criminal forum from 1826-30, but 1-3 during the period of 1856-60.

Oettingen ("Moralstatistik") quotes 136 cases of assault on children committed in France in 1826, but 805 in 1867.

Moreau ("Aberrations du sens génésique") quotes, for the year 1872, 682 cases of immoral attacks on children in France, for the year 1876 their number was 875.

In England similar delicts on children numbered 167 for the period 1830-34, and 1395 for the period 1855-57.

In Prussia, according to *Oettingen*, sexual attempts were in the proportion of 325:925; sexual crimes in the proportion of 1477:2945. *Ortloff* also finds ("die strafbaren Handlungen") a considerable increase in immoral offenses on children under the age of fourteen. We are indebted to *Thoinot* for interesting statistics of moral offenses dealt with by the criminal courts of France (Attentats aux moeurs et perversions des sens génital, 1898, Paris). Sexual criminal cases seem to have been on the wane in France. There were in 1860 830 (2.3 to a population of 100,000) offenders sentenced; in 1892 only 679 (1.7 to a population of 100,000). The proportion of crimes committed on adults and children was in 1860 180:650 (1:3.6), whilst in 1892 it rose to 78:601 (1:7.7). In 1885 it reached the highest point, viz.: 1:9.5.

The moralist sees in these sad facts nothing but the decay of general morality, and in some instances comes to the conclusion that the present mildness of the laws punishing sexual crimes, in comparison with their severity in past centuries, is in part responsible for this.

The medical investigator is driven to the conclusion that this manifestation of modern social life stands in relation to the predominating nervous condition of later generations, in that it begets defective individuals, excites the sexual instinct, leads to sexual abuse, and, with continuance of lasciviousness associated with diminished sexual power, induces perverse sexual acts.

It will be clearly seen from what follows how such an opinion is justified, especially with respect of the increasing number of sexual crimes committed on children.

The relative increase of sexual delicts on children seems to point to an advance in the physical decadence (impotence) and psychical degeneration of the adult population.

This view seems to be supported by *Tardieu, Brouardel* and *Bernard,* who find that attacks on children are more frequent in large cities, whilst those on adults, especially rape, occur more often in the country.

The statistical facts compiled by *Tardieu* and *Brouardel,* according to which the proportion of sexual offenses on children is in ratio with the age of the offender, *i.e.,* the older the criminal the younger the victim, and the circumstance that acts of immorality by very old men are only committed on children, seem to demonstrate that impotence and moral decay (senile dementia) are the fundamental causes of these horrible crimes.

It is at once evident, from the foregoing, that neuropathic, and even psychopathic, states are largely determinate for the commission of sexual crimes. Here nothing less than the responsibility of many of the men who commit such crimes is called in question.

Psychiatry cannot be denied the credit of having recognized and proved the psycho-pathological significance of numerous monstrous, paradoxical sexual acts.

Law and Jurisprudence have thus far given but little attention to the facts resulting from investigations in psycho-pathology. Law is, in this, opposed to Medicine, and is constantly in danger of passing judgment on individuals who, in the light of science, are not responsible for their acts.

Owing to this superficial treatment of acts that deeply concern the interests and welfare of society, it becomes very easy for justice to treat a delinquent, who is as dangerous to society as a murderer or a wild beast, as a criminal, and, after punishment, release him to prey on society again; on the other hand, scientific investigation shows that a man mentally and sexually degenerate from the first, and therefore irresponsible, must be removed from society for life, but not as a punishment.

A judge who considers only the crime, and not its perpetrator, is always in danger of injuring not only important interests of society (general morality and safety), but also those of the individual (honour).

In no domain of criminal law is co-operation of judge and medical expert so much to be desired as in that of sexual delinquencies; and here only anthropological and clinical investigation can afford light and knowledge.

The *nature of the act* can never, in itself, determine a decision as to whether it lies within the limits of mental pathology, or within the bounds of mental physiology. *The perverse act does not of itself indicate perversion of instinct.* At any rate, the most monstrous and most perverse sexual acts have been committed by persons of sound mind. *The perversion of feeling must be shown to be pathological.* This proof is to be obtained by learning the conditions attending its development, and by proving it to be part of an existing general neuropathic or psychopathic condition.

The species of act is important; but it, too, allows only presumptions, since the same sexual act, according as it is committed by an epileptic, paralytic, or a man of sound mind, takes on other features and peculiarities, in accordance with the manner in which it is done.

Periodical recurrence of the act under identical circumstances, and an impulsive manner in carrying it out, give rise to weighty presumptions that it is of pathological significance. The decision, however, must follow after referring the act to its psychological motive (abnormalities of thought and feeling), and after showing this elementary anomaly to be but one symptom of a general neuropathic condition—either an arrest of mental development, or a condition of psychical degeneration, or a psychosis.

The cases discussed in the portion of this work devoted to general and special pathology will certainly be useful to the medical expert, in assisting him to discover the motive of the act.

To obtain the facts necessary to allow a decision of the question whether immorality or abnormality occasioned the act, a medico-legal examination is required—an examination which is made according to the rules of science; which takes account of both the past history of the individual and the present condition,—the anthropological and clinical data.

The proof of the existence of an *original*, congenital anomaly of the sexual sphere is important, and points to the need of an examination in the direction of a condition of psychical degeneration. An *acquired* perversity, to be pathological, must be found to depend upon a neuropathic or psychopathic state.

Practically, syphilitic dementia and epilepsy must first come to mind. The decision concerning responsibility will depend on the demonstration of the existence of a psychopathic state in the individual charged with a sexual crime.

This is indispensable, to avoid the danger of covering simple immorality with the cloak of disease.

Psychopathic states may lead to crimes against morality, and at the same time remove the conditions necessary to the existence of responsibility, under the following circumstances:—

1. To oppose the normal or intensified sexual desire, there may be no moral or legal notions, owing to (*a*) the fact that they may never have been developed (states of congenital mental weakness); or to (*b*) the fact that they have been lost (states of acquired mental weakness).

2. When the sexual desire is increased (states of psychical exaltation), consciousness simultaneously clouded and the mental mechanism too much disturbed to allow the opposing ideas, virtually present, to exert their influence.

3. When the sexual instinct is perverse (states of psychical degeneration). It may, at the same time, be so intensified as to be irresistible.

Cases of sexual delinquency that occur outside of states of mental defect, degeneration, or disease, can never be excused on the ground of irresponsibility.

In many cases, instead of an abnormal psychical condition, a neurosis (local or general) is found. Inasmuch as the transitions from a neurosis to a psychosis are easy, and elementary psychical disturbances are frequent in the former, and constant in profound perversion of the sexual life, the neurotic affection—*e.g.*, impotence, irritable weakness, etc. —exerts an influence on the motive of the incriminating act; and a just judge, notwithstanding the lack of legal irresponsibility due to mental defect or disease, will recognize the circumstances which ameliorate the heinousness of the crime.

For various reasons the practical jurist will, in all cases of sexual crimes, call medical experts to make a psychiatric examination.

To be sure, his own conscience and judgment must be the guides when necessity makes them his only reliance. Under the following circumstances *indices* are given which point to a pathological condition:—

The accused is senile. The sexual crime is committed openly, with remarkable cynicism. The manner of obtaining sexual satisfaction is silly (exhibition), or cruel (mutilation or murder), or perverse (necrophilia, etc.).

From what experience teaches, it may be said that, among the sexual acts that occur, rape, mutilation, pederasty, lesbian love, and bestiality may have a psychopathological basis.

In case of lust-murder—in as far as its ulterior object goes beyond the murder itself—and likewise in cases of mutilation of corpses, psychopathic conditions are probable.

Exhibition and mutual masturbation seem to indicate the probable existence and pathological conditions. Masturbation of another and passive onanism may occur in connection with senile dementia and inverted sexual feeling, but also with mere sensuality.

Cunnilingus and *fellatio* (placing the penis in the mouth of a woman) have not thus far been shown to depend upon psychopathological conditions.

These horrible sexual acts seem to be committed only by sensual men who have become satiated or impotent from excessive indulgence in a normal way. Placing the penis in the mouth of a woman does not seem to be psychopathic, but rather a practice of married men of low morality, who wish to prevent pregnancy; and of satiated cynics in non-marital sexual indulgence.

The practical importance of the subject makes it necessary that the sexual acts threatened with punishment as sexual crimes be considered by jurists from the standpoint of the medico-legal expert. Thus there is an advantage gained, in that the psycho-pathological acts, according to circumstances, are placed in the right light by comparison with analogous acts that fall within the domain of physiological psychology.

1. OFFENSE AGAINST MORALITY IN THE FORM OF EXHIBITION.[3]

(Austrian Statutes, § 516; Abridgment, § 195. German Statutes, § 183.)

In man's present condition of civilization, modesty is a characteristic and motive so firmly fixed by centuries of education that presumption of a psycho-pathological element necessarily arises when *public* decency is coarsely offended.

The presumption is justifiable that an individual who has in this way offended public decency and his own self-respect was incapable of (idiots) or had lost the feelings of morality (states of acquired mental weakness); or that he acted while in a clouded state of consciousness (transitory insanity, states of partial consciousness).

A very distinctive act which belongs here is that of exhibitionism. The cases thus far recorded are exclusively those of men who ostentatiously expose their genitals to persons of the opposite sex, whom in some instances they even pursue, without, however, becoming aggressive.

The silly manner of this sexual activity, or really sexual demonstration, points to intellectual and moral weakness; or, at least, to temporary inhibition of the intellectual and moral functions, with excitation of *libido* dependent upon a decided disturbance of consciousness (abnormal unconsciousness, mental confusion), and at the same time calls the virility of these individuals in question. Thus there are various categories of exhibitionists.

The first category includes *acquired states of mental weakness* in which, owing to the causative cerebral (or spinal) disease, consciousness is clouded, and the ethical and intellectual functions are interfered with; and in which there can be no resistance made to a sexual desire that has either always been intense or that has been intensified by the disease-process. At the same time impotence exists, and no longer permits expression of the sexual instinct in violent acts (rape), but only in acts that are silly.

The majority of reported cases [4] fall in this category. They are those of individuals afflicted with senile dementia, paretic dementia, or mental defects due to alcoholism, epilepsy, etc.

CASE 198. Z., high official, aged sixty; widower, father of a family. He gave offense in that, during fourteen days, he had repeatedly exposed his genitals at his window, to a girl of eight years who lived opposite him. After a few months, under like circumstances, this man repeated his indecent act. At his examination he acknowledged the depravity of his action, and could give no excuse for it. Death, a year later, due to cerebral disease (*Lasègue, op. cit.*).

CASE 199. Z., aged seventy-eight; seaman. He had repeatedly exhibited his genitals on children's playgrounds and in the neighbourhood of girls' schools. This was the only way in which he was active sexually. He was married, and the father of ten children. Twelve years previously he had suffered a severe head-injury, which left a deep scar, indenting the bone. Pressure on this scar caused pain; at the same time his face would flush, his expression become fixed, and he would grow somnolent, with convulsive movements in the right upper extremity (apparently epileptoid state in connection with cortical disease). Moreover, there was senile dementia and advanced senility. It is not reported whether the exhibition coincided with epileptoid attacks or not. Senile dementia proved; pardoned (Dr. *Schuchardt, op. cit.*).

Pelanda (*op. cit.*) has reported a number of cases of this kind:—

1. Paralytic, aged sixty. At the age of fifty-eight he began to exhibit himself to women and children. In the asylum at Verona, for a long time thereafter, he was lascivious, and also attempted *fellatio*.

2. A drinker, aged sixty-six, suffering with circular madness. (The suggestion seems to be that the patient likes to go round, or *circulate*, exhibiting himself.) His exhibition was first noticed in church during divine service. His brother was likewise an exhibitionist.

3. A drinker, predisposed, aged forty-nine. He was always very excitable sexually; in an asylum on account of chronic alcoholism. He exhibited himself whenever he saw a woman.

4. A man, aged sixty-four; married; father of fourteen children. Great predisposition. Rachitic, microcephalic head. For years he had been an exhibitionist, in spite of repeated punishment.

CASE 200. X., merchant, born in 1833; single. He had repeatedly exhibited himself to children, or even urinated at the same time; once, under these circumstances, he had kissed a little girl. Twenty years previously X. had had a severe attack of mental disease, lasting two years, in which he was said to have had an apoplectic attack. Later, after loss of his fortune, he gave himself to drink, and of late years had often appeared absent-minded. His condition was that of alcoholism, presenile dementia and mental weakness. Penis small; phimosis; testicles atrophic. Proof of mental disease; pardoned (Dr. *Schuchardt, op. cit.*).

Such cases recall the lasciviousness of youthful, sexually excited persons that are still more or less boyish; but also that of many mature cynics of low morality, who find pleasure in defiling the walls of public closets, etc., with drawings of male and female genitals,—a kind of ideal exhibition which, however, is still widely separated from actual exhibition.

Another category of exhibitionists is made up of *epileptics*.[5] This category is *essentially* to be distinguished from the foregoing, because a conscious motive for the exhibition is wanting; and it appears much more like an *impulsive* act which, without any consideration of external circumstances, is performed as if it were an abnormal organic necessity.

At the time of the act there is always a state of imperfect consciousness; and thus is explained the fact that the unfortunate individual, without consciousness of the meaning of his act, or at least, *without cynicism*, does it in obedience to a blind impulse. On regaining consciousness, he regrets and abhors it if there is not permanent mental weakness.

The prime motive in this state of imperfect consciousness, as with other impulsive acts, is a feeling of apprehensive oppression. If a sexual feeling becomes associated with it, then the ideas are given a certain direction in the sense of a corresponding (sexual) act.

How sexual ideas very easily arise temporarily in epileptics may be understood from the discussion on p. 313.

If however, such an association has once been formed; if a particular act has taken place in an attack—it is the more easily repeated in every subsequent attack; for, so to speak, a known track has been established in the path of motivity.

The feeling of anxiety, with the state of imperfect consciousness, causes the associated sexual impulse to appear as a command—an inner force, which is acted upon in a purely impulsive manner and in a state of absolute irresponsibility.

CASE 201. K., a subordinate official, aged twenty-nine; of neuropathic family; living in happy marriage; father of one child. He had repeatedly, especially at dusk, exhibited himself to servant-girls. K. was tall, slim, pale, nervous and hasty in manner. *There was imperfect memory of the crimes.* Since childhood there had been frequent severe congestive attacks, with intense flushing of the face, a rapid, tense pulse, and a fixed, absent stare. At the same time there were, now and then, confusion and vertigo. In this (epileptic) exceptional state K. would answer only after repeated questioning, and then *it was as if he were waking from a dream.* K. stated that he had always felt excited and restless for some hours before his criminal acts, and experienced a feeling of fear, with oppression, and congestion of the head. In this condition he had often been giddy, and experienced an indistinct feeling of sexual excitement. At the height of such states he had left the house, without any purpose in view, and exposed his genitals anywhere. When he had reached home again, he had had but a dreamy remembrance of what had occurred, and felt very weak and depressed. It was also remarkable that, while exhibiting his genitals, he had used lighted matches to make them visible. The opinion was to the effect that the criminal acts depended upon epilepsy, and were imperative impulses; but he was, nevertheless, sentenced, with the assumption of extenuating circumstances (*Dr. Schuchardt, op. cit.*).

CASE 202. L., aged thirty-nine; single; tailor. His father was probably a drinker; he had two epileptic brothers, one of whom was insane. The patient himself had slight epileptic attacks, and from time to time states of imperfect consciousness, in which he ran about aimlessly, and thereafter did not know where he had been. He was considered a moral man, but he was now accused of having exhibited and played with his genitals in a strange house five or six times. His remembrance of these acts was very imperfect.

On account of repeated desertion from the army (probably likewise in epileptic states of imperfect consciousness), L. had been severely punished. In imprisonment he became insane with "epileptic insanity," was sent to the Charité, and from there discharged "cured." As far as the criminal acts were concerned, cynicism and wantonness could be excluded. That they were committed in a state of imperfect consciousness was probable from the fact among other things, that to the police-man who arrested him, the "imbecile" appeared to be in a remarkably cloudy state of mental consciousness (*Liman*, "Vierteljahrsschrift f. ger. Med.," N. F. xxxviii., Heft 2.)

CASE 203. L., aged thirty-seven. From 15th October to 2nd November, he had many times given offense by exhibiting himself to girls in daylight in the open street, and even in schools, into which he forced himself. It happened occasionally that he wanted the girls to perform masturbation or allow coitus, and, when refused, he performed masturbation before them. In G., in a public-house, he rapped with his exposed penis on the window so that the children and servant-girls in the kitchen were forced to see it.

After his arrest it was ascertained that since 1876 L. had very frequently caused trouble by exhibitions, but had always escaped punishment, owing to the demonstration of mental disease by physicians. On the other hand, he had been punished for desertion and theft in the army, and, later, once, as a civilian, for stealing cigars. L. had repeatedly been in asylums on account of insanity (attacks of insanity?). Besides, he was often remarkable on account of his changeable, quarrelsome character, occasional excitement and inconstancy.

L.'s brother died of paralysis. He himself presented no degenerative signs; no epileptic antecedents. At the time of observation he was neither insane nor mentally weakened.

He behaved himself very well, and expressed great regret for his sexual crimes, which he explained in this wise: though not a drinker, he occasionally had an impulse to drink. Soon after he began, congestion of the head, vertigo, restlessness, anxiety and oppression came on. He then passed into a dreamy state. An irresistible impulse now forced him to expose himself; and he then experienced a feeling of relief and breathed more easily. When he had once exposed himself, he knew nothing more of what he had done. As precursors of such attacks, he had often, a short time before, had flames before the eyes and vertigo. Of the time of his clouded state of consciousness he had but an obscure, dreamy memory.

It was only after a time that sexual ideas and impulses had become associated with these apprehensive, cloudy states of consciousness. Years ago, in such states, without motive and with great danger, he had deserted; once he had jumped from a third-story window; on another occasion he had left a good position to wander about aimlessly in a neighbouring country, where he was at once arrested for exhibition.

When outside of his abnormal periods, L. once became intoxicated, there was no exhibitionism. In the lucid state his sexual feeling and intercourse were perfectly normal (*Dr. Hotzen*, "*Friedreich's* Blätter," 1890, Heft 6).

A clinical group that very nearly approaches the epileptic exhibitionists is made up of certain *neurasthenic* individuals, in whom, likewise, there may occur attacks (epileptoid?) of imperfect consciousness [6] in connection with a feeling of apprehensive oppression; and with this sexual impulses may be associated, resulting in acts of exhibition having an impulsive character.

CASE 204. Dr. S., academic teacher, had aroused public indignation by being seen repeatedly running about in the Zoological Garden at Berlin, before ladies and children, with his genitals hanging out. S. admitted this, but denied all thought or consciousness of causing public offense, and excused himself by saying that his running about with exposed genitals afforded him relief from nervous excitement. Mother's father was insane, and died by suicide; his mother was constitutionally neuropathic, a somnambulist, and had been temporarily insane. He was neuropathic, had been a somnambulist, and had had continuous aversion to sexual intercourse with females. In his youth he practiced onanism. He was a neurasthenic man, shy, torpid and easily became embarrassed and confused. He was sexually always much excited. Frequently he dreamed that he was running about with exposed genitals, or that, dressed only in a shirt, he hung from a horizontal bar with his head downward, so that the shirt fell down, exposing his erected penis. His dreams would induce pollution, and he would then have rest for a few days or an entire week.

In his waking state also the impulse would often come upon him, just as in his dreams, to run about with exposed genitals. As he was about to expose himself, he would become very hot, and then he would run aimlessly about. The member would become moist with secretion, but pollution was never induced. Finally, when it had become flaccid, he would put it up, and then come to himself, glad if no one had seen him. In such conditions of excitement *he seemed to be in a dream, as if intoxicated*. He had never had the intention to offend women. S. was not epileptic. His declarations had the impress of truth. He had actually never followed or spoken to women while in this condition. Frivolity and coarseness were excluded. No doubt S.'s act was due to pathological sensation and idea, and S. was in a condition of pathological disturbance of mental action at the time of the commission of his acts (*Liman*, "Vierteljahrsschrift für gerichtl. Med.," N. F. xxx. viii., Heft 2).

CASE 205. X., aged thirty-eight; married; father of one child. Always sullen and silent. Suffered frequently with headache. *Very neurasthenic*, though not insane. He was troubled much at night by pollutions. He had repeatedly followed shop-girls, for whom he had lain in wait, exposing and handling his genitals. In one case he even followed a girl into a shop (*Trochon*, "Arch. de l'anthropologie criminelle," iii., p. 256).

In the following case the exhibition seems subsidiary to the impulsive desire to satisfy sudden, intense *libido* by means of masturbation:—

CASE 206. R., coachman, aged forty-nine; Vienna; married since 1866; childless. Father neuropathic and given to sexual excesses; died of cerebral disease. He presented no degenerative signs.

At the age of twenty-nine he suffered a severe concussion by falling from a height. Up to that time his sexual life had been normal. Since then, however, every three or four months he had been seized with very painful sexual excitement, accompanied by an intense desire to masturbate. A feeling of weariness and discomfort, with a desire for alcoholic indulgence, preceded this. In the intervals he was sexually cold, and had but very infrequent desire for his wife, who, moreover, for five years had been sick and incapable of cohabitation.

He gave the assurance that, as a young man, he never masturbated, and that, in the intervals between his attacks, he had never thought of satisfying himself sexually in this way.

The impulse to masturbate during the attack was always excited by certain feminine charms—short cloak, pretty foot and ankle, elegant appearance. Age made no difference; even little girls excited him. The impulse was sudden and unconquerable. R. described the situation and act as characteristically impulsive. He had often tried to resist it; but then he would grow hot, terribly frightened, his head would burn, and he would seem to be in a fog; but he never lost consciousness. At the same time he would have violent, darting pain in the testicles and spermatic cords. He regretted it, but had to confess that the impulse was stronger than his will. In such a situation it forced him to masturbate, no matter where he might be. After ejaculation he would become calm, and regain his self-control. He regarded it as a terrible affliction. Defense showed that R. had been punished six times for similar offenses—exhibition and masturbation in the open street. Although an examination into his mental condition by experts was demanded by his counsel, the court refused it on the ground that the proceedings had raised no doubt as to his responsibility.

On 4th November, 1889, R., while in his worst condition, happened to be in the street as a crowd of schoolgirls went by. This awakened his unconquerable impulse. There was not time to run to a closet, he was too excited. There was immediate exhibition, masturbation in front of a house—great scandal and immediate arrest. R. was not weak-minded, and had no ethical defect. He bemoaned his fate, deeply regretted his act, and feared new attacks. He regarded his condition as abnormal—as a fate against which he thought he was powerless.

He thought himself still virile. Penis abnormally large. Cremasteric reflex present; patellar reflex increased. Weakness of the sphincter of the bladder, that had existed for some years. Various neurasthenic difficulties.

The opinion showed that R. was subject to the influence of abnormal conditions, and had acted impulsively. Patient was sent to an
asylum, from which he was discharged after a few months.

In the foregoing case the important point, clinically, lies not in
the neurosis that is present, but rather in the impulsive character of the
act (exhibition dependent on masturbation).

With the enumeration of the categories of imbeciles, of mentally
weakened individuals, and of the exhibitionists that are in a neurotic
(epileptic or neurasthenic) state of benumbed consciousness, apparently
the clinical and forensic side of this phenomenon is still unexhausted;
in addition to these, there is another class, the representatives of which,
owing to deep hereditary taint (hereditary degenerative neurosis?), are
impelled to periodical and very impulsive exhibition.

With reference to these conditions of *psychopathia sexualis periodica*
(*cf.* "Periodical Insanity"), in which the accidentally awakened impulse
to exhibition is but a partial manifestation of a clinical whole, like in
dipsomania periodica the craving for drink, *Magnan,*[7] from whom I
borrow the following instructive cases, justly lays the greatest stress upon
the impulsive, periodical feature of these abnormal impulses; and no
less upon the fact that they are often accompanied by terrible anxiety,
which, after the realization of the impulse, gives place to a feeling of
relief.

These facts, and, no less, the clinical picture of degeneracy that,
for the most part, is referrable to injurious conditions that are hereditary, or that exercise an injurious effect on the development of brain in
early years (rachitis, etc.) are, medico-legally, of decisive importance.

CASE 207. G., aged twenty-nine, waiter in a *café*. In 1888, while
standing under a church-door, he exhibited himself to several girls
working opposite. He confessed the act, and also that, many times, in
the same place and at the same time of day, he had been guilty of the
same crime, having been punished for it the year before with imprisonment for one month.

G. had very nervous parents. His father was mentally unstable and
very irascible. His mother was at times insane, and suffered with severe
neurotic affection.

G. had always had nervous twitching of the face, and constant
alternation of causeless depression, with weariness of life and periods
of elation. At the ages of ten and fifteen, for slight cause, he wished
to commit suicide. When excited, he had similar twitching of the extremities. He presented constant general analgesia. In prison he was at
first beside himself with shame about the disgrace he had brought on
his family, and said he was the worst of men, deserving the severest
punishment.

Until his nineteenth year G. had satisfied himself with solitary and mutual masturbation, and, on one occasion, he had practiced onanism with a girl. From that time, working in a *café*, the female customers had excited him so intensely that ejaculation was often induced. He suffered with almost constant *priapism*, and, as his wife stated, in spite of coitus, it often disturbed his rest at night. For seven years he had repeatedly exhibited himself at his window, and also exposed himself naked to female neighbours living opposite.

In 1883 he married for love. Marital intercourse did not satisfy his needs. At times his sexual excitement was so intense that he had headache, and seemed confused, like one drunk, strange and incapable of work.

In one of these attacks he had recently exhibited himself before ladies in two streets of Paris (12th May, 1887). Since then he was fighting a desperate battle against these morbid impulses which had now become almost permanent, and when at their height made him morose and confused, and caused him to weep all night. In spite of all efforts he backslided again and again. *Opinion:* Proof of hereditary degeneration with delusions and irresistible impulses ("perversion délirante du sens génital"). Pardon (*Magnan*, "Arch. de l'anthropologie criminelle," v., No. 28).

CASE 208. B., aged twenty-seven; of neuropathic mother and alcoholic father. He had one brother who was a drinker; and a hysterical sister. Four blood relations on paternal side were drunkards, one female cousin is hysterical.

After his eleventh year, onanism, solitary or mutual. After his thirteenth year, impulses to exhibition. He attempted it at a street urinal; he felt pleasure in it, but also immediately twinges of conscience. If he attempted to oppose his impulse thereafter, he became apprehensive, and had a feeling of oppression in his chest. When a soldier, he was often impelled to expose himself, under various pretexts, to his comrades.

After his seventeenth year he had sexual congress with women. It gave him great pleasure to show himself naked before them. He continued his exhibition on the street. Since he could but infrequently count on female spectators at urinals, he changed his place to churches. In order to exhibit himself at such places, he always had to strengthen his courage by drinking. Under the influence of spirits, the impulse, at other times controllable with difficulty, became irresistible. He was not sentenced. He lost his position, and then drank more. Not long after, he was again arrested for exhibition and masturbation in a church (*Magnan, ibid.*[8])

CASE 209. X., aged thirty-five; barber's assistant. Repeatedly punished for offense against decency, he was again arrested; for, during three weeks he had been hanging around girls' schools, trying to attract the attention of the pupils, and, when he had succeeded in this, had exhibited himself. Occasionally he had promised them money, with the words, "I have a beautiful penis. Come to me and stroke it."

At his examination X. confessed everything, but did not know how it had come about. He was the most reasonable of men in other respects, but had the impulse to commit this crime, and could not overcome it.

In 1879, when in the army, he was once out on leave, and had run around exhibiting himself to children: imprisonment for a year. The same crime in 1881. He chased the crying children, and "stared" at them: imprisonment of one year and three months. Two days after his discharge, he said to two little girls: "If you want to see my penis, come with me into this inn." He denied these words, and claimed drunkenness; imprisonment for three months.

In 1883 renewed exhibition; during the act he said nothing. At his examination he stated that, since a severe illness, eight years previously, he had suffered with such excitations: imprisonment for one month.

In 1884 exhibition before girls in a churchyard; again in 1885. He declared: "I understand my crime, but it is like a disease. When it comes over me, I cannot keep from such acts. It sometimes happens that, for quite a long time, I am free from these inclinations." Imprisonment for six months.

Discharged on 12th August, 1885, he had a relapse on 15th August. The same excuse was given. This time he underwent medical examination. The examination revealed no mental disturbance. Sentenced to three years. After discharge, a series of new exhibitions. On this occasion, examination revealed the following:

His father suffered from chronic alcoholism, and was said to have been guilty of the same crime. Mother and a sister nervously ill, and the whole family of excitable temperament.

From his seventh to his eighteenth year X. *suffered with epileptic convulsions.* First cohabitation at sixteen; later, gonorrhoea and, it was stated, syphilis. After that, normal sexual intercourse until his twenty-first year. At that time he often had to pass a playground, and at times would urinate there; and it happened that the children watched him out of curiosity.

He noticed, occasionally, that being watched in this manner caused him sexual excitement, induced erection and even ejaculation. He now found more pleasure in this kind of sexual gratification, and became indifferent about coitus; satisfying himself only in this manner. He felt that all his thought was ruled by this, and he dreamed only of exhibitions, with pollutions. His attempts to control his impulse became more and more ineffectual. It came over him with such force that he noticed nothing around him, and saw and heard nothing, and was like one "devoid of reason"—like "a bull trying to butt his head through a wall."

X. had an abnormally broad head; small penis; the left testicle deformed. Patellar reflex absent. Symptoms of neurasthenia, especially cerebral. Frequent pollutions. For the most part, his dreams were about normal coitus, only infrequently about exhibition before little girls.

With reference to his sexual acts, he stated that the impulse to seek and approach little girls was primary; only when he had succeeded in exposing his nude genitals to them did he have an erection and ejaculation. He did not lose consciousness in the act. After it he was troubled about his deed, and, if undiscovered, said to himself, "Once more I have escaped the authorities."

In prison he did not have the impulse; there, he was troubled only with dreams and pollutions. When free he had daily sought opportunity to satisfy himself with exhibition. He would give ten years of his life to be free from the thing; "this life of constant anxiety, this alternation between freedom and imprisonment, is unendurable."

The opinion assumed a congenital (?) perversity of the sexual instinct, with unmistakable hereditary taint, neuropathic constitution, asymmetry of cranium, and defective development of the genitals.

It is also worthy of remark *that the exhibition began when the epilepsy ceased; so that one might think of a vicarious phenomenon.*

The sexual perversity developed, with predisposition, through accidental association of ideas of sexual content (children looking at him urinating) with an act that, in itself, was purposeless.

The patient was not sentenced, but sent to an asylum (*Dr. Freyer,* "Zeitschr. f. Medicinalbeamte," 3 Jahrg., No. 8).

CASE 210. At nine o'clock at night, in the spring of 1891, a lady, in great trepidation, came to the policeman in the city park of X., with the statement that a man, absolutely naked in front, had approached her from the shrubbery, and she had run away frightened. The officer went at once to the place indicated, and found a man, who exposed his nude front and genitals. He attempted to escape, but was overtaken and arrested. He stated that he had been sexually excited by alcohol, and had been on the point of going to a prostitute. On his way through the park, however, he recalled the fact that exhibition gave him much greater pleasure than was afforded him by coitus, in which he seldom, and only for want of something better, indulged. After drawing up his shirt, he posted himself in the shrubbery, and when two women came up the path he approached them with exposed genitals. In such exhibition he had a pleasurable feeling of warmth, and the blood mounted to his head.

The accused worked in a factory, and his employer stated that he was faithful, thrifty, sober and intelligent.

In 1886 B. had been punished because he had twice exhibited himself publicly—once in broad daylight and once at night, under a street lamp.

B., age thirty-seven, single, made a peculiar impression owing to his dandified dress and affected manner. His eyes had a neuropathic, languishing expression; around his mouth played a smile of self-satisfaction. He was said to come of healthy parents. A sister of his father and one of his mother's were insane. Others of their relatives were thought religiously eccentric.

B. had never had any severe illness. From childhood he was eccentric and imaginative. He loved romances about knights and others, was entirely absorbed by them, and even went so far as to identify himself in fancy with the heroes. He always thought himself a little better than others, and thought much of elegant dress and ornaments; and when he strutted about on Sundays he imagined himself a high official.

B. had never shown epileptic symptoms. In youth moderate indulgence in masturbation; later, moderate indulgence in coitus. Previously, never any perverse sexual feelings or impulses. Retired manner of life; in leisure hours, reading (popular novels, heroic tales, Dumas and others). B. was not a drinker. Exceptionally he made himself a kind of punch, by which he was always excited sexually.

For some years, with marked decrease of *libido*, after such alcoholic indulgence, he had developed the "accursedly silly thought" and the desire to exhibit his genitals publicly to women.

If he got into this state he felt warm, his heart beat violently, blood rushed to his head, and he could then no longer resist the impulse. He heard and saw nothing more, and was absolutely absorbed in his lust. Afterward he had often pounded his crazy head with his fists, and firmly resolved never to do such a thing again; but the crazy ideas had always returned.

In his exhibition his penis became only half-erected, and ejaculation never occurred; even in coitus it was always tardy. In exhibition he was satisfied with inspection of his genitals, and he had the lustful thought that this sight must be very pleasant to women, since he himself liked so much to see the genitals of women. He was capable of coitus only when the girl showed herself very partial to him; without this he preferred rather to pay and go without doing anything. In his dreams he exhibited himself to young, voluptuous women.

The medico-legal opinion recognized the hereditary psychopathic character of the culprit, and the perverse, impulsive desire to perform the incriminating acts; and pointed out, further, the remarkable fact that in B., who was otherwise sober and saving, the impulses to indulge in alcohol depended on abnormal conditions that recurred periodically and forced him to indulge. That, during his attacks, B. was in an exceptional psychical state, in a kind of mental confusion, and absolutely absorbed in his perverse sexual fancy, was clearly shown by the dossier. Thus was explained the fact that he became aware of the approach of the police only when it was too late to try to escape. In this hereditary and degenerate impulsive exhibitionism, it is interesting to note how the perverse sexual impulse is awakened from its latency by the influence of alcohol.

The foregoing cases seem to justify the assumption of a psycho-pathological meaning of "exhibition" in the sense of sexual demonstration.

A forensically important variety of exhibition, which, clinically speaking, rests for certain upon a similar neurotic and degenerate foundation, and which expresses itself in a peculiar act, conditioned by violent *libido* excessive sexual desire, associated with diminished virility, is made up of the so-called *frotteurs* (those who rub against others).

The three following cases, borrowed from *Magnan* (*op. cit.*), are typical:

CASE 211. D., age forty-four; hereditarily predisposed; drinker, and suffering with lead poisoning. Until the last year he had masturbated much, and often drawn pornographic pictures and shown them to his acquaintances. He had repeatedly dressed himself as a woman in secret.

For two years, after becoming impotent, he had felt desire, while in crowds at dusk, to bare his penis and rub it hard against the buttocks of a woman. Once, when discovered in the act, he had been sentenced to imprisonment for four months.

His wife kept a milk-shop. Again and again he could not restrain himself from completely immersing his genitals in a jar of milk. In the act he felt lustful pleasure, "as if touched with velvet." He was cynical enough to use this milk for himself and the customers. During imprisonment alcoholic persecutory insanity developed in him.

CASE 212. M., age thirty-one; married six years; father of four children; badly predisposed; subject to melancholia at times. Three years before, he was discovered by his wife with a silk dress on, masturbating. One day he was discovered, in a shop, in the act of rubbing on a lady. He was very repentant, and asked to be severely punished for his irresistible impulse.

CASE 213. G., age thirty-three; badly predisposed hereditarily. At an omnibus station he was discovered in the act of rubbing with his penis on a lady. Deep repentance; but he stated that at the sight of a lady's noticeable buttocks, he was irresistibly impelled to practice rubbing, and that he became confused and knew not what he did. Sent to an asylum.

CASE 214. A *frotteur*. Z., born in 1850; of blameless life previously, of good family; private official. He was well to do financially; untainted. After a short married life he became a widower, in 1873. For some time he had attracted attention in churches, because he crowded up behind women, both old and young indifferently, and toyed with their "bustles." He was watched, and one day he was arrested in the act. Z. was terribly frightened, and in despair about his situation; and, in making a full confession, he begged for pardon, for nothing but suicide remained for him.

For two years he had been subject to the unhappy impulse to go in crowds of people—in churches, at box-offices of theatres, etc.—and press up behind females and manipulate the prominent portion of their dresses, thus producing orgasm and ejaculation.

Z. stated that he was never given to masturbation, and had never been in any way perverse sexually. Since the early death of his wife, he had gratified his great sexual desire in temporary love-affairs, having always had an aversion for prostitutes and brothels. The impulse to rubbing had suddenly seized him, two years ago, while he happened to be in church. Though he was conscious that it was wrong, he could not help yielding to it immediately. Since then he had been excited by the buttocks of females, and had been actually impelled to seek opportunities for rubbing. The only thing on women that excited him was the "bustle"; every other part of the body and attire was a matter of indifference to him; neither did he mind whether the woman was old or young, beautiful or ugly. Since this began, he had had no more inclination for natural gratification. Of late rubbing scenes had appeared in his dreams.

During his acts he was fully conscious of his situation and the act, and tried to perform it in such a way as to attract as little attention as possible. After his act he was always ashamed of what he had done.

The medical examination revealed no sign of mental disease or mental weakness, but symptoms of neurasthenia—deficient libido (?)—which was also proved by the circumstance that even the mere touch of the fetich with the unexposed genitals sufficed to induce ejaculation. Apparently Z., weakened sexually and distrusting his virility, and yet libidinous, had come to practice rubbing by having noticed a woman's behind accidentally at the same time that he felt sexual excitement; and this associative combination of a perception with a feeling permitted the former to attain the significance of a fetich.

Whether these *frotteurs* (if considered as men who in consequence of disturbed virility have become either temporarily or permanently hypersexually degenerated) should come under the category of exhibitionists, or should be classified with the fetichists, as *Garnier* does ("Les fétichistes," p. 73), can hardly be decided on account of the limited number of cases thus far observed.

The point whether exposure of genitals takes place or not, cannot affect this decision, for it may depend in the *frotteur* on the intensity of the orgasm which may lead even to lustful ecstasy, or also from external circumstances favourable to this loathesome impulse. The very fact that up till now in pathological fetichism the fetich has never had reference to genital parts or the surrounding parts seems to upset *Garnier's* theory as to fetichism of woman's genitals (*cf.* p. 218).

The simplest explanation seems to be that *"frottage"* is a masturbatorial act of a hypersexual individual who is uncertain about his virility in the presence of women. This would also explain the motive of the assault being made not anteriorly but posteriorly (*cf.* case 211). That fetichism may be involved seems to follow from case 212, which clearly proves silk-fetichism. Very likely the lady in question wore a silk gown, and the indecent attack was directed upon the dress, not the buttocks. In case 214 the act is evidently qualified by the "bustle" and not by the particular part of the body.

As an act which offends public morals, and which is, therefore, punishable, the *violation of statues*—a whole series of cases of which *Moreau* (*op. cit.*) has collected from ancient and modern times—may be enumerated here. They are, unfortunately, given too much like anecdotes to allow satisfactory judgment of them. They always give the impression of being pathological—like the story of a young man (related by *Lucianus* and *St. Clemens*, of Alexandria) who made use of a Venus of Praxiteles for the gratification of his lust; and the case of Clisyphus, who violated the statue of a goddess in the Temple of Samos, after having placed a piece of meat on a certain part. In modern times, the "Journal L'événement" of 4th March, 1877, relates the story of a gardener who fell in love with a statue of the Venus of Milo, and was discovered attempting coitus with it. At any rate, these cases stand in etiological relation with abnormally intense *libido* and defective virility or courage, or lack of opportunity for normal sexual gratification.

The same thing must be assumed in the case of the so-called *"voyeurs"* [9]—i.e., men who are so cynical that they seek to get sight of coitus, in order to assist their virility; or who seek to have orgasm and ejaculation at the sight of an excited woman. Concerning this moral aberration, which, for various reasons, cannot be further described here, it will suffice to refer to *Coffignon's* book, "La Corruption à Paris." The revelations, in the domain of sexual perversity, and also perversion, which this book makes, are horrible.

2. RAPE AND LUST-MURDER.

(Austrian Statutes, §§125, 127; Austrian Abridgment, §192; German Statutes, §177.)

By the term rape, the jurist understands coitus, outside of the marriage relation, with an adult, enforced by means of threats or violence;

or with an adult in a condition of defenselessness or unconsciousness; or with a girl under the age of fourteen years. Insertion of penis, or, at least, joining of members (*Schütze*) is necessary to establish the fact. Today, rape on children is remarkably frequent. *Hofmann* ("Ger. Med.," i., p. 155) and *Tardieu* ("Attentats") report horrible cases.

The latter establishes the fact that, from 1851 to 1875 inclusive, 22,017 cases of rape came before the courts in France, and of these 17,657 were committed on children.

The crime of rape presumes a temporary, powerful excitation of sexual desire, induced by excess in alcohol or by some other condition. It is highly improbable that a man morally intact would commit this most brutal crime. *Lombroso* (*Goltdammer's* "Arch.") considers the majority of men who commit rape to be degenerate, particularly when the crime is done on children or old women. He asserts that, in many such men, he has found actual signs of degeneracy.

It is a fact that rape is very often the act of degenerate male imbeciles,[10] who, under some circumstances, do not even respect the bond of blood.

Cases as a result of mania, satyriasis and epilepsy have occurred, and are to be kept in mind.

The crime of rape may be followed by the murder of the victim.[11] There may be unintentional murder, murder to destroy the only witness of the crime, or murder out of lust (see below). Only for cases of the latter kind should the term *lust-murder* [12] be used.

The motives of lust-murder have been previously considered. The cases given in illustration are characteristic of the manner of the deed. The presumption of a murder out of lust is always given when injuries of the genitals are found, the character and extent of which are such as could not be explained by merely a brutal attempt at coitus; and, still more, when the body has been opened, or parts (intestines, genitals) torn out and are wanting.[13]

Lust-murders dependent upon psychopathic conditions are never committed with accomplices.

CASE 215. W*eak-mindedness; epilepsy; attempt at rape; murder.* On the evening of 27th May, 1888, a boy eight years old, Blasius, was playing with other children in the neighborhood of the village of S. An unknown man came along and enticed the boy into the woods.

The next day the boy's body was found in a ravine, with the abdomen slit open, an incised wound in the cardiac region and two stab-wounds in the neck.

Since, on 21st May, a man answering to the description given of the murderer of the boy had attempted to treat a six-year-old girl in a similar manner, and had only accidentally been prevented, it was presumed to be a case of lust-murder.

It was proved that the body was found in a heap, with only the shirt and jacket on; also that there was a long incision in the scrotum.

Suspicion fell upon a farm-hand, E.; but, on confrontation with the children, it was not possible to identify him with the stranger who had enticed the boy into the woods. Besides, with the help of his sister, he provided an *alibi*.

The untiring efforts of the officers brought new evidence to light, and finally E. confessed. He had enticed the girl into the woods, thrown her down, exposed her genitals, and was about to abuse her; but, as she had an eruption on her head and was crying loudly, his desire cooled, and he fled.

After he had enticed the boy into the woods, under the pretext of showing him a bird's nest, he was taken with a desire to abuse him. Since the boy refused to take off his trousers, he did it for him; and when the boy began to cry out he stabbed him twice in the neck. Then he made an incision, just above the pubes, in imitation of female genitals, in order to use it to satisfy his lust. But, since the body grew cold immediately, he lost his desire, and, cleaning his knife and hands near the body, he fled. When he saw the boy dead, he was filled with fear, and his member became flaccid.

During his examination E. toyed apathetically with a rosary. He had acted in a state of mental weakness. He could not understand how he came to do such a thing. He must have been beside himself; for he often became so weak in his head that he would almost fall down. Previous employers report that he had periods when he was confused and stubborn, doing no work all day, and avoiding others.

His father stated that E. learned with difficulty, was unskilful at work, and often so obstinate that one did not dare to punish him. At such times he would not eat, and occasionally ran away and remained from home for days. At such times he also seemed quite lost in thought, screwed his face up, and said senseless things.

When a youth, he still sometimes wetted the bed, and often came home from school with wet or soiled clothing. He was very restless in sleep, so that no one could sleep beside him. He had never had playmates. He had never been cruel, bad, or immoral.

His mother gave similar testimony; and further, that, in his fifth year, E. had convulsions for the first time, and once lost the power of speech for seven days. Sometime about his seventh year he once had convulsions for forty days, and was also afflicted with dropsy. Later, too, he was often seized in sleep, and he often then talked in his sleep; and mornings, after such nights, the bed was found wet through.

At times it was impossible to do anything with him. Since his mother did not know whether it was due to viciousness or disease, she did not venture to punish him.

Since the convulsions in his seventh year, he had failed so in mind that he could not learn even the common prayers; and he also became very irascible.

Neighbors, persons prominent in the community, and teachers state that E. was peculiar, weak-minded, and irascible; that at times he was very strange, and apparently in an exceptional mental state.

The examinations of the medical experts gave the following results:

E. was tall, slim, and poorly nourished. His head measured 53 centimetres in circumference. The cranium was rhombic, and in the occipital region flattened.

His expression was devoid of intelligence; his glance was fixed, expressionless; his attitude was careless, and his body was bent forward. Movements were slow and heavy. Genitals normally developed. E.'s whole appearance pointed to torpidity and mental weakness.

There were no signs of degenerative marks, no abnormality of the vegetative organs, and no disturbances of motility or sensibility. He came from a perfectly healthy family. He knew nothing of convulsions or of wetting his bed at night, but he stated that, of late years, he had had attacks of vertigo and loss of mind.

At first, he denied the murder point blank. Later, in great contrition, before the examining judge, he confessed all, and gave a clear motive for his crime. He had never had such a thought before.

He had been addicted to onanism for years; he even practiced it twice daily. He stated that, for want of courage, he had never ventured to ask coitus of a woman, though in dreams such scenes exclusively passed before him. Neither in dreams nor in the waking state had he ever had perverse instincts; particularly no sadistic or antipathic sexual feelings. The sight of the slaughter of animals had never interested him. When he enticed the girl into the woods, his desire, of course, was to satisfy his lust with her; but how it happened that he tried such a thing with a boy, he could not explain. He thought he must have been out of his mind at that time. The night after the murder he could not sleep on account of fear; he had twice confessed already, to ease his conscience. He was only afraid of being hanged. This should not be done, as he had done the deed in a weak-minded condition.

He could not tell why he had cut open the boy's abdomen. It had not occurred to him to grope among the intestines, smell them, etc. He stated that, after the attempt on the girl in the day time, and in the night, after the murder of the boy, he had convulsions. At the time of his crime he was indeed conscious, but he had given no thought to what he was doing.

He suffered much with headache; could not endure heat, thirst, or alcohol; there were times when he was confused. The test of his intelligence showed mental deficiency.

The opinion (*Dr. Kautzner*, of Graz) showed the imbecility and neurosis of the accused, and made it probable that his crime, for which he had only a general recollection, had been committed in an exceptional (pre-epileptic) mental state, explained by the neurosis. Under all circumstances, E. was considered dangerous, and probably would require commitment to an asylum for life.

CASE 216.[14] *Rape on a little girl by an idiot. Death of the victim.*

On the evening of the 3rd of September, 1889, Anna, aged ten years, daughter of a labourer, went to the village church, distant about two miles, but did not return. The following day her body was found about fifty paces from the main road, in a copse. The face was turned to the ground; the mouth was gagged with moss; signs of a criminal assault about the anus.

Suspicion fell upon a young labourer, K., nineteen years of age, because he had on the 1st of September attempted to entice the child in the wood when she was returning from church.

K. was arrested. At first he denied the deed; but afterwards made a complete confession. He had strangled the child, and when she stopped kicking and resisting, he had perpetrated an act of sodomy upon the anus of the child.

During the preliminary examination no one had raised the question as to the mental condition of this monster; in consequence, when shortly before the trial counsel defending him asked for an examination of the mental condition of his client, his request was refused on the ground "that the previous proceedings contained nothing which could warrant the plea of insanity."

By accident, counsel for the defense succeeded in establishing the fact that the great grandfather and the paternal aunt of the accused had been insane; that the father was an inveterate alcoholic since earliest youth and a cripple on one side of the body. These facts were verified during the trial.

But it made no impression. The defense finally prevailed upon the medical adviser of the court to suggest that K. be sent for observation to an insane asylum for a period of six weeks.

The opinion of the physician at the institute established K.'s idiocy, thus rendering him irresponsible for his deed.

He appeared insipid, stolid, apathetic; had forgotten nearly all he had ever learned at school; neither by voice or mien did he betray the slightest emotions of compassion, contrition, shame, hope, or fear of the future. His face was immovable as a mask.

Head quite abnormal; bullet-shaped. Proof that the brain was diseased already during the foetal period or during the earliest years of development.

Upon this report K. was permanently interned at the asylum.

Through the indefatigable efforts of a brave lawyer the court was saved from committing a judicial murder, and the honour of society was sustained.

CASE 217. *Lust-murder; moral imbecility.* A man of middle age; born in Algeria; said to be of Arabic descent. Had served for several years in the colonial troops; had then shipped as a sailor between Algeria and Brazil, and later on, in the hope of finding lighter employment, had gone to North America. He was known among his acquaintances as being lazy, cowardly and brutal. Several times he had been sentenced for vagrancy; it was said that he was a thief of the lowest kind; that he knocked about with women of the lowest class, and made common cause with them. His perverse sexual relations and acts were also well known. On several occasions he had bitten and beaten women with whom he had sexual converse. According to the description given of him, the authorities thought they had secured a certain unknown party who had scared at night the women in the streets by embracing and kissing them, and had acquired the nickname of "Jack the Kisser."

He was a tall man (over six feet), slightly bent forward. Low forehead, very prominent cheek bones, massive jawbones; small, narrow, inflamed eyes, piercing look; big feet, hands like birds' claws; shambling gait. His arms and hands were tattooed all over. Remarkable was the picture of a woman in colours, around which the name "Fatima" was inscribed, because tattooing the female form upon the body is considered to be disgraceful among the Arabs of the Algerian army; and prostitutes generally have a cross tattooed in their skin. His general appearance gave the impression of a low grade of intelligence.

N. was convicted of the murder of an elderly female with whom he had spent the night. The corpse bore various wounds, some remarkable for their length; the abdomen was ripped open, pieces of the intestines were cut out, so was one of the ovaries; other parts were strewn around about the corpse. Several of the wounds were like crosses; one was in the shape of a crescent. The murderer had strangled his victim. He denied the deed, and every inclination to commit such an act (*Dr. MacDonald*, Clark University, Mass.).

3. BODILY INJURY, INJURY TO PROPERTY, TORTURE OF ANIMALS DEPENDENT ON SADISM.

(Austrian, §§152, 411; German, §223 [bodily injury]. Austrian, §§85, 468; German, §303 [injury to property]. Austrian Police Regulations; German statutes, §360 [torture of animals].)

Aside from lust-murder, described in the foregoing section, as milder expressions of sadistic desires, impulses to stab, flagellate or defile females, to flagellate boys, to maltreat animals, etc., also occur.

The deep degenerative significance of such cases is clearly demonstrated by the series of examples given under "General Pathology." Such mentally degenerate individuals, should they be unable to control their perverse impulses, could only be objects of care in asylums.

CASE 218. *Sadism on boys and girls committed by a moral idiot.*

K., fourteen years and five months old; killed a small boy in a cruel manner. The trial developed the following details: Two cases of murder; a long series of cases (seven) in which K. had cruelly tortured little boys. All these children ranged in age from seven to ten years. K. would lure them into a hidden place, strip them naked, bind them hand and foot, tie them against some object, gag the mouth with a handkerchief and then beat them with a stick, a strap or a piece of rope, slowly, pausing for minutes—grinning all the time without uttering a word. One of the boys he forced under threat of death to repeat the Lord's Prayer twice, to promise under oath secrecy and to repeat curse words and oaths after him. In another instance he pricked the boy's cheeks with a needle, played with his genitals, and stabbed him in the pubic region; he then ordered him to lie on his stomach when he would jump on his back, dancing all over the body; finally he stabbed him in the buttocks and dug his teeth into them. Another boy he bit in the nose and stabbed him with a knife.

The eighth victim, a little girl, he enticed into his mother's shop, fell upon her from behind, and clapping one hand over her mouth, cut her throat with the other. The body was found in a dark corner, covered over with ashes and manure. The head was severed from the body, the flesh cut away from the bones, the whole body covered with cuts and wounds. The largest cut was on the inner side of the left thigh, penetrating through the genitals into the abdomen. Another cut extended from the iliac fossa obliquely across the abdomen. The clothes and linen were torn and cut into shreds.

The corpse of the ninth victim was found with the throat cut across, blood was flowing from the eyes, the heart was pierced by innumerable stabs. A number of thrusts were found in the abdomen. The scrotum was ripped open, the testicles were hanging out, and the glans penis was cut off.

K. had first lured the boy to him as he had done the little girl, cut his throat and then stabbed him all over.

K., whose hereditary conditions were not known, had been suffering from a severe illness during the whole of his first year's existence, and thus had become very much emaciated. He began to recover, and it is claimed that since then he had not been afflicted with bad health, excepting frequent complaints about pain in the head and eyes and vertigo, until he was eleven, when he went through a "severe illness," which made him delirious. Headaches would suddenly seize him, so that he would run away from play, and return only after a considerable interval. When asked on such occasions about his conduct, he would slowly answer, "My head, my head."

He was intractable, disobedient and beyond control. Showed sudden and extreme moods, desires and opinions. When three years old he was one day seen to torture a chicken with a knife. He lied with every appearance of truth. At school he was a disturbing element, making faces, constantly talking to himself; was obstinate and disrespectful. Punishment to him was injustice; he was unrepentant. In the house of correction he was secluded, preoccupied with himself, suspicious, disliked by his comrades—in fact without any chum. His intellectual powers were good; he possessed sagacity, reason and a good memory. He showed great defect in the ethical direction. He betrayed not the slightest signs of sorrow or penitence for his deeds, or the least consciousness of his responsibility. Only for his mother he seemed to have a sort of tender feeling. He could assign no reason for his actions. He calmly discussed his chances: "they would not condemn him to death because he was only fourteen years of age; heretofore they had not been wont to hang boys of his age, and surely they would not make a beginning with him." What motive he had in his deeds cannot be ascertained from him. Once he said that reading a description of the tortures visited upon their victims by Red Indians had tempted him to imitate them. He had even once thought of running away from home to join the Indians. Whenever he espied a victim his imagination would be filled with pictures of cruel actions.

On the morning of such days he would always wake up with vertigo and pressure in the head, which condition would last all day.

As physical anomalies only an exceptionally large penis and very big testicles are mentioned. Mons veneris completely and thickly covered with hair; in fact, the genitals were fully developed like those of an adult. No symptoms of epilepsy (Dr. MacDonald, Clark University, Mass.).

CASE 219. Sadism; bodily injury. B., seventeen years of age, tinsmith, bought on the 4th January, 1893, a long knife; went to a prostitute, had repeatedly sexual intercourse with her, gave her money, and made her sit undressed on the edge of the bed. He now stabbed her slightly three times in the chest and abdomen whilst his member was erect. When the girl began to shout and people came to her assistance, B. fled, but immediately gave himself up to the police. At first he said he had stabbed the girl in a quarrel, but afterwards stated he had had no motive for his deed. Several blood relations of his father had been insane. B. was not tainted, not a drunkard, had not gone through any severe illness, never masturbated, but had practiced coitus for two years. Genitals normal. Seemed, under observation, mentally normal; was ashamed of his action, to which the experts properly ascribed a sexual motive. In spite of definite proof of mental sanity, he was released (*Coutagne*, "Annal. méd. psych.," 1893, July, Aug.).

CASE 220. *Acts of violence emanating from sadism.* M., sixty years of age, owner of several millions, happily married, father of two daughters, one eighteen, the other sixteen years of age, was convicted of seduction of minors and acts of violence on females. He was accustomed to go to the house of a procuress, where he was known as "the man who stabs," and there, lying upon a sofa in a pink silk dressing-gown, lavishly trimmed with lace, would await his victims—three nude girls. They had to approach him in single file, in silence and smiling. They gave him needles, cambric handkerchiefs and a whip. Kneeling before one of the girls, he would now stick about a hundred needles in her body, and fasten with twenty needles a handkerchief upon her bosom; this he would suddenly tear away, whip the girl, tear the hair from her *mons veneris* and squeeze her breasts, etc., whilst the other two girls would wipe the perspiration from his forehead and assume lascivious positions. Now excited to the highest pitch, he would have coitus with his victim. Later on, for the sake of economy, he was satisfied to perform his brutality with one girl alone. This girl fell in consequence into a severe illness, and in her distress asked him for help. He reported this "extortion" to the police, who, on their part, made inquiries, and brought a charge against him. At first he denied the facts, but convicted, expressed his surprise that such a fuss should be made about a mere trifle. M. was described as a man of repulsive appearance, with receding forehead. He was sentenced to six months' imprisonment, a fine of 200 francs, and 1000 francs damages to his victim ("Journal Gil Blas," Aug. 14 and 16, 1891).

A less revolting case, that of a young man, is related by *Ferrioni*, "Archivio delle psicopatie sessuali," i., p. 106, 1896. This young sadist would first wrestle with the girl in order to bring about virility and would, in the act, bite and pinch her in order to produce satisfaction. But one day he bit the girl so hard that she brought an action against him.

CASE 221. *Murder through sadism.* Married man, at the time of this crime thirty years of age. He had lured a girl to the bell tower of the church of which he was the sexton and there killed her. Circumstantial evidence forcing him to admit the deed, he confessed to another similar murder. Both corpses showed numerous contusions about the fleshy parts of the head, fractures of the skull, extravasations under the *dura mater* in the brain. No other bodily injuries were found; the genital organs were intact.

Spermal stains were found on the underwear of the criminal, who was arrested soon after the deed was committed. L. was described as of pleasing appearance, of dark complexion, beardless. No details about his hereditary relations, antecedents, previous sexual life, etc.

His motive, according to his own admission, was "lust of the cruellest and most abominable kind" (*Dr. MacDonald*, Clark University, Mass.).

Guillebeau,[15] Professor at the Veterinary College of Berne, has collected a number of cases of horrible sadistic acts of violence on dumb brutes.

1. Injuries to the vagina in six cows. Offender unknown.

2. Mortal injuries on four calves and goats, committed by a youth, nineteen years of age, with the sharp point of a stick. He had become an imbecile at the age of four due to meningitis. He confessed that the act was one of sexual lust. Considered irresponsible.

3. Repeated and numerous injuries to cows and goats in the anus and in the vagina, by a stable-boy (age twenty-four) with a stick. He confessed that when milking or otherwise attending the animals he became sexually excited, had violent erections and sensations of fear. At first he used his hand, and then a stick, which he would introduce into the orifice. It was always an impulsive act and only at such times when he suffered from sleeplessness and nervous and sexual excitement. After the act he was always tormented by pangs of conscience but could not help relapsing into the same fault. Considered irresponsible.

4. A similar offense (in imitation of the former) in the same stable by a feeble-minded cowherd, eighteen years old, on the rectum of an ox.

CASE 222. X., age twenty-four. Parents healthy, two brothers died from tuberculosis, one sister suffered from periodical fits. X. began to experience at the age of eight pleasurable feelings with erection when he pressed his abdomen against the desk in school. He often did this. Later he practiced mutual masturbation with a schoolmate. First ejaculation at the age of thirteen. In the first attempt at coitus (when eighteen) he was impotent. He continued auto-masturbation. When reading a popular book describing the dreadful consequences of onanism, he became very neurasthenic. A water cure brought improvement, but a second attempt at coitus proved unsuccessful. Return to masturbation. In time this failed him, too. He would now pick up a living bird by the tail and swing it around in the air. The sight of the tortured animal provoked erection and when the flapping wing touched his penis, ejaculation would ensue with enormous sexual lust (Dr. *Wachholz, Friedreich's* Blätter, f. gerichtl. Med. 1892, 6 Heft, p. 336.).

See also, Murder through Sadism. Rivista Sperimentale, 1897, xxiii., p. 702, and 1898, xxiv., fasc. 1.—*Kölle*, ger. psych. Gutachten, Fall 4. p. 48.

4. MASOCHISM AND SEXUAL BONDAGE.

Masochism [16] may under certain circumstances attain forensic importance, for modern criminal law no longer recognizes the principle *volenti non fit injuria*, and the present Austrian statute in §4 says expressly: "Crimes may also be committed on persons who demand their commission on themselves."

Psychologically speaking, the facts of *sexual bondage* are of greater criminal importance (*cf.* p. 120).

If sensuality is predominant, or in other words, if a man is held in fetich-thralldom and his moral power of resistance is but weak, he may by an avaricious or vindictive woman into whose bondage his passion has led him be goaded on to the very worst crimes. The following case is a striking instance:

CASE 223. *Murder of a family through sexual bondage.* N., soap manufacturer in Catania; thirty-four years of age; previously of good character; stabbed his wife to death in her sleep on the 21st of December, 1886, and strangled his two daughters, one seven years old and the other six weeks old. At first he denied the deed, tried to throw suspicion upon others, but finally confessed to all the details and begged to be hanged.

N. came of a sound family, was healthy himself, a good business man and highly respected; married well, but for several years was under the fascinating influence of a mistress who had captivated and completely controlled him.

He had kept this matter a secret from the world and his wife.

By playing on his jealousy and declaring that by marriage alone he could for the future possess her, this monster of a woman had brought the weak and infatuated N. to become the murderer of his wife and children. After the deed he had induced his young nephew to fetter him as if he himself were the victim of the villains and under the threat of death commanded him to silence. When the neighbours came in he played the *rôle* of the unhappy, maltreated father.

After a full confession he showed the deepest contrition. During the two years of the subsequent trial, N. never showed signs of mental derangement.

His mad love for the mistress he could only explain as an infatuation. He never had cause to find fault with his wife. There were no traces of abnormal or perverse sexual instinct in this exceptional criminal. His sorrow and contrition over the deed gave proof that no moral defect was present. His mental condition was declared to be sound. Exclusion of irresistible impulse (*Madalari,* "Il morgagni," 1890, Feb.).

CASE 224. *Sexual bondage in a lady.*

Mrs. X., thirty-six years of age; mother of four children. Came from a neuropathic and heavily-tainted mother. Father psychopathic. She began to masturbate at the age of five, had an attack of melancholia at the age of ten, during which period she was troubled with the delusion that she could not go to heaven on account of her sins. This made her nervous, excitable, emotional, neurasthenic. At the age of seventeen she fell in love with a man who was denied her by her parents. She now showed symptoms of hysteria. When twenty-one she married a man by many years her senior who had but little sexual appetite. Her conjugal relations with him never satisfied her; coitus produced severe genital pain which she could not satisfy with masturbation. She suffered tortures from this unsatisfied desire, yielded more and more to onanism, became heavily hystero-neurasthenic, capricious and quarrelsome, so that marital relations grew ever colder.

After nine years of mental and physical anguish, Mrs. X. succumbed to the blandishments of another man in whose arms she found that gratification for which she had so long languished.

But now she was tormented with the consciousness of having broken her marriage vow, often feared she would become insane, and only the love for her children prevented her from committing suicide.

She scarcely dared to appear before her husband whom she highly esteemed on account of his noble character, and felt dreadful qualms of conscience because she had to conceal the awful secret from him.

Although she found full gratification and immense sensual pleasure in the arms of the other man, she had repeatedly made attempts to give up this *liaison.* Her efforts were in vain. She got deeper and deeper into the bondage of this man, who recognizing and abusing his power had merely to dissemble as if he would leave her in order to possess her without restraint. He abused this bondage of the miserable woman only to gratify his sexual appetite, gradually even in a perverse manner. She was unable to refuse him any demand.

When Mrs. X. in her despair came to me for professional advice she declared that she could no longer continue such a life of misery and anguish. An insuperable *libido,* disgusting to herself, drew her to this man, whom she could not love but could not do without, while on the other hand she was constantly tormented with the danger of discovery, and with self-reproach because of her offense against the law of God and man.

The greatest mental pain was caused by the thought of losing her paramour, who often threatened to leave her if she did not yield to his wishes, and who controlled her so thoroughly that she would do anything and everything at his bidding.

The soundness of mind in the horrible case 223 and in many other analogous cases cannot be called in question. As matters now stand, when the public cannot comprehend the more refined analysis of the motives in a tragedy and when the law profession rejects psychology in favour of logical formalism, it can hardly be expected that judge and jury will regard the weight of *sexual bondage*—especially as in this condition the incentive to the crime is not a morbid one and the intensity of the incentive itself cannot be dealt with.

Nevertheless in such cases we must consider whether the accused was possibly still susceptible to counter-motives or whether these were excluded. If the latter be the case it would be equivalent to a disturbance of the psychical equilibrium.

No doubt in these cases a sort of acquired moral weakness is produced which impairs the soundness of mind. *Sexual bondage* should certainly constitute a cause for leniency in crimes committed through its agency.

5. BODILY INJURY, ROBBERY AND THEFT DEPENDENT ON FETICHISM.

(Austrian, §190; German, §249 [robbery]. Austrian, §§171, 460; German, § 242 [theft].)

It is seen from the section on fetichism, under "General Pathology," that pathological fetichism may become the cause of crimes. There are now recognized, as such, hair-despoiling (cases 81, 82, 83); robbery or theft of female linen, handkerchiefs, aprons (cases 86, 87, 91, 93); shoes (cases 66, 93, 94), and silks (case 99). It cannot be doubted that such individuals are the subjects of deep mental taint. But, to assume an absence of mental freedom and consequent irresponsibility, it must be proved that there was an irresistible impulse, which, either owing to the strength of the impulse itself or to the existence of mental weakness, rendered control of the criminal perverse impelling force impossible.

Such crimes and the peculiar manner in which they are carried out —whereby they differ very much from common robbery and theft— always demand a medico-legal examination. But that the act by itself does not by any means have to arise from psycho-pathological conditions is shown by the infrequent uses of hair-despoiling [17] simply for the purpose of gain.

CASE 225. P., labourer, age twenty-nine. Family heavily tainted. Emotional, irritable, masturbated since childhood. When ten years old he saw a boy masturbate into a woman's handkerchief. This gave the direction to P.'s sexual life. He stole handkerchiefs from pretty girls and masturbated into them. The mother tried every means to break him of this habit; she admonished him, took the stolen handkerchiefs away and bought him new ones, all in vain. He was caught by the police and punished for theft. He then went to Africa and served in the army with an excellent record. On his return to France he resumed his old practices. He was only potent if the girl held a white handkerchief in her hand during the act. He married in 1890 and sustained his virility by grasping a handkerchief during coitus.

The fetichistic crisis always came suddenly, like a paroxysm, especially at moments of laziness. He would feel out of sorts, psychically moody and sexually excited and impelled to masturbate. Soon the fancy-picture of a handkerchief would appear and take full possession of his thoughts and feelings. If at that period he should catch sight of a woman's handkerchief he would choke with fear, palpitation of the heart would set in, he would tremble and profuse perspiration would break out all over his body. Although conscious of the risk involved, he was irresistibly forced to steal the handkerchief. He was arrested on one such occasion, but the examining physician declared him irresponsible. During the time of detention he was free from the obsession. He hoped to master his weakness in future. The number of handkerchiefs he had stolen he estimated to be one hundred. He used each handkerchief only once and then threw it away. (*Magnan* in *Thoinot*, attentats aux moeurs, p. 428.)

CASE 226. *Handkerchief-fetichism; repeated thefts of handkerchiefs belonging to women.*

D., forty-two years of age, man-servant, single, was sent on 11th March, 1892, by the police to the district asylum of Deggendorf (Niederbayern) for observation of his mental faculties.

He was 1.62 m. high, muscular and well fed. Head submicrocephalic; expression of face blank. The eye distinctly neuropathic. Genital organs normal. With the exception of a moderate degree of neurasthenia and increased patellar reflexes, there was nothing abnormal in D.'s nervous system.

In 1878 D. received his first sentence of one and a half years' imprisonment at Straubing for stealing handkerchiefs.

In 1880 he stole a handkerchief from a tradeswoman in the yard of an inn, and was sentenced to fourteen days.

In 1882 he made an attempt in the public road to pull the handkerchief from the hand of a peasant girl. Charged with attempted robbery, he was found not guilty on the strength of medical opinion, which stated weakness of mind and a morbid disturbance of the mental faculties at the time of the crime.

In 1884 he was tried before a jury for having committed, under similar circumstances, robbery of a woman's handkerchief, found guilty, and sentenced to four years' imprisonment.

In 1888 he took in the public market-place a handkerchief from the pocket of a woman. Sentence, four months.

In 1889, for a similar offense, nine months.

In 1891, ditto, ten months. Otherwise his record shows only a few fines or detentions at the police station for carrying a concealed weapon (a knife) and for vagrancy.

All the thefts of handkerchiefs were committed from young females, chiefly in broad daylight, in the presence of other people, and so clumsily and impudently that each time he was arrested on the spot. In the proceedings not the slightest traces of theft of other articles, ever so small, can be found.

On the 9th December, 1891, D. was once more released from jail. On the 14th he was caught stealing the handkerchief from a peasant girl in a crowd at the annual fair. He was at once arrested, and upon searching him the police found two more white handkerchiefs belonging to women.

On former occasions also whole collections of women's handkerchiefs had been found on his person (1880, thirty-two pieces; 1882, fourteen, nine of which he wore next his skin; on another occasion twenty-five. In 1891 seven white handkerchiefs were found upon him).

When questioned as to the motive for stealing handkerchiefs, he always said that he was drunk at the time, and had taken the handkerchiefs for a joke.

The handkerchiefs found upon him he claimed to have bought or swapped for something else, or he said women with whom he had relations had given them to him.

Under observation D. showed weakness of mind, appeared run down through vagrancy, drink and masturbation, but good-natured, obedient, and by no means afraid of work.

He knew nothing of his parents, grew up without supervision; when a child he made a living by begging; at thirteen he was a stable-boy, and was used at fourteen by others for pederasty. He declared that at a very early period he felt the sexual instinct very strongly; began early to have coitus and to practice masturbation. When he was fifteen, a coachman had told him that great pleasure could be derived by applying the handkerchiefs of young women to the genitals. He tried it, found it to be true, and now sought to obtain handkerchiefs in any manner possible. This craving became so strong that wherever he saw a pleasing young woman with a handkerchief in her hand or visible in her pocket violent sexual excitement would seize him, and he was impelled to make his way to this woman and take the handkerchief away from her.

When sober he generally succeeded in resisting this impulse for fear of punishment. But when he had drink in him he could not resist. When serving in the army he had often induced young and pleasing girls to give him their handkerchiefs that had already been in use, and to exchange them for others after he had used them for a while.

When he slept with a girl he generally exchanged his own handkerchief for the girl's. Often he had bought handkerchiefs that he might exchange them with those used by women.

New and unused handkerchiefs had no effect on him. The girl must have carried it about and used it before it excited him sexually.

In order to bring unused handkerchiefs into contact with women, he would at times throw them in the road in front of a woman coming towards him, that she might step on it (this is taken from the proceedings). Once he fell upon a girl, pressed a handkerchief against her neck, and ran away.

As soon as he came into possession of a handkerchief that had been touched by a woman, he would have erection and orgasm. He would then put the handkerchief to his nude body, or preferably to the genitals, and thus produce a pleasurable ejaculation.

He never asked such women to have coitus with him, partly because he feared a refusal, chiefly, however, because he preferred the handkerchief to the girl.

D. made all these confessions with great reserve, and sporadically. Repeatedly he broke into tears and refused to say more because "he was so ashamed of himself." "I am not a thief, and have never stolen a penny's worth even when I was in dire distress. I never could have brought myself to sell one of these handkerchiefs. I am not a bad man. Only when I do these stupid things I am beside myself."

The favourable opinion given by the authorities of the asylum attributed his misdeeds to an abnormal mental condition producing a morbid, irresistible impulse to commit these acts, coupled with weakness of intellect in a moderate degree. Free pardon from theft.

CASE 227. *Violation of ladies' toilets emanating from stuff-fetichism.*

X., heavily tainted (great uncle insane, father a drunkard, sister an idiot) was arrested in an office while pushing up against ladies where he was cutting with a pair of scissors pieces of fur, velvet or cloth from their apparel. In his pockets and in his room a big lot of such cuttings was found.

X. had shown since his tenth year a weakness for woolly and fluffy materials. Even the very sight, but especially the touch, of them would bring on orgasm and ejaculation. Fur particularly had this effect on him, and after that satin. The latter accounted for the fact that in his collection a number of cuttings of satin ribbons were found.

He induced lustful emotions by placing the stolen pieces of stuff next to his skin. If ejaculation was not spontaneous he assisted with masturbation. Woman in her capacity as woman, or sexual intercourse with her, had no charm for him (*Garnier*, "Les Fétichistes pervertes," p. 49, Paris, 1896).

NOTES ON THE QUESTION OF RESPONSIBILITY IN SEXUAL OFFENSES CAUSED BY DELUSION.[18]

The question of delusion in those sexual feelings which occur in fetichism, sadism and exhibition, offers many difficulties. The all important point is to find the motive for the act resulting either from fetichism or sadism, for it is a sexual motivation—likely an equivalent for impossible coitus—and not a theft for instance, that claims our attention. The offender, from shame over his act, is apt to mislead the examining judge. Particular stress should be laid upon the fact that the act emanated from an irresistible impulse, a delusion which voids responsibility. The patient, although not fully bereft of consciousness, is yet unable to shake off the delusion and finds relief only in committing the imperative act, which as a rule is accompanied by strong paroxysms of fear and anxiety. The organic source of this fear may be found in powerful somatic vasomotoric manifestations. Of psychical importance is the consciousness that the mind is inhibited in its power of forming free thoughts, that the will power is impaired and quite impotent in the presence of the delusion. This may be accompanied by hypersexuality, and the affect of fear may be overcompensated by an anticipated pleasurable feeling. Thus the patient, though conscious of the wrongfulness of the act and its consequences determines to end the situation by yielding to the impulse, which is, after all, the only psychologically possible way out of the difficulty. The offender is merely an automaton, the slave of a driving idea.

The situation is an organic force, an impulse to rid himself of an intolerable position involving his very existence. As a matter of fact, with the committal of the deed, beneficent freedom from the constraint and the predominating idea is experienced. Delusions in the narrower sense, cardinal symptoms of which are the presence of consciousness, struggle against the prevailing impulse and fear, must not be confounded with:

1. *The sexual acts of psychically defective individuals* in whom the sensual appetite by virtue of ethical and intellectual insufficiency finds prompt satisfaction in some adequate sexual act, but without psychical affects, or a conflict with moral principles.[19]

2. *Impulse sexual acts committed by heavily degenerated individuals* by virtue of pre-eminent sexual feelings in hyperactive desire. These feelings suddenly grow, when they first begin to exist, into a powerful sexual

affect to the occlusion of the spheres of will power and consciousness, and into a sexual delusion coloured with the character of a psychical reflex, or a quasi psychical convulsion.

Alcohol and prolonged sexual abstinence are the provocative causes of such affects in many degenerates. The corresponding acts of violence consist, as a rule, in rape.[20] They originate from epileptical [21] and hysterical neuroses or from over-indulgence in alcohol, whilst acts emanating from delusions maintain clinical relations to neurasthenia.

3. *The sexual acts* (chiefly exhibition) *which are committed under exceptional episodical psychical conditions* with or without delirium and hallucinations. These occur in individuals afflicted with general neuroses (epilepsy, hysteria) or alcoholism, when consciousness is clouded and memory paralyzed. They generally present the character of an impulsive act.[22]

These perversions may be observed in heterosexual as well as in homosexual individuals; likewise in those who are sexually impotent or otherwise.

The perversions occurring in the performance of the sexual act or any other act that serves as an equivalent for coitus consist (*a*) in heterosexual, potent individuals: in imaginary representations of the female sexual organs. (*Raymond* et *Janet,* nécroses et idées fixes ii., p. 162); gazing at the genitals of women (Petres et Régis, "obsessions," p. 40); holding their own genitals to the feet of women (case 76); a woman's urinating into the patient's mouth (case 68); bestiality (cases 199, 201, 203); periodical pederasty (*Tarnowsky*).

(*b*) In heterosexual, impotent individuals in sadistic acts.

In homosexual individuals the same manifestations may be observed only with due alteration of details.

The question of responsibility in the individual case depends on the psychical conditions by which the offender was motivated. In many instances the culprit is devoid of all moral worth and ethical and intellectual understanding, is, in fact, in the transitory stage of becoming a psychically defective sexual criminal. In other instances prolonged sexual abstinence was the motive power which led to the criminal act, or the complicating influences of alcohol with its erogenous and demoralizing effects (chiefly in exhibition cases). *Forensic responsibility* in these cases is determined by the question whether the offender succumbed to an irresistible impulse or not. In how far the offender is to be held accountable for having consciously and in reckless manner impaired his moral will power by intoxication, it is for the jurist to decide. If the act is the result of a delusion, it cannot be considered in the light of a punishable act.

An episode of psychical perversion especially when manifested in the form of a delusion, cannot be designated as a mental disease; it is rather a temporary confusion of consciousness, a morbid state of the mind, a transitory disturbance of the psychical life.

Nevertheless the offender is a danger to the common weal and welfare and the interests of society are best served by his confinement in an insane asylum, where abstinence from alcohol is enforced and proper treatment (if necessary hypnotic suggestion) offers promises of a final cure.

6. VIOLATION OF INDIVIDUALS UNDER THE AGE OF FOURTEEN.

(Austrian Statutes, §§ 128, 132; Austrian Abridgement, §§ 189, 191 [3]; German Statutes, §§ 174, 176 [3].)

By violation of sexually immature individuals, the jurist understands all the possible immoral acts with persons under fourteen years of age that are not comprehended in the term "rape." The term violation, in the legal sense of the word, comprehends the most horrible perversions and acts, which are possible only to a man who is a slave to lust and morally weak, and, as is usually the case, lacking in sexual power.

A common feature of these crimes, committed on persons that really still belong more or less to childhood, is that they are unmanly, knavish, and often silly. It is a fact that such acts, excepting pathological cases, like those of imbeciles, syphilitics, and senile dements, are almost exclusively committed by young men who lack courage or have no faith in their virility; or by *roués* who have, to some extent, lost their power. It is psychologically incomprehensible that an adult of full virility and mentally sound should indulge in sexual abuses with children.

Non-Psychopathological Cases.

Non-psychopathological cases of immoral acts with children may be summarized as under:

1. Debauchées who have tasted all the pleasures of normal and abnormal sexual pleasures with woman. The only motive for the infamous act can be found in a morbid psychical craving to create a novel sexual situation and to revel in the shame and confusion of the child victim. A subordinate motive may be sexual impotence with the adult seeking a new stimulus in the extraordinary coitus with an immature female. If virility also fails in this instance, sexual contact with boys is very likely resorted to, especially in the form of pederasty. In large cities the markets for these filthy needs are well stocked. (*Cf. Tardieu's* revelations of Paris, and *Tarnowsky's* of St. Petersburg.) *Casper* tells us that lewd mothers often prepare their little daughter for the use of these libertines.

2. Young men who are afraid of the adult female or are diffident about their own virility. These are chiefly recruited from the bands of masturbators suffering from psychical impotence or some irritable weakness of the sexual organs which render coitus with a woman impossible and seek a compensating equivalent in the manipulation of the female organs in the child which as a rule suffices to produce orgasm and ejaculation in themselves. If potency is still unimpaired, insertion of the penis will be attempted in almost every case.

Casper in his "Clinical Novels," [23] cases 4 and 5, shows that even brothers have proved dangerous fiends towards their little sisters.

3. A large percentage of cases is represented by lewd servant girls, governesses and nursemaids, not to speak of female relatives, who abuse the little boys entrusted to their care, for sexual purposes[24] and often even infect them with gonorrhea.

The cases in which lascivious tutors, governesses, etc., cane or spank their pupils without provocation, are open to investigation as to the pathological condition of the malefactor.[25]

The manner in which acts of immorality are committed on children differs widely, especially where libertines are concerned. They consist chiefly in libidinous manipulations of the genitals, active masturbation (using the child's hand for onanism), flagellation, etc. Less frequent is cunnilingus, perversion of girls, intercourse between the thighs, exhibitionism. The possibilities in this direction are inexhaustible.

The finer feelings of man revolt at the thought of counting the monsters among the psychically normal members of human society. The only presumption is that these individuals have suffered injury in the sphere of morality and potency. This should not, however, preclude the moral responsibility of the perpetrator, as sheer moral depravity may be at the bottom of the act, especially in individuals oversated with natural sexual intercourse, in lascivious characters or drunkards. Judgment of the act should ever be guided by the monstrosity and the degree in which it psychically and physically differs from the natural act.

Psychopathological Cases.

A great number of these cases, however, certainly depend upon pathological states.

A review of the psycho-pathological cases of immorality with children shows that the largest number may be reduced to conditions of *acquired* mental weakness. First of all we must mention senile dementia [26] (*Kirn*, "Allg. Zeitschr. f. Psychiatrie," 39, p. 217), then chronic alcoholism,[27] paralysis,[28] mental debility due to epilepsy,[29] injuries to the head and apoplexy,[30] syphilis.[31] Then follow the *original* mental defects,[32] and states of degeneration.[33]

The cause of these offenses may also be found in states of morbid unconsciousness.

Not infrequently these outrages on morality are due to overindulgence in alcoholic stimulants or epilepto-psychical conditions of an exceptional character, at times also to a mistake as to sex or as to person. They may be explained on the ground of the sexual excitement concomitant with these conditions, especially in epileptic subjects.[34] Rape and pederasty are of frequent occurrence under these circumstances. In the states of psychical weakness the point whether virility is present decides as to the quality of the sexual act.

In addition to the aforesaid categories of moral renegades, and those afflicted with psychico-moral weakness—be this congenital or superinduced by cerebral disease or episodical mental aberration—there are cases in which the sexually needy subject is drawn to children not in consequence of degenerated morality or psychical or physical impotence, but rather by a morbid disposition, a *psycho-sexual perversion*, which may at present be named erotic paedophilia (love of children).[35]

In my own experience I have only come across four cases. They all refer to men. The first case is of more value than the others for it appears in the form of platonic love; but it manifests its sexual character in the fact that this (paranoic) lover of children is only stimulated by little girls. He is quite callous towards the grown-up woman and, as it appears, is a hair-fetichist. (In the other cases it came to libidinous acts.)

Observation No. 2 represents a man tainted by heredity. Since the time of puberty (which came very late at the age of twenty-four) sensual emotions towards little girls of five to ten years of age. The very sight of such a girl brought on ejaculation; a touch from her absolute sexual paroxysm with only a succinct recollection as to its duration. The marital act gave a slight gratification, thus enabling him to control his desire for little girls for a time. But a heavy neurasthenia supervened (chiefly due to *coitus interruptus*) when he became a criminal either because his moral powers of resistance slackened, or his sexual appetite increased in intensity.

The third case is a man tainted by heredity and constitutionally neurasthenic; cranium abnormal, never had a normal inclination to the adult woman; but in coitus was like an animal at rutting time. To immorally touch little girls gave this man the highest possible pleasure. He became paedophilic only at the age of twenty-five.

My fourth case is a man, tainted, who has ever found sexual charm only in immature girls. Mature women had but little attraction for him. When impotence (tabes and syphilitic dementia) set in he could no longer resist the morbid impulse.

The cases quoted here under the head of erotic paedophilia in the sense of sexual perversion have the following traits in common:—

(1) The individual afflicted is tainted.

(2) The affection for immature persons of the opposite sex is of a primary nature (quite in opposition to the debauchée); the imaginary representations are in an abnormal manner and very strongly marked by lustful feelings.

(3) The libidinous acts—if you exclude the one case in which virility was present—consist only in immodest touches or masturbation of the victim. Nevertheless they adduce the gratification of the subject, even though ejaculation be not attained.

The following cases taken from *Magnan* ("Lectures on Psychiatry") show clearly that this erotic paedophilia occurs also in women.

Magnan's first case is a lady twenty-nine years of age, tainted by heredity; has delusions and phobias.

Since eight years strong desire for sexual union with one of her (five) nephews. First her desire is directed towards the oldest when he was five years of age. She transferred this desire to each of them in turn as they grew up. The sight of the child in question was sufficient to produce orgasm and even pollution. She was able to resist her inclination, which she cannot explain. She had no inclination for mature men.

The second case is a woman thirty-two years of age, mother of two children; heavily tainted by heredity; separated from her husband on account of brutal treatment.

For several months she had neglected her children, had visited a friend's house every day, and always at the time when the son of the house was returning from school. She hugged and kissed the child, and at times said that she was in love with him and wanted to marry him.

One day she told his mother that the boy was ill and unhappy. She wanted to cohabit with him in order to cure him.

She was forbidden entrance to the house, but laid siege to it.

One day she tried to force her way in, when she was sent to an asylum, where she continued to rave about the boy.

That erotic love of children may occur periodically is demonstrated by *Anjel's* observation (see above, cases 187 and 188).

In the sphere of antipathic sexual instinct this perversion is by no means rare. In the same measure in which the former is an equivalent of the heterosexual instinct, so in this instance the predilection for the immature is equally abnormal and exceptional. Practically speaking, acts of immorality committed on boys by men sexually inverted are of the greatest rarity.

I have already laid stress upon this fact in my pamphlet "Der conträr Sexuale vor dem Strafrichter," second edition, p. 9. I have pointed out there that the real seducer of youth is the weak-minded man, though born sexually normal; the *roué* who is impotent or at least sexually perverted and morally depraved; the senile man who is morally enfeebled but sexually excited.

Under such accidental conditions, the sexually inverted individual may also eventually become a danger to boys (*cf.* case 127 of the present and 109 of the ninth edition of this book); but this has nothing to do with paedophilia, for the very reason that in these cases the boys were past puberty, whilst in cases of genuine paedophilia the subject is drawn only to the sexually quite immature. The second case of *Magnan* seems to be the most instructive in this regard, for in it the desire turned in each instance from the older boy to the younger one as he grew to the age of three to five years.

The following case, reported by *Pucotte* and *Raynaud* ("Archives d'Anthropologie criminelle," x., p. 435), may be looked upon as a proof that erotic love of children may also occur in cases of antipathic sexuality.

CASE 228. X., thirty-six years of age, journalist; heavily tainted by heredity; ethically and intellectually defective; since early youth afflicted with epileptoid spells; intolerant of alcohol; face asymmetrical; never cared for woman; masturbated since he was eighteen; attempts at coitus found him cold and impotent.

But boys of ten to fifteen years of age excited him very much. Although he was conscious of the criminality of the act, he could not resist the impulse to have relations with them. Oftentimes he was sated with their "enchanting looks and their sweet smiles."

Neither adult nor little girls possessed any charms for him. Only at the age of twenty-two, when a boy twelve years old forced sexual intercourse upon him, he became paedophilic. At that time he refused his seducer, but soon he could resist no longer the desire awakened in him by that incident, although he was repeatedly sentenced and imprisoned for this offense. His life was blighted by this unfortunate weakness, and he made several attempts at suicide.

Expert opinion established congenital sexual inversion, and, within the limits of homosexuality, a special anomaly, *viz.*, exclusive love for boys of a certain age and of delicate constitution.

It was claimed that degenerative mental disturbance affected the soundness of his mind and rendered him a danger to the community.

X. was inconsolable over the result of his trial, for he was sent to an insane asylum. He had anticipated a free pardon.

In my "Collected Works" (Heft 4, pp. 119-124) I have published three other cases of erotic paedophilia, which came under my personal observation. Two other cases in my files have never been published. It seems to me as if all these cases might be explained by fetichism. This would at once account for the paradox apparent in the manifestations of erotic love of children. It can only be explained on the ground of heavy taint, for a strongly marked degenerative predisposition can always be found in these individuals. That these cases are not of every-day occurrence and require a fetichistic impulse, may also account for their rarity.

False erotic love of children occurring in indviduals who have lost *libido* for the adult through masturbation and subsequently turn to children for the gratification of their sexual appetite—is much more frequently observed. (*Cf.* case 106 of the tenth edition of this book.)

Another classical case may be found in my "Collected Works," Heft 4, p. 125.

Irresponsibility should, as a rule, not be claimed in these cases, for experience teaches that paedophilic impulses can be mastered, unless a weakening or total loss of will power has been superinduced by pathological conditions, such as neurasthenia or syphilitic dementia. A plea for ameliorating circumstances, however, may be indicated. Nevertheless a criminal enquiry should always be made in flagrant cases of erotic love of children. The question of responsibility depends entirely on the comprehension of all the characteristics of the individual involved. Hypersexuality, overindulgence in alcoholic drinks, moral weakness, etc., should be carefully considered as they frequently counteract freedom of choice.

At any rate these unfortunate beings should always be looked upon as a common danger to the welfare of the community, and put under strict surveillance and medical treatment. The proper place for such persons is a sanitarium [36] established for that purpose, not prison. [37]

That a cure is possible is evidenced by two severe cases which came under my observation and treatment.

Unfortunately the presumption that psycho-pathological conditions are present cannot always be proved. But the fact that pathological characteristics are not lacking, should be carefully weighed. At any rate, a thorough investigation of the mental status of the individual must be made. This is especially the case when old men seduce children. Moral and intellectual idiocy, heavy psychical degeneration, defects springing from acquired organic causes and mental aberrations are frequently at the bottom of these excesses. The beginning of senile or syphilitic dementia is not always sufficiently pronounced to allow a proper diagnosis. Proper care must therefore be exercised.

7. UNNATURAL ABUSE (SODOMY). [38]

(Austrian Statutes, § 129; Abridgement, § 190; German Statutes, § 175.)

(a) VIOLATION OF ANIMALS (BESTIALITY). [39]

Violation of animals, monstrous and revolting as it seems to mankind, is by no means always due to psycho-pathological conditions. Low morality and great sexual desire, with lack of opportunity for natural indulgence, are the principal motives of this unnatural means of sexual satisfaction, which is resorted to by women as well as by men.

To *Polak* we owe the knowledge that in Persia bestiality is frequently practiced because of the delusion that it cures gonorrhoea; just as in Europe an idea is still prevalent that intercourse with children heals venereal disease.

Experience teaches that bestiality with cows and horses is none too infrequent. Occasionally the acts may be undertaken with goats, bitches, and, as a case of *Tardieu's* and one by *Schauenstein* show ("Lehrb.," p. 125), with hens.

The action of Frederick the Great, in a case of a cavalryman who had committed bestiality with a mare, is well-known: "The fellow is a pig, and shall be reduced to the infantry."

The intercourse of females with beasts is limited to dogs. A monstrous example of the moral depravity in large cities is related by *Maschka* ("Handb.," iii.); it is the case of a Parisian female who showed herself in the sexual act with a trained bull-dog, to a secret circle of *roués*, at ten francs a head.

CASE 229. In a provincial town a man was caught in intercourse with a hen. He was thirty years old, and of high social position. The chickens had been dying one after another, and the man causing it had been "wanted" for a long time. To the question of the judge, as to the reason for such an act, the accused said that his genitals were so small that coitus with women was impossible. Medical examination showed that actually the genitals were extremely small. The man was *mentally quite sound.*

There were no statements concerning any abnormalities at the time of puberty, etc. (*Gyurkovechky*, "Männl. Impotenz," 1889, p. 82).

CASE 230. On the afternoon of 23d September, 1889, W., aged sixteen, shoemaker's apprentice, caught a goose in a neighbour's garden, and committed bestiality on the fowl until the neighbor approached. On being accused by the neighbour, W. said, "Well! Is there anything wrong with the goose?" and then went away. At his examination he confessed the act, but excused himself on the ground of temporary loss of mind. Since a severe illness in his twelfth year, he had attacks several times a month, with heat in his head, in which he was intensely excited sexually, could not help himself and did not know what he was doing. He had performed the act during such an attack. He answered for himself in the same way at the trial, and stated that he knew nothing of the species of act except from the statements of the neighbour. His father states that W., who comes of a healthy family, had always been sickly since an attack of scarlet fever in his fifth year, and that, at the age of twelve, he had a febrile cerebral disease. W. had a good reputation, learned well in school, and later helped his father in his work. He was not given to masturbation.

The medical examination revealed no intellectual or moral defect. The physical examination revealed normal genitals; penis relatively greatly developed; marked exaggeration of the patellar reflexes. In other respects, negative result.

The history of the condition at the time of the deed was not to be depended upon. There was no proof of previous attacks of mental disturbance, and there were none during the six weeks of observation. There was no perversion of the sexual life. The medical opinion allowed the possibility that some organic cause (cerebral congestion), dependent upon cerebral disease, may have exercised an influence at the time of the commission of the criminal act. (From the opinion of Dr. *Fritsch*, of Vienna.)

But there is another group of cases falling well within the category of bestiality, in which decidedly a pathological basis exists, indicated by heavy taint, constitutional neuroses, impotence for the normal act, impulsive manner of performing the unnatural act. Perhaps it would serve a purpose to put such cases under the heading of a special appellation; for instance, to use the term "bestiality" for those cases which are not of a pathological character, and the term "Zooerasty" for those of a pathological nature.

CASE 231. *Impulsive sodomy.* A., aged sixteen; gardener's boy; born out of wedlock; father unknown; mother deeply tainted, hystero-epileptic. A. had a deformed, asymmetrical cranium, and deformity and asymmetry of the bones of the face; the whole skeleton was also deformed, asymmetrical and small. From childhood he was a masturbator; always morose, apathetic, and fond of solitude; very irritable, and pathological in his emotional reaction. He was an imbecile, probably much reduced physically by masturbation, and neurasthenia. Moreover, he presented hysteropathic symptoms (limitation of the visual field, partial color blindness; diminution of the senses of smell, taste and hearing on the right side; anaesthesia of the right testicle, clavus, etc.).

A. was convicted of having committed masturbation and sodomy on dogs and rabbits. When twelve years old he saw how boys masturbated a dog. He imitated it, and thereafter he could not keep from abusing dogs, cats and rabbits in this vile manner. Much more frequently, however, he committed sodomy on female rabbits,—the only animals that had a charm for him. At dusk he was accustomed to repair to his master's rabbit-pen in order to gratify his vile desire. Rabbits with torn rectums were repeatedly found. The act of bestiality was always done in the same manner. There were actual attacks which came on every eight weeks, always in the evening, and always in the same way. A. would become very uncomfortable, and have a feeling as if some one were pounding his head. He felt as if losing his reason. He struggled against the compulsive idea of committing sodomy with the rabbits, and thus had an increasing feeling of fear and intensification of headache until it became unbearable. At the height of the attack there were sounds of bells, cold perspiration, trembling of the knees, and, finally, loss of resistive power, and impulsive performance of the perverse act. As soon as this was done he lost all anxiety; the nervous cycle was completed, and he was again master of himself, deeply ashamed of the deed, and fearful of the return of an attack. A. stated that, in such a condition, if called upon to choose between a woman and a female rabbit, he could make choice only of the latter. In the intervals, also, of all domestic animals he is partial only to rabbits. In his exceptional states simple caressing or kissing, etc., of the rabbit sufficed, as a rule, to afford him sexual satisfaction; but sometimes he had, when doing this, such sexual passion that he was forced to perform sodomy wildly on the animal.

The acts of bestiality mentioned were the only acts which afforded him sexual satisfaction, and they constituted the only manner in which he was capable of sexual indulgence. A. declared that, in the act, he never had a lustful feeling, but satisfaction only, inasmuch as he was thus freed from the painful condition into which he was brought by the imperative impulse.

The medical evidence easily proved that this human monster was a psychically degenerate, irresponsible invalid, and not a criminal (*Boeteau*, "La France médicale," 38th year, No. 38).

CASE 232. X., peasant, aged forty; Greek-Catholic. Father and mother were hard drinkers. Since his fifth year patient had epileptic convulsions—*i.e.*, he would fall down unconscious, lie still two or three minutes, and then get up and run aimlessly about with staring eyes. Sexuality was first manifested at seventeen. The patient had inclinations neither for women nor for men, but for animals (fowls, horses, etc.). He had intercourse with hens and ducks, and later with horses and cows. Never onanism.

The patient painted pictures of saints; was of very limited intelligence. For years, religious paranoia, with states of ecstasy. He had an "inexplicable" love for the Virgin, for whom he would sacrifice his life. Taken to hospital, he proved to be free from infirmity and signs of anatomical degeneration.

He always had an aversion for women. In a single attempt at coitus with a woman he was impotent, but with animals he was always potent. He was bashful before women; coitus with women he regarded almost as a sin (*Kowalewsky*, "Jahrb. f. Psychiatrie," vii., Heft 3).

CASE 233. T., thirty-five years of age. Father an inebriate; mother psychopathic. Never had a severe illness; never showed special peculiarities. At the age of nine immorality with a hen; later on with other domestic animals. When he began to have sexual relations with women his bestial desires disappeared. Married when twenty, and found sexual satisfaction.

When twenty-seven he began to drink. Then his former perverse inclinations were awakened. One day he took a she-goat to a neighbouring village to have her covered. He felt a strong desire to commit sodomy with her, but he at first overcame the impulse. Palpitation of the heart, pain in the chest, and a violent orgasm made him succumb. T. declared that these bestial acts gave him greater lustful gratification than intercourse with a woman.

His acts of bestial remained unnoticed. He was finally sent to an insane asylum on account of *delirium tremens,* when, during his examination upon admission, he made the above revelations (*Boissier et Lachaux,* "Annal. médico-psychol.," July-August, 1893, p. 381).

In the explanation of zooerasty great difficulties are encountered. The attempt to reduce it to fetichism, as is possible in erotic feeling for animals (*cf.* p. 185), has utterly failed.

It is questionable whether *zoophilia* can ever lead to sexual acts with beasts (eventually bestiality). If it be in reality a fetichistic manifestation, this possibility cannot be based upon the present knowledge of fetichism.

Even in the case of fetichistic erotic feeling for animals (p. 185), acts of bestiality were never committed; in fact, the sex of the animals there in question was never considered. The only thing that at present can be done is to consider zooerasty as an original perversion of the sexual life, and place it on the same level with antipathic sexuality.

The following case, although it is only rudimentary and abortive, seems to support this theory and to establish complete unconsciousness of the motive of the impulse.

CASE 234. Y., twenty years of age, intelligent, well educated; claimed to be free from taint by heredity; physically sound except evidences of neurasthenia and hyperactive urethra; said he never masturbated. Always fond of animals, especially dogs and horses. Since the age of puberty increased love for animals, but sexual ideas in connection with sport seem to have been absent.

One day when he mounted a mare for the first time he experienced a sensation of lust; two weeks later, on a similar occasion, the same sensation with erection.

During his first ride he had ejaculation. A month after the same thing happened. Patient felt disgusted at the occurrence, and was angry with himself. He gave up the saddle. But from now on pollutions almost daily.

When he saw men on horseback, or dogs, he had erections. Almost every night he had pollutions accompanied by dreams in which he rode on horseback or was training dogs. Patient came for medical advice.

Treatment with sounds removed the hyperactivity of the urethra and diminished pollutions. The patient reluctantly followed the advice of the physician to have coitus, partly on account of dislike for women, partly on account of lack of confidence in his virility.

He made abortive attempts at coitus, but could not even bring about an erection, which, however, took place the moment he saw a man on horseback. This depressed him; he considered his condition abnormal beyond remedy.

Continued medical treatment. A further attempt at coitus was successful with the assistance of fancied images of riders and dogs, which stimulated erection.

Patient grew more virile; his love for animals waned; erections at the sight of riders and dogs disappeared, nocturnal pollutions with dreams of animals became less frequent; he dreamed now of girls. Erection, which at first did not support premature ejaculations, and pathological coitus grew normal under treatment with sounds. Patient found normal sexual gratification, and was freed from his perverse sexual impulse (Dr. *Hanc*, "Wien. med. Blätter," 1887, No. 5).

The preceding case justifies the assumption of an original perversion, for instead of the idea of the normal object (woman), it is the idea of animals (dogs and horses) frequently seen which awakens sexual feelings and desires. There may have been a latent sadistic element in the case, for at least in the sexual life of the dreams, the riding of horses and the training of dogs played a prominent part.

The following case, that of a violator (rapist) of animals, is of pathological interest.

CASE 235. Mr. X., forty-seven years of age, of high social position, came to me for advice on account of a troublesome anomaly of his sexual life. He was about to be married and in his present condition considered it morally impossible to enter upon matrimony.

X. was evidently heavily tainted—his father, two of his sisters and one brother were highly neurotic. The mother was presumed to have been a healthy woman.

The sexual instinct awoke early in X.; he began to masturbate spontaneously at the age of eleven.

He was decidedly hypersexual, practiced masturbation with passion, and at the age of fourteen he forgot himself so far as to sodomize bitches, mares and other female animals. He ascribed these acts to excessive sexual desire and to want of opportunity to satisfy his cravings in the normal way—he spent his childhood and boyhood in a lonely part of the country and later on he visited a boarding school.

X. admitted that he was quite conscious of the abomination of his acts, and said that he fought with all his will power against these bestial impulses. But the greed, the lust, the pleasure which they gave, always overpowered him. When grown up to manhood he never had homo-sexual desires, nor did he feel an inclination for woman.

Up to this part of his case history the opinion seems justified that his bestiality was not a perversion, but only a perversity which found root in his habits.

But it strikes one as peculiar that his erotic dreams were always about bestial intercourse, and that when at the age of twenty-five he sought to improve his condition by coitus with a woman, he derived not the slightest gratification from it, although he was quite potent and the girl pleasing and sympathetic.

He had the same experience at other attempts which he repeatedly made during the subsequent twenty-two years. He described coitus as a mere mechanical act devoid of lustful excitement. He might as well have coitus with a piece of wood. It simply disgusted him, while during coitus with an animal he experienced the height of pleasure.

The mere sight of animals excited him wildly. The society of ladies caused him *ennui*. When he went with a girl she had to resort to all kinds of manipulations to prepare him for the act.

For two months previous to his first visit to me X. had exerted all his will power to resist the impulses to masturbation and bestiality.

He was physically a peculiar being, evidently a superior degenerate. There were no symptoms of anatomical degeneration, no traces of neurasthenia.

I made strong suggestions to be on his guard against masturbation and bestiality, and to seek more the society of ladies; prescribed anaphro-disiacs, advised frugality, slight hydrotherapy, plenty of open-air exercise, steady occupation, and had the satisfaction to learn that the patient at the end of ten months experienced a slight gratification in repeated sexual intercourse with a woman and that he was almost free from his former perverse desires.

An analogous case is reported by *Moll,* "Libido sexualis," p. 421.

Another remarkable case of zooerasty is published by *Howard* ("Alienist and Neurologist," 1896, vol. xvii., 1.). It refers to a young man of sixteen years of age who found sexual gratification only with pigs.

The rarity of cases of real zooerasty seems to be remarkable. But this may be explained by the ease with which they are kept secret.

The present state of our knowledge does not permit of a final judgment as to whether zooerasty is an original anomaly or a perverse condition acquired through fetichistic influences.

Moll (Libido sexualis, p. 432) is inclined to the belief that it is an arrest of unindifferentiated sexuality coupled with hypersexuality directed to beasts (analogous to masturbatory impulses) and that this craving for sexual dealings with beasts is permanent and does inhibit the development of libido towards the human female. Practically speaking, sexual feeling and psychical potency seem to be absent, even the power to differentiate between the male and female beast as an object for sexual accomplishment. *Cf. Howard's* case, in which only a certain species of animal was preferred.

The forensically important distinction between bestiality and zooerasty can never be difficult.

Whoever seeks and finds sexual gratification exclusively with animals, although the opportunities for the normal act are at hand, must at once be suspected of a pathological condition of the sexual instinct. At any rate more so than the sexually inverted person, for in sexual acts with animals the psychical condition is wanting, *i.e.*, the possibility of the perversion of one part leading to the perversity of the other.

It may be assumed, however, that the number of cases of zooerasty as compared with those of sexual inversion is unequally smaller. This follows *a priori* from the character of both these perversions. The zooerast as compared with the sexual invert is much farther removed from the normal object. This would qualify the perversion of the former as a much graver condition—because it is more degenerative—than that of the latter.

(b) WITH PERSONS OF THE SAME SEX (PEDERASTY; SODOMY IN ITS STRICT SENSE).

German law takes cognizance of unnatural sexual relations only between men; Austrian, between those of the same sex; and therefore, unnatural relations between women are punishable.

Among the immoralities between men, pederasty (inserting the penis into the anus) claims the principal interest. Indeed, the jurists thought only of this perversity of sexual activity; and, according to the opinions of distinguished interpreters of the law (*Oppenhoff,* "Stgsb.," Berlin, 1872, p. 324, and *Rudolf* and *Stenglein,* "D. Srafgesb. f. d. Deutsche Reich,*" 1881, p. 423), insertion of the penis into the living body must take place to establish the criminal act covered by § 175.

According to this interpretation, legal punishment would not follow other improper acts between male persons, *so long as they were not complicated with offense to public decency, with force, or undertaken with boys under the age of fourteen.* Of late this interpretation has again been abandoned, and the crime of unnatural abuse between men is assumed to have been committed when acts *similar to cohabitation* are performed.[40]

The study of antipathic sexual instinct has placed male love for males in a very different light from that in which it, and particularly pederasty, stood at the time the statutes were framed. The fact that there is no doubt about the pathological basis of many cases of inverted sexual instinct shows that pederasty may also be the act of an irresponsible person, and makes it necessary, in court, to examine not merely the deed, but also the mental condition of the perpetrator.

The principles laid down previously must here be adhered to. Not the deed, but only an anthropological and clinical judgment of the perpetrator can permit a decision as to whether we have to do with a perversity deserving punishment, or with an abnormal perversion of the mental and sexual life, which, under certain circumstances, excludes punishment.

The next legal question to settle is whether the antipathic sexual feeling is congenital or acquired; and, in the latter case, whether it is a pathological perversion or a moral perversity.

Congenital sexual inversion occurs only in predisposed (tainted) individuals, as a partial manifestation of a defect evidenced by anatomical or functional abnormalities, or by both. The case becomes clearer and the diagnosis more certain if the individual, in character and disposition, seems to correspond entirely with his sexual peculiarity; if the inclination towards persons of the opposite sex is entirely wanting, or horror of sexual intercourse with them is felt; and if the individual, in the impulses to satisfy the antipathic sexual instinct, shows other anomalies of the sexual sphere, such as more pronounced degeneration in the form of periodicity of the impulse and impulsive conduct, and is a neuropathic and psychopathic person.

Another question concerns the mental condition of the homosexual. If this be such as to remove the possibility of moral responsibility, then the pederast is not a criminal, but an irresponsible insane person.

This condition is apparently less frequent in congenital homosexuals. As a rule, these cases present elementary psychical disturbances which do not remove responsibility.

But this does not settle the question of responsibility in the homosexual. The sexual instinct is one of the most powerful organic needs. There is no law that looks upon its satisfaction outside of marriage as punishable in itself; if the homosexual feels perverse, it is not his fault, but the fault of an abnormal condition natural to him. His sexual instinct may be aesthetically very repugnant, but, from his morbid standpoint, it is natural. And again, in the majority of these unfortunates the perverse sexual instinct is abnormally intense, and their consciousness recognizes it as nothing unnatural. Thus moral and aesthetic ideas fail to assist them in resisting the instinct.

Innumerable normally constituted men are in a position to renounce the gratification of their *libido* without suffering from it in health. Many neuropathic individuals,—and homosexuals are almost always neuropathic,—on the contrary, become nervously ill when they do not satisfy the sexual desire, either as Nature prompts or in a way that to them is perverse.

The majority of homosexuals are in a painful situation. On the one hand, there is an impulse towards persons of their own sex that is abnormally intense, the gratification of which has a good effect, and is natural to them; on the other hand, there is public feeling, which stigmatizes their acts, and the law which threatens them with disgraceful punishment. Before them lies mental despair,—even insanity and suicide, —at the very least, nervous disease; behind them, shame, loss of position, etc. It cannot be doubted that, under these circumstances, states of stress and compulsion may be created by an unfortunate natural disposition and constitution. Society and the law should understand and appreciate these facts. The former should pity, and not despise, these unfortunates; the latter must cease to punish them,—at least while they remain within the limits which are set for the activity of their sexual instinct.

As a confirmation of the opinions and demands concerning these step-children of Nature, it is permissible to reproduce here the memorial of a homosexual to the author. The writer of the following lines is a man of high position in London:—

"You have no idea what a constant struggle we all—particularly those of us who have the most mind and finest feelings—must endure, and how we suffer under the prevailing false ideas about us and our so-called 'immorality.'

"Your opinion that the phenomenon under consideration is primarily due to a congenital 'pathological' disposition will, perhaps, make it possible to overcome existing prejudices, and awaken pity for poor, 'abnormal' men, instead of the present repugnance and contempt.

"Much as I believe that the opinion expressed by you is exceedingly *beneficial* to us, I am still compelled, in the interest of science, to repudiate the word 'pathological'; and you will permit me to express a few thoughts with respect to it.

"Under all circumstances the phenomenon is anomalous; but the word 'pathological' conveys another meaning, which I cannot think suits this phenomenon; at least, as I have had occasion to observe it in very many cases. I will allow, *a priori*, that, among homosexuals, a far higher proportion of cases of insanity, of nervous exhaustion, etc., may be observed than in other normal men. Does this increased nervousness necessarily depend upon the character of homosexuality, or is it not, in the majority of cases, to be ascribed to the effect of the laws and the prejudices of society, which prohibit the indulgence of their sexual desires, depending on a congenital peculiarity, while others are not thus restrained?

"The youthful homosexual, when he feels the first sexual promptings and naïvely expresses them to his comrades, soon finds that he is not understood; he shrinks into himself. If he tells his parents or teacher what moves him, that which is as natural to him as swimming is to a fish is described as wrong and sinful, and he is told it must be fought and overcome at any price. Then an inner conflict begins, a powerful repression of sexual inclinations; and the more the natural satisfaction of desire is repressed, the more lively the fancy becomes, and paints the very pictures that the wish is to banish. The more energetic the character that carries on this inner conflict, the more the whole nervous system must suffer. Such a powerful repression of an instinct so deeply implanted in us, in my opinion, develops the abnormal symptoms which are observed in many homosexuals; but this does not necessarily follow from the homosexual's disposition.

"Some continue the conflict for a longer or shorter time, and thus injure themselves; others at last come to the knowledge that the powerful instinct born in them cannot possibly be sinful, and, therefore, they cease to try to do the impossible—the repression of the instinct. Then, however, begins constant suffering and excitement. When a normal man seeks satisfaction of sexual inclination, he knows how to find it easily; it is not so with the homosexual. He sees men that attract him, but he dares not say—nay, not even betray by a look—what his feelings are. He thinks that he alone of all the world has such abnormal feelings. Naturally he seeks the society of young men; but he does not venture to confide in them. Thus he comes to provide himself with a satisfaction that he cannot otherwise obtain. Onanism is practiced inordinately, and followed by all the evil results of that vice. When, after a time, the nervous system has been injured, the abnormality is again not the result of homosexuality, but it is produced by the onanism to which the homosexual resorts, as a result of the public sentiment that denies him opportunity to satisfy the sexual instinct that is natural to him.

"Or let us suppose the homosexual has had the rare fortune to soon find a person like himself; or that he has been introduced by an experienced friend to the events of the world of homosexuals. Then he is spared much of the inner conflict; but, at the same time, fearful cares and anxieties follow his footsteps. Now he knows that he is not the only one in the world that has such abnormal feelings; he opens his eyes and wonders that he meets so many of his kind in all social circles and in all callings; he also learns that, in the world of homosexuals, as in the other, there is prostitution, and that men as well as women can be bought. Thus there is no longer any want of opportunity for sexual satisfaction. But here how differently the experience is gained from that obtained in the normal manner of sexual indulgence!

"Let us consider the happiest case. After longing all one's life, the friend of like feeling is found. But he cannot be approached openly, as a lover approaches the girl he loves. In constant fear, both must conceal their relations; nay, even intimacy that might easily excite suspicion—especially should they not be of like age, or should they belong to different classes—must be kept from the world. Thus, even in this relation, is forged a chain of anxiety and fear that the secret will be betrayed or discovered, which leaves them no joy in the indulgence. The slightest thing that would not affect others makes them tremble with fear that suspicion might be excited and the secret discovered, and destroy social position and business. Could this constant anxiety and care be endured without leaving a trace, without exerting an influence on the entire nervous system?

"Another less fortunate man does not find a friend of like feeling, but falls into the hands of a handsome man, who sought him until the secret was discovered. Now the most refined blackmail is extorted. The unfortunate, persecuted man, brought to the alternative of paying or of losing his social position, and bringing disgrace on himself and his family, pays; and the more he gives, the more voracious the blackmailer becomes; until at last there remains nothing but absolute financial ruin or dishonour. Who can wonder that nerves are not equal to such a terrible struggle!

"They give way; insanity comes on, and the miserable man at last finds the rest in an asylum that he could not find in the world. Another, in the same situation, driven to despair, finds relief in suicide. It cannot be known how many of the suicides of young men are to be attributed to this combination of circumstances.

"I do not think that I am in error when I declare that at least one half of the suicides of young men are due to such conditions. Even in those cases where homosexuals are not persecuted by a heartless villain, but where a happy relation between two men exists, discovery, or even the fear of it, very often leads to suicide. How many officers, how many soldiers, having such relations with their subordinates or companions, in the moment when they have believed themselves discovered, have sought to escape the threatened disgrace by means of a bullet! And it is the same in all callings.

"Therefore, if it must be admitted that, among homosexuals, more mental abnormalities and more insanity are actually observed than other men, yet this does not prove that the mental disturbance is a *necessary* accompaniment of the homosexual's condition, and that the latter induces the former.

"According to my firm conviction, *by far* the greater number of cases of mental disturbance or abnormal disposition observed in homo-sexuals are not to be attributed to the sexual anomaly; but they are caused by the existing notions concerning homosexuals, and the result-ing laws, and dominant public sentiment concerning the anomaly. Any one with an adequate idea of the mental and moral suffering, of the anxiety and care that the homosexual must endure; of the constant hypocrisy and secrecy he must practice in order to conceal his inner instinct; of the difficulties that meet him in satisfying his natural desire, —can only be surprised that more insanity and nervous disturbance does not occur in homosexuals. The greater part of these abnormal states would not be developed if the homosexual, like another, could find a simple and easy way in which to satisfy his sexual desire,—if he were not for ever troubled by these anxieties!"

With regard to established law, as far as the homosexual is con-cerned, the paragraph with reference to pederasty should not be applied *without the proof of actual pederasty*; and psychical and somatic abnor-malities should be examined by experts with respect to an estimate in the individual of the question of guilt.

With regard to proposed law, the homosexuals wish a repeal of the paragraph. The jurist could not consent to this, if he is to remember that pederasty is much more frequently a disgusting vice than the result of a physical and mental infirmity; and that, moreover, many homosexuals, though driven to sexual acts with their own sex, are yet in nowise compelled to indulge in pederasty,—a sexual act which, under all cir-cumstances, must stand as cynical, disgusting, and, when passive, as decidedly injurious. *Whether for reasons of expediency* (difficulty of fixing the guilt, encouragement of blackmail, etc.), *it would not be opportune to strike from the statutes the legal punishment of the male-loving man is a question for the jurists of the future.*[41]

My reasons for advocating the abolition of the laws above referred to are the following:—

(1) The offenses referred to in these laws generally spring from an abnormal psychical condition.

(2) Only a most careful medical examination can distinguish cases of sheer perversity from those of pathological perversion. As soon as the individual is charged with the offense he is socially ruined.

(3) The majority of homosexuals are the victims of a perverse instinct of abnormal quality. In qualifying the sexual instinct they are irresistibly forced by physical compulsion.

(4) Many homosexuals are incapable of considering their sexual instinct as unnatural; on the contrary, their own appears to them the natural act, and that permitted by law as contrary to nature. The moral means of correction which might prevent the sexual transgression are therefore wanting.

(5) The definition as to what constitutes an immoral offense is

defective, and allows the judge too much latitude. In Germany, for instance, the interpretation of § 175, growing more subtle and ingenious every day, gives direct proof of the uncertainty of its proper legal understanding.

The deed in itself ought to be decisive in this matter, and the verdict should be in accordance with it. (As a rule, the motive is scarcely ever scrutinized.) But how is this to be established? For the deed is, as a rule, committed in secret and in the absence of witnesses.

(6) Theoretical criminal reasons for the retention of the paragraph are never advanced. It does not deter crime and has no corrective influence, for pathological manifestations are not removed by penal remedies. Decidedly it is not an atonement for a criminal act which can only under certain and mostly false presumptions be considered as criminal, and thus may lead to acts of gross injustice. It must be remembered that in many civilized countries this paragraph no longer is in vogue, that in Germany it only exists as a concession to public morality, whilst the latter is based on false principles, and frequently confuses perversion with perversity.

(7) In my opinion, public morality and youth are sufficiently protected, in Germany at any rate, by other paragraphs of the statutes; and I incline to the belief that paragraph 175 does more harm than good, in so far as it favours and abets blackmail—one of the basest and vilest vices.

Of course, the blackmailer may be punished, but he has always the one chance in his favour, that his victim will never resort to the extreme measure of appealing to the law. If it comes to the worst, the scoundrel is confined to prison for a short time without running the risk of losing the honour which he never possessed, whilst his victim has lost all, *i.e.*, his good name and the respect of others, is thus ruined and often brought to self-destruction.

(8) If the German law-maker should deem public morality endangered by the abrogation of § 175, surely the extension of § 176, 1, to *male* persons as well should be sufficient (at present this paragraph deals only with immoral acts committed on females either with force or under threats). The French penal code has such a paragraph. Eventually the age of fourteen years mentioned in this paragraph 176, 3, and beyond which immoral actions committed on youthful persons go unpunished, might be raised to a higher figure. This would also benefit the female portion of society, who scarcely possess at the age of fifteen sufficient maturity of mind and judgment to protect themselves against the evil. Moreover by this act a more efficient protection would be given to young people in general (say up to the end of the sixteenth year) than is now granted by § 175, which after all is only directed against pederasty (and according to more recent interpretation against other acts of a coitus-like nature) while it regards onanism and other immoral

acts with impunity. Perverse people but seldom endanger the morality of the young by pederasty, but much more frequently by other acts of immorality. Beyond a certain age, say eighteen, when a sufficient degree of moral and intellectual maturity has been attained, the law has neither the right nor the duty to impugn immoral acts which are committed between married people, behind closed doors, and by mutual consent. The individual himself is responsible for such acts, for they do not violate either public or private interests.

What has been said *de lege lata* concerning congenital sexual inversion and its relation to the law is also applicable to the *acquired* abnormality. The accompanying neurosis or psychosis should have much diagnostic and forensic weight with reference to the question of guilt.

It is of high psychopathological and, under the circumstances, also of criminal interest that individuals of antipathic sexuality when unfortunate in their love affairs, or when meeting with deception on the part of the beloved, are subject to all those psychical reactions in the shape of jealousy and vindictiveness which occur in the love affairs between man and woman; nay, these often lead to deeds of violence to revenge the affront or to punish the robber of happiness.

Nothing else could prove more clearly the constitutional determination of these inverted sexual feelings; their dominating power over sense, thought and aspiration, and their complete substitution for hetero-sexual normal feeling and development. A case of such unrequited and betrayed love is the following taken from recent American criminal acts, the report of which was sent to me by Dr. *Boeck* of Troppau.

CASE 236. A *sexually inverted girl kills the girl she loves because she was rejected.*

In January, 1892, Alice M., a young girl belonging to one of the best families of Memphis, Tennessee, U.S.A., killed in the public street of that town her girl friend, Freda W., also of the best society. She made several deep gashes in the neck of the girl with a razor.

The trial elicited the following facts:—

Alice inherited taint from her mother—an uncle and several cousins in the first degree were insane—the mother herself was psychopathic, had post partum psychosis after each confinement, the worst attack following the birth of the seventh child, *i.e.*, Alice, now a prisoner—afterwards she declined mentally, suffering from persecutory dementia.

A brother of the accused suffered from mental derangement for some time after an alleged sunstroke.

Alice was nineteen years of age, of medium height, not pretty. The face was childlike and "almost too small for her size," and asymmetrical, the right facial side was more developed than the left, the nose "of striking irregularity," the eye piercing. She was left-handed.

With the beginning of puberty, severe and continued headaches were of frequent occurrence; once a month she suffered from nose bleed, often up to within the very latest period from attacks of tremor. On one occasion she lost consciousness during one of these attacks.

Alice was a nervous, irritable child, and very slow in physical development. She never enjoyed children's or girls' games. When she was four to five years old she took much pleasure in tormenting cats, suspending them by one leg.

She preferred her younger brother and his games to her sisters; she vied with him in spinning tops, playing baseball and football, or shooting at targets, and in many silly pranks. She loved to climb trees and roofs, and was very clever in this sport. Above all things she loved to amuse herself in the stable among the mules. When she was six to seven her father had bought a horse, and she took great delight in feeding and tending it, and rode about the paddock astraddle on its back like a boy, without a saddle. Later on she would also groom the horse and wash his hoofs. She would lead him along the street by the halter, gear him up in the buggy, and became quite an expert in harnessing him when required.

At school she was slow and faulty, incapable of continued occupation with the same subject, did not grasp things easily, and had little memory. For music and drawing she had not the slightest talent, and hated feminine occupations. She never cared for reading, and could bear neither books nor newspapers. She was stubborn and capricious, and was considered by her teachers and friends as an abnormal youngster.

When a child she did not care for boys, and had no companions among them; later on she never cared for men, and had no lovers. She was quite indifferent towards the young men, even abrupt, and they looked upon her as being "cracked."

But "as far as she can remember" she had an extraordinary love for Freda W., a girl of her own age, daughter of a friend of the family. Freda was a tender and sweet girl; the love was mutual, but more violent on the part of Alice. It increased from year to year until it became a passion. A year previous to the catastrophe Freda's family moved away to another town. Alice was steeped in sorrow; a very tender love correspondence now ensued.

Twice Alice went to visit Freda's family, during which time the two girls, as witnesses attested, showed "disgusting tenderness" for each other. They were seen to swing together in a hammock by the hour, hugging and kissing each other—"they hugged and kissed to the point of nausea." Alice was ashamed of doing it in public, but Freda upbraided her for this.

When Freda paid a return visit, Alice made an attempt to kill her; she tried to pour laudanum down her throat while she slept. The attempt failed because Freda woke up in time.

Alice then took the poison herself in front of Freda, and was taken violently ill. The reason for the attempted murder and suicide was that Freda had shown some interest in two young men, and Alice declared she could not live without Freda's love, and again "she wanted to kill herself in order to find release from her tortures and make Freda free." After recovery they both resumed the amorous correspondence, even with more fervour than before.

Soon after this Alice proposed marriage to Freda. She sent her an engagement ring, and threatened death if she proved disloyal. They were to assume a false name and fly to St. Louis. Alice would wear men's clothes and earn a living for both; she would also grow a moustache, if Freda were to insist upon it, as she felt confident that by shaving frequently she could succeed in this.

Just before the attempted elopement the plot was discovered and prevented; the "engagement ring" was returned together with other love tokens to Alice's mother, and all intercourse between the two girls was stopped.

Alice was completely shattered. She lost sleep, refused food, became listless and confused (at the shops had the purchased goods put down to the name of her beloved). The ring and other love tokens —among them a thimble of Freda's filled with the latter's blood—she concealed in a corner of the kitchen, where she spent hours in contemplating these objects, now bursting into peals of laughter, now into floods of tears.

She became emaciated, her face assumed an anxious expression, her eyes showed "a peculiar strange lustre." When she learned of an intended visit by Freda to Memphis she firmly resolved to kill her *if she could not possess* her. She stole a razor from her father and carefully concealed it.

In the meantime she started a correspondence with Freda's admirer, simulating friendship for him in order to find out about his relations with Freda, and kept herself informed about them.

All attempts to see her or hear from her made by Alice during Freda's sojourn in Memphis failed. She waylaid Freda in the street and once almost succeeded in carrying out her purpose had not an accident prevented her. On the very day, however, when Freda was leaving town and on her way to the steamboat Alice overtook her.

She felt mortally hurt because Freda, although walking alongside of the buggy in which she herself was riding, never spoke a word to her, but only gave her a glance now and then. She jumped from the vehicle and cut Freda with the razor. When Freda's sister tried to beat her off she became frantic and blindly cut deep gashes into the poor girl's neck, one reaching almost from ear to ear. While everybody was busy helping Freda she drove off furiously through the streets. Upon reaching home she immediately told her mother what had happened. She could not comprehend the awfulness of the deed; she was cold and unmoved at the consequences pointed out to her. But when she heard of the death and the funeral of her beloved and realized her loss she burst into tears and passionate wailings, kissed the picture of the dead girl and spoke as if she were not dead but still alive.

During the trial her callous behaviour struck every one; the deep sorrow of her own family did not affect her in the least; she showed absolute indifference to the ethical points of her deed.

At moments, however, when her passionate love for Freda and her jealousy became evident, she yielded to boundless grief and emotion. *"Freda has broken her faith!"* "I have killed her because I loved her so!" The experts called in the case found her mental development on a level with that of a girl of thirteen to fourteen years. She comprehended that no children could have sprung from her "union" with Freda—but that a "marriage" between them would have been an absurdity she would not admit. She absolutely denied that sexual intercourse between the two (even mutual masturbation) ever took place. But nothing definite about this point or about her previous sexual life could be learned. A gynaecological examination of her person was not made.

The verdict was insanity ("Memphis Medical Monthly," 1892).

CULTIVATED PEDERASTY.[42]

This is one of the saddest pages in the history of human delinquencies.

The motives that bring to pederasty a man orginally sexually normal and of sound mind are various. It is used temporarily as a means of sexual satisfaction for want of something better—as in infrequent cases of bestiality—where abstinence from normal sexual indulgence is enforced.[43] It thus occurs on shipboard during long voyages, in prisons, in watering-places, etc. It is highly probable that, among men subjected to such conditions, there are single individuals of low morals and great sensuality, or actual homosexuals, who seduce the others. Lust, imitation, and desire further their purpose.

The strength of the sexual instinct is most markedly shown by the fact that such circumstances are sufficient to overcome repugnance for the unnatural act.

Another category of pederasts is made up of old *roués* that have become supersatiated in normal sexual indulgence, and who find in pederasty a means of exciting sensual pleasure, the act being a new method of stimulation. Thus they temporarily renew their power, that has been psychically and physically reduced to so low a state. The new sexual situation makes them, so to speak, relatively potent, and renders pleasure possible that is no longer found in the normal intercourse with women. In time power to indulge in pederasty also flickers out. The individual may thus finally be reduced to passive pederasty as a stimulus to make possible temporary active pederasty; just as, occasionally, flagellation or looking on at obscene acts (*Maschka's* case of mutilation of animals) is resorted to for the same purpose.

The termination of sexual activity expresses itself in all kinds of abuse of children—*cunnilingus, fellatio,* and other enormities.

This kind of pederasts is the most dangerous, since they *deal mostly with boys,* and ruin them in body and soul.

In reference to this, the experiences of *Tarnowsky* (*op. cit.,* p. 53 *et seq.*), gathered from society in St. Petersburg, are terrible. The places where pederasty is cultivated are the institutes. Old *roués* and homosexuals play the *rôle* of seducers. At first it is difficult for the person to carry out the disgusting act. Fantasy is used to assist by calling up the image of a woman. Gradually, with practice, the unnatural act becomes easy, and at last the individual, like one *debased* by masturbation, becomes relatively impotent for women, and lustful enough to find pleasure in the perverse act. Such individuals, under other circumstances, give themselves for money.

As *Tardieu, Hofmann, Simon* and *Taylor* show, such fiends are not infrequently found in large cities. From numerous statements made to me by homosexuals, it is learned that actual prostitution and houses of prostitution for male-loving men exist in large cities. The arts of coquetry used by these male prostitutes are noteworthy—ornament, perfumes, feminine styles of dress, etc., to attract pederasts and homosexuals. This imitation of feminine peculiarities is spontaneous and unconscious in congenital and in some acquired cases of (abnormal) antipathic sexual instinct.

The following lines are of interest to the psychologist, and may give the officers of the law important clues concerning the social life and practice of pederasts:—

Coffignon, "La Corruption à Paris," p. 327, divides active pederasts into *"amateurs," "entreteneurs"* and *"souteneurs."* [I have taken the liberty of not translating the French words appearing on these pages, since they are mostly not used in their normal meaning, but are a special type of slang used by the homosexuals of Paris at the time the book ("La Corruption à Paris"—see page 587) was written. Furthermore, these terms are all explained by the English context. Otherwise, I myself should not have understood them completely.—Translator.]

The *"amateurs"* (*"rivettes"*) are debauched persons, frequently of congenital sexual inversion, of position and fortune, who are forced to guard themselves against detection in the gratification of their homosexual desires. For this purpose they visit brothels, lodging-houses, or the private houses of female prostitutes, who are usually on good terms with male prostitutes. Thus they escape blackmail.

Some of these *"amateurs"* are bold enough to indulge their vile desires in public places. They thus run the risk of arrest, but in a large city little risk of blackmail. Danger is said to add to their secret pleasure.

The *"entreteneurs"* are old sinners who, even with the danger of falling into the hands of blackmailers, cannot deny themselves the pleasure of keeping a (male) "mistress."

The *"souteneurs"* are pederasts that have been punished, who keep their *"jesus,"* whom they send out to entice customers (*"faire chanter les rivettes"*) and who then, at the right moment if possible, appear for the purpose of using the victim.

Not infrequently they live together in bands, the members, in accordance with individual desire, living together as husbands and wives. In such bands there are formal marriages, betrothals, banquets and introductions of brides and grooms into their apartments.

These *"souteneurs"* train up their *"jesus."*

The *passive* pederasts are *"petits jesus," "jesus,"* or "aunts."

The *"petits jesus"* are lost, depraved children, placed by accident in the hands of active pederasts, who seduce them, and reveal to them the horrible means of earning a livelihood, either as *"entretenus"* or as male street-walkers, with or without *"souteneurs."*

The slyest and choicest *"petits jesus"* are those trained by persons who instruct these children in the art of female dress and manner.

Gradually they emancipate themselves from teacher and master, in order to become *"femmes entretenues,"* not infrequently by means of anonymous denunciation of their *"souteneurs"* to the police.

It is the object of the *"souteneur"* and the *"petit jesus"* to make the latter appear young as long as possible by means of all the arts of the toilet.

The limit of age is about twenty-five years; when they all become *"jesus"* and *"femmes entretenues,"* and are then often sustained by several *"souteneurs."* The *"jesus"* falls into three categories: *"filles galantes,"* i.e., those that have fallen again into the hands of a *"souteneur"*; *"pierreuses"* (ordinary street-walkers, like their female colleagues); and *"domestiques."*

The *"domestiques"* hire themselves out to active pederasts, either to gratify their desires or to obtain *"petits jesus"* for them.

A sub-group of these *"domestiques"* is formed by such of them as enter the service of *"petits jesus"* as *"femmes de chambre."* The principal object of these *"domestiques"* is to use their positions to obtain compromising knowledge, with which they later practice blackmail, and thus assure themselves ease in their old age.

The most horrible class of active pederasts is made up of the *"aunts"* —i.e., the *"souteneurs"* of (male) prostitutes—who, though normal sexually, are morally depraved, and practice pederasty (passive) only for gain or for the purpose of blackmail.

The wealthy "*amateurs*" have their reunions and places of meeting, where the passive ones appear in female attire, and horrible orgies take place. The waiters, musicians, etc., at such gatherings, are all pederasts. The "*filles galantes*" do not venture, except during the carnival, to show themselves on the street in female attire; but they know how to lend to their appearance something indicative of their calling by means of style of dress, etc. They entice by means of gesture, peculiar movements of their hands, etc., and lead their victims to hotels, baths, or brothels.

What the author says of blackmail is generally known. There are cases where pederasts have allowed their entire fortune to be blackmailed from them.

That these monstrosities of large cities in the shape of "*petits jesus*" are not only the productions of professional training, but rather of a degenerated mental condition is apparent from the researches made by *Laurent* ("Les bisexués," Paris, 1894). He described on page 175 of his book under the title of "Hermaphroditisme artificiel" manifestations of "*effemination*" and "*infantilisme*." They refer to boys who at incipient puberty show no further development of the frame and the genital organs, have no growth of hair about the face or pubes, do not change the voice and are retrograde in their mental faculties. Often it happens that in such cases secondary physical and psychical female characteristics of sexuality are developed. A *post mortem* of such "*petits garroches*" (*Brouardel*) reveals a small bladder, mere rudiments of the prostate, absence of the *ischio* and *bulbo cavernosi* muscles, infantile penis, and a very narrow pelvis.

They are beyond doubt heavily tainted individuals who have experienced at the time of puberty a sort of rudimentary sexual change.

Laurent (p. 181) makes the interesting remark, *that from the ranks of these "Infantiles" and "Effeminates" the professional passive pederasts ("petits jesus") are recruited.*

It is evident, therefore, that these human monstrosities are predestined for and trained, so to speak, in their abominable career by degenerative and anthropological factors.

The following notice from a Berlin newspaper, of February, 1884, which fell into my hands by accident, seems suited to show something of the life and customs of pederasts and homosexuals:

"*The Woman-haters' Ball.*—Almost every social element of Berlin has its social reunions—the fat, the bald-headed, the bachelors, the widowers—and why not the woman-haters? This species of men, so interesting psychologically and none too edifying, had a great ball a few days ago. 'Grand Vienna Fancy Dress Ball'—ran the notice. The sale of tickets is well controlled; they wish to be very exclusive. Their rendezvous is a well-known dancing-hall. We enter the hall about midnight. The merry dancing is to the strains of a fine orchestra. Thick tobacco-smoke, veiling the gaslights, does not allow the details of the moving mass to become obvious; only during the pause between the dances can we obtain a closer view. The masks are by far in the majority; black dress-coats and ball-gowns are seen only now and then.

"But what is that? The lady in rose-tarletan, that just now passed us, has a lighted cigar in the corner of her mouth, and puffs like a trooper; and she also wears a small, blonde beard, lightly painted out. And yet she is talking with a very *décolleté* 'angel' in *tricots*, who stands there, with bare arms folded behind him, likewise smoking. The two voices are masculine, and the conversation is likewise very masculine; it is about the 'd—— tobacco smoke, that permits no air.' Two men in female attire! A conventional clown stands there, against a pillar, in soft conversation with a ballet-dancer, with his arm around her faultless waist. She has a blonde 'Titus-head' sharp-cut profile, and apparently a voluptuous form. The brilliant ear-rings, the necklace with a medallion, the full, round shoulders and arms, do not permit a doubt of her 'genuineness,' until, with a sudden movement, she disengages herself from the embracing arm, and, yawning, moves away, saying, in a deep bass, 'Emile, you are too tiresome today!' The ballet-dancer is also a male!

"Suspicious now, we look about further. We almost suspect that here the world is topsy-turvy; for there goes, or, rather, trips, a man— no, no man at all, even though he wears a carefully trained moustache. The well-curled hair; the powdered and painted face with the blackened eyebrows; the golden ear-rings; the bouquet of flowers reaching from the left shoulder to the breast, ornamenting the elegant black gown; the golden bracelets on the wrist; the elegant fan in the white gloved hand —all these things are anything but masculine. And how he toys with the fan! How he dances and turns and trips and lisps! And yet kindly Nature made this doll a man. He is a salesman in a large sweet shop, and the ballet-dancer mentioned is his 'colleague.'

"At a little corner-table there seems to be a great social circle. Several elderly gentlemen press around a group of *décolleté* ladies, who sit over a glass of wine and—in the spirit of fun—make jokes that are none too delicate. Who are these three ladies? 'Ladies!' laughs my knowing friend. 'Well, the one on the right, with the brown hair and the short, fancy dress, is called "Butterrieke," he is a hairdresser; the second one— the blonde in a singer's costume, with the necklace of pearls—is known here by the name of "Miss Ella of the tight-rope," and he is a ladies' tailor; and the third—that is the widely celebrated "Lottie." '

"But that person cannot possibly be a man? That waist, that bust, those classic arms, the whole air and person are markedly feminine!

"I am told that 'Lottie' was once a bookkeeper. Today she, or, rather, he, is exclusively 'Lottie,' and takes pleasure in deceiving men about his sex as long as possible. 'Lottie' is singing a song that would hardly do for a drawing-room, in a high voice, acquired by years of practice, which many a soprano might envy. 'Lottie' has also 'worked' as a female comedian. Now the quondam bookkeeper has so entered into the female *rôle* that he appears on the street in female attire almost exclusively, and, as the people with whom he lodges state, uses an embroidered night-dress.

"On closer examination of the assembly, to my astonishment, I discover acquaintances on all sides: my shoemaker, whom I should have taken for anything but a woman-hater—he is a 'troubadour,' with sword and plume; and his 'Leonora,' in the costume of a bride, is accustomed to place my favorite brand of cigars before me in a certain cigar-store. 'Leonora,' who, during an intermission, removes her gloves, I recognize with certainty by her large, blue hands. Right! There is my haberdasher, also; he moves about in a questionable costume as Bacchus, and is the swain of a repugnantly bedecked Diana, who works as a waiter in a beer-restaurant. The real 'ladies' of the ball cannot be described here. They associate only with one another, and avoid the woman-hating men; and the latter are exclusive, and amuse themselves, absolutely ignoring the charms of the women."

These facts deserve the careful attention of the police, who should be placed in a position *to cope with male prostitution, as they now do with that of women.*

Male prostitution is certainly much more dangerous to society than that of females; it is the darkest stain on the history of humanity.

From the statements of a high police official of Berlin, I learn that the police are conversant with the male *demi-monde* of the German capital, and do all they can to suppress blackmail among pederasts—a practice which often does not stop short of murder.

The foregoing facts justify the wish that *the law-maker of the future may, for reasons of utility, at least, abandon the prosecution of pederasty.*

With reference to this point, it is worthy of note that the French Code does not punish it so long as it does not become an offense to public decency. Probably for politico-legal reasons, the new Italian Penal Code passes over the crime of unnatural abuse in silence, as do the statutes of Holland and, as far as I know, Belgium and Spain.

In how far such cultivated pederasts are to be regarded as mentally and morally sound may remain an open question. The majority of them suffer with genital neuroses. *At least in these cases there are the stages of transition to acquired pathological antipathic sexual instinct* (see p. 188). The responsibility of these individuals, who are certainly much lower than the women who prostitute themselves, cannot, generally speaking, be questioned.

The various categories of male-loving men, with respect to the manner of sexual indulgence, may be thus characterized in general:

The *congenital* homosexual becomes a *pederast only exceptionally,* and eventually resorts to it after having practiced and exhausted all the possible immoral acts with males.

Passive pederasty is to him the ideally and practically adequate form of the sexual act. He practices active pederasty only to please another. The most important point here is the congenital and unchangeable perversion of the sexual instinct.

It is otherwise with the pederast *by cultivation*. He has once acted normally sexually, or at least had normal inclinations, and occasionally has intercourse with the opposite sex. His sexual perversity is neither congenital nor unchangeable. He begins with pederasty and ends in other perverse sexual acts, induced by weakness of the centres for erection and ejaculation. At the height of his power his sexual desire is not for passive, but only for active pederasty. He yields to passive pederasty only to please another; for money, in the *rôle* of a male prostitute; or as a means, when virility is declining, to make active pederasty still occasionally possible.

A horrible act, that must be alluded to, in conclusion, is pederasty, insertion of the penis into the anus of women,[44] and even wives. Sensual individuals sometimes do it with hardened prostitutes, or even with their wives. *Tardieu* gives examples where men, usually practicing coitus, sometimes indulged in pederasty with their wives. Occasionally fear of a repetition of pregnancy may induce the man to perform and the woman to tolerate the act.

CASE 237. *Imputation of pederasty that was not proved. Résumé* from the legal proceedings:

On 30th May, 1888, S., chemist, of H., in an anonymous letter, was accused by his stepfather of having immoral relations with G., aged nineteen, the son of a butcher. S. received the letter, and, astounded by its contents, hastened to his master, who promised to proceed discreetly in the matter, and to ascertain from the authorities what was being said about it by the public.

On the next morning, G., who lived in the house of S., was arrested. At the time he was suffering from gonorrhoea and orchitis. S. tried to induce the authorities to release G., and advised caution, but he was refused. In his statement to the judge, S. said that he became acquainted with G. on the street, three years previously, and then saw no more of him until the fall of 1887, when he met him in his father's shop. After November G. supplied S.'s kitchen with meat—coming in the evening to get the order, and bringing the meat the next morning. Thus S. gradually got well acquainted with G., and came to have a very friendly feeling for him. When S. fell ill and was, for the most part, confined to his bed until the middle of May, 1888, G. gave him so much attention that S. and his wife were much attracted to him on account of his harmless, child-like and happy disposition. S. showed and explained to him his collection of curiosities, and they spent the evenings pleasantly together, the wife also being usually present; besides, S. and G. experimented in making sausages, jelly, etc. In February, 1888, G. fell ill with gonorrhoea. S., being his friend, and having studied medicine for several terms, took care of G., procured medicine for him, etc. In May, G. being still ill, and, for several reasons, inclined to leave home, S. and his wife took him into their own home to care for him. S. denied the truth of all the suspicions that had been raised by this revelation, and defended himself by pointing to his life of previous respectability, his education, and to the fact that G., at the time, was suffering with a disgusting, contagious disease, and that he himself had a painful affection (kidney stones, with occasional attacks of colic).

Opposed to this statement of S.'s must be mentioned the facts that were brought out in court, and which led to conviction in the first trial.

The relation of S. to G. had, by reason of its obviousness, given cause for remarks by private individuals, as well as by those in public houses. G. spent almost all his evenings with S.'s family, and, finally, came to be quite at home there. They took walks together. Once, while out on such a walk, S. said to G. that he was a pretty fellow, and that he (S.) was very fond of him. On the same occasion, there was also talk of sexual matters, and also of pederasty. S. said he touched on these subjects only to warn G. With reference to the intercourse at home, it was proved that occasionally S., while sitting on a sofa, embraced G., and kissed him. This happened in the presence of the wife, as well as of the servant-girls. When G. was ill with gonorrhoea, S. instructed him in the method of using a syringe, and, at the time, took the penis in his hand. G. testified that S., in answer to his question why he was so fond of him, said, "I don't know myself." When, one day, G. remained away, S., with tears in his eyes, complained of it to him when he returned. S. also told him that his marriage was unhappy, and, in tears, begged G. not to leave him; that he must take the place of his wife.

From all this resulted the just accusation, that the relation between the two men had a sexual direction. The fact that all was open and known to everybody, according to the complaint, did not speak for the harmlessness of the relation, but more for the intensity of the passion of S. The spotless life of the accused was allowed, as well as his honesty and gentleness. The probability of an unhappy marriage, and that S. was of a very sensual nature, was shown.

During the course of the trial, G. was repeatedly examined by the medical experts. He was scarcely of medium size, pale, and of powerful frame; penis and testicles were perfectly developed (large).

In consonance with the accusation, it was found that the anus was pathologically changed, in that there were no wrinkles in the skin about it and the sphincter was relaxed; and it was presumed that these changes pointed to the probability of passive pederasty.

The conviction was based on these facts. The judgment passed recognized that the relation existing between the culprits did not necessarily point to unnatural abuses, any more than did the physical conditions found on the person of G.

However, by reason of the combination of the two facts, the court was convinced of the guilt of both culprits, and held it proved: "That the abnormal condition of G.'s anus had been caused by the frequently repeated introduction of the penis of S. and that G. voluntarily permitted the performance of this immoral act on himself."

Thus the conditions of §175, R. St. G. B., seemed to be covered. In passing sentence there was consideration of S.'s education, which made him appear to be G.'s seducer; in G.'s case, this fact and his youth were given weight; and the previous respectability of both was held in view. Thus S. was sentenced to imprisonment for eight months, and G. for four months.

They appealed to the Supreme Court at Leipzig, and prepared themselves, in case the appeal should be denied, to collect evidence sufficient to call for a new trial.

They subjected themselves to examination and observation by distinguished experts. The latter declared that G.'s anus presented no signs of indulgence in passive pederasty.

Since it seemed of importance to those interested to make clear the psychological aspects of the case, which was not touched on at the trial, the author was intrusted with the examination and observation of S. and G.

Results of the Personal Examination, from 11th to 13th December, 1888, in Graz: "S., aged thirty-seven; two years married, without children. Ex-director of the City Laboratory of H. He comes of a father who is said to have been nervous, owing to great activity; who had an apoplectic attack in his fifty-seventh year, and died, at the age of sixty-seven, of another attack of apoplexy. His mother is living, and is described as a strong person, who has been nervous for years. Her mother reached an old age, and is said to have died of a cerebellar tumor. A brother of the mother's father is said to have been a drinker. The paternal grandfather died early, of softening of the brain.

"S. has two brothers, who are in perfect health.

"He states that he is of nervous temperament, and has been of strong constitution. After rheumatoid arthritis, which he had in his fourteenth year, he suffered with great nervousness for some months. Thereafter he often suffered with rheumatic pains, palpitation, and shortness of breath. These symptoms gradually disappeared with sea-bathing. Seven years ago he had gonorrhoea. This disease became chronic, and for a long time caused bladder difficulty.

"In 1887 he had his first attack of renal colic, and he had such attacks repeatedly during the winter of 1887 and 1888, until 16th May, 1888, when quite a large renal calculus was passed. Since then his condition had been quite satisfactory. While suffering with stone, during coitus, at the moment of ejaculation, he felt severe pain in the urethra and the same pain when urinating.

"With reference to his life, S. states that he attended the Gymnasium until he was fourteen, but after that, owing to the results of his severe illness, he studied privately. He then spent four years in a chemist's shop, and then studied medicine for six semesters at the University, serving, in the war of 1870, as a voluntary hospital assistant. Since he had no certificate of graduation from the Gymnasium, he gave up the study of medicine, and obtained the degree of doctor of philosophy. Then he served in the Museum of Minerals in K., and later as assistant in the Mineralogical Institute of H. Thereafter he made special studies in the chemistry of food-stuffs, and five years ago became director of the City Laboratory.

"He makes all these statements in a prompt, precise manner, and does not hesitate about his answers; so that one is more and more led to think that he is a man who loves and speaks the truth—the more, since, on the following day, his statements are identical. With reference to his sexual life, S., in a modest, delicate and open way, states that in his eleventh year he began to have a knowledge of the difference of the sexes, and for some time, until his fourteenth year, was given to onanism. He first had coitus at eighteen, and thereafter indulged moderately. His sensual desire had never been very great, but, until lately, the sexual act had been normal in every way, and accompanied by gratifying pleasurable feeling and full virility. Since his marriage, two years ago, he had cohabited with his wife exclusively. He had married his wife out of love, and still loved her, having coitus with her at least several times a week. The wife, who was also at hand, confirmed these statements.

"All cross-questioning with reference to a perversion of sexual feeling towards men S. answered repeatedly in the negative, to repeated examination, and that without contradiction or any thought of the answers. Even when, in order to trap him, he is told that the proof of a perverse sexual instinct would be of avail in the trial, he sticks to his statements. One gains the important impression that S. has not the slightest knowledge of the facts of homosexuality. Thus it is learned that his lascivious dreams have never been about men; that he is interested only in female nudity; that he liked to dance with ladies, etc. No traces of any kind of sexual inclination for his own sex can be discovered in S. With reference to his relations with G., S. expresses himself exactly as he did at his examination before the court. In explanation of his partiality for G., he can only say that he is nervous, and a man of feeling and great sensibility, and very sensitive to friendliness. During his illness he had felt very lonesome and depressed; his wife had frequently been with her parents; and thus it had happened that he had become friendly with G., who was so gentle and kind. He still had a weakness for him, and felt remarkably quiet and contented while in his society.

"He had had two such close friendships previously: when he was yet a student, with a corps-brother, a Dr. A., whom he also embraced and kissed; later, with a Baron M. When it happened that he could not see him for a few days, he became depressed, and even cried.

"He also had a similar feeling and attachment for animals. Thus he had mourned the loss of a poodle that died a short time ago, as if it had been a member of the family; he had often kissed the animal. (On relating this, the tears came to his eyes.) His brother confirmed these statements, with the remark, with reference to his brother's remarkable friendship for A. and M., that in these instances there was not the slightest suspicion of sexual colouring or relation. The most careful and detailed examination of S. gave not the slightest reason for such a presumption.

"He states that he never had the slightest sexual feeling for G., to say nothing of erection or sexual desire. His partiality for G., which bordered on jealousy, S. explained as due merely to his sentimental temperament and his inordinate friendship. G. was still as dear to him as if he were his son.

"It is worthy of note that S. stated that when G. told him about his love adventures with girls, it had hurt him only because G. was in danger of injuring himself and ruining his health by dissipation. He had never felt hurt himself by this. If he knew a good girl for G., he would be glad to rejoice with him and do all he could to promote their marriage.

"S. states that it was first in the course of his legal examination that he saw how he had been careless in his intercourse with G., by causing gossip. His openness he explained as due to the innocence of their friendship.

"It is worthy of note that S.'s wife never noticed anything suspicious in the intercourse between her husband and G., though the most simple wife would instinctively notice anything of that nature. Mrs. S. had also made no opposition to receiving G. into the house. On this point she remarked that the spare-room in which G. lay ill was on the second floor, while the living apartments were on the fourth; and, further, that S. never associated alone with G. as long as he was in the house. She states that she is convinced of her husband's innocence, and that she loves him as before.

"S. states freely that formerly he had often kissed G., and talked with him about sexual matters. G. was much attracted to women, and in friendship he had often warned him about sexual dissipation, particularly when G., as often happened, did not look well. He had once said that G. was a handsome fellow; it was in a perfectly harmless relation.

"The kissing of G. had been due to inordinate friendship, when G. had shown him some particular attention, or pleased him especially. In the act he had never had any sexual feeling. When he had now and then dreamed of G. it was in a perfectly harmless way."

It appeared of great importance to the author to form also an opinion of G.'s personality. On 12th December the desired opportunity was given, and G. was carefully examined.

G. was a young man, aged twenty, of delicate build, whose development corresponded with his years; and he appeared to be neuropathic and sensual. The genitals were normal and well developed. The author thought he might be permitted to pass over the condition of the anus, as he did not feel called upon to pass judgment upon it. Prolonged association with G. gave one the impression that he was a harmless, kind, and artless man, light-minded, but not morally depraved. Nothing in his dress or manner indicated perverse sexual feeling. There could not be the slightest suspicion that he was a male courtesan.

When G. was introduced in the course of the case, he stated that S. and he, feeling their innocence, had told the matter as it actually was, and on this the whole trial had been based.

At first, S.'s friendship, and especially the kissing, had seemed remarkable, even to him. Later he had convinced himself that it was merely friendship, and had then thought no more about it.

G. had looked upon S. as a father-like friend; for he was so unselfish, and loved him so.

The expression "handsome fellow" was made when G. had a love-affair, and when S. expressed his fears about a happy future for G. At that time S. had comforted him, and said that his (G.'s) appearance was pleasing, and that he would make an eligible match.

Once S. had complained to him (G.) that his wife was inclined to drink, and burst into tears. G. was touched by his friend's unhappiness. On this occasion S. had kissed him, and begged for his friendship, and asked him to visit him frequently.

S. had never spontaneously directed the conversation to sexual matters. G. once asked what pederasty was, of which he had heard much while in England; and S. had explained it to him.

G. acknowledged that he was sensual. At the age of twelve he had been made acquainted with sexual matters by schoolmates. He had never masturbated, had first had coitus at the age of eighteen, and had since visited brothels frequently. He had never felt any inclination for his own sex, and had never experienced any sexual excitement when S. kissed him. He had always had pleasure in coitus normally performed. His lascivious dreams had always been of women. With indignation, and pointing to his descent from a healthy and respectable family, he repelled the insinuation of having been given to passive pederasty. Until the gossip about them came to his ears, he had been innocent and devoid of suspicion. The anal anomalies he tried to explain in the same way that he did at the trial. Auto-masturbation denied.

It should be noted that Mr. J. S. claimed to be no less astonished by the charge against his brother of homosexuality than those more closely associated with him. Yet he could not understand what attached his brother to G.; and all the explanations which S. made to him concerning his relation to G. were vain.

The author took the trouble to observe S. and G., in a natural way, while they were dining, in company with S.'s brother and Mrs. S., in Graz. This observation revealed not the slightest sign of improper friendship.

The general impression which S. made on me was that of a nervous, sanguine, somewhat overstrained individual, but, at the same time, kind, open-hearted, and very emotional.

S. was physically strong, somewhat corpulent, with a symmetrical, brachycephalic cranium. The genitals were well developed; the penis somewhat bellied; the prepuce slightly hypertrophied.

Opinion.—Pederasty is, unfortunately, not infrequent among mankind today; but still, occurring among the peoples of Europe, it is an unusual, perverse, and even monstrous manner of sexual gratification. It presumes a congenital or acquired perversion of the sexual instinct, and, at the same time, defect of moral sense that is either original or acquired, as a result of pathological influences.

Medico-legal science is thoroughly conversant with the physical and psychical conditions from which this aberration of the sexual instinct arises; and in the concrete and doubtful case it seems requisite to ascertain whether these empirical, subjective conditions necessary for pederasty are present. It is essential to distinguish between active and passive pederasty.

Active pederasty occurs:—

I. As a *non-pathological* phenomenon:

1. As a means of sexual gratification, in case of great sexual desire, with enforced abstinence from natural sexual intercourse.

2. In old debauchees, who have become satiated with normal sexual intercourse, and more or less impotent, and also morally depraved; and who resort to pederasty in order to excite their lust with this new stimulus, and aid their virility that has sunk so low psychically and physically.

3. Traditionally, among certain barbarous races that are devoid of morality.

II. As a *pathological* phenomenon:—

1. Upon the basis of congenital sexual inversion, with repugnance

for sexual intercourse with women, or even absolute incapability of it. But, as even *Casper* knew, pederasty, under such conditions, is very infrequent. The so-called homosexual satisfies himself with a man by means of passive or mutual onanism, or by means of coitus-like acts (coitus between the thighs); and he resorts to pederasty only very exceptionally, as a result of intense sexual desire, or with a low or lowered moral sense, out of desire to please another.

2. On the basis of acquired pathological sexual inversion:

(*a*) As a result of onanism practiced through many years, which finally causes impotence for women with continuance of intense sexual desire.

(*b*) As a result of severe mental disease (senile dementia, brain-softening in the insane, etc.) in which, as experience teaches, an inversion of the sexual instinct may take place.

Passive pederasty occurs:—

I. As a *non-pathological* phenomenon:—

1. In individuals of the lowest class, who, having had the misfortune to be seduced in boyhood by debauchees, endured pain and disgust for the sake of money, and became depraved morally, so that, in more mature years, they have fallen so low that they take pleasure in being male prostitutes.

2. Under circumstances analogous to those of I., 1—as a remuneration to another for having allowed active pederasty.

II. As a *pathological* phenomenon:—

1. In individuals affected with sexual inversion, with endurance of pain and disgust, as a return to men for the bestowal of sexual favours.

2. In male homosexuals who feel towards men like women, out of desire and lust. In such female-men there is fear of women and absolute incapability for sexual intercourse with women. Character and inclinations are feminine.

The empirical facts that have been gathered by legal medicine and psychiatry are all included in this classification. Before the court of medical science, it would be necessary to prove that a man belonged to one of the above categories in order to carry out the conviction that he was a pederast.

In the life and character of S., one searched in vain for signs which placed him in one of the categories of active pederasts which science has established. He was neither one forced to sexual abstinence, nor one made impotent for women by debauchery; neither was he congenitally male-loving, nor alienated from women by masturbation, and attracted to men through continuance of sexual desire; and, finally, he was not sexually perverse as a result of severe mental disease.

In fact, the general conditions necessary for the occurrence of pederasty were wanting in him—moral imbecility or moral depravity, on the one hand, and inordinate sexual desire on the other.

It was likewise impossible to classify the accomplice, G., in any of the empirical categories of passive pederasty; for he possessed neither the peculiarities of the male prostitute nor the clinical marks of effemination; and he had not the anthropological and clinical stigmata of the female-man. He was, in fact, the very opposite of all this.

In order to make a pederastic relation between the two plausible medico-scientifically, it would have been requisite for S. to present the antecedents and marks of the active pederasts of I., 2, and G., those of the passive pederasts of II, 1 or 2.

The assumption lying at the basis of the verdict was from a psychological standpoint, legally untenable.

With the same right, every man might be considered a pederast. It remains to consider whether the explanations given by Dr. S. and G. of their remarkable friendship are psychologically valid.

Psychologically it is not without parallel that so sentimental and eccentric a man as S.—without any sexual excitement whatever—should maintain borderline friendships. It suffices to recall the friendship of schoolgirls, the self-sacrificing friendship of sentimental young persons in general, and the partiality which this sensitive man sometimes showed even for domestic animals—where no one would think of sodomy. With S.'s mental character his extraordinary friendship for the youth G. may be easily comprehended. The openness of this friendship permitted the conclusion that it was innocent, much rather than that it depended upon sensual passion.

The defendants succeeded in obtaining a new trial. The new trial took place on 7th March, 1890. There was much evidence presented in favour of the accused.

The previous moral life of S. was generally acknowledged. The Sister of Charity who cared for G. in S.'s house, never noticed anything suspicious in the intercourse between S. and G. S.'s former friends testified to his morality, his deep friendship, and his habit of kissing them on meeting or leaving them. The anal abnormalities previously found on G. were no longer present. Experts called by the court allowed the possibility that they had been due simply to digital manipulations; their diagnostic value in any case was contested by the experts called for the defense.

The court recognized that the imputed crime had not been proved, and exonerated the defendants.

LESBIAN LOVE.[45]

Where the sexual intercourse is between adults, its legal importance is very slight. It could come into consideration only in Austria. In connection with male homosexuality, this phenomenon is of anthropological and clinical value. The relation is the same, in detail, as between men. Lesbian love does not seem to approach male homosexuality in frequency. The majority of female homosexuals do not act in obedience to an innate impulse, but they are developed under conditions analogous to those which produce the homosexuality by cultivation.

These "forbidden friendships" flourish especially in penal institutions for females.

Kraussold (*op. cit.*) reports: "The female prisoners often have such friendships, which, when possible, extend to mutual manustupration.

"But temporary mutual gratification is not the only purpose of such friendships. They are made to be enduring—entered into systematically, so to speak—and intense jealousy and a passion for love are developed which could scarcely be surpassed between persons of opposite sex. When the friend of one prisoner is merely smiled at by another, there are often the most violent scenes of jealousy, and even beatings.

"When the violent prisoner has been put in irons, in accordance with the prison regulations, she says 'she has had a child by her friend.' "

We are indebted to *Parent-Duchatelet* ("De la prostitution," 1857, vol. i., p. 159), for interesting communications concerning Lesbian love.

According to this experienced author, repugnance for the most disgusting and perverse acts (coitus in axilla, ore, between breasts, etc.) which men perform on prostitutes is not infrequently responsible for driving these unfortunate creatures to Lesbian love. From his statements it is seen that it is essentially prostitutes of great sensuality who, unsatisfied with intercourse with impotent or perverse men, and impelled by their disgusting practices, come to indulge in it.

Besides these, there are prostitutes who let themselves be known as given to tribadism; persons who have been in prison for years, and in these hot-beds of Lesbian love, because of abstinence, acquired this vice.

It is interesting to know that prostitutes hate those who practice tribadism—just as men abhor pederasts; but female prisoners do not regard the vice as indecent.

Parent mentions the case of a prostitute who, while intoxicated, tried to force another to Lesbian love. The latter became so enraged that she denounced the indecent woman to the police. *Taxil* (*op. cit.*, pp. 166, 170) reports similar instances.

Mantegazza ("Anthropol. culturhistorische Studien," p. 97) also finds that sexual intercourse between women has especially the significance of a vice which arises on the basis of unsatisfied excessive sexual desire.

In many cases of this kind, however, aside from congenital sexual inversion, one gains the impression that, just as in men, the cultivated vice gradually leads to acquired antipathic sexual instinct, with repugnance for sexual intercourse with the opposite sex.

At least *Parent's* cases were probably of this nature. The correspondence with the lover was quite as sentimental and exaggerated in tone as it is between lovers of the opposite sex; unfaithfulness and separation broke the heart of the one abandoned; jealousy was unbridled, and led to bloody revenge. The following cases of Lesbian love, by *Mantegazza*, are certainly pathological, and possibly examples of congenital antipathic sexual instinct:—

(1) On 5th July, 1777, a woman was brought before a court in London, who, dressed as a man, had been married to three different women. She was recognized as a woman, and sentenced to imprisonment for six months.

(2) In 1773, another woman, dressed as a man, courted a girl and asked for her hand; but the trick did not succeed.

(3) Two women lived together as man and wife for thirty years. On her death-bed the "husband" confessed her secret to those about her.

Coffignon (*op. cit.*, p. 301) makes later statements worthy of notice.

He reports that this vice is, of late, quite the fashion, partly owing to novels on the subject, and partly as a result of excessive work on sewing-machines, the sleeping of female servants in the same bed, seduction in schools by depraved pupils, or seduction of daughters by depraved servants.

The author declares that this vice ("saphism") is met with more frequently among ladies of the aristocracy and prostitutes.

He does not differentiate physiological and pathological cases, nor, among the latter, the acquired and congenital cases. The details of a few cases, which are certainly pathological, correspond exactly with the facts that are known about men of inverted sexuality.

The saphists have their places of meeting, recognize each other by peculiar glances, carriage, etc. Saphistic pairs like to dress and ornament themselves alike, etc. They are then called "little sisters."

Moraglia makes a strong distinction between *Cunnilingus* and *Tribady*.

The former (*Cunnilingus*) he generally finds in woman with normal sexual instinct but hypersexual feelings, *i.e.*, in girls who have no opportunity for, or are afraid of coitus, pregnancy, or in married women whose sexual desires remain unsatisfied in consequence of the husband's impotence or of failure of sexual feeling due to masturbation. Here it is not a matter of love or intense jealousy, unless it be in individuals with *acquired* antipathic sexual instinct—but only an ephemeral union for the purpose of mutually to satisfy libido, coupled with all sorts of other concomitant acts to obtain the means desired.

Tribady is according to this author, practiced only by women of antipathic sexual instinct as a means of sexual satisfaction in a permanent bond of love in which the active individual always assumes the male character towards the female consort. These women are much more subtle and persevering in their campaigns of conquest and coquetry with heterosexual women than man ever can be under similar (reversed) circumstances.

If this assumption be true, this method of sexual intercourse would establish at once an easy means for diagnosing perversity from perversion. The individuals referred to by the author were, without exception, either viragos or gynandrics.

Chevalier very drastically characterizes the perversity and distinguishes it from the perversion in the following words (*cf.* "L'inversion sexualle," p. 268, Paris, 1895):

". . . whether one is a pederast or a lesbian through over-excitement of exhausted senses, by mercenary corruption, because one needs to deceive oneself as to one's 'appetite,' through weakness of mind or for amateurism, it can be concluded from this analysis that the anomaly is not born with the individual, that childhood knows nothing of it, that it seldom shows itself all at once, but little by little, gradually, at a certain age, after normal sexual practices. Furthermore, it is neither permanent, nor absolute; it can be reconciled with the full knowledge and integrity of the intelligence, it may become modified and disappear, it is originally associated with no physical or psychic taint of any consequence, it knows no objective standard other than itself, it is neither fatal nor irresistible in its urges, and, finally, it constitutes a peculiar state whose roots lie rather in society than in the individual.

"A lack of instinctiveness, of spontaneity, of incoercibility, of immutability; the absence or later development of organic defects and co-related mental ones; acquisition late in the day and by artificial means, premeditation of the acts, conscience; a genesis of a semi-logical kind, the necessity for a preliminary initiation and, above all, no trace of heredity: all these are most certainly the characteristic of pure passion and of unadulterated vice. To sum up: there is nothing pathological; the anomaly should therefore be prevented, or else it can be suppressed."

8. NECROPHILIA.[46]

(Austrian Statutes, §306.)

This horrible kind of sexual indulgence is so monstrous that the presumption of a psychopathic state is, under all circumstances, justified; and *Maschka's* recommendation, that the mental condition of the perpetrator should always be investigated, is well founded. In any case, an abnormal and decidedly perverse sensuality is required to overcome the natural repugnance which man has for a corpse, and permit a feeling of pleasure to be experienced in sexual congress with a cadaver.

Unfortunately, in the majority of the cases reported, the mental condition was not examined; so that the question whether necrophilia is compatible with mental soundness must remain open. But any one having knowledge of the horrible aberrations of the sexual instinct would not venture, without further consideration, to answer the question in the negative.

9. INCEST.

(Austrian Statutes, §132; Abridgment, §189; German Statutes, §174.)

The preservation of the moral purity of family life is a product of civilization; and feelings of intense displeasure arise in an ethically intact man at thought of lustful feeling towards a member of the same family. Only great sensuality and defective ideas of laws and morals can lead to incest.

Both conditions may, in tainted families, be operative. Drinking and a state of intoxication in men; weak-mindedness which does not allow the development of the feeling of shame, and which, under certain circumstances, is associated with eroticism in females—these facilitate the occurrence of incestuous acts. External conditions which facilitate their occurrence are due to defective separation of the sexes among the lower classes.

As a decidedly pathological phenomenon, the author has found incest in states of congenital and acquired mental weakness, and infrequently in cases of epilepsy [47] and paranoia.

In many of the cases, probably a majority, it is not possible, however, to find a pathological basis for the act which so deeply wounds not only the tie of blood, but also the feeling of a civilized people. But in many of the cases reported in literature, to the honour of humanity, the presumption of a psychopathic basis is possible.

CASE 238. Z., age fifty-one, superintendent, enamored with his own daughter since her puberty. She had to leave home and reside with relatives abroad. He was a peculiar, nervous man, somewhat given to drink, without manifest taint. He denied being in love with his daughter, but the latter stated that he acted and behaved towards her like a lover. Z. was very jealous of every man who ever approached his daughter. He threatened to commit suicide if she ever married, and on one occasion proposed to her that they should die together. He knew how to arrange things so that he could be always alone with her, and over-whelmed her with presents and caresses. No signs of hypersexuality. Did not keep a mistress and was looked upon as a very decent man.

In the *Feldtmann case* (*Marc-Ideler*, vol. i., p. 18), where a father constantly made immoral attacks on his adult daughter, and finally killed her, the unnatural father was weak-minded and, besides, probably sub-ject to periodical mental disease. In another case of incest between father and daughter (*loc. cit.*, p. 247), the latter, at least, was weak-minded. *Lombroso* ("Archiv. di Psichiatria," viii., p. 519) reports the case of a peasant, aged forty-two, who practiced incest with his daughters, aged, respectively, twenty-two, nineteen, and eleven; he even forced the young-est to prostitute herself, and then visited her in a brothel. The medico-legal examination showed predisposition, intellectual and moral imbe-cility, and alcoholism.

There was no mental examination in the case reported by *Schür-meyer* ("Deutsche Zeitschr. für Staatsarzneikunde," xxii., Heft 1), in which a mother laid her son of five and a half years on herself, and prac-ticed abuse with him; and in that given by *Lafarque* ("Journ. Méd. de Bordeaux," 1874), where a girl, aged seventeen, laid her brother, aged thirteen, upon herself, brought about joining of members, and performed masturbation on him.

The following cases are those of tainted individuals:—

Legrand ("Ann. méd.-psych.," May, 1876) mentions a girl, aged fifteen, who seduced her brother into all manner of sexual excesses on her person; and when, after two years of this incestuous practice, her brother died, she attempted to murder a relative. In the same article there is the case of a married woman, aged thirty-six, who hung her open breast out of a window, and indulged in abuse with her brother, aged eighteen; and also the case of a mother, aged thirty-nine, who practiced incest with her son, with whom she was madly in love, became pregnant by him, and induced abortion.

A second case published by *Kölle* and taken from a criminal psy-chiatric opinion of the psychiatric clinic of Zurich refers to incest com-mitted by a father on his imbecile adult daughter. This man suffered from chronic alcoholism.

Thoinot (*op. cit.*) reports a case of a nymphomaniac (age 44), who made an attempt at suicide on account of unrequited love to her own son, 23 years old. She pestered him with kisses and caresses, tried one night to force him to coitus, which he refused. Other similar attempts followed with periodical spells of sanity. When all her efforts had failed she made an attempt on her own life.

Another case reported by *Tardieu* is still more horrible. A chronic nymphomaniac mother, apparently homosoxual, often masturbated her little daughter, 12 years of age, for hours in the middle of the night, in the vagina and anus. During that time she was highly excited.

Through *Casper* we know that depraved mothers in large cities sometimes treat their little daughters in a most horrible fashion, in order to prepare them for the sexual use of debauchees. This crime belongs elsewhere.

10. IMMORAL ACTS WITH PERSONS IN THE CARE OF OTHERS AS WARDS; SEDUCTION (AUSTRIAN).

(Austrian Statutes, § 131; Abridgment, § 188; German Statutes, § 173).

Allied to incest, but still less repugnant to moral sensibility, are those cases in which persons seduce those entrusted to them for care or education, and who are more or less dependent upon them, to commit or suffer vicious practices. Such acts, which especially deserve legal punishment, seem only exceptionally to have psychopathic significance.

NOTES

NOTES FOR PREFACE

1. *Hartmann's* philosophical conception of love ("Philosophy of the Unknown," Berlin, 1869, p. 583) is: "Love causes more pain than pleasure. Pleasure is only an illusion. Reason would demand the avoidance of love were it not for that fatal sexual instinct. Hence it would be better to be castrated." *Schopenhauer* expresses the same view in his work: "Die Welt als Wille und Vorstellung," third edition, vol. ii. p. 586, etc.

NOTES FOR CHAPTER I

1. Cf. *Lombroso*, "The Criminal"; *Westermarck*, "The History of Marriage"; *Ploss*, "Das Weib in der Natur- und Völkerkunde," third edition, vol. ii, p. 413-90. *Joseph Müller*, "Das sexuelle Leben der Naturvölkur," 2 Aufl. 1902; *derselbe*, "Das sexuelle Leben der alten Kulturvölker, 1902 (Leipzig, Grieben).

2. According to *Westermarck, op. cit.*, it was "not the feeling of shame which suggested the garment, but the garment engendered shame. The desire to make themselves more attractive originated the habit among men and women to cover their nakedness."

3. This assertion may be modified in so far as the symbolical and sacramental character of matrimony was clearly defined only by the Council of Trent, although the spirit of Christianity always tended to raise woman from the inferior position which she occupied in previous centuries and in the Old Testament.

   The tradition that woman was created from the rib of the sleeping man (see Genesis) is one of the causes of delay in this direction, for after the fall she is told "thy will shall be subject to man." According to the Old Testament, woman is responsible for the fall of man, and this became the corner-stone of Christian teaching. Thus the social position of woman had to be neglected, as it were, until the spirit of Christianity had conquered tradition and scholastic tenets.

   It is a remarkable fact that the gospels (barring divorce, Matt. xix. 9) contain not a word in favour of woman. The clemency shown towards the adulteress and the penitent Magdalen does not affect the position of woman in general. The epistles of St. Paul definitely insist that no change can be permitted in the position of woman (2 Cor. xi. 3-12; Eph. v. 22, "woman shall be subject to man," and 23, "woman shall fear man").

   How much the fathers of the Church are prejudiced against woman on account of Eve's part in the temptation may be easily learned from *Tertullian*, "Woman, thou shouldst ever go in mourning and sackcloth, thy eyes filled with tears. Thou has brought about the ruin of mankind." *St. Jerome* has nothing good to say about woman. "Woman is the gate of the devil, the road of evil, the sting of the scorpion" ("De Cultu Feminarum," i. 1).

   Canon law declares: "Man only is created to the image of God, not woman; therefore woman shall serve him and be his handmaid."

   The Provincial Council of Macon (sixth century) seriously discussed the question whether woman had a soul at all.

These opinions of the Church had a sympathetic influence upon the peoples who embraced Christianity. Among the converted Germanic races the *dower value* of woman fell considerably (*J. Falke,* "Die ritterliche Gesellschaft," Berlin, 1862, p. 49. *Re* the valuation of the two sexes among the Jews, *cf.* 3 Moses, xxvii. 3-4).

Even polygamy, which is distinctly recognized in the Old Testament, (Deut. xxi. 15) is nowhere in the New Testament definitely prohibited. In fact many Christian princes (*e.g.* the Merovingian kings: Chotlar I., Charibert I., Pippin I. and other Frankish nobles) indulged in polygamy without a protest being raised by the Church at the time (*Weinhold,* "Die deutschen Frauen im Mittelalter," ii., p. 15; *cf. Unger,* "Marriage," etc., and *Louis Bridel,* "La Femme et le Droit," Paris, 1884).

4. *Cf. Friedländer,* "Sittengeschichte Roms"; *Wiedemeister,* "Der Cäsarenwahnsinn"; *Suetonius, Moreau,* "Des aberrations du sens génésique."

5. *Friedreich* ("Hdb. der gerichtlichärztlich, Praxis," 1843, i. p. 271) is of a different opinion, for according to him the Red Indians of America are addicted to the practice of pederasty. *Cf.* also *Lombroso,* p. 42, and *Bloch,* Beiträge zur Etiologie der Psychopathia Sexualis, 2. Theil, 1903.

6. *Cf. Freidreich* ("Gerichtl. Psychologie," p. 389) who quotes numerous examples. For instance, *Blankebin,* the nun, was constantly tormented by the thought of what could have become of that part of Christ which was removed in circumcision.

Veronica Juliani, beatified by Pope Pius II., in memory of the divine lamb, took a real lamb to bed with her, kissed it and suckled it on her breasts.

St. Catherine of Genoa often burned with such intense inward fire that in order to cool herself she would throw herself upon the ground crying, "Love, love, I can endure it no longer." At the same time she felt a peculiar inclination to her confessor. One day, lifting his hand to her nose, she noticed a peculiar odour which penetrated to her heart "a heavenly perfume that would awaken the dead."

St. Armelle and *St. Elizabeth* were troubled with a similar longing for the Infant Jesus. The temptations of *St. Anthony, of Padua,* are known to the world. Of significance is an old Protestant prayer: "Oh! that I had found thee, bless'd Emanuel; that thou wert with me in my bed, to bring delight to body and soul. Come and be mine. My heart shall be thy resting place."

7. *Cf. Friedreich,* "Diagnostik der psych. Krankheiten," p. 247 etc.; *Neumann,* Lehrb. d. "Psychiatrie," p. 80.

8. This may be observed in the actual life as well as in the fiction and the plastic arts of degenerate eras. For instance, *Bernini's* carving, which represents St. Teresa "sinking in an hysterical faint upon a marble cloud, whilst an amorous angel plunges the arrow (of divine love) into her heart."—*Lübke.*

9. *Cf. Max Müller* who derives the word fetich etymologically from *factitius, i. e.,* artificial, insignificant.

10. "Deutsches Montagsblatt," Berlin, 20, 8, 80.

11. *Magnan's* "spinal cérébral postérieur" who finds gratification with any sort of woman, is only animated by lust. Meretricious love that is purchased cannot be genuine (*Mantegazza*). The power to perform love's act is by no means a guarantee of the noblest enjoyment of love.

There are homosexuals who are potent with women—men who do not love their wives, but are nevertheless able to perform the marital "duty." In the majority of these cases even lustful pleasure is absent; for it is simply an onanistic act rendered possible by the aid of imagination which substitutes another beloved being. This deception may, indeed, superinduce sexual pleasure, but, rudimentary gratification as it is, it can only arise from a psychic trick, just as in solitary onanism, voluptuous satisfaction is obtained chiefly with the assistance of fancy. As a matter of fact that degree of orgasm which completes the lustful act is entirely dependent upon the intervention of fancy.

Where psychic impediments exist (such as indifference, disgust, aversion, fear of contagion or impregnation, etc.) the feeling of sexual gratification seems to be wanting altogether.

NOTES FOR CHAPTER II

1. The olfactory centre is presumed by *Ferrier* ("Functions of the Brain") to be in the region of the *gyrus uncinatus*. *Zuckerkandl* ("Ueber das Riechcentrum," 1887), from researches in comparative anatomy, concludes that the olfactory centre has its seat in the Hippocampus major.

2. Later researches by *Müller* (Klin. u. experiment. Studien, etc., Deutsche Zeitschr. f. N. heilkunde xxi.) seem to render it more probable that the centre of erection does not lie in the conus medullaris of the spinal cord, but rather in the sacral ganglia, thus constituting a sympathetic *reflex*.

3. Cf. *Albert Hagen,* "Die sexuelle Osphresiologie," Charlottenburg, 1901 (Verlag H. Basdorf, a most interesting monograph on the relations between the olfactory senses and odours and the sexual acts in man. *Albert Moll,* "Untersuchungen über libido sexualis," p. 377. (Literature and studies on the olfactory sense as a stimulating cause of the sexual instinct.)

4. See also further interesting observations on the aphrodisiac effects of sweat on both sexes. *Féré,* l'instinct sexuel, p. 127. (Paris, 1899).

5. Cf. *Laycock,* who ("Nervous Diseases of Women," 1840) found that in women the love for musk and similar perfumes was related to sexual excitement.

6. The following case, reported by *Binet,* seems to be in opposition to this idea. Unfortunately nothing is said concerning the mental characteristics of the person. In any event, it is certainly confirmatory of the relations existing between the olfactory and sexual senses:—

   D., a medical student, was seated on a bench in a public park, reading a book (on pathology). Suddenly a violent erection disturbed him. He looked up and noticed that a lady, redolent with perfume, had taken a seat upon the other end of the bench. D. could attribute the erection to nothing but the unconscious olfactory impression made upon him.

7. *Meibomius,* "Of the practice of flagellation in medical cases," London, 1765; *Boileau,* "The History of the Flagellants," London, 1783; *Doppet,* "Aphrodisiaque externe," Paris, 1788; *Cooper,* "Der Flagellantismus u. d. Flagellanten; *Hansen,* Stock u. Peitsche in xix. Jahrhundert (Dohrn, Dresden), 2 vols.

8. *Corvin,* Hist. Denkmale des christlichen Fanatismus, II., Leipzig, 1847; *Foerstemann,* Die christlichen Geisslergesellschaften, Halle, 1828.

9. It is a common proceeding for blasés and impotents to have themselves whipped. A few years ago much noise was made about one such amateur who died whilst being whipped by several women in a house of prostitution at Moscow. (*Ibankow,* Archives d' Anthropol. criminelle. xiv. p. 697).

10. Cf. *Roubaud,* "Traité de l'impuissance et de la stérilité," Paris, 1878.

NOTES FOR CHAPTER III

1. Bardach, Die Physiologie als Erfahrungswissenschaft, 1826-40; *Ploss,* Das Weib, 1891, 3d edition; *A. Moll,* Die conträre Sexualempfindung, 3d ed. p. 3; *Idem,* Untersuchungen über die Libido sexualis, 1897-98.

2. *Laurent,* les bisexués, Paris, 1894; *Idem,* de l'hérédité des gynécomastes. Annales d'hygiene, publ. 1890.

3. Cf. *Moll*, Libido sexualis, p. 335-350, where he gives a large number of cases of perverted sexual characteristics, of a physical as well as psychical nature, even of sexual inversion.

NOTES FOR CHAPTER IV

1. Literature: *Parent-Duchatelet*, "Prostitution dans la ville de Paris," 1837. *Rosenbaum*, "Entstehung der Syphilis," Halle, 1839—also, "Die Lustseuche im Alterthum," Halle, 1839. *Descuret*, "La médécine des Passions," Paris, 1860. *Caspar*, "Klin. Novellen," 1860. *Bastian*, "Der Mensch in der Geschichte." *Friedländer*, "Sittengeschichte Roms." *Wiedemeister*, "Cäsarenwahnsinn." *Scherr*, "Deutsche Kultur und Sittengeschichte," Bd. i., cap. ix. *Jeannel*, "Die Prostitution," deutsch von Müller, Erlangen, 1869. *v. Krafft*, "Neue Forschungen auf dem Gebiete der Psychopathia sexualis," 2. Aufl., Stuttgart, 1891. *Taxil*, "La Prostitution contemporaine," Paris, 1884. *Frank Lydston*, "Philadelph. Med. and Surg. Reports, 1889. *Urquhardt*, Journal of Mental Science, Jan. 1891. *Antonini*, "Archiv. di Psichiatria," xxi., 1, 2. *Cantarano*, Zeitschr. "La Psichiatria," v., 2, 3. *Krauss*, "Psychologie des Verbrechens," 1884. *Kiernan*, "Medic. Standard," Nov., 1889. *Delcourt*, "Le Vice à Paris," 1889. *Lombroso*, "L'uomo Delinquente," 2 Aufl., 1878. *Toulmouche*, "Annal. d'hygiène," 1868. *Giraldès* et *Horteloup*, ibidem, 1876, p. 419. *Eulenburg*, "Klin. Handb. d. Harn- und Sexuelorgane," 1894, 4 Abthl., p. 36. *Moll*, "Untersuchungen über die Libido sexualis," 1897; "Archivio delle psicopatie sessuali," Naples (1896) volume unico. *Tardieu*, "Des attentats aux moeurs," 7 édit., 1878. *Emminghaus*, "Psychopathol.," pp. 98, 225, 230, 232. *Schüle*, "Handbuch der Geisteskrankheiten," p. 114. *Marc*, "Die Geisteskrankheiten," ii., p. 128. *v. Krafft*, "Lehrb. d. Psychiatrie, 6 Aufl. i., p. 77; "Lehrb. d. ger. Psychopathol.," 3 Aufl., p. 279; "Archiv f. Psychiatrie," vii., 2. *Moreau*, "Des aberrations du sens génésique," Paris, 1880. *Kirn*, "Allg. Zeitschr. f. Psychiatrie," 39, Heft 2 u. 3. *Lombroso*, "Geschlechtstrieb und Verbrechen in ihren gegenseitigen Beziehungen." (*Goltdammer's* "Archiv." Bd. 30). *Tarnowsky*, "Die krankhaften Erscheinungen des Geschlechtssinnes," Berlin, 1886. *Ball*, "La folie érotique," Paris, 1888. *Sérieux*, "Recherches cliniques sur les anomalies de l'instinct sexuel," Paris, 1888. *Hammond*, "Sexual Impotence," 1889. *v. Krafft*, "über sexuale Perversionen." *Leyden's* deutsche Klinik, 1901, vi. *v. Schrenk-Notzing*, Die Suggestionstherapie, 1892; also, Zeitsch. für Hypnotismus, vii., H. 1 & 2, viii., H. 1. (Literatur.) *Moll*, die conträre Sexualempfindung, 3 Aufl. 1889; also, Untersuchungen üb. d. Libido sexualis, 1897-98. *Hirschfeld*, Jahrb. f. sexuelle Zwischenstufen, Jahrg. i.-iv. *Bloch*, Beiträge z. Aetiologie der Psychopathia sexualis, ii., Theil, 1903.
   Among modern novelists who deal with the subject of sexual perversion the French are most pre-eminent, *viz.*: *Catulle Mendés, Péladan, Lemonnier, Dubut de la Forest* ("L'homme de joie"), *Huysmans* ("La bas"), *Zola*.

2. An interesting instance of how an imperative conception of non-sexual content can exert an influence is related by *Magnan* ("Ann. Méd. Psych.," 1885): Student, aged twenty-one, strongly predisposed hereditarily, previously a masturbator, constantly struggles with the number thirteen as an imperative conception. As soon as he attempts coitus the imperative idea inhibits erection and renders the act impossible.

3. *Douyer-Villermay* speaks of masturbation in a girl of three or four years, and *Moreau* ("aberrations du sens génésique," 2 édit., p. 209) of the same in one of two years. See further *Maudsley*, "Physiology and Pathology of Mind"; *Hirschsprung* (Kopenhagen), Berlin. klin. Wochenschr.," 1886, Nr. 38; *Lombroso*, "The Criminal," cases 10, 19, and 21.

4. Cf. *Kirn*, "Zeitschr. f. Psych.," Bd. xxxix. *Legrand du Saulle*, "Annal. d'hyg.," Oct., 1868.

5. Cases, *vide Laségue;* "Les exhibitionistes," Union médicale, 1871: 1st May.
6. *Legrand du Saulle,* "La folie devant les tribunaux," p. 530.
7. *Kirn, Maschka's* "Handb. d. ger. Med." pp. 373, 374; "Allg. Zeitschrift f. Psychiatrie," Bd. xxxix., p. 220.
8. "Die Welt als Wille und Vorstellung," 1859, Bd. ii., p. 461 *et seq.*
9. No doubt Swift's, the greatest satirist, was a case of anaesthesia sexualis. *Adolf Stern* says in his biography of Swift ("Aus dem 18. Jahrhundert; Biographische Bilder und Skizzen," Leipzig, 1874): "It seems that he was totally devoid of the sensual elements of love; his candid cynicism, found in many of his letters, is almost definite proof of this. Whoever properly grasps certain passages in 'Gulliver's Travels,' and especially the account which Swift gives of the marriage and progeny of the Houyhnhorses, the noble steeds of the last chapters, can scarcely doubt that this great satirist abhorred marriage, and never felt the impulse which draws the sexes together." Practically speaking, the enigmatical side of Swift's character, and several of his works, *viz.,* "Diary to Stella," and "Gulliver's Travels," can only be understood if Swift is considered sexually anaesthetic.
10. "Ueber männliche Sterilität," Wiener med. Presse, 1878, Nr. 1. "Ueber Potentia generandi et coëundi," Wiener Klinik, 1885, Heft 1, S. 5.
11. In individuals in whom intense sexual hyperaesthesia is associated with acquired irritable weakness of the sexual apparatus, it happens that simply at the sight of a pleasing female figure, without peripheral irritation of the genitals, the psycho-sexual centre may excite into action not only the mechanism of the erection, but also that of ejaculation. For such individuals, all that is necessary to induce orgasm or even ejaculation, is to imagine themselves in a sexual situation with a female that sits opposite them in a railway carriage or a drawing-room. *Hammond* (*op. cit.,* p. 40) describes several cases of this kind that came to him for treatment or subsequent impotence, and he mentions that these individuals used the term "ideal coitus" for the act. Dr. *Moll,* of Berlin, told me of a similar case, and in this instance the same designation was chosen for the act.
12. So named from the notorious *Marquis de Sade,* whose obscene novels treat of lust and cruelty. In French literature the expression "Sadism" has been applied to this perversion. *Eulenburg* ("Klin. Handb. der Harn und Sexualorgane") uses the term "active algolagnia" in connection with these phenomena.
13. *Moll,* Contr. Sexualempfindung, 3d ed., p. 160; *Krafft-Ebing "Arbeiten"* iv., p. 106; *Idem, Leyden's German clinic,* vi. Sect. 2, p. 137; *Eulenburg, Grenzfragen des Nerven-und Seelenlebens,* xxi. p. 1.
14. *Cf.* also *Alfred de Musset's* famous verses to the Andalusian girl: How superb she is in her disorder—when she falls, her breasts naked—how one sees her, wide open, twisting in a kiss of passion and biting—while howling unknown words.
15. During the excitement of battle the idea of lust forces its way into consciousness. *Cf.* the description of a battle, by a soldier, by *Grillparzer:*—
    "And as the signal rang out, the armies met, breast to breast—lust of the gods—here, there, the murderous steel slays enemy, friend. Given and taken—death and life—with wavering change—wildly raging in frenzy" ("Dream a Life," Act i.).
16. *Schulz* ("Wiener Med. Wochenschrift," No. 49, 1869) reports a remarkable case of a man, aged twenty-eight, who could perform coitus with his wife only after working himself into an artificial fit of anger.
17. Concerning analogous acts in rutting animals, see *Lombroso,* "The Criminal."
18. Among animals it is always the male who pursues the female with proffers of

love. Playful or actual flight of the female is not infrequently observed; and then the relation is like that between the beast of prey and the victim.

19. The conquest of woman takes place to-day in the social form of courting, in seduction and deception, etc. From the history of civilization and anthropology we know that there have been times, as there are savages to-day that practice it, where brutal force, robbery, or even blows that rendered a woman powerless, were made use of to obtain love's desire. It is possible that tendencies to such outbreaks of sadism are atavistic.

In the "Jahrbücher für Psychologie," ii., p. 128, *Schäfer* (Jena) refers to the reports of two cases by *A. Payer*. In the first case states of great sexual excitement were induced by the sight of battles or of paintings of them; in the second, by cruel torturing of small animals. It is added: "The pleasure of battle and murder is so predominantly an attribute of the male sex throughout the animal kingdom that there can be no question about the close relation existing between this side of the masculine character and male sexuality. 1 believe, too, that by unprejudiced observation I can show that, in men who are mentally and physically absolutely normal, the first indefinite and incomprehensible precursors of sexual excitement may be induced by the reading of exciting scenes of the chase and war—*i. e.*, they give rise to unconscious longings for a kind of satisfaction in warlike games (wrestling), in which the fundamental sexual impulse to the most perfect and intense contact with a companion is expressed, with the secondary thought of conquest more or less clearly defined."

20. It sometimes happens that an accidental sight of blood, etc., puts into motion the preformed psychical mechanism of the sadistic individual and awakens the instinct.

21. *Cf. "Metzger's* ger. Arzneiw., herausgegeben von Remer," p. 539; *"Klein's* Annalen," x., p. 176; xviii., p. 311; *Heinroth*, "System der psych. Med., p. 270; *Neuer Pitaval*, 1855, 23 Th. ("Fall Blaize Ferrage").

22. *Michéa*, Union méd. 1849,—*Brierre*, Gaz. méd. 1849, July 21; Moreau (op. cit.) p. 250,—*Epaulard*, "Vampyrisme (nécrophilie, nécrosadism, nécrophagie), Lyon, 1901.

23. A similar case is related by *Neri* ("Archivio delle psicopatie sessuali," 1896, p. 109). A man, fifty years of age, used in a Lupanar only girls who, clad in white, lay motionless feigning death. He violated the body of his own sister, by inserting his penis into the body of the dead woman until ejaculation was produced! This monster also had fits of fetichism for the pubic hairs of girls, and the trimmings of their fingernails; eating them caused strong sexual emotions.

24. *Simon* ("Crimes et délits," p. 209) mentions an experience of Lacassagne's, to whom a respectable man said that he was never intensely excited sexually except when a spectator at a funeral.

25. *Taxil* (*op. cit.*) gives more detailed accounts of this sexual monster, which must have been a case of habitual satyriasis, accompanied by perverse sexual instinct. Sade was so cynical that he actually sought to idealize his cruel lasciviousness and to be the apostle of a theory based upon it. He became so bad (among other things he made an invited company of ladies and gentlemen erotic by causing to be served to them chocolate bonbons which contained cantharides) that he was committed to the insane asylum at Charenton. During the revolution of 1790 he escaped. Then he wrote obscene novels filled with lust, cruelty and the most lascivious scenes. When Bonaparte became Consul, Sade made him a present of his novels, magnificently bound. The Consul had the works destroyed and the author committed to Charenton again, where he

died at the age of sixty-four. Sade was inexhaustible in his lascivious publications, which were markedly intended for advertisement. Fortunately it is difficult to-day to obtain copies. Extant are: "Histoire de Justine," 4 vols.; "Histoire de Juliette," 6 vols.; "Philosophie dans le boudoir," London, 1805. Interesting is Sade's biography by *J. Janin*, 1835.

A scientific and very thorough study of Sadism has recently been made by Dr. *Marciat*, "Bibliotheque de criminologie" xix., 1899 (Paris, Masson). It gives an analysis and table of contents of Sade's writings.—*cf.* also *Dühren*, "The Marquis de Sade" 1900.

26. *Cf. Krauss*, "Psychologie des Verbrechens," 1884, p. 188; *Dr. Hofer*, "Annalen der Staatsarzneikunde," 6 Jahrgang, Heft 2; "*Schmidt's* Jahrbücher," Bd. 59, p. 94.

27. According to newspaper reports, in December, 1890, several similar attacks were made in Mainz. A young fellow between fourteen and sixteen years of age pressed against women and girls and stabbed them in the legs with a sharp-pointed instrument. He was arrested, and seemed to be insane. Further details of the case are not known.

28. *Leo Taxil* ("La Corruption," Paris, Noiret, p. 223) makes the same statements. There are also men who demand the introduction of the tongue of a harlot into the anus.

29. *Leo Taxil* (*op. cit.*, p. 224) relates that in Parisian brothels instruments are kept ready which look like knouts, but which are merely tubes filled with air, such as clowns use in circuses. Sadistic men use them to create for themselves the illusion that they are whipping women.

30. Dimitri, the son of Ivan the Cruel, derived unspeakable pleasure when witnessing the death struggles of sheep, chickens and geese. (Bibliothèque de Criminologie, xix., p. 278.)

31. The legend is especially spread throughout the Balkan peninsula. Among the modern Greeks it has its origin in the myth of the *lamioe* and *marmolykes*—blood-sucking women. *Goethe* made use of this in his "Bride of Corinth." The verses referring to vampirism, "suck thy heart's blood," etc., can be thoroughly understood only when compared with their ancient sources.

32. Another case of *Sadismus feminae* is given by *Moll*, 3rd edit. of "Die Contr. Sexualempfindung," p. 507, case 29. It is the exact counterpart of Masochism in man and represents the ideal desire of the Masochist.

33. The gifted *Henry von Kleist*, who was beyond doubt mentally abnormal, gives a masterly portrayal of complete feminine sadism in his "Penthesilea." In scene xxii., *Kleist* describes his heroine pursuing Achilles in the fire of love, and when he is betrayed into her hands, she tears him with lustful, murderous fury into pieces, and sets her dogs on him: "Tearing the armour from his body, she strikes her teeth in his white breast—she and her dogs, the rivals, Oxus and Sphynx—they on the right side, she on the left; and as I approached blood dripped from her hands and mouth." And later, when Penthesilea becomes satiated: "Did I kiss him to death? No. Did I not kiss him? Torn in pieces? Then it was a mistake; kissing rhymes with biting [in German, *Küsse, Bisse*], and one who loves with the whole heart might easily mistake the one for the other." In recent literature we find the matter frequently treated, but particularly in *Sacher-Masoch's* novels, of which mention is made later on, and in *Ernest von Wildenbruch's* "Brunhilde," *Rachilde's* "Le Marquise de Sade," etc.

34. *Literature. v. Krafft*, Neue Forschungen aus dem Gebiete der Psychopathia Sexualis, 2 Aufl.—*Idem*, Arbeiten aus d. Gesammtgebiete d. Psychiatrie u. Neuropathol., iv., p. 127-160.—*Moll*, Die Conträre Sexualempfindung, 3. Aufl.,

276—*Eulenburg*, Grenzfragen des Nerven- und Seelenlebens, xix., Sadismus u. Masochismus, 1902. *Fuchs*, Therapie der anomalen *vita sexualis* (Stuttgart, Enke) Beob. 5 and 6.—*v. Schrenk-Notzing*, Die Suggestions-Therapie, 1892.— *Seydel*, Vierteljahrschr. f. gerichtl. Med., 1893, iv. 2 (Interessante Briefe von Masochisten).—*Bloch*, Beiträge z. Aetiol. d. Psychop. sexualis, 2 Theil, Dresden, 1903.

35. Cf. for corroboration Sacher-Masoch, biography by *v. Eulenburg:* Grenzfragen des Nerven- und Seelenlebens, 1902, xxix., pp. 46-57.

36. *Cf.* above, Introduction.

37. This difference of courage in the face of events in nature, on the one hand, and in the face of conflict with will-power, on the other, is certainly remarkable, even though it is the only indication of effeminacy apparent in this case.

38. "Transactions of the Colorado State Medical Society," quoted in the "Alienist and Neurologist," April, 1883, p. 345.

39. Instructive instances are given by *Seydel*, "Vierteljahrsschr. f. ger. Med.," 1893, Heft 2, pp. 275, 276.

40. *Léo Taxil* (*op. cit.*, p. 228) describes masochistic scenes in Parisian brothels. The man affected with this perversion is there also called "slave."

   Coffignon ("La corruption à Paris") has a chapter in his book entitled "Les Passionels" which contains contributions to this subject.

   The strongest proof of the frequency of masochism lies in the fact that it openly appears in newspaper advertisements. For instance, the following advertisement appeared in the "Hannoversches' Tageblatt," 4th December, 1895:—

   "*Sacher-Masoch.* 109,404. Ladies interested in the works, and who embody the female characters, of this author are requested to send their address, under No. R. 537, to the offices of this paper. Strictest discretion." Another similar advertisement appeared in the same number.

41. However, the domain of masochism must be sharply differentiated from the principal subject of that work, which is, that love contains an element of suffering. Unrequited love has always been described as "sweet, but sorrowful," and poets speak of "blissful pain" or "painful bliss." This must not be confounded, as Z. does, with the manifestations of masochism, any more than should be the characterization of any unyielding lover as "cruel." It is remarkable, however, that *Hamerling* ("Amor und Psyche," iv. Gesang) uses perfect masochistic pictures, flagellation, etc., to express this feeling.

42. *Cf.* his recent paper on "Passivisimus" in the "Archives d'Anthropologie Criminelle," 1892, vii., p. 294.

43. (*Moll*, "Untersuchungen über *Libido Sexualis*, Bd. i., 2 Thiel, Beob. 36, p. 320.) However, against the theory that foot- and shoe-fetichism is a manifestation of (latent) masochism, Dr. *Moll* (*op. cit.*, p. 136) raises the objection that it is still unexplained why the fetichist so often prefers boots with high heels, to boots and shoes of a particular kind—buttoned or laced. To this objection it may be remarked that in the first place, the high heels characterize the shoes as feminine, and in the second place, that in spite of the sexual character of his inclination, the fetichist demands all kinds of aesthetic qualities in his fetich; also the interesting theories advanced by *Restif de la Bretonne* [himself a foot-fetichist], and quoted in *Moll's* work, *op. cit.*, pp. 498 and 499, footnote.

44. Compare the instructive case of *Moll*, Libido sexualis, p. 320.

45. There is apparently a connection between foot-fetichism and the fact that certain persons of this kind, whom coitus does not satisfy, or who are unable to perform it, find a substitute for it in rubbing their member between the feet of a woman.

46. This disgusting impulse is also referred to in case 68 of the eighth edition of this work. It seems to occur especially with coprolagnists and fetichists.

47. The laws of the early middle ages gave the husband the right to kill the wife; those of the later middle ages, the right to beat her. The latter right was used freely, even by those of high standing (*cf. Schultze*, "Das höfische Leben zur Zeit des Minnesangs," Bd. i., p. 163 *et seq.*). Yet, by the side of this, the paradoxical chivalry of the middle ages stands unexplained (see below, p. 132).

48. *Cf.* Lady Milford's words in *Schiller's* "Kabale und Liebe": "We women can only choose between ruling and serving; but the highest pleasure power affords is but a miserable substitute, if the greater joy of being the slaves of a man we love is denied us!" (Act II, Scene l.).

49. *Seydel*, "Vierteljahresschr. f. ger. Med.," 1893, vol. ii, quotes as an instance of masochism the patient of *Dieffenbach*, who repeatedly and purposely dislocated her arm in order to experience lustful sensations when it was being reduced, anaesthetics not being known then.

50. Analogous facts are found in the animal kingdom. *Pulmonata Cuv.*, for instance, possess a small calcareous staff which lies hidden in a special pouch of the body, but is at the time of mating projected and used as a means of sexual excitement, producing, beyond doubt, pain.

51. *Cf.* the author's article, "Uber geschlechtliche Hörigkeit und Masochismus," in the "Psychiatrische Jahrbücher," Bd. x., p. 169 *et seq.*, where this subject is treated in detail, and particularly from the forensic standpoint.

52. The expressions "slave" and "slavery," though often used metaphorically under such circumstances, are avoided here because they are the favourite expressions of masochism, from which this "bondage" must be strictly differentiated.

The expression "bondage" is not to be construed to mean *J. S. Mill's* "Bondage of Woman." What *Mill* designates with this expression are laws and customs, social and historical facts. Here, however, we always speak of facts having peculiar individual motives that even conflict with prevalent customs and laws. Besides it has reference to either sex.

53. Perhaps the most important element is, that by the habit of submission a kind of mechanical obedience, without consciousness of its motives, which operates with automatic certainty, may be established, having no opposing motives to contend with, because it lies beyond the threshold of consciousness; and it may be used by the dominant individual like an inanimate instrument.

54. Sexual bondage, of course, plays a *rôle* in all literature. Indeed, for the poet, the extraordinary manifestations of the sexual life that are not perverse form a rich and open field. The most celebrated description of masculine "bondage" is that by *Abbé Prévost*, "Manon Lescault." An excellent description of feminine "bondage" is that of "Leone Leoni," by *George Sand*. But first of all comes *Kleist's* "Käthchen von Heilbronn," who himself called it the counterpart of (sadistic) "Penthesilea." *Halm's* "Griseldis" and many other similar poems also belong here.

55. Cases may occur in which the sexual bondage is expressed in the same acts that are common in masochism. When rough men beat their wives, and the latter suffer for love, without, however, having a desire for blows, we have a pseudo form of bondage that may simulate masochism.

56. It is highly interesting, and dependent upon the nature of bondage and masochism, which essentially correspond in external effects, that to illustrate the former certain playful, metaphorical expressions are in general use; such as "slavery," "to bear chains," "bound," "to hold the whip over," "to harness to the triumphal car," "to lie at the feet," "henpecked," etc.,—all things which, literally carried out, form the objects of the masochist's desire. Such similes are frequently used in daily life and have become trite. They are derived

from the language of poetry. Poetry has always recognized, within the general idea of the passion of love, the element of dependence in the lover, who practices self-sacrifice spontaneously or of necessity. The facts of "bondage" have also always presented themselves to the poetical imagination. When the poet chooses such expressions as those mentioned, to picture the dependence of the lover in striking similes, *he proceeds exactly on the same lines as does the masochist, viz.,* to intensify the idea of his dependence (his ultimate aim), he creates such situations in reality. In ancient poetry, the expression "domina" is used to signify the loved one, with a preference for the simile of "casting in chains" (*e.g., Horace,* Od. iv., 11). From antiquity through all the centuries to our own times (*cf. Grillparzer,* "Ottokar," act v.: "To rule is sweet, almost as sweet as to obey") the poetry of love is filled with similar phrases and similes. The history of the word "mistress" is also interesting. But poetry reacts on life. It is probable that the courtly chivalry of the middle ages arose in this way. In its reverence for women as "mistresses" in society and in individual love-relations; its transference of the relations of feudalism and vassalage to the relation between the knight and his lady; its submission to all feminine whims; its love-tests and vows; its duty of obedience to every command of the lady—in all this, chivalry appears as a systematic, poetical development of the "bondage" of love. Certain extreme manifestations, like the deeds and sufferings of *Ulrich von Lichtenstein* or *Pierre Vidal* in the service of their ladies; or the practice of the fraternity of the "Galois" in France, whose members sought martyrdom in love and subjected themselves to all kinds of suffering—these clearly have a masochistic character, and demonstrate the natural transformation of one phenomenon into the other.

57. If it be considered that, as shown above, "sexual bondage" is a phenomenon observed much more frequently and in a more pronounced degree in the female sex than in the male, the thought arises that masochism (if not always, at least as a rule) is an inheritance of the "bondage" of feminine ancestry. Thus it comes into a relation—though distant—with antipathic sexual instinct, as a transference to the male of a perversion really belonging to the female.

It must, however, be emphasized that "bondage" also plays no unimportant *rôle* in the masculine sexual life, and that masochism in man may also be explained without any such transference of feminine elements. It must also be remembered here that masochism, as well as its counterpart, sadism, occurs in irregular combination with antipathic sexual instinct.

58. Cf. cases 57 and 58.

59. Cf. case 70 in *Schrenck-Notzing;* case 20 in *Féré,* l'instinct sexuell, p. 262.

60. Cf. case 67 in *Schrenck-Notzing; Moll,* Contr. Sexualempfindung, 3rd edition, p. 265 (gentleman who pestered an officer with letters in which he begged him to be allowed to clean his boots); *ibidem,* p. 281 (gentleman who was agitated by two wishes, viz.: (1) to be a woman that he might have coitus with the man he loved, (2) to be maltreated by the same); *ibidem,* case 17; ditto, p. 283 (man who finds satisfaction in the act with another man only when the latter rubs his back with a hard brush till the blood flows); p. 284 (coprolagnia); p. 317; *v. Krafft,* Psycop. sexual., 6th edit., case 43; 8th edit., cases 46, 114, 115; *item,* Jahrb. f. Psychiatrie, xii., pp. 339 and 351; *item,* "Arbeiten," iv., p. 134.

61. Of course, both have to contend with opposing ethical and aesthetic motives in their own minds. After these have been overcome, active sadism immediately comes in conflict with the law. This is not the case with masochism, which accounts for the greater frequency of masochistic acts. But the instinct of self-preservation and fear of pain prevent the realization of the latter. The

practical significance of masochism lies only in its relations to psychical impotence; while that of sadism lies beyond this, and is principally forensic.

62. *Schrenck-Notzing*, who in his explanation of all perversions lays particular stress upon the "occasional momentum," gives preference to the theory of acquired perversions over the congenital, and allows the manifestations of sadism and masochism only a subordinate position. Although he admits that many cases can only be explained on the assumption of congenital predisposition, yet he contends that circumstances or a timely coincidence control their acquirement (*op. cit.* p. 170).

His arguments are based upon observations. Quoting two cases of *psychopathia sexualis* (29 and 37 of the seventh edition) he contends that the accidental sight of a girl bleeding or a boy being whipped coinciding with a strong sexual emotion may be sufficient cause for continued pathological associations.

Against this it may, however, be decisively held that in every hyper-aesthetic individual early and strong sexual emotions have often coincided with numerous heterogeneous things, whilst the *pathological associations are always coupled with but few definite* (sadistic and masochistic) *things.* Numerous pupils indulge in sexual emotions or gratifications during lessons in grammar and mathematics in the class-room, as well as elsewhere, without thereby contracting perverse associations.

From this clearly follows that the sight of a whipping or similar scenes may provoke pathological associations already present but latent, but that it cannot produce them. Moreover, the aroused sexual instinct is not associated with the numerous *indifferent* things that are ever present, but only with such as normally excite disgust.

The same argument refers to the opinion of *Binet*, who also seeks to explain these manifestations by accidental associations.

63. Every attempt to explain the facts of either sadism or masochism owing to the close connection of the two phenomena demonstrated here, must also be suited to explain the other perversion. An attempt to offer an explanation of sadism, by *J. G. Kiernan* (Chicago) (*see* "Psychological Aspects of the Sexual Appetite," Alienist and Neurologist, St. Louis, April, 1891) meets this requirement, and for this reason may be briefly mentioned here. *Kiernan,* who has several authorities in Anglo-American literature for his theory, starts from the assumption of several naturalists (*Dallinger, Drysdale, Rolph, Cienkowsky*) which conceives the so-called conjugation, a sexual act in certain low forms of animal life, to be cannibalism, a devouring of the partner in the act. He brings into immediate connection with this the well-known facts that at the time of sexual union crabs tear limbs from their bodies and spiders bite off the heads of the males, and other sadistic acts performed by rutting animals with their consorts. From this he passes to lust-murder and other lustful acts of cruelty in man, and assumes that hunger and the sexual appetite are, in their origin, identical; that the sexual cannibalism of lower forms of animal life has an influence in higher forms and in man, and that sadism is an atavistic rebound.

This explanation of sadism would, of course, also explain masochism; for if the origin of sexual intercourse is to be sought in cannibalistic process, then both the survival of one sex and the destruction of the other would fulfil the purpose of nature, and thus the instinctive desire to be the victim would be explained. But it must be stated in objection that the basis of this reasoning is insufficient. The extremely complicated process of conjugation in lower organisms, into which science has really penetrated only during the last few years, is by no means to be regarded as simply a devouring of one individual by another (*cf. Weismann,* "Die Bedeutung der sexuellen Fort-pflanzung für die Selectionstheorie," p. 51, Jena, 1886).

64. In *Zola's* "Thérèse Raquin," where the lover repeatedly kisses his mistress's boot, the case is quite different from that of shoe- and boot-fetichists, who, at the sight of every boot worn by a lady, or even alone, are thrown into sexual excitement, even to the extent of ejaculation.

65. Cf. "Arbeiten," iv., p. 172. Case of ring fetichism; p. 174, mourning crape fetichism in homosexual persons.

66. Though *Binet* (*op. cit.*) declares that every sexual perversion, without exception, depends upon such an "accident acting on a predisposed subject" (where, under predisposition, only hyperaesthesia in general is understood), yet such an assumption for other perversions than fetichism is neither necessary nor satisfactory. For example, it is not clear how the sight of another's chatise-ment could excite sexually even a very excitable individual, if the physiological relationship of lust and cruelty had not been developed into *original* sadism in an abnormally excitable individual. As the sadistic and masochistic associa-tions are performed in the mind of the subject from homogeneous elements in adjacent spheres, in the same measure is the possibility of fetichistic asso-ciations prepared by the idiosyncrasies of the object and thus easier under-stood. In nearly every instance it is impressions of parts of the female form (including garments) that are in question. Fetichistic association which originated only by mere accident can only be traced in a few special cases.

67. When young husbands who have associated much with prostitutes feel im-potent in the face of the chastity of their young wives—a thing of frequent occurrence—the condition may be regarded as a kind of (psychical) fetichism in a wider sense. One of my patients was never potent with his beautiful and chaste young wife, because he was accustomed to the lascivious methods of prostitutes. When he now and then attempted coitus with girls he was perfectly potent. *Hammond* (*op. cit.* pp. 48, 49) reports a very similar interest-ing case. Of course, in such cases, a bad conscience and hypochondriacal fear of impotence play an important part.

68. Great sexual hyperaesthesia.

69. This is also sexual hyperaesthesia. Any intense excitement affects the sexual sphere (*Binet's* "Dynamogénie générale"). Concerning this *Dr. Moll* communi-cates the following case: "A similar thing is described by Mr. E., aged twenty-seven; merchant. While at school, and afterwards, he often had ejaculation with pleasurable feeling when he was seized with a spell of intense anxiety. Besides, almost every other physical or mental pain exerted a similar influence. E., as he stated, had a normal sexual instinct, but suffered with nervous impotence."

70. Exceptions are the cases of latent masochism in the form of Coprolagnia in which case the fetichistic stimulus is not to be found in the clean naked foot but the contrary *cf.* case 80.

71. *Garnier* (Sadi-fetichism, Annal. d'hyg.) knew a degenerate whose fetich was the hair of the *Mons Veneris*. His greatest delight was to tear them out with his teeth. He collected specimens and used them for renewed sexual gratification by biting and chewing them. He bribed housemaids of hotels to let him search the beds in which ladies had slept for such hairs. Whilst searching for them he became erotically excited and trembled with happiness when he made a successful find.

72. *Moll* (*op. cit.*, p. 131) reports: "A man, X., becomes intensely excited sexually whenever he sees a woman with the hair in a braid; loose hair, no matter how beautiful, cannot produce this effect."

Of course, it is not justifiable to consider all hair-despoilers fetichists, for in a few cases such acts are done for the purpose of gain—*i. e.*, the stolen hair is not a fetich.

73. *Cf.* Goethe's remarks about his adventure in Geneva ("Briefe aus der Schweiz," 1. Abtheil, Schluss).

74. The fact that the partly veiled form is often more charming than when it is perfectly nude, is, as far as object goes, similar, but quite different psychically. This depends upon the effect of contrast and expectation, which are common phenomena, and in no sense pathological.

75. On page 161 (*op. cit.*) Dr. *Moll* writes concerning this impulse in hetero-sexual individuals: "The passion for handkerchiefs may go so far that the man is entirely under its control. A woman tells me: 'I know a certain gentleman, and when I see him at a distance I only need to draw out my handkerchief so that it peeps out of my pocket, and I am certain that he will follow me as a dog follows its master. Go where I please, this gentleman will follow me. He may be riding in a carriage or engaged in important business, and yet, when he sees my handkerchief he drops everything in order to follow me,— *i. e.*, my handkerchief.'"

76. Another case of temporary, *i. e.*, periodical handkerchief-fetichism, accompanied by anxiety and severe sweating, is related by Dr. *Moll* in the "Centralblatt f. d. Krankheiten der Harn- und Sexual-organe," v., 8. This might be a case of latent epilepsy. (Head injury at the age of ten, imbecility, repeated fainting fits, later on partial amnesia for fetichistic conditions, accompanied by anxiety and sweating, etc.) In these attacks of morbid impulse to steal ladies' handkerchiefs, which set in after an attack of typhus at the age of thirty, the patient would wipe his face with the stolen article, which act produced erection, and at times also ejaculation. A physician whom he consulted had given him the advice never to wear linen shirts again, as his peculiar impulse was caused by them.

77. Other cases of shoe-fetichism without distant relations to masochism are given by *Alzheimer*, "A Congenital Criminal," "Archiv f. Psychiatrie u. Nerven Krankheiten," Bd. 28, p. 350. This same case was declared by *Kurella*, "Fetischismus oder Simulation," *ibid.*, Bd. 28, p. 964, to be simulation; but the reasons given are trivial and easily refuted. See also *Moll*, "Untersuchungen über libido sexualis," case 32.

78. In the novels of *Sacher-Masoch*, fur plays an important *rôle;* in fact, it serves as a title in some of them. The explanation given that fur (ermine) is the symbol of sovereignty, and therefore the fetich of the men described in these novels, seems unsatisfactory and far-fetched.

79. *Garnier* ("Anomalies Sexuelles," Paris, pp. 508, 509) reports two cases (cases 222 and 223) that are apparently opposed to this assumption, particularly the first, in which despair about the unfaithfulness of a lover led the individual to submit to the seductions of men. But the case itself clearly shows that this individual *never found pleasure in homo-sexual acts.* In case 223, the individual was effeminated *ab origine*, or was at least a psychical hermaphrodite.

Those who hold to the opinion that the origin of homo-sexual feelings and instinct is found to be exclusively in defective education and other psychological influences are entirely in error.

An *untainted* male may be raised ever so much like a female, and a female like a male, but they will not become homo-sexual. *The natural disposition is the determining condition; not education and other accidental circumstances, like seduction.* There can be no thought of antipathic sexual instinct save when the person of the same sex exerts a psycho-sexual influence over the individual, and thus brings about *libido* and orgasm,—*i. e.*, has a psychical attraction. Those cases are quite different in which, for want of something better, with great sensuality and a defective aesthetic sense, the body of a person of the same sex is used for an onanistic act (not for coitus in a psychical sense).

In his excellent monograph, *Moll* shows very clearly and convincingly the importance of original predisposition in contrast with exciting causes (*cf. op. cit.*, pp. 212-231). He knows "many cases where early sexual intercourse with men was not capable of inducing perversion." *Moll* significantly says, further: "I know of such an epidemic (of mutual onanism) in a Berlin school, where a person, who is now an actor, shamelessly introduced mutual onanism. Though I now know the names of very many urnings in Berlin, yet I could not ascertain, even with anything like probability, that among all the pupils of that school at that time there was one that had become an urning; but, on the other hand, I have quite certain knowledge that many of those pupils are now normal sexually in feeling and intercourse.

80. *Cf.* author's "Experimental Study in the Domain of Hypnotism," third edition, 1893.

81. *Cf. Sprengel*, "Apologie des Hippokrates," Leipzig, 1792, p. 611; *Friedreich*, "Literargeschichte der psych. Krankheiten," 1830, p. 31; *Lallemand*, "Des pertes séminales," Paris, 1836, i., p. 581; *Nysten*, "Dictionn. de médecine," xi. édit., Paris, 1858, Art. "Eviration et Maladie des Scythes"; *Marandon*, "De la maladie des Scythes"; "Annal. médico-psychol.," 1877, Mars, p. 161; *Hammond*, "American Journal of Neurology and Psychiatry," August, 1882.

82. An abstract of this may be found in case 103 of the ninth edition of this book.

83. *Cf. ibid.*, cases 104 and 105.

84. Bibliography (besides works-mentioned hereafter): *Tardieu*, "Des attentats aux moeurs," 7 édit., 1878, p. 210.—*Hofmann*, "Lehrb. d. ger. Med.," 6 Aufl., pp. 170, 887.—*Gley*, "Revue philosophique," 1884, No. 1.—*Magnan*, "Annal. med-psychol.," 1885, p. 458.—*Shaw* and *Ferris*, "Journal of Nervous and Mental Diseases," 1883, April, No. 2.—*Bernhardi*, "Der Uranismus," Berlin (Volks-buchhandlung), 1882.—*Chevalier*, "De l'inversion de l'instinct sexuel," Paris, 1885.—*Ritti*, "Gaz, hebdom. de médecine et de chirug.," 1878, 4. Januar.—*Tamassia*, "Rivista sperim," 1878, pp. 97-177.—*Lombroso*, "Archiv. di Psichiatr.," 1881.—*Charcot* et *Magnan*, "Archiv. de neurologie," 1882, Nr. 7, 12. *Moll*, "Die conträre Sexualempfindung," Berlin, 3rd edit., 1899 (numerous bibliographic references).—*Chevalier*, "Archives de l'anthropologie criminelle," vol. v., No. 27; vol. vi., No. 31.—*Reuss*, "Aberrations du sens génésique," "Annales d'hygiène publique," 1886.—*Saury*, "Etude clinique sur la folie héréditaire," 1886.—*Brouardel*, "Gaz. des hôpitaux," 1886 and 1887.—*Tilier*, "L'instinct sexual chez l'homme et chez les animaux," 1889.—*Carlier*, "Les deux prostitutions," 1887.—*Lacassagne*, art. "Pédérastie," in the "Diction. encyclo-pédique."—*Viberta*, art. "Pédérastie," in the "Diction. med. et de chirurgie."—*Coutagne*, "Lyon medical," 1880, Nos. 35, 36.—*Blumer*, "Americ. Journ. of Insanity," July, 1882.—*V. Krafft*, "Zeitschr. f Psychiatrie," No. 38.—*Blumen-stock*, art. "Conträre Sexualempfindung," "Realencyclop. d. ges. Heilkunde," 2 Aufl. vi.—*Brouardel*, "Gaz. des hôpiteaux," 1887.—*Kriese*, "Inaugural dissert.," Würzburg, 1888.—*Hofman*, art. "Paederastie," Realencyclop. d. ges. Heilkunde," 2 Aufl. xv.—*Tarnowsky*, "Die krankhaften Ercheinungen des Geschlechtsinnes," Berlin, 1886.—*Magnan*, "Séance de l'académie de médecine du 13 Janvier," 1885, *idem*, "Annales médico psychol.," 1886 ("Anomalies du sens génital"; "Discussion sur la folie héréditaire").—*Serieux*, "Recherches cliniques sur les anomalies de l'instinct sexuel," Paris, 1886.—*Chevalier*, "L'inversion sexuelle," Lyon, Paris, 1893.—*Ladame*, "Revue de l'hypnotisme," Sept., 1889.—*Peyer*, "Münch. med. Wochenschrift," 1890, No. 23.—Lewin, "Neurolog. Central-blatt," 1891, No. 18.—*V. Schrenck-Notzing*, "Die Suggestions-therapie," etc.,

Stuttgart.—*Eulenburg, op. cit.,* p. 66, "Homo-sexuelle Parerosie."—*Raffalovich,* "Die Entwickelung der Homo-sexualität," Berlin, 1895,—*idem,* "Uranisme et Unisexualité," Paris, 1886.—*V. Schrenck-Notzing,* "Klin. Zeit- und Streit-fragen," ix. 1 (Wien, 1895).—*Laupts,* "Perversion et perversité sexuelles," Paris, 1896.—*Legrain,* "Des anomalies de l'instinct sexuel," etc., Paris, 1896.

85. Dr. *Moll,* of Berlin, called my attention to the fact that in *Moritz's* "Magazin f. Erfahrungsseelenkunde," vol. viii., Berlin, 1791, references are made to antipathic sexual instinct in man. In fact, two biographies of men are there reported who manifested an enthusiastic love for persons of their own sex. In the second case, which is particularly noteworthy, the patient him-self explains his aberration by the fact that, as a child he was caressed only by grown persons, and as a boy of ten or twelve years only by his school-fellows. "This, and the want of association with persons of the opposite sex, in me caused the natural inclination towards the female sex to be entirely diverted to the male sex. I am still quite indifferent to women."

It cannot be determined whether such a case is one of congenital (psycho-sexual hermaphrodisia?) or acquired antipathic sexual instinct.

86. "Vindex, Inclusa, Vindicta, Formatrix, Ara spei, Gladius furens" (Leipzig, H. Matthes, 1864 and 1865); *Ulrichs,* "Kritische Pfeile," 1879, in Commission, by H. Crönlein, Stuttgart, Augustenstrasse, 5.

87. *Tarnowsky* (*op. cit.,* p. 34) records a case which shows that antipathic sexual feeling, as a concomitant manifestation with neurotic degeneration, may also affect the descendants of parents having no neurotic taint. In this instance, lues of the parents played a part, as in a similar case of *Scholz* ("Vierteljahrs-schr. f. ger. Med."), in which the perversion of the sexual desires stood in causal relation with an arrest of psychical development, caused by traumatism.

88. The researches in zoology, by *Klaus* ("Zoology," 1891, p. 490) show that, in the lower grades of the animal world, not only hermaphroditism exists, but that also (physiological?) sexual exchange in one and the same individual may take place. *Klaus* states that the *cymothoideae* (classified under crustacea) perform in the first part of their life the functions of the male, and in the second part under many, even secondary, changes of the sexual character those of the female.

89. A mono-sexual psychic apparatus of generation, in a monosexual body which belongs to the opposite sex, does, of course, not mean a "feminine soul in a masculine brain," or *vice versa*—this would simply contradict all monistic and scientific thought; neither a feminine brain in a masculine body—this contradicts every anatomical fact—but only a feminine psycho-sexual centre in a masculine brain, and *vice versa*.

90. *Joseph Müller,* in a clever *brochure* ("Ueber Gamophagy," Stuttgart, 1892) offers an inducement for further research in this direction. He advances the opinion that by a certain law, established by necessity, and transcending in normal fashion, a union of the organs and their qualities is effected. This union would explain how, in the struggle of the development of mono- and bi-sexuality, those organs and their qualities suffer the common fate of conquest or defeat which belong together as a whole with regard to their functional capacity. The defect of the elements connecting the organs during the struggle for superiority in beings subject to organic taint could only be explained as a negative result of this hypothetical law.

91. That inversion of the sexual instinct is not uncommon is proved, among other things, by the circumstance that it is frequently the subject in novels. The neuropathic foundation of this sexual perversion does not escape the writers. This theme is treated in German literature in "Fridolin's heimliche Ehe," by *Wilbrand;* in "Brick-a-Brack oder Licht im Schatten," by *Emerich*

Graf Stadion; also by *Balduin Groller,* "Prinz Klotz." The oldest urning romance is probably that published by *Petronius* at Rome, under the Empire, under the title "Satyricon."

92. *Cf.* author's work, "Ueber psychosexuales Zwitterthum," in the "Internationales Centralblatt f. d. Physiologie u. Pathologie der Harn- und Sexualorgane," Bd. i., Heft 2.

93. This idea is supported by the statements of an unmarried homosexual, which *Dr. Moll,* of Berlin, kindly communicated to me. He could report a number of cases of his acquaintance, in which married men had also "relations" with men.

94. Literature: *Havelock Ellis,* "Alienist and Neurologist," April, 1895; *Moll,* "Conträre Sexualempfindung," second edition, p. 322.—*Moll,* Conträre Sexualempfindung, 3rd ed., p. 504.—*Moraglia,* Neue Forschungen aus d. Gebiet der weiblichen Criminalität,—v. *Krafft,* Jahrb. f. sexuelle Zwischenstufen, iii., p. 20.

95. Observations: (1) *Westphal,* "Arch. f. Psych.," ii., p. 73;—(2) *Gock, op. cit.,* No. 1.;—(3) *Wise,* "The Alienist and Neurologist," January, 1883;—(4) *Cantarano,* "La Psichiatria, 1883," p. 201;—(5) *Sérieux, op. cit.,* obs. 14;—(6) *Kiernan, op. cit.;*—(7) *Müller, Friedreich's* "Blätter f. ger. Med.," 1891, Heft 4.;—(8-19) *Moll,* "Conträre Sexualempfindung," 2 Aufl. Beob., 18, 19, 20, 21, 22, 23;—(20) *Meyhöfer,* "Zeitsch. f. Medicinalbeamte," v., 16;—(21-22) *Zuccarelli,* "Inversione congenita in due donne," Napoli, 1888;—(23-33) *Moll,* "Untersuchungen über Libido sexualis," Fälle 10-12, 40-44, 47, 56, 57; —(34-36) *Havelock Ellis, op. cit.;*—(37) *Penta e Urso,* "Archiv. delle psichopatie sexuali," p. 33;—(38) *Penta, ibid.,* p. 94.—(39-40) *Féré,* l'instinct sexuelle, observ. 15, p. 242, observ. 22, p. 291.—(41) Case *Urban* of the 18th century, reported by *Moll,* Contr. Sexualempfindung, 3rd ed. p. 533.—(42-43) v. *Krafft,* Jahrbücher für sexuelle Zwischenstufen, iii, p. 27 and 29.

96. *Paul,* Epist, ad Rom.

97. *Ploss, op. cit.*

98. It is remarkable fact that in fiction, lesbian love is frequently used as the leading theme, *viz., Diderot,* "La Religieuse"; *Balzac,* "La fille aux yeux d'or"; *Th. Gautier,* "Mademoiselle de Maupin"; *Feydeau,* "La Comtesse de chalis"; *Flaubert,* "Salammbo"; *Belot,* "Mademoiselle Giraud, ma femme"; *Rachilde,* "Monsieur Venus."

The heroines of these lesbian *novelles* appear to the beloved persons of the same sex in the character and the *rôle* of a *man;* their love is most intense.

The oldest case of sexual inversion recorded thus far in Germany is one of viraginity dating as far back as the beginning of the eighteenth century. It is that of a woman who was married to another woman cohabiting with the consort by means of a leathern priapus. See *Dr. Müller* in *Friedreich's* "Blätter f. ger. Med.," 1891, Heft 4.

99. *Cf.* the expert medical opinion of this case, by *Dr. Birnbacher,* in "*Friedreich's* Blätter f. ger. Med.," 1891, Heft 1.

NOTES FOR CHAPTER V

1. For numerous cases, "*v. Henke's* Zeitschr.," xxiii., "Ergänzungsheft," p. 147; *Combes,* "Annal. méd. psychol.," 1866; *Liman,* "Zweifelh. Geisteszustände," p. 389; *Casper-Liman,* "Lehrb., 7, Auflage," Fall 295; *Bartels,* "*Friedreich's* Blätter f. gerichtl. Med.," 1890, Heft 1.

2. Other cases of pederasty, *v. Casper,* "Klin. Novellen," Fall 5; *Combes,* "Annal. méd. psychol.," July, 1866.

3. *V. Sander*, "Vierteljahrsschr. f. ger. Med.," xviii., p. 31; *Casper*, "Klin. Novellen," Fall 27.
4. *Arndt* ("Lehrb. d. Psych.," p. 410) especially emphasizes the passionate element in epileptics: "I have known epileptics who behaved in a most sensual way towards their mothers, and others who were suspected by their fathers of sexual intercourse with the mothers." But when *Arndt* declares that, wherever there is a peculiarity of the sexual life, thought of an epileptic element should come into consideration, he is in error.
5. *Cf.* also *Liman*, "Zweifelhafte Geisteszustände," Fall 6; *Lasègue*, "Exhibitionists, Union méd.," 1877; *Ball* and *Chambard*, "Art. Somnambulisme" ("Dict. des scienc. méd.," 1881).
6. Literature: *Bienville*, Traité de la nymph., Amsterdam, 1771; *Louyer-Villermay*, art. nymphomanie, dict. des sciences med., xxx., p. 563; *Magnet*, dict. en 60 vol. (vol. xxxvi., p. 580); *Meyer Alexis*, des rapports conjugaux, Paris, 1882, 7 éd.; *Guibout*, traité clinique des malad. des femmes, Paris, 1886; *Icard*, la femme pendant la période menstruelle, 1890; *Marc*, die Geisteskrankheiten, übersetzt von *Ideler*, ii., p. 138; *Ideler*, Grundriss der Seelenheilkunde, ii., p. 488; *Foville*, dict. de méd. et de chirurch. pratique; *Legrand du Saulle*, la folie devant des tribun., 1864; *Ball*, la folie érotique, 1888; *Moreau*, aberrations du sens génésique, 1884; *Thoinot*, attentats aux moeurs, p. 487; *Legrand du Saulle*, les hystériques, 1883.
7. *Thoinot*, Attentats aux moeurs, p. 498.
8. See case of *Merlac*, in the author's "Lehrb. d. ger. Psychopathol.," 2 Aufl., p. 322; *Morel*, "Traité des malad. mentales," p. 687; *Legrand*, "La folie," p. 337; Process La Roncière, in "Annal. d'hyg.," I Serie, iv.; 3 Serie, xxii.
9. The incubus in the witch-trials of the middle ages depended on them.

Notes for Chapter VI

1. *S. Weisbrod*, "Die Sittlichkeitsverbrechen vor dem Gesetz," Berlin, 1891; *Dr. Pasquale Penta*, "I pervertimenti sessuali nell'uomo," Napoli, 1893; *Seydel*, "Die Beurtheilung der perversen Sexualvergehen in foro," "Vierteljahrsschr. für ger. Med.," 1893, Heft 2; *Viazzi*, "reati sessuali" ("Biblioteca antropologico-giuridica"); Archivio di Psichiatria, vol. xix., fasc. 1., "Strafgesetzbücher und Unzuchtsdelikte."—*v. Schrenck-Notzing*, Archiv f. Kriminalanthropol. Bd. 1, H. I.
2. *Cf. Casper*, "Klin. Novellen"; *Lombroso*, "Goltdammer's Archiv," Bd. xxx.; *Oettingen*, "Moralstatistik," p. 494.
3. *Boissier* et *Lachaux*, "Perversions sexuelles à forme obsédante," "Archives de Neurologie," 1893, October; *Schäfer*, "Vierteljahrsschr. f. gerichtl. Med.," 3 Folge, x., 1.—*Thoinot*, attentats aux moeurs, 1898, p. 366-398;—*Seiffer*, Arch. f. Psych. Bd. 31, H. 1 and 2.—*Cramer*, Die Beziehungen des Exhib. zum §51. des deutsch. Stfgsb., Zeitschr. f. Psych. 54, p. 481.—*Bassenge*, Der Exhibitionismus, Inaug.-Dissert., Berlin, 1896.—*Hoche*, Neurolog. Centralbl., 1896, 2.
4. *Lasègue*, "Union Médicale," 1877, May; *Laugier*, "Annal. d'hygiéne publ.," 1878, No. 106; *Pelande*, "Pornopaths," "Archivio di Psichiatria," viii.; *Schuchardt*, "Zeitschr. f. Medicinalbeamte," 1890, Heft 6.—*Duchateau*, Bulletin de la société de médecine de Gand, 1897, Febr.-March.—*Garnier*, Annal. médico-psychol. 1894, Jan.-Feb.—*Vigouroux*, ibidem.—*Hoppe*. Vierteljahrsschr. f. gerichtl. Med., 3. Folge xx., 2.—*Leppmann*, Die Sachverständigenthätigkeit, p. 101.—*Rayneau*, Annal. méd.-psych. 1895, May-June.—*von Schrenck-Notzing*, Arch. f. Criminalanthropol. Bd. i., H. 2 and 3, Fall 4 u. 5.—*Strassmann*, Vierteljahrs. f. geriehtl. Med., 3. Folge, 10 Bd.

5. Instructive case reported by *Morselli*, "Bolletino della R. Accademia medica di Genova," vol. ix. (1894), fasc. 1.
6. *Cf. v. Krafft*, "Ueber transitorisches Irresein bei Neurasthenischen," "Irrenfreund," 1883, No. 8; and "Wiener klin. Wochenschr.," 1891, No. 50.
7. "Recherches sur les Centres Nerveux," 2e série, Paris, 1893.
8. Analogous case: *Boissier* et *Lachaux*, "Archives de Neurologie," 1893, October.
9. *Dr. Moll* calls this perversion (?) mixoscopia (from μιξις, cohabitation; and σκεπτειν, to look). Merzejewsky in his "Gynécologie médicolégale," relates the case of an old Castellan who, in order to excite himself, made his servants violate women and girls in his presence. (*Ivankow*, Archiv. d'Anthropolog. criminelle, xiii., p. 697.)
10. "Annal. médico-psychol.," 1849, p. 515; 1863, p. 57; 1864, p. 215; 1866, p. 253.
11. *Cf.* the cases of *Tardieu*, "Attentats," pp. 182-92.
12. *Cf. Holtzendorff*, "Psychologie des Mords."
13. *Tardieu*, "Attentats," case 51, p. 188.
14. *Cf.* the complete medico-legal opinion on this case reported in *"Friedreich's Blätter,"* 1891, Heft 6.
15. (Schweizer Archiv f. Thierheilkunde, Heft 1, Jahrg. 1889.)
16. As *Herbst* ("Handb. d. österr. Strafrechts, Wien," 1878, p. 72) remarks, there are, nevertheless, crimes conditioned by the absence of assent on the part of the injured individual which cease to be such as soon as the injured individual has given consent—*e. g.*, theft, rape.
   But *Herbst* also enumerates here the limitation of personal freedom (?).
   Of late a decided change of views on this point has taken place. The German criminal law regards the consent of a man to his own death of such importance that a very different and much milder punishment is inflicted under such circumstances (§ 216); and it is the same in Austrian law (Austrian Abridgment, § 222). The so-called double suicide of lovers was the act considered. In bodily injury and deprivation of freedom, the consent of the victim must also receive consideration at the hands of the judge. Certainly a knowledge of masochism is of importance in making a judgment of the probability of asserted consent.
17. According to Austrian law, this crime should fall under § 411, as *slight* bodily injury; according to the German criminal law, it is bodily injury (*cf.* Liszt, p. 325).
18. Abstracts from a paper read before the International Congress at Paris.
19. *Cf.* cases 211, 212, 213, 214, 221, 225, 226, 228. (Cases by *Marc, Ideler, Friedreich, Giraud.*)
20. *Cf.* cases 10, 23.
21. *Cf.* cases 12, 172, 174, 175, 176.—*Chevalier*, l'inversion sexuelle, p. 362; les epileptiques, p. 81.
22. *Cf.* cases 196-200.
23. *Tardieu*, Attentats aux moeurs; *Casper*, Klinical Novels, case 1; *Maschka*, Handbuch, ii., p. 175; *Casper*, Vierteljahrschr., 1852, Bd. 1.
24. *Lop*, Archives d'antropol. crimin., x., 55, Annales d'hygiéne, xxxv., p. 462; *Bernard*, attentats à la pudeur sur les petites filles. Thèse de Lyon, 1886; New York Med. Journ., 1893, 13 December.
25. *Albert*, Friedreich's Blätter f. ger. Med., 1859, p. 17.
26. Cases, No. 163, 164, 165 quoted in this book.
27. *Leppmann*, "Die Sachverständigenthätigkeit," p. 96; *Lombroso*, "Archivio di psichiatria," viii., p. 519.
28. *Cf.* above, page 468, and my "Arbeiten," Heft 4, p. 96 (*Incest*, immorality with children.)

29. Cases 181, 182, above; *Liman,* "Zweifehafte Geisteszustände," case 6.
30. Cases 174, 175.
31. Case 176.
32. *Casper's* "Klin. Novellen," p. 161, 193, 272; *Leppmann, op. cit.,* p. 115; *Henke's,* "Zeitschr." xxiii., "Ergänzungsh.," p. 147; *cf.* above, pp. 445, etc.; 501, etc.
33. See above, cases 193 and 194, 10th ed. and 209 above, "Vierteljahrsschr, f. ger. Med., N. F. xlix., 2.
34. See above, cases 178, 179, 184, 185.—Also *v. Krafft,* "Arbeiten," iv., p. 97 (Schändung von Kindern im epil. Dämmerzustand des Thäters).
35. *Cf.* author's original article in *Friedreich's* "Blätter f. ger. Med.," 1896, and "Arbeiten," Heft 4, p. 105.
36. *Fuchs,* Therapie der anomalen vita sexualis, p. 11.
37. Cf. Zeitschrift f. Psychiatrie, 58, 4.
38. I follow the usual terminology in describing bestiality and pederasty under the general term of sodomy. In Genesis (chap. xix.), whence this word comes, it signifies exclusively the vice of pederasty. Later, sodomy was often used synonymously with bestiality. The moral theologians, like St. Alphonsus of Ligouri, Gury and others, have always distinguished correctly, *i. e.,* in the sense of Genesis, between sodomy, *i.e.,* intercourse with a person of the same sex, and bestiality, *i. e.,* intercourse with a beast. (*cf.* Olfers, "Pastoral-medicin," p. 78).

    The jurists brought confusion into the terminology by establishing a sodomy by virtue of the sex and a sodomy by virtue of the species. Science, however, should here assert itself as *ancilla theologiæ,* and return to the correct usage of words.
39. For interesting histories, see *Krauss,* "Psychol. d. Verbrechens," p. 180; *Maschka,* "Hdb.," iii., p. 188; *Hofmann,* "Lehrb. d. ger. Med.," p. 180; *Rosenbaum,* "Die Lustseuche," 5th edition, 1892.
40. How difficult, unpleasant, and dangerous it may be for the judge to form a proper judgment of these "coitus like" acts for the establishment of the objective fact of the crime is well shown by an article on the punishableness of male intercourse, in the "Zeitschr. f. d. gesammte Strafrechtswissenschaft., Bd. vii., Heft 1, as well as by a similar one in *Friedreich's* "Blätter f. ger. Medicin, 1891, Heft 6. See, further, *Moll,* "Conträre Sexualempfindung, p. 223 *et seq.,* and *Bernhardi,* "Der Uranismus," Berlin, 1895; *van Erkelens,* "Strafgesetz u. widernatürl. Unzucht," Berlin, 1895.—*Schäfer,* "Vierteljahrs. f. gerichtl. Med.," 3 Folge, xvii., Heft 2.
41. *Cf.* the author's pamphlet "Der conträr Sexuale vor dem Strafrichter." Leipzig and Vienna (Deutike), 2 Aufl., 1895.
42. For interesting histories and notes, *v. Krauss,* "Psychol. des Verbrechens," p. 174; *Tardieu,* "Attentats"; *Maschka,* "Handb.," iii., p. 174. This vice seems to have come through Crete from Asia to Greece, and, in the times of classic Hellas, to have been widespread. Thence it spread to Rome, where it flourished luxuriantly. In Persia and China (where it is actually tolerated) it is widespread, as it also is in Europe (*cf. Tardieu, Tarnowsky, et al.*).
43. *Lombroso* ("Der Verbrecher, p. 20 *et seq.*) shows that also, in case of animals, intercourse with the same sex occurs where normal indulgence is impossible.
44. *Cf. Tardieu,* "Attentats," p. 198; *Martineau,* "Deutsche Med. Zeitung," 1882, p. 9; *Virchow's* "Jahrb.," 1881, i., p. 533; *Coutagne,* "Lyon Mèdical," Nos. 35, 36. *Eulenburg* in "Zülzer's Klin. Handb. d. Harn- u. Sexual-organe," iv. Abtheil., p. 45, relates cases of his own experience, in which women brought actions for divorce on the ground that the husband, in order to avoid offspring, practiced *paedicatio* only.

45. *Cf. Mayer,* "*Friedreich's* Blätter," 1875, p. 41; *Krausold,* "Melancholie und Schuld," 1884, p. 20; *Andronico,* "Archiv di psich. scienze penali ed anthropol. crim.," vol. iii., p. 145; *Chevalier,* "L'inversion sexuelle," Paris, 1893, p. 217 (searching description of "sapphic love" in modern Paris).—*Moraglia,* op. cit., p. 24.
46. *Cf. Maschka,* "Hdb.," iii., p. 191 (good historical notes); *Legrand,* "La folie," p. 521.
47. *Vallon,* Annal. Méd. Psych., 1894, p. 116. (Immoral assault by a father on his own little daughter.)

INDEX